MW01058621

THE NEW

care &
TRAINING

OF THE
TROTTER
& PACER

U.S.T.A.

THE NEW
CARE and *TRAINING of*

the *TROTTER* and *PACER*

written by CURT GREENE

in conjunction with

NORMAN CHRIS BORING

JOHN D. CAMPBELL

CARTER H. DUER

PER K. ERIKSSON

THOMAS L. HAUGHTON

JOHN LEW, Ph.D.

ROBERT A. MCINTOSH

BRUCE K. NICKELLS

GENE RIEGLE

CHARLES A. SYLVESTER

RONALD WAPLES

written by DEAN A. HOFFMAN

in conjunction with

DOUGLAS J. ACKERMAN

HOWARD BEISSINGER

GARY R. LEWIS

RAY REMMEN

Plus a special section on lameness

by KENNETH P. SEEBER, D. V. M.

Illustrated by William A. Orr

THE UNITED STATES TROTTING ASSOCIATION

Published by

THE UNITED STATES TROTTING ASSOCIATION

750 Michigan Avenue
Columbus, OH 43215

Library of Congress Catalog Card Number: 96-60792

PHOTO CREDITS: All photographs by Ed Keys, USTA *Photography* Department or the USTA Photo Files, with the following exceptions: pages 16, 20, 32, 34 by Tony Leonard; pages 550, 563 by Monica Thors; and page 547 by Stephen Smith.

All illustrations by William A. Orr, except for the illustration appearing on page 585 which was done by Barbara DeGraves.

Please note that records and earnings shown in this book are current through January 1, 1996.

Table of Contents

FOREWORD

Since its formation in the late 1930s, the United States Trotting Association has served the Standardbred industry in many ways, but I doubt if any single USTA service has been more valued than the 1968 publication of the *Care and Training of the Trotter and Pacer.*

The book became so widely read that it became known as "the green bible" because it was virtually indispensable for any aspiring trainer, driver, breeder, owner, or groom. Parts of the book were translated into many foreign languages and helped spread the insight of experts on how to succeed in the Standardbred sport.

This book is the sequel to the 1968 version and I am certain that it will join its predecessor as a valuable tool for thousands of people in the sport. Writing a sequel to a classic like the 1968 volume is always a challenge, but I think that Curt Greene has done an outstanding job. Carol Cramer, Dean Hoffman, and Ed Keys of the USTA staff have assisted in the compilation of the book. We were particularly pleased to have the services of William A. Orr as illustrator since he had done the illustrations for the 1968 volume.

While the previous version of the *Care and Training of the Trotter and Pacer* is still quite useful and a classic in its own right, harness racing has changed over the decades and it was essential that we publish a book that offers the knowledge of the leading horsemen of today.

The fact that so many top horsemen and experts would give willingly of their valuable time to contribute to such a book speaks volumes for their class and character. They were not compensated in any way except with the knowledge that they have made a significant contribution to the body of knowledge about harness racing. On behalf of the readers of this book and on behalf of the U.S.

Trotting Association, I want to thank these gentlemen for sharing their knowledge so willingly.

I know you will find this book to be extremely useful and I wish you the best of luck with your Standardbred.

July, 1996

Corwin M. Nixon, President
The United States Trotting Association

INTRODUCTION AND ACKNOWLEDGEMENTS

Early on a summer morning in 1993, the phone rang in the office I have in my home in Lexington. It was my good friend Dean Hoffman, executive editor of *Hoof Beats*, calling to see if I would be interested in completing a project under the aegis of the U.S. Trotting Association.

Dean proposed that I be commissioned to complete a re-write of the *Care and Training of the Trotter and Pacer*. I knew that the idea of a re-write had been pondered for some time and that Dean himself had written four new chapters with the idea of serializing them in *Hoof Beats*, then publishing a new book when the cycle of new chapters was complete.

What Dean was proposing now was a different plan. The serialization plan was being replaced with the idea of finishing the re-write and publishing a totally new book.

I told Dean I was flattered by the request, but humbled by the enormity of the assignment. I knew the original was the most successful harness racing publication in history, having survived a quarter-century as an acclaimed classic. Doing the sequel, so to speak, seemed somewhat like a no-win situation. How could I improve upon a classic?

But then I was inspired.

I began to think about how much harness racing has changed since the late 1960s. And I recalled the delightful mornings of my youth when I grabbed a pitchfork in one hand and a lead shank in the other. I remembered the people who had taught me the basics of horsemanship. I also recalled how excited I had been at age 19 when I read *Care and Training...* for the first time.

The summers of my teenage years were spent on the dusty backstretches of Illinois county fair tracks at outposts such as Jerseyville, Carlinville, Mount Sterling, Lincoln, Pana, Champaign-Urbana, Farmer City, Newton, Taylorville, and my home track at Decatur.

It was not a misspent youth. Even then, I was serious about horses and wanted to learn more about them. I progressed from groom to trainer and from trainer to driver. I drove a few times and won my share of races, but I realized a career as a race driver was probably out of the question.

On the advice of a high school English teacher, I went to college and earned a degree in journalism. The plan was to write about horses and stay as close to the business as possible. I never imagined my career would take me to Lexington, then Chicago and Du Quoin, and then back to Lexington.

I certainly never imagined that I would be able to put to such constructive use the 30 years of observation of horses and horsemanship that has culminated with the writing of this new book.

So I agreed to undertake the completion of the re-write project.

There are many people whose contributions must be acknowledged, beginning with Dean Hoffman. Dean passionately wanted to complete this project himself. I understood this from the outset. It heightened my desire, knowing that Dean had essentially hand-picked me to complete the re-write. It has placed me forever in his debt.

Then there are the authors. I found it absolutely inspiring that our sport's most accomplished horsemen would be willing to sit down and unselfishly outline what it is that they do and how they do it. Like the original authors, none of the participants were paid for their time and, to their credit, none asked for compensation.

The interviews were conducted over the space of a year and a half. Some transpired in the comfort of a living room. Others were taped sitting at a kitchen table. And, of course, there were several completed in a backstretch tackroom or track kitchen. The rest were done over the telephone. Copies and drafts filled the mail for months, and my word processor hummed into the night on many occasions.

The information gleaned from these contributing "authors" will tell the reader in rather dramatic ways how harness racing has changed since the late 1960s. From John Campbell, who was my first interview subject, to Tommy Haughton, who was my last, I found the authors to be incisive, bright, articulate, confident, and, most amazingly, ready to share many of their most important trade secrets. As with the original book, there are contradictions and differences of opinion on some subjects. This, I believe, is one of the defining characteristics of our business. There is more than one way to breed, feed, train, shoe, and drive a good horse!

I was also very conscious of the history represented by these men and the horses they have touched. Each of the authors was asked to relate specifics about some of our most accomplished horses of the past 25 years. The historical importance of this information was apparent to me and was one of the goals I constantly kept in focus in the drafting and completion of each chapter.

I also spoke with many owners, breeders, and farm personnel, gathering information for my own chapter on bloodlines and breeding. It was not necessary or possible to offer attributions for all those who contributed their personal insights. It would require a virtual index of nearly everyone at the very highest levels of our industry. All I can do at this time is offer my thanks to everyone who answered the questions put to them or whose opinions were solicited during the course of my inquiry.

There are many others at the USTA who also must be singled out for praise. David Carr, chief of the good-gaited and speedy Information and Research Department, provided unlimited access to the wealth of data in his department and allowed me to roam the USTA's information highway when the re-write was commenced.

Bruce Brinkerhoff, a valuable member of the USTA's Information and Research department, answered hundreds of my inquiries, and provided advice and guidance on the maternal families sires research and spent countless hours in the final proofing of the book. Bruce was enthusiastic and willing to share his own unique brand of interest and knowledge with a fellow Illini.

Dick Jones, retired associate editor of *Hoof Beats*, did much of the editing and is responsible for the clarity of many of the chapters. Dick's command of the language, which is amazing, was much-needed here. In many cases, he saved me from errors of both context and content.

Carol Cramer, editor of the *Stakes Guide* and a member of the USTA Publicity Department, reprised her role in the original *Care and Training* book performing many of the same duties. Once again, her technical knowledge of the sport proved invaluable. Her altogether-rare ability to collate and organize a great deal of information was again on ample display.

Ed Keys, head of the USTA Photography Department brought his considerable knowledge of the human and equine photo inventory to bear on this project. Ed's editorial expertise was a key element in refining the chapters. Ed and Carol then pulled all the chapters together for final proofing and subsequent printing.

Artist Bill Orr was again asked to provide his wonderful artwork for the book. Bill proved that the years have been kind to him as he updated and provided new drawings for all the chapters.

The work of all these dedicated folks was thorough and professional.

Well-known Swedish writer Lars Palm also provided much information on the history, lineage and accomplishment of many American stars now performing overseas, and was responsible for much of the information gleaned for the "Leading Sires Throughout The World" addendum near the back of the book.

Personally, the re-write was sometimes entertaining and pleasant, but at other times it was troublesome, tedious and just slightly overwhelming. In the end, however, I am intensely proud of the finished product. I believe the reader will find the advice, ideas and perspectives of each of the horsemen represented here interesting, informative and thought-provoking.

If only one person reads this book and is persuaded to enter or widen his or her involvement with this wonderful breed of horse, I will consider it to have been a worthwhile endeavor.

Curt Greene
Lexington, Kentucky

1

PERSPECTIVES ON BLOODLINES & BREEDING

CURT GREENE

I t is nearly 150 years since the birth of Hambletonian, and as we near the close of the 20th century, the Standardbred has evolved from modest beginnings into a contemporary racing machine capable of producing and carrying speed over a mile distance at a rate once thought unattainable.

It will be my mission in this chapter to update the work of my predecessor, James Harrison, in his landmark, *Care and Training of the Trotter and Pacer*, published by the United States Trotting Association in 1968. It is not my intention here to re-trace Harrison's steps, or to re-draw the history of the Standardbred horse. Harrison's eloquence on the beginnings of our breed is so wonderful, so full of historical character and intimate background, that to attempt to cover the same ground seems foolhardy.

However, the Standardbred of today is a far different animal from the one Harrison analyzed. This development of the breed, while outstanding, should not come as a surprise to anyone who has made even a cursory examination of history. This is a young breed of horse and we have only begun to tap the potential development that lies down the evolutionary path. Where that road will lead is not of interest here, for to spend a great deal of time on speculation about the future seems an unwise path. I am, instead, focusing this effort on the reporting of recent history.

I will be exploring the four basic sire lines that have dominated Standardbred pedigrees for many years and will be updating their respective status.

I also will be commenting on the most productive maternal families in the breed. I believe it is intensely interesting to discover the source of many of our champions and to understand that many of them sprang from the same set of maternal ancestors. It is a well-documented fact that a very few of these families are disproportionately responsible for many of our most accomplished horses.

I will close with a subjective overview of the modern trotter and his pacing counterpart. This examination will include observations on the key pacers and trotters of the past quarter century and a discussion relative to developments and trends within each group of sires and maternal families.

EVERYTHING FLOWS FROM HAMBLETONIAN

All racing Standardbreds in North America trace their male line heritage to four sons of Hambletonian. This important quartet is comprised

Electioneer, a foal of 1868, and son of Hambletonian, founded the male line which eventually produced Meadow Skipper, Adios and Good Time, among others. Electioneer was a trotter, but his siring line was transformed to the pace by his grandson The Abbe. Modern pacing super sires Cam Fella and Abercrombie trace directly to Electioneer through nine generations.

of Hambletonian's 1856 foal, George Wilkes; his 1863 foals, Dictator and Happy Medium; and his 1868 son, Electioneer.

Electioneer, like all the early sires, was a trotting horse. He became, however, one of the most important horses in the history of the breed in the establishment of a pacing dynasty. In the latter part of the 19th century, the Electioneer trotters were everywhere. Electioneer's son, May King, a foal of 1886, sired the brilliant Bingen, and he, in turn, was the sire of the world champion gelding Uhlan 1:58. Electioneer's son, Conductor, was the grandsire of 1908 Kentucky Futurity winner and world champion The Harvester, undefeated at three and later the fastest aged trotting stallion in the world.

After the turn of the century, however, a funny thing happened. The trotters in the family disappeared and the Electioneer pacers emerged to dominate all pacing bloodlines. The conversion to the pace began with The Abbe, a 1903 son of Chimes, and, therefore, a great grandson of Hambletonian. The Abbe was a horse who raced at three on the trot and was campaigned by the legendary trotting horse master, Ben White. The Abbe got a modest record on the trot and was later raced on the pace by

Ed (Pop) Geers, another of that era's leading horsemen. The Abbe sired two sons who would change the breed.

One of them was Abbedale, foaled in 1917. The other was Bert Abbe, born in 1922. The Abbedale line, the most dominant of the two, leads eventually to Adios, Good Time and Meadow Skipper, while the Bert Abbe line has a contemporary stronghold with Big Towner.

In 1968, with the first foals of the charismatic Bret Hanover arriving, the Electioneer male line dominated the breed, and looked to have a lock on the future of this sire line from the offspring of Bret and his male relative Good Time.

DALE FROST—THE SIRE OF MEADOW SKIPPER

Bret Hanover was a son of Adios, a sire who dominated the 1950's and 1960's pacing stakes. Good Time was an early 1950's racing hero. Adios and Good Time were both sons of Hal Dale, a 1926 foal of Abbedale.

On the fringe of the Hal Dale family was a horse named Dale Frost, foaled late in Hal Dale's career. The family patriarch was 25 the spring that Dale Frost suckled up to his dam.

Dale Frost was an accomplished racehorse, although not by today's standards. His two-year-old mark of 2:00.1 seems modest, but was, in fact, a world record race mile for a freshman colt pacer. He finally got an aged mark of 1:58. Certainly, his racing and siring careers in total did not promise the delivery of a magnificent son. Dale Frost, after all, sired only seven 2:00 offspring! He did sire one horse, however, whose progeny would come to dominate pacing in the 1970's and whose towering legacy continues today through his sons and grandsons. That horse was Meadow Skipper.

Like his own sire, Meadow Skipper was a horse who would be an unlikely choice to become one of the most important sires in the history of the breed.

As a racehorse, Meadow Skipper was not the equal of his chief racetrack adversary, the handsome Overtrick, a Volomite-line pacer. Meadow Skipper did get a race mark of 1:55.1 at three, taken in a memorable battle at The Red Mile with Overtrick.

Meadow Skipper was not a particularly good-gaited horse and often put in steps, particularly on a half-mile track. There was little mile track racing in those pre-Meadowlands days, but had there been, it is a fair supposition that Meadow Skipper's racing career would have been far different.

Racing for Norman Woolworth's Clearview Stable at three, Meadow Skipper won the Wm. Cane Futurity in a then stakes-record 1:58.4h for trainer Earle Avery. In 86 lifetime starts over four seasons, Meadow Skipper won $428,057, with 38 career victories.

It is difficult to look at the other get of Dale Frost and find any clue

Meadow Skipper's get transformed the pacing breed. An attractive son of Dale Frost, he was responsible for many changes in the appearance and gait of the contemporary pacer. His sons and grandsons dominate the siring ranks, and his blood appears prominently in nearly every modern pacing champion.

that would lead to his being the sire of such a grand horse as Meadow Skipper. Dale Frost's only other son of note in the breeding ranks is the rugged Mountain Skipper, p,T1:56.1, whose lone major accomplishment is as the sire of the dam of Presidential Ball p,3,1:50 ($3,021,363.)

MEADOW SKIPPER—BOTTLED LIGHTNING

Meadow Skipper, however, had bottled lightning in his genes.

From his first crop, in 1967, to his final crop, foaled in 1982, Meadow Skipper sent forth a stream of champion males and females that was unprecedented. Meadow Skipper literally and simply took over the pacing breed. In his glorious 16-year stint at Stoner Creek Stud, he sired more than four hundred fifty 2:00 performers.

Meadow Skipper's initial crop in 1967 included the Triple Crown champion Most Happy Fella, a horse also destined for siring stardom.

Subsequent crops included one of the finest racehorses and sires in history, Albatross, foaled in 1968. Then came a litany of champions (listed

Albatross was a racing star, and is one of the breed's top stallions. Stanley Dancer raced him at three and four and considers him the finest racehorse he ever campaigned. Albatross possessed a flawless gait and has done much to improve the modern pacer. He was one of the early stars sired by the legendary Meadow Skipper.

here with records and year of foaling) such as Nero p,4,T1:55.1, in 1972; Windshield Wiper p,3,T1:53.2 in 1973; Governor Skipper p,3,1:54 in 1974; Falcon Almahurst p,3,T1:52.2 in 1975; Scarlet Skipper p,3,1:56.2, General Star p,3,1:54.3 and Genghis Khan p,1:51.4 in 1976; Landslide p,3,1:54.1 and French Chef p,2,1:54 in 1978; Trenton p,3,1:51.3 and Mr. Dalrae p,1:52.2 in 1979; Ralph Hanover p,3,1:53.4 in 1980 and, finally, Chairmanoftheboard p,3,1:53.2f in 1982.

In between, there was a host of champion fillies as well, such as the lustrous world champion Handle With Care p,3,T1:54.2, giving Meadow Skipper a siring record comparable to the most prepotent sires in history. His offspring have transformed the breed.

Meadow Skipper was as important to the breed as any of the other seminal stallions of history. Like that of the truly great sires, one of the hallmarks of Meadow Skipper's stud career was his ability to lift a seemingly obscure pedigree to championship status. Some of his champion offspring had maternal pedigrees that must be appraised as weak.

For instance, his most successful racing and siring son, Albatross, was out of Voodoo Hanover, a Dancer Hanover matron whose immediate maternal family had been culled by Hanover Shoe Farms years earlier.

ALBATROSS—TALENT AND GAIT

Albatross was a wonderful, talented colt, whom Stanley Dancer still regards as the finest horse he ever campaigned. Albatross' two-year-old season, when he won 14 of 17 starts, was directed by the noted horseman Harry Harvey, who broke the colt and developed him into a champion. Dancer got Albatross at three, and raced him for his final two seasons.

Albatross is a small horse, with a long barrel and a short, stocky neck, and what seems like an unusually large head. He was, however, a great-gaited horse with high speed, good racing manners and uncommon durability.

Part of the reason for his soundness was the fact that his gait was his most dominant and desirable characteristic. He seemed to float over the ground with a minimum of effort. He was also capable of performing free-legged. Dancer is convinced that Albatross could have raced free-legged—such was the reliability of his gait. Albatross was a world champion at three in two memorable 1:54.4 miles at Lexington (he was momentarily off-stride in both heats!) and took his p,4,1:54.3f mark at Sportsman's Park in Chicago.

Albatross won 59 races from 71 starts and $1.2 million in three remarkable seasons, with victories in nearly every major stake. He was denied the Triple Crown when he inexplicably dropped the Little Brown Jug to Nansemond, but he retired as the leading money-winning pacer of all time. He was Harness Horse of the Year in both 1971 and 1972 in his three- and four-year-old seasons.

A wonderful racing career does not always foretell greatness as a sire, but Albatross delivered in the breeding shed just like he did on the track. I have always believed that Albatross' greatness lay in his ability to transmit his fluid gait. I also feel this is the main reason that Albatross became a successful broodmare sire. His fillies are among the sport's best and they have transmitted many of their desirable traits, including their gait, to their offspring. Albatross seems to dominate any pedigree in which he appears.

MEADOW SKIPPER'S FIRST STAR

Most Happy Fella, on the other hand, was not a good-gaited horse and was somewhat of an adventure to drive. He had a chip in a hock and was withdrawn by his breeder, Stoner Creek Stud, from its annual yearling consignment to Tattersalls.

Stanley Dancer broke him and then purchased him for a mere $12,500 at a sale at Pompano Park in the winter of his two-year-old year.

At two, Most Happy Fella was bothered by the hock and was, to be honest, a rough-gaited colt. He had a habit of putting in steps, much like his sire Meadow Skipper, and was not as willing or as aggressive a horse as Albatross. He suffered from an infected stifle which cut short his two-year-old season. In fact, Most Happy Fella did not have a 2:00 record at two; his freshman mark was a modest 2:01.3f. He made 14 starts at two, winning six.

At three, however, racing in a crop which included the amazing colt pacers Columbia George and Truluck, Most Happy Fella emerged as winner of pacing's Triple Crown, and Dancer marked him at T1:55 at The Red Mile at the conclusion of his sophomore season. He was Pacer of the

Year in 1970 and earned more than $400,000 while winning 22 of 40 lifetime starts. At three, he won 16 races.

Most Happy Fella was a much bigger horse than Albatross and a completely different type. Whereas Albatross was from a Dancer Hanover mare, Most Happy Fella was from Laughing Girl, an unusually large mare by Good Time. He was taller and rangier than Albatross, and his foals tended to be bigger and more coarse, particularly in the hind limbs.

MULTIPLE CROSSES TO HAL DALE

The two horses, however, had much in common. They both carried multiple crosses to their paternal ancestor Hal Dale. Albatross' Dancer Hanover dam and Most Happy Fella's Good Time dam gave each of them a large dose of Hal Dale blood. Most Happy Fella carried a 3x3 generation inbred cross to Hal Dale. Albatross' relationship is a 3x4 generation linebred cross to the same horse.

Let us pause for a moment here to define our terms.

Inbreeding in this context means a horse has a common ancestor in his pedigree that appears either in the third generation of both the sire and dam, or in a closer relationship. A horse is said to be inbred if the common ancestor appears in the third generation of both parents. A 2x3 generation cross is also considered to be an inbred cross. A 2x2 cross would be described as an incestuous relationship.

Linebreeding means the relationship to a common ancestor may appear in the third generation of one parent, but is outside of that with the other. A 3x4 generation cross would be defined as being linebred. A 4x4 generation cross is also described as being linebred, as is a 2x4 or 4x2 cross. Common crosses that appear outside of the fourth generation are not considered to be either inbred, or linebred. These crosses are sometimes described as outcrosses, although this is technically inaccurate since real outcrosses are not available in a closed genetic pool like the Standardbred.

There are many horses, particularly stallions, who are advertised as "outcross horses," but, to be honest, they are not. A real outcross now occurs in our breed only when bloodlines are mixed between countries. For instance, an American-bred female trotter bred to one of the top European horses, whose pedigree is not of U.S. origin, would produce an outcrossed foal. Interestingly enough, some of this Franco-American breeding has been done, and with considerable success.

The linebreeding to Hal Dale of Albatross and Most Happy Fella interests us for a number of reasons. Of primary interest is the fact that the Most Happy Fella male line has found great success when mated with mares by Albatross. This is the branch of the Meadow Skipper sire family which appears to have the ability to carry on in succeeding generations.

For instance, Most Happy Fella's son Cam Fella is out of a mare by

Cam Fella was one of the standout racehorses of the 1980's, and became a leading money-winning sire. A son of Most Happy Fella, he was from a Bret Hanover dam and had four major crosses to Hal Dale. A short-coupled horse with a compact frame, Cam Fella sires long-gaited, fast and durable performers.

Bret Hanover, a grandson of Hal Dale. Cam Fella's second dam is a mare by Dale Frost, the sire of Meadow Skipper.

Cam Fella, therefore, carries a total of four crosses to Hal Dale in the fourth generation. This sort of cross is described by saying he is double-linebred. This concentration of blood is very interesting, since Cam Fella was one of the most astounding racehorses in history and has become one of the breed's most successful sires.

Cam Fella was not a particularly fast horse, as his lifetime record of 1:53.1, taken in 1983, was not remarkable in his day and seems absolutely pedestrian by today's standards. He was, however, brilliantly brave and courageous. He found a way to win races. Resolute and strong on the front end, he could come first-over or race out of a hole and he won 58 times at three and four, earning more than $2 million. His 1:53.1 mark was taken at four at The Meadowlands for Canadian trainer-driver Pat Crowe. In a memorable three-year-old season, Cam Fella won 28 races!

As a sire, Cam Fella has more than duplicated his own racetrack brilliance, sending out a stream of champions that have dominated pacing headlines in the late 1980's and early 1990's. Beginning with Camtastic in his first crop, and continuing with the likes of Goalie Jeff, Camluck, Precious Bunny, Cambest, Presidential Ball, Village Jiffy, Cam's Card

Shark, and Village Connection in subsequent crops, Cam Fella has achieved a unique status.

Conventional breeding theory would dictate that a horse such as Cam Fella, with a double-linebred cross to Hal Dale, would require an infusion of hybrid vigor, or blood from another unrelated pacing family, in order to become a successful sire.

Just the opposite is true.

It appears that Cam Fella cannot get enough of the Hal Dale blood. Precious Bunny, his second fastest racing offspring at p,3,1:49.4, is from a mare by B.G's Bunny, a son of Albatross who is also linebred to Hal Dale. Cam's Card Shark p,3,1:50 is also bred this way.

Precious Bunny's second dam is by Romeo Hanover, a grandson of Adios also inbred to Hal Dale. And Precious Bunny's third dam, a Bye Bye Byrd mare, is herself linebred to Hal Dale. This means that the mating that produced Precious Bunny has eleven separate crosses to Hal Dale! Cam Fella has shown a unique affinity for Albatross-line mares, as that same cross has also produced Camtastic, p,4,T1:49.3; Goalie Jeff p,3,1:51.2; and Carlsbad Cam, p,3,1:51—all major stakes performers, and all winners in excess of $1 million.

Cam Fella's other successful sons, such as Presidential Ball p,3,1:50; Cambest p,T1:46.1 and Camluck p,T1:48.4, also share common ancestors, but not to the same degree. Presidential Ball, an electrifying two-year-old, $3-million winner, and divisional champion at both two and three, is out of a mare by Mountain Skipper, a son of Dale Frost. Camluck, who came to top form as an aged horse, is from a Striking Image dam, with a distant connection to Hal Dale through Striking Image's grandsire Bret Hanover. World champion and millionaire Cambest, who was not only fast but durable, is the relative hybrid of the group, since his Harold J. dam has only a smattering of Hal Dale maternal blood.

Perhaps one of the most intriguing developments of the next decade will be to witness the siring abilities of these sons of Cam Fella to see if the Cam Fella x Albatross sires are more successful than the Cam Fella sons with somewhat hybrid maternal influences.

COMPLEMENTARY CROSSES

A possible explanation for the success of Cam Fella on Albatross-line mares is that this mating matches the complementary virtues of both sire and dam.

I have the feeling that the courage, strength, determined personality and physical qualities of Cam Fella are complementary to the gait and speed that is typical of the Albatross-line female. This is not an isolated occurrence. In another branch of the Most Happy Fella siring family, we find a similar circumstance.

One of Most Happy Fella's fastest sons was Oil Burner, a horse with a Shadow Wave dam. This produces in Oil Burner, like Cam Fella, a concentration of Hal Dale blood. Unlike Cam Fella, however, Oil Burner was not a courageous, dominating horse. He had high speed, earning a 1:54.2 race mark, but he was not a very cheerful, willing horse and lacked the strength and stamina of Cam Fella.

Oil Burner's first crop included a colt named No Nukes, foaled in 1979. No Nukes was a big, handsome, dark horse blessed with exceptional ability. He could, like his sire, rip off a string of spectacular fractions. The problem with No Nukes was that his speed was not entirely manageable. The night he started in the Woodrow Wilson at two for Benny Webster and trainer Steve Demas at The Meadowlands he forced two recalls and was allowed to race only after he was removed from the betting pools.

No Nukes' poor gate manners followed him throughout his racing days, and although he earned a T1:52.1 record for Glen Garnsey at three, it was clear that he went to stud with gas still left in the can.

Like Cam Fella, No Nukes has a lot of Hal Dale blood coursing in his veins. No Nukes is out of a mare by the Little Brown Jug winner Overtrick, a horse with a Hal Dale dam. No Nukes' second dam is a Tar Heel mare whose own dam is by Good Time.

Therefore, No Nukes has five significant crosses to Hal Dale in his immediate pedigree. This is an even larger concentration of Hal Dale blood than we find in Cam Fella. This becomes even more interesting when we consider that No Nukes, like Cam Fella, also has crossed well with mares with strong Hal Dale influences.

No Nukes' son, Western Hanover p,3,1:50.4 ($2,541,647), for instance, also has a dam by Albatross. Western's second dam, a Best Of All mare, offers additional Hal Dale blood because Best Of All is a son of Good Time. The Hal Dale loop is widened with the third dam, who is by Bullet Hanover, a champion colt pacer by Adios.

Western Hanover was a sharp, glib-gaited colt who won two of the three legs of the 1992 Triple Crown before dropping the Little Brown Jug in an exhausting three-heat battle with Fake Left. He has nine crosses to Hal Dale in his immediate pedigree. This phenomenon is also repeated in No Nukes' world champion filly Immortality p,3,1:51, who has four maternal crosses to Hal Dale to complement No Nukes' five crosses.

No Nukes' Woodrow Wilson-winning son, Die Laughing p,3,1:51.1f ($2,164,386), a foal of 1988, has a similar genetic background since he, too, is out of an Albatross dam with a second dam by Shadow Wave and a fourth dam by Good Time.

Die Laughing was quite a freshman pacer, despite the fact he was a June foal. When he won the Woodrow Wilson at two at The Meadowlands for Richie Silverman, he did so in world record time, and then came back at three to win the Messenger, Prix d'Ete and the New Jersey Classic, racing in a crop which included world champions Precious Bunny, Artsplace and Cambest. Die Laughing's first crop, foals of 1993, includes world champion Live Or Die p,2,1:51.4, who is from a mare by Temujin, a son of Race Time.

Dexter Nukes p,3,1:51.3 ($1,027,620), a foal of 1986, was yet another son of No Nukes who came from an Albatross dam. His second dam was the Fulla Napoleon mare Bacall, in another pedigree dominated by multiple Hal Dale influences. Before injury sidelined him at mid-season, Dexter Nukes had dominated the 1989 three-year-old stakes, winning the New Jersey Classic and the Meadowlands Pace in a season eventually claimed by Little Brown Jug and Breeders Crown winner Goalie Jeff.

JATE LOBELL, STAR OF NO NUKES' FIRST CROP

Jate Lobell, an established, successful sire of early speed, also has a similar cross to Good Time in his maternal background. "Jate the Great" was a dynamic, exciting two-year-old and went undefeated in 15 starts for trainer Mark O'Mara in 1986. At two and three, he was voted the top colt of his year and won $2,231,402. His 1:53 mark at two was taken over a rain-soaked Red Mile, a performance which earned him near-deity status. He was certainly one of the top five two-year-old pacers in history, and included among his victories the Fox Stake and Kentucky Pacing Derby.

At three, racing in a talented crop which included Call For Rain, Laag, Run The Table and Frugal Gourmet, Jate Lobell won 15 times in 25 starts, his biggest victory coming in the North America Cup in Canada. He retired with a 1:51.2 mark and has shown himself to be an outstanding sire of two-year-old speed. Jate's son Riyadh won two legs of the 1993 Triple Crown, winning the Cane Pace and the Messenger. Jate has also produced the 1995 star David's Pass p,3,1:50.4 ($1,652,500) and Breeders Crown winner Kingsbridge.

There is one major difference, however, in comparing the mating of Albatross-line mares to Cam Fella and the mating of Albatross-line mares to the Oil Burner male line. The Albatross-line mares bred to Cam Fella produce better three-year-olds, (e.g. Goalie Jeff, Precious Bunny, Cam's Card Shark) while the No Nukes-line stallions bred to Albatross mares produce the better two-year-olds (e.g. Die Laughing, Immortality). The mating of Albatross-line mares to the Oil Burner line is an example of male-line speed bred to female speed, while the Albatross mares bred to Cam Fella match male-line stamina with female speed.

Although the Most Happy Fella male-line stallions cross very well with Albatross-line mares, the inverse breeding has not worked as efficiently. The Albatross-line stallions have not crossed well with Most Happy Fella-line mares. In fact, the chief broodmare credits for Most Happy Fella have come when his mares were bred to horses such as Big Towner, Direct Scooter and Abercrombie. Of that group, only Abercrombie has a Hal Dale male-line presence.

The success of the Albatross broodmares with both Cam Fella and No Nukes might lead us to believe that the Albatross mares only cross well under these kinds of circumstances. Nothing could be farther from the truth. Like all of history's top broodmare sires, Albatross has produced mares who have been complementary with a number of stallions. For example, Abercrombie's best sons—Artsplace, Life Sign and Albert Albert—have Albatross dams. In addition, an Albatross mare is the dam of the Walton Hanover world champion mare Caesars Jackpot, p,T1:49.2.

Albatross mares have also enjoyed success with Big Towner, Direct Scooter, On The Road Again and Storm Damage. Although the Albatross sire line has been weakened in the past five years, the broodmare credits continue to mount up. Albatross is, by far, the leading broodmare sire in history.

How far might we be able to extend this Hal Dale concentration before inbreeding weakens the offspring? That is a good question which only history will be able to answer. It is clear, however, that the successful sons of Cam Fella and No Nukes have been and will be matched with mares from similar backgrounds, providing a further pooling of Hal Dale blood.

Consider a horse such as Precious Bunny when he is bred to a mare by Abercrombie, whose dam might be an Albatross x Bret Hanover cross. This foal will be carrying as many as 12-15 crosses to Hal Dale. Or, look at the courageous Little Brown Jug champion Life Sign, a son of Abercrombie, whose dam Three Diamonds is an Albatross x Bret Hanover combination. Life Sign is going to be bred to a lot of No Nukes and Cam Fella mares and these matings will produce a unique and unprecedented concentration of Hal Dale blood. The top colt from Precious Bunny's first crop, Breeders Crown winner John Street North p,2,1:53.3 is from an Abercrombie mare whose second dam is by Albatross, a pedigree which has Hal Dale blood oozing from nearly every single pore.

ALBATROSS MALE LINE HAS NOT PROSPERED

Albatross' success as a broodmare sire is interesting when we consider that the Albatross male line has not prospered. There was a time when every major Standardbred nursery either had a son of Albatross or was looking to get one. Now the decline of the Albatross male line is obvious.

Albatross' son Niatross, p,3,T1:49.1 was one of the great racing champions of the breed, winning 37 of 39 lifetime starts and more than $2 million. Undefeated at two, he was the first to conquer the 1:50 barrier in a historic Red Mile time trial in 1980 for trainer Clint Galbraith.

However, Niatross was a very high-going horse in front. He is also slightly back on his knees, a trait he passed on to many of his offspring. Put into the stud in Kentucky at Castleton Farm, Niatross produced major stakes winners such as world champion Nihilator p,3,1:49.3 and Barberry Spur p,3,T1:50.2 while in residence in the Bluegrass state. After only two seasons, the syndicate controlling Niatross moved him to New York and, for some reason, the championship train was derailed. He has not sired a major, high-level stakes colt since he left Kentucky. His fall from grace has been both stunning and puzzling.

Niatross' two foal crops in Kentucky did not lack for depth. They included not only Nihilator and Barberry Spur, but a whole supporting cast of stakes winners.

Nihilator, Niatross' top son, had a shortened stud career and succumbed due to complications from a bout with laminitis, but the evidence is that he, too, was not destined for siring greatness. Trained superbly by the late Billy Haughton and raced by Haughton and Bill O'Donnell, Nihilator was a very high-going horse in front and not particularly good-gaited, except at a very high rate of speed. Even then, Nihilator was a hard-going horse. He overcame these deficiencies and was a truly powerful, aggressive, dominating racehorse. However, many of the flaws in his gait were passed on.

Niatross' and Nihilator's inabilities to sustain siring careers is also characteristic of the other Albatross-line horses. Two of Albatross' best early offspring were the incredibly fast pair of B.G's Bunny and Sonsam. Both were good individuals and had extreme speed, but neither became a truly successful sire.

B.G's Bunny is a successful broodmare sire, but he did not sire a dominant son. Sonsam was a beautiful colt, was out of a stakes-winning Bret Hanover mare and was equipped with a great gait and breathtaking speed.

The winning move Sonsam made in the 1979 Meadowlands Pace for George Sholty remains one of the most electric efforts in the history of the breed. Sonsam and his offspring, however, failed to continue the Albatross line. His best son was the Fox Stake- and Adios-winning Marauder, a handsome colt pacer who competed against Nihilator, Dragon's Lair and Pershing Square, but failed to provide siring power, and was exported. Nobleland Sam, another son of Sonsam, has become a prominent Ohio sire but lacks national opportunities.

Another of Albatross' sons with a glowing racetrack reputation was Jaguar Spur p,4,T1:49.2 ($1,806,473). He is bigger than most of the other successful sons of Albatross and, as this is written, his oldest foals are only four-year-olds. He appears to have some siring ability, but lacks the opportunities for success that some of the others sons of Albatross enjoyed.

It may be that somewhere down the line a grandson or great-grandson may rekindle the Albatross siring fire.

THE OTHER MEADOW SKIPPER-LINE STALLIONS

Some of the other Meadow Skipper-line horses have also not sustained the greatness of their family patriarch.

Falcon Almahurst, who stands in Ohio, has produced a number of quality performers, particularly champion fillies, who have and will continue
to make valuable broodmare contributions. Falcon Almahurst, however,
has not left a son who appears to have the siring power to sustain Falcon's
national influence.

Nero, one of the best two-year-old pacers I ever saw, did not possess
the magic to continue his line either, although he was a successful sire of
several top racing fillies. His lone top male performer was the $1 million
winning Runnymede Lobell, a contemporary of Matt's Scooter. Governor
Skipper, the Adios and Little Brown Jug winner, started his siring career
brilliantly, producing the Woodrow Wilson winner Fortune Teller in his
first crop and later the Breeders Crown champion mare Follow My Star.
But then he went sterile.

It appears that the Meadow Skipper line has its most promising stronghold through the sons and grandsons of Most Happy Fella. The two
branches leading from Most Happy Fella that we have already examined
through Cam Fella and Oil Burner are supplemented with those from
Most Happy Fella's son, Tyler B, a foal of 1977 and a racing nemesis of
both Niatross and Storm Damage.

Tyler B stood at Hanover Shoe Farms before his untimely death at age
13 and sired just ten crops, but he produced some outstanding stakes
horses, most notable of which are the world champion Dragon's Lair, a
member of his initial crop in 1982, Magical Mike p,3,1:50.2, a member of
his last crop foaled in 1991, and Tyler's Mark, sire of world champion
Nick's Fantasy.

Dragon's Lair was a magnificent two-year-old, whose memorable battle
with Nihilator in the 1984 Breeders Crown ranks as one of the sport's
greatest races. He was a beautifully-gaited horse, elegant and refined
like a Thoroughbred. He was capable of extreme speed with seemingly
little effort.

In winning the Breeders Crown for Jeffrey Mallet, Dragon's Lair was
parked to a seemingly suicidal :26.3 opening quarter only to go on, grab
the racetrack, turn back a first-over challenge from Nihilator, and still
win in then world record time of 1:54.1f. It was an epic performance.

Dragon's Lair failed to return to this championship level at three, however, and the balance of his racing career was anti-climactic. He did accumulate more than $1 million in earnings, and earned a mark of 1:51.3
at age five for John Campbell, a mile which was then an all-age track
mark at Vernon Downs.

Dragon's Lair's pedigree provides further evidence that this branch of
the Most Happy Fella line also prospers from the doubling of Hal Dale
blood, since Dragon's Lair is out of a mare by Race Time, with a third dam
by Adios. This produces in Dragon's Lair, as in Cam Fella and No Nukes, a
massive concentration of Hal Dale blood. It is also noteworthy that this
kind of breeding utilizes three separate male-line branches of the Hal

Dale family, since the blood of Dale Frost, Good Time and Adios are all present here.

Dragon's Lair's stud career, like his racing career, has been something of an enigmatic adventure. It was first thought the horse was unable to breed a large number of mares. However, the few mares he did impregnate produced outstanding foals and, thus, a persistent effort was made to continue breeding the horse even after a short comeback effort on the track was completed.

The final fate of Dragon's Lair as a stallion is unknown. The early results, however, do indicate that he, too, prefers mares from the Meadow Skipper male line in addition to the Hal Dale blood he already possesses.

Magical Mike's major victories at two included the Woodrow Wilson and the Governor's Cup. At three, in 1994, a late-season surge produced victories in the Oliver Wendell Holmes, the Little Brown Jug and the Breeders Crown. He has a pedigree that is remarkably similar to both Tyler's Mark and Dragon's Lair, since he is by Tyler B and out of a Race Time dam.

FRENCH CHEF WAS TOP TWO-YEAR-OLD

French Chef, p,2,1:54, a son of Meadow Skipper, was an exceptional juvenile for owner-breeder Norman Woolworth and trainer Stanley Dancer, winning 21 of 23 starts. It is generally forgotten that French Chef retired as the fastest two-year-old in history on mile and five-eighths mile tracks.

Like his sire, French Chef stood at Stoner Creek Stud before his exportation to Australia and his subsequent untimely death. He sired three millionaire offspring from his eight U.S. crops and his Australian get quickly came to prominence.

The first two U.S. champions sired by French Chef were Amity Chef p,3,1:51.1, foaled in 1983, followed by Frugal Gourmet p,3,1:51.3, born in 1984. Both of these successful horses were among the best of their years and accumulated high-level stakes wins and many dollars. Amity Chef, in turn, sired the wonderful world champion filly Miss Easy p,3,1:51.1 ($1,777,656) in his first crop, but failed to provide an encore star.

Despite this kind of success on the racetrack, there was a lack of respect for French Chef and his offspring, and his yearlings never commanded top dollar. He was not a consistent sire of stakes winners. Part of this lack of appreciation came from the fact that French Chef was the result of mating a Nevele Pride mare with Meadow Skipper, thereby introducing trotting blood into a pacing equation. While we have known historically for years that speed on the pace has been acquired from speed on the trot, there was still a groundswell of disrespect for French Chef and his offspring. The horse never attracted a big book of mares.

In 1987, French Chef sired a colt named Beach Towel, also bred by

Stoner Creek Stud, and sold by that farm as a yearling to Seth Rosenfeld's Uptown Stable. Beach Towel had a stunning career, winning 29 of 36 career starts and more than $2.5 million. He got his p,3,1:50 tag at Du Quoin after pacing to the three-quarters in 1:20.1!

Beach Towel is as good a racing pacer as the breed has ever produced. He was 22 times first or second in 23 starts as a sophomore for trainer-driver Ray Remmen. Beach Towel's lone off-the-board blemish came when he made a break in the first turn of the North America Cup. Remmen drove Beach Towel in all of his starts, a rather remarkable statistic in today's racing world.

A wonderfully-conformed individual with as near a hybrid pedigree as is available in a high-profile horse, Beach Towel could inherit some of Meadow Skipper's greatness. Like Dragon's Lair, this would not be a surprise. Beach Towel's first crop, foals of 1992, included the 2-time Breeders Crown-winning Jenna's Beach Boy p,2,1:51.4; 3,1:48.4, the fastest racing three-year-old in history.

THE LEGACY OF ADIOS AND GOOD TIME

The rest of the Hal Dale male line rests with Adios and Good Time, giants of their time whose paternal influences have been diminished in the last two decades. The dominance and superiority of the Meadow Skippers made it all but impossible for the Adios and Good Time pacers to compete.

I have always believed that one of the reasons for this is that both Adios and Good Time raced well beyond their colt form and did not go to stud until they were fully mature horses. Adios' first major crop was foaled in 1950 when he was already ten years old. Good Time's first crop hit the ground in 1954 when the "Mighty Mite" was eight.

Compared to today's stallions, whose first foals are born in the stallion's fifth or sixth years, Adios and Good Time got late starts. I have the feeling that both Adios and Good Time suffered from this. The practical effect was that both horses were at an advanced age when their fastest male foals performed, unlike today's champions whose first crops often perform well, enabling a horse to attract a better book of well-bred mares, and improve his chances to sustain his siring career.

Good Time's first really spectacular colt was Castleton Farm's home-bred Race Time, a foal of 1961. Race Time began his racing career in 1963. This meant that Good Time, a foal of 1946, was already 17 before his first real colt champion raced. Further, Good Time was 21 when Best Of All was three; 24 when Columbia George was racing on even terms with Most Happy Fella; and 30 when Crash, his final major stakes performer, won the Fox Stake.

Similarly, Adios was an older horse before the world took note of his siring ability. He barely had 100 foals total in his first five crops! Adios was already into his mid-teens before his sons Adios Harry and Adios

Good Time was a superb racehorse and a marvelous pacer with great physical quality. However, he did not leave a lasting male-line legacy, and his major contributions were maternal. His best sons were racing stars Best Of All and Race Time, both of whom also became successful broodmare sires.

Boy alerted the world to their sire's ability. Adios was 18 when his son Shadow Wave won the Little Brown Jug and was 25 when he died in 1965, in the midst of Bret Hanover's and Adios Vic's memorable three-year-old seasons.

While Good Time did produce memorable horses, of which Best Of All and Race Time were by far the best, he does not have a male-line presence in today's upper-echelon pacing pedigrees. His major contribution is that he appears prominently in the maternal pedigrees of many top horses, such as Jate Lobell, Western Hanover, Dragon's Lair and Die Laughing.

Adios and Good Time were also adversely affected by the fact that neither ever had large foal crops. Adios' largest foal crop was but 51 foals. Good Time never had a crop with more than 57 foals, and he had only two seasons with as many as 50 offspring. Adios' average annual foal count over his 19 seasons at stud was only 31 offspring—and Good Time's average was a mere 29 in his 23 years at Castleton!

Good Time's legacy is strongest with the daughters of Race Time, a horse with a very strong, but largely unappreciated record, as a broodmare sire. A number of prominent stakes horses, most notably Dragon's Lair, Magical Mike, and the Cam Fella mare Ellamony, have Race Time dams.

Bret Hanover is one of history's most famous Standardbreds. A legendary world champion racehorse and multiple world champion sire, his most profound legacy is that of a broodmare sire. A physically coarse horse that stood 16.2 hands, Bret Hanover was a son of Adios from the royally-bred Tar Heel matron Brenna Hanover.

Race Time also has begun to appear frequently in the maternal pedigrees of many other successful stakes horses.

Adios had, and still has, a very strong siring presence, through both an expected source—Bret Hanover—and an unexpected source—Abercrombie.

In my opinion, Bret Hanover, who was campaigned by Hall of Fame great Frank Ervin, is the finest racehorse in the history of our breed, since he extended his brilliance over the course of three spectacular seasons. He won 62 of 68 career starts, was undefeated through his first 35 races, won the Triple Crown and amassed nearly $1 million in earnings. He is the only pacer ever to be voted Harness Horse of the Year three times.

As a sire at Castleton Farm, Bret Hanover was expected to carry on the legacy of his own sire and, to a large extent, he did that. Like the other stallions of his time, he found it difficult to compete with Meadow Skipper, but that does not diminish his profound influence on the breed. To be certain, Bret Hanover had more success in the stud than all of the other sons of Adios combined.

Bret's sons Storm Damage, Warm Breeze and Strike Out were world champion racehorses and each produced a world champion son. Storm Damage has Call For Rain p,4,1:49.3 ($1,065,919); Warm Breeze sired Falcon Seelster p,3,1:51h ($1,121,045); and Strike Out sired Striking

Image p,2,1:55, the first 1:55 juvenile.

Falcon Seelster was an incredibly fast horse. He had a high-headed, quick, staccato gait, a trait repeated in his multiple world champion daughter Shady Daisy. However, his son, Falcons Future, a foal of 1991, was an attractive horse and came equipped with a classically efficient gait. Falcon Seelster is a handsome individual, but Falcons Future is one of the more attractive Standardbreds in history, pacer or trotter. As a two-year-old, Falcons Future showed flashes of mature brilliance. At three, he won the Cane Pace in impressive style. He was a high-quality horse who got a 1:51f mark at three and earned $1,054,761, but never realized his full racing potential.

Certainly, the Bret Hanover sons do not compare with any of the more fashionable branches of the Meadow Skipper dynasty. Part of the problem with Bret Hanover's siring career was the fact that Bret represented the most productive cross of his time. He was a son of Adios from a royally-bred Tar Heel mare. Therefore, Bret was closed out on the most fashionable and productive bloodlines of that era. Many of the top females were bred just as he was. Albatross, the horse who was the top stallion of the following decade, crossed mightily with Bret Hanover's daughters.

It is as a broodmare sire that Bret Hanover's legacy is most profound. A few broodmare sires of his time produced slightly larger overall numbers, but the depth of quality from Bret Hanover broodmares is hard to ignore. Among the many stars with Bret Hanover dams are Cam Fella, Miss Easy, Three Diamonds, Nihilator, Town Pro, B.G's Bunny, Fan Hanover, Troublemaker, Barberry Spur and Jaguar Spur. That's quite a group! Bret is the leading broodmare sire of $1 million winners.

It should be noted that, from this list of performers, Nihilator and Miss Easy are among the top money-winning male and female pacers in history. In addition, Cam Fella is a leading sire of pacers; Fan Hanover is the only filly ever to win the Little Brown Jug; and Three Diamonds, a wonderful champion racing filly, is the dam of Life Sign, winner in miraculous style of the 1993 Little Brown Jug. B.G's Bunny became a leading broodmare sire, producing the dams of Precious Bunny and Cam's Card Shark.

The Good Time male line has not fared as well as the Bret Hanover blood—and this is a puzzlement. Good Time was a wonderful pacer, and he sired good horses. No finer colt pacer ever lived than Best Of All, a long-gaited, fast and attractive horse. But Best Of All's problems also lay somewhat with his historical timing. Standing at Hanover Shoe Farms, he was bred to a number of that farm's wonderful Tar Heel mares, a cross which did not fare well. Only one of his good sons, the exported Boyden Hanover, was out of a Tar Heel mare.

Good Time's other sons, such as Crash and Columbia George, did not have successful stud careers, and the Good Time male line, without an apparent savior, appears headed for the history books.

Henry T. Adios, shown in this conformation study, was a son of Adios whom historians initially overlooked until his grandson Abercrombie became a successful sire. Henry T. Adios had high speed for a short distance, but became the forebearer of a modern male line noted for its stamina, durability and courage.

THE ADIOS COMEBACK

The Adios male line is a different story, for it has witnessed an interesting comeback in recent years.

One of Adios' early stars was his 1958 foal Henry T. Adios, a son of the Nibble Hanover mare Greer Hanover. Developed and raced by Stanley Dancer, "Henry T." was an attractive, smallish horse with tremendous gate speed, but he lacked the courage or dominance of a wire-to-wire performer. He was, to be honest, a horse who preferred a trip to win.

In his five-year racetrack career, during which he won the 1961 Little Brown Jug, earned more than $700,000 and a mark of 1:57 (at age six), Henry T. Adios displayed great durability and tenacity. He was sent to Stoner Creek Stud in that nursery's pre-Meadow Skipper days.

One of the mares he bred in the spring of 1968 (his fourth year at stud) was Stoner Creek's Tar Heel matron Hobby Horse Tar, a daughter of the Wilmington dam Wilellen in a branch of the famed Miss Duvall

Silent Majority was the top three-year-old of his year, racing for Billy Haughton (as shown here) and Stanley Dancer. A son of Henry T. Adios, the handsome horse earned a niche in history by being the sire of Abercrombie, the horse who revived the Adios sire line.

maternal family. The resulting foal was Silent Majority, purchased as a yearling by Canadian trainer Roger White. Silent Majority became a stakes winner at two, winning 17 of 21 starts.

Following White's tragic death, Silent Majority raced at three for both Billy Haughton and Stanley Dancer, acquiring a mark of 1:56.3 in a late-season stake at The Red Mile for Haughton. He was the leading money-winning three-year-old of his year, racing in a crop which included the likes of Strike Out. He also won the 1972 Messenger for Haughton. Silent Majority was a fast colt, but, like his sire, he was not a dominant, overpowering type. He was, frankly, also in need of a journey. He could pin his ears and was a bit foul-tempered at times, with a notorious kicking habit. He was a bigger horse than Henry T. Adios, was an attractive light bay and had an efficient gait and high speed.

Like his sire, Silent Majority entered the stud in Kentucky at the conclusion of his racing days, but took up residence at Walnut Hall Farm. His first crop, foaled in 1975, included a handsome, bulldog-type colt christened Abercrombie, whose dam was the Duane Hanover mare Bergdorf.

Abercrombie was sold to Indiana attorney Keith Bulen for $9,500 as a yearling. Later, Bulen sold a half-interest in the colt to his friend Morris Mitchell, who had been diagnosed with cancer. Bulen hoped that if the horse raced well, it might prolong his friend's life. Originally given only months to live, Mitchell lived to see Abercrombie named Harness Horse of the Year.

Abercrombie was developed at two by Indiana horseman Jerry Landess

Abercrombie is one of the best conformed stallions in the history of the breed. His excellent type and clean, efficient gait have allowed him to produce offspring with a combination of early speed and enduring soundness. A foal of 1975, he crossed best with mares by sons of Meadow Skipper, most notably with Albatross.

and was later trained by both Cecil Peacock and Harold Barnes before he landed in the stable of the late Glen Garnsey at the conclusion of his juvenile season. He had first burst upon the national scene by winning the Standardbred stake during the Grand Circuit meeting at Delaware in season's record time, and Garnsey gave the colt a 1:56 mark at Lexington that same fall. Abercrombie stayed in Garnsey's shedrow through his four-year-old season, which he climaxed by winning in a then world record 1:53 at The Meadowlands. At three, Abercrombie won the Messenger, Adios, Prix d'Ete and the Dancer and Murphy Memorials.

Abercrombie retired with earnings just shy of $1 million, winning exactly half of his 72 lifetime starts. He is a handsome, dark-hued horse and is bigger than he is perceived to be. He stands at least 15.3 hands and is a marvelous individual, with a wonderful head and eye. He is one of the most physically correct Standardbreds in history.

Abercrombie went low-headed and was somewhat quick-gaited, but his action was very efficient in that his gait had no sideways motion. He was a "line-gaited" pacer. This efficiency, plus excellent physical type, is thought to have allowed Abercrombie to over-achieve. He entered the stud at Castleton Farm in Kentucky at the conclusion of his racing days. Since Abercrombie represented a branch of the Adios sire line that had not been productive, not much was expected of his stud career.

Abercrombie, however, attracted a number of quality mares from his first year in the stud. There were two reasons for this. His syndicate had a number of prominent breeders, and more importantly, he arrived on the scene at the same time that mares by Meadow Skipper and his sons— most notably Albatross—were becoming available. His pedigree invited the mating of Meadow Skipper-line mares.

It is an acknowledged historical fact that the leading sire of one generation will become one of the leading broodmare sires of the following generation. And some stallion, from a different but still compatible sire line, can benefit if he crosses well with the mares available to him.

Not every horse will accept that challenge, but Abercrombie could, and did. From his very first crop, which included the handsome colt, Panorama (sire of 1993 Horse of the Year Staying Together), it was clear that Abercrombie was going to make it as a sire. Subsequent crops included Breeders Crown winner Armbro Emerson p,4,T1:51.4; the gray champion Laag p,3,1:51.2; the Fox Stakes winner Albert Albert p,3,1:52.1; Breeders Crown winner Kentucky Spur p,3,1:52; and millionaire Topnotcher p,4,1:52.2f. He also sired wonderful fillies, such as Breeders Crown winners Anniecrombie p,1:52.3 ($1,414,477) and Leah Almahurst p,3,1:52.3 ($1,053,201).

However, as good as the performances of those horses were, there was still the feeling that Abercrombie lacked the punch to sire a really dominant racing son. Each of the aforementioned horses had moments of brilliance, but none were the dominant, overpowering type. He had not produced a Meadowlands Pace or Little Brown Jug winner.

The speculation about Abercrombie's ability to sire a really great horse ended with not one champion, but two: Artsplace and Life Sign.

Artsplace is a homebred of Chicago breeders George Segal and Brian Monieson and was the result of the mating of the well-bred Albatross mare Miss Elvira with Abercrombie in 1987. It should be noted that Segal and Monieson had given more than $200,000 for Miss Elvira as a yearling. Her first Abercrombie colt, Artsplace, was named after a cultural center in downtown Lexington, Kentucky.

Artsplace was first noticed in the Fox Stake at Indianapolis at two, finishing second in Deal Direct's world record 1:51.4 mile though parked the whole mile from the second tier. He won 11 of 15 starts at two, taking the Metro Stakes in Canada and the Governor's Cup at Garden State Park for John Campbell. Artsplace also stunned everyone with an amazing 1:51.1f world-record mile in the Breeders Crown at Pompano Park for Campbell, an effort that certainly ranks among the top five single performances by a two-year-old in the history of the breed. Six years later, it is still the fastest mile in history by a freshman pacer over any size track. Artsplace was voted Two-Year-Old Pacer of the Year in 1990.

At three, Artsplace won 10 of 18 starts, with victories in the American-National and the Gaines and Dancer Memorials, but was second-best most of the year to the Cam Fella colt Precious Bunny. He did set a world record of 1:50.4f for Campbell in an elimination of the Adios in a memorable duel with Precious Bunny.

At four, with Precious Bunny off to stud, Artsplace won all 16 of his appearances, including a 1:49.2 race mark at The Meadowlands for catch driver Catello Manzi. Artsplace also had major wins at four for John Campbell, Bill O'Donnell and Dave Magee. Campbell steered him to a second Breeders Crown triumph.

Artsplace, developed for his two- and three-year-old seasons by Hall of Fame trainer Gene Riegle, was a sensationally fast horse, as his world record two-year-old mile at Pompano Park will attest. As noted above, his four-year-old season, in the barn of Canadian trainer Bob McIntosh, was unblemished.

Artsplace is the definitive Abercrombie archetype. He went low-headed, had a powerful and efficient gait and was built like a bruising fullback. He was a horse who matured a great deal from his colt form into his four-year-old season.

At four, Artsplace was a dominant force who could take over a race and dictate the fractions with such power that no one dared pull on him. He never lost a race in his entire career when he was on top at the half-mile pole. He was rewarded for this domination by following in his sire's footsteps as Harness Horse of the Year in 1992 after accumulating more than $3 million in three memorable seasons, with 37 lifetime wins.

While Artsplace was dominating the free-for-all ranks in 1992, trainer Gene Riegle had another Segal homebred Abercrombie colt in his barn, the handsome Life Sign, who wound up with a p,3,1:50.3 mark and nearly $2 million in purses.

Life Sign was always accorded special respect in the Riegle stable, for his dam was the world champion Three Diamonds p,3,1:53.1, who had been selected and trained by Gene Riegle, and raced by Gene's son Bruce Riegle for George Segal. Three Diamonds won the Jugette, Countess Adios, Debutante, Mistletoe Shalee, Adioo Volo, American-National, Helen Dancer Memorial, and Tarport Hap stakes, and is considered to be one of the best pacing fillies in history.

Three Diamonds' maternal heritage is as outstanding as her racing career, since she is by Albatross, the leading broodmare sire in history. Her mother is the Bret Hanover mare Ambiguity, from the super-successful Nora Adele branch of the Miss Duvall maternal family founded by breeder William Shehan.

Life Sign, foaled in 1990, was one of the most courageous champions of the modern era. Gifted with a great gait, an imposing pedigree and outstanding conformation, the Abercrombie horse represents the continued evolution of his branch of the Adios sire line, once thought to be headed toward oblivion.

Life Sign possessed two rather extraordinary racing gifts. He had both wonderful, raw courage and an amazing, and altogether rare ability to accelerate in the final stages of a race. This splendid bravery and timely speed were never more amply displayed than in the final heat of the 1993 Little Brown Jug, where Life Sign was parked through three turns and yet visibly rallied in deep stretch to win one of the most dramatic and exciting races in the history of the breed.

Life Sign took three of his most important victories in the Little Brown Jug, the Breeders Crown at Freehold and the Art Rooney Memorial at Yonkers. Remarkably, in each of those three races, all on half-mile tracks, Life Sign won from the first-over position!

Many, this writer included, believe Life Sign to be the epitome of pacing excellence. Indeed, he may provide the best combination of exquisite pedigree, efficient gait, outstanding conformation and racetrack bravery available to the contemporary breeder.

The willing fortitude of the Abercrombie offspring is an interesting development for the breed, since it is well known that his grandsire Henry T. Adios and Silent Majority were, to be diplomatic, horses who preferred a covered-up trip. Yet, Abercrombie was a wonderfully tough horse, and his offspring are characteristically brave, with tremendous tenacity and stamina.

Despite his numerous successes, there is a criticism of Abercrombie in some corners that stems from the fact that nearly all of his champion sons and daughters have splendid maternal pedigrees. Among his nine $1 million-winning offspring, all come from mares by Meadow Skipper or one of his sons.

This has never bothered me when considering the future of the Abercrombie male line, since a number of stallions get a crack at blueblood mares and fail to become successful sires. To put it another way, I would be concerned only if the stallion bred good mares and couldn't produce. Abercrombie has produced with the chances given to him.

The dominant Abercrombie characteristics of durable soundness, efficient gait, outstanding conformation and splendid courage, allow his offspring to race through many productive seasons. If these characteristics cannot carry a horse into succeeding generations, then there is no way to predict a future for any sire.

THE BERT ABBE PACERS

The remaining Electioneer-line pacers trace paternally to Bert Abbe, a 1922 son of The Abbe. Bert Abbe's son, Gene Abbe, stood most of his career in Ohio and was the first horse to be bred using extensive artificial insemination.

A prolific and fertile horse, he sired a host of successful racehorses, male and female. Near the end of Gene Abbe's siring career, a particular colt appeared just when it looked as if the Gene Abbe male line might disappear.

The colt was Big Towner.

He was a refined, athletic-looking racehorse, earning a mark at four of 1:54.4 for the late John Chapman, with earnings over $540,000. He was an exceptionally good half-mile track horse. His dam is a Shadow Wave mare from the immediate maternal family of Good Time. (See Kathleen Maternal Family)

Put into stud at Hanover Shoe Farms, Big Towner was an immediate success, getting the good stakes colt Walton Hanover p,3,1:53.2 ($802,741) in his second crop. Walton Hanover also had early successes, siring the world champion pacing mare Caesars Jackpot p,T1:49.2 ($969,494) and the handsome colt pacer Totally Ruthless p,2,1:55.1f ($1,150,964). Another of his successful sons was the two-year-old star Apache Circle p,2,1:55.2, who is from the immediate family of Race Time, Storm Damage and Warm Breeze. Apache Circle subsequently sired the handsome millionaire star Apaches Fame p,4,1:51.4f, whose first crop of two-year-olds were stars of the 1995 Ontario Sire Stakes. Big Towner's other successful sons include midwestern sires Broadway Express and Towner's Big Guy.

Big Towner was raced by Hall of Famer John Chapman and was very much at home on the half-mile tracks of New York. An athletic pacer, Big Towner was a very attractive, well-conformed racehorse who became a successful sire, most noted for champion fillies Town Pro and Hardie Hanover.

Big Towner is also an exceptional filly sire; his female offspring include his top money-winner to date, the outstanding Town Pro p,3,1:51.4 ($1,229,582), a daughter of the Bret Hanover mare Programmed. His Breeders Crown-winning daughter Hardie Hanover p,3,1:51.3 sold for $500,000 at public auction at the end of her three-year-old season at the 1994 Harrisburg mixed sale. Hardie Hanover is out of an Albatross mare, a cross which also produced the world champion Breeders Crown winner Central Park West p,2,1:53.3f ($534,863).

Like Abercrombie, Big Towner is a good individual and his offspring are correct, good-gaited horses. I suspect that Big Towner will appear in a number of prominent pedigrees for years to come, since his sire, Gene Abbe, was a very successful broodmare sire.

The only other Gene Abbe-line horse who has been prominent is the modestly-bred Dorunrun Bluegrass p,1:49.4 ($1,880,235). Bred in Tennessee by Paul Shelton, this horse emerged from obscurity to win 52 races in five successful seasons, racing for Kentucky breeder Dr. Luel Overstreet.

Dorunrun Bluegrass was sired by Dr. Overstreet's stallion Fortune Richie p,3,2:00.1f, a son of Gene Abbe, who is from the immediate maternal family which also produced the world champion colt pacers Laag p,3,1:51.2 and Trim The Tree p,2,1:53.3. The dam of Dorunrun Bluegrass is a mare by Sir Carlton, a son of Meadow Skipper. This is the nearest that the breed has come to producing a hybrid champion in a long, long time.

THE PETER THE GREAT SIRE LINE

Another of Hambletonian's prominent sons was Happy Medium, a foal of 1863. Happy Medium has an interesting historical background, as he is not only an important horse in the Peter The Great sire line, he was also the sire of one of the sport's early female stars, the brilliant mare Nancy Hanks, first trotter to beat 2:05.

This is the paternal trail that leads to trotting champions Super Bowl, Nevele Pride, Speedy Crown, Mack Lobell, Pine Chip, Speedy Somolli and Valley Victory.

Happy Medium's grandson, Peter The Great, was a foal of 1895 and first caught the attention of the trotting horse world when he won a new stakes race in 1898. Called the Kentucky Futurity, the race had been inaugurated only five years before and had not yet achieved its lofty status as a major test for three-year-olds.

Peter The Great has two trumpeting claims to fame, his sons Peter Scott and Peter Volo, both of whom founded successful siring families of their own. Each of these horses was sired by Peter The Great when the great family founder stood at Patchen Wilkes Stock Farm near Lexington, Kentucky, as was Peter The Great's pre-eminent female, the storied Volga E.

The imposing success of the Peter The Great line was foretold by an earlier branch of the family that has faded from the pages of history, but nonetheless produced a champion who gave us a glimpse of what was to follow.

In 1908, Peter The Great sired a son, Azoff, who had a dam by Axworthy and thus carried what we know today was the best blood available in the trotting horse world at that time.

Azoff had little success overall, but in 1916 sired a horse many years ahead of his time, the brilliant gelding champion, Peter Manning, who trotted in 1:56 3/4 for Thomas W. Murphy in 1922! Azoff also sired Siskiyou, a horse who appears close-up in the maternal pedigree of pacing star No Nukes.

THE PETER SCOTT BRANCH

Thomas W. Murphy, the famous "Wizard of the Reins," raced Peter Scott. Like many of the stars of his day, Peter Scott was not a precocious colt performer, but instead developed into a champion older horse, trotting in 2:05 on the Grand Circuit at an advanced age. In one season, however, he showed how good he was — by winning 16 races. He was the leading money-winner sired by Peter The Great.

One of Peter Scott's early successful racing sons was the good colt Sam

Williams, who earned a 2:01 3/4 mark before being exported to France. Of historical interest is the fact that Sam Williams, foaled in 1922, founded the male line which leads to the French trotting champions Ourasi, Ideal du Gazeau, Coktail Jet and Fakir du Vivier.

Peter Scott was also the sire of Scotland, born in 1925 and a horse destined to found his own branch of the sport's deepest siring family. Scotland then produced Spencer Scott, and that top racehorse produced Rodney in a male line which leads directly to both Speedy Crown and Pine Chip. Let us focus on Rodney for a moment.

In an all-too-brief siring career, Rodney produced a slate of champion trotters, among them the Canadian star Tie Silk, classics winner Duke Rodney, and 2:00 trotter Porterhouse, the wonderful filly Elaine Rodney, FFA star Express Rodney and world champion Speedy Rodney. A grandson of Rodney, the late Rex Rodney, was bred in Europe and became a celebrated star, winning the famed Elitlopp.

However, none of the males in that group played a prominent role in the continuation of the Rodney male line. World champion Speedy Rodney did sire the world champion Hambletonian winner Green Speed 3,1:55.3, but that branch of the family abruptly stopped when Green Speed died after only five modest seasons at stud.

This sire line came to depend on a colt from one of Rodney's early crops. He was Speedster, who raced with moderate success on the Grand Circuit, and whose main attribute was his very clean gait. In fact, his gait was so solid that he raced without hind shin boots.

Speedster's gait, pedigree and overall appearance were such that he was nabbed by Castleton Farm as a sire prospect, since it was thought he would cross well with the get of the farm's other sires, most notably the champion Victory Song. The wisdom of this move is pretty convincing. The mating of a Victory Song mare named Scotch Love to Speedster in 1959 produced a colt destined for stardom.

He was Speedy Scot.

Foaled in the spring of 1960, Speedy Scot was retained by Castleton Farm and expertly managed by the venerable Ralph Baldwin, one of the great trainers in history, who was then under contract as the farm's head trainer.

Speedy Scot became one of the most accomplished colt trotters in history, winning the Triple Crown and racing on through age five. His mark of 1:56.4, taken at three, was a world record when made. He was a strong-willed, powerfully-gaited and handsome horse who was a perfect match for Baldwin's cool, professional horsemanship.

Speedy Scot, like his own sire, did not wait long in the stud to produce a champion. From only his second crop, Speedy Scot sired Speedy Crown, a wonderful colt trotter who was one of the most handsome, good-gaited stars to ever grace an American racetrack.

Speedy Crown is a light bay horse who went low-headed and possessed

Speedster was such a good-gaited horse that he raced without hind shin boots, as shown in this photo from Du Quoin. A son of Rodney, Speedster became an important link in the siring male line that eventually produced modern trotting star Valley Victory.

a wonderful, classic stroke. He was fast, good-mannered and very reliable. He seemed the perfect racehorse. He could jog, warm up and race, and never really tighten a line beyond the point where he was manageable. Trained by Hall of Fame horseman Howard Beissinger, Speedy Crown was a champion in every way, because his conformation, too, was flawless.

At three, he won the Hambletonian, and at four, he captured the Roosevelt International, American Trotting Championship and the Realization, retiring with $545,495 earned. He was a classy, perfect racehorse.

Like many successful horses, Speedy Crown wasted no time in showing he would be a sire as well, bestowing upon the trotting world a son named Speedy Somolli in only his second crop. It is hard to describe just how fast a horse Speedy Somolli was. He was a real hot rod. Unlike his sire, however, he lacked the manners to temper and shape his speed. Speedy Somolli was like the proverbial sorcerer's apprentice. He had all

Speedy Crown was one of the best-conformed and best-gaited trotters in history. A son of Speedy Scot and a Florican dam, Speedy Crown became one of the most successful sires and broodmare sires in history. A splendid individual, his major contribution is that he has greatly improved the physical quality and type of the trotter.

the magical skills, but lacked the manners that would have allowed him to maximize his many gifts.

Still, Speedy Somolli trotted in 1:57.2 at two (a world record which never made the history books, because it was broken the same day when Brisco Hanover trotted in 1:57) for Howard Beissinger at Du Quoin and was the breed's first 1:55 trotter in a race a year later, over the same racetrack, in the first heat of the classic 1978 Hambletonian.

This was one of the most competitive Hambletonians in history. The first heat was won in 1:55 by Speedy Somolli, and Florida Pro won the second heat with a courageous first-over mile, also in 1:55. This was the first time the 1:55 barrier had been conquered by racing trotters, and here was a pair of them in a single afternoon! Speedy Somolli finally prevailed after a totally remarkable, day-long, three-heat contest with Florida Pro, Brisco Hanover and Doublemint. Speedy Somolli also won the Yonkers Futurity, but was denied the Triple Crown in the Kentucky Futurity by Doublemint.

I always had the feeling that, like No Nukes and a few other soon-to-be successful sires, Speedy Somolli went to the stud with unfulfilled potential. Gifted with great ability, he was a difficult horse at the gate, where he would take a serious hold, robbing him of some of his vast gift. Speedy Somolli entered the stud after his three-year-old season, joining his sire at Lana Lobell Farms.

His son Baltic Speed, a foal of 1981 in Speedy Somolli's second crop, won the Breeders Crown; his 1982 crop included Kentucky Futurity winner Flak Bait 3,1:55.2 ($880,576), and his 1983 crop featured Hambletonian winner Nuclear Kosmos 3, 1:55.4 ($985,687). Baltic Speed showed his quality in his first crop, getting Peace Corps and Valley Victory in his initial season.

PEACE CORPS—HISTORY'S TOP TROTTING MARE

It is hard to hide or disguise my admiration for Peace Corps, Baltic Speed's outstanding daughter.

From her two-year-old season, when she rose to prominence, winning the Merrie Annabelle and Breeders Crown, through her World Trotting Derby, Kentucky Futurity and Breeders Crown wins at three, and her aged victories in the Elitlopp and the Yonkers International, Peace Corps had an amazing career. Even given the vagaries of currency exchange rates converting her international earnings to U.S. dollars, it is agreed that she won nearly $5 million, making her the leading money-winning Standardbred of all time, regardless of gait or sex.

Peace Corps' brilliance was not fashioned with God-given tools. She is not a pretty mare, being downright plain, with a long, unattractive head. She is also rather homely through the body, and her gait was not that of some of our more noted trotting stars. She did not have a classic stroke, nor did she trot all that cleanly. However, she had wonderful determination and desire. I saw all of her major victories and was continually amazed at her resilience and accomplishment, despite not having the natural abilities one associates with a horse of her caliber.

Peace Corps' race mark of 1:52.4 made her the fastest three-year-old trotting filly in history and was taken barefooted in the second heat of the 1989 World Trotting Derby at Du Quoin. During her illustrious American career, she was superbly conditioned by Tommy Haughton and raced almost exclusively by John Campbell. Mike Lachance drove her to her Merrie Annabelle triumph at two, but Campbell was in the seat for all her remaining wins at two and three.

Her victory in the mile-and-a-quarter Yonkers International in 1991, at age five, for Stig Johansson ranks as one of the most amazing efforts in the history of the breed. Her three-wide rally around the final turn in stakes-record equalling time of 2:28.3h was the stuff of legend. That same year she defeated Europe's best in the Elitlopp at Solvalla in Sweden. In 1992, Peace Corps returned to North America to capture her fourth Breeders Crown. She is the only four-time winner in the initial decade of Breeders Crown competition. In my estimation, no trotting mare of any previous generation has ever had a comparable career.

Peace Corps' pedigree is full of the blood of Star's Pride and Volomite. Baltic Speed, her sire, is line-bred 3x4 to Star's Pride. Her grandsire Speedy Somolli has a Star's Pride dam, and her sire Baltic Speed is from a mare by Carlisle, a grandson of Star's Pride. Peace Corps' dam, Worth Beein', is by Super Bowl, a son of Star's Pride. Worth Beein' also has four crosses to Volomite in her immediate pedigree.

Peace Corps was bred by Stanley Dancer and Rosehild Breeding Farm and raised at Stoner Creek Stud in Kentucky, then sold as a yearling to Lou Guida, who raced her at two and then sold her before her three-year-old season to Swedish owner Bjorn Pettersson. Of historical interest is the fact that nearly all of the horses in Peace Corps' maternal pedigree have strong links to Stanley Dancer. Dancer raced Super Bowl, the sire of her dam, and Noble Victory, the sire of her second dam. He also trained all three of Peace Corps' first three dams!

Peace Corps' maternal pedigree is full of championship females. Super Bowl is the most outstanding male representative of a very successful family of females, including the Hambletonian winner Kerry Way and her daughter, the international star Classical Way. Peace Corps' second dam Aunt Hilda is by Noble Victory, a son of the Hambletonian-winning Star's Pride filly Emily's Pride. Peace Corps' third dam, Worth Seein, 3,T1:58, by Worthy Boy, was a world champion trotting filly at three for Dancer. Looking even further back into her maternal lineage, Peace Corps traces directly to the legendary Miss Bertha Dillon in the most successful branch of the breed's largest and most successful family. (See Medio Maternal Family) It is no wonder that such a great filly emerged from such a splendid maternal background.

VALLEY VICTORY WON EARLY ADMIRERS

Peace Corps was not the only star of Baltic Speed's first crop. While the brilliant filly was winning the Breeders Crown distaff event, Baltic Speed's son Valley Victory was winning the colt division.

Valley Victory first caught the attention of observers when he won at The Red Mile earlier that same fall, trotting the final quarter in :27.1 in a late closer for Bill O'Donnell.

Trotters don't often close up in 27 seconds at any level and when a green two-year-old did it, everyone took notice.

His Breeders Crown victory for owner Arlene Traub set the stage for what should have been a successful three-year-old season. He started his undefeated sophomore campaign winning several New Jersey Sires Stakes and he also captured the Yonkers Trot in 1:58.3h for trainer Steve Elliott and driver O'Donnell. At that time, only Mack Lobell had a faster Yonkers Trot win. Valley Victory had only 14 lifetime starts, winning 11 of

Valley Victory became one of the siring stars of the late 20th century. A world champion race colt at two when he won the Breeders Crown for Bill O'Donnell, the son of Baltic Speed has made a dramatic impact on world trotting. His get are long-barrelled, clean-going and extremely determined. Valley Victory hails from one of the leading maternal families, tracing to the foundation mare Mamie.

them. All three of his losses were early, at two.

However, illness on the very eve of the Hambletonian forced him to miss the remaining classics, and a major interest in the horse was sold in the fall of that season to a syndicate headed by the late Tony Pedone and George Segal, for stud duty at Southwind Farms in New Jersey.

Bred by New Jersey breeder William Weaver's Valley High Stable, Valley Victory was a gifted horse with speed and gait and he, too, went to the breeding shed with unrealized potential. His early stud career is full of exciting promise; his first crop, foals of 1991, includes World Trotting Derby, Yonkers Trot and Kentucky Futurity winner Bullville Victory 3,1:53.1 ($759,285) and the Hambletonian winner Victory Dream, 3,1:53.2 ($1,016,537), a gifted and courageous colt who also won heats of the World Trotting Derby and Kentucky Futurity. Merrie Annabelle winner Armbro Monarch 3,1:54.3 ($670,374) was the top money winning filly, followed closely by the fast and impeccably-bred Armbro Mascara 4,1:53 ($100,903).

His second crop, foals of 1992, featured the Peter Haughton-winning colt Donerail 2,1:55.4, and filly stars such as Breeders Crown winner (twice) Lookout Victory 3,1:54.3 and New Jersey Sire Stakes winner Lifelong Victory 3,1:54.1. His third crop, foals of 1993, feature the Peter Haughton-winning Dancer's Victory 2,1:57, Valley Victory stake winner

Lindy Lane 2,1:56 and Mr. Vic 2,1:57.1. He also sired impressive fillies in this crop, including Breeders Crown winner Continentalvictory 2,1:55.3 and Act Of Grace 2,1:55.3.

There are some parallels here to the earlier discussion of common crosses to Hal Dale that have produced such dramatic results with Cam Fella, No Nukes and company. The same can be observed with respect to the Speedy Scot, Speedy Crown, Speedy Somolli sire line. The point is what occurred in the Hal Dale line by doubling up of Hal Dale blood from separate branches of the same sire family has also occurred in this male line by doubling up to Star's Pride. The important point of this example is that the strongest ancestor in the pedigree is the one which has been doubled. It is a necessary element of inbreeding that you inbreed to strength.

Speedy Somolli is a definite Star's Pride type, and physically is much more representative of the male line of his dam than that of the bigger, stronger Speedy Scot-Speedy Crown males. This is noteworthy, because it is his sire line that appears destined to last. He has also become a successful broodmare sire, since such trotters as American Winner, Pine Chip, CR Kay Suzie, and Giant Force are all from Speedy Somolli dams.

For all of Speedy Crown's great success, including champion sons such as Hambletonian winners Prakas and Armbro Goal, World Trotting Derby winner Royal Prestige, Dexter Cup winner Defiant Yankee, and the precocious Crowning Point, the Speedy Crown legacy appears to be funneled into this one male line branch, although it would not surprise anyone to see a grandson or great-grandson of Speedy Crown pop out with an excellent showing sometime in the next decade.

I have always found it interesting that Speedy Somolli's most successful son, Baltic Speed, has a dam by Carlisle, a grandson of Star's Pride. Valley Victory, Baltic Speed's top son, is out of a mare by Bonefish, another grandson of Star's Pride, thereby tripling the Star's Pride influence on this pedigree. Speedy Somolli's leading money-winning son, Mr. Lavec 3,1:54.3. ($1,985,998) is from a mare by Allen Hanover, a son of Super Bowl, which again triples the Star's Pride influence

This is the same theme developed with success in the Hal Dale line when the strongest ancestor was doubled and sometimes tripled in the pedigree.

This sort of linebreeding has been part and parcel of successful horse breeding for years. Many of the ancestors of these horses were stallions who were inbred or linebred in a significant way, including both Star's Pride and Speedy Scot in this particular instance.

THE SIRE LINE OF PINE CHIP

Speedy Scot's laurels do not rest singularly with his son, Speedy Crown. This male line is also responsible for Pine Chip, one of the most gifted trotting horses in history.

One of Speedy Scot's most enigmatic offspring was the pure-gaited but erratic Arnie Almahurst. Arnie was a big, powerful horse who very much resembled his sire Speedy Scot. Trained by Gene Riegle, Arnie Almahurst had a wonderful gait, but also inherited his sire's strong-willed attitude. After a bad gate experience at two, Arnie was a poor post horse throughout his career. He was the favorite for the 1973 Hambletonian, but made a costly break after the first quarter in the first heat. Arnie Almahurst was another horse who went to stud with something left to prove. His T1:57.2 record, taken in a Red Mile time trial for Joe O'Brien the week before Arnie won the 1973 Kentucky Futurity, was no indication of the horse's true ability.

Arnie Almahurst was at stud for nine seasons at Castleton's Florida and Ohio farms before his death, but in that short time frame, he sired many stakes winners, headed by a quartet of stakes-winning colts. His siring feats are rather remarkable, because he never bred a big book of mares.

The first Arnie to succeed was the world champion Florida Pro 3, 1:55; the second was the World Trotting Derby winner Diamond Exchange 4,1:55; the third was the brilliantly fast Arndon 3,T1:54 and finally, there was the classics-winning Power Seat 3,1:55.4. Florida Pro, who stood at Hanover Shoe Farms before his export to Sweden, sired the $1.7 million-plus winner Sugarcane Hanover, 4, 1:54.3 while still in the U.S., but he was not a horse destined to leave a dramatic impact on American bloodstock. Diamond Exchange and Power Seat did not fare well either, while at stud in the U.S., as each failed to produce a single son who could compete at the higher stakes levels. Arndon, however, was a different story.

The late trainer-driver Ned Bower told this writer that Arndon was the fastest trotter that ever lived and predicted that one day Arndon would sire a trotter so fast that people would not believe it. Bower, an astute trainer and developer of champion trotters, could not have been more prophetic.

Speed is a valuable tool for a stallion—and Arndon had it. He also suffered from terrible unsoundness most of his life. The day he trotted in 1:54 for Delvin Miller in a Red Mile time trial, he lugged badly the entire mile. Although he rarely took a sound step, Arndon was always capable of extraordinary speed. Bower reported that Arndon could trot an eighth in 12 seconds on demand!

Arndon's sometimes spectacular, but wholly unpredictable racetrack career did not attract much attention to him as a stallion candidate and, therefore, he was eventually exported to Italy.

In 1989, Arndon was bred to the Speedy Somolli mare Pine Speed by breeders Fred Kayne, Robert Muh and Sig Wolkomir (the KMW Stable), and the foal was named Pine Chip. Breeding a Speedy Somolli mare to Arndon might seem like throwing gas on an open flame. It can generate a lot of heat, but can be very dangerous if not managed properly!

Pine Chip, trained masterfully by Chuck Sylvester, was unraced at two,

Pine Chip was developed by trainer Chuck Sylvester and became the fastest trotter in history with a T1:51 effort at The Red Mile in 1994 for John Campbell, the same year he also set a half-mile track world record of 1:54 at Delaware in a race. A son of Arndon, Pine Chip traces to Speedy Scot through his paternal grandsire Arnie Almahurst.

but rose through the ranks at three to become one of the fastest racing trotters in history with a mark of 1:52.3 taken in a heat of the 1993 Kentucky Futurity, a race where he trotted both heats faster than 1:53 for John Campbell. He is the only trotter ever to do that. On the day Pine Chip won the Futurity, ending American Winner's Triple Crown bid, he likely could have trotted below 1:51, such was the ease of his victory.

At four, Pine Chip returned to the races and, although he did not totally recapture the magical form he displayed late in his three-year-old season, he did trot in 1:51 in a Red Mile time trial for John Campbell. He also raced in 1:52.4, a world race mark for older males, in winning The Nat Ray at The Meadowlands, and lowered the world half-mile mark to an astounding 1:54 in a race at Delaware, Ohio, during the 1994 Grand Circuit meeting just two weeks ahead of his 1:51 effort at Lexington. Pine Chip was the fulfillment of Ned Bower's prophecy, and was Trotter of the Year in both 1993 and 1994.

Pine Chip has a linebred 4x4 generation cross to Star's Pride and a 3x4 linebred cross to Speedy Scot, since both Arndon and Speedy Somolli trace paternally to the "Castleton Cannonball." It is important to note, too, that the linebred cross to Speedy Scot is in different branches of the Speedy Scot male lineage. Arndon is a grandson of Speedy Scot through

Arnie Almahurst, and Speedy Somolli, sire of Pine Chip's dam, is a son of Speedy Crown. This, again, is a repetition of a common theme, that of linking up male lineages from different branches of the same sire line.

On the other hand, Pine Chip's common cross to Star's Pride is completely maternal, since it appears on the dam's side of both Arndon (Super Bowl dam) and Speedy Somolli (Star's Pride dam).

Pine Chip resembles his grandsire Arnie Almahurst more than any other horse in his pedigree. He is a scaled-down version of Arnie, had Arnie's pure gait and a speed-on-speed pedigree. He got all the best aspects of both Arndon and Speedy Somolli, two of the fastest trotters ever, and none of their worst.

THE LINE THROUGH SPEEDY COUNT

Speedster also sired Speedy Count 3,1:58.4, a major two-year player on the Grand Circuit for Billy Haughton in 1963 and 1964. Speedy Count could not go with the world champion Ayres at three, but he was a very good trotter, and found a useful home in the stud barn at Hanover Shoe Farms before his eventual exportation to Germany.

Speedy Count sired two Hambletonian winners in Steve Lobell and Burgomeister. He also produced the great mare Delmonica Hanover, and is the sire of Matina Hanover, dam of Mack Lobell. But it is Speedy Count's son, Dream Of Glory, which carries this branch of the Speedster family.

A world champion racehorse, Dream Of Glory 3,1:57.2 ($473,316) went to stud at Armstrong Brothers in Canada following his racing days in the barn of his Ohio breeder Leo Soehnlen. He sired a number of successful trotters in Canada and is acquiring a considerable reputation as a broodmare sire.

Dream Of Glory's daughters, although still very young, have already produced the world champion colt Wesgate Crown 2,T1:55.1; 4,1:54.3 and Breeders Crown champions Earl and Lifetime Dream. They also provide a productive nick with Canada's leading trotting sire, Balanced Image.

The other branch of Peter Scott's family is that leading from Scotland and his sons, including Darnley and Hoot Mon. Each of these horses, most notably Hoot Mon, were exceptional broodmare sires, but neither left a son to carry on the male lineage. The death blow may have been delivered when Hoot Mon's most accomplished son, Scott Frost, went sterile after only a short time at stud. Hoot Mon was a Hambletonian and Kentucky Futurity winner and produced three Hambletonian-winning sons: Scott Frost, Blaze Hanover and A.C.'s Viking.

Hoot Mon's lasting legacy is as a broodmare sire, since his fillies have produced some of the breed's most luminous stars, including Nevele Pride and Armbro Flight.

THE PETER VOLO FAMILY—TROTTERS & PACERS

In 1911, only two years after Peter Scott was foaled, Peter The Great sired a son named Peter Volo from the famous Nervolo mare Nervolo Belle, who was also dam of the brilliant undefeated filly Volga E.

Peter Volo was a somewhat coarse, black stallion who was campaigned by Thomas W. Murphy and came along when Peter The Great was 16. It was not that Peter The Great lacked celebrity at this point, for his fillies included some of the sport's best. In fact, his fastest offspring were fillies, and would later prove their excellence as broodmares. For instance, a Peter The Great mare was the dam of Greyhound.

But the knockers felt that Peter The Great lacked the siring power to produce a son who could carry on his male line, a knock we are still quick to put on a horse in modern times.

Peter Volo was a different case, however, and his stardom on the racetrack foretold a solid career as a sire. He helped build on the status that Guy Axworthy had brought to Walnut Hall Farm and he made a perfect consort for the mares already in residence at the historic Kentucky nursery.

PETER VOLO & MISS BERTHA DILLON

Peter Volo's early success in the stud came as a result of his matings with the brilliant filly, Miss Bertha Dillon, herself a racing champion, and founder of a famous maternal family that is unparalleled in its excellence.

Peter Volo and Miss Bertha Dillon had 11 foals, and their offspring and the descendants flowing from them have provided the breed with some of its more famous performers. Peter Volo and Miss Bertha Dillon's 1924 foal, Sandy Flash, for instance, is the sire of classics winner Bill Gallon in a branch of sires that produced Hambletonian champion Harlan Dean and the successful midwestern sire and broodmare sire B.F. Coaltown.

Later matings of Peter Volo and Miss Bertha Dillon produced the first trio of sibling 2:00 trotters, Charlotte Hanover 3,T1:59 1/2; Hambletonian winner Hanover's Bertha 3,T1:59 1/2, and Miss Bertha Hanover 4,T2:00. Each of these mares founded significant families of her own and made a huge imprint on the breed. As noted in the Maternal Family Study which appears elsewhere in this book, the Miss Bertha Dillon descendants have included, at one time or another, the fastest horses in the history of the breed at both gaits.

In 1926, the San Francisco mare Cita Frisco had a son born from a mating with Peter Volo. The son was Volomite, who raced on the trot in the powerful stable of William H. Cane. He was the second- or third-string horse in that stable in 1929, the best being the ill-fated Walter Dear, winner of both the Hambletonian and the Kentucky Futurity for driver Walter Cox before being exported to Germany.

However, Volomite followed his sire into residency at Walnut Hall Farm, standing next to Guy Axworthy. He eventually was joined by Scotland, giving Walnut Hall a troika of siring stars.

To imagine the stranglehold that Walnut Hall Farm had on the industry at that time, one would have to imagine a single farm concurrently standing Meadow Skipper, Speedy Crown and Star's Pride. No farm before or since has been the parallel of Walnut Hall Farm at that point in history.

Volomite's siring career began with some success at both gaits. His daughter Princess Peg won a heat of the 1934 Hambletonian and won the Kentucky Futurity for driver Sep Palin. But much of Volomite's early success was on the pace, with his sons Chief Counsel and Blackstone.

In 1940, however, when bred to the Peter The Brewer mare Warwell Worthy, Volomite produced a handsome colt named Worthy Boy for breeder Henry Warwick, the same breeder who would later produce Worthy Boy's talented son Star's Pride.

Warwell Worthy was a well-bred mare, since she was a half-sister to the world champion trotting mare Rosalind. Therefore, Worthy Boy had the paternal blood of Peter The Great and Peter Volo, coupled with the maternal influences of one of the breed's best families. This has always intrigued me, because this meant that Peter Volo, Worthy Boy's grandsire, is from the same maternal family as Worthy Boy himself. Nervolo Belle, the dam of Peter Volo, is the fifth dam of Worthy Boy. (See Mambrino Beauty Maternal Family) Worthy Boy has a single claim to lasting fame, but oh what a claim it is! He is the sire of Star's Pride, a horse responsible for a magnificent trotting dynasty.

Star's Pride, raced by E. Roland Harriman and Lawrence Sheppard, was an accomplished racehorse, a contemporary of stablemate Florican on the track. However, Star's Pride far outdistanced Florican in the breeding shed, getting eight Hambletonian winners and ten Kentucky Futurity champions while in stud at Hanover Shoe Farms, those champions including such accomplished trotters as Nevele Pride, Lindy's Pride, Kerry Way, Armbro Flight and Super Bowl.

THE STAR'S PRIDE LEGACY

Star's Pride was a foal of 1947, and after racing for Harry Pownall went into stud at Hanover Shoe Farms where he found a great number of outstanding mares awaiting him.

One of the interesting legacies of the Star's Pride line is the ability of its descendants to stay on the trot through interference. Star's Pride hit his shins, and none of the leading Star's Pride horses were clean-going, but they were very determined and successful.

Such was the case in 1965 when the Hoot Mon mare Thankful delivered a Star's Pride colt eventually named Nevele Pride. No better racing

Star's Pride became the most successful trotting sire in history, siring eight Hambletonian winners and ten Kentucky Futurity champions. Bred by Henry Warwick, Star's Pride also left an indelible mark as a broodmare sire. Super Bowl was his most successful siring son.

trotter ever lived! Nevele Pride was the first trotter to beat 1:55. He was a spectacular performer, winning everything in sight for trainer-driver Stanley Dancer. He was a world champion every year he raced (2,1:58.2; 3,1:56.3) and retired as the fastest trotter ever, eclipsing Greyhound's long-standing world mark in a 1:54.4 time-trial effort at Indianapolis as a four-year-old.

Following Nevele Pride, Star's Pride sired Lindy's Pride, who also stormed through the Triple Crown races, this time for Howard Beissinger. Lindy's Pride was followed by the $1 million-winning gelding, Savoir. Nevele Pride and Lindy's Pride both went to stud in Kentucky, with Nevele Pride taking up residence at Stoner Creek Stud and Lindy's Pride beginning at Almahurst Farm.

With Star's Pride's advancing age came one of his greatest champions, Super Bowl, foaled in 1969 in Kentucky at Stoner Creek Stud and sold by them as a yearling. It could not be known at the time, but the destiny of the Star's Pride male line would rest with Super Bowl and not with Nevele Pride or Lindy's Pride.

Super Bowl was a wonderful racehorse who, in fact, was much better as a three-year-old than he was at two, a trait seen in some of his notable

Super Bowl is the most successful son of trotting kingpin Star's Pride. A tall, and athletic racehorse, Super Bowl has produced nearly a dozen $1 million earners and six Hambletonian winners. A foal of 1969, the Hanover Shoe Farm stallion crossed best with mares by his contemporary Speedy Crown.

offspring. He captured the Triple Crown in 1972—the last trotter to accomplish the sweep of the Yonkers Trot, the Hambletonian and the Kentucky Futurity. He took his 1:56.2 world mark in the Hambletonian at Du Quoin for Stanley Dancer.

Unlike Nevele Pride and Lindy's Pride, Super Bowl is a big, rangy horse, who had a wonderful round stroke and a powerfully built frame that propelled him to the heights of his division. In his physical type, he embodies his broodmare sire Rodney, one of the more robust sires in history.

Super Bowl was also a breeding departure from most of Star's Pride's other accomplished offspring, since he did not have a drop of the Hoot Mon blood on which Star's Pride seemed to flourish. Star's Pride on Hoot Mon mares was that era's most effective cross. Super Bowl, however, is out of a Rodney mare.

This observation must be tempered by the fact that Hoot Mon and Rodney are from the same male line. Hoot Mon is by Scotland, and Rodney is by Spencer Scott, a son of Scotland. Lindy's Pride, coincidentally, is out of a mare by Spencer Scott. It is clear now that the Rodney male line had more going for it than that of Hoot Mon, whose male and female contributions have been diminished by history's cruel stare.

But while the blood may be the same, the physical appearance is remarkably different. Ayres, Nevele Pride and Lindy's Pride were all smaller than Super Bowl. Nevele Pride, particularly, always looked big when fashioning those world record miles through his three Horse of the Year seasons, but in truth he was barely 15.2 hands and was extremely short-coupled.

Like most of the Star's Pride offspring, Nevele Pride was a horse who touched his shins throughout his career, particularly on a half-mile track. His short-coupled frame also betrayed Nevele Pride in the stud, as trotting horse trainers and owners flocked to the quicker, bigger, stronger (and longer) Super Bowl and Speedy Crown offspring.

The fact that Nevele Pride's stud career lagged has always puzzled me, because he was one of the most sensational colt trotters in the history of the breed. He won 57 races! Yet, he was only an average sire who could not reproduce his own exciting brand of speed. Nevele Pride did not sire a sub-1:56 trotter in a stud career that spanned 23 years at Stoner Creek Stud!

Like Bret Hanover, though, Nevele Pride represented the best blood available and was shut out on the many top mares that carried pedigrees similar to his. The best mares of his time, the Star's Pride x Hoot Mon crossed females, went to, and prospered with, horses like Speedy Crown.

None of Nevele Pride's colts had his quickness or tenacity. His most accomplished son, the Hambletonian winner Bonefish 3,1:58.1, never raced on a half-mile track. Bonefish stood at Castleton Farm for most of his stud career and was an exceptional filly sire, including among them world champions Winky's Gill and Filet Of Sole, and Hambletonian Oaks winners Nan's Catch and Conch. He also sired the dams of Valley Victory and Supergill. Bonefish's sons, for the most part, were not successful. His only quality males were the $1-million winner Firm Tribute 3,1:54.3, the European star Sea Cove and Beacon Course winner Netted 3,1:56.2.

The only one of Nevele Pride's sons who appeared to have his championship fire was the handsome Incredible Nevele 3,1:56, but he fizzled at three after a world championship two-year-old season that saw him trot in 2:00h at Delaware for Glen Garnsey, the first juvenile trotting performance of its kind. Nevele Pride did find some fame during his stud career, however, because his offspring were excellent distance horses and became highly sought-after in Europe. Among Nevele Pride's expatriate notables were Madison Avenue (sire of Meadow Road), Zoot Suit, Pershing, Snack Bar and Messerschmitt.

Nevele Pride also earned a reputation as a broodmare sire. His daughters produced such successful stars as Hambletonian winner Duenna 3,

1:56.3 and World Trotting Derby winners Royal Prestige 3,1:55.1 and Diamond Exchange 4,1:55.

It appears the future of the Star's Pride line rests with Super Bowl and his sons.

Super Bowl's siring career can be summed up in two phases. The first phase of his career at Hanover Shoe Farms covers the time period from his first foal crop in 1974 through the end of that decade. During this period, Super Bowl sired such performers as Kentucky Futurity winner Texas 3,1:57.3; world champion juvenile Brisco Hanover 2,1:57; Hambletonian winner Legend Hanover 3,1:56.1; Kentucky Futurity champion Final Score 3,1:56.3; successful sire Worthy Bowl 2,1:58; Hambletonian winner Speed Bowl 3,1:56.2; Yonkers Trot winner Joie De Vie 3,1:56.3 and world champion Express Ride 4,1:53.

All of these horses had notable accomplishments, most especially the well-bred Texas, who sired the $1 million-winning mare Grade's Singing while at stud in the U.S. and the two-time Elitlopp winner Copiad after being exported. None of Super Bowl's other early champions, however, look to have the staying power to carry on the Super Bowl line.

That power appears to come from the second half of Super Bowl's stud career, or post-1983. Anyone looking at these two periods in Super Bowl's siring career would rate the second group a much stronger and more attractive bunch.

SPEEDY CROWN MARES WITH SUPER BOWL

Beginning with the brilliant millionaire filly Davidia Hanover 4,1:56, Super Bowl started getting more Speedy Crown mares. The string of champion trotters by Super Bowl from Speedy Crown dams includes such stars as Hambletonian winners Probe 3, 1:54.3; Giant Victory 3,1:54.4; and Tagliabue 3,1:54.4; the two-year-old star Cumin 3,Q1:57.1; Breeders Crown winner and world champion sire Royal Troubador 2,1:57.1 and World Trotting Derby winner Somatic 3,1:53.

The cross of Speedy Crown mares to Super Bowl appears far superior, however, to the mating of Super Bowl mares to Speedy Crown. The only high-level son of Speedy Crown from a Super Bowl mare is Peter Haughton champ Giant Chill 3,1:55.4. This cross has been responsible for quite a few filly stars, though, including the Breeders Crown winners Armbro Fling 3,1:55.3 and Armbro Flori 3,1:57, as well as the Breeders Crown and Hambletonian Oaks-winning Gleam 3,1:55.3. However, the numbers for Super Bowl mares bred to Speedy Crown do not even begin to match the performance of Speedy Crown mares with Super Bowl.

There are only two sons of Super Bowl who reached stardom that are not from Speedy Crown-line mares, but each is a very significant horse. The first was Napoletano, who is from a mare by Noble Victory. The second is Supergill, who is from the world champion Bonefish mare Winky's Gill.

NAPOLETANO—A TRUE CLASSIC TROTTER

Napoletano was a true classic trotter, winning the World Trotting Derby, Kentucky Futurity and the Elitlopp, Europe's top mile test for older horses. He got a mark at three of 1:53.2 and won nearly $2.5 million as an international star. His defeat of Mack Lobell in the 1987 Kentucky Futurity, when he trotted the final quarter in :26.1, is one of history's outstanding trotting performances. Napoletano is Super Bowl's leading money-winning son and is a tall, athletic-looking dark bay horse with a wonderful reach and stroke. He had some unsoundness due to a fracture at two, but developed throughout his three-year-old season, closing the gap between himself and arch-rival Mack Lobell. He first up-ended Mack Lobell in the World Trotting Derby at Du Quoin. The general feeling at the time was that Napoletano had won the Trotting Derby only because Mack Lobell jumped offstride. In truth, however, Napoletano was every bit the trotter that Mack Lobell was at that time. For the month of September and early October in 1987, Napoletano was as good a trotter as ever lived.

Napoletano's pedigree is of great interest because both his sire and dam are linebred to Volomite. Thus, Napoletano has the same relationship to Volomite that a pacing horse such as Cam Fella has to Hal Dale—he is double-linebred to a prominent ancestor.

Super Bowl is by Star's Pride, a grandson of Volomite. His second dam Bewitch is by Volomite. On the maternal side, Napoletano's dam Noble Sarah is by Noble Victory, a grandson of Volomite, and Napoletano's third dam Victory Miss is by Victory Song, a son of Volomite. In addition, Napoletano has a 2x4 generational linebred cross to Star's Pride, and a 3x3 inbred cross to Rodney. Napoletano also has a deep maternal heritage, since his fifth dam is a sister to Peter Volo. (See Mambrino Beauty Maternal Family.)

SUPERGILL—PEDIGREE AND PERFORMANCE

Supergill is another of Super Bowl's sons with a strong license to succeed as a sire. He also has a 2x4 generational linebred cross to Star's Pride. Unlike Napoletano, however, Supergill's common cross to Star's Pride is in the male line of both his sire and dam, which is most unusual in a successful horse.

He is by Super Bowl, a son of Star's Pride, and his dam is by Bonefish, a grandson of Star's Pride. An extremely handsome horse, Supergill was a $500,000 yearling. His attractiveness to yearling buyers was well-deserved, for he is one of the best bred and best looking trotters in history. Supergill's dam, Winky's Gill, was a world champion in her racing days, trotting in 1:57 at two and in 1:55.2 at three for trainer-driver Hakan Wallner. This mare, one of trotting's super-elite, has a venerable pedigree, as she is inbred 3x3 to Speedster and is from the maternal family tracing from the vaunted Lady Ann Reed.

Winky's Gill is another mare for whom there are not enough superlatives. A beautiful, dark bay mare with a wonderful gait, flawless conformation and manageable racing personality, she was the best of the many fine fillies sired by Bonefish. In addition to being the dam of Supergill, Winky's Gill is the dam of the fine Armbro Goal filly Winky's Goal 3,1:54.4 ($844,924), exported at four by her Italian owners.

Supergill, therefore, brought a lot of armor to the battle and earned a 1:53.3 mark at three, taken at Springfield for trainer-driver Berndt Lindstedt. It was the fastest trotting mile of 1988. Bothered by foot soreness during his racing career in which he won $664,194, Supergill enjoyed early successes in the stud at Castleton Farm with Speedy Crown-line mares. After six seasons in the U.S., Supergill was exported to Italy, joining Napoletano as an expatriate.

AMERICAN WINNER—SUPER BOWL'S FASTEST SON

By almost any yardstick, however, American Winner is Super Bowl's finest racing son to date.

Victorious in two of the three legs of the 1993 Triple Crown, American Winner was a great-gaited horse who very much resembled the male-line blood of his dam, who was by Speedy Somolli. In his appearance and gait, he was Speedy Somolli reincarnated.

Like Napoletano and Supergill, American Winner carries the same 2x4 generation linebred cross to Star's Pride: He is by Super Bowl, and his dam BJ's Pleasure is a daughter of Speedy Somolli, who has a Star's Pride dam.

It would be hard to improve on American Winner's racetrack presentation. His stakes records in the Yonkers Trot (1:56.2h) and the Hambletonian (1:53.1), both for driver Ron Pierce, are strong barometers of his greatness.

American Winner came to the Kentucky Futurity, the final leg of his Triple Crown quest, compromised by injury, but it is doubtful that any trotter could have beaten Pine Chip that day. American Winner took his 1:52.3 mark in a courageous, parked-out effort at Syracuse in the Zweig Memorial (over Pine Chip) and won just under $1.3 million.

Like Napoletano and Supergill, he also hails from a strong maternal family; his dam, BJ's Pleasure 3,1:59.4f is an older half-sister to world champion Mack Lobell. This mare also produced two other quality trotters. Her first foal was the stakes-winning Super Pleasure 3,1:58f ($827,238) and her second foal was the Peter Haughton-winning BJ's Mac 2,1:57.4 ($376,210). This is the Miss Bertha Hanover branch of the vast Medio maternal family, the same tribe which also produced Peace Corps. American Winner's stud career, as well as that of his two accomplished full brothers, should be interesting.

FROM VOLOMITE TO MACK LOBELL AND BALANCED IMAGE

Among Volomite's most successful matings were those with the Nelson Dillon mare Evensong, one of the breed's most productive females. Her son Volo Song, by Volomite, is still acknowledged by those who saw him as one of the best-gaited trotters who ever lived.

Volo Song died before his stud career ever got underway, however, and it was left to his full brother Victory Song, foaled in 1943, to carry this branch of the family into history.

Victory Song raced for Castleton Farm and trainer-driver Sep Palin, and was the first of many post-World War II heroes. Standing at Castleton, his overall stud career lacked its anticipated success, although his daughters have been successful broodmares, having produced the Triple Crown champion Speedy Scot, among others.

The Victory Song line comes to the end of the 20th century with a question mark next to it. Although the Victory Song male line has had success in Europe, most notably in France, the North American future of this branch of the Volomite sire line appears to rest with the Canadian sire Balanced Image, a son of Noble Gesture and a great-grandson of Victory Song.

One of Victory Song's finest sons, Noble Victory 4,1:55.3, was a wonderful colt trotter, but like many of the Victory Songs, he was a light-framed, small horse who was difficult to condition. His dam, the Hambletonian and Kentucky Futurity winner Emily's Pride 3,T1:58, insured that Noble Victory possessed one of history's deepest pedigrees. Both his sire and his dam were racing stars with royal blood in their trotting veins. (See Midnight Maternal Family)

Noble Victory stood his entire stud career at Lana Lobell Farms. For a horse with such a pedigree and ample opportunity, his siring abilities must be appraised as falling below expectation. He was not a fertile horse, and his best high-profile performer was the brilliant two-year-old Noble Gesture 2, 1:59.1.

Noble Gesture raced for his breeder K.D. Owen of Houston, Texas and was a spectacular colt trotter for trainer Sonny Graham. Although very fast, he was a horse who was very hard on himself. He was nervous and high-strung and was his own worst enemy, so tightly wound that, as a stallion, he could not be turned out alone in his stud paddock for fear of injuring himself. He had to be exercised by a handler.

Noble Gesture stood at Castleton Farm and sired several good trotters, one of them being the 1979 foal Mystic Park, who had a brief flirtation with greatness both as a racehorse and sire. Early in his three-year-old form, after his Yonkers Trot win, Mystic Park was conceded to be the best trotter in the land. But by Hambletonian Day, his bubble had already burst.

Mystic Park made a lot of friends while racing, and also took up resi-

Balanced Image, shown in his colt days for Steve Waller at Indianapolis, became a successful sire in Canada. A tall, rangy, athletic horse, Balanced Image provided trotting breeders a much-needed dosage of his Volomite male line.

dence at Lana Lobell Farms. He wasted no time showing that his racetrack prowess could be transmitted, as his very first crop included a smallish brown colt named Mack Lobell who would one day become the fastest and richest racing American-bred male trotter in history.

Trained by Chuck Sylvester, Mack Lobell first became the fastest two-year-old in history, trotting in 1:55.3 at The Red Mile in 1986 for driver John Campbell. The following year, he won two of three legs of the Triple Crown, setting stakes records in the Yonkers Trot and Hambletonian. Only a monstrous effort by Napoletano in the historic 1987 Kentucky Futurity denied him trotting's highest prize.

Between the Hambletonian and World Trotting Derby, Mack Lobell ventured to Illinois and trotted in 1:52.1 in a heat of the Review Stake at the Illinois State Fair's lightning mile track. Sold later to Swedish interests, he went on to have a successful European campaign and retired as the richest American-bred trotter ever, with earnings just short of $4 million. His stud career in Sweden began with considerable success, and he was returned to the U.S. for the 1996 breeding season after siring six crops in Europe.

Mystic Park's moment in the sun, however, was short-lived, as he was beset with all sorts of medical problems that effectively stopped his American stud career. He, too, was eventually sold for export after several seasons. He did produce another top colt in the 1990 Kentucky Futurity winner Star Mystic, but that colt died from a twisted intestine less than a year after winning the Futurity.

The best chance for the continuation of the Noble Victory male line seems to rest with Balanced Image, a son of Noble Gesture foaled in

1978, and trained and raced by the late Glen Garnsey. Most of the off-spring of Noble Gesture were fast horses, but, like their sire, were nervous, hard-to-manage horses.

Such was the case with Balanced Image. He was an adventure to train or jog, because he pulled badly. Unlike the rest of the members of this sire family, Balanced Image is a wonderful individual, with great size, power and presence. His record of 1:58.4 was taken at three in winning a Kentucky Sires Stake. At four, he won the American-National Maturity. Garnsey recommended Balanced Image to breeders right from the start, because he alone knew how fast a horse Balanced Image really was. Garnsey always thought that Balanced Image could have been a 1:55 trotter, despite being unmanageable.

Balanced Image has more than lived up to Garnsey's prophecies, having become one of the most successful trotting sires in the industry. His sons A Go Go Lauxmont, Natural Image, Elitlopp star Billyjojimbob, Breeders Crown winners Earl and Armbro Officer, Beacon Course winner Whiteland Image and Canadian stars Armbro Leader and Armbro Marshall have brought him to the attention of trotting horse breeders everywhere. He certainly has the opportunity to produce a champion trotter to extend his struggling male line, although it is most interesting, given the aggressive nature of the sire line, that Billyjojimbob, Armbro Officer, Whiteland Image, Armbro Leader and Armbro Marshall are all geldings!

FROM VOLOMITE TO MATT'S SCOOTER

One of the unique aspects to Volomite's stud career was his ability to found more than one successful line of pacers to complement his trotting influences. The only other notable sire in history who could parallel this phenomenon was Nibble Hanover, who sired a winner of both the Little Brown Jug (Knight Dream) and the Hambletonian (Miss Tilly).

Volomite's first really successful pacers were Chief Counsel, Blackstone and King's Counsel. Chief Counsel was the world's fastest three-year-old pacer from 1938 to 1951, while Blackstone won the Fox Stake in 1938.

King's Counsel was a contemporary of Adios and waged many memorable battles with Adios that are a unique part of the sport's lore. Its lone representative is the handsome Overtrick, the 1963 Little Brown Jug winner. Overtrick did not leave a son to carry on the Volomite pacing line on the national level, but he did leave his mark on the breed as a prominent broodmare sire. His daughters have produced, among others, the top sire No Nukes and the world champions Falcon Seelster and Trenton.

The major pacing branches of the Volomite family emanate from his 1944 foal, Poplar Byrd and his 1947 foal Sampson Hanover.

Poplar Byrd's claim to fame was his son, the rugged Bye Bye Byrd, a star of the late 1950's and a successful sire who produced a number of high-quality sons. However, none of Bye Bye Byrd's sons sustained the Poplar Byrd male line.

It is not that Bye Bye Byrd lacked depth as a sire, because from the very start of his career he produced many fast, useful horses. Stakes winners such as Nardin's Byrd, Bye And Large, Bye Bye Sam and world champion Entrepreneur p,2,1:56.4 (the sport's first sub-1:57 two-year-old) made it appear as though Bye Bye Byrd would stay around for a long, long time.

Midway in his stud career, Bye Bye Byrd got the wonderful colt pacers Armbro Nesbit p,3,1:56 and Keystone Ore p,3,1:55.2. Both of these horses were outstanding stakes winners. Keystone Ore, particularly, was a handsome, good-gaited horse who had abundant class. However, Armbro Nesbit died after a couple of seasons in the stud at Hanover Shoe Farms, and Keystone Ore's siring career has disappointed.

The one observation to make about Bye Bye Byrd's stud career is that he always had a fondness for Adios-line mares, and many of his better-producing daughters had Adios dams. It seems that whenever I trace a pedigree which has a strong Bye Bye Byrd influence, Adios is never far away. This is particularly interesting because Bye Bye Byrd's dam, the Billy Direct mare Evalina Hanover, was a daughter of a Hal Dale mare named Adieu, who was a full sister to Adios!

The most obvious example of this phenomenon is the Hanover Shoe Farms modern foundation mare Keystone Sandra, dam of four 1:55 pacers, including the midwestern sire Good To See You. This mare, who has produced six 1:58 two-year-olds, is a daughter of Bye Bye Byrd from Keystone Squaw, by Adios.

THE SAMPSON HANOVER LINE

Unlike the Bye Bye Byrd line, however, the Sampson Hanover line is going strong. Sampson Hanover sired Sampson Direct in 1957 and he, in turn, sired Direct Scooter, whose siring strength cannot be discounted.

Direct Scooter, who has stood his entire career at Walnridge Farm in New Jersey, is one of the breed's upper echelon sires, having produced such stalwarts as world champions Matt's Scooter p,3,T1:48.2 and In The Pocket p,3,T1:49.3.

Like Abercrombie and Big Towner, Direct Scooter is a horse whose siring career has been influenced heavily by the availability of Meadow Skipper-line mares. His three-year-old world champion son Matt's Scooter is out of a Meadow Skipper mare and many of his other major stakes winners, such as Scoot Outa Reach, OK Bye, W R H, Tooter Scooter, Armbro Maneuver and Expensive Scooter, are from mares that trace paternally to Meadow Skipper. In The Pocket is from a Tar Heel mare, but his second dam is by Meadow Skipper.

The major difference with Direct Scooter lies in the fact that his paternal and maternal lines are full of trotting blood! His grandsire Sampson

Hanover is a grandson of the trotting foundation mare Isotta, a daughter of Peter The Great. Direct Scooter's dam is by Noble Victory and his subsequent dams are by Scotland and Guy Abbey. The presence of trotting blood in Direct Scooter's pedigree accounts for the tendency of his offspring to be high-going horses in front, as seen most dramatically in Matt's Scooter.

It will be interesting to watch the Direct Scooter male line in the coming decade to see if it can maintain the strong showing it flashed in the 1980's and early 1990's. Matt's Scooter's first crop included the champion filly Freedoms Friend p,2, 1:53.1 ($637,622) and his second crop, foals of 1992, featured the classy, but ill-fated colt Stand Alone p,2,1:52.4.

THE FAMILY OF AXWORTHY

In the 1920's, the trotting world was dominated by the get of Guy Axworthy, a foal of 1902 whom Lamon Harkness tabbed for stud duty at Walnut Hall Farm in the infant years of the Kentucky nursery.

Guy Axworthy became the dominant trotting sire of his time, producing a slate of champion trotters led by the world champions Lee Axworthy and Mr. McElwyn. However, Lee Axworthy, whose T1:58 1/4 mark in 1916 stood for more than 25 years, died after only a couple of seasons in the stud at Castleton Farm.

Mr. McElwyn, raced by the noted trainer Ben White, was also a champion, but he, too, has disappeared from the siring scene, his lone significant contribution being that he sired the dam of Star's Pride.

The Axworthy line is of great interest to historians because it refuses to go away. The demise of this sire line has been predicted for the better part of the last 50 years, but it remains a significant factor in the production of both our modern trotters and several prominent pacing lines.

Let us first examine the Axworthy trotters.

There have been three significant Axworthy male line trotters of note in the past 60 years. The earliest of these was the sport's first 2:00 two-year-old, the fabled Titan Hanover.

Titan Hanover was not only the first 2:00 two-year-old trotter, he also beat the pacers to the punch, by almost a full decade. Titan trotted in 2:00 in 1944, and the first 2:00 two-year-old pacer (Adios Boy p,2,T1:58.3) did not arrive on the scene until 1953. Titan Hanover was a son of Calumet Chuck, who was by the exported Guy Axworthy stallion Truax, and was a handsome horse with a great gait and racing attitude. He also had an impeccable pedigree, since his dam Tisma Hanover was by Peter The Brewer, a son of Peter The Great who was a full brother to Elizabeth, the dam of Greyhound. This is also the immediate family of Nibble Hanover. (See Miss Copeland Maternal Family)

The male-line blood of Titan Hanover, however royal, did not last. His lone notable accomplishment at stud was the Hambletonian winner Hickory Smoke 4,T1:58.2, a sire who fashioned a modestly successful career at Hanover Shoe Farms, but did not leave a son to carry on the family.

The second significant Axworthy-line trotting family to develop was that tracing from Axworthy's 1910 son, Dillon Axworthy. Dillon Axworthy earned a lasting spot in history through his daughter Miss Bertha Dillon, founder of the sport's largest and most successful maternal family. In addition, a number of Dillon Axworthy's other daughters show up in many of the leading maternal families, including such household names as Volga Hanover, Isabel Hanover and Irene Hanover. Duane Hanover, for instance, is from Dorsh Hanover, a daughter of Dillon Axworthy. Irene Hanover is the dam of Sampson Hanover, sire of Sampson Direct.

But Dillon Axworthy also had another brief moment of fame as a sire. He produced the sensational colt trotter Dean Hanover 3,T1:58 1/2, a horse who appears prominently in a great many successful maternal pedigrees, but whose only noteworthy accomplishment as a sire was the ill-fated Hambletonian champion Demon Hanover, T1:59.4.

The only Axworthy trotting blood that has survived the twists and turns of history is that leading from Guy Axworthy's son, Guy McKinney, winner of the inaugural Hambletonian in 1926.

Guy McKinney is the grandsire of Florican, who stood at Castleton Farm and sent forth a large number of good-gaited sons and daughters to populate the sport's leading broodmare bands. The Axworthy line has been praised historically for its purity of gait and the clean physical qualities of the offspring.

Florican was a good representative, for he was a handsome, good-gaited horse. This clean gait and quality of the Axworthys was also obvious in Titan Hanover and in Dean Hanover. But for some reason, these qualities, which should have carried the line, failed to do so, and it was left to Florican alone to shoulder the burden of perpetuating his male line.

Florican sired a number of quality horses, including Florlis 3, 1:57.3, who had the misfortune to be born in the same year as Speedy Scot. Florlis was Speedy Scot's main nemesis at both two and three, and beat Speedy Scot in the opening heat of the 1963 Hambletonian at Du Quoin.

Florlis subsequently stood at Walnut Hall Farm and sired the excellent Flower Child, a U.S. and international star. Flower Child did not find a home at a major farm, and died after a brief and uneventful stud career. Florican also had wonderful fillies, and a Florican mare, Missile Toe, is the dam of super-sire Speedy Crown, one of the purest-gaited and best-conformed champions in history. Much of the excellent physical type of Speedy Crown and his offspring must be attributed to Florican.

In addition to his maternal influences, Florican also sired a horse who would help to sustain the Axworthy male line. That horse was Songcan, a foal of 1969 and a racetrack adversary of none other than Super Bowl, with whom he waged many a memorable battle. Songcan was actually a much faster two-year-old than Super Bowl. I remember, vividly, seeing

Sierra Kosmos is a son of Nearly Perfect, and grandson of Songcan, therefore representing the sole perpetuation of the historic Axworthy male line of trotters. Gifted with tremendous speed, Sierra Kosmos was trained and raced by Rick Beinhauer and trotted in 1:53.4 in 1992.

Songcan defeat Super Bowl and the rest of the top juveniles of 1971 in the Castleton Farm stake at Du Quoin in 2:00 for driver Gilles LaChance. Songcan was a glib-gaited, sure-footed juvenile trotter who had enormous potential.

This great promise went largely unfulfilled at three, since Super Bowl improved so dramatically and Songcan was compromised by illness and injury. At three, Songcan did get a 1:58.3h mark, a world record when made, winning the Old Oaken Bucket at Delaware for his trainer-driver George Sholty. Songcan's great ability found him a home at Pine Hollow Stud in New York following his racing days and sired Nearly Perfect, a foal of 1982.

A handsome, virile-looking horse, Nearly Perfect was the result of a mating which crossed Songcan with the Super Bowl mare Exciting, a descendant of the Kashmary trotting tribe which has produced so many of our past and present trotting stars. (See Maggie H. Maternal Family)

Nearly Perfect earned a mark of 1:55.2 in a heat of the Kentucky Futurity for Mickey McNichol in 1985 and, at four, blossomed into the top trotter in the land, winning the Breeders Crown and the Nat Ray. There is no question that Nearly Perfect could have trotted far below his 1:54 mark at four, but repeated rains washed out a scheduled time trial at Lexington that fall.

Nearly Perfect's promise, however, has been delivered in the stud, as he has already produced one of the most exciting colt trotters of this or any decade, the unbelievably fast Sierra Kosmos 3, 1:53.4.

Sierra Kosmos rose from modest beginnings to be one of the sport's genuine stars of the early 1990's. On the day he took his 1:53.4 mark at Lexington for trainer-driver Rick Beinhauer, Sierra Kosmos set the crowd abuzz with a spectacular opening half in :54.3! He also trotted in 1:56.3h at Delaware, and had 15 wins in only 30 lifetime starts at two and three, winning $558,710. Sierra Kosmos' light frame can be attributed to the fact that his dam is by Noble Victory, who, like most of the Victory Song trotters, was a small-boned horse.

Nearly Perfect has also shown the ability to deliver champion fillies and mares, getting the Breeders Crown champion Imperfection 4,1:54.1; the exported Kentucky Futurity winner Whiteland Janice 3, 1:54.1; and the world champion Sunbird Groovey, 1:55 in his early crops.

Of particular interest to trotting historians is the fact that Nearly Perfect and several of his most successful offspring, including Sierra Kosmos, Imperfection and Sunbird Groovey, all share the same maternal roots— a very rare and interesting occurrence. (See Maggie H. Maternal Family)

Sierra Kosmos has a unique opportunity to prolong the Axworthy sire line, as his initial books at Hanover Shoe Farms attracted a large number of the sport's best trotting mares. He is an attractive outcross for many mares, including those by Speedy Crown and Super Bowl and their sons.

THE AXWORTHY PACERS

While the Axworthy trotters have found renewed life in the past decade, the Axworthy pacers have not fared as well.

The Axworthy pacing line developed from Nibble Hanover's 1945 son Knight Dream, who produced the handsome Duane Hanover in 1952. Duane Hanover, who stood at Walnut Hall Farm, had some limited success, siring the good colt pacer True Duane, conqueror of Bret Hanover in the 1966 American Pacing Classic.

Duane Hanover's only lasting claim to fame is as the sire of the dam of Abercrombie. Duane Hanover is given some of the credit for Abercrombie's success, since it is his attractive physical type that Abercrombie inherited and that has proven so useful in re-awakening the Adios sire line.

Knight Dream's other significant contributions were also maternal, since he was a valuable broodmare sire who appears prominently in the pedigrees of many current champions.

The Knight Dream sire line, however, has disappeared.

THE DIRECT FAMILY OF SIRES

Hambletonian's only other sire line remaining at this time is that tracing from his 1863 son Dictator. This family of sires might already be considered extinct, since no prominent male-line member has emerged in more than 20 years.

The last prominent Direct male-line pacer was Armbro Ranger, a foal of 1973 and a son of the free-legged world champion Steady Star p,4,T1:52.

This is a male line which gave every indication that it would have the legs to continue for generations. The collapse of this family is perplexing, because it had what every family needs. It had a seemingly dominant horse who could sire both successful sons and productive daughters. That horse was Tar Heel, one of the most successful and well-bred horses in the history of the breed.

Tar Heel was a son of world champion Billy Direct, the first 1:55 pacer. He also had an extremely attractive maternal pedigree, since his dam Leta Long was by Volomite and his third dam Rose Scott, was a full sister to Scotland. (See Jessie Pepper Maternal Family)

Tar Heel was also a good racehorse and was trained by Delvin Miller for his breeder, North Carolina tobacco magnate W.N. Reynolds. Tar Heel won the 1951 Little Brown Jug for catch driver Del Cameron, but he was not a good-gaited horse and was a rough, physically coarse individual.

Despite this, his daughters became prized broodmares, the best examples being the royally-bred Brenna Hanover, dam of Bret Hanover, and modern foundation mares such as Romola Hanover, who produced nine 2:00 offspring. Tar Heel mares dominated the broodmare-sires lists for more than a decade in the 1960's and early 1970's.

While his daughters "did their thing," Tar Heel was also siring useful racing sons in such numbers that it would have been easy to predict a lasting future for this sire line. In the late 1950's and 1960's, Tar Heel's successful sons included such horses as Thorpe Hanover, Steady Beau, Bengazi Hanover, Golden Money Maker, Laverne Hanover, Isle Of Wight, Kentucky, Nansemond and Otaro Hanover.

From this list, Steady Beau sired the world champion Steady Star, and the future of the sire line appeared hearty. But, one by one, these horses all failed as sires. Of the aforementioned group, only the well-bred Kentucky found fame as a sire—and that came in Australia. The Direct sire line is all but extinct in North America.

THE STUDY OF MATERNAL FAMILIES

An important adjunct to the study of the prominent sire lines is the review of the prominent maternal families which have consistently produced the best horses.

Many observers dismiss the importance of maternal families in discussing the backgrounds of successful horses, citing the fact that many of the most prominent stallions and successful racehorses do not have solid maternal pedigrees. This is a historical fact which is readily and commonly acknowledged. For instance, important sires such as Adios, Star's Pride, Albatross, Abercrombie and Speedy Crown do not possess royal maternal pedigrees.

The importance of the leading maternal families to the breed, however, must be recognized. It is no freak occurrence that many of the sport's stars trace their maternal heritages to the same tap roots. While it is possible for a truly great male to rise above questionable parentage and still become an accomplished performer, the great mass of data suggests that the best females from the best families will be the ones who consistently and more frequently produce the most useful, successful horses.

I believe that a knowledge of the leading families is an important tool for anyone who wishes to breed horses successfully over a long period of time. Through study of these families, a better understanding of history can be acquired.

MANY FAMILIES ARE IN DECLINE

It is also clear that many of these leading families are in decline, or have branches which are no longer competitive. I am constantly amazed year after year to see colts and fillies from previously successful families selling for very high prices at the various yearling sales, even though it may have been many years since that family produced an outstanding horse.

However, a slumbering branch of a good family can also be awakened by an outstanding sire. I would not be hesitant, for instance, to recommend a yearling from a dormant family if I considered the sire to be the dominant type.

One such instance is the top pacing colt Die Laughing, one of No Nukes' top-performing sons. A contemporary of Precious Bunny, Artsplace and Cambest, Die Laughing is from the Albatross dam Makin Smiles, an unraced mare from a family which had produced many good horses through the 1960's and early 1970's. This is a family which emanates from the Good Time mare Way Wave, and the branch leading to Die Laughing went through her daughter, the Painter mare Seascape. This family went on hiatus during much of the late 1970's and most of the 1980's, only to return with a splash with Die Laughing when Makin Smiles was sent to the speed sire No Nukes.

If yearling buyers are going to consistently purchase horses who will not only make it to the races, but be productive money-winners, a knowledge of the family ties of that yearling is an important part of the equation used to determine what the buyers will look at and buy. A dominant sire mated with a solid maternal family often produces an outstanding foal.

MATERNAL FAMILY PRODUCTION

One of the aspects of the maternal family study which I discovered in doing research for this chapter is a characteristic of most of the good families.

Regardless of what family it may be, one of the recurring trends is that a mare often produces one outstanding foal—often an early foal—but then has little else. She might have a filly or two who are full or half-sisters to her performing foal, and they may not be successful racehorses, but more often than not these fillies often show up later down the line in the pedigree of a very good horse. I would never hesitate to recommend a foal out of a full or half-sister to a very good horse, even if the mare had no record.

Another phenomenon of many maternal families is that a full sister to an outstanding race mare often out-produces her more accomplished racing sister. There are many examples of this, none better than the great pacing mare Belle Acton, generally considered one of the top racemares ever.

Belle Acton had limited success as a broodmare, but her full sister Bonnie Belle became a far more successful producer, establishing a family branch which accounts for many good horses.

There are numerous other examples.

In the Medio maternal tribe, the fastest racing daughter of Miss Bertha Dillon was the gifted Hambletonian and Kentucky Futurity winner Hanover's Bertha 3,T1:59 1/2, who raced for the British-born trainer-driver Tom Berry. This branch of the Medio tribe is replete with successful trotters, but many of them do not trace from Hanover's Bertha. Instead, they trace from Hanover's Bertha's less-accomplished siblings.

Miss Bertha Hanover and Charlotte Hanover were full sisters to Hanover's Bertha, and all three of these fillies earned 2:00 marks, but Hanover's Bertha was by far the best racehorse. Yet, the Miss Bertha Hanover branch of the family is far more successful than that of Hanover's Bertha. So is Charlotte Hanover's branch.

Hanover's Bertha also had two half-sisters, Miss Bertha Worthy and Bertha Hanover, who out-produced the female racing star of the family. Miss Bertha Worthy's family produced Bret Hanover, and the Bertha Hanover branch accounted for Artsplace and Cambest.

MATERNAL FAMILIES NOT IMPORTANT FOR SIRES

I am always a little amused to see stallion advertisements which trumpet the particular maternal background of a new stallion candidate. I believe the maternal pedigree of a sire candidate is of little value in determining whether that horse will become a successful stallion. The evidence is pretty overwhelming that a stallion is an individual whose male line is more valuable than his maternal heritage.

Some of the most influential stallions in history are horses whose maternal families are very weak. Adios, Albatross, Speedy Crown and Abercrombie all have weak maternal backgrounds. Gait, on the other hand, may be a far more important factor in predicting success as a sire. Bad-gaited horses, or horses who accomplished a great deal but were hard-going, have historically not made successful sires.

I do believe, however, that a filly or mare's success may be predicted with some certainty, based on her maternal family. With a female, family is far more important than the individual. I also believe it is absolutely imperative that any horse who hopes to succeed as a stallion must have access to broodmares from the leading compatible families. Many of the great sires of the past, whose own maternal lineage may have been weak, found their best success when mated with mares from the leading families.

For example, the leading broodmare sire of the past decade has been Albatross, whose mares have produced many of the sport's most dominant stars. Albatross, standing at Hanover Shoe Farms, had access to their abundant supply of mares from the leading families. Hanover Shoe Farms did not achieve its lofty status without an adequate understanding that maternal families are all-important to a successful breeding operation. Sires have come and gone with the passage of time, but the leading maternal families of previous decades are still around.

Albatross mares that have produced the most outstanding offspring— mares such as Three Diamonds (dam of Life Sign); Miss Elvira (dam of Artsplace); Lushkara (dam of Camtastic); Lismore (dam of Albert Albert); Perette Hanover (dam of Carlsbad Cam); Park Avenue Bell (dam of Central Park West); and Tracy's Jackpot (dam of Caesars Jackpot)—all hail from the sport's leading female families.

In compiling a study of the leading maternal families for this book, it became apparent that all of the most successful breeders acquired mares from the very best families. The leading breeders have understood that the acquisition and/or retention of females from the leading families gives them a huge, long-term edge in the competitive marketplace.

THE TOP PERFORMING FEMALES

While it is true that many of the best racing and siring males do not have strong maternal families, nearly all of the leading racing females in history do have strong maternal ties.

Look at a list of the top performing trotting and pacing females in history:

On the trotting side, Peace Corps, Armbro Flight, Impish, Winky's Gill, Rosalind, Fancy Crown, Emily's Pride, Colonial Charm, Classical Way and Elma are generally considered to be the top ten mares the sport has produced. Every one of these high-performance females has a strong and successful maternal pedigree. Beat The Wheel, the fastest racing trotter of all time, hails from the Maggie H. maternal family, one of the breed's oldest and strongest trotting tribes.

Among pacers, female stars such as Miss Easy, Fan Hanover, Three Diamonds, Handle With Care, Silk Stockings, Shady Daisy, Belle Acton, Armbro Feather, Tarport Hap and Caesars Jackpot are considered to be the top performing mares in history. Each of them has a strong maternal pedigree as well.

Look at any chronicle of winners of the most important filly stakes in the breed, and you will discover a group of blueblood mares.

BREEDING FOR GAIT AND TYPE

I also believe that not enough breeding is done on the basis of gait and type. By this, I mean that not enough attention is paid to the way a mare travels and how her gait characteristics will match with a stallion. The same can be said for the mare's type, or her physical characteristics.

The late Bill Shehan was acknowledged as one of the leading individual breeders of the past 30 years and one of the most successful breeders in history. His accomplishments put him on a historical par with such breeders as Charles W. Phellis, K.D. Owen and Norman Woolworth. Shehan's success as a breeder of champion horses is astounding, given the fact that he never had a large broodmare band and often bred his mares in puzzling ways.

Shehan had only two criteria for breeding his mares. He wanted to breed for gait and type. If he had a bad-gaited mare, he would breed her to the best-gaited stallion he could find. If he didn't like her type, he would breed her to a horse whose conformation he admired. He wanted to breed out flaws in the physical horse.

At the same time, he always said he was not overly concerned about the fashionable crosses of the day, the leading families or the leading stallions. His best families have some of the most obscure stallions represented at the tap roots, although many of his best producing mares were from branches of already successful families. His affection for the Maggie H. trotters was evident, and he also had great success in single-handedly developing a prolific branch of the vast Miss Duvall family of pacers.

However, Shehan's first great success as a breeder was fashioned by the purchase of an Ensign Hanover mare named Golden Miss, whom he had seen race on the Grand Circuit. Golden Miss was a successful racemare, getting a mark of p,4,2:02.1h in 1959. Shehan saw something in her that led him to believe she would be an outstanding broodmare. He loved her look and her gait. For him, that was enough. He wanted to own her.

Golden Miss's maternal pedigree was very weak, and she was by Ensign Hanover, a wholly unsuccessful son of Billy Direct who stood at Castleton Farm. She was a full sister to Plutocrat p,3,1:59.2, one of the few accomplished sons Ensign Hanover ever produced.

Shehan bred Golden Miss, a chestnut, to the Little Brown Jug winner Shadow Wave, a chestnut son of Adios. That mating produced a filly Shehan named Shifting Sands and she, in turn, through her daughters Shifting Scene and Whispering Sands (both by Race Time) founded a small, but very successful pacing family.

In 1968, Shehan bred Golden Miss to Bret Hanover and the result of that mating was the 1972 Little Brown Jug champion Strike Out p,3,1:56.3h, a superb race-colt and high-percentage speed sire. Later, Shehan bred Golden Miss to a son of Bye Bye Byrd named Bye And Large, who was only a couple of years away from exile to Australia. The result of that mating was a non-record filly named Malaysia who is the dam of the gifted colt pacer Riyadh p,3,1:49.4 winner of more than $2 million and two legs of the pacing Triple Crown in 1993.

Shehan, for instance, would never breed a big mare to a big stallion. He would never breed a small mare to a small horse. He always wanted to breed to get away from faults and to emphasize strengths. I think more breeders would succeed if they followed the same formula.

Shehan believed that too much of our breeding has been done by politics and geography, among our friends and neighbors, with little attention to the inherent physical qualities of a prospective mating. For Shehan, there was no substitute for high speed, clean gait and good physical quality on both sides of the pedigree.

In nearly every champion's pedigree that I peruse, I find the melding of compatible characteristics, not only from the point of pedigree, but also from the gait and physical type of both the mare and the stallion.

THE MODERN TROTTER

The recent history of the trotting horse has been dominated by the get of Speedy Crown and Super Bowl, two racing champions who carried their racetrack prowess to the breeding shed. Each has made valuable contributions to the further development of the breed.

The major attribute of Speedy Crown is that he is such a wonderfully made horse that his sons and daughters have contributed to an overall improvement in the body type of the contemporary trotter. The Speedy Crown offspring have been good-gaited, clean-going, long-barrelled horses. This excellent type has also allowed the Speedy Crown blood to be inbred successfully.

Super Bowl, on the other hand, added his wonderful determination and courage to the equation. The Super Bowls are not as naturally gifted, nor as clean-gaited as the Speedy Crowns, but they have great attitudes and want to go forward.

Speedy Crown prospered from the mating of the many Star's Pride x Hoot Mon mares that were the stars of the late 1950's and mid-1960's. For instance, one of his high-profile sons, the Hambletonian winner Armbro Goal 3,1:54.3, is out of the brilliant race mare Armbro Flight 3,1:59, and her maternal pedigree is Star's Pride on a Hoot Mon dam. Speedy Somolli, one of the most important racing and siring trotters in history, is also out of a Star's Pride x Hoot Mon mare.

Speedy Crown's other successful sons, such as Crysta's Crown, Prakas, Royal Prestige and King Conch, all had Star's Pride-line dams. Of Speedy Crown's notable sons, only the exported Breeders Crown champion Workaholic and his full brother Rule The Wind have non-Star's Pride-line dams.

SPEEDY CROWN LINE HEADED THROUGH SPEEDY SOMOLLI

The Speedy Crown male line appears headed forward through his most successful son, the blazingly-fast Speedy Somolli. Speedy Somolli enjoyed great success when he was mated with mares from the Star's Pride male line—which is interesting in light of the fact that Speedy Somolli has a Star's Pride dam.

Speedy Somolli's most successful siring son, Baltic Speed, is the sire of the star-crossed Valley Victory, whose initial crops hit the racetracks like a D-Day invasion. Valley Victory has already established himself as a quality young sire, and has found great success with mares by, of all horses, Speedy Crown. His Hambletonian-winning son Victory Dream and his Yonkers Trot-, World Trotting Derby- and Kentucky Futurity-winning son Bullville Victory are both from Speedy Crown mares, as is the star of his second crop, the Peter Haughton-winning Donerail.

Since Valley Victory is a great-grandson of Speedy Crown, his apparent "nick" (affinity between bloodstrains of certain sires) with Speedy Crown mares is particularly interesting. This produces a 4x2 generational cross to Speedy Crown in the male line of both sire and dam, which is most unusual.

Successful crosses almost always employ a close-up relationship between the female side of the stallion and the male line of the dam. For example, it has been known for years that a very good way to breed a successful horse is to return to a stallion the male-line blood of his dam. What Valley Victory has done is to alter that equation in a novel way. He apparently wants his own male-line blood returned to him. We might have expected this to occur, but in a much different way.

We might have thought that Valley Victory would have done well with mares from the Speedy Crown male line that does not pass through Speedy Somolli. We might think, for instance, that Valley Victory would prosper from a mating with a mare by one of the other successful sons of Speedy Crown. This might include a mare by Royal Prestige, Armbro Goal or Prakas, for instance. That may yet happen.

Past breeding history also might predict that Valley Victory, who has a Bonefish dam, would be very successful with mares from the Star's Pride line, particularly those by Super Bowl and his sons. There is some evidence that the Super Bowl mare cross to Valley Victory is a good one (his daughter, Lookout Victory, is from a mare by Joie De Vie, a son of Super Bowl), but the Speedy Crown cross back to him has produced the better horses up to this point.

SUPER BOWL'S LEGACY

The Super Bowl male line has apparently accepted the task of perpetuating Star's Pride's legacy. This is another case of one of the strongest sons taking on the task of extending the male line.

Nevele Pride, for many years considered the heir apparent, did not sire a son who could continue the male line in the U.S. Other successful sons of Star's Pride, such as Hickory Pride, Matastar, Ayres, Egyptian Candor and Lindy's Pride, also lacked the siring power to extend the line.

Supergill has already given an indication of his siring ability, and the glib-gaited American Winner received a wonderful book of mares in his initial season in the stud at Hanover Shoe Farms in 1994. North American breeders received a setback when Napoletano, Super Bowl's best racing son, was exported at four to Sweden. He would have provided a perfect cross for mares by Speedy Crown and his sons. Supergill's export to Italy after six seasons in the U.S. is also a blow to the Super Bowl male line. It is difficult to accept that the Star's Pride male line has diminished, and a great deal is riding on the ability of American Winner and his brothers to perpetuate their male ancestry.

History has taught us that these male lines narrow in their advancing age and that the number of successful family branches withers with time. This is the trend in the breed since Hambletonian's day. It may be that the Star's Pride line will disappear, although it is certainly premature to offer a funeral dirge just yet. As this book is written, a granddaughter of Super Bowl, the gifted Royal Troubador lass, CR Kay Suzie, has rampaged through memorable 1994 and 1995 seasons, establishing numerous world records on all size tracks, and was named Harness Horse of the Year for 1995.

WHAT IS THE FUTURE OF THE TROTTER?

What will happen to trotting bloodlines as they continue to narrow in the coming decades?

Will it be the Speedy Crown line which dominates?

Will it be a son or grandson of Super Bowl?

Will Sierra Kosmos continue to carry the Axworthy flame?

Will Balanced Image prolong Volomite's other trotting influence?

The only other exciting possibility on the horizon is the stud career of the gifted Pine Chip 3,1:52.3; 4,T1:51. He is by Arndon, a Speedster male-line horse who does not pass through Speedy Crown. Pine Chip could extend the Speedster line and give breeders an outlet for the mares by Speedy Crown and Super Bowl and for mares by the sons of these horses. The fact that Pine Chip has a Speedy Somolli dam only heightens his chances to succeed in the stud, since there is no substitute for that kind of racing class and speed inheritance in a pedigree that invites the breeding of Speedy Crown-line mares.

EXPORTS HURT THE NORTH AMERICAN TROTTER

During the decade of the 1980's and early 1990's, there was a mass export of trotting bloodstock from North America. It is estimated that as many as 6,000 broodmares and stallions were exported to Scandinavia and the rest of continental Europe during this period.

This exodus of mares, particularly, has weakened the North American trotter. It has placed a huge hole in the gene pool available to breeders. A very high percentage of the exports were females, and the loss of mares is much more devastating than the loss of stallions. In several instances, as many as two generations of some of our leading trotting families have been exported, a blow from which it will take years to recover.

It is clear that we can still produce a champion trotter in North America, but the overall depth of the trotting stakes is weaker now than it has been for more than three decades.

The exportation of trotters to overseas destinations is not a modern phenomenon. Some of our most prominent trotting bloodlines have gone overseas since well before the turn of the 20th century. The first official export certificates were issued in the late 1800's. John Hervey, writing in his landmark work *The American Trotter*, reported that more than 6,500 horses were exported from the U.S. between 1890 and 1947.

Germany and Italy have long favored American breeding, and the explosion of interest in Scandinavia in the 1980's took many prominent North American sires and broodmares overseas. In 1988, for instance, nearly 1,000 export certificates were issued by the U.S.Trotting Association, a great percentage of them to Scandinavia. To illustrate the depth of the export exodus, the entire field from the 1989 Kentucky Futurity, including the winner Peace Corps, was exported, at least temporarily. Happily, Peace Corps returned to American soil in 1994 and foaled a filly by Mack Lobell early in 1995, but the Europeans have always admired and acquired North American breeding whenever and wherever they could.

THE MODERN PACER

Unlike the trotting horse, the modern pacer has not had to contend with the export problem. The only pacers that have been exported over the past 15 years are horses who either could not find homes at North American farms or who failed in their early years to produce high-caliber stakes horses.

There are two important developments in pacing that I wish to discuss. One is the speed at which pacers now race. The other is the development of a different type of pacer who can carry his speed over the full mile distance.

One of the chief characteristics of world-record pacing miles, pre-1980, was that nearly all those efforts included a slow quarter somewhere within the mile. For many years, it was thought that a horse could not sustain his maximum speed over the full mile. In Bret Hanover's then-epic T1:53.3 mile at Lexington in 1966, for instance, he paced three quarters in 1:24 and the final quarter was in :29.3. All other record attempts contained at least one slow quarter somewhere in the mile.

We now know that this theory was folly, for the top-flight pacers today are capable of brushing to the first quarter in 26-27 seconds, going a half in :54 and whistling the back two fractions in 56 seconds with regularity. A 1:50 race mile no longer elicits special excitement!

Niatross was the first to carry his speed over the full mile in his historic 1:49.1 time trial at Lexington in 1980. On the day Cambest paced in 1:46.1 at Springfield for Bill O'Donnell, he went four fractions of :26.1-:25.3-:27.1-:27.1! Matt's Scooter paced his final quarter in 27 seconds after averaging 27 seconds for the first three quarters on the way to his record T1:48.2 mile as a three-year-old at Lexington in 1988.

The modern pacing horse has become a mile sprinter! Very few races at a high level are won from off the pace, such is the strength of front-end speed. This development has occurred almost simultaneously at all levels of the pacing breed, regardless of what stallions are represented or where the racing is conducted. Whether the winners are the offspring of Cam Fella, Direct Scooter, Abercrombie, No Nukes or Jate Lobell, the results are the same. The pacers go faster and faster with each succeeding generation.

There were two major developments which ushered in this style of racing for pacers. One was the explosion of speed and quality associated with the dominant blood of Meadow Skipper and his sons and grandsons. These horses brought both a purity of gait and unprecedented speed to the industry.

At the same time, the way we race pacers was changed dramatically by the opening of The Meadowlands in New Jersey in 1976, where, for the first time, major pacing races were contested on a mile track. Prior to that, all the major pacing classics were half-mile track races, like the Little Brown Jug, Messenger and Cane Pace.

The Meadowlands style of racing, which dictated constant movement and aggressive driving, was the perfect match for the emerging Meadow Skipper line. It dovetailed with the arrival on the scene of horses such as No Nukes, Cam Fella and Niatross.

The success of these horses in new races such as the Woodrow Wilson, Meadowlands Pace and New Jersey Classic earned them spots in the breeding paddocks of the major farms, and their offspring have changed the North American pacer. This did not happen with trotters because the Hambletonian and other significant trotting races, such as the midwestern Grand Circuit features and the historic Kentucky Futurity, have always been raced on mile tracks.

The Meadow Skipper line which dominates world pacing will narrow over time, as all lines do. In what way it will narrow is not known, nor can it be anticipated. We have already seen, for instance, that the Albatross male line appears weakened by its inability to compete with the get of Most Happy Fella's sons and grandsons—Cam Fella, Dragon's Lair and No Nukes.

Cam Fella is currently the dominant pacing sire in North America. However, if history teaches us anything, it is that the dominant pacer of the next generation will probably not be a son of Cam Fella, but rather a horse who will cross with mares from his male line. A young Cam Fella mare has already produced the exceptional pacing colt Jenna's Beach Boy, no doubt a harbinger of success down the road for the Cam Fella mares.

Who will that horse be?

It could be a son or grandson of Abercrombie, such as Life Sign or Artsplace. It could be a son or grandson of No Nukes, such as Jate Lobell, Die Laughing or Western Hanover—or one of their sons. It could be a Direct Scooter-line horse, or some re-emerging Meadow Skipper-line horse, such as Beach Towel.

WHAT IS THE FUTURE OF THE PACER?

There are several questions to ponder concerning the future of the North American pacer.

Will nature provide us with an outlet that will infuse some hybrid vigor into converging sire lines?

Will the two-year-old speed of the No Nukes sire line stand up under history's gaze?

Will the sons of Cam Fella continue the domination established by their own sire?

It is apparent that nearly all of our major pacing champions of the current decade are doubly- and sometimes triply-inbred to Hal Dale. What long-term effect will this produce? Will this massive inbreeding weaken the pacing breed?

The total demise of the Billy Direct sire line due to the failure of Tar Heel to leave a son was a huge setback for the pacing horse because it has narrowed the gene pool. It may have been that the Billy Direct-line horses were all just too coarse and rough to compete with the refinement found in the more successful male lines. The same inference could be drawn on the failure of the Bye Bye Byrd male line.

However, when the Billy Direct male line disappeared, along came Direct Scooter to provide a little hybrid vigor, and the Adios line reawakened with Abercrombie. The latter two developments could not have been forecast by even the most sage observers.

TODAY'S SUCCESSFUL HORSE IS SMALLER

Another trend in the breed is obvious as we examine the state of the

Standardbred in the mid-1990's.

The breed is evolving toward a smaller, more refined, athletic, and attractive horse. It is clear from the exploits of pacers such as Presidential Ball, Jate Lobell, Abercrombie and Cam Fella that the really successful horses of today are smaller than their ancestors. The speeds at which horses must race now have put a premium on gait and size. A big, heavy horse will break down under the demands of the modern pacer, particularly during the early money-winning years.

This can also be observed with the trotters. Pine Chip, American Winner, Valley Victory's sons Victory Dream and Bullville Victory, and the entire Speedy Somolli male line appear to be downsizing the trotter. The big, hulking, hard-going trotter of the past has been replaced by a smaller, longer, more efficiently-gaited horse.

IN SUMMARY

These issues are the same haunting ones that have perplexed breeders from the time of Hambletonian's first success. The successful breeders of the next few decades will be those who can stay on the cutting edge of change, and who recognize or anticipate the trends and utilize them to their advantage. Nature always seems to provide a solution to our breeding problems. The ability to recognize nature's solutions is what separates the successful breeder from the masses.

The answers to the issues raised here will befuddle and bemuse us. The mystery of successful horse breeding remains just that—a mystery! I believe this is where some of the attraction of our industry lies. We are constantly amazed by the ironic twists and puzzling turns of horse breeding, and are continually surprised by what happens around the next corner.

We should not be, really, for it is the surprise that we all seek. It has always been said that we breed the best to the best and hope for the best. I always thought it would be more accurate to say that we breed the best to the best. . .and then hope it will work anyway! Sometimes, this theory delivers a splendid horse.

I am quite sure that when George Segal envisioned the mating of his world champion mare Three Diamonds to Abercrombie, he conjured up the vision of a magnificent colt who could compete in the classics and maybe even win one. He got that with Life Sign.

What Segal accomplished, however, is very rare.

More often than not, the successful breeding of a good horse—one capable of performing at a high level—often appears to be more a combination of luck, politics, geography and historical timing than an exercise in careful planning.

This is what makes horse breeding the optimistic and enigmatic pursuit that it is, and why it has continued to intrigue us through all of history.

I n 1996, Curt Greene embarked on his fourth decade in the horse business. His experience has covered all facets of harness racing, including such down-to-earth jobs as caretaker, trainer, driver, and track announcer. For 10 years, Greene was manager of The Red Mile and Tattersalls sale company. Prior to that, he was a public relations and marketing executive for the Du Quoin State Fair and was instrumental in the establishment of the World Trotting Derby after the Hambletonian was moved from Du Quoin to New Jersey.

Greene also has been a commentator on telecasts of the Breeders Crown, the Little Brown Jug, and the Kentucky Futurity.

His primary interest in Standardbreds is as a student of pedigrees, providing consultations on yearling purchases, and recommending breeding and racehorse acquisitions. Since 1991, Greene has been a bloodstock agent operating under the name of Greene Speed, Ltd. and has authored numerous articles on breeding and racing performance for *Hoof Beats* and *The Horseman and Fair World*. He also serves as executive director of the American Classic Series, Ltd.

This work is the second book by the 1971 news/editorial journalism graduate of Southern Illinois University. His first was a 100-year history of the Kentucky Futurity, published in 1992.

2
YEARLING SELECTION

DOUGLAS J. ACKERMAN

Anyone who has ever had to buy a new or used car has been confronted with a decision. How much do you spend? Which one do you buy? Are the extremely expensive ones all that much better than the moderately-priced ones? We're all drawn to the sleek, racy-looking cars with lots of pizzazz, but invariably they're the most expensive. But not everyone wants or can afford the high-priced cars. Maybe you've had good luck driving Fords in the past, while another person is a loyal Chevrolet customer.

In the end, your decision will be dictated by your budget and by your personal preferences based upon your own experience. And, frankly, that's pretty much the same way it is when it comes to buying yearlings. We all see things a little differently. The only difference is that you can check an automobile engine by raising the hood, but, unfortunately, we can't do that when we select yearlings.

Different people see horses differently. I remember that my good friend Joe O'Brien would frequently buy horses that were big, rugged individuals, even a little on the coarse side. No one would question Joe's ability as a horseman, but he often bought yearlings that wouldn't have appealed to me. But he frequently made them into stakes winners, and that's what really counts.

Bearing in mind that yearling selection is a highly subjective topic and that no one has a lock on wisdom, I will present some of the ideas and preferences I've developed in a lifetime of working with harness horses. My ideas may not work for you. In fact, they don't always work for me because, like every other trainer in this business, I've bought my share of duds. I do hope, however, that my ideas might serve as a guideline for people who are actively involved in yearling selection.

For many years, there were two major yearling sales: Tattersalls in Lexington and the Standardbred Horse Sale in Harrisburg. The racing season wasn't as busy as it is now and trainers had more opportunity to spend time at the breeding farms looking over yearlings.

All that has changed. There are quality yearling sales in many different states and they stretch over several months. Plus, the racing season, which once pretty much ended with Lexington, now stretches into the fall with major races such as the Breeders Crown. Trainers are busier than ever, and the chance to spend adequate time inspecting yearlings is a thing of the past.

I try to attend as many sales as possible, but I make no pretense about trying to inspect every yearling. Only Billy Haughton with his great eye and his endless energy had the ability to do that, and I think even Billy became more selective in his later years.

One of the dangers inherent in trying to look at every yearling is that after a while they all begin to look alike. You begin to think that every yearling you see is a good one. Or that every yearling is bad. With me, if I've looked at too many yearlings in one day, they all begin to look pretty good and then I know I'm losing my judgment. I find that I'm personally much sharper and more critical in my inspections in the morning.

So prior to the sale I try to go through a sale catalog and sort out the yearlings I'm interested in. I mark those catalog pages with little clips, then I can set about the business of examining yearlings with appealing pedigrees.

There is nothing special about my system of marking a catalog. I simply circle the parts of a pedigree that appeal to me and I put a line under anything that I deem to be a weak spot in the yearling's family.

It is my practice to avoid looking at colts whose pedigrees don't seem to have enough power. That way I don't get tempted to bid on a great-looking individual with mediocre breeding. I've got to like both the pedigree and the individual, but I first eliminate them on the basis of pedigree. And the first part of the pedigree that I notice, of course, is the sire of the yearling.

I have the same prejudices and feelings about certain sires and certain families that any horseman has. If you've raced an outstanding colt by Tyler B, chances are that you're going to be in the market for another Tyler B. We're all influenced by our experiences with horses by a certain sire or from a certain family.

If you've had a bad experience with a yearling, you can't help being affected by that. I know it's dead wrong, but if I train a colt or filly from a family, and that horse is just simply no good, I'm reluctant to plunge back into that same family the following year. I know that's wrong, because if it's a solid maternal family, chances are it will produce speed. But I'm afraid of getting stung twice.

By the same token, I have no problem whatsoever drinking from the same cup several times if I like the first taste. That is, I'll buy a full brother or sister to a horse I've raced successfully. I suppose the best example I can cite here is that I raced Noble Hustle in 1979 when he was named two-year-old Trotter of the Year. That same fall I bought his full brother Noble Traveler and he earned $263,137 and won in 1:57.4 before we sold him for export.

(I will admit here that I almost missed a chance to buy Noble Hustle. I didn't have him marked in my sale catalog, but I was wandering around Tattersalls one night looking to buy a horse and I just happened to look in a stall in the Gay Acres Farm consignment and saw Noble Hustle. I told myself then that if I liked him as much outside the stall as I did looking at him inside the stall, I'd be the last bidder. He was a nicely-

The author was an early and enthusiastic patron of Valley Victory yearlings. From Valley Victory's first crop he selected the superb filly Prolific Lady 3,1:56.2 ($373,925) and the fast gelding Federal Yankee 4,1:54. Prolific Lady, above, appealed to Ackerman because she stood so nicely. She was a little lower in the back than he liked but that was offset by the fact that she had high withers.

made colt and, fortunately, I was able to buy him for my owner Richard Staley.)

Then there was the trotter Speeds Right who raced successfully for me in Michigan. I bought his full brother Rocket Force, and both horses won right around $100,000 before we sold them.

In 1993, I bought Stonewall Kosmos, a full brother to Sierra Kosmos, for $145,000, on behalf of Mr. Staley.

I knew that Sierra Kosmos could trot fast, but I also knew that he was a little hot on the track. But Stonewall Kosmos was the nicest yearling on the end of a lead shank that I ever saw in my life. And he was that way after I started training and racing him.

He will just stand there with his groom holding him and pose with his ears up and his head where it should be. He'll never offer to bite, pin his ears, or do anything wrong.

I really think that Stonewall is a better-looking individual than Sierra Kosmos. I know he's got a better head and ear on him. Stonewall has an exceptional head.

If I had to fault him, maybe his legs could have been a little longer when I bought him, but he grew and overcame that flaw.

Overall, Stonewall Kosmos is the most perfect-standing horse I've ever bought, but probably the worst-training horse I've ever had.

Stonewall Kosmos was a problem to train from the moment we broke him. He did just about everything wrong. But when he got to the races, he did just about everything right. He only broke stride once as a two-year-old.

Stonewall is a horse who trained badly but raced good. Don't ask me to explain that because I can't. Maybe he just doesn't like training.

Because I was afraid that Stonewall might get too hot and become a runaway on me, I never really taught him speed as a two-year-old. I just hung on to him and let him plunk along wherever he wanted to go.

I won't spend a lot of time dwelling on sires because it doesn't take a genius to recognize the leading sires in the business. I should add one note about first-crop sires: I'm willing to buy a yearling by a first-crop sire, but only if the sire was a horse I truly admired.

When Valley Victory's first crop went to the sales in 1992, I bought three yearlings. I was a big believer in Valley Victory. He had high, high speed, and a pure gait. He was a great horse who never really got a chance to show it. I thought he was as good as any three-year-old I've ever seen. He could really go!

Those three Valley Victory yearlings were Prolific Lady 3,1:56.2 ($373,925); Federal Yankee 4,1:54, who finished fifth in the 1994 Hambo final; and Time Power, a mare I put on the pace in early 1995.

I remember looking at Prolific Lady when she was a yearling. Of course, the bloodlines on the bottom side of her pedigree were super. She was a big filly, which surprised me, but I thought that since Valley Victory was such a little horse it was a good sign that he produced a big filly in Prolific Lady. Don't ask me why, but I liked that.

I remembered her dam Keystone Profile as a racehorse and she was a big mare. It seems that if you breed a big mare to Valley Victory, you get a big colt or filly.

Prolific Lady had a nice big, brown eye and stood nicely on her feet. Everything was square about her.

The only place I would fault her is that I thought she was a touch low in the back. But since she had high withers, I didn't let her low back turn me away.

I never saw Prolific Lady turned out in a paddock. I think I saw a videotape of her, but videotapes, as you will read later, don't mean that much to me. I know darn well that a consignor wouldn't show anything bad on a videotape. Anything that would detract from the yearling would wind up on the cutting room floor.

For my money, I like a horse who can do his own work. By that I mean that he can race on top and still win. I like to see a horse who's dead game, the kind who can cut his miles and draw off to win. I'm a bit less impressed by those who need cover and by those who benefit from some canny driving. A horse who can march right down the road and win races on his own is the horse who appeals to me as a stallion.

Let me point out here that I've been wrong just as often as anyone else in predicting whether a sire is going to make it. I can remember that I wasn't too high on Meadow Skipper's chances as a sire, and I don't suppose a person could have been more wrong on a stallion. He didn't have the greatest gait and I never thought he was a great, great horse. And I wasn't the first trainer to recognize that Bret Hanover mares would be great broodmares, either. Some of Bret's foals weren't the best racehorses, and I just didn't have too much faith in his fillies as broodmares, but I was wrong.

Diamond Hal, a horse who Joe O'Brien raced back in the 1950s, taught me a lesson. I thought he'd be a top sire, and I even bred my own mares to him, but I can see now that Diamond Hal didn't have the ability to whack out his own miles and still win. He had to come from behind after other horses had done all the work up front.

You should also pay attention to the kind of Sires Stakes program to which a yearling will be eligible. I might be shooting for a Grand Circuit performer when I buy a yearling, but I'm realistic enough to keep in mind that many yearlings won't be that good, so it's nice to have a good Sires Stakes program to fall back on.

Naturally, the female side of a pedigree is important, too. When I'm appraising a mare, I look first for the money earnings of her produce. I tend to throw out the fast records that horses get these days because literally hundreds of horses can get fast records. But how many of them can earn their keep? That's why I think it's imperative that the emphasis be on how much money a horse has won. It's so expensive to train a horse these days, and I want to see if a mare is producing profitable horses or unprofitable horses.

Once a mare has a few foals old enough to race, you can judge her production record, but that surely shouldn't discourage you from buying foals from young mares or even the first foals of mares. Billy Haughton popularized buying first foals, and I personally prefer to buy yearlings from young mares because I've had success in doing so.

There are some horsemen who will see a mare whose first few foals were blanks or mediocre horses at best, then the mare comes up with a nice yearling. The trainer will try to excuse the mare's lack of production by saying that the first few foals didn't get in the hands of good trainers and, therefore, this yearling will be a steal. Frankly, he'd have to be quite a steal to interest me, because I don't believe that horses get into "bad hands." That might be true every once in a while, but I believe that top horses have a way of becoming top horses no matter who trains them.

I make it a practice to take a copy of the *Sires and Dams* book to a sale. Even if I don't carry it with me when I'm looking at yearlings at the sale, I'll have it back at my motel room. It's a handy reference to have because it will answer questions that the sale catalog doesn't.

The prevalence of inbreeding in Standardbreds today bothers me, but I guess I've been wrong all these years because I thought it was bad and yet many good horses today are inbred. I still admit, however, that I don't like too many crosses to the same sire in a pedigree. Even if that horse was a great sire, you run the risk of the bad traits being exacerbated and you might have a real problem horse on your hands.

It would be nice if every yearling had a world champion for his dam, but I'm not afraid to buy a yearling out of a non-record dam if I like the colt and I like the mare's family. Now if I had trained the mare and knew her, I'd probably be less inclined to bid on the colt because my own bad memories of the mare might influence me.

I will relate two examples I can recall involving non-record mares who produced fast-record horses and how the trainers of those mares were affected by their memories of the mare.

Billy Haughton had trained a Bret Hanover filly named Uncanny Ability and he said that she was absolutely no account and showed him no ability whatsoever. So in the fall of 1981 when Stoner Creek Stud was offering a Governor Skipper colt from Uncanny Ability, Haughton wanted no part of that yearling. All he could remember was how common the yearling's mother had been.

The yearling colt was named Fortune Teller, and Eldon Harner bought him for $19,000—and the colt won $1.3 million as a two-year-old! Eldon hadn't trained Uncanny Ability, so he wasn't prejudiced by her lack of ability.

The next incident occurred just a year later at the same Tattersalls sale, and I was involved. I had taken a liking to a Speedy Crown colt and bought him for $50,000. My friend Howard Beissinger came over to me after the sale and seemed a bit dismayed that I had bought this yearling. He told me that he had trained this colt's dam and that she couldn't do anything right.

I wasn't too worried, because I liked this colt very much, and I turned out to be fortunate because this colt was Crowning Point 3,1:54, by far the fastest trotter I've ever sat behind.

Crowning Point also illustrates a point that I would like to make about a pedigree. I naturally would like to see a yearling's pedigree loaded with world champions up close, but I'm content if I can find some hint of class in the first three generations of a pedigree.

For example, Crowning Point was the first foal of his dam, and his second dam showed only two record performers. (Both were stakes winners, however.) It was Crowning Point's third dam Noel that appealed to me, because I had driven her in races many years ago and I knew her to be a quality mare.

I should add here that I have no problem whatsoever purchasing a yearling from a small consignor. I know that some horsemen prefer to pick their stock from established breeding farms, but I think you can often shop around and get some good buys from the smaller, lesser-known consignors. Crowning Point was bred and sold by Killydonnell Farm in Ohio.

However, I am not nearly as keen about bidding on yearlings from a consignor who has a history of bidding on his own stock. I suppose that a consignor should be allowed to protect his investment, but I don't want to feel as if the consignor is trying to run up the price at my expense. An unfortunate amount of this occurs at sales.

First of all, inspecting yearlings takes time if you're going to do it properly. You need to drag an awful lot of horses out of the stall, pick up a lot of feet, and look at a lot of legs if you're going to be a serious buyer. I usually try to establish a price limit in my mind before a yearling enters the ring. And I just don't like the feeling of doing all that work, establishing a fair price on the yearling, then discovering that the colt brings twice what I had estimated because the consignor is bidding on him. I won't bother going back to that consignment in the future.

I will touch on how I establish a price limit and my philosophy on bidding later in this chapter, but let's start now with the actual examination of the yearling.

When the yearling comes out of the stall, the most important thing is that you first get an overall impression of the colt. Forget about his sesamoids and splints for a moment. Look at the whole horse.

Does he fit together? Do all the parts seem to be symmetrical, or is he one of those horses that seems to be packaged in several different parts—front, middle, and rear? Is his neck proportional to his body? Does his head fit in with the rest of him?

This is a critical phase of the examination. So many times I see a colt walk out of a stall and the people looking at him have their heads bowed. You might think that they're praying (which, incidentally, isn't a bad idea for anyone trying to select yearlings), but they are, in fact, so caught up in looking at a horse's feet and lower legs that they never stand back and get an overall impression of the horse.

I'm not saying that the feet and legs aren't important; obviously, they are very important. However, the most frequent mistake I see people making is that they get so caught up in examining the individual parts of a horse that they never take time to see how the parts fit together.

Now you might wonder why it is important that the neck be the right length or that the fore and hind quarters blend in smoothly with the barrel, but remember that the yearling you are inspecting is bred to be an athlete. That yearling will be subjected to rigorous training, and just the least little problem can often spell the difference between disaster and success.

Proportion and balance are critical. One yearling with long, fine cannon bones might be highly desirable if he shows a lot of refinement throughout his entire body. However, put those same light cannon bones on a heavy-bodied horse and you've almost surely got the formula for future lameness.

The importance of balance can be hard to describe, but look around at

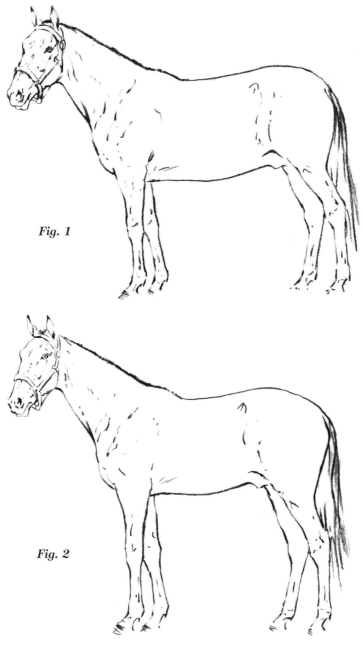

Fig. 1

Fig. 2

These illustrations show the difference between a well-proportioned and a poorly proportioned horse. Fig. 1 shows a horse with short legs and a short neck. Fig. 2 shows a short coupled horse with long legs.

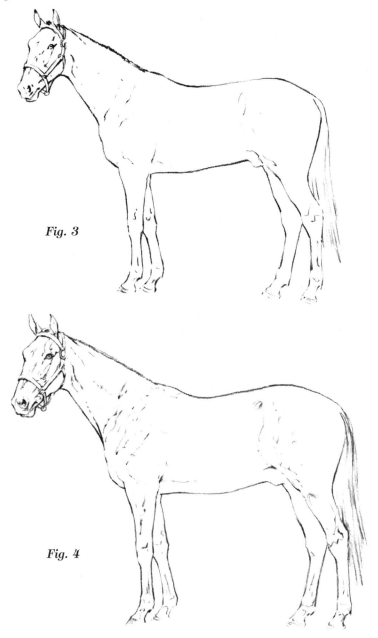

Fig. 3

Fig. 4

*Fig. 3 shows a horse with an overall weakness and shallow heart girth.
Fig. 4 shows a well-proportioned horse.*

the horses in the paddock whenever a major stakes race is contested. Most of them will exhibit excellent balance; otherwise, they wouldn't be stakes-caliber horses. You won't, for example, see a top trotter with a short neck very often. A good horseman can easily spot a horse who is out of balance; the horse simply won't look "finished." A badly proportioned horse is like a car with the fenders off.

While you're looking at the overall horse, you might take time to check his hair. Depending upon the time of year the sale is being held, you often might find a yearling with dull, shaggy hair. That won't bother me as much if the sale is being held late in the year and the yearling hasn't been blanketed, but if the sale is held during the warm weather months, the horse shouldn't have long hair. We all like to see a yearling with a gleaming coat, with his hair as fine as mouse hair.

If you do find a colt with dull or long hair, take a look around at the other yearlings in the same consignment. If they all have the gleaming coats we admire, then something went wrong with the yearling with the dull hair. I wouldn't absolutely reject such a yearling, but I'd mark him down for that.

The same principle applies to the weight a yearling is carrying. I know that some yearlings come to the sale with too much weight, but that won't bother me nearly as much as seeing a thin yearling. If I see a thin yearling, I automatically ask myself, "What's been wrong with him? Has he been sick?"

Each breeder has a little different idea on how much flesh a yearling should be carrying at sale time. Again, it helps to look at the other yearlings in the same consignment. If the yearling I'm considering is not carrying very much flesh and I discover that the entire consignment is on the trim side, then maybe it wouldn't bother me so much. But if the remainder of the consignor's colts are robust, fat colts, then something must be wrong with the thin yearling.

Size, too, is a very subjective matter with yearlings. Many people are unduly impressed with size in a yearling, but the object is to win races and not to be the tallest or broadest. There have been dozens of outstanding small horses in our breed, and I've raced some good small horses myself.

I do not, however, favor small horses. You can come to expect that in yearlings by some sires such as Albatross, for example. He is not a big horse himself and he naturally doesn't sire many big horses. It is ironic, however, that Niatross, the best horse he ever sired, was quite an atypical Albatross in that he was much taller and had more substance than most horses by Albatross.

I will not buy what I consider to be a tiny horse. I try to give an unusually small yearling every consideration, but if I think I'm dealing with a horse that is small all over and will remain small all over, then I'd just as soon let someone else train him.

Homer Walton, a great old horseman from Indiana whom I got to know when I was quite young, once told me, "Doug, a small horse can be a real pleasure to race—until you have to race him against a big horse!"

When you're looking at yearlings, it's important that you be able to discern the difference between a truly tiny horse and one who is simply immature. The foaling date of the yearling and the date of the sale will often give you some clues. In some cases, we've seen yearlings in the ring who are barely 15 months old, and those yearlings are at a real disadvantage.

An immature yearling will often have a look to him that can only be described as "unfinished." You'll notice it most in his shoulders and hind quarters. He just hasn't come together properly in those areas and hasn't filled out and muscled up.

Tiny horses tend to have tiny bones, short legs, and be short in the back, too. There is an old trick that horsemen have used for years to predict the ultimate height of a yearling. You simply measure a yearling from the point of his elbow to the ground. Let's say that distance is 32 inches. Then you measure 32 inches above the point of his elbow and you will have the horse's mature height. I've seen horsemen do that for years, so there must be some validity to it.

If you're able to distinguish a truly small yearling from a yearling which is simply immature, you can often find bargains. It's amazing what another month or two will do to the physical appearance of many yearlings.

I know it has been proven that the average horse gets 90 percent of its height in the first 12 months of life, but that is the average horse. Some will really grow and fill out even after you buy them at auction. And keep in mind, too, that the 10 percent of growth can make a big difference in the yearlings you're looking at.

Allow me another comment with regard to size and the overall physical appearance of a yearling. If a sire has gained fame by siring smallish, racy performers, as Albatross did from the very beginning of his career, that's probably the type you want to seek when you're hunting for Albatross yearlings. I want a yearling to look like the other good ones his sire has produced. There are exceptions, of course, and I have already mentioned Niatross, but most of the Albatross yearlings I've seen are solid, sound-looking yearlings. I recall looking at one well-bred Albatross filly and I couldn't really fault her physically, but she didn't look too racy nor did she show any resemblance to the great fillies Albatross has sired. I passed on her.

Like Albatross yearlings, the colts and fillies sired by Speedy Crown tend to run to a type. They are good-sized horses with very pleasant heads and strong stifles and hind ends.

I might mention here that I'm like most trainers and have some prejudices on color in a yearling. While many trainers don't care for chestnut yearlings, I have nothing against them. I'm certain my feelings stem from the fact that my grandfather went to a sale at Indianapolis in 1933 and bought three chestnut horses, and all three were good horses.

There aren't many chestnut Standardbreds in comparison to Thoroughbreds. That is probably the result of the dominance of horses such as Volomite and Scotland years ago; neither of those stallions sired chestnut performers. Chestnuts, however, are quite prevalent in the Thoroughbred business and there isn't any prejudice against them.

There are some people who believe that chestnut horses tend to be hotter than bay or brown horses, but I don't think that color has anything to do with temperament.

By contrast, I do not particularly like a light bay yearling; that real light bay, almost yellowish in color. Yet Speedy Crown is a light bay and he sires a lot of the same color and that hasn't stopped him from being a great sire. However, I won't buy a horse with light-colored, yellowish hair in his flanks. I've never had a good one with that physical trait.

After getting a good overall impression of the total horse, the next thing I do when I'm examining a yearling is to stand directly in front of him and see how he's going to look out through the bridle. Francis McKinzie, a great farm manager who raised many top horses at several Kentucky farms, taught me this. You get a good chance to see how the yearling strikes your fancy. Does he have an intelligent head and eye? Is he alert and attentive to what's going on around him?

Look at the horse's eye because that is often the sign of his intelligence. I like a good-sized eye and I like it to be properly placed on the forehead, not too high up near the ears. Naturally, I like some width between the eyes, too, because the horse with a narrow head isn't pleasant to look at and he's often a little bit of a slow learner.

I don't care for a horse with a lot of white around his eyes. We call those horses "chalk-eyed" and you notice horses with those eyes. I won't buy one. Maybe that doesn't mean anything, but I just prefer to avoid a horse that shows me a lot of white around the eye. It may be likened to my distaste for horses with Roman noses. They're simply not very attractive, and I think you will often find that a Roman-nosed horse has a small eye and a small nostril, too.

You like to see a horse with his ears up, a sure sign that he's alert and interested in what's going on during the inspection process. But I'll be more apt to excuse a filly with large, floppy ears than I will a colt. I'm not talking about a filly who pins her ears back while you look her over; that's another problem altogether. But if a filly stands there and has one ear pointing north and the other pointing south and she even looks a little dumb, that won't particularly bother me. Often those kinds of fillies go on to be the tough race mares.

Some horsemen say they want their fillies to look feminine. Not me. I want them to look rough and tough, because it has been my experience that the petite fillies with fine little ears aren't the top performers on the

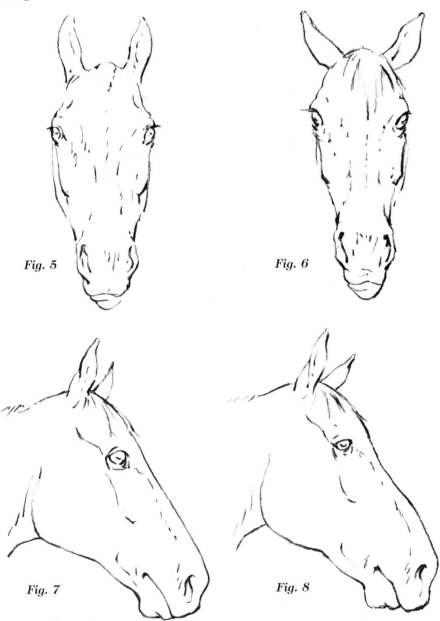

Fig. 5

Fig. 6

Fig. 7

Fig. 8

By standing directly in front of a horse, you can see how he will look out thru the bridle. Fig. 5 shows a pleasant head with adequate space between the eyes while Fig. 6 shows an unattractive, narrow head with the eyes set too high. Fig. 7 shows an attractive head viewed from the side while Fig. 8 shows a coarse head with a Roman nose.

track. I know that mares such as Tarport Hap, Duenna, and my mare Albaquel weren't exactly pretty, but they were bearcats on the track.

The ears are one area that I will distinguish between my standards for colts and for fillies. I plain don't like big floppy ears on a colt. I think you'll find colts with big ears to be slow learners, and you'll usually find that colts with big ears have bad eyes and big, ugly heads, too.

It's also a very good idea to make certain that a yearling isn't parrot-mouthed; that is, you want to make certain that the horse's jaws protrude to the same point and that his teeth meet.

Often you can't miss a parrot-mouthed horse because his muzzle will come to a bit of a point. If you see one whose muzzle seems a bit more pointed than normal, take a look at his teeth and mouth.

Many parrot-mouthed horses go on and race satisfactorily. I know that a lot of horsemen say that they don't eat properly because they can't chew their feed, but the yearlings who are parrot-mouthed must be able to eat satisfactorily or they wouldn't be in sale condition! If a yearling isn't able to eat properly, chances are he'll be in such poor condition that you won't like him from the moment he walks out of the stall.

If I like everything else about a yearling and find he's parrot-mouthed, I wouldn't be afraid to take a chance on him. After all, he must have been able to derive sufficient nutrition from his feed, and I don't see any major problems he might incur if he's made it to sale time.

In his chapter on yearling selection in *Care and Training of the Trotter and Pacer,* Billy Haughton revealed his technique of checking a colt's air passage by seeing if he could insert four fingers between the blades of the colt's jawbones. After that book appeared, you'd see all sorts of people checking a yearling's air passage with the four-finger test.

The ironic thing about that test, however, was that Billy Haughton had an exceptionally small hand and the width of four fingers for him might not be the width of four fingers for other people with larger hands. For example, if you had tried shaking hands with Charlie Keller, former baseball great who bred so many outstanding horses at his Yankeeland Farms, you'd realize his hands were huge. I remember the first time I ever shook hands with Charlie; I thought my hand had been caught in a bear trap!

It is essential, however, to check how the head fits onto the horse's neck and to make certain that the horse isn't thick-jowled. You want to make certain there is clearance so that if you take a snug hold of the horse, he won't be a prime candidate to have his air supply shut off. That's how horses choke down.

Now let's move down to the horse's chest. No trainer likes to see an exceptionally narrow-chested horse where both front legs seem to come out of the same hole. But I think that some yearlings, particularly a trotter, can also be too wide-chested in front.

Many times I will chuckle to myself when a trotting-bred yearling with

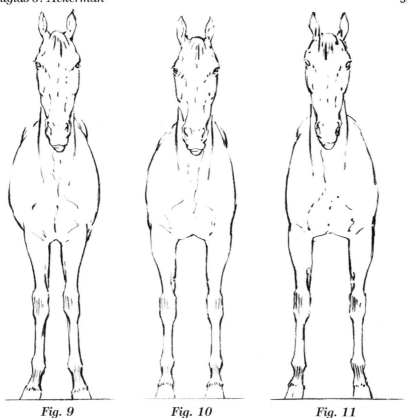

Fig. 9   Fig. 10   Fig. 11

Fig. 9 shows a horse with a very narrow chest. This horse might hit his knees depending on how he picks up his feet. Fig. 10 shows a normal chest width. Fig. 11 is a horse whose chest is too wide. Trotting yearlings with wide chests might develop the habit of hitting their shins.

a wide chest is led out of the stall and someone says, "Well, as wide as he is in front, he'll never hit his knees."

I'm always tempted to speak up and say, "No, he might not hit his knees, but he'll probably clobber his hind shins with every stride he takes!" The ideal trotter moves with his front legs coming back just to the inside of his hind shins, when going at high speed, and those horses with wide chests often bring their front feet back directly toward the shin and hit it a pretty good lick.

Of course, the critical element with either a wide-chested or a narrow-chested yearling is how he picks up his feet and whether the foot travels in toward the opposite knee or whether it travels out. A horse might stand fairly close in front as a result of being narrow-chested, but if he picks up his front feet straight, then the narrowness might not bother him at all.

When examining the yearling's front legs, your attention should be directed from the knee down. Incidentally, that is where Albatross excels as a sire, in my estimation. Over the years, I've always enjoyed looking at Albatross yearlings because he sires such sound horses from the knee down, a critical area for all horses. Albatrosses aren't always the biggest or the prettiest horses in a sale, but they generally have a very sound set of legs underneath them. And they go fast, too!

Stand directly in front of the horse and notice how the leg comes out of the horse's chest and passes through his knee and ankle. It should make a straight line, and the line should pass right through the center of the knee. The bulge of the knee shouldn't be to the inside or the outside of the center. It should be balanced.

Now watch how the cannon bone comes out of the knee. Does it come out in a straight line with the arm bone above the knee? Or is it placed just outside the line of the arm bone? That's what we call bench-kneed, and although you don't see much of it these days, it's something best avoided.

Also, it's a good idea to look at both knees at the same time. Are they the same size and shape? They should be. That's easy to spot if you glance at one knee and then the other.

I'm a stickler on knees, and any horseman should be a stickler on knees, considering the speeds we ask of our young horses today. I want a nice clean knee joint which is flat in front and doesn't evidence any filling whatsoever. However, as in any other aspect of yearling selection, you can be fooled. I remember in the fall of 1985 I put a homebred filly by Gay Skipper in training without much hope of success. I told my wife that, with the knees this filly had, she would never stay sound. Her knee joints were off-center and the line definitely didn't pass through the center of the joint itself.

That filly's name was Cleverness and all she did as a two-year-old was get a mark of 1:58 and win 11 of 19 starts!

Of course, the most critical part of examining a knee comes when you stand facing the horse's shoulder and determine how his leg comes out of the shoulder and passes through the knee and ankle. Again, we are concerned with straight lines. From the point where the leg joins the shoulder, there should be a straight line passing through the middle of the knee joint, and through the center of the ankle joint, and touching the ground at the back of the horse's heel.

If you envision that imaginary line when looking at a horse from the side, and his knee joint is behind the line, that horse is said to be calf-kneed. There are varying degrees of this defect. I know that the great pacer Niatross was slightly calf-kneed, but that still doesn't change my mind. I avoid a calf-kneed horse at all costs. I know some of the better Niatross colts and fillies have been a little calf-kneed, but I think that the percentages are definitely against you if you lower your standards and buy calf-kneed yearlings. You might get one who will stay sound, but the odds are against them.

Some trainers feel that you can help a horse overcome the problems associated with being calf-kneed if you'll only keep a high angle on his front feet. I don't buy that. It's never worked for me. I also know many trainers feel that the high angle of the foot will help take some of the stress off the tendons of a calf-kneed horse. However, I think that high angle will cause you just as many, if not more, problems than the calf knees will. The shock of the foot with the high angle hitting the track time after time will more likely cause a bowed tendon or other problems than the strain usually endured by a calf-kneed horse.

The cannon bone between the knee and the ankle is one of the most important bones in a horse's body, and much of a trainer's time will be spent dealing with problems associated with that cannon bone. I like to see a long cannon bone in a yearling. I like that length. I think if you look at many of our best basketball players who are so fast and quick, you'll see that they have exceptionally long shin bones (comparable to the horse's cannon bone).

You not only want the cannon bone to have some length to it, you want to make certain that the bone itself is more flat than it is round because the tendons and ligaments will lie better around a flat cannon bone. I don't automatically rule out a yearling with a round cannon bone, but I do prefer a flat bone. You should be suspicious of any filling in the tendon or any thickness or "meatiness" to the tendon. It should tie in nicely to the cannon bone itself.

Notice how the tendon comes out of the knee. You can almost see a weak attachment there, if there is one. I don't like to see the cannon bone and tendon be real narrow right behind the knee. It just looks weak.

You're bound to encounter yearlings with splints if you do much horse hunting, and I'm afraid that I'm a bit out of the mainstream in my thinking on splints. I think they indicate a weakness in a horse. Occasionally I will buy a yearling with splints, as long as the splints are not up near the knee or under the suspensory ligament. If the splint is around on the front of the cannon bone and down from the knee so that it isn't rubbing against anything, maybe it won't bother the horse, but I still think splints are a sign of weakness.

Moving down the leg to the ankle, you want to make certain the sesamoid bones, those tiny bones at the back of the ankle, aren't prominent. You want them to fit into the contour of the ankle joint itself. Horses are so prone to fracturing sesamoid bones that you don't want to start out with a pair of prominent sesamoids just waiting to fracture. Actually, the problem of fractured sesamoids might be caused more by improper conditioning than by the prominent placement of the bones themselves, but I would shy away from a yearling with prominent sesamoid bones.

The ankle is connected to the foot by the pastern and here again you

get into the fact that everything must be in proportion on a horse. Nobody likes short stubby pasterns, even though Tar Heel sired many horses
with short pasterns and it didn't ruin them. I prefer to see a horse with
a long pastern, but not one whose pastern is so long that the angle of the
pastern is excessively low.

We talked earlier about the imaginary line which bisects the leg by
travelling through the knee and ankle and hitting the ground at the back
of the horse's heel. If that line goes through the center of the knee and
ankle and touches the ground an inch or two behind the heel, then you're
looking at a horse who is excessively back on his ankles and you're asking for tendon troubles.

Now let's talk about the most important part of the horse's anatomy:
his foot. When you consider the size of the horse, his weight, the pressure he brings to bear on his feet during a fast mile, and realize how
small his feet are, you begin to understand the importance of a sound
foot.

Most of the yearlings presented for sale today by the major consignors
have been properly trimmed by a competent blacksmith. However, if you
go to some of the smaller sales, you will see examples of what bad trimming can do to a colt. They're easy to spot. Just look at the way the
ridges in the yearling's feet line up. The ridges on a badly-trimmed foot
won't be parallel to the ground; they'll be crooked and very easy to spot.

You might notice fever rings on a yearling's feet, although I don't think
they always mean that the horse has been sick. A fever ring that seems
excessively deep into the foot will disturb me, but if I see mild fever
rings and the horse has an otherwise healthy foot, those rings won't
deter me from bidding on him, because I don't think the rings are always
a bad sign.

You will occasionally see a foot that is dished in front. That means the
front of the hoof wall is concave, instead of coming straight down. Many
farms try to have a blacksmith rasp out the dish in a yearling's foot, but,
in doing so, the blacksmith must often leave the front of the foot a little
seedy, meaning the shell of the foot is cracking. No one likes a seedy foot
because it's not healthy and it's difficult to keep a shoe on a horse with a
seedy foot. Also, if you suspect that a horse has a dished foot, check the
bottom of the foot; horses with dished feet often have contracted heels,
and that's not a difficult condition to spot.

You should also eyeball both front feet of a horse to make certain that
they're basically the same size and shape. If they are not mates or near
mates, then the horse probably has sustained some type of injury to the
affected foot—and you want to avoid that.

Every horse trainer would like to have horses whose front legs point
absolutely straight and who don't toe out or toe in. Since horses aren't
produced out of a mold, however, you're going to get yearlings whose
front legs aren't perfectly straight.

If you stand directly in front of a horse, the toe of his foot should fall directly beneath the point of his shoulder. The leg should be perfectly straight when it comes out of the shoulder and remain straight through the knee, cannon bone, ankle, and foot. If everything is pointed straight ahead, the horse is more likely to be efficiently gaited.

While I don't recommend buying a horse that toes out, I have done it on occasion. I think a distinction must be made in *where* the horse actually toes out. If the entire leg toes out from the point where it leaves the shoulder, then you're looking at a loser and you'd best avoid him. However, if the entire leg is straight from the shoulder through the ankle and the horse toes out only from the ankle down, you should not automatically reject him. Those horses probably won't hit their knees. If the leg is straight from shoulder to ankle, the horse mechanically *can't* hit his knees; the leg won't fold that way. But these horses are prone to lameness, so buyer beware.

Of course, you will see horses who toe in from the ankle down or toe in from the shoulder down. Those horses won't hit their knees, but they will become paddlers; that is, they will swing their feet out away from their body in a motion similar to a person paddling a canoe. Paddling puts a lot of strain on a horse and is merely wasted motion.

Let me dispense with the age-old controversy about white feet on horses by saying that I have never found any reason to be prejudiced against white feet. So that doesn't really enter into my consideration.

The most critical part of a horse's foot is the bottom, because that is what comes in contact with the track surface. I see many people look at yearlings and never bother to bend over and pick up a horse's foot. To me, that's inexcusable. It would be like a doctor trying to diagnose an illness without bothering to take your temperature. It's so very basic that it must be an indispensable part of looking at every yearling you intend to bid upon.

To pick up a horse's foot, simply walk carefully up to the horse's shoulder. You might calm the yearling just a bit by putting your hand on his shoulder to let him know you're there and that you're not going to hurt him. Then run your hand down his leg and grab the horse by the front of the ankle and help him pick up the foot.

Many horses resist this and initially refuse to pick up their front feet, but if you use your shoulder to lean into the horse a little bit, you will shift his weight over to the opposite front foot and make it easier for him to pick up the foot you want.

When you pick up that foot, you want to see a nice, slightly oval foot. You do not want to pick up the foot and find yourself looking at one that is narrow and contracted in the heels. That spells trouble. Neither do you want a big, platter-footed horse. It's important to check to see that the horse has a normal, healthy frog (the triangular section in the sole of the hoof).

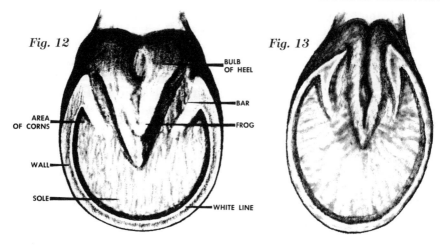

Fig. 12 shows a normal foot with a healthy frog while Fig. 13 shows a narrow foot with a contracted heel. Note the difference in the width of the frog.

While you have the foot in your hand, you want to make certain not only that the frog is normal, but that the sole appears to be free of any defects or injuries.

I think the frog of a horse's foot is one of the key indicators of how he will pick up his feet. Also, the direction that the "V" of the frog points is very important, but I will come back to that later in our discussion.

Once you have completed your inspection of a horse's front legs and feet, you should stand back and take a look at his withers. I do not like a low-withered horse. It has been my experience that a horse with low withers can't carry speed as far as one with higher withers. You will often find that a horse with low withers has a very straight shoulder, too.

I had an Albatross filly named Lady Lynn J who had low withers and, despite the fact that she had extreme speed, she couldn't carry it. She got a record of 1:59 and earned $31,921, but I wonder how fast she might have gone if she'd been able to carry her speed farther.

We call low-withered horses "mutton-withered" because they look like sheep; sheep have low withers. Did you ever watch sheep try to run? They take little mincing strides and don't go very fast. Horses with low withers don't seem to have an adequate stride to become top horses.

I remember that Eddie Davis raced a filly named Sales Girl who had very low withers. She was a good filly, however, and scored a major upset when she was a three-year-old by defeating Anniecrombie at Lexington. Sales Girl proved that low withers aren't an impediment to every horse. For every rule in yearling selection there is an exception, and much of what I have written is merely opinion.

Fig. 14 shows a mutton-withered or low-withered horse while Fig. 15 shows a horse with normal withers. The author believes that low-withered horses seldom are able to carry their speed very far.

When you find a horse whose rump is noticeably higher than his withers, that horse is said to "run downhill" in appearance and I don't care for those horses because they often have low withers. You must appreciate, however, that a horse grows one end at a time, and young horses will often be high behind because the rump grows first, then the withers catch up. You can spot these horses because you'll see that the horse has the potential for high withers, but that he really hasn't grown up into them yet. Personally, I like to see a horse whose withers are as high or higher than his rump, because that means I'm dealing with a high-withered horse.

Now examine the horse through his middle. Everyone knows that you'd prefer to have a long-barrelled trotter, but you really don't want an exceptionally long-barrelled horse or what we call a "two saddle horse." Again, the horse's middle should be in proportion to the overall horse. You definitely don't want a short-barrelled trotting prospect, because those kinds hit their shins.

The length of the barrel doesn't make as much difference with a pacing-bred yearling. My son Doug won the 1985 Fox Stake driving Happy Chatter and he was a colt who wasn't very long through his barrel. Of course, with a pacer you're not concerned about him hitting his shins, you're worried about cross-firing. However, you will find that even some long-barrelled pacers cross-fire. It all depends on how they're gaited.

While examining the length of the horse's barrel, you should pay particular attention to the depth of the horse's heart girth. The heart girth is right behind the horse's shoulders, and you want to make certain that there is plenty of room—top to bottom—for the horse's heart and lungs.

While I believe that depth is the most important part of the heart girth, you don't want a yearling that looks like a sunfish—plenty of depth top to bottom, but no width. We call such yearlings slab-sided horses, and you want to avoid them. You want what are called well-sprung ribs.

(One yearling that fooled me badly was Dancer's Crown. I looked at him and thought he was too slab-sided or flat-ribbed for my taste. Stanley Dancer sure outfigured me, because the colt developed into a great-looking horse and a champion trotter before he died.)

Note, too, the top of the horse's back from his withers to his rump. You don't want to buy a yearling with a low back. At least I don't. I've never seen a good low-backed horse and, although you're going to have a little "dip" in the back, you don't want it to be too pronounced.)

I once bought a well-bred yearling filly whose problem was the opposite problem of a low back; she was hog-backed, or roach-backed. She had a humped back just like a hog. She trained down to 2:12 on the trot, but she couldn't stay at it and I think her back had something to do with her problems. She got a record around 2:00 on the pace, and I thought she might make a broodmare, but when I saw her full brother was also hog-backed, I decided that this must be a genetic flaw and I sold the mare.

Now let's move to the horse's hind quarter, a section which is particularly important because a Standardbred derives his propulsion from the strength of his hind quarters.

Stand off to the side and look at the horse's hind leg. It should have a nice set to it; that is, it shouldn't be too straight or too sickled or curved. The hind leg acts as a lever to propel the horse forward, and if the leg is too straight there won't be enough leverage to enable the horse to stride properly or forcefully enough. Conversely, if the leg has too much curve to it, you're risking the possibility of curby hocks.

Some horsemen and veterinarians think that curbs are a minor problem, a nuisance that's easily overcome. Just treat the curb, rest the horse a week or two, and go right on with him.

I don't agree at all. I hate curbs. A curby hock is a sign of internal weakness just as surely as a boggy hock is. Horses do race with curbs and bogs, but I hate to see a yearling come equipped with such obvious problems.

Once you treat a curb, the horse may appear to get over the problem and may not evidence any pain, but I have found that horses with curbs often will not carry their speed as far as they did before the curb appeared. They still have their speed, but they'll go only so far in a race, then stop. I attribute that to the unseen effect of the curb.

A boggy hock is one that is filled with fluid and will not have the neat and trim look that a hock joint should have. I know many boggy-hocked yearlings go on to make racehorses, but I think you're asking for trouble when you buy one.

I don't think we see many horses with true cow hocks any more. That's a situation where the horse stands toed out behind and his hocks point

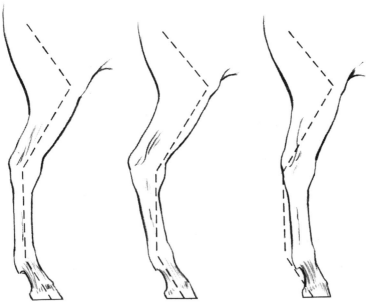

A proper "set" or angle to the hind leg is important. Shown at left is a normal hock and hind leg while the center shows a hock which is sickled and thus prone to curbs, a serious flaw in the authors opinion. The hind leg at the right is too straight and will not give the horse the proper thrust in its stride.

in toward each other when viewed from behind. My grandfather told me that we got rid of cow hocks when the Axworthys started to disappear, and I suppose it's a fault that has been bred out of our horses over the decades. I don't think you need to worry about it much.

I do think that you should pay some attention to the horse's gaskin or, more properly, the portion of the hind leg from the stifle down to the hock. Again, proportion is important, but I hate to see a yearling who is "slight" in this area and doesn't appear to have the muscle and substance he needs.

When you stand behind a yearling, you want to see some width across his rump. You'd be surprised how many horses look good when you're standing next to them, but when you stand directly behind them you'll notice that their hind quarters practically come to a point. You want to avoid that; you want some breadth to the hind quarter because this is where the horse gets his driving power.

Also, when you're standing behind a yearling, you should be able to see the bulge of the horse's stifle; it shouldn't be obscured by the hind quarters. Make certain, too, that there is good width to the stifle when viewed from the side. You don't want a weak-stifled horse.

Ironically, I mentioned previously how much I liked Albatross yearlings from the knee down, but I don't think Albatross generally sires horses with good stifles. That is a fault that you could overlook a little bit with colts or fillies by Albatross, because their weak stifles don't seem to stop many of them from winning the big races.

The trainer is accustomed to sitting behind a horse and looking up over its hind quarters at the neck and head. If you stand behind a yearling, you'll get a pretty good idea of what you'll be looking at when you sit in the jog cart behind him.

I do not care for a yearling that has too much slope in his rump. By that I mean a horse whose hind quarters just seem to fall off abruptly from the top of his rump or whirlbone area. I think a horse with a severely-sloped rump will have an awkward gait behind and carry his hind legs too far underneath himself.

Neither do I like a horse with a big, butterball rump that is too round. I find that these horses sometimes will show speed, but they can't carry it that far.

While we're on the horse's hind quarters, it's essential that you check each yearling colt to make certain that he has two testicles. Many horsemen contend that we're seeing more ridgelings than ever, but I think that simply results from the fact that there are so many more horses these days. A ridgeling, of course, is a male horse with only one descended testicle. The other testicle is often still in the horse's abdomen. Ridgelings can be difficult, but not impossible, to geld.

One of the fastest pacers I ever trained was a ridgeling when I bought him as a yearling. That horse was Leopard, and his undescended testicle was in such a position that he could be castrated without difficulty. I did that even before starting to break him.

Gelding Leopard might not have been the best decision I ever made, because he paced in 1:54.1 as a three-year-old (then a world record for age, sex, and gait) and won over $325,000. He was by Most Happy Fella, and I might have had another Cam Fella (another ridgeling by Most Happy Fella) if I hadn't castrated Leopard.

I'm not afraid to buy a ridgeling, but you must keep in mind there is a very good chance that the horse might have to be gelded if he's going to amount to anything on the track. So I wouldn't want to buy a ridgeling if I had any idea of using the horse as a future stallion. To be frank, however, such a small percentage of male horses are ever used for stallion duty that this is seldom a consideration when buying a yearling.

I remember a Star's Pride trotter named Kerry Pride that Eddie Wheeler raced in the late 1960s. He was a ridgeling, and when Eddie started breaking him at Del Mar, in California, the horse was just terrible. He trotted with his leg way out to the side and he just had a terribly awkward way of going. He was obviously bothered by that undescended testicle, so Eddie had him gelded.

Within 30 days, Kerry Pride was trotting square and progressed to the point where he was a Grand Circuit stakes performer and often raced against Nevele Pride and other top colts of his generation.

While you are subjecting the yearling to your physical examination, you should take note of the yearling's attitude, too. Any trainer will tell you that attitude is important with a horse. It's one thing to have ability; it's quite another to have a horse who really wants to win. That extra heart and desire is often what separates the good horses from the ordinary ones. It's not always easy to determine a horse's attitude at a sale, because that is such an artificial environment for a horse. But I think you should be alert for some telltale signs.

I don't mind a yearling showing a little spunk while being shown. In fact, you want to see some life in the horse. You want to do your best to avoid yearlings who seem soured on the whole process. This is especially true with fillies. (Ironically, one of the best fillies I ever trained, Albaquel p,3,1:53.3, could be a sour filly, but she got sour after being placed in training.) Watch a filly or colt while it submits to examination by other trainers. Watch its ears. Are they laid back against its neck? If so, you've got an unhappy horse and that horse might become a lot more resentful when subjected to the rigors of training. And if you ever see a handler go into a filly's stall and she squeals just as soon as someone touches her, go on to the next yearling on your list. You don't need that kind of aggravation.

You'll often see a yearling get nervous or excited at a sale and kick just a little bit. That doesn't bother me. That's just the excitement and unusual surroundings getting the best of the horse. But when a yearling, particularly a filly, stands there flat-footed and kicks at everyone within ten feet, then you might want to be wary of her. She might start kicking when she's hooked to a sulky or jog cart and I frankly don't want to put up with that kind.

(On the subject of kicking, I might say here that it's a wonder to me that more people aren't seriously injured at sales. You often have congested conditions, nervous yearlings, and buyers interested in everything except their own safety. It pays to keep your eyes open and watch your step whenever you're around horses. Don't get so caught up in what you're doing that you get injured. It's not worth it.)

I mentioned about fillies having a sour attitude, and I should emphasize that colts can be sulky and sour, too. The stress of pre-sale inspections can produce a bad attitude in a colt.

I recall going to Stoner Creek Stud in 1981 and looking at a pacing colt that really caught my eye. I liked everything about his breeding and conformation, but I noticed that he had to be pushed back into the stall whenever he was done being shown. Every time I watched the grooms push him back in the stall, I liked him less and less, and I said to myself, "I sure don't want this sulky so-and-so."

The colt's name, by the way, was Umbrella Fella and all he did was win $669,474, and it turned out that I was the one who sulked when I saw what kind of racehorse he became!

Before you end your physical examination of a yearling's conformation, take a minute to stand back and reinforce your overall impression of him. If you look at enough yearlings, you can often get a little confused.

I sometimes think that the people who buy cows have an advantage over horse buyers in that they aren't at all reluctant to bring out two or three cows and stand them side-by-side and compare them. You occasionally see a really nice-looking yearling and then someone will bring out the colt in the next stall. The second colt might be so superior to the first one that you forget all about the colt you came to see. Often it isn't until you see two yearlings on a comparative basis that you're able to realize how much better one is than the other.

Correct conformation is important, of course, but Standardbreds don't compete in halter classes. They compete on a racetrack and, therefore, it is of the utmost importance that the yearling moves properly.

Just about every aspect of yearling selection is open for debate. Every horseman sees things a little differently. There is one point, however, on which you won't get any disagreement: the more you can see a yearling in action, the better you'll be able to judge his potential.

It's better to see a yearling standing in an aisle than it is to see him standing in a stall. It's better to see a yearling walking than it is to see him standing in an aisleway. It's better to see a yearling turned out in a paddock than it is to see him walking. It's better to see a yearling led by a pony or golf cart than it is to see him turned out.

In fact, it would be better yet if you could hook a yearling and drive him for 30 days. Then you'd know a lot more about him!

Of course, it's not practical for a trainer to "test-drive" a yearling, nor is it practical to see a yearling on a lead strip or turned out, because many breeders simply don't do that. As I mentioned earlier in this chapter, time constraints preclude trainers from getting around to the farms before a sale, so most buyers will wind up inspecting their yearling prospects at the sale facility itself.

I know that it's customary to have a yearling walked up and down an aisle to see how he picks up his feet, but I frankly question how much this tells you. For one thing, I think a horse will pick up his feet entirely different on an artificial surface than he will on a racetrack. Many of the aisles in sale barns are covered with indoor-outdoor carpeting or canvas, and horses don't pick up their feet naturally on such surfaces. In many facilities, the ground surface isn't even, and the yearling's groom often doesn't walk the horse properly. These factors inhibit your ability to judge a yearling's action, too.

Years ago, Bob Tosh, a very good blacksmith, told me that a horse's frog is a virtually foolproof indicator of how the horse is going to carry his

When holding the horse's leg by the cannon bone, the V of the frog should point straight up and down. If the frog points in underneath the horse's body you could be looking at a knee-knocker.

front feet. The frog, as I noted, is the V-shaped section of the sole in a horse's foot. Over the years, I've found that Bob Tosh was right. I consider examination of a horse's frog a keystone in my evaluation of a horse.

Just pick up a horse's front leg and hold it by the front of the cannon bone. Don't hold it by the ankle or pastern or you'll wind up forcing the foot and frog to turn in one direction or another. Just hold the leg by the bottom of the cannon bone and let the pastern and foot fall naturally from the ankle.

Now note the direction of the frog. It forms a V, so check to see if that V is pointing straight up and down, as it should be, or if it points to the inside. If it points toward the inside, you're probably dealing with a potentially serious knee-knocker and you'd best avoid that horse.

I know that a lot of people are going to tell me about all the great horses who have worn knee boots. Sure, there have been a lot of good horses who wore knee boots, but there aren't nearly as many as there were in the past. In the 1950s and 1960s, far more horses wore knee boots and they really used those boots. Today, you might see a top horse wearing knee boots, but they're usually worn only as a precaution. At the speeds we race today, a horse can't be bouncing off his knees with every step.

Just because I have faith in the horse's frog as an indicator of how he will pick up his front feet doesn't mean that I don't bother to watch a horse walk. I do think it's important that you watch a horse walk, even at a sales arena, but I think your primary concern should be focused on the yearling's hind legs rather than his front legs.

Watch closely and note if the yearling walks too close behind or if he walks too sprawled out. You can often get a little indication of how the yearling will walk by noting the way he stands, but watch how he walks anyway.

I recall seeing a Most Happy Fella yearling filly at a sale several years ago and she walked all spraddled behind and, since I liked everything else about her, I decided to buy her. I figured that once she started wearing hobbles, the hobbles would draw her hind legs in and give her a normal gait.

I was dead wrong. When she was going at any kind of speed, she would travel so wide behind that she hit the stirrups of the sulky and wasn't worth 25 cents.

So you should be wary if you see a yearling walking with its hind legs noticeably wider than its front legs. It's fairly easy to spot. You can look between the hind legs as a horse walks away from you and see a big gap. That's bad.

When you're watching a yearling on a lead strip or turned out in a paddock, the best vantage point from which to appraise him is directly behind or in front. In that way, you can see whether he travels in toward his knees when he picks up his front feet. You can't discern that if you're watching a yearling from the side. All you can see from the side is how he folds his front feet.

Don't be misled or overly impressed if a trotting-bred yearling is turned out and puts his tail up over his back and struts off in a nice trot. That might be pretty, but it doesn't mean a thing. I'll guarantee you that the best pacer in the country can put his tail up over his back and trot through a paddock, too.

If you're watching a colt on the lead strip, take note of how he carries his front feet, how he folds in front, and whether he seems to be enjoying his work. If he's laboring on the lead strip, what's his attitude going to be when he has to train three trips in one morning?

It's nice to see a colt show a little speed on a lead strip, but I don't really know how much it means. What I really like to see at Hanover and other places that lead yearlings is a colt who will bump the lead pony, be knocked offstride for a moment, and then bounce right back on gait. That yearling knows what he's supposed to do.

Regardless of the circumstances under which you see a horse move, you want to see an athletic horse, not one who is stumbling around in the paddock or on the lead strip. And with trotters, make certain that they're not stabbing a hind leg or putting a leg where it doesn't belong.

Incidentally, it's a good idea to take note of what kind of shoes a yearling has on when he's being shown on the lead strip or turned out in a paddock. I remember one consignor telling me to be sure to watch a certain colt because he had such a wonderful trotting stroke out in the paddock. He was right; the colt folded like a good-gaited trotter and was impressive. When I picked up his feet, I saw that he was wearing 3/4-inch half-round shoes on his front feet. Those shoes must have weighed 10-12 ounces each. No wonder he was folding so impressively! With all that weight, he was bound to pick up his feet.

There are trainers who will shy away from yearlings who carry so much weight just for show. They think that excessive weight will predispose a yearling to lameness because his bones, ligaments, and tendons aren't mature. I don't really think this weight will hurt a yearling, because I don't think they're stressed enough, but I do know that excessive weight will make a yearling do things he's not naturally going to do. For example, I don't break my trotting yearlings in a heavy 3/4-inch half-round shoe, so I wonder how a yearling will be gaited when I put a lighter shoe on him?

Of course, most often you won't have an opportunity to see a yearling on a lead strip or turned out. Consignors know this and many of them have made videotapes of their yearlings being turned out. The videotapes make for nice diversions, but I'm not sure they're really all that helpful to a person buying horses. Maybe they're useful as attention getters, but let's be realistic: a consignor isn't going to show you anything bad on the tape, is he?

I don't think I'd ever buy a yearling just off what I saw on a videotape. Sure, it helps to see if a yearling has some knee action when he moves, but I'd want to make sure I liked the individual, too. But if I saw something bad on a videotape, that might cause me to reject a yearling.

Sometimes it's what you don't see that can set off alarms. For example, if you're watching a yearling videotape and you don't see a front or rear view of the yearling in motion, you can be pretty sure that he has a tendency to go toward his knees, and the consignor simply didn't want you to see that. I'd be suspicious there.

My advice regarding videotapes is that you should watch them and

Consigned by Brittany Farms, Versailles, Kentucky

VV'S FIRST LADY

BARN 9

(NEW JERSEY ELIGIBLE)

Third foal of world champion **KEYSTONE PROFILE** 3,1:55.1 ($158,064); three-quarter sister to world champion, 1977 USTA "3YO Trotter & Horse of the Year" **GREEN SPEED** 3,1:55.3 ($953,013), **PALM BAY** 3,2:03.3h, **PERIDOT PRIDE** 2,2:04.2 ($116,684), to the dams of **PAMELA'S PRIDE** 3,1:58.3 and **KEYSTONE HAPPY** 3,2:02f and grandam of **KEYSTONE NIGHTHAWK** 4,2:00.3f; half-sister to **ANDIAMO** 4,1:59.3f (Finland) and to the dam of **A WORTHY LAD** 3,1:57.3f ($446,858), etc.

BAY FILLY Foaled February 23, 1991 Tat. No. K2955

	Baltic Speed 3,1:56	Speedy Somolli 3,1:55
Valley Victory 3,1:55.3		Sugar Frosting 2,2:13h
	Valley Victona 3,2:00.3f	Bonefish 3,1:58.3
VV'S FIRST LADY		Victorious Lou 3,T1:59
	Speedy Crown 3,1:57.1	Speedy Scot 3,1:56.4
Keystone Profile 3,1:55.1 (Third foal)		Missile Toe 3,2:05/2h
	Pendot 2,2:14.2h	Hickory Pride T1:59.2
		Cha Cha Hanover

Dam of 6 winners, incl:
Keystone Profile 3,1:55.1
Green Speed 3,1:55.3
Andiamo 4,1:59.3f
Palm Bay 3,2:03.3h
Pendot Pride 2,2:04.2
Grandam of:
A Worthy Lad 3,1:57.3f
Pamela's Pride 3,1:58.3
That's Great 2:01.1f
Cap D'Antibes 3,2:02.1h

Dam of:
Peridot 2,2:14.2h
Grandam of:
Riklis 3,T1:56.2

By **VALLEY VICTORY** 2,1:57.2; 3,1:55.3. Career at 2 and 3 of 14-11-1-0; $485,307. At 2 winner in elimination & Final Breeder's Crown, etc. At 3, 7-7-0-0, winner in elimination & Final Yonkers T., 3 NJSS & NJSS Final, etc. Oldest foals now yearlings.

1st dam

KEYSTONE PROFILE 2,2:00.2; 3,1:55.1 (1:11.5KR) by Speedy Crown 3,1:57.1. 7 wins at 2 and 3; $158,064. World champion at 3. At 2, winner of Frank Ervin T., heat of Bluegrass S. and New York Sires S. at Syracuse; second in Bluegrass S. and New York Sires S. at Syracuse. At 3, winner in heats & Finals of World Trotting Derby and Horseman Futy.; second in Bluegrass S. and heat of Lexington Filly S.; third in Breeder's Crown. This is her third foal. Dam of:
Joe Palooka (Meadow Road). Now 3 and racing.

2nd dam

PERIDOT 2,2:14.2h by Hickory Pride T1:59.2. Record at 2; $9,365. At 2, second in National Capital S., Reading Futy and Pennsylvania Sires S. at Pocono; third in Reynolds Memorial. Dam of 6 winners, including:
KEYSTONE PROFILE (M) 2,2:00.2; 3,1:55.1 (Speedy Crown). As above.
GREEN SPEED 2,2:01f; 3,1:55.3 (Speedy Rodney). 37 wins, 2 thru 4; $953,013. World champion. 1977 USTA "3YO Trotter & Horse of the Year", etc. At 2, 15-8-0-3, winner of Hanover S., Westchester T., heat & Final of Harriman Cup and 4 New York Sires S. including Yonkers and Roosevelt, etc. At 3, 21-16-2-0, winner in heats & Finals of Hambletonian and Currier & Ives S., Yonkers T., Beacon Course T., Colonial T., Leland Stanford T., Batavia S., heat of Founder's Gold Cup, etc. At 4, 20-13-2-3, winner of American-National S., Marques d'Lafayette T., 5 New York Sires S., etc.
ANDIAMO 3,2:05f; 4,1:59.3f -Finland (Carlisle). 3 wins at 3 prior to export; $7,449. Stakes winner in Europe.
PALM BAY 3,2:03.3h (Speedy Rodney). 2 wins at 3; $9,756. At 3, winner in Final of Saratoga July Championship; second and third in legs of July Championship.
PERIDOT PRIDE 2,2:04.2 (Speedy Rodney). 10 wins at 2 and 3, prior to export; $116,884. At 2, winner in New York Sires S. at Roosevelt, Yonkers, Buffalo (twice), Batavia, Syracuse and Saratoga. At 3, winner in New York Sires S. at Yonkers and Monticello.
Producers: Fragrance (dam of **A WORTHY LAD** 3,1:57.3f -$446,858), Keystone Pamela (dam of 1 foal: **PAMELA'S PRIDE** 3,1:58.3), Hopefull (dam of **KEYSTONE HAPPY** 3,2:02f; grandam of **KEYSTONE NIGHTHAWK** 4,2:00.3f) and Semalu Bleue (dam of **MAGNA SEMALU** 3,2:01.1f).

3rd dam

CHA CHA HANOVER by Hoot Mon 3,2:00. From 5 foals, dam of:
THAT'S GREAT 2,2:05; 2:01.1f (Great Lullwater). 16 wins, 10 at 2; $131,432. At 2, winner of Hanover-Hempt S. and 6 New York Sires S., etc.
CAP D'ANTIBES 2,2:05.4; 3,2:02.1h (Star's Pride). 8 wins at 2 and 3; $52,847. At 2, second in Hoosier Futy., etc. At 3, winner of Reynolds Memorial, Final of Hilltop Series and heat of Historic Dickerson T.
Producer: Lady Carlisle (dam of **RIKLIS** 3,T1:56.2 -$515,898).

ENGAGEMENTS

Arden Downs	Dancer Trot	Historic Series	Matron	Old Oaken Bucket	Standardbred
Bloomsburg Fair	Dexter Cup	Hoosier Futy.	New Jersey Futy.	Review Futy.	Tompkins-Geers
Bluegrass Series	Flamboro Brdrs.	Horseman Futy.	New Jersey Sires	Reynolds Mem.	World Trot Derby
Champlain	Hambletonian	Kentucky Futy.	New Jersey Fairs	Simcoe S.	Yonkers T.
Colonial	Hanover Filly	Landmark	Northfield GC	Smith Classic	Zweig Mem.
Currier & Ives	Hanover Shoe				

The author makes notes in his yearling sales catalog to help him remember the strengths and weaknesses of each yearling he appraises. VV'S First Lady was renamed Prolific Lady and she won $373,925 and was a major Grand Circuit star for owner Richard Staley. The author liked her "good

Douglas J. Ackerman   111

Consigned by Preferred Equine Marketing, Agent, Hasbrouck Heights, NY

STONEWALL KOSMOS

BARN 3
Aisle E
Stall 4

(PENNSYLVANIA ELIGIBLE)

Full-brother to world champion **SIERRA KOSMOS** 3,1:53.4 ($558,710), **DEAR CORNELIA** 2,2:00.2, etc. Fifth foal of **Sunkiss Bel** 3,2:06.4f; half-sister to the dam of **SABATOGE KOSMOS** 2,2:05f. Second dam a full-sister to **SONATA HILL** 2,2:01.2 ($297,778; dam of **SELENA LOBELL** 4,1:57 -$424,473), **SUTTON LOBELL** 3,1:58, **SUERAT LOBELL** 3,1:59.2 -$186,079, **SASHAY LOBELL** 2,T2:01.4). Third dam, **STARLETTE HILL** 2,2:04; full-sister to **FASHION HILL** 2,2:02.3; half-sister to the dam of **QUANDO HILL** 3,T2:01.3, etc and grandam of **BUCKY'S PRIZE** 2:01f ($236,720), etc.

BAY COLT Foaled January 22, 1992 Tat. No. L78497

	Songcan 3,1:58.3h	Florican 1:57.2
Nearly Perfect 4,1:54		Ami Song
	Exciting	Super Bowl 3,1:56.2
STONEWALL KOSMOS		Gypsy Slipper 2,T2:03.1
	Noble Victory 4,1:55.3	Victory Song 4,1:57.3
		Emily's Pride 3,T1:58
Sunkiss Bel 3,2:06.4f		B F Coaltown T2:00.1
	Sunday Hill 3,2:07.4f	Starlette Hill 2,2:04

Dam of:	Dam of:	Dam of:
Sierra Kosmos 3,1:53.4	Sunkiss Bel 3,2:06.4f	Sonata Hill 2,2:01.2
Dear Cornelia 2,2:00.2	Oscar RG 4,2:06.4f-'93	My Boy Hill 4,2:04.2f
Stuart Kosmos 4,2:00.2f	Grandam of:	Sunday Hill 3,2:07.4f
(From 4 foals)	Sabatoge Kosmos 2,2:05f	(From 4 foals)

By **NEARLY PERFECT** 4,1:54.4. Sire of SIERRA KOSMOS 3,1:53.4, WHITELAND JANICE (M) 3,1:54.1, 1992 USTA "3YO Trotting Filly of the Year" IMPERFECTION (M) 4,1:54.1, SUNBIRD GROOVEY (M) 1:55, JACK 3,1:57, SPEED PINE 4,1:57.3f, etc.

1st Dam

SUNKISS BEL 2,2:09.2f; 3,2:06.4f (1:18.8KR) by Noble Victory 4,1:55.3. 6 wins at 2 and 3; $13,383. At 2, third in Canadian Juvenile S. At 3, second in Canadian Juvenile S. From 4 previous foals, dam of 3 winners, 1 in 1:54, including:
    SIERRA KOSMOS 2,1:56.4; 3,1:53.4 (Nearly Perfect). 15 wins at 2 and 3; $558,710. World champion. At 2, winner Harriman Cup, Reynolds Memorial, Arden Downs S., heat & Final Horseman S.; second in Tompkins-Geers, heat Review S.; third in Final of Review S. At 3, winner Beacon Course, Old Oaken Bucket, Northfield Grand Circuit S., heats Bluegrass S. and World Trotting Derby; second in Zweig Memorial, etc.; third in Final World Trotting Derby.
    DEAR CORNELIA (M) 2,2:00.2 (Nearly Perfect). 2 wins at 2; $30,645. At 2, winner heats Bluegrass S. and Review S.; second in Arden Downs S. Now 3.
    Stuart Kosmos 2,2:06.3f; 3,2:01.4f; 4,2:00.2f (Lindy's Crown). 5 wins at 3 and 4; $17,220.

2nd Dam

SUNDAY HILL 3,2:07.4f by B F Coaltown T2:00.1. 2 wins at 3. Exported to Italy. Dam of:
    Sunkiss Bel (M) 2,2:09.2f; 3,2:06.4f (Noble Victory). As above
    Oscar RG 4,2:06.4f-'93 (Nearly Perfect). Now 4 and a winner in Italy.
    Producer: Saville Kosmos (dam of **SABATOGE KOSMOS** 2,2:05f).

3rd Dam

STARLETTE HILL 2,2:04 by Star's Pride 1:57.1 15 wins at 2 and 3; $31,733. At 2, 28-14-5-1, winner National Capital S., Reynolds Memorial, Parshall Memorial, Hanover-Hempt S., heat & Final Ohio State Fair S., etc.; second in Goldsmith Maid S.; third in Buckeye Futy. At 4, winner Ohio Colt S. at Hilliard; third in Grandview Futy. From 4 foals, dam of 3 winners, including:
    SONATA HILL (M) 2,2:01.2 (B F Coaltown). 26 wins, 2 thru 6; $297,778. At 2, winner Arden Downs S., Flora Temple S., Lou Dillon T., In Free S., Reading Futy., Ohio State Fair S., heat & Final Hoosier Futy., Delaware Standardbred S.; second in Reynolds Memorial; third in R Horace Johnston T. At 3, second in Hanover S., heat Ohio Governors Cup; third in Blue Bonnets Grand Circuit S., Final Ohio Governor's Cup. At 4, winner Old Glory T., etc. Dam of **SELENA LOBELL** 4,1:57 ($424,473), **SUTTON LOBELL** 3,1:58, **SUERAT LOBELL** 3,1:59.2 ($186,079), **SASHAY LOBELL** 2,T2:01.4.
    Producer: Starry Hill (dam of **STARRY SEELSTER** 3,2:07.4h).

4th Dam

GAY HILL 4,2:06.4h by Scotland T1:591/4. 2 wins at 4. Half-sister to **MODEL** 2:04.3f (dam of **ROAMER 4** T1:59.1), to the dam of **WINSTON HANOVER** 1:59.1 ($224,528), etc. From 9 foals, dam of 7 winners, including:
    FASHION HILL 2,2:02.3 (Star's Pride). 11 wins at 2 and 3; $87,825. At 2, 19-8-3-3, winner Reading Futy., Scioto Challenge S., heats and Finals Buckeye Futy., Hoosier Futy. At 3, winner Scioto Challenge S.; second in Yonkers Futy. etc.
    DEMON HILL p,2,2:14.1h; 3,2:09.2h; 2:08.3h (Demon Hanover). 14 wins; $6,243.
    Producer: Queen Hill (dam of **QUANDO HILL** 3,T2:01.3, **QUILLIE HILL** 3,T2:02.3, **QUENTIN HILL** 2:03.2f, **QUAKER HILL** 4,2:03.2; grandam of **PAULA PAULA** 2:00.4, **BUCKY'S PRIZE** 2:01f -$236,720, **RUFFIAN ROSE** 2:02.4f, **CARLI'S MIA** 3,2:03f).

ENGAGEMENTS

Amer-Nat'l	Currier & Ives	Hayes Mem.	Kentucky Futy.	Pa Sires Fairs	Standardbred
Arden Downs	Dexter Cup	Historic Series	Metron S.	Review	Tompkins-Geers
Bluegrass Series	Great Midwest	Hoosier Futy.	Northfield GC	Reynolds	World Trot. Derby
Breeders Crown	Hambletonian	Horseman S.	Old Oaken Bucket	Simcoe	Yonkers Trot
Champlain	Hanover Colt	Intn'l Stallion	Pa Sires P-M	Simpson S.	Zweig Mem.
Colonial					

withers - high," but noted that she was a little low in the back. He thought that the Nearly Perfect colt named Stonewall Kosmos was a "little short in the back" but marked that the colt displayed "super manners." Stonewall Kosmos earned $142,197.

pay particular attention to any head-on views, but you should never use a videotape as a substitute for seeing a yearling and inspecting it first-hand.

Once I've given a yearling a thorough examination, I will rate that yearling on a 1-10 basis. This rating is an overall assessment of the horse's conformation and pedigree. I make it a practice not to bid on any yearling unless it is rated at least a 9 or a 10 on my scale. I don't buy that many yearlings annually, so I can afford to be selective. Anyone who buys yearlings must learn to be selective.

After I've given a yearling a numerical rating, I will put an estimated price in my catalog page. Keep in mind that I'm probably going to be looking at a couple dozen yearlings, and I need that price estimate as a reminder at sale time. I'm like everyone else in the horse business; I've been known to go over my price limit once in a while, but I think you need a figure in your catalog as a rough gauge for you when the bidding starts.

Whenever I go to a yearling sale, I like to get there early and do some of my looking before the sale gets underway. Once the sale starts, I find it helpful to sit down and see what the first dozen or so yearlings bring. That will give you a pretty good feel for the market.

If the sale is exceptionally strong, you might have to adjust your price estimates up a bit, but I find that getting a sense of the market guides you in determining how likely you are to get a yearling for the price you've estimated.

For example, let's say that you're interested in purchasing two yearlings in a given sale. By getting an early idea of what the market is like, you can tell how many yearlings you might have to look at in order to successfully buy two. And if a market is unusually strong, that yearling you've estimated as worth $20,000 might bring a few thousand more, so you should factor that into your considerations.

At just about every yearling sale you attend, there is sure to be a yearling in the ring that seems to be selling for considerably less than he's worth. After all, just about every yearling looks good in the ring, especially if you're sitting a hundred feet away.

You'll sit there and wonder why this colt is selling so cheap. You look him over from where you're standing or sitting and he seems to be O.K. The bidding is still less than half of what you think he should be bringing, but you're nervous because you didn't bother to inspect him before the sale. You're tempted to bid. He might be the greatest bargain of all time.

Stop! If you follow only one piece of advice I offer in this chapter, please heed this: Don't buy a yearling without looking it over before the horse steps into the sale ring.

I speak from experience. I did this one time before and got burned badly. I wanted to help someone out and bought the horse without looking it over. When I went back to the horse's stall after I'd signed the sales slip, I discovered that I had the unique honor of buying the worst-looking horse in the whole world.

I know that good horses have been bought by bidders who didn't bother to look at them prior to the time they came into the ring. In fact, I think one of Chuck Sylvester's owners bought the 1:55 trotter Diamond Exchange in that fashion. That's the exception, however, rather than the rule.

If a yearling is bringing substantially less than what his pedigree says he should bring, there usually is a good reason. There aren't many blind people buying yearlings these days. Maybe that yearling's four feet point north, south, east, and west. That's not always so easy to tell when you're sitting in the stands. So avoid the temptation and don't bid on a horse unless you have inspected him thoroughly first. You might occasionally miss a good horse, but the odds are far better that you'll avoid buying a lot of bad horses.

When I do bid on a yearling, I generally like the bidding to get established before I jump in. Of course, it seems as if no one wants to make the first bid at an auction and we all know that. (Occasionally, the first bid will come from the auction stand. Otherwise all the prospective buyers would just sit on their hands waiting for someone else to make the first bid.)

When I do start bidding, however, I make it a practice to bid quickly and with determination up to my price estimate. For example, if I'm willing to pay $50,000 for a yearling and I get in the bidding at $25,000, I won't hesitate when it comes my turn to counter another bid. I bid quickly and without hesitation.

I don't know enough about the psychology of auctions to know if this is an effective method of bidding, but I do believe that it might tend to discourage other bidders. Most auctions come down to two or three bidders after a certain point, and if I bid promptly whenever I'm asked for a bid, the other person might begin to think I'm going to buy the yearling regardless of the cost. He doesn't know, of course, that I've set a limit of $50,000; he might think I'm so determined to buy the yearling that the sky's the limit.

My bid of $50,000 would be given just as quickly as my bid of $30,000 or $35,000. I don't want the other bidders to know that $50,000 is my limit. I don't want to show any hesitation. I think if I show hesitation and bid very deliberately, it signals the other bidder that I've run out of money. So the other bidder figures, "One more bid will stop the other guy." And if he bids $52,000, then I'm in the position of having to bid even higher.

I don't have a degree in psychology and I really have no idea if my method of bidding is effective, but I do know that it would work against me. I'm certainly more reluctant to keep bidding if the other bidder makes me think he's got an unlimited bankroll.

I've touched on many different aspects of yearling selection and the bidding process, but I have by no means exhausted the subject. We all see horses a little differently and, therefore, another horseman might disagree with my ideas on yearling selection, and his ideas might be just as valid.

Buying horses is serious business. Even if you're only buying a so-called "cheap" yearling, you must remember that the ultimate cost will include not only the purchase price, but the training, staking, shipping and all the incidentals that go into this business. So even buying a "cheap" yearling can turn out to be very costly. Buying a yearling is such serious business that I recommend you work at it and never buy one on a whim or without knowing a great deal about the particular horse as an individual.

You'll undoubtedly have to compromise your standards at some point in your selection of yearlings. If you're looking for a perfect horse, you'd better have either deep pockets or a lot of patience (or both). And remember not to get so absorbed with the individual parts of a yearling that you don't take time to stand back and appraise how the parts fit together.

In the end, make certain that you buy a horse that you like. You can get all sorts of advice at a yearling sale, much of it bad. If you're going to pay for the yearling and you're going to pay the training bills, make certain that you're happy with the choice.

D oug Ackerman is one of the most respected and popular horsemen active in the sport today. He is respected by his peers for his basic horsemanship and he is liked for his easy-going personality and his sense of humor.

In the words of Shakespeare, Doug Ackerman was "to the manner born." He grew up around horses. His father Rollin was an active trainer and driver in Michigan in the 1930s and '40s.

Doug Ackerman went west as a young man and began making a name for himself in the post-World War II boom years in California harness racing. He attracted the attention of Richard Staley, another midwesterner who had moved to the Golden State, and the partnership of Staley and Ackerman has been one of harness racing's most enduring success stories.

For Staley, Ackerman has developed such Grand Circuit stars as Crowning Point, Self Confident, Noble Hustle, Armbro Cadet, Prolific Lady, Albaquel, Noble Traveler, and Wall Street Banker.

Ackerman is particularly respected for his keen eye in spotting potential in an untried yearling. He summons his lifetime of experience with horses to spot the youngsters who have the physical and mental makeup to be a champion.

Doug Ackerman is the patriarch of a family that is totally involved in the sport. His wife Ada Jean is the daughter of trainer Foy Funderburk. Son D.R. Ackerman is a driver, and daughter Connie Hochstetler, a racing official and amateur driver, is married to driver Homer Hochstetler.

3
BREAKING THE YEARLING

CHRIS BORING

Regardless of the level at which horses are raced, every horseman involved in racing must, at least one time in his career, deal with teaching young horses the ways of the track by getting them used to the sights and sounds of the training centers, and learning their respective gaits.

This is one of my favorite times of the year. I have just come out of a busy racing season. Late fall is when I normally return to my winter training headquarters in Florida. It is the first time in months that I have been able to really put my feet up and look forward to beginning another season with a green crop of yearlings.

I have been asked in this chapter to detail the breaking process as it has worked for me over the years. As with most aspects of the horse business, this is an entirely subjective area and many of the ideas I have about this will, no doubt, be questioned by others. Still, these are the techniques and practices that have worked for me and allowed me to have some success.

Breaking yearlings is a far easier task to accomplish these days than it was when I was a youngster in Michigan. My dad and grandfather were both horsemen, and from a very early age I was educated in horsemanship. Much of my success today comes from the fact that I was raised to respect a horse, to like a horse and to appreciate its athletic talent. I do not see how anybody could be a successful horse trainer and not like horses.

Much of the tension associated with breaking yearlings these days has been removed because we have learned a lot as an industry about how to raise young horses and how to accustom them to human contact. I remember a time when yearlings coming in to be broken to harness may not have been handled a great deal. It was a real adventure, replete with a lot of frustration and broken equipment.

I cannot recall, however, the last time I had a really tough yearling in my barn. I do not know if I have just been lucky, or if I am attracted to yearlings who are smart-looking with good attitudes. I generally am turned-off if I come across a colt or filly at the sales who looks as though he or she may sulk or be hard to manage. I like a horse with a good smart look and a good head and eye.

Generally speaking, most of the colts that arrive for winter training in Florida are ones that have been handled a great deal since the time of their birth. They are comfortable with human contact and generally have had good experiences with people. Couple this with the fact that the Standardbred horse is pretty docile by nature, and you have a very good situation.

DON'T BE IN A HURRY

I think every trainer is anxious to get his young horses broke and moving. This is human nature. However, the rush to get them going often leads to trouble. A good piece of advice here is to just take your time and not be in a hurry.

I know there are trainers who bring a colt in, throw some harness on him, line-drive him a few minutes, and then hook him. Sometimes, they get along fine. Other times, they go along O.K. for a day or two, but then end up in trouble somewhere down the road. A little patience with a young horse can pay big dividends at all steps of his training, and this is as true of the initial breaking period as in all the other plateaus of training. Don't ever be in a hurry to get a yearling hooked! They will see plenty of the track in the next few months. A few days of patient handling at this point can alleviate a lot of frustration in the coming weeks and months. If there is anything I have learned in 40 years in the horse business, it is that you had better learn early to be patient.

TAKE STOCK OF THE STATUS OF EACH HORSE

Every horse who comes into your stable has not been through the same experience. At my winter training headquarters in Florida, I get colts who are homebred and I get colts who have been through either the Kentucky or Harrisburg sales.

What I do with each group of colts depends on where they were raised, how they were raised, and what circumstances were involved in their shipping to Florida.

For instance, I do not start with my yearlings until around December 1. I really do not see any reason to start much earlier than that. I know a lot of trainers want to break a colt in October and get him going, but I am comfortable with a late start— and would be regardless of where I winter trained. This still gives you seven or eight months to get a colt to the races and that should be adequate for any competent trainer.

I like to have all the yearlings assessed once they get to Florida. After the Kentucky sales, the yearlings purchased for my clients are turned out at the farms where they were raised. I simply ask all the farms to take those colts and fillies back, then send them down when I am ready for them.

First of all, I am a hands-on trainer, and I do not like to have horses spread all over North America. After the Kentucky sales, I am still managing a couple of racing horses and travelling quite a bit, so I ask my assistants not to begin the breaking process without me. Instead, I wait until my racing season is over when I can give full attention to the youngsters just coming in.

The Harrisburg yearlings are shipped down immediately after the sale and I try to coordinate their arrival with the other colts from Kentucky, or with any homebred yearlings. These yearlings are watered-out after their trip and turned out on a daily basis in the paddocks that adjoin the shedrow stables in Florida. I take their temperature each day. Most of the time, these yearlings arrive with some sickness. It is the first big trip of their lives; they have been hauled more than 1,000 miles and they often get a cold and run a fever for a day or two after arriving. I want to make sure every yearling is good and healthy before I begin the breaking process.

If a yearling is sick, the first thing I do is take its grain away. I will give it hay, but I take the grain away because I have found that a colt seems to get better quicker if his diet is a little leaner. And if a colt is sick, I want to avoid any possible colic. By giving him a good hay ration, but keeping the grain away, I am avoiding any problem with colic.

In fact, I think it is a very good idea to avoid graining with all your yearlings, even the ones who are not sick after shipping. This is something I have done for many years, and I find the colts are a lot more docile and a lot easier to handle if I hold back their grain during the initial breaking period of four to six weeks.

I would also recommend this for anyone who is breaking a yearling and is having a lot of trouble with it kicking or running out draw gates or balking. I have found that a yearling who has his grain withheld has a lot less energy and is much easier to handle than one on a full ration. After the breaking process is complete, you can begin throwing the yearling some grain a couple of times per day. Since grain products are the principal sources of energy for a horse, I think any trainer will get along better with his youngsters if he withholds grain during the breaking process. It just keeps them quieter and more accepting of everything that faces them.

There are several other recommendations before the process of breaking any yearling begins. I think it is vitally important to have a yearling's teeth checked by a qualified equine dentist. This is important because it can go a long way toward determining what kind of mouth a horse will have. I have the equine dentist float all the teeth and remove any wolf teeth.

Floating the teeth with a dental rasp is an effective way to remove any sharp edges from teeth. Removal of the wolf teeth is also a good idea, because if you leave them in they may be a source of irritation and cause a horse to grab one line and not drive straight. This can ruin a colt's mouth in the first few weeks. It is very important to pay attention to the condition of a horse's mouth at all times, but it is critical at the yearling stage, because that is when a horse's mouth is "set."

Additionally, I feel that yearlings should be de-wormed before you ever start with them and that all the fillies should be sutured vaginally by a qualified veterinarian. This will prevent a filly from "sucking air" through her vagina and will assist in keeping her from becoming infected. De-worming should continue on a monthly basis unless a severe worm problem exists that is not responsive to general de-worming products.

BE VERY CAREFUL WITH FILLIES

This is as good a time as any to talk about the differences in handling colts versus fillies.

Fillies generally have a much different disposition than colts. I have had a number of good fillies and some of them shared a common characteristic. They were all pretty tough to be around. I do not know why this is, but many fillies who turn out to be above average in ability will give you some trouble when you start out with them. This may continue after the breaking process is completed. I do not think a trainer should be concerned if a filly offers to misbehave, as long as you are careful in response to the problem. A filly should never be punished harshly for what she does. A trainer will accomplish a lot more with fillies if he teaches them what he wants by patience and repetition rather than by harsh treatment. A colt will respond to punishment—but a filly generally will not.

BREAKING TO HARNESS AND BRIDLE FIRST

Before a yearling can be hooked, it must be fitted with a set of harness. Over the years, I have used " breaking" harness, but in recent years I have found I make out just as well with an older set of regular racing harness—the same kind used in jogging and training every day.

Just about every yearling we get is already broken to the crossties, but in the event they are not, this is a relatively easy process. I start out putting just one crosstie on a yearling from one side, then add the second crosstie after a day or two. Again, you should be as quiet around a yearling as possible. You should let it know every move you make in the stall, by speaking to it, and touching it with your hands whenever you want to move around. In this way, the horse develops some confidence that you will not hurt him. Everything that he is going to be confronted with is brand new, so it is important to build his trust as soon as you can.

Most yearlings will accept the harness right away if you take your time placing it on their backs. I try to always have two grooms working on a horse the very first time we harness him. In this way, one can work from either side.

The harness should be placed just in back of the withers at the beginning of the horse's backbone. Placement here is very important since the harness will not fit well if it is too far forward or too far to the back. It should rest comfortably on the horse's back.

Next, you will want to put the crupper under the horse's tail. Since most yearlings are used to having their tails grabbed for grooming purposes, this is normally not a problem anymore, but in the past this was sometimes an issue with some horses. In most cases, the harness should

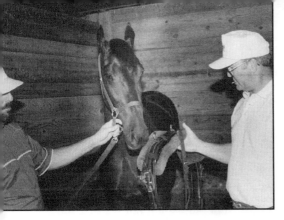

The author recommends that yearlings be broken to the harness in the following sequence. First, the author introduces the horse to the harness. Note that the author recommends that two men be used during this process, one to actually place and fit the harness, the other to hold the horse's head.

After the saddle pad is placed on the horse's back, the author recommends this procedure to place the crupper under the yearling's tail. The author is standing off to the side and not directly behind the yearling in order to avoid being kicked. The right hand holds the tail and the left hand pulls the crupper into position.

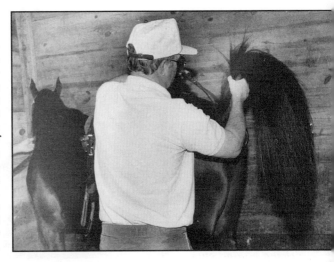

The author checks to see if the crupper is properly placed under the horse's tail. Special attention should be taken to see that all tail hairs are free of the crupper as this will lead to irritation and problems.

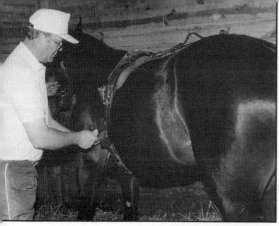

After the crupper is in place, pull the saddle forward and cinch the girth. The girth should be snugged up comfortably but should not bind a yearling.

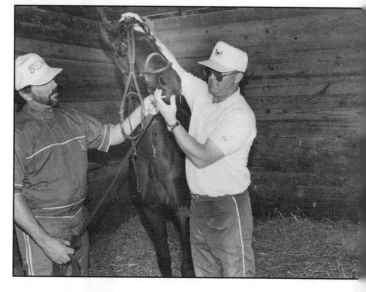

Special attention and care should also be taken in the first few days when the bridle is placed in position. Note again that a handler holds the yearling while the author positions the driving bit and chin strap. The bridle should initially be placed over the regular stall halter.

After the bridle is in place, the author recommends the use of a "bitting rig" in order to acclimate the horse to tension on the bit. This is done by simply tying a piece of twine on the driving bit and then attaching the other end to the saddle pad. Note also that the author recommends an open bridle during this initial phase of breaking.

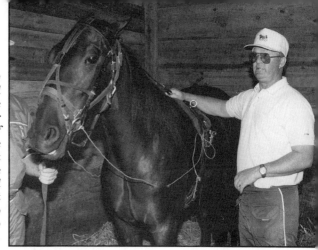

After the bitting rig has been attached (note slack in the twine line) the author adjusts the height of the overcheck. Note that the head is not lifted at any time except to a natural level. A yearling that is initially checked too high may develop balking tendencies.

The author recommends that a yearling be turned loose in the stall when the harness has been placed into position, the bitting rig attached and the overcheck fastened into place. The yearling should be encouraged to move around in the stall to become accustomed to the harness before an attempt to line-drive is made.

be slid backwards across the horse's back, and the tail should be grabbed from the left side of the horse and pulled toward you. The tail should be felt and picked up at a point just below the end of the tail bone. The tail bone will, in most cases, be about six to eight inches long, extending at the root of the tail. The tail is then fed through the loop of the crupper and you are ready to place it under the tail.

I recommend at this point that you be very patient and quiet with this procedure, since the horse may be a little apprehensive about what is going on. If you are not patient and careful, you may discover it is very easy to get kicked. You want to build trust and confidence in the animal. Take your time!

You should continue to work from the left side of the horse. You want to avoid getting behind the horse because you can be struck if the horse should begin to kick. You may wish to rotate the tail sideways first to see how the horse reacts before you attempt to raise the tail. If the horse accepts this sideways action readily, then slowly raise the tail once without attempting to set the crupper loop. If the horse is uncomfortable or offers some firm resistance, you will want to work quietly to gain its confidence. Normally, in just a few minutes, the horse will relax and you can get the tail crupper set properly. It is important that all tail hairs are free of the crupper loop.

An easy check is made by running your fingers down either side of the crupper loop to see if any tail hairs have been snagged. If any are, simply pull them loose and make sure that none are caught under the crupper loop. Again, move slowly and quietly; do not ever attempt to force a young horse to do something. After you have patiently done this step for a couple of days and the horse is accepting the harness without fear, you can move on to bigger hurdles.

After the tail crupper is in place, slide the harness forward to its position just behind the withers. At this time, you will want to buckle the girth. It is important that you proceed slowly here. If anything, I recommend that the girth be a little loose at first. I do not recommend trying to cinch a colt up too tight, because he will resent it and it may cause problems. It is a good idea to fasten the girth loosely at first in a comfortable position, wait a couple of minutes for the horse to relax, then come back and take the harness up a hole before proceeding. The girth should be cinched tight enough that it will not slip backwards, but not so tight as to bind a horse's mid-section.

USE AN OPEN BRIDLE TO BEGIN

I know most horsemen use a blind bridle to break their yearlings, but for many years now, I have used an open bridle at the beginning to acclimate my yearlings to the initial breaking process. I think an open bridle lets a colt see more and allows him to be more comfortable in these initial days. I do recommend a blind bridle when a colt is to be hooked for the first time, but I use an open bridle the first few days to help gain his confidence and to avoid trouble.

Most yearlings have also had work done around their heads by grooms and handlers and they will accept having a bridle put on. As with most things, there is a right and a wrong way to place a bridle on a horse.

The correct way is to again approach the horse from the left side and bring the bit up into the horse's mouth with the left hand, while holding the bridle in position with the right. After the bit is in place, the bridle is pulled over the right ear first then pulled into position over the left ear. This should be done as smoothly and quietly as possible, and a yearling should never be forced to comply. All this movement around the head can cause a colt to shy sometimes, but I have found that if you move slowly, this can be accomplished in most cases without trouble.

In some cases, it may be necessary to unfasten the bit on the left side, place the bridle in position around the ears, then pull the bit into position. You also may wish to let the cheek pieces on the bridle out a notch or two to allow the bridle to slip on easily, but the cheek pieces should be readjusted to allow the bit to sit correctly in the horse's mouth once the bridle is in place.

The bit ought to be able to be moved around in the horse's mouth, and the cheek pieces of the bridle should have a little "play" in them. If the bit is too tight, the horse will resent it and give you problems in your initial teaching sessions. I do recommend that the stall halter be left on during the initial breaking process, and also recommend that it be a nylon halter in good repair. The reasons for this will be discussed a little later in this chapter.

While talking about bridles, and about fitting them to a yearling, I want to stress the importance of this period. These early days of every-day contact with humans in a totally new environment may often have an impact that could carry into a horse's entire career. Never try to force a yearling into anything. Do not attempt, for instance, to force a yearling to accept a bridle. Find a way to get it done without incident. I have seen a number of horsemen who were anxious to get their work done and wanted to rush through everything. In this way, you could end up spoiling a colt. This must be avoided.

I prefer not to trim the foretop of a yearling. I know a number of horse-men like to do this because they do not want to fool with it every day, and it sometimes can be a problem blowing around a horse's ears. But I feel that the foretop should be left alone. If the horse does not like it blowing around the ears, you can always braid the foretop.

I make two adaptations to my racing harness on yearlings. First, of course, I remove the conventional leather racing lines and I also attach a leather strap from the turrets that will act as a loop to accept the long lines used in teaching a horse to drive. I want this loop to hang down about 8-10 inches from the turrets and to be tied around the belly band. This will allow the long lines, when used, to ride at about flank level to the horse.

Next, after the harness is on and the bridle is in place, I will attach what is called a "bitting rig." This is simply a light piece of clothesline or twine that is attached to the driving bit on either side of the horse and then tied to the girth of the harness. There should be plenty of play in these lines. They should not pull the horse's head back in any way. He should be allowed to move his head from side to side before he feels any pressure on the bit. This will get him used to feeling the bit in his mouth and feeling the pressure when he turns his head in either direction.

The last thing to be done at this point is to fasten the overcheck. It is very important that the overcheck be as loose as possible. As a guide, I try to lift a colt's head only to a natural standing position. If I have to lift his nose at all to fasten the overcheck the first time, it is very likely the overcheck is too short.

I also recommend that no overcheck bit be used the first few days that a yearling is to be driven. Simply fasten the overcheck into the top of the driving bit or use an overcheck fastened with a chin strap. I do not recommend trying to break a yearling without using an overcheck. This can be very dangerous. A colt who can get his head down can be a real problem to handle. Just be careful and do not make the overcheck too short.

The driving bit itself is not a complicated issue. I prefer to use a conventional, jointed, snaffle driving bit. I know a lot of trainers who use latex or rubber coating on their bits, or who use the old "Frisco June" colt driving bits, which are covered with leather. I have had good results, however, simply using a plain snaffle bit. I think it puts a better mouth on a horse, and will make him more responsive in the future.

After the harness is placed, the bridle is on, the bitting lines are attached to the bit and the overcheck is fastened, I like to turn a colt loose in the stall for a period of time. In most cases, I will let a colt wear this rigging for the better part of an hour. I think this helps him to get acclimated to the equipment. Normally, a colt will stand still for a period of time with all this new equipment on and then will take a few tentative steps. If a colt does not move readily, I go back in the stall and ask him to move a step or two in either direction. This can be accomplished by simply leading him around in the stall. Once the colt learns he can move with confidence, he will begin to relax and move about the stall.

THE PRACTICE OF LINE-DRIVING

As I indicated earlier, many trainers have abandoned the practice of line-driving a yearling for a few days before it is hooked. I do not recommend this, although it probably would be acceptable for a large percentage of the yearling population. For the yearling that may cause you trouble, however, a few days spent line-driving can overcome a multitude of sins later on down the training path.

When a colt is ready to line-drive, I recommend that the bitting rig be removed and that the long lines be fastened to the bit and run through the leather straps that have been hung from the harness turrets. Up until the creation of the quick-hitch harness, these long lines were run through the shaft holders, but most of our racing harness does not have shaft holders anymore.

At this point, I recommend that the yearling be led out of the stall, and the overcheck be fastened. Two words of caution are appropriate here: If the overcheck is too high, a colt will be uncomfortable and may balk and refuse to walk off. Remember, if you must lift a colt's nose to attach the overcheck, then the overcheck is too short. Let it out until you can attach it without lifting a colt's head at all.

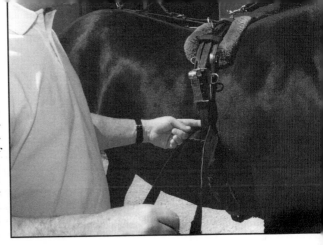

When the yearling is ready to be driven for the first time, the author recommends the use of long lines. The long lines can be run through the quick-hitch on the harness, or as shown here can simply be run under the quick-hitch.

When starting out, the handler should lead the yearling before joining the driver at the rear of the animal. Note that the yearling is led from the left side and that the driver walks a few paces behind in order to avoid being kicked. It is important that the yearling be taught to step off briskly and to walk in a straight line.

If the yearling progresses rapidly, the handler, with the third line attached to the stall halter on the left side, joins the driver behind the horse. It is important at this point that the driver have as light a touch on the lines as possible. The lines should not sag below the horse's stomach line as this may create a situation where a horse could get a leg over a line and make it difficult to steer or control, or lead to a kicking incident.

Another way to determine that the overcheck may be too high is if it results in a yearling balking on the track. I see a lot of this and often times a yearling that is checked too high is uncomfortable and unwilling to go forward.

Secondly, it is very important that the colt be taught to enter and exit his stall properly. He should not run in, or out, of his stall. The handler should have specific instructions to always center the colt in the doorway when entering and exiting. This is another reason I prefer an open bridle at this point. The colt can see more, and teaching him the proper way to enter and exit his stall is made much easier. If a yearling learns to walk calmly into and out of the stall, he will be a much nicer horse to be around. This should be repeated every time a horse enters or leaves his stall for any reason. There are enough opportunities for injury during the course of the training period, so avoid anything that might lead to an injury that is wholly preventable.

With the two long lines attached to the driving bit, I also want a third line attached to the side ring of the nylon stall halter mentioned earlier. Some trainers like to attach this third line to the bottom ring of the halter, but I prefer to have it attached to the side ring. This allows some extra leverage for the trainer who will be handling the third line.

After the long lines and third line are attached, I ask the yearling to step off. I like a yearling to walk off readily. The trainer handling the long lines should be careful to stay back a good ways to avoid being kicked if the yearling should stop and "fire off a volley or two." The long lines should be long enough to allow the trainer to have about six feet between himself and the yearling, with enough extra line to be comfortable.

I recommend that all yearlings be driven by one person, assisted by another on the third line. A yearling should be allowed to walk off, and the person on the third line should remain at the side of the yearling to keep him moving. If the yearling walks off and keeps moving, the person with the third line can work his way back near the same point as the one driving.

During the initial line-driving, I do not recommend using two men with long lines attached on either side of the colt's stall halter. This is another problem which can be avoided. I think this overpowers a colt and makes him feel like he is in a vise. Both men can end up pulling on him at the same time, and the colt can get confused about what he is to do.

The only real reason for the third line is to prevent a colt from getting loose. The person on the third line should try to keep some slack in his line at all times. There should also be some slack in the driving lines.

I do not like to see a yearling being line-driven with a taut line. Let him have a little slack in these lines as well. I think a taut line begins to harden a colt's mouth right away and will lead to a colt who is difficult to drive later on. Putting a good mouth on a yearling is a very important item for me and it starts the first day a colt is driven. Try to make your touch as light as possible.

Line-driving should be done in an area that is as open as possible. I try to line-drive my yearlings right on the track. Our track has neither an inside nor outside rail, which makes it a very safe place to break a yearling. I cannot tell you how many injuries to horses have been avoided and how much equipment has been saved due to the fact that we have no hub rail or outside fence.

The first day a colt is line-driven, I do not want to accomplish a lot. I want to keep a yearling moving and let him look around and get acquainted with his surroundings. I also want to avoid trouble. There is nothing more discouraging than having trouble with a yearling the very first time he is line-driven. You must be patient and take the time to manner a colt properly.

I also want to teach a colt from the very first day that I want him to stay straight. The long lines can be useful in this, which is why you want them to hit a colt at about flank level. This way, you can move back and forth with him to let him know that you wish him to move straight down the track.

You must keep your yearlings from becoming scared. This procedure is all new to a yearling, and a little fear is to be expected. Sometimes, I think we ask too much too quick of a young horse, and that can create some serious problems later on.

On the first day out, I like to walk a yearling about a mile. This should take about 30-35 minutes. I want to get out and back without frightening it. I also don't want to get a yearling too tired. Depending on how well we are getting along, I might try to teach a yearling to turn the very first day.

If a colt is walking along O.K., shows no signs of fright and is willing, I might try to turn him in the direction in which the third line can assist me. If the third line is attached on the left side, I will try to turn him in that direction. In this way, I can communicate with the third-line person, and he knows when to apply some pressure to teach the colt that he is to turn when he feels the pressure on the left side. I am constantly amazed at how quickly a yearling learns this. If a colt learns to turn to the left, but is reluctant to turn to the right, the third line can be attached on either side to assist in teaching.

The principal reason for the third line, as indicated earlier, is to prevent a colt from getting loose if he should happen to break a bridle by rearing or throwing himself. The last thing you want is having a colt get loose the very first day.

The overall purpose of line-driving is to accomplish four goals. You wish to teach a horse to stop, go, stand and turn on your command. Each of these should be accomplished before you ever contemplate hitching a colt for the first time. He should learn to stop when you apply light pressure on the lines and say "whoa" to him. He should learn to go when the pressure is released from the lines and you speak to him softly.

He should also be taught to stand a few moments quietly on the track, although this should not be overdone. There will be circumstances when a colt needs to stand on the track, but generally I only want to teach a colt this to avoid trouble. Generally speaking, I like to keep my yearlings moving on the track. I even teach them from day one that they must learn to empty out their bowels on the move. This is a safety matter as much as anything. If a colt does not learn to empty out on the move, he may stop in front of somebody and get his driver run over on a busy training track!

When teaching a colt to turn, try to make the turns as wide and easy for him as possible. Do not attempt to turn a colt sharply; you will only create a situation where he begins to fight you. Try to make the turn as gradual as possible and to duplicate what you will ask him to do once he is hooked to a cart.

I do not like to see a colt turned with his head pulled around sharply. Try to coax him into the turn gently. Once a colt learns that what is expected is a gradual, safe turn, that is what you will get. It is also important to note that he should be taught how to turn in both directions. This works in concert with everything else you are doing in order to put a good mouth on your yearling.

For instance, if you are breaking a colt to turn, do not attempt to put him into a tight spot while turning. If your training track has either an inside or outside fence, make sure you are a good distance away from the fence before you begin your turn. If you have to bend him too tightly to keep from hitting the fence, he can get to going sideways with you and will not learn to turn properly.

READY TO HOOK FOR THE FIRST TIME

After the four basic commands of stop, go, stand and turn have been taught, the yearling is ready to hook for the first time.

Again, this is a very important time for a yearling. I am often asked about this with regard to how many times a yearling should be line-driven before he is driven to a cart. There is no pat answer. Every horse will be a little different. Some are ready to drive after only a couple of days. Some will require a week of line-driving. A simple recommendation here is that if you are not completely comfortable with a yearling during line-driving, do not attempt to hook him for the first time. You want to avoid trouble, and to keep yourself and the yearling in a safe situation.

When a colt is ready to be hooked, I think he should be turned out in the morning, line-driven a short period and then introduced to the jog cart. On the morning he is to be hooked to the cart for the first time,

When the yearling has successfully completed line-driving, the author recommends that a blind bridle be used when a colt is hooked for the first time. Also note that an overcheck bit has been added, replacing the chin strap that had been used in the line-driving process. The equipment change from chinstrap to overcheck bit is optional.

The author recommends that every yearling be hooked by three handlers. One should remain at the horse's head. The driver should approach the horse on his left side, and another handler should approach from the opposite side. Please note the author recommends the yearling should have his overcheck attached during the initial hitching process.

After the driver swings into position, the yearling should be led off briskly by the handler. The author believes that a yearling should be taught to step off quickly, but not jump or buck during the first few steps.

I recommend an equipment change—I replace the open bridle with a blind bridle.

While it is to your advantage during the line-driving process to allow a horse to see everything, you want to restrict his vision somewhat the first day you hook him. In this way, you will have more control and he will be a little more dependent on you for cues about what to do. If he has learned his preliminary lessons well, this will not create a problem.

When a colt is to be hooked for the first time, I want it done as quickly as possible. The quick-hitch harness is wonderful in that respect because a yearling does not have to stand a long time waiting to be hooked. There is, however, something that should not be overlooked at this point. The first time that the cart approaches the horse from the rear, it is important to keep the cart shafts raised and pointed upwards until you have cleared the horse's flanks. In this way, if the horse should move, the horse's hind quarters will not be struck by the shafts. Simply raise the shafts until the hips are cleared, and then lower the shafts into the correct position to be tied down or snapped into the locking devices on the quick-hitch harness.

I believe the hooking process should be a three-man exercise. I think there should be a person on each side of the yearling (the driver being one of the three) and one at his head. The person at the horse's head should have a hold of the third line, which is attached to the stall halter, and he will be the one to assist with this yearling on the track the first time. The yearling should also have his overcheck fastened at this point.

It is also important the first time the yearling is to be driven, that it is not during a heavy traffic period on the track. This would seem like common sense to most people, but I have seen instances where trainers get a first-time yearling out on a busy training track. This only invites trouble. Try to save the yearlings until the last part of the morning's work, or save them entirely until the afternoon if you are the least bit concerned about their behavior.

If quick-hitch harness is not being used, and the conventional harness is, a colt needs to be tied in as quickly as possible. It is also important that the harness and tie-downs are not too tight. This is especially true with fillies, and is another reason that I recommend use of the quick-hitch harness. It takes much of the guesswork out of tying a horse in.

When a yearling is hooked, I want the driver to take his seat and then ask the colt to move off on a quick, lively walk. In many cases, the assistant on the long line will need to help coax the colt to move off, but once the colt learns what is expected, he will move off quickly.

I also think it is very important to teach a colt to walk to and from the track. This is so important because it teaches them to relax and accept their work without getting too excited. It will also aid in mannering a colt, something which is vitally important in my operation.

Once the track is reached, I will normally ask the colt to break into a jog. If a colt wants to walk, I let him walk for an eighth of a mile or so, but then I ask him to jog. In most instances, colts take to this readily, but in some cases, they are reluctant to accept the weight of the cart the first time they feel it. This is when the assistant with the third line is valuable as well, since he can encourage the colt to keep moving. Generally speaking, once colts get accustomed to the little pull involved, they get along quite nicely.

I like to start off by jogging about a mile and a half the first day. I want to go far enough to teach something, but not so far as to get the yearling too tired. Over the next six weeks, I will add about a half-mile per week, until I get up to jogging about four miles per day. I usually will go a different direction each day. This aids in teaching a yearling to carry his head straight, another important fundamental of good horsemanship.

If you come out every morning and go the same way all the time, a young horse may learn to carry his head toward one side of his body. This is extremely poor horsemanship. A good horse must learn to carry his head in front of him at all times. During this early period, I want to keep working at putting a good mouth on a colt and teaching him to carry his head straight. These are two very important items.

I am not so much concerned in making speed with a yearling right now; enough of that will come later. In these early stages, I am more interested in manners. I want a yearling to learn to turn in both directions and respond to all the different commands. Remember, in teaching a colt to turn, do not attempt to turn him too short. In the old days this was a bigger problem than now because the cart shafts used to dig into a horse's neck when he turned sharply. This problem has generally been alleviated by the quick-hitch harness and the bobbed shafts used in connection with them, but it should remain an issue with anyone using a long-shafted jog cart. Always make the turn as slow and deliberate as possible. You want a colt to keep moving when he is learning to turn because you do not want him to stop sideways in the track, for safety reasons.

WHAT TO DO WITH A KICKER

Many yearlings, at one time or another, are going to offer to kick. This is natural, and should be anticipated by anyone working around them. Yearlings are young, they feel good and have a lot of energy. It is natural for them to offer to kick. Once you hook them you should be alert for this possibility. Let me say something about this right at the start. I do not like kicking straps. I have no use for them. I have always thought they were ill-designed to stop horses from kicking and, in fact, I always thought they contributed to making a horse kick.

A horse generally kicks because he feels good, not because he is looking to do something wrong. If a horse offers to kick, but never does, I do

The author does not recommend the use of a kicking strap. Instead, the use of a cotton rope is advised. The rope is tied around the shafts of the breaking cart at a point ahead of the crossbar and mud apron. The mud apron may be removed. The rope should be tied in such a way so it touches the horse only if he kicks.

The cotton rope should be wrapped with a stall bandage or other similar material.

The kicking rope, properly wrapped, is shown in place.

not take any precautions with him. If I know one has kicked, or will kick in certain circumstances, I can then anticipate the kick and maybe work out of the situation.

A yearling will always kind of swell up and gather himself before he kicks, and this is a telltale sign. He will also attempt to get his head down. You want to anticipate all of this and try to keep him moving. You can also turn his head in one direction or another. It will be hard for him to kick if his head is being turned.

If a horse is a persistent, habitual kicker, I like to tie a soft, cotton rope behind him between the shafts, ahead of the crossbar on the jog cart. This should be a half-inch, cotton rope that is wrapped with a stall bandage. When the horse kicks, he feels that rope and does not like it. It will help teach him not to kick again, in most cases.

Another practice that is very useful with a kicker is to put an effective overcheck bit in his mouth. For this purpose, the Burch overcheck is the most recommended one. It has a spoon that rides up into the roof of a horse's mouth and it is very effective with a kicker. When his head is lowered against that Burch overcheck, the spoon raises up into the roof of the horse's mouth and should make a gentleman out of him pretty quickly. The combination of a rope tied between the shafts and the Burch overcheck has been far more effective for me than any kicking strap ever could be.

SCHOOLING AROUND DRAW GATES

I am lucky at my Florida training center because I do not have any draw gates to contend with on the training track. There is no outside or inside rail on our track, and that is the way I like it. As I said earlier, it has saved a lot of equipment from being destroyed over the years and saved a lot of horses from possible injury.

But most training centers have outside rails and certainly any raceway must have them, so some discussion about yearlings and draw gates is appropriate.

This is a matter of repetition in teaching a horse that a draw gate is not something to be abused. Nearly every yearling will learn where "home" is pretty quick, and will want to get out of his work and get back to the barn. Teaching a yearling proper draw gate etiquette is very important, primarily for safety reasons.

I have found, over the years, that the most effective method of teaching a horse not to run out of draw gates is make him understand that the draw gates are only to be used when he is walking. I make it very clear to always repeat the same pattern with every yearling. When a yearling is coming off the track, it will be slowed to a walk and will come out the gate at the walk. A young horse should never exit the track at a jogging rate. Teach them to walk off the track on a loose line.

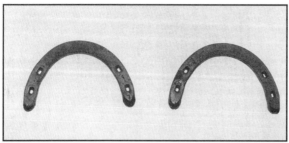

The author recommends the use of toe clips, or half shoes, on a pacing yearling that is cross-firing, or who needs a little weight to find his proper gait.

If you have trouble with a yearling who wants to run out a draw gate, try to position him so he cannot see the gate. If he wears a blind bridle, steer him away from the gate just as you get there. This will cause him to have his head turned and he may not see the gate. Or, put some other horses between you and the gate. If you are having trouble with a colt, never come right up to the gate and allow the horse to make the decision as to when to leave the track. Teach him that you, not he, will give the cue to come off the track. A good rule is to always drive past a draw gate, stop, turn and come back to it before going out.

This is a very good rule to use in the initial phases of training because, just as in going in and out of a stall, you also want to avoid getting a cart caught on a draw gate which could happen if the colt cuts a corner with you too sharply. I think it is a very good idea, if possible, to come out gates head-on the first few times to avoid trouble.

THE FIRST PAIR OF SHOES

I start all my yearlings off barefooted. I have done this for years and do not see a reason to add shoes before they are necessary. Shoes are not needed, it seems to me, until the initial breaking process has been successfully concluded and you are ready to go to work gaiting a colt and finding his natural action. When a colt is ready for shoes, I like to put only two shoes on the first time. With my trotters, I start with front shoes and with my pacers, I like to put the hind shoes on first.

There are a couple of reasons for this. First of all, I am always conscious of managing a yearling to avoid trouble of any kind. If you take a yearling to the blacksmith for the first time and leave it in there long enough to get four shoes made and fitted, it will probably be in there too long and may have a bad experience. Thereafter, that horse will be a problem in the blacksmith shop. By making and fitting only two shoes in the first few visits, the blacksmith helps you stay out of trouble because the horse will be in the shop only for a short period of time.

Secondly, at this early phase of training, the shoes are relatively unimportant and two shoes are all that is required in most cases.

I try to start all my trotting yearlings in a 9/16-inch, half-round shoe.

When I tack the first set of shoes on, I generally add a pair of bell boots and roll a pair of brace bandages on a colt's hind legs. I do this for protection, as I do not want a colt to hit himself first without covering him up to avoid the development of gaiting problems later on. A colt who starts off hitting himself without any protection might get to snatching a leg or stabbing or trotting sideways. It is very important from the beginning to teach a horse to trot cleanly and to trot straight in the shafts.

With pacing colts, I tend to lean toward putting their hind shoes on first; a pair of light, half-round, half-swedge shoes. A pacer's action behind is a little more critical to his development than that of the trotter and I want to make certain from the start that he is handling his hind limbs in the right way.

If I feel a pacing colt needs shoes in front very soon to assist him in establishing his gait, I prefer a pair of "toe clips," which are basically just half-shoes that cover only the toe of the foot. A common problem with pacers is that of "cross-firing," where the rear leg interferes with a front leg on the opposite side.

A cross-firing pacer may strike himself with his left-hind shoe either on the bottom or side of his right front hoof. This often results in a full-sized shoe being yanked off. The rear leg catches the shoe right at the heel and pulls it off. By using toe clips, there is no shoe sticking out over the heel and you avoid a shoe being pulled off and avert any potential hoof damage as well.

Most of my yearlings wear these shoes until it is time to reset or replace them, and at that time I add the missing pair depending upon how the yearling has established his gait and whether I have made an assessment of his natural abilities.

PUTTING HOBBLES ON THE PACERS

I like to put hobbles on my pacing yearlings as soon as possible after the initial phases of breaking. I do not recommend putting them on a colt the first time he is to be driven. In most cases, the colt should tell you when he is ready for something new.

If a yearling has successfully learned to go back and forth from the track like a gentleman, does not show an inclination to kick maliciously, and has learned the rudiments of steering, I think the hobbles can be added without causing any big problems.

It is very important that the first time hobbles are used, great pains should be taken to ensure that they are not too short. The hobbles should be hung and worn the first time with the colt outside of his stall. I like to get a horse outside, have one attendant hold the horse at the head, and another work to place the hobbles on the first time.

Quite often, a yearling will feel pretty constricted if the hobbles are placed on for the first time in a closed-in space such as a box stall. I

After a pacing yearling has been driven for a few days, it is time to add hobbles. The author recommends that this be done outside and not in a box stall. Again, working with a handler, the process begins by adding the hobble spreader over the back, left. After this, the side hangers are hung from the back strap, above. Not shown is the addition of the front hanger.

The side hobble hangers should be attached to the hobble first, below left. After attaching the two side hangers to the hobble you should then go to the rear hobble loop. In the center photo, the author demonstrates the correct way to approach the horse and ask him to lift his rear leg. The horse then steps into the hobble loop and the hanger is attached. The front hanger is attached in the same way, below, right, with the horse being asked to lift his foot so the handler can guide it through the hobble loop. The front hanger should be adjusted so that the hobble loop hangs midway between the horse's chest and his knee joint.

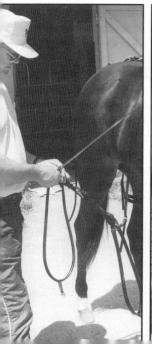

After the hobbles are placed in the same manner on both sides, the author suggests that a yearling be asked to move out under the handler's control to get used to wearing hobbles. Note that the driving lines have been removed. This is a safety precaution. If the horse does act up, this will prevent him from stepping over a line and becoming entangled in the harness. The driving lines are then threaded through the turrets on the saddle pad and attached to the driving bit.

When the yearling is ready to be hooked, the handler stands at the head, the driver waits on the left side, and a third handler brings the cart into position. The cart shafts are held high in order to avoid striking the horse while the cart is brought into position, above, right.

After the horse is hitched, the handler again steps off with the yearling with the driver in position.

think colts are more comfortable if the hobbles are hung outside where everybody can see what is happening. Also, you have the room outside to deal with any problems without getting anyone hurt or breaking up any equipment.

If you wear a very short hobble on a yearling to start with, and that length hobble burns him, you will soon have a very reluctant horse on your hands. It is a good practice to ensure that the hobbles you use for the first time are longer than may be thought necessary. If an error is made, let it be because the hobbles are too long. It is much easier to take them up and help a colt establish his gait naturally, than it is to use a short hobble and burn a colt from the first day. Rest assured that you will probably not get them on right the first time, and you can adjust them the next day.

Most yearlings are fairly docile about accepting the hobbles, but occasionally you run across a yearling who does not like the hobbles and becomes a real problem.

What I do with a horse like this is go back to line-driving him in the hobbles until he gets his "play" out, then hook him when I feel the edge has been taken away. You may also find it necessary to go back to using an assistant with a third line if the colt balks at wearing the hobbles.

I like to use a plastic hobble because of its light weight and durability. Nearly every trainer I know has an old pair of leather hobbles around the barn for a colt who might be tough to gait. I do not recommend leather hobbles for the colts making good progress, as they tend to burn a colt more than a plastic hobble, but they can be very effective in gaiting a colt who is having trouble hitting the pace.

Remember that in all phases of training horses you are dealing with patience and repetition. Any trainer who asks too much too soon of a horse at any level of his training is asking for trouble. Take your time. Have some patience. A horse learns through patience and the repetition of his tasks. If you learn to wait and establish good fundamental groundwork, you will have a much more successful career as a horseman.

WHEN CAN YOU ASK FOR A LITTLE SPEED?

After a horse has been taught the basics, it will be natural to start to teach it a little speed. I believe that speed in a yearling is not an acquired talent. They either have it or they do not. I consider myself a pretty competent trainer, but I have to admit I have never found a way to teach speed to a colt who did not have any ability. Some of my horses in the past had what I call "manufactured" speed. A lot of pacers had to have their heads up high and had to wear a really tight hobble to learn any speed. A lot of trotters needed to wear heavy shoes and be driven by someone with great experience in keeping a trotter steady and going forward.

Today's horses, however, are not manufactured in this way. They are much more natural athletes, and due to their genetic background, are capable of high speed.

But how soon should this speed come out? That is a fair question, and a good one. I see nothing wrong with letting a yearling find out that it can go fast. It will be natural during the initial phases of training for a colt to get spooked and get its tail up and strut a little. I generally do not attempt to restrain a colt much at this time. If he wants to ramble out a little and stretch for a quarter of a mile or so, I just let him. I think a colt likes to learn a little speed. This is a very effective way, when a colt is willing, to let him know that he can go fast and that, in fact, is encouraged to do so.

Also, if you restrain a yearling at this time, a good deal of trouble can develop. This is when a pacer will get a little sideways and possibly cross-fire. A trotter can get to interfering if he is "doubled-up." If a yearling gets spooked, keep him straight, but let him go on a little. It won't hurt a thing as long as he doesn't go too far.

After the first few weeks of training, I will ask a colt for speed about two days a week. This begins to establish a twice-weekly training routine which will be repeated throughout the period leading to the first race. I prefer to ask a colt for a little speed or allow him to take off if he is spooked, when I am headed the right way of the track. I do not like to brush a colt going the wrong way (clockwise). I want him to learn to relax when he jogs and I cannot do that if I am brushing him while jogging the wrong way.

On the other hand, I want him to learn that the counter-clockwise motion is an acceptable time for him to try and learn a little speed.

HORSES TEND TO BE SOCIAL—WORK THEM IN SETS

I like to work my colts in sets. If you have ever observed young horses in the field, you will notice that they like to run and play together and socialize. I think a yearling will learn more, and learn it quicker, if he is cheerful about his work. I have found that if a young horse is on the track with a number of other yearlings, he stays more focused on what he is doing and has a better time.

If you do not have a number of yearlings to break, send an older horse out with the colt. This socialization on the track is an important psychological move in keeping a horse cheerful and willing to learn.

I also do not believe a yearling should be forced to jog faster than he wants to. If you have to "chase" a yearling to jog, you are probably asking him to jog faster than he likes. Horses are individuals, and their abilities need to be developed in individual patterns. The successful horse trainer is one who realizes this and does not attempt to fit the horse into a strict program. At the early stages of development, a horse who is uncomfortable will not learn to do anything and will not develop his ability the same way as one who is comfortable.

In summary, breaking yearlings is very much like taking your kids to school for the first time. We are horsemen, but we are really more like school teachers. We are looking to teach a colt fundamentals that he can use the rest of his racing life, just as kids are taught the basics of education that they may use the rest of their lives. A child must learn to read and write. A horse must learn the fundamentals of racing. We must always remember that we are dealing with finely-bred athletes that ultimately may be capable of some pretty outstanding feats. Treat them with the respect they deserve.

Keep it simple. Stay out of trouble. Keep a colt from becoming frightened. Teach him manners. Put a good mouth on him. Allow him to enjoy his unique gifts and abilities. And that will allow him to develop whatever natural talent he possesses.

Highly regarded by his peers for his ability to break yearlings and develop young colts and fillies, Norman Chris Boring has made the Grand Circuit his harness racing home for many years.

The Indianapolis native, whose stable is based in Michigan, stepped into the harness racing spotlight initially in the mid-1960s. The colt responsible for the early attention was True Duane whose most notable accomplishment was knocking off Bret Hanover and Cardigan Bay in the 1966 American Pacing Classic in what turned out to be Bret's last race.

In 1984, Boring enjoyed a banner year behind Colt Fortysix, as the colt paced to a 1:50.3 record race mile and later won the Little Brown Jug.

More recently, Boring has been associated with the hard-nosed pacing colt Albert Albert who captured the Fox Stake and Kentucky Pacing Derby at two, then nailed down the Slutsky Memorial and final of the Oliver Wendell Holmes at three. However, the most memorable race of the Boring-trained colt's career may have been the final heat of the 1988 Little Brown Jug in which Albert Albert engaged eventual winner B J Scoot through a blistering :53.4 first half.

Delaware, Ohio, in fact has been very good to Chris Boring. He won the Old Oaken Bucket with Dr. Guillotine, the Buckette with Narva Hanover, and the Ohio Breeders Championship with Ms. La Mirage at the famed half-mile oval.

He and his wife, Joyce, own several Standardbreds and their son, Troy, is a promising young reinsman.

4

SHOEING AND HOOF CARE

HOWARD BEISSINGER

hen I was a youngster, we had a gray mare named Dolly at our family farm. She was half-Standardbred and half-draft horse. She was a good mare to work around and I would spend hours pulling shoes off her and nailing them back on, just to get practice in shoeing a horse.

While I am a trainer, not a farrier, I don't regret that time I put in with Dolly because I think it behooves every horse trainer to understand shoeing and foot care and to be able to communicate your wishes to your horseshoer. (The proper term for a person who shoes horses is farrier or horseshoer, but I have always used the term blacksmith, and will do so in this chapter.)

Many young trainers think that harness horses have evolved so far and developed to a point where shoeing is pretty much automatic. Frankly, I couldn't disagree more. Sure, our breed has evolved significantly in the past few decades; I've seen great changes during my career. That doesn't mean, however, that shoeing and foot care are any less important. Many trainers today don't seem to understand the importance of these aspects of horsemanship.

It's been my experience that shoeing and foot care are the most neglected areas in the training of harness horses today. The trainer who will devote time to properly breaking a horse or who will attend to the business aspects of his stable in a professional manner will often ignore the shoeing needs of his horses. He just doesn't seem interested in this area. That's inexcusable, and sooner or later it will catch up to that trainer unless he's very lucky.

Let me say right up front in this chapter that if a trainer doesn't go to the blacksmith's shop when his horses are being shod, the rest of what I have to say won't mean much. I think it's essential that a trainer be there when the horse's shoes are pulled, so he can see how the shoes have been worn, note the condition of the feet, personally supervise the trimming and leveling of the feet, tell the blacksmith what length of toe and angle of foot the trainer wants, and explain what changes might be needed.

I've been fortunate enough in my career to attain some success, and people often ask me my opinion of young trainers in the Standardbred business. It's never easy to judge another person's abilities or talents unless you have been able to observe his operation, but I can say categorically if a trainer does not make a regular practice of going to the blacksmith's shop with his horses, he's simply not a professional horse trainer.

I know that sounds harsh, but I've got to tell it like it is and I feel that a trainer should learn the techniques of shoeing and find the time to get to the shop with his horses.

Yes, I know trainers are busy today, as many stables are quite large and horses are on the road frequently. We have all heard the expression, "No foot, no horse," and no trainer has ever questioned its validity. A horse will probably be shod every few weeks, and the only time he has his shoes off is for that short period of time he's in the blacksmith's shop. It's very important for the trainer to be there to inspect the foot and look for corns, cracks, or any other defect that might require care.

If a trainer can spare only a few minutes, he should be there when the blacksmith pulls the horse's shoes and measures and trims the horse's feet. That's the critical part of a trip to the blacksmith shop. If the trainer is busy, let him do something else when the shoes are being shaped and nailed on. It is far more important to be there when the shoes are pulled than it is to be there when the shoes are being nailed on.

Nailing the shoes on is an important part of shoeing, and I'll touch on that later, but you only need to communicate your ideas on nailing once to a blacksmith, and then he'll be the one doing the work.

Shoeing and balancing is a matter of fractions of inches, weight measured in ounces, and angles that might vary from 45° to 60°. I will attempt to cover the basics and not be too detailed for the novice or too boring for the experienced horseman.

The chapters on shoeing written by Johnny Simpson and Frank Ervin in *Care and Training of the Trotter and Pacer* which was published in 1968 were both excellent, and I heartily recommend that you consider reading them, as well as my comments. Both were great horsemen and, despite the fact that the breed has evolved over the years, the basics are still the same. I have great admiration for the men who were training back in the 1930s and 40s, because harness horses then were tougher to handle and were far less natural in their gait. The trainers had to be real horsemen in that era.

There is no mystique or magic to the shoeing of horses. It is mostly just good common sense, a keen eye, and attention to detail. You must have a good working rapport with your blacksmith so that he fully understands what you expect to be done. The blacksmith should make every effort to accommodate the trainer even if he doesn't agree with the trainer's methods, because the trainer is usually paying the bill for the owner.

I have heard from other people that I am a hard trainer to shoe for, and some blacksmiths don't like working for me. I don't feel as if I'm hard to please, but I do want the blacksmith to do exactly as I ask him, and I will not tolerate a sloppy shoeing job. Perhaps it makes some blacksmiths uncomfortable to have me in the shop, but I think a good blacksmith appreciates having the trainer there when the shoes are pulled. If there are problems with the feet or in trimming the feet, the trainer and the blacksmith can discuss those problems right on the spot and decide upon a good approach. If the trainer is not in the shop, the blacksmith must simply guess what the trainer wants done. If the trainer is too easy to shoe for, he is probably too easy to groom for. Consequently, the blacksmith and grooms are pretty much on their own, so why do you need a trainer?

A blacksmith once told me that a so-called prominent trainer ordered him to trim all his pacers with a 3 1/2-inch toe and a 50° angle in front and to not worry about their feet behind. The trainer gave those instructions to the blacksmith in advance because he simply didn't know any better. Maybe it would be nicer to say that this trainer simply couldn't spare the time to be present when the horses were shod. That negligence will show up in the stable's racing performance sooner or later.

That just amazed me. In any stable you're going to have big horses, small horses, horses with long pasterns, and horses with straight pasterns. How a trainer can expect them all to be trimmed and shod alike is beyond my comprehension.

If I could simplify things, I would say that your two goals in shoeing a horse—trotter or pacer—are (1) to have the horse going clean-gaited so that he isn't hitting his knees, shins, or wherever; and (2) to have the horse feel "solid" and free-going on the lines.

If you stop to think how many strides a horse takes in a race mile, you begin to understand the importance of shoeing and balancing and why a horse will go faster and farther and be easier to drive if he is good-gaited.

Any trainer worth his salt knows how a horse will feel when it is not balanced properly. When you have to use the lines to steady a horse that is uncertain in his gait, he is not balanced. A properly balanced horse will feel solid enough that a trainer will feel as though he does not have to hold the horse together. A trainer can close his eyes and hear the 1-2-3-4 cadence of a balanced trotter as well as feel that balance through the lines. That is a feeling that a person on the bench or in the grandstand cannot have.

Many times a trainer will make a change in shoeing and balancing based strictly on his intuition. It might be difficult for the trainer to explain his reasons for the change, but from his experience, he simply senses it is the proper thing to do. Remember, natural instinct plus experience will often tell you what to do.

You must face up to the fact that some horses are going to be foul-gaited and no trainer in the world is going to be able to help them. You have only yourself to blame for picking out a bad-gaited horse to train. And you have only yourself to blame if you don't get a consignment blank for the next sale in your area. The best remedy for some foul-gaited horses is to sell them and let someone else worry about getting them gaited. I'm not advocating that you give up entirely when a horse doesn't

Breeders Crown winner Defiant One was a star trotting pupil developed by the author. He is a son of Defiant Yankee, a Speedy Crown stallion also developed by Beissinger.

show a natural, fluid gait, but some horses simply come equipped with a foul gait, and no trainer has enough magic to cure these horses.

Occasionally, I hear a horseman say that he had a colt who stood badly and was foul-gaited, but that he corrected the horse with corrective trimming. In those cases, I just tell that horseman it's been nice to know him, and I walk away.

If a horse naturally has short, straight pasterns and is back on his knees, you're not going to eliminate those conformation flaws by corrective trimming. You might be able to alter the way the horse stands a little bit, but no trainer or blacksmith can change the way the cannon bone comes out of the knee or the way the pastern comes out of the ankle. That determines how the horse will fold up with his front feet. You just can't vary some horses too much, and anyone who claims that he can isn't telling the truth.

Time is a great healer in many aspects of the horse business, but the chances are very slim that time will heal a bad-gaited horse. Years ago, when a colt or filly couldn't seem to get balanced or gaited, the trainer would just say, "Let's turn him out for a year and let him mature. He'll be better-gaited next year."

But, with very few exceptions, if a horse is not good-gaited as a two-year-old, he won't be any better at three. With so much emphasis on early speed today, the most popular stallions were usually top two-year-olds and tend to sire horses who come to their gait and speed early. A stallion whose offspring tend to develop into good older horses just isn't very appealing in our business today.

Often when you try to change the gait of a horse too drastically, you will actually cause more problems than you solve. You can seldom affect any significant changes from a horse's natural way of moving.

Again, let me emphasize that you simply can't afford to wait forever on every slow learner in your stable. Most of them will never amount to anything. Once in a great while, a decent horse will be slow to develop, so you sell him and someone else goes on to do well with your discard. It's happened to me and it's happened to every top trainer in the business. Don't let it worry you. If you insist on sticking with every slow learner in your stable, you'll go broke.

Every trainer has picked out a bad-gaited yearling, so you won't be the first. It does help immensely when you can see a yearling turned out or led prior to the sale. I supervised the leading process for the Lana Lobell Farm yearlings for many years and I think this offers buyers a big edge when assessing a horse's gait. Of course, there are some horses who moved beautifully on the lead strip, then seemed like a different horse once they were between the shafts.

Whenever you are watching a yearling move, it is important that he have his head straight in front of him. Any trainer will tell you that you can't gait and balance a colt if his head is off to one side and neither can you accurately judge a yearling's gait this way. That's one of the problems you encounter when a yearling is led next to a pony. Often the yearling's head is pulled around to the side and it's difficult for him to go naturally this way. That's why I prefer to use golf carts, jeeps, or another method that allows you to keep a yearling's head straight in front of him.

Since I have been fortunate enough to break, develop, and drive three Hambletonian winners and later train their offspring, I should mention that gait is usually a trait a sire passes along to his foals. That is, I don't want to buy any yearlings by a trotter who was not good-gaited. I don't care how fast the horse could go, because a bad-gaited trotter is at a handicap right from the start.

A good example would be the Hickory Smoke stallion Dayan. I raced against Dayan many times with Lindy's Pride in the 1969 trotting classics and he was always a formidable opponent because he had very high speed. He was, however, a foul-gaited son-of-a-gun, and I have to give Fred Bradbury a lot of credit for the job he did in racing Dayan because driving him was no day at the beach. He was a tough horse to drive.

Dayan later went to stud and sired some decent horses, but overall he simply didn't sire good enough trotters to become a success as a sire. He was later exported.

By contrast, Speedy Crown was a wonderfully-gaited horse and his offspring are the most naturally gaited trotters I've ever worked with— and other trainers tell me the same thing. They have such a natural gait

A.C.'s Princess, dam of ABC Freight, sire of Hambo winner Historic Freight, was one of the few stabbing trotters able to overcome her gait problems and go on to enjoy a moderately successful career. As this photo shows, however, Beissinger had her hind shins well protected, and also used knee boots on her.

and always seem to carry their heads just right. Speedy Crown's good manners and disposition are other traits he passed on.

Curiously, however, his own sire Speedy Scot was not especially good-gaited, to my way of thinking, nor did he have a good mouth for driving. His action in front was too much up and down for my taste, and I think if Speedy Scot had been trained by anyone other than a master such as Ralph Baldwin we might never have heard of him.

Speedy Crown did not have many of the characteristics of Speedy Scot as far as gait went. He did go close to his elbows, as I mentioned earlier, but he also reached out. I think the fact that Speedy Crown was out of a Florican mare offset the tendency of some Speedy Scots to hit their elbows. The Floricans tended to be lower-gaited.

There are two measurements that are extremely important in properly shoeing and balancing a harness horse. Those measurements are the length of the horse's toe and the angle formed by the front of the hoof wall and the ground.

The length of the toe is measured with a caliper by measuring the front of the foot from the coronary band to the ground. A blacksmith will use a foot level to find out the angle of the foot.

The average mature harness horse will have a toe that measures between 3 1/2 to 4 inches. What is normal for one horse won't necessarily be normal for another horse, because a big horse will almost always have a bigger foot and longer toe than a small horse.

The length of toe will affect a horse's balance and gait. A longer toe will act the same as more weight in the foot and that may act to steady a young horse in his gait, but it will also create more stress on his tendons and ligaments. Therefore I'm like most trainers in that I like to have a horse go with his toes as short as possible.

A shorter toe will cause the horse's foot to break over quicker than a longer toe and, yes, every variation, such as 1/8-inch, makes a critical difference in how a horse breaks over. That might make the difference between a trotter hitting his shins and not hitting his shins.

A trotter will usually require a slightly longer toe in front than a pacer, because the trotter's gait requires the extra balance that the longer toe gives him. Both trotters and pacers usually go with their hind toes about 1/4-inch to 1/8-inch shorter than their front toes.

The angle of the foot is extremely important, too, because it also affects a horse's balance and stride and how the foot breaks over. The average foot of a harness horse will range from a 48-52° angle in front to a 52-56° angle behind.

The rule of thumb is that the higher the angle of the foot, the quicker the foot will break over and the higher the foot will travel in its stride. That is quite easy to imagine, as you can see that a horse must exert more leverage to lift a low-angled foot off the ground than he would to lift a high-angled foot.

It is a good idea to keep a record of your horse's trips to the blacksmith's shop and what changes you have made. Almost every stable maintains shoeing cards on horses, and they're excellent if they are kept up to date.

However, I should point out that blacksmiths often measure differently, so if you have to ship your horses around to different tracks, you might find that two competent blacksmiths might vary as much as 1/8-inch in measuring the toe length and as much as two degrees in measuring the angle. Those can be critical differences. The measurements depend upon the gauge the blacksmith is using and how the foot is held when it's being measured.

Therefore, when you're dealing with different blacksmiths, you often might be well-advised to ignore the shoeing card and tell him to raise or lower the angle, shorten the toe, or simply leave the horse the way he is, irrespective of what appears on the shoeing card. This is an area where the trainer's instinct is critical.

A shoeing card that is updated every time the horse goes to the shop

Horse:	DEFIANT ONE			Year:	1987	
			Stable: Beissinger Stable			
Date			**Front**			**Back**
	Length	Angle	Type of Shoe	Length	Angle	Type of Shoe
1-5	3 3/4	49	3/4 H.R.	3 1/2	54	1/4 x 1/2 Flat
2-2	3 5/8	50	5/8 H.R.	3 1/2	54	Same
3-3	3 5/8	50	5/8 H.R.	3 3/8	54	Same
4-1	3 5/8	50	5/8 H.R. - Bar	3 3/8	54	Full Swedge Bar
5-4	- Same -		- Same - - - - -	- - -	Same	- - - - - - -

All trainers should maintain shoeing cards, and this card shows minor changes made in the shoeing of Breeders Crown winner Defiant One.

is an important source of information for the trainer, particularly if you're using the same blacksmith all the time.

Now let's start talking about the actual shoeing process itself.

A horse's foot will grow about 1/4-inch each month if the horse is shod and in training. If a horse is turned out and the ground is wet from rain, then its foot might grow more than if the ground in the pasture were dry and hard. On hard, dry ground, an unshod horse may wear his feet off as fast as they grow.

A trainer should not let a horse go much more than four weeks between trips to the blacksmith shop, and that interval should be maintained as a maximum, regardless of the condition of a horse's shoes. Even if the shoes are still adequate, you can't let a horse go more than four weeks without having its feet trimmed. For example, a horse might grow more toe and very little heel; thus, the angle of his feet will change between shoeings. Or one foot might grow differently from the other. Frankly, when a horse is actively racing, it's best to shoe him every three weeks.

If the horse's shoes are still holding up O.K. and the swedges, for example, are still sharp, then you might ask your blacksmith to simply reset the same shoes. But make sure you get those feet trimmed! Actually, I usually go ahead and get new shoes virtually every time I send a horse to the shop for trimming, because most blacksmiths charge almost as much to reset an old pair of shoes as they do to make a new set.

(I could never quite understand their logic, because I always considered the floor work about equal to the fire-and-anvil work.)

It is essential that your blacksmith have a clean and level surface for the horse to stand on when its feet are being examined. The shop should be well-lit, because you need to take this opportunity to look not only at the horse's feet, but also his legs and overall condition.

I had great respect for the late Ralph Baldwin, who was a superlative horseman and a master of every little detail it takes to be a trainer. I remember Ralph was strong in his belief that he could notice things in a blacksmith's shop that he might otherwise miss elsewhere. You get a horse in the shop on a clean surface without any harness, boots, or bandages on him and you might notice a curb or splint starting, or some other problem.

I trained Castleton Memo when she was a four-year-old. She was a good Arnie Almahurst filly who had competed in many Grand Circuit stakes at two and three. Just before she was ready to race as a four-year-old, I was with her in the shop and picked up her front feet to inspect them after the blacksmith pulled the shoes. I noticed that she had a minor crack starting in the wall of her foot back toward the heel.

Castleton Memo had shown no evidence whatsoever of any soreness on that heel crack during her training miles, and the groom hadn't called it to my attention. So if I hadn't been there in the shop, it might have slipped past us. Then it would have progressively worsened to the point where she would be lame on it. By finding that crack when it was just starting, I got the blacksmith to cut it out and thus prevent it from getting any worse.

I should say here that a trainer cannot rely on grooms to spot problems with horses. A good experienced groom can be very helpful, but good grooms are getting harder and harder to find. Remember, the owner is paying the trainer to supervise the horse's care, so the trainer shouldn't rely entirely on the groom. I tell my grooms that if they notice anything unusual about the horse, they should bring it to my attention or tell one of the assistant trainers. It might not be serious, but I'd rather have the groom point it out than risk missing a potentially serious problem.

When the blacksmith pulls the horse's shoes off, study the shoes and feet carefully. Is one angle lower than the other? Is there a dish (a concave area) in the front of one foot? Study the condition of the feet. Notice whether they are brittle, soft, or just right.

If you take time to study feet, you will notice, as I have, that many horses have front feet that are not mates. That is, they are not the same size and shape. Some of the better horses I've trained have had front feet that were not mates, but usually the hind feet on horses will be mates. Lindy's Pride, for example, had front feet that weren't mates and so did his son Lindy's Crown. Look for this when you go to purchase a yearling. Some of the defects are pretty well-hidden by a blacksmith.

Lindy's Pride was practically club-footed in one of his front feet. That foot had a dish in the front, a high heel, and was unusually narrow. The other front foot was a more normal round foot with no dish in the toe, but it had a low angle and never grew much heel.

I never went by a gauge when I shod Lindy's Pride because you really couldn't measure the foot accurately. I would just have the blacksmith work on his bad foot first and get it in as good shape as possible, then we'd try to make the other foot as close to it as we could. It was a problem, because we had to cut off heel on one front foot and toe on the other front foot.

To compound the situation, Lindy's Pride had quarter cracks in front and one quarter crack behind. I firmly believe that his cracks—and most quarter cracks, as a matter of fact—are caused by internal injuries or disease. I think that a quarter crack starts inside the hoof and works out, not the other way around. Often the cause of a quarter crack is an infection in the foot. The infection has to find a way to break out and that's how nature takes care of it.

The concussion of a horse hitting the track so hard with each stride is another important factor in causing quarter cracks.

Lindy's Pride had fertility problems, as is well known, and he sired some bad-footed horses. I frankly expected that he would. Lindy's Crown didn't have the best feet, as he had quarter cracks in addition to some problems with curbs. Fortunately, most of the colts and fillies I saw by Lindy's Crown had good feet and very few curbs, and he went on to be a well-respected sire.

(Incidentally, I had Lindy's Crown's curbs pin-fired twice when he was a young horse. The second time his curbs were fired, they looked so bad that a prominent veterinarian in Lexington told me that Lindy's Crown wasn't worth the cost of the pin-firing, in his opinion. I said, "Just go ahead and fire him," and the rest is history. Fortunately, the horse had the size, gait and manners you want in a trotter and he won in 1:54.4 and earned over a quarter-million.)

I've been told that Fancy Crown and Toy Poodle, two outstanding race mares of the 1980s, both had front feet that weren't mates and yet they managed to overcome that, just as Lindy's Pride and Lindy's Crown did. There is an old saying that "you can't shoe a good horse bad and a bad horse good," and there might be a grain of truth to that because good horses do seem to have a way of overcoming problems that would stop ordinary ones.

When trimming and shaping a foot, I always want my blacksmith to try to shape it nearly the way nature should have done it. For example, if a horse has an exceptionally thick wall around the toe and a thin wall at the heel, I tell the blacksmith to dress down the toe with his rasp (from the top side) until the toe appears to be a more normal thickness. If a foot has a thick wall on one side and a thinner wall on the other side,

I would have the thick wall dressed down from the top side to match the thinner wall.

Very few blacksmiths will do this unless you ask them to.

One important tip, however, should be remembered if you do any rasping on the toe of your horse. The rasping will alter the reading of the horse's angle on the blacksmith's gauge. If you're rasping off the wall in the toe area, you will invariably alter the reading of the angle. Actually, the angle of the foot won't change any, but the gauge reading will be altered. The same is true if your blacksmith tries to rasp out a dish in your horse's toe.

Therefore, it is important to measure the angle before you try to rasp off the wall or work on taking out a dish.

Perhaps the key word in shoeing is "natural." The horse should be shod as close to nature as possible. You must remember that what is natural for one horse won't necessarily be natural for another horse. It might be quite "natural" for one horse to carry a 47° angle in front while another horse might carry a "natural" 53°. Each horse must be treated individually and what works on one might not work on another. That's why the question-and-answer columns you see in magazines won't always be helpful to every horse.

Stand next to a horse and closely note how the pastern comes out of the ankle joint. The angle of the pastern should be about the same as the angle formed by the grain in the hoof.

I probably like my horses to go with a slightly higher angle than other trainers do. I think that a higher angle will help a horse break over quicker, develop good knee action, and prevent a trotter from hitting his shins. With my trotters, I try to develop a rolling action in front that resembles a barrel rolling downhill.

The first thing a blacksmith will do after he pulls the shoes is measure the feet to determine the length of the toe and the angle of the foot. He should call these off to you. He might say, "Forty-nine and three-eighths," when measuring the front foot of a pacer, and that will tell you that the angle is 49° and that the toe is 3 3/8-inches long. You will then have to tell the blacksmith if you want the foot trimmed differently or if you want the angle higher or lower or whatever special instructions you might have for him.

If your horse's front feet do not match—as I pointed out was the case with Lindy's Pride—then the blacksmith must first try to do as much as possible to correct the problems with the bad foot and then try to make the better foot match it. For example, if you have a pacer who might carry an unusually low angle, such as 46°, in one front foot and a more normal angle of 50° in the other foot, the blacksmith should work on the foot with the 46° angle first. Bring it up as much as possible.

Remember, you can always trim off more of the foot or lower the angle, but you cannot add once you have taken off.

When a horse has an unusually low angle, the blacksmith won't want to trim anything off the heel, but will trim off the toe of the foot. That should help raise the horse's angle, but it may well be that you cannot get this horse up any higher than a 48° angle on that bad foot. It may be physically impossible to trim the foot in such a manner as to raise the angle any higher. So, in that case, you should leave that foot at 48°, then try to bring the other foot down from 50 degrees to 48 degrees to match the other one.

With some horses who have unusually low angles, you can use a specially-designed pad that will help raise the angle of the foot. It's called a degree pad. It works just like a normal pad in that it fits between the shoe and the wall of the foot, but it is wedge-shaped so that it is thicker back toward the heel and, thus, it effectively raises a horse's angle.

I trained the top trotting mare Nadir's Pride for a brief time when she was a four-year-old, and she carried an unusually low heel, so I had decided to use a 2 degree rim pad on her. That would have raised her angle from 48° to 50 °.

While the blacksmith is measuring the toes and angles after he has pulled the shoes, it's a good idea for the trainer to look at the old shoes to see how the horse is wearing down the shoe. Just as a person wears down his shoes in a unique way, depending upon his gait, so does a horse. The part of the shoe showing the most wear in the toe will be the part where the horse is breaking over when its foot leaves the ground. If it is worn excessively elsewhere, that will tell you that the horse is landing on the worn part of the shoe first when it hits the ground in its stride.

You would like to have a horse breaking over near the middle of a shoe, but often that isn't the case. All horses travel a little differently. How the horse is breaking over will help you determine if you want the blacksmith to trim the feet any differently.

For example, if you have a horse whose shoes show more wear on the outside of the shoe as opposed to the inside, that is a sure indication that your horse is not landing flat when it hits the ground. He is landing on the outside of his foot first and that could ultimately lead to lameness.

In that case, you should ask your blacksmith to trim the outside of the foot a bit lower. You might start by having him use his rasp to brush just a little extra off that outside section of the foot. When you put a new shoe on, the horse should be landing flat on the ground with every stride.

If you're training a horse who has a tendency to go close to his knees, you might also want to trim the front feet just a little lower on the outside. That is a standard prescription for getting a horse away from its knees, but it doesn't always work, and you must be careful not to make any drastic changes in trimming or you could adversely affect a horse's gait and cause unsoundness problems. Some horses are just born to hit their knees. You can try to get a knee knocker to go above or below his knees by using different types and weights of shoes. Most horsemen generally try to get a trotter to go above his knees and a pacer to go below his knees. I'll elaborate on this later when I discuss shoeing problems that you may encounter with trotters and pacers.

FOOT CARE

It is important that you take note of the overall condition of a horse's foot while he is in the shop. This should be done before the blacksmith begins nailing the new shoes back on. Is the frog firm, yet pliable? Is it able to take some of the concussion when the horse's foot hits the ground? Are there any signs of thrush? Is the foot hard or brittle?

When I train my stable in Florida, I bed my horses on sawdust. I find it is wonderful for keeping a horse's feet in good condition. The turpentine in pine sawdust does the trick.

Clay is the natural way to keep moisture in a horse's foot and it is the recommended packing material when your horses are bedded on straw. A horse's feet may not need to be packed every day. You should inspect his feet to see their condition. It is a good idea to pack feet on a frequent basis, however. You can buy clay in a powder form. I add a handful of Epsom salts to the clay and moisten this mixture with cider vinegar to use as a packing material.

A few years ago, I remember that Freddy Bach, the trainer from Lexington, got some clay from Mayfield, Kentucky, which he called Old Hickory Clay. It would stay moist for a long time. He sold it for $5 a bucket and it was real clay, not a powder. He had it dug right out of the banks of a river down there. If you have a spot where you can dig your own blue clay, I would recommend it.

Incidentally, if you have a horse turned out, one of the best things you can have is a mud puddle near the watering trough, because every time a horse comes up to get a drink, it must stand in that mud puddle and that will help prevent its feet from drying out.

My father trained horses when I was a youngster and, although he didn't have Grand Circuit stock, he was a good horseman and tried to be a perfectionist. He taught me that walking a horse through dew-covered grass early in the morning is wonderful for a horse's foot. Dew is the most penetrating moisture available. My father made me walk horses out in a grassy area or hay field early in the morning, and he would even check my shoes to see if they were wet when I came back. That way he knew I'd had the horses out in the dew. The coronary band of the foot would be white because of all the moisture in the foot.

Of course, today at pari-mutuel tracks you can't exactly walk a horse in the dew when the entire barn area is blacktopped, but if you train on a farm track or at a fairgrounds, you might want to get your horses out in the morning dew.

I know that there are many hoof greases and oils available which

purportedly keep the feet in good condition, but I would much rather
rely on good clay instead of the commercial products. Much of the hoof
dressing that I have seen is made to sell, not to use.

I'm especially amazed when I see a groom or trainer who paints the
sole of the horse's foot with a greasy dressing, then packs the foot with
clay. That's just plain stupid. It's defeating the purpose of the clay. That
greasy foot dressing seals the foot, and the moisture from the clay can't
penetrate and do any good. If you wish to use a hoof dressing, a mixture
of equal parts of fish oil and lanolin is the best, because lanolin is the
only kind of oil that is water-soluble.

Some trainers and grooms like to use Reducine along the coronary
band and down in the heel a little, and that is O.K. That will help stimulate growth, but if a foot is growing normally I see no purpose in using
these products. Just try to keep the feet with a natural texture.

There are all sorts of tricks which people use to help a horse's foot,
and I suppose some of them have merit. We've all heard that gelatin will
make a person's fingernails grow, so some trainers feed their horses gelatin to make the hoof grow. But you'd have to feed a horse gelatin for a
long time for that to do any good.

I cannot overemphasize the importance of preserving the horse's feet.
It takes a year to grow a new foot, and you simply can't afford that luxury.
There is never a good time to get lax with foot care, even when a horse is
turned out and away from the races.

I recall racing a trotting filly one season and she performed extremely
well, so I gave her a little turn-out time at the end of the year. During
that time, her feet were trimmed (butchered, I should say) far too short,
and I had a real problem on my hands when she started back in training.
It took me two months to get her feet grown out properly to where I
could get her properly shod. Preserve the feet at all times! Never trim
them too short. You're much better off to leave some foot for the blacksmith to work with.

Many of the lameness problems a trainer encounters today are the
result of poor foot care or, sad to say, no foot care. Even if the lameness
shows up in the knee or shoulder, that problem might have started when
a horse's feet got to stinging him and he began adjusting his gait to get
away from that soreness. Pretty soon a foot problem can become a knee
problem. And track conditions can be a major factor in creating foot problems. When I started training and driving professionally in the years
right after World War II, we raced almost exclusively over clay tracks.
They were great when they were dry, but terrible when it rained. Since
tracks cannot afford to have racing programs rained out, they have had
to develop all-weather surfaces that enable them to race in any kind of
weather. Consequently, the racing surfaces we have today often consist
of stone dust or a gritty material which causes more shoe wear and usually isn't as fast as a well-maintained clay track.

Many trainers make use of leather or synthetic pads in shoeing both trotters and pacers to cushion the feet, but I think pads should be used sparingly. Whether a horse needs pads or not will depend upon the condition of his feet and, more importantly, the condition of the track.

A full pad will cover the entire sole of the foot, while a rim pad fits only under the shoe itself, leaving the sole of the foot open. I generally use a rim pad when the track is off just a little or if it is deep. But when I have to race on a hard, clay track, I may go to a full pad. I will usually use a leather pad on a trotter and a plastic pad on a pacer.

A leather pad is wonderful on a trotter when it is first put on because it is thicker than a plastic pad and thus will absorb more of the concussion. (A trotter hits the ground harder than a pacer.) Once a leather pad gets wet and starts to dry out, it becomes hard and loses its ability to cushion a foot. And it's very difficult to prevent a leather pad from getting wet with horses being bathed and exposed to so much moisture.

TYPES OF SHOES

Let's assume that you have inspected the feet and the previous set of shoes and the blacksmith has properly trimmed the feet. Obviously, the next step is to decide what kind of shoes to put on your horse. This may seem very elementary, but I have had blacksmiths tell me that many trainers don't even know what different shoes are available, nor do they know the reasons for using various shoes. That's just hard to believe.

The simplest type of shoe is a plain, flat, steel shoe; you will hear it called a flat shoe; a plain shoe, or sometimes just a plate. It comes in two standard thicknesses: 1/4-inch and the thinner 3/16-inch.

The 1/4-inch-thick flat shoe comes in widths of 1/2-inch, 5/8-inch, and 3/4-inch.

The 3/16-inch flat shoe comes in widths of 9/16-inch and 5/8-inch. Another very simple shoe is the half-round shoe, and its name is very descriptive of its shape. Draw a circle and then draw a line through its middle from left to right. Each half of that circle would look like a half-round shoe. The flat part of the shoe, of course, is the part which is nailed to the hoof wall while the rounded part is what hits the ground.

The half-round shoe comes in widths of 1/2-inch, 9/16-inch, 5/8-inch, 11/16-inch, and 3/4-inch. The wider the shoe, of course, the heavier it is, and usually the only half-round you see on pacers is a 1/2-inch half-round because pacers generally don't require much weight.

(Do not think that it is impossible for all pacers to wear weight, however. I remember that Harry Fitzpatrick, one of the best horsemen who ever pulled a line over a horse, put 3/4-inch half- round front shoes on the great pacer King's Counsel many years ago and they engaged in some great battles with Adios. That's just one example why there aren't any set rules in training horses.)

The next shoe with which you should familiarize yourself is the swedge

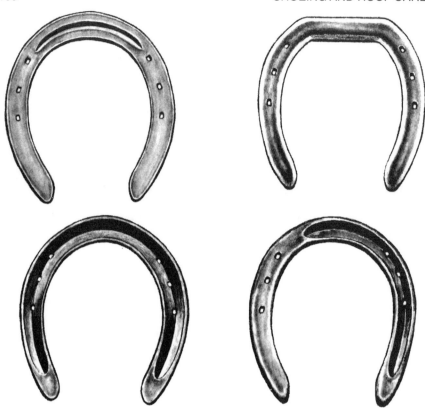

Four very common shoes are shown here. (Top row): Flat shoe with a creased toe and a half-round shoe with a squared toe. (Bottom row): Full swedge and a half-round half-swedge shoe.

shoe. This is a shoe with a V-shaped crease or swedge running through the middle of the shoe from heel to heel. The outside and inside surfaces are the only part of the shoes that come in contact with the track, and thus the swedge acts as a "brake" to stop the foot when it hits the track.

The "braking" action of the swedge is caused when the swedge fills with dirt, and that dirt acts as a non-slippery surface to "grip" the track surface.

Another way to illustrate the stopping ability of a swedge shoe is to think of the horseshoes in the same way you think of your own shoes. A smooth-soled shoe won't give you the "grip" that a shoe with a ridged sole will. The swedge shoe simply gives the horse that grip on the track.

Swedge shoes come in three sizes. The most-commonly used is the shoe which is 7/16-inch wide and 1/4-inch thick. Swedges also come 3/8-inch wide and 1/2-inch wide.

There are variations of swedge shoes. The half-round half-swedge shoe is the most common and it is often the standard shoe on the hind feet of pacers. The swedged section of this shoe is placed to the outside.

You will often see a flat shoe with a shallow swedge in the toe of the shoe. This is called a crease, not a swedge, because it isn't as deep nor does it extend as far around the shoe. Many times a trainer will put a crease in the toe of a front shoe to provide just a bit of hesitation to the horse's action and prevent him from going too high in front or to prevent him breaking over too quickly. A crease in the toe also prevents the horse from slipping when breaking over.

Putting a grab on a shoe is another way, besides a swedge or crease, to slow down a horse's action in front or to give him a better grip on the track. A grab is just a thin piece of metal extending across the toe of the shoe. A grab might be easily compared to the spikes that a track athlete wears. The spikes give the track athlete a better grip on the track than a smooth-soled shoe would. However, I should point out that a grab can be quite severe on the muscles and ligaments, especially of a young horse.

A flat, half-round, or swedge shoe can be made into a bar shoe by extending a flat piece of steel across the back of the shoe. This is often done with horses who have low heels or who have a problem maintaining a proper angle. A properly made bar shoe will allow the frog to absorb some of the shock, but the bar will run across the frog, not the length of it, and thus the pressure won't be as harmful.

Bar shoes are often used on a low-heeled horse because they will add some support in the back of the foot and effectively preserve the horse's angle. Also, you will find some horses with normal heels who land on the ground heel first; thus, it's almost impossible to keep a good heel on such a horse. That's when a bar shoe can help out by preventing the heels from getting pounded down. To my way of thinking, there is a lot more involved in making a bar shoe than simply putting a piece of steel across the heel of the shoe. When a blacksmith makes a bar shoe, I like him to make a regular open shoe first, then weld the bar onto the shoe. It is extremely important that the bar be fitted into the shoe so that it runs across the strongest point of the frog. With that fitting, it can support more of the jarring and, in turn, protect the heel of the foot.

Many blacksmiths just automatically put a bar at the back of the shoe and don't pay much attention to what part of the frog the bar is resting on. Make certain that the bar is resting on the strongest part of the frog, and make certain that the frog has been trimmed so that the frog and the heel of the foot are level and each carries its equal share of the weight.

This might result in a shoe that has the bar placed as much as a half-inch from the heel of the shoe. Don't worry about that. Make sure the bar rides in the right place.

Also, it is important that the bar not be made out of a narrow piece of

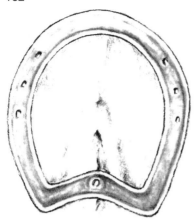
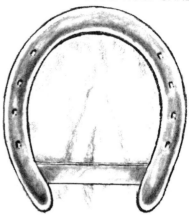

A bar shoe can be made with a bar fitted at the back of the shoe (left), but placement of the bar depends upon the horse's frog. The bar must rest on the strongest part of the frog. Thus, if a frog sits forward in a foot (right), the bar must be inset from the heels.

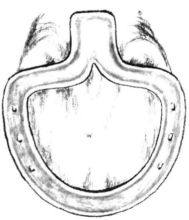

Two relatively new types of shoes discussed by the author are the heart-bar shoe (left) and the mushroom shoe (right). The author prefers the heart-bar shoe to the mushroom.

steel, because if the bar is too narrow, the steel has a way of burrowing into a horse's frog and I don't like that. For me, a bar on a shoe should be 9/16-inch wide and 3/16-inch thick. That gives a good bearing surface.

A bar shoe, of course, places some extra weight in the heel of the foot, but that extra weight amounts to very little. The opposite of weight in the heel is weight in the toe. Although toe weights have been used since time immemorial on trotters, I can't say that I am in favor of using toe weights extensively. I try to stay away from them whenever I can. I firmly believe if a horse indicates to me that he would benefit by having a little more weight up front, he will be better off with a heavier shoe instead of a toe weight. It will depend upon the gait of the horse.

An egg-bar shoe is a form of bar shoe in which the bar does not extend straight across the back of the shoe, but forms a rounded heel instead and gives the shoe the shape of an egg.

An egg-bar shoe is ideal for many low-heeled horses if such a horse has a foot which is shaped to accommodate an egg-bar shoe. Generally, you will find that feet which are shaped a bit more round than normal feet are best for an egg-bar shoe. Also, when using an egg-bar, you want to make certain that the frog sits back from the end of the heel.

Egg bar shoes mostly are used behind, but I have used them in front on horses if their feet are shaped to accommodate an egg-bar shoe.

During the 1970s, trainers from Europe introduced the mushroom shoe in the United States and it gained acceptance quite rapidly. The front part of the shoe is shaped normally, but the ends of the shoe are bent inward toward the frog, then straightened at right angles to form the "stem" of the mushroom. An illustration of a mushroom shoe is helpful in understanding it. You can readily detect the mushroom-like shape of the shoe.

I don't care much for a mushroom shoe because the heel of the shoe rests entirely on the frog of the foot and takes all of the impact. I doubt if that is the way nature intended it to be.

Another shoe which has gained popularity in recent years is the heart-bar shoe. It is shaped like a heart, with the bar made to fit the frog of the foot. The bar should be extended down to within a 1/4-inch of the point of the frog.

The theory with a heart-bar shoe is to apply pressure to the frog, and I find that the heart-bar shoe is effective with horses that have sore feet or those who may have been foundered. It is more effective on a flat-footed horse than it is on a mule-footed or narrow-footed horse. The heart-bar shoe has an effect similar to a mushroom shoe, but I like it better. However, you should hope that you never use it because it indicates a horse has a problem.

The shoes I've described up to this point are all steel or aluminum shoes, but plastic shoes were introduced by a French farrier about two decades ago and they were used extensively for a while. As with many fads, the plastic shoes then went out of favor for various reasons. I am not that fond of plastic shoes and will use them only in very special situations.

The colts and fillies I train are aimed primarily at stakes competition on the Grand Circuit, and seldom do I train a horse older than three. Earlier in my career I trained more raceway horses, but in later years I have concentrated on developing young stock. Let me explain my shoeing procedures with young horses.

Some trainers prefer to start out with a short foot and a light-weight shoe. For example, they might start with a 3 1/2-inch toe and a 1/2-inch half-round shoe on their trotters in front. Then they can add a heavier shoe or a toe weight or allow the horse to grow some more foot as they see how the trotter progresses in training.

I prefer to start the other way, with a longer toe and more weight than you will get from a little 1/2-inch half-round shoe. My preference might be to start a trotter out with a 3 3/4-inch toe in front and a heavy, 3/4-inch half-round shoe that will weigh about 11 ounces. I would rather begin to take the weight and toe off a trotter as he learns to trot than to have to add weight or resort to a longer toe.

This early stage of training is really just experimental and yet it may last for several months. I think a young trotter will develop better knee action and a better overall gait if I gradually peel the weight off him.

Again, I want to emphasize that every horse is different and must be treated according to his individual needs. For example, if a colt showed me some natural gait, I would be more inclined to try a 3 5/8-inch toe and a 5/8-inch half-round after his first shoeing.

You don't want to leave the heavier shoes on a young horse any longer than necessary. The weight should come off gradually, as a horse learns his gait and learns to trot fast. Using a heavy 3/4-inch half-round shoe isn't usually a problem in the early stages of training, but as you progress, the combination of weight and speed will often set your trotter up for lameness problems.

Getting a trotter (or pacer) to go with a light shoe will not only help you avoid lameness problems, but it will also lessen the potential damage if a horse hits a shin or a knee. To illustrate this point: Suppose I were doing some carpentry work and accidentally hit my finger with a hammer. I'd much rather hit it with a small, light-weight hammer than with a large, heavy one. It wouldn't hurt as much. The same principle applies to horses interfering. The less foot they have and the lighter the shoe is, the less damage they will do if they hit a knee or a shin.

Usually, I would start my trotters out behind wearing just a flat shoe that is 1/2-inch wide and 1/4-inch thick behind. Although many of my trotters will ultimately wind up wearing swedge shoes behind, I do not like to start them out in swedges, because a swedge will anchor a horse so much that it can be bad on his legs.

Generally, I prefer not to put swedges on my trotters behind until they get to the 2:30 stage, although that will depend not only upon the horse, but also upon the track surface.

With my pacers, I will start them out with a 9/16-inch by 3/16-inch flat shoe in front and 1/2-inch by 1/4-inch shoe behind. That will give them about equal weight in front and behind. Again, most of my pacers will wear half-swedge shoes behind when they race, but they don't need those swedges early in training.

It is well known that adding weight in front generally will help encourage a horse to trot, and adding weight behind will usually help to make a horse pace. That's not always the case, but it's a sound enough rule that many horsemen tend to leave their trotters barefoot behind early in training while allowing their pacers to go barefoot in front.

That practice is O.K. while you're breaking a yearling or in the early stages of training on soft ground, but I don't like to have a horse go barefoot on rough or hard surfaces. First of all, when you get a yearling right from the sale, many times his feet will be trimmed down so short that you have to put some shoes on the horse simply to protect his feet.

I know that some horsemen will even race horses barefoot, but that sure bothers me. It's against my principles. In fact, if I have a horse throw a shoe at the half-mile pole in a race, I'm tempted to just pull him up right there to avoid breaking up his foot. Again, I'm a believer in preserving a horse's feet.

I am aware that in 1986 the Nordins raced Buckfinder barefooted in front at Indianapolis and the track was hard that day. Yet he trotted in 1:55.4 to set a world record for two-year-old trotters. In 1987, Berndt Lindstedt raced Express Ride barefooted all around at Chicago and Lexington, and he trotted better than ever.

It appears to me that this practice is mostly for horses that are interfering extensively, and should only be considered as a last resort.

If I were going to pull the shoes on a horse, I'd be more likely to try it with a pacer than with a trotter because pacers hit the ground so much lighter. Occasionally, I have known trainers to pull the front shoes off a pacer who hits his knees pretty bad. Eliminating the weight will make the horse go lower, possibly below the knees, but even if he does hit his knees he won't have as much to hit them with if you pull his front shoes.

I make extensive use of the 1/2-inch by 1/4-inch and 9/16-inch by 3/16-inch flat shoe early in training, as they are medium-weight flat shoes and give adequate protection to the foot. They weigh about the same, but the 9/16-inch by 3/16-inch shoe gives you a slightly wider bearing surface for the foot. The 1/2-inch by 1/4-inch shoe will wear longer since it is 1/16-inch thicker.

SHOEING THE TROTTER

Since the problems you will encounter with a trotter are often different than those you encounter with a pacer, let's talk about how I might gait a young trotter first. Then we'll touch on some important aspects in shoeing a young pacer.

As I indicated, I start most of my trotters in a 5/8-inch or 3/4-inch half-round shoe in front, and I think that most trainers do the same. Either shoe has a rounded edge and this facilitates the breaking-over process with front feet. It is very important to teach those young trotters to break over quickly and to develop a rolling knee action.

If I find that one of my trotters is not folding up properly in front in the early stages of training, I will often take those same half-round shoes and simply turn them around on the horse's front feet. I'll just nail them on backwards, leaving the toe open and the heel closed.

Putting a shoe on backwards is an effective way to get a horse folding, because the open toe will encourage a horse to break over faster and the weight in the heel will force him to pick his feet up higher in front.

Whenever you are about to put a shoe on backwards, you should first examine the way the horse is wearing down his shoes to determine where he is breaking over. You want to put the open part of the shoe right where he is breaking over. For example, if you have a horse breaking over a little to the outside, as most do, you want to have the open part of the shoe there instead of right in the middle of the toe.

In the very early stages of training, you'll also begin to see if you have a line-gaited or a passing-gaited trotter.

A passing-gaited trotter is one who goes wide enough behind that when his back feet are extended forward they are passing on the outside of the front feet as the front feet swing backwards.

A line-gaited trotter will trot narrower behind so that his front feet are about in line with the back feet when they travel.

There are very few rules in horse training to which there are no exceptions, but I dare say that if a trotter starts out as a line-gaited trotter he will be a line-gaited trotter for the rest of his life no matter how you trim his feet or what kind of shoes you put on him. Often this will run in families, as certain sires tend to produce trotters that are line-gaited while others produce more passing-gaited trotters.

The above description of the trotting gait is good evidence why it is usually important for a trotter to have good length to his barrel and why it is essential for a trotter to have some reach to his stride so he doesn't trot back under himself.

That is not to say that horses don't change their gait. They sometimes do, but the change does not occur overnight. A young horse will often change in gait as he learns to go faster. It is not unlike a golfer who is first learning to swing a club. At first, he might feel a little awkward holding the club and standing over the ball, but as he practices and becomes more comfortable he will often alter his swing to fit his own style.

So it is with horses. I can recall that Speedy Crown wore 5/8-inch half-round shoes when he won the Hambletonian, but he started going too close to his elbows to suit me and I had to put a 5/8-inch x 1/4-inch flat shoe on him to bring him down off his elbows. The weight of the flat shoe was about the same as the half-round shoe, but the flat shoe had the effect of making him go just a little lower.

Speedy Crown was a passing-gaited trotter, but he was not a horse who went extremely wide behind like, for example, Scott Frost did. Speedy Somolli was also passing-gaited and tended to go a little wider behind than his sire. Both Speedy Crown and Speedy Somolli had no problems getting around turns, but generally I would prefer a line-gaited trotter on a half-mile track. I find that they usually get around the turns better than the typical passing-gaited trotter, especially if the latter horse is real wide and sprawly-gaited behind.

Incidentally, almost all line-gaited trotters wear down the outside of their hind feet. So when the blacksmith trims their feet, he should leave the outside of their hind feet just a little low out there. Do not try to level the foot.

One of the most important things with a young trotter is to get one breaking over properly in front so he doesn't start the habit of interfering with his hind leg. That can lead to the far more serious problem of stabbing. Every trainer has had trotters like this.

A stabber is a trotter who will not extend his hind legs directly forward with each stride, but who instead will stab or jab a hind leg to the inside or to the outside of its normal line of travel. A stabber usually is a horse who has had the misfortune to whack his hind shins with his front feet early in training, and he's simply trying to re-position his hind legs to avoid a recurrence.

If a young trotter starts to misplace a hind leg or simply can't seem to figure out where to put his hind leg, you have a problem that you'd better solve quickly before this habit becomes permanent. With a stabber, after I put his half-round shoes on backwards on his front feet, if he persists in stabbing I would put plastic shoes on his hind feet or at least let him go barefoot behind for a while.

As I indicated earlier, I seldom use plastic shoes, but they do serve a purpose with stabbers. I'll try putting plastic shoes on a stabber's hind feet. For a horse to wear a plastic shoe behind is practically like going barefoot.

I will leave those plastic shoes on behind long enough for the trotter to regain his confidence and to overcome his problems of stabbing. With the combination of the shoe on backwards in front and the plastic shoes behind, the horse may trot clean. If so, he soon will learn that he can move along without hitting himself. Once I think the horse is set and is beyond remembering his stabbing problems, I will go back to using a 1/2-inch by 1/4-inch flat shoe behind, or possibly even a swedge shoe.

Whenever you're trying to solve a gait problem on a horse—trotter or pacer—make your adjustments on one end at a time. If a trotter is hitting his shins, I'll work on the end that is doing the hitting first. That is, I will change a horse's shoeing in front to see if he's better, before I start experimenting with his hind shoes. If you work on both ends at the same time, you'll never know which change helped him the most.

The only stabbing trotter I've ever had much luck with was A.C.'s Princess, the dam of ABC Freight. She was by A.C.'s Viking and she stabbed right from the very beginning; nothing seemed to help her. Amazingly, however, that filly would stay trotting and could go fast. I even won some stakes with her. You just didn't want to look down at her legs when she was trotting.

Some trainers will square the toes on any trotter that begins to stab a hind leg, on the principle that the squared toes in front will help the horse break over easier and will thus get the front feet out of the way faster and avoid interference. That practice is all right for some horses, but I generally prefer a round toe in front. I do not like to square toes, because I don't think they're natural. Instead of squaring a toe, I might ask my blacksmith to "blunt" the toe just a bit; that's not as extreme as squaring the toe. When I tell my blacksmith to "hit it in the face" he knows that I mean to blunt the horse's front shoes right where the horse tends to break over.

I will be more likely to square a trotter's hind toes than his front toes. A horse's hind feet are shaped differently than his front feet. The front feet are rounder, whereas the hind feet tend to be more oval. I think you can square a hind toe more effectively than you can a front toe. I never like a pointed toe behind on a trotter, whereas I don't mind it on a pacer.

Most horsemen believe that stabbing is caused by the horse's fear of hitting itself. That's probably true in most cases, but I have known trotters to stab even before they had a chance to hit their shins. They would stab in the very early stages of training before we started to make speed. So I believe some horses are just born to stab. And they are a real headache.

Let's assume that your horse is not stabbing and is beginning to trot on, but has not developed that nice front stroke you'd like to see on a trotter. If the trotter has adequate knee action, but simply isn't extending far enough in his stride, then you might try adding a toe weight.

However, if the trotter is striding out far enough, but goes stiff-legged and does not have that nice knee action most trotters have, you'll probably be better off putting a heavier shoe on the colt.

It's sometimes difficult to know whether a colt will benefit more from the addition of a toe weight or a heavier shoe or from having a longer toe, so that's where you need to experiment a little. Your first option, however, should be adding a toe weight.

The advantage that a toe weight offers, of course, is that you can add and subtract toe weights very easily and, therefore, you can determine if a horse will benefit by the addition of some weight. Toe weights come in sizes ranging from one ounce up to four ounces. A toe weight may help a horse extend his stride more than the extra weight in the shoe—and you don't have to get your trotter reshod to find out.

Actually, you can often find out if a horse will benefit from having more weight simply by putting heavy-ribbed bell boots on his front feet. Or you can put two pair of bell boots on the same foot to see if the extra weight will help the horse. I really believe that the feel the horse gets from the flopping of the boots is what makes the change, rather than the boots' weight.

Now you have your young trotter developing a nice stroke in front. You found that you had to go to a slightly heavier shoe to get the horse to develop that stroke, but your experience tells you that, as the horse learns to trot, the weight can come off. Another consideration in your mind every time you sit behind your trotter should be how he handles his feet after they leave the ground.

Horse trainers would have fewer problems if every horse broke over near the middle of his toe and folded his front foot up straight, and it traveled in a straight motion at every point in the stride. Unfortunately, that often isn't the case. Many horses will not fold their front feet straight and instead will fold inward toward their knees or, conversely, fold outward.

Horses who swing their front feet to the outside are called paddlers. I would much rather have a line-gaited trotter paddle than I would a passing-gaited trotter. Usually with a paddling gait in front and a wide gait behind, the passing-gaited trotters just clobber their shins. Paddlers not only have lost motion, but it is extra strain on their ankles and knees.

If a trotter paddles with his front feet and tends to be narrow-gaited behind, he can often scoot his hind feet up between his front feet and thus avoid interfering. That's not the most desirable gait, but it is sometimes the best you can hope for with a confirmed paddler.

Pershing, a son of Nevele Pride who went on to be so successful in Europe, was a paddler when I trained him as a two-year-old. Fortunately, he was a high-going colt and that's often a blessing for a paddler because his gait is such that he will get his front feet up and out of the way, thus missing his shins. I might have even raced Pershing with elbow boots because I would rather have had him going too high and hitting his elbows than clobbering his shins.

The worst kind is a horse who paddles in front and who is wide-gaited behind. Neither of those traits is fatal alone, but in combination they make a horse virtually odds-on to clobber his shins.

The opposite of a paddler, of course, is a horse who folds up to the inside with his front feet and thus can bring his foot around to hit his knee on the opposite leg.

Knee knockers are not as serious a problem as they were years ago, and the problem is not as serious with trotters as it is with a pacer. Many trotters who fold up to the inside often go above their knees and thus avoid interference. Some of these horses will hit the arm just above the knee, but that doesn't concern me too much because hitting the muscle of the arm is infinitely preferable to hitting the bone of a critical joint like the knee.

If your trotter does fold up to the inside and hits his knees, you often can make some adjustments to get him to go above his knees. There are five approaches to getting a trotter to go above his knees: (1) a longer toe; (2) a heavier half-round shoe; (3) a higher angle to his front feet; (4) the addition of bell boots; and (5) adding a thick, full leather pad under his shoes with silicone between the foot and pad. I really like to use silicone under a full pad because it forms to the shape of the sole of the foot and stays pliable and never gets hard. Thus it helps tremendously to absorb any sting the horse might feel from hitting the track. It also keeps the foot in good condition, and seldom lets it dry out. Silicone is easier, cleaner, and better for the blacksmith to use instead of some other products, such as oakum and pine tar.

For example, if your horse is going with a 3 1/2-inch toe in front and is brushing his knees just a little, you might let his front feet grow out a little and not trim so much off during his next shoeing. Let him go with a 3 5/8-inch toe and see what happens to his gait.

Another simple solution would be to simply go to a heavier half-round shoe. If you're using a 1/2-inch half-round shoe on your horse in front and he's brushing his knees, try a 5/8-inch half-round shoe or a 9/16-inch half-round shoe. A 5/8-inch half-round shoe weighs about two ounces more than a 1/2-inch half-round shoe, and that extra weight might get your horse to go above his knees.

A higher angle on a horse's front feet will always result in the horse going higher in front. That is another adjustment that can be made at the time the horse is taken to the blacksmith's shop. If your trotter has a 48° angle in front, try raising it to 50° and I can almost assure you that your horse will clear his knees.

Perhaps the easiest remedy to get a horse above his knees is the addition of bell boots. You can start with one pair of light-weight bell boots and if that isn't sufficient to get him above his knees, you might try using two sets of bell boots or go to the heavy-ribbed bell boots that were used by so many trainers years ago.

It is essential that I emphasize strongly that many trotters will begin to hit their knees only after they start the habit of hitting their shins. So it is important for you to prevent your trotter from starting to hit his shins.

What will happen is that the trotter's front foot will come back and hit the inside of the hind shin, and that interference will often redirect the flight of the foot and deflect it in toward the knee. If the horse were trotting clean and not hitting his shins, he would probably not hit his knees, either.

Before leaving the horse's front feet and shoes, I want to make one additional point. I will address the subject of nail placement in greater detail later because I think it is an extremely important part of shoeing that somehow gets sloughed off by many blacksmiths and trainers, but I should mention that I like to use eight nails, instead of the customary six, on a trotter's front shoe.

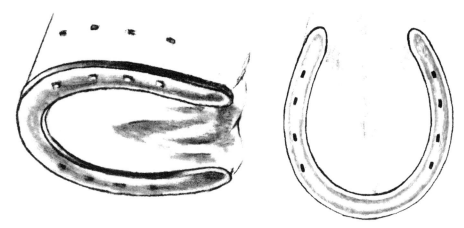

The author will often use eight nails to secure the front shoes of trotters as they enter the latter stages of training. Trotters, he notes, have a greater tendency to throw a front shoe, and the extra nails provide greater holding power. Nails should exit the hoof wall at least three-quarters of an inch from the bottom of the foot. In positioning the nails in the hoof wall, note that the rear nails are placed closer to the outside of the shoe.

It's not unusual to see a trotter throw a shoe during a race. This is especially true if a trotter is wearing pads and racing on a wet or muddy track. A trotter carries more weight in front than a pacer and its gait is higher; thus a trotter is more likely to lose a shoe. That usually means losing a race, and no trainer likes to sacrifice his chances because of a lost shoe.

I do this only on my trotters, not my pacers, and I only put the eight nails in their *front* shoes, not their hind shoes. Those two extra nails in each front shoe are a little insurance policy with my trotters. I might add that this isn't necessary in the early stages of training, but I start adding the extra nails when I have a horse about ready to race.

Now let's return to our trotting colt who has that good stroke in front and yet is starting to brush his shins a bit. You don't want that to become habit-forming, because it will affect the trotter's speed and may cause him to start hitting his knees.

If your trotter is line-gaited and is folding up straight in front and still hitting his shins, this might be the time to square his front toes a bit. That will not only help him break over a little quicker, but since it is the front part of his foot that is making contact with the shin, squaring the front toe might enable him to go clean.

However, if your trotter is passing-gaited and folding up straight and hitting his shins, I would rasp off the outside toe of his front feet, leaving just enough wall to nail a shoe on securely. Again, merely by rasping down the outside of the wall which is making contact with the hind shin, you might enable your trotter to go clean.

(This same practice will work when a horse is hitting his knees. If you rasp off the inside wall of the front foot, you reduce the part of the foot that makes contact with the knee and that might allow your horse to clear his knees.)

In trying to get your trotter to clear his shins or to go above his knees, as we discussed earlier, you may worry that your trotter will hit his elbows. That doesn't worry me too much since the ideal trotter will have good knee action and go within a couple inches of his elbows anyway.

You will know when your trotter does start to hit his elbows because you'll often see a little dirt on his elbows after a fast mile. I should add that often a trotter doesn't really hit the point of his elbow, but instead hits the muscle just below the point.

While on the subject of high-gaited trotters, let me say that I use elbow boots only as a last resort. I'll try just about anything to shoe a horse off his elbows. In my opinion, elbow boots are the hardest boots to fit properly on a horse. When you do get them fitted properly, they look as if they're too sloppy. But when they look sloppy, that's when they are usually about right for the horse trotting at high speed.

Sanders Russell is one horseman I admired very much and he used a lot of elbow boots. I also know that many good horses, Speedy Scot being one of them, wore elbow boots. But I think you are better off trying to *shoe* your horse off his elbows.

If you have a trotter going toward his elbows and you want to bring him down lower, the first thing I would do is cut some toe off him, if he has any excess, and see what effect that has. Often, just trimming an eighth-inch off a horse's front toes will help. Or you can blunt his front toes, as I described earlier, because that is usually the part of the foot that makes contact with the elbow.

If that didn't help me, I would then lower the horse's angle on his front feet a little. That should also serve to bring a horse's front action down. Just a degree or two is usually enough.

A lighter shoe of the same type may also help bring a horse down off his elbows. Naturally, I never use any heavier shoe than is necessary with a horse, but let's say my trotter was wearing a 5/8-inch half-round shoe in front. Trying this trotter in either a 9/16-inch or possibly even a 1/2-inch half-round shoe might get him off his elbows. Or you could do as I did with Speedy Crown and use a 5/8-inch by 1/4-inch flat shoe.

If going to a lighter shoe doesn't get the horse off his elbows, I would try changing the type of shoes. If the horse had been wearing a half-round shoe, I would try a flat shoe on him. If the horse was wearing a flat shoe, I would put a crease in the toe of that shoe to see if that would hold him on the track any longer. If the flat shoe with the creased toe didn't get the job done, I would try using a full swedge shoe in front, although you usually don't have to go to that extreme.

Keep in mind that as you're making adjustments to overcome one problem, you might actually be creating another problem. Make certain that you keep your horse trotting clean and feeling solid to you.

Ideally, a trotter's hind leg should travel close to the ground and scoot up under his front feet. I dislike a trotter with a high, hocky gait behind because he is wasting a lot of motion and he is also a candidate to interfere.

Usually, the standard shoe for a trotter behind is a full swedge shoe, and you will find that this is the best shoe for most of your trotters. Most blacksmiths will extend the heels of a hind shoe just a bit beyond the edge of the foot. This extra edge helps keep a scalper in place if you need to use one, as you frequently do, on the hind foot of a trotter. As long as the trailer part of a swedge shoe isn't too long, you need not worry about it affecting the gait of your horse.

Incidentally, I have used a standard half-swedge behind on my trotters, with the swedge on the outside and the half-round section on the inside. This may widen out a trotter behind. I would use a standard half-swedge instead of a full swedge if a trotter has a swinging motion to his hind legs, similar to a pacer.

For the past few years, I have raced many of my young horses at The Meadowlands and I use a lot of borium there, not necessarily to give the horse's shoes a better grip on the track, but to prevent the shoes from wearing out so fast. Every time you shoe a horse you are putting new nail holes in the foot, and that will eventually weaken the wall of the foot. Common sense tells you that you can't put holes in the foot without having some effect. Those nail holes will not grow shut, they just have to grow out.

When you apply borium to a shoe of a horse racing at most pari-mutuel tracks, you don't need a big bead of borium or a borium grab. On a half-round or flat shoe that I might wear on a horse in front, I need only run the borium around the toe from nail hole to nail hole and from the last nail back to the heel. If I have a horse who tends to wear one side of his shoe more than the other, I will even dot some borium in between the nail holes on that side of the shoe.

On a swedge shoe behind, I will run the borium on the inside of the swedge and even back along the heel of the shoe.

Before I leave the subject of hind shoes, let me add that I often have my blacksmith put clips on a horse's hind shoes because I find that the shoes are more likely to stay in place if clips are used. This is particularly important if a horse is in the habit of kicking the wall of its stall. Kicking will often loosen a shoe or slide it back, but the groom or trainer may not realize the shoe is loose until the shoe flies off during a training or race mile. So the clips are sort of a cheap form of shoe insurance. I will also use clips on feet that are shelly and not so solid and, therefore, do not hold nails well.

174

SHOEING A PACER

Let me switch gaits now and talk a bit about the problems you might encounter shoeing a young pacer. As I stated before, I start all my pacers off with either a 1/2-inch x 1/4-inch or 9/16-inch x 3/16-inch flat shoe in front. Behind they will wear a 1/2-inch x 1/4-inch flat shoe.

The 1/4-inch-thick flat shoe will always outwear the 3/16-inch shoe, of course, but the 9/16-inch x 3/16-inch shoe has a little more bearing surface, and I find that desirable.

Those shoes usually will be steel shoes, because I am not that fond of using aluminum shoes on my horses—although I might occasionally use aluminum shoes if a pacer starts out too climby-gaited in front. A lighter aluminum shoe will tend to make him go lower. Many aluminum shoes come with a grab in the toe, and I would be very careful about using a grab on the toe of a shoe worn by a young horse. The grab will accomplish your goal of eliminating his tendency to climb in front, but the grab will also exert severe stress on the ankles. You might ask your blacksmith to grind off the grab altogether or to grind it down so that it isn't quite so severe.

One important precaution in using a grab in the toe of any shoe is that you must remember it will change the horse's angle by raising his toe.

If I had a pacer who had the opposite problem and who was going so low to the ground that he couldn't even pace over a corncob, I would perhaps try him in a 1/2-inch half-round shoe. That will generally encourage the horse to fold a little bit in front. Don't think that half-round shoes are only for trotters. With a low-going or "daisy-cutting" pacer I may also try a heavier flat shoe, such as 3/4-inch x 1/4-inch shoe, to get him to pick up his feet more.

The ideal pacer should have good knee action, although not as much as a trotter and not so much that he hits the bottom of his hobbles. It's also important that a pacer reach out and not pace underneath himself.

Once in a while, a trainer will have a pacing-bred colt or filly who doesn't show any inclination toward pacing initially. I would prefer not to strap a tight hobble on a horse like this right away because the colt or filly will often fight the hobbles and then you've got problems. Sooner or later, the pacing-bred youngster usually will hit a decent pace and show his breeding, but you can help one along by letting his hind feet grow out to about four inches and cutting down the front toes. You can also add a side-weight shoe behind, but I haven't had to use many of them in recent years.

Frankly, horses who fit this category are quite rare, but if I have a youngster who is pacing-bred and wants to trot, I'll just let him trot for a while and see what happens. Don't get yourself into a situation where you're forcing or fighting the colt this early in training.

Don't get discouraged if you have a pacer who doesn't seem to come to a natural gait. Many horses, both trotters and pacers, will get better-gaited as they learn to go faster in those first months of training. It's just the maturity and experience that helps them.

For example, many pacers will show signs at first of being what we call trappy-gaited. That is, they will often go with their front legs reaching up too high and not extending far enough. They just pace underneath themselves and don't cover any ground. Such a horse might benefit by having a full swedge shoe in front or maybe even an aluminum shoe with a mild grab, but many trappy-gaited horses will improve as they go faster miles.

I should add that pacers as well as trotters can go too high. I recall that Paulsboro p,3,1:54.1 was climby-gaited in front and I put a full swedge shoe on him to take some of that action away. I shortened his toes a little and dropped the front angle, and he was fine from that point forward.

When a pacer is marking the bottom of his hobbles, then you know he is going a little too high in front.

In my comments on trotters, I indicated the problems a trainer could have with a paddler, but I don't find a pacer who paddles to be nearly as troublesome. At least you know that a pacer who paddles will not hit his knees, although the paddling action is a strain on a horse's ankles.

Pacers hitting their knees can be quite a problem, and there are some methods a trainer can employ to help a pacer miss his knees. But there also are some pacers just destined to hit their knees.

Before I get into discussing the various methods, let me emphasize the importance of having a horse's head in front of him when he travels. I mentioned this briefly when talking about how you can judge a yearling's gait. A horse who might normally be good-gaited will often start hitting his knees if he gets his head around to the right, for example, going into a turn.

Your horse might need a headpole or gaiting strap to keep him going straight, and it is only when you have a horse moving with his head straight that you can adjust his gait. A horse with his head off to the right will often flip his right foot in and hit his left knee, and you might be able to eliminate that problem if you get the horse to carry his head straight.

If your horse is carrying his head straight and still hitting his knees, there are several things you can do to help this horse. They might not work if you have a confirmed knee knocker, but there are some remedies you can try.

For example, if you have a pacer that hits one knee but not the other, you can often help this horse by keeping his head turned slightly toward the side he is hitting. If your pacer hits his left knee but not his right, you might try to turn his head slightly to the left so that he's less likely to hit that left knee.

If the pacer were just slightly brushing his knees, I would ask the blacksmith to rasp off a little of the inside wall of his front foot. After all, that is the part of the foot which is brushing his opposite knee and you might be able to take off enough to enable the pacer to go clean. You need to leave enough of the hoof wall to nail the shoe on, of course, but no more than that.

If the pacer persists in hitting his knees, the time-honored remedy is to lower the foot on the outside. Let me caution you, however, that you should ask your blacksmith to lower the horse's foot only slightly, as an abrupt change would lead to lameness and might even cause worse problems. I've found that lowering a horse on the outside might not eliminate the problem altogether, but it might cause the horse to merely brush his knees instead of hitting them hard.

Actually, since some horses are going to fold in toward their knees no matter what you do, your efforts are best directed toward getting a pacer to go lower than his knees just as you might try to get a trotter to go above his knees. And if all else fails, get a pair of well-padded knee boots.

Many pacers will race quite satisfactorily with knee boots, and many of them will require knee protection no matter what you try. I do think, however, that you should try whatever you can to avoid using boots, because I have had some pacers who came close to their knees, but never showed that they touched a hair. Many horsemen, including myself, think, "Well, I might as well just put a pair of knee boots on him for protection in case he does hit a knee."

In some cases, that pacer who was merely getting close to his knees in the past will mark his newly-fitted knee boots rather severely, and then he'll probably need those boots for the rest of his career.

The same is true of a horse going to his elbows. I've had trotters go so close to their elbows that I couldn't tell if they were hitting or not, but if I put a pair of elbow boots on such a horse, I can assure you he'd mark them up pretty good.

I think that when a horse—pacer or trotter—is going clean, he never gives any thought to the prospect of interference. He is going free and naturally. But once he hits a knee, elbow, or shin for the first time for whatever reason, he begins to think about hitting. Even though the horse may be trying to avoid interference, he actually is so afraid of it recurring that he simply can't prevent himself from hitting.

Pacers generally aren't as likely to require pads, as trotters are, because they don't hit the ground as hard. I will use a plastic rim pad on some of my pacers if we're racing over a hard track.

Don't think, however, that pacers can't wear full pads, because often it is necessary to go to a full pad if a horse has bad feet. Bardot Lobell, for example, wore full pads when she was a three-year-old because she had bad feet, thin soles, and corns. Those pads helped protect her feet. I like to use silicone underneath pads; it has a lasting, rubbery effect and it will shape to the sole of the foot and prevent any foreign matter from

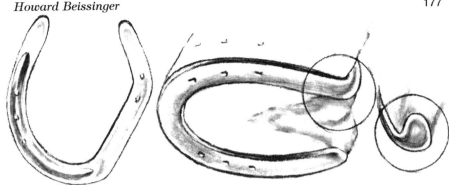

Cross-firing is often a problem with pacers, and one traditional remedy is the diamond-toe shoe (left). The author also notes that the inside heel on a pacer's front shoe can be "spooned" or turned up to prevent it from being grabbed by a cross-firing hind foot.

getting between the pad and the sole of the foot.

The rear end is where the driving power of a horse is, so I like a pacer whose hind legs travel forward with the normal swinging motion. I do not like a wide, sprawly-gaited pacer with too much swinging to his hind legs. As with a hocky-going trotter, that is wasted motion. Unless the horse is cross-firing, the hind legs of a pacer usually follow his front legs and there isn't much you need to worry about.

As I indicated earlier, virtually all my pacers will wind up with a half-swedge shoe behind, with the swedge portion to the outside. That swedge section acts to widen up a horse to prevent it from cross-firing. We don't see nearly as much cross-firing in pacers today as we did years ago. Cross-firing is a problem where the hind feet of the pacer will swing in underneath the body so far that they will clip the front feet on the opposite side. The natural swinging motion of a pacer contributes to this, and many older trainers would use a trailer on the outside to prevent cross-firing. Putting caulks on the end of a trailer was popular years ago, too. Another trick many trainers have used is to lower the inside of a pacer's hind feet. Our horses are more naturally-gaited today and cross-firing is seldom a serious problem.

If you do have a pacer who cross-fires, a traditional remedy is to put a diamond-toe half-swedge shoe on the horse behind. That is simply a standard half-swedge shoe with the inside toe of the hoof wall blunted so the shoe is not round but instead comes to a diamond point.

Also, since the inside heel of the front shoe is often clipped by a cross-firing pacer, I will have the blacksmith "spoon" or turn up the heel of that shoe. The blacksmith will simply turn up the end of the shoe and fit it to the outside of the wall so the end of the shoe will look much like a clip used on a hind shoe. The cross-firing pacer then can't grab the heel of his front shoe as easily.

NAIL PLACEMENT

Now that I have talked about the different ways to shoe a trotter and a pacer, let me address a subject to which few trainers give any consideration. I'm referring to the manner in which a shoe is nailed on the foot. That may sound so very elementary that it isn't even worth discussing, but I think it is an important part of shoeing and I have some strong opinions on this subject.

My lifetime of working with harness horses has taught me that the placement of nails in shoeing is extremely important. After all, the nails are what hold the shoe on and the shoe is what protects the foot. Today, we have so many shoes that come with pre-punched nail holes, but those nail holes simply aren't in the proper place for some horses. That is why I like to have my blacksmith punch his own nail holes. That way, the nails go where they should go and where I want them to go.

I realize that the trainer will seldom be the person nailing the shoes on a horse, but this is an area where he must communicate his wishes to the blacksmith and then supervise the work to make certain it is done according to his wishes.

There seems to be an unwritten rule among blacksmiths that you should not punch a nail hole any farther back than the widest part of the foot. I don't buy that. I think that you not only can put a nail back farther than the widest part of the foot, but I like to have a nail back toward the heel of the foot, as long as there is sufficient wall to nail to there.

I know that some trainers will throw up their hands and say, "You'll cripple a horse doing that," but I say, "Not if you're using a competent blacksmith and common sense."

Not only is it important to have at least one nail hole back toward the heel, I would recommend that you space your nail holes out. Don't let the blacksmith punch the nail holes too close together. By spacing your nail holes out farther, you will have more holding surface for the shoe and also preserve the foot.

When you trim the foot, you can see how thick the wall of the foot is, and that will determine your nail placement. The wall of the foot is thicker toward the toe, then tapers off back toward the heel. So when you punch a nail hole in the shoe back toward the heel, it should be toward the outside of the shoe.

White feet are usually softer than black feet, so horses with white feet are good candidates for clips on their shoes. White feet, however, don't really require any more care than black feet. Both need to be preserved as much as possible.

When your blacksmith pulls the shoes of a horse, check to see where the nail holes are on the horse's feet and tell your blacksmith to put the holes in the new shoes in between the holes from the previous shoeing. You should never let your blacksmith get into a pattern of putting the nail holes in the same place shoeing after shoeing. If you don't watch this, the blacksmith will often fall into a pattern naturally and when you drive the nails into the same part of the hoof wall each time you're going to weaken the foot and compromise the ability of the nail to hold the shoe in place.

There may be times when the blacksmith cannot avoid putting the nail holes in much the same spot as they were in the previous shoeing, but just because the nail enters the foot in the same spot doesn't mean that it must come out of the foot in the same place. A good blacksmith can angle his nails a little forward or back and get the nails to come out in a different place. And, believe me, where the nails come out of the foot is every bit as important, or more important, as where they go in.

I like to have the nail come out high on the foot, preferably three-quarters of an inch up from the bottom of the foot. Once again, I can just picture trainers saying, "You'll 'quick' a horse by getting a nail hole too high." And my response is, you should have no problem with putting your nails high if your blacksmith is competent.

To avoid quicking a horse, the critical part is where the nail goes in, not where it comes out. That is very important.

If the nail comes out of the foot low, then you won't have as much hoof wall holding the nail and your shoes won't be as secure. You've got to get the nail holes up high enough so that you have plenty of foot to hold on to. That will also help preserve the foot.

Another often-overlooked part of shoeing is how much clinch the black-smith leaves on the nail. When the nail has been driven up through the hoof wall, the blacksmith must use his nippers to cut off the pointed end of the nail, then clinch or flatten the exposed nail so that it is secure in the foot.

Some blacksmiths will leave a clinch that is too big and rough for my taste. Be aware that a happy medium should be reached between too little clinch and too much clinch. The large clinch might hold the shoe in place securely, but if the track is muddy and the slop just literally pulls the shoe off the foot (as often happens), the big clinches just take part of the foot with them.

Don't make the mistake of thinking that a big clinch will hold the shoe in place if a horse should happen to grab the shoe during a race. If your horse's hind foot reaches up and grabs a front shoe, that shoe is probably going to come off, no matter how big the nail clinch is. And when a horse grabs a shoe that's been nailed on with big clinches, it really breaks up the foot.

With a more moderate clinch, if a horse should grab a shoe, the nails will probably pull out clean and not destroy so much of the hoof wall.

Some blacksmiths don't pay much attention to this area of shoeing, but a trainer should. If a blacksmith files off the nail clinches altogether, then the horse is a prime candidate to throw a shoe. There must be some clinch, but make certain it isn't too much.

In this chapter, I have touched on many different aspects of shoeing and foot care, and I still haven't nearly exhausted the subject. I wouldn't hesitate to say that it's certainly one of the most important aspects of training a horse. The time you spend paying attention to every detail of shoeing and foot care will usually pay great dividends when it comes time to race.

In closing, I would like to point out that I have acquired my ideas through experience and knowledge that I picked up from great horse-men such as Ralph Baldwin, Joe O'Brien, Sanders Russell, Frank Ervin, Clint Hodgins, Harry Fitzpatrick, and others. I didn't always agree with their ideas, but I certainly gained some good ones from them.

People occasionally will compliment me on having good-gaited horses and then ask me to divulge my secrets for shoeing horses. There really are no secrets, but certainly one key to having good-gaited horses is sim-ply picking out yearlings with good conformation. You simply can't im-prove too much on nature, so if you pick out horses who stand and move properly, and use common sense and stick close to nature in shoeing them, those horses will probably be good-gaited and they'll make you look good when they're on the track.

Howard Beissinger is one of the best all-around horsemen harness racing has ever known. His attention to detail and his strong work ethic vaulted him to success early in his career and led the Ohio native to the Hambletonian winner's circle on three separate occasions.

Beissinger selected Lindy's Pride as a yearling in 1967 and trained and drove the Star's Pride colt to victory in the Trotting Triple Crown in 1969. As that trotter's career was ending, Beissinger had another future star in his stable, this one named Speedy Crown. The youngster, who was bred by Beissinger's wife Ann and foaled at the Beissinger family farm in southwestern Ohio, swept to victory in the 1971 Hambletonian.

When Speedy Crown went to stud, Beissinger spotted a colt from his second crop who seemed to possess extraordinary quickness and athletic ability. His name was Speedy Somolli and Beissinger chalked up his third Hambletonian behind this colt in 1978.

Speedy Crown and Speedy Somolli, of course, went on to become sires of enormous influence in the breed.

It was attention to detail in areas such as hoof care and shoeing that made Beissinger successful with these horses and many others, such as Dance Spell, Defiant One, Bardot Lobell, Lindy's Crown, Widower Creed, Entrepreneur, South Bend, Super Juan, and Torway.

5

CHOOSING THE RIGHT EQUIPMENT

TOMMY HAUGHTON

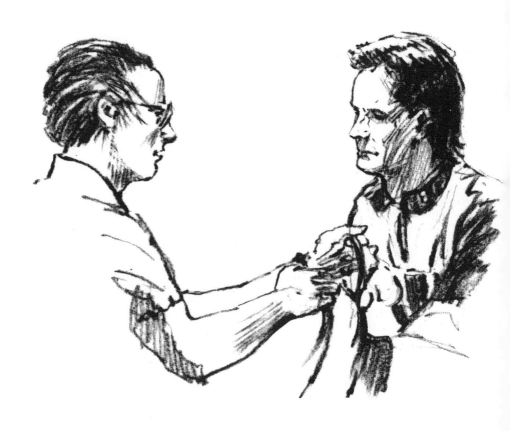

I am pleased to be able to contribute to the effort to rework the original *Care and Training of the Trotter and Pacer*. My dad, Bill Haughton, contributed a couple of chapters to that book. I am honored to be the only son of one of the original authors to contribute to the new book.

Dad was an outstanding all-around horseman. He could break horses, shoe them, train them and drive them at a very high level. He loved what he did and he taught me a lot about horsemanship. The great thing about the way he taught is that he let me learn by making my own mistakes. He encouraged me to experiment. He let me try almost anything if a horse was having trouble. This was important to my foundation as a horse trainer.

One of the important lessons in growing up in the W.R. Haughton Stable related to the proper use of equipment. This was an area where my dad had pretty specific ideas, even though he let me have a free rein, so to speak. Dad believed a horse should be rigged as simply as possible to go as straight as possible.

Even though the breed has improved dramatically in the past few years, I have found that I spend an incredibly large amount of my time as a horse trainer trying to do the same things my dad dealt with. I want a horse to be as relaxed as possible, to be as quiet as possible and to be as sound as possible.

The Standardbred of today is an aggressive horse, and it is very important to be able to temper this natural, in-bred aggressiveness. The aggressiveness reveals itself in speed. Horses today can do things naturally that no one ever imagined. The breed has improved greatly, even in just the past decade. This improvement, however, has made the job of horse training a lot different than it used to be.

For instance, a lot of my dad's time in his early years was spent in trying to manufacture horses' gaits and trying to teach them speed. Today, I am not concerned about any lack of speed. My main concern relates to keeping a horse toned down to where he can use his natural speed at the proper times and in the proper way.

In this chapter, I will discuss the various methods I employ to keep a horse quiet and comfortable. I will outline the various bits, boots and bridles used in the current Haughton Stable. Much of the equipment in use today is virtually the same as it has been for many, many years. There have been but a few significant changes in the kinds of equipment used on horses, with respect to bits, boots and bridles. There have been significant alterations to harness design since the original book was written, however, and I will touch briefly on the design changes in that area.

The main focus of this chapter will be on the everyday equipment used by the everyday horseman. I am going to attempt to give practical guidelines on the proper use of bits, boots and bridles.

I have been fortunate to have managed the careers of some truly outstanding horses, and will, when applicable, relate how equipment changes affected the careers of those horses, including such stars as Peace Corps, Nihilator, Napoletano and Magical Mike.

GENERAL ATTITUDE ABOUT EQUIPMENT

I would say that my general philosophy about equipment is pretty simple. I want to make a horse comfortable. I want a horse to be as relaxed, quiet and confident as possible. I want them to drive straight, to carry their heads in front of them, and to use only the equipment that is absolutely necessary.

Horse trainers are as much creatures of habit as the horses they train. Sometimes a trainer finds a little success with a certain piece of equipment, and pretty soon all the horses in his stable are wearing the same rigging. Look at the number of horses that started wearing leverage overchecks after Jate Lobell came along. Or look at all the Mack Lobell imitators that had sheepskins on their bridles after Mack won the Hambletonian.

Equipment on any horse should fit that horse's individual needs. It is a mistake to imitate what a famous horse wore. Every horse has to be treated as an individual. It is also important not to add equipment simply for appearance's sake. A number of horse trainers are guilty in this area. Everyone wants their horses to be as attractive as possible on the track, but the horse trainer who adds a piece of equipment simply because he likes the way it looks is headed for trouble. If it works, use it. But honestly ask yourself, "Do I really need this on this horse?" If not, take it off.

BE PATIENT

Another key to the entire subject of equipment relates to patience. A really successful horse trainer must be a patient person, for it is as true today as ever that no one can train a horse in anger. There are no "quick fixes" in a stable of horses, no panaceas that will work the same way every time. Sometimes, it takes a while before a change may begin to help a horse. What I look for when I make a change on a horse is just a little gradual improvement. I don't hope to solve all of a horse's problems immediately.

A lot of people feel that if a change is made on a horse and the horse does not immediately react to the change and improve, the change has done him no good. This is not a theory that is endorsed in my stable.

The two most-used driving bits are the plain snaffle (left) and the Swedish snaffle (right). Both are recommended. The Swedish snaffle is a little kinder to a horse's mouth, because of the larger tapering of the bit towards the outside.

When I make a change, I always try and give a horse some time to adjust to what I have done. What happens a lot of times is that gradual changes will occur, and I end up down the road with a horse much better prepared for a season at the races.

What works on one horse may not necessarily help another. The more I train, the more I am around, the more I learn that the basics of the business are unchanged from my father's time. The guy who is the best horseman, who has the most success, will be the guy who uses the best feed, has the best help, uses good animal practices and employs a lot of common sense.

There are few exotic remedies that will affect a large population of horses. An occasional horse may be helped by some exotic bit or bridle, but the average horse is going to be happier and more productive if he is rigged as simply as possible.

DRIVING BITS

A number of different types of driving bits have been invented over the years through some horseman's attempt to create a greater degree of control.

Actually, there are only a couple of driving bits used in my stable. The first is the common snaffle bit, which is usually sold with every bridle unless otherwise specified. The snaffle bit is made of a light metal and has a jointed hinge in the middle. It is a useful, practical tool which has been successfully used by horsemen for many years. It comes in a standard size, which is actually too long for most young horses, but it can be used successfully in spite of this.

The other bit I use a lot is the so-called "Swedish snaffle," which is a cousin, so to speak, of the traditional snaffle bit. This bit has the traditional jointed center, but has thicker metal which tapers larger toward the outside. This makes the bit thicker at the outer edges and is easier on a horse's mouth in most instances. The major advantage of this bit, as opposed to the traditional snaffle bit, is that the Swedish snaffle will not pinch a horse at the corners of the mouth. A plain snaffle bit, particularly an ill-fitting one, can create some irritation by pinching a horse's mouth.

Straight driving bits are also available. The bit on the left is a straight, unjointed driving bit while the bit on the right is the same bit with a rubber covering. These bits may be used if a horse is reluctant to take hold of a snaffle bit.

Any competent horseman should be able to adjust any bit in a horse's mouth. This is done by simple visual inspection. Having said that most bits are overly long for young horses, I must emphasize that it is vital that the driving bit be fitted properly. This is accomplished by making sure the cheek pieces of the bridle are adjusted to the correct length. The cheek pieces should be adjusted to allow the bit to be centered in the horse's mouth with a minimum of "play" possible in either direction.

The bit should fit like a pair of shoes, I suppose. It should be tight enough to be felt, but not so tight that it creates a pinching sensation. A bit that is too tight will create a sore mouth on a horse and may get a horse to carry his head one way or another in an attempt to get away from the soreness. A bit that is too loose will slide back and forth in the horse's mouth and you will not have much control.

Nihilator and Peace Corps both wore plain snaffle bits throughout their careers. Peace Corps had a better mouth than Nihilator, who was a pretty aggressive horse at both two and three. People are amazed when I tell them that Nihilator raced in a plain snaffle bit, but it is really a testimony to the efforts of my dad and Bill O'Donnell. Nihilator was a horse who was always on the line between being alert and strong and being hard to control.

Over the two years we trained Nihilator a lot of effort was concentrated on keeping him from becoming too aggressive, and Bill O'Donnell did a great job racing him. Bill often got a lot of criticism because he would lay off the gate with Nihilator, but he knew that if he took Nihilator right to the gate and got him rolling and up on the bit, there would be no rating him.

By staying off the gate and teaching him to relax behind it, Bill was able to maximize Nihilator's great strengths. I think the only time Bill ever raced him wire-to-wire was in the Little Brown Jug, but that's a race where you don't surrender the lead unless you have to. Bill would generally take Nihilator off the gate or just let him float out of there, then put him in gear after a quarter-mile or so.

Nihilator was the kind of horse who might have become a real problem to drive if we had not been careful with him. He could have been ruined after only a couple of starts because he had such high speed. Dad drove Nihilator in his early starts. A less competent driver would have busted him out the gate once or twice and would have been in big trouble. Nihilator was the kind of horse who could have gone a couple of amazing races, then never been heard from again.

We were lucky with Nihilator, because he never advanced to being a hard-mouthed horse. He got to a certain point where he would take a hold and never went beyond that.

If a horse is taking a serious hold in training, you must be extremely careful not to let him get away with it. There could be a number of explanations for this type of behavior. Often times, a horse will begin to take a hold if some soreness is present. A horse only knows to get away from pain. This is often seen in young horses that start out quiet and relaxed, but begin to take hold in training. A good, overall examination by a veterinarian may be desirable to determine the level of soundness.

If it is determined that a horse is sound, and just aggressive, then a number of solutions should be tried. The first is the use of earplugs. If that fails, you can use a hood with the earplugs to keep as much noise as possible away from the horse. If a horse is wearing a blind bridle and is acting aggressively when another horse comes alongside, I might switch to a Kant-See-Bak or even an open bridle to try and calm him down.

If that does not work, I would consider changing the overcheck bit and going to a more severe bit, particularly if the horse hogged down into the overcheck when he took a hold.

Peace Corps, on the other hand, wore a plain snaffle when I had her. She had a real good mouth and never needed anything exotic. She was unlike a lot of good fillies in that she never took much hold. She would train or jog, and early on learned to relax on the track. She was a hellion around the barn, but was all business on the track. When people ask about her rigging, I often joke with them that Peace Corps rigged us, we didn't rig her!

UNJOINTED DRIVING BIT NOT RECOMMENDED

One of the driving bits available to trainers is the unjointed bit. I do not like to use an unjointed, straight driving bit on most horses because I believe it creates a tough-mouthed horse if used over a long period of time.

There is an instance, however, when I recommend the use of a straight, unjointed driving bit.

Every trainer has a yearling who won't grab the bit at all. This is a problem which should be addressed early. Some colts are just lazy. Others might have a problem with a tooth that needs attention. The lazy yearling needs to be taught to take a nice hold of the bit. If a yearling does not take hold of the bit, his progress in training will be retarded. I

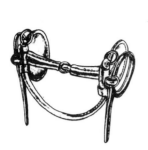 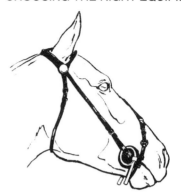

The Frisco June "colt bit" is highly recommended. This is a snaffle driving bit covered with leather pieces which help the bit rest comfortably in a young horse's mouth. It also comes with a built-in chin strap which attaches to an overcheck, as shown in the illustration at right.

like to teach a colt to take a comfortable hold in training. You cannot help a colt who will not take a hold of the bit. I do not want him to "latch on" to me, but I want him to take a comfortable position with the bit.

If a colt is reluctant to grab the traditional snaffle bit, I often make a switch to a rubber-coated straight bit. This allows for a lot more natural contact in the horse's mouth and I feel it gives a yearling an extra measure of confidence.

A yearling can be afraid of many things, including other horses and track equipment. A yearling who will grab the bit when he's scared is easier to manage, because he can be steered. If a yearling gets scared and backs out of the bit and goes sideways on you, there isn't much you can do to help him avoid trouble with other horses or fences.

USING A "COLT BIT" TO START OUT

While the traditional snaffle is my bit of choice, I start out all my yearlings in a leather-covered snaffle bit called a Frisco June. This is a very useful bit because it combines the advantages of the snaffle and the larger diameter bits.

This bit is especially useful with young horses. Because of its design, it will not slip back and forth in a horse's mouth, nor pinch his cheek. It also acts as a combination chin strap and overcheck, because the overcheck straps are incorporated into the chin strap.

I use this bit almost exclusively with my young horses for the first month or two and find that it helps to establish very good touch and driving habits with most of the yearlings. A lot of yearlings learn to grab or "hang" on a line right from the first. The use of the Frisco June bit overcomes a lot of this and helps to put a real good mouth on the colts. It also helps us to teach them to carry their heads straight.

Sidelining, or "sidereining" bits are useful when a horse wants to carry his head to one side or the other. The illustration on the left shows a sidelining bit with an extension on one side. The driving line attaches to the small ring. This bit may be used on either the right or left side. The illustration on the right shows a slip-mouth, sidelining bit.

USE GOOD DENTAL PRACTICES

Any discussion of the use of bits should also include something about good dental practices. I recommend a dental examination for each and every horse in a stable on a regular basis. Wolf teeth should be removed as soon as possible, because they can create sharp edges in the mouth than can lead to problems later on.

There are two indications that a horse might have some dental problems. The first is when a horse who has been a good eater begins to leave some of his feed. The second is when the horse starts to hang on a line during training.

When I get a colt who starts hanging on one line in his early training, I first look for trouble in his mouth. It is vitally important that a horse not be allowed to carry his head crooked for an extended period of time. If dental problems do not exist, or have been attended to, and a horse still wants to carry his head around to one side or the other, a veterinarian should be consulted to look for other, more serious medical explanations.

HORSES DON'T GET SOUND WITH EQUIPMENT

This is as good a time as any to say there is not a single piece of equipment ever made that can get a sore horse sound. A lot of good things can be accomplished with different bits, headpoles, gaiting straps and the like, but an unsound horse will not be helped with simple equipment changes. A number of trainers seem to overlook this practical fact and will try some new piece of equipment on a horse who is going a little crooked. The new equipment doesn't work, because the horse is unsound. Yet the trainer feels disappointed, because what he tried did not produce the desired result. The problem lies with the fact that the horse is lame and needs veterinary attention!

THE SIDELINING BIT

Another common driving bit for young horses is the sidelining bit. It comes in several different varieties and can be a useful bit in some instances, although I do not like it for most horses.

A sidelining driving bit is my method of last resort for most of my

The steering bar sidelining bit is shown here on the left. This bit is effective with a horse who may bear out in the stretches or in on the turns. The driving bit shown on the right is a snaffle bit with a curb chain.

young horses. I prefer to correct a colt who may be grabbing one line by using other measures first. I will use a sidelining bit after other remedies are exhausted. There are several different types of sidelining bits.

The conventional sidelining bit is built with extensions on each side and creates special leverage for those situations where a horse may bear in during one part of a mile and bear out at another.

A slip-mouth, sidelining bit is designed to allow the bit to slide back and forth in a horse's mouth. If the horse bears in on a turn, the bit will slide through to the right side, providing extra leverage on that line. The opposite is supposed to happen when the horse bears out, with the bit sliding through on the left side, giving you extra leverage to help hold the horse straight. My experience with this particular bit has not been too good. It usually does not work as well as I would like.

The sidelining bit I prefer is the so-called "steering bar" sidelining bit. This is a bit which does not slide back and forth. It is leather-covered and has an extension to which the line attaches. This bit can be used for a horse who either bears in or bears out habitually, but does not do both. For a horse who bears in habitually, the steering bar would be placed on the right side to provide extra leverage.

Magical Mike wore a steering bar when he was two and, in fact, wore it in a race for the first time the night he won the Woodrow Wilson. Mike Lachance had been driving Magical Mike for us coming up to the Wilson and had recommended that I give the steering bar a chance. Magical Mike had learned to go hanging on the left line. He did this most of his life, bearing out a little in the stretches.

In the Wilson, John Campbell catch-drove for us and reported that the steering bar made Magical Mike a much more manageable horse. The fact that John was able to steer him effectively was vitally important in that it may have saved Magical Mike some ground somewhere in the mile. He won the race in a very tight photo!

Another variation on the traditional driving bit utilizes a small-caliber chain with the regular snaffle bit. This is the kind of bit I used on Napoletano as a three-year-old. He was a horse who did not want his mouth totally shut. He also liked to play with the bit in his mouth. I tried to pull his head halter up a little snug to help him keep his mouth shut, but he did not like his mouth totally closed. So I let Napoletano

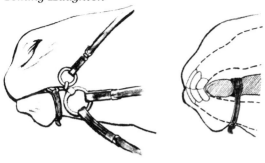

Tongue ties are needed by almost every horse. The proper placement of a tongue tie is illustrated here. The tongue tie should not interfere with either the driving or overcheck bit. Proper placement of the tongue tie is also shown relative to teeth and jaw.

play with his bit, but also put a little curb chain in his mouth to give him something to play with. Napoletano liked this setup and became a real easy horse to drive. He was rigged this way at three when he won the World Trotting Derby, and during both weeks at Lexington where he set a stakes record in winning The Transylvania the first week, then beat Mack Lobell in the Kentucky Futurity the following week.

Although there are a number of other driving bits available, I really do not recommend their use. Most of them are too severe for a horse. In this class, I would place the Dr. Bristol, the Crescendo bit, the Simpson bit and the old single and/or double wire bits. There may be occasionally a horse that these bits could be used on, but they have no home in my stable. Many of these bits were used before we began to tie horses' tongues on an every day basis, and thus they have gone out of fashionable use. Besides, a really severe driving bit is resented by most horses and will only create additional problems later on. A severe bit is only going to toughen a horse's mouth over time.

Tongue ties are very important. I start tying the tongues of my young horses after jogging reaches three miles per day. Tying a horse's tongue will cut down on the number and variety of problems associated with driving bits. However, tongue ties should never be too tight on a horse. A horse will learn to resent his tongue being tied if the tie is habitually too tight. A tongue tie should be tight enough to hold the tongue in place under the driving bit, but not so tight as to cut off circulation.

A number of the older bits came into play only because they provided remedies for horses who may have been "tongue-lolling" the driving bit. Many horses learn to manipulate their driving bits with their tongues, and a number of horses get their tongues on top of the driving bit, rendering them almost uncontrollable.

By tying the tongue down, you remove one of the major problems faced by horse trainers on an every day basis. I recommend the use of either the traditional flannel tongue ties, or some kind of non-porous elastic, which should be washable and not accept moisture.

There are horses who will refuse to wear a tongue tie; most resent it at first, but learn to accept it over time. However, there are horses that will never learn to relax and will shake their heads and never get comfort-

 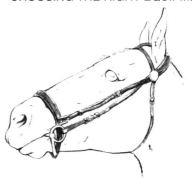

Head halters should be positioned correctly to be used most effectively. The horse on the left shows a head halter correctly positioned at the midpoint of the nose. The head halter on the right is too low on the nose and will interfere with the driving and overcheck bits.

able with a tongue tie. If this happens, it is better to keep the horse relaxed and quiet than to try to force him into wearing a tongue tie. Sometimes, you simply have to live with that kind of problem.

Magical Mike had problems late in his two-year-old season of 1993 when he choked down in the Presidential at Rosecroft. I was already tying his tongue down, but he liked to get his tongue out of his mouth to one side. What I had to do with Magical Mike after he choked down was to not only tie his tongue down, but to take a second string and tie his tongue a second time to the ring on his head halter. Magical Mike had his tongue tied in this manner for most of his three-year-old season, including the day he won the Little Brown Jug and the night he won the Breeders Crown.

PROPER USE OF HEAD HALTERS

With horses who develop bad habits around their heads, one of the common causes is that the head halter may be fitted improperly.

Head halters should be worn on a horse so the bottom loop (nose band) of the halter fits the horse a couple of inches above the mouth and does not interfere with the action of the driving bit. The nose band buckles under the horse's jaw and should be pulled snug, but not tight, after the bits are in place. This last item is very important.

You can create real problems with a horse who may need to wear a severe overcheck bit if you pull the head halter up snug before you put the bridle on. A horse may need to open his mouth to get a driving bit and a fairly severe overcheck bit, such as a Burch or Crit Davis, in place.

The proper procedure is to place the head halter in position, buckle it loosely, put the driving and overcheck bits in place, pull the bridle over the ears, and position everything before the head halter is pulled snugly into place.

 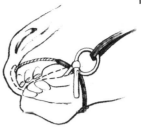

A mini-bit, left, is a most useful driving bit for a horse who is difficult to control. The mini-bit employs two driving bits, one inside the other. The driving lines are attached to both bits. The illustration at the right shows the proper position and use of a lip cord. Note that the lip cord is placed behind the driving bit and above the gum line.

YOU MAY NEED A MINI-BIT

Another effective bit to use on an aggressive horse is the so-called "mini-bit." This is a bit that Keystone Pioneer wore during her great trotting career. A mini-bit is very effective with any horse who likes to take a little extra hold at some point in the mile. Keystone Pioneer wore it only to race in, but it was the only way we found to control her during a race.

What this amounts to is the use of an overcheck bit in conjunction with the driving bit. The regular driving bit and overcheck, sometimes a jointed bit, are used in combination. The driving lines are buckled into the overcheck, or mini-bit, which is placed on top of the regular driving bit.

This combination of bits should give the driver a little more control than what he has with just a driving bit. It is important to remember that while the driving line is fastened to the mini-bit, the cheek piece of the bridle should remain buckled into the driving bit. I carry a mini-bit in my driving bag at all times. It can be very useful in keeping a horse calm during the early warm-up miles before racing.

Another common remedy for a horse who wants to pull is the use of a lip cord. I have not used one a great deal, but will if necessary. Bill O'Donnell recommended that we use a lip cord on Pershing Square, a Niatross colt who raced in our stable the same season as Nihilator. Pershing Square took a good hold, especially when he was sitting in a hole, and O'Donnell thought a lip cord would help make him be more manageable.

A lip cord is a round, nylon cord that goes over the gums beneath the upper lip, and it can be used with any combination of driving and overcheck bits. The ends of the cord go behind the driving bit on either side of the mouth and are then brought out and buckled under the chin.

What you are looking for is a situation where the pressure on the driving bit pulls against the lip cord and exerts pressure on the gums. This should make a horse back off the bit, because the gums are a very sensitive area of a horse's mouth. It worked great on Pershing Square because he really respected that lip cord.

There is a word of caution here. Any lip cord that is tight enough to create bleeding from the gums is too tight. And a driver must be aware that a horse is wearing a lip cord. Any sharp movement one way or the other can pull the lip cord across the gums and create bleeding. What you are looking for is direct pressure on the gums, not a situation where the gums bleed.

THE PROPER USE OF OVERCHECK BITS

As I indicated earlier, most of my colts start off with the Frisco June driving bit. This bit allows the overcheck to be strapped right into a chin strap which is built right into the bit assembly. After the yearling gets broken to the harness and begins to establish his gait, it may be necessary to place an overcheck bit in his mouth.

If not, a regular chin strap can be used without any overcheck bit in place. If this is done, simply remember to keep the chin strap in front of the driving bit. A chin strap may also be used in connection with an overcheck bit.

When a yearling is ready for an overcheck bit, the Frisco June driving bit is no longer used and a yearling is transferred into a plain snaffle driving bit. At the same time, a standard, unjointed overcheck bit is also put into use.

While on this subject, I would like to speak directly to the issue, somewhat controversial, of how high a horse's head should be. This is regulated by every trainer, who can adjust the overcheck to either pull a horse's head up or let it down. Throughout the sport, there have been a number of prominent horses who have had unusually long overchecks. These horses raced with great success with their heads down, and this created quite a stir in the training community.

Personally, I have not had much success with letting a horse have his head down at chest level. I wore a long overcheck for a time on Magical Mike when he was a two-year-old, but I felt that he was a better horse, was better-gaited and more comfortable with his head up. As I mentioned earlier, Magical Mike choked down in the Presidential at Rosecroft when he was two. His driver, Mike Lachance thought one of the contributing factors was that Magical Mike got his head down too far with a long overcheck.

After that incident, I took Magical Mike's head up a couple of holes and it stayed that way the rest of his racing career.

I also feel that any horse with breathing problems (and there are a great many of those in our breed) will be better with its head higher. I can assure you that none of the successful horses who raced with their heads down ever had significant breathing problems.

Having said that, I think anyone who postulates that any training

The illustration, above left, shows a plain overcheck bit, while the overcheck on the right is a McKerron bit. The McKerron bit is recommended for many young horses who are trying to get their heads down, or are a little too aggressive in early training.

method — whether related to the length of the overcheck or any other remedy — can be applied to an entire population of horses is simply way off base.

Horses are individuals and need to be trained that way. The sooner a horseman learns this lesson, the better a horse trainer he will become. Some horses can learn to go with their heads down; of that I am certain, because I have seen them do it. Others need to have their heads a little higher. Experiment with your stable. Find out what works for each horse. Never apply something universally to your stable, or you will be asking for trouble.

PROGRESSION OF OVERCHECK BITS

The first overcheck bit of choice is the plain overcheck. In reality, not many horses are going to race with a plain overcheck, but it is a very useful bit for a young horse early in the training cycle. The plain overcheck can be very helpful in setting a horse's head.

When it becomes necessary to use a more severe overcheck bit, my next choice is the McKerron. The McKerron bit is very well-designed, and I have had very good results with this overcheck. Dad used one on Nihilator throughout his career, and it helped Nihilator because, like most horses, he respected that bit. Using a McKerron on Nihilator allowed him to tuck his neck a little, but did not allow him to hog down into the overcheck. It "made a gentleman of him," as the saying goes.

Nihilator was always a very aggressive horse and walked the line between being alert and responsive and being too aggressive. He always seemed to be on the verge of becoming unmanageable, but he never did. I think the McKerron overcheck had a lot to do with that. It allowed us to control him without being too severe, and it did not make Nihilator mad or resentful.

The McKerron is designed to sit well in a horse's mouth because it has a spoon right in the bit's center. The McKerron has two sets of rings. The smaller set of rings fastens into a nose band that is part of the McKerron design, and the overcheck straps fasten into the larger set of rings on the front of the bit. This creates a lifting action of the spoon in the center of the bit when the horse attempts to get his head down. As overchecks go, it is not a severe bit, but on the right horse—such as Nihilator—it provides just the right kind of control.

If a McKerron does not produce the desired result, I like to go to a Crit

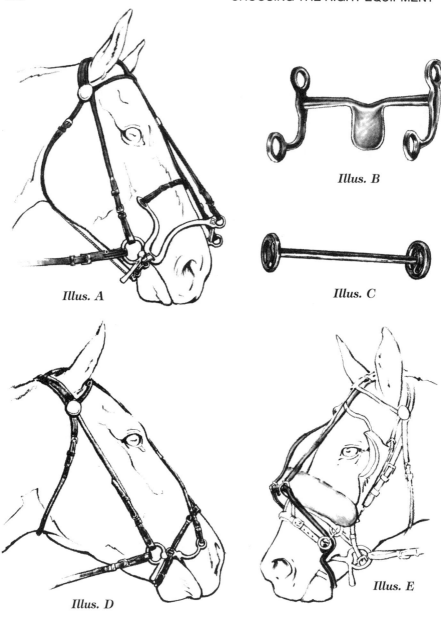

Illus. A

Illus. B

Illus. C

Illus. D

Illus. E

Illustration A shows a Raymond overcheck and its proper placement.
Illustration B is a Crit Davis overcheck. Illustration C is a Speedway
overcheck. Illustration D shows the correct positioning of a Crit Davis
overcheck, while illustration E is an O'Mara overcheck used in combination
with a shadow roll and a Kant-See-Bak bridle.

Davis. Magical Mike wore a Crit Davis almost exclusively at three because he had a tendency to duck his head down. The design of the Crit Davis is very similar to the McKerron in that there are two sets of rings, one for the nose band and another for the overcheck straps.

The Crit Davis overcheck has a single bar which has a U-shaped curve directly in the center of the bit. It is designed in such a way that the U-shaped bar will rotate up into the roof of a horse's mouth if the horse attempts to lay into the overcheck. The Crit Davis is a very useful bit for any horse who is better with his head up.

If I am unhappy with the results on a particular horse with both the McKerron and the Crit Davis, the next overcheck bit to be tried would be no overcheck bit at all. Instead, it would be a leverage overcheck, which comes under various trade names, including Raymond and O'Mara. As I said earlier, Jate Lobell wore an O'Mara leverage bit named after its adaptor, trainer Frank O'Mara.

I wore a leverage overcheck like this on Golden Greek, an Abercrombie colt who raced with great success for me a few years back and is now one of the leading young sires in Australia. Golden Greek was a typical Abercrombie in that he was not an overly aggressive horse; he liked to be able to get his head down and go.

The leverage bit is actually misnamed, since it does not use an overcheck bit which goes in the horse's mouth. The leverage assembly comes with a longer than normal nose band which is used in connection with a V-shaped metal assembly that attaches to the noseband on one end and to the overcheck straps on the other. The nose band rides higher up on a horse's nose than other traditional overchecks, and the bottom of the V-shaped metal should lay just ahead of the driving bit. This assembly should be used in concert with either a chin strap or chain to help it stay in place.

The leverage assembly is a good idea with a horse who wants his head down, because a driver can retain control through the leverage created by the V-shaped metal assembly. When a horse attempts to get his head down, the nose band presses down on the nose and the chin strap lifts at the same time. This creates the leverage action which earned this contraption its name. This is a good bit to use on a horse who may need his head at a certain level, but resents a severe overcheck.

Next in line of preference in the use of overcheck bits is the simple Speedway bit, which is nothing more than a straight bit used in connection with a chin strap. In reality, not many horses can wear this bit when they race, because it simply does not provide any resistance to horses who want to hog down in their overchecks, or who want to take a good hold.

One of the more effective overcheck bits, especially for that good-feeling colt or filly who offers to kick, is the Burch overcheck bit. The Burch overcheck bit is very effective with kickers and any horse who needs

A Burch overcheck bit (left) is most effective for kickers and horses who want to "hang" on the overcheck. The Hutton overcheck bit (right) is recommended for a horse who wants to get his mouth open. The double bar Crabb bit (center) is used on horses who are unwilling to keep their heads up in training.

more than a normal overcheck, but doesn't require the severity of a Crit Davis or double-bar Crabb.

The Burch has a single pair of rings which attach to the overcheck straps and it is normally used without a chin strap. It has a single bar that curves upward in the middle and has a little horizontal bar in the center of the bit. Since the raised section is designed to exert pressure on the roof of the mouth, this bit will not tolerate much hogging from any horse.

The Burch overcheck bit is a very effective bit to use with kickers because a horse wants to get his head down when he kicks. When he does, the horizontal bar on the Burch rides right up into the roof of the mouth, and not many horses can tolerate this. The Burch overcheck is far more effective in keeping a horse from kicking than all the kicking straps ever used.

The final overcheck bit in use in my stable is the Hutton. McKinzie Almahurst wore a Hutton overcheck. McKinzie was a very aggressive colt, like most of the B.G's Bunny offspring, and needed his head up to be manageable. But he was not comfortable with his head up; he wouldn't go that way. An important lesson for any horse trainer can be learned from the situation we faced with McKinzie. He would get mad if we tried to get his head up, and he just wouldn't pace. But he still needed his head up to go, so we finally decided on the Hutton overcheck for him. He was wearing a Hutton the night he won the Woodrow Wilson.

Sometimes, you have to reach sort of a compromise with a horse. If a horse is comfortable a certain way and wants to go that way, you may find it is more productive in the long run to find a way to get along than to try and force a horse into a situation where he cannot be productive.

The Hutton overcheck is wonderfully designed to fit the contours of a horse's mouth and comes with a special bridle assembly that goes over the nose, runs through each side of the overcheck bit, and up between the eyes and ears and through the top of the bridle.

When a horse exerts downward pressure, the strap over the nose presses down, forcing the overcheck bit to be pulled up in the mouth. The chin strap helps to keep the mouth shut and provide a little extra leverage.

The only remaining overcheck bits I have not discussed are the Crabb bits, including single and double-bar Crabbs, and double-bar Crabbs with spoons. It is my opinion that these bits are pretty severe for most young horses, and I do not normally recommend their use. These bits were designed for use on the hard-mouthed, tough-minded horses of another era. The double-bar Crabb overcheck bit can be used for a horse who needs to respect an overcheck, but it would be a matter of last resort for me. I have not used a Crabb overcheck of any kind for many years, but would if a special situation presented itself. I would have to have a real bad horse to ever use one again.

Another piece of equipment relegated to storage in my stable is the four-ring overcheck. I cannot remember the last time I used a four-ring. I am not fond of it and do not recommend its use for most horses.

It is basically designed to use on horses that pull a lot. The concept behind the four-ring overcheck is that it creates extra leverage for the driver by creating different angles of pull for the driving lines. It is also effective in some cases with horses who need to have their heads higher at certain times, but do not like to be checked higher. By using a four-ring overcheck, a trainer enables a horse to get his head up at the start of a race by exerting pressure on the lines, then allows the horse to get his head down later when the pressure is relieved. As with the Crabb overchecks, it takes a bad horse to wear one of these things.

MARTINGALES ARE EFFECTIVE

One of the pieces of equipment I like on both trotters and pacers is a martingale. They come in several different types, including the Buxton martingale, the standing martingale and the combination (ring) martingale.

The Buxton martingale is used primarily in the place of a breast collar. It is a simple device that attaches to the bottom of the girth and then splits in a "Y" configuration at the horse's chest.

There is also a yoke piece that goes over the horse's withers and two straps on either side which then attach to the backpad. It is available in both leather and nylon models. The primary purpose of the Buxton is to insure that the backpad and girth cannot slip back from their desired position.

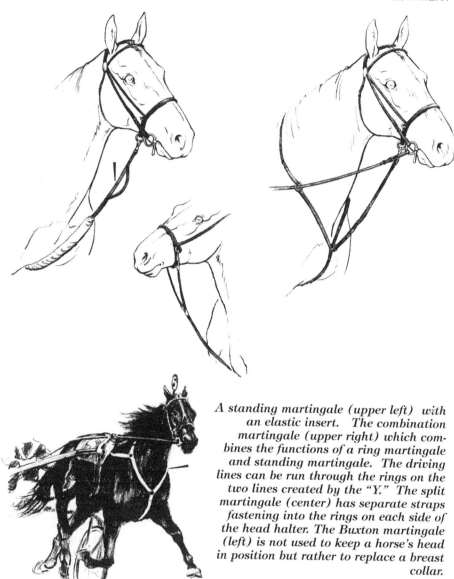

A standing martingale (upper left) with an elastic insert. The combination martingale (upper right) which combines the functions of a ring martingale and standing martingale. The driving lines can be run through the rings on the two lines created by the "Y." The split martingale (center) has separate straps fastening into the rings on each side of the head halter. The Buxton martingale (left) is not used to keep a horse's head in position but rather to replace a breast collar.

The standing martingale comes in two styles, and is sometimes simply called a "tie down," because in effect, the horse's head is tied down. The first style is a single, long strap fastened to the bottom of the girth that extends between the horse's front legs and attaches to a ring in the center and at the bottom of the head halter. The strap is adjustable, and also can be ordered with an elastic insert which allows some up and

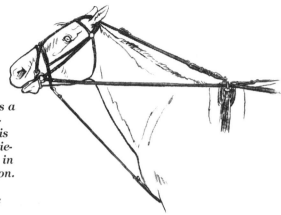

The illustration above shows a horse who had been improperly rigged. The overcheck is too short in relation to the tie-down, therefore the horse is in a very uncomfortable position. The overcheck and the tie-down should allow for some freedom of movement.

down movement of the head. The second type of standing martingale splits into a Y-shape before it reaches the head halter and attaches to the head halter ring on either side. This type of martingale is recommended when a nose cord or chain is to be used to provide resistance when a horse attempts to lift his head, although the single martingale can also be used with a chain or cord over the nose. Both types may also be used without a chain or nose cord. The standing martingale of either type is recommended when a horse wants to throw his head.

The combination, or ring martingale, fastens to the girth in a similar way and comes up between a horse's legs as a single strap, but then separates in a Y-shape at the mid-point of a horse's chest in the same way as the standing martingale. The difference comes in the fact the two lines created by the "Y" have rings, and the driving lines may be run through these rings. As with the Buxton, there is a yoke piece over the horse's withers. This was a very popular piece of equipment on my dad's trotters. Dad liked this very much because he thought it helped set the head, develop a good, soft mouth and helped keep the head straight.

The ring martingale can also be used with a strap that runs from the split chest piece up to the bottom ring of the head halter, thereby combining the positive aspect of the standing martingale and Buxton martingale. The ring martingale may also be useful with a horse who may not be taking a proper hold. This type of martingale helps hold the lines in position and can assist in putting a good mouth on a colt reluctant to grab the bit.

There is something to watch, however, whatever type of martingale is chosen. You must avoid putting a horse in a vise. I have seen trainers who use martingales with a very short overcheck. The horse is in a vise because he cannot lower or raise his head. Ideally, there should be a little play in both the overcheck and the martingale so the horse feels some freedom and is more comfortable.

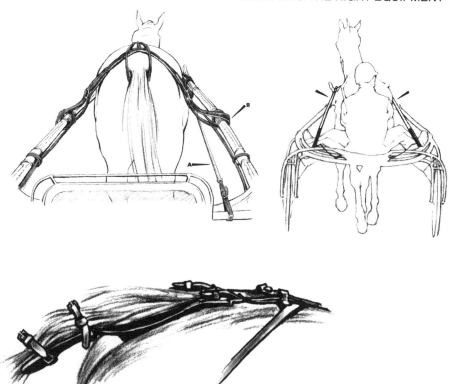

Kicking and gaiting straps are very effective training tools. Gaiting straps (A, upper left) can be used on both jog carts and sulkies and help keep a horse tracking straight. A kicking strap (B, also upper left) may be used, but are not recommended by the author. Gaiting poles (upper right) are often used on trotters to help keep them straight in the shafts. A tail-set crupper (center) may be used for a horse who wants to swish its tail, a sure signal that it is thinking about kicking.

KICKING STRAPS NOT RECOMMENDED

Every trainer has to learn to deal with a horse who is a real good feeler and who, on those mornings when there is a little wind blowing or there has been a change in the weather, will offer to kick.

If this occurs repeatedly and becomes a problem, a lot of trainers use kicking straps. I do not, and I do not recommend their use; more horses than not will kick when wearing them. What is more effective is what I described in preceding paragraphs: the use of a Burch overcheck. Another good remedy is to increase the workload by adding a few extra jog miles. When a horse gets tired, he will be a lot less likely to kick.

Nearly every horse is going to offer to kick at least once somewhere

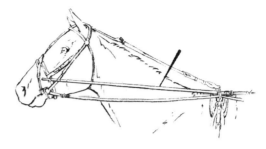

The proper position of a headpole is illustrated here. The headpole attaches to a small ring on the head halter on one end and to the back pad on the other. The headpole should not be placed under the bridle cheek pieces and should not interfere in any way with the driving bit.

along the way. If the horse persists, another remedy which can be tried is the use of a tail-set crupper. A lot of horses, particularly fillies, can be helped by using a tail-set crupper. It prevents them from swishing their tails, which is a sure signal that a horse is thinking about kicking. The tail can also be tied, but in most cases this will not be needed. I have never seen a kicker who could not be helped by the addition of a Burch overcheck, a tail-set crupper and a few extra-tough jog miles.

GAITING STRAPS AND GAITING POLES

One type of strap which is very useful is the gaiting strap. I make extensive use of gaiting straps in my stable and recommend their use.

The gaiting strap is a plastic-coated, nylon strap which affixes to the jog cart or sulky at the tip of the shaft and runs back to the arch of a sulky or the crossbar of a jog cart. The strap must be pulled very tight so it will not sag if a horse gets his hind end against it. By providing tension, the gaiting strap encourages the horse to carry his hind end straight.

Gaiting poles were brought to this country by the Scandinavian trainers and serve the same basic purpose as the gaiting strap, except that gaiting poles are designed so the pole can be moved on a horse during a training session or during a race.

For instance, a trotter may have a tendency to trot a little crooked during the few moments right before he comes to the gate. The pole can be adjusted by the driver's leg and moved to a useful position. During the race, the pole can be moved again to free a horse up or provide additional stimulus for it to stay straight.

On many horses, the use of two gaiting straps, one for each side, is desirable. This is recommended for those horses that need help staying straight in the turns and the stretches. The most common occurrence is when a horse needs help because it gets its hind end over to the left in the turns (bearing in), then to the right (bearing out) in the straightaway.

THE PROPER USE OF HEADPOLES

One of the most commonly used pieces of equipment in our industry nowadays is the headpole.

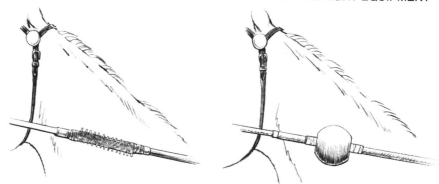

The headpole with the leather studded burr (left) and the headpole with a
ball attachment, right are used when a horse wants to lean into the
headpole.

I think the headpole is one of the great inventions in our industry, and
cannot imagine training a stable of horses without using it. Nearly every
horse in my stable wears a headpole at one time or another, and a lot of
them wear two headpoles to race.

Headpoles should be used judiciously, and I want to say again that the
use of a headpole to keep a horse's head straight should only be contemplated when other veterinary reasons have been exhausted.

A great many horses need a headpole simply to help them keep their
head straight, particularly around half-mile track turns. I don't know of
very many horses who could race at the speeds we do today, and not wear
a headpole. This is true even at the upper levels of our sport. I remember
racing in the North America Cup at Greenwood in Canada a few years
ago; of the nine horses starting in the $1 million final, seven wore two
headpoles.

Most of the horses in my stable start wearing a headpole very early in
their training period. Some will resent it at first, but if you are patient,
they will learn to wear it in time. Sometimes, a yearling will have to be
driven on long lines at first in order to get it to accept the headpole, but
generally a headpole is pretty well accepted by most horses.

One of the tricks that can be used when a headpole is added to a
horse's equipment list is to not put the headpole on too tight to begin
with. I recommend using an additional small ring on the head halter
side ring to allow the headpole to flop around a little at first. In this way,
the horse does not resent it and eventually accepts it.

Headpoles are a very valuable piece of equipment and can be used in
combination with lots of other equipment as well. Burrs or a small diameter ball can be added to the headpole to help keep a horse's head straight.

Here is a story which will explain how a trainer sometimes must compromise regarding what he wants to do with a horse.

Several years ago, I trained and raced a very fast Trenton colt named How Bout It. He developed a habit in his first few races of getting his head toward his right side around the last turn. He would carry his head straight most of the time, but when he really was asked to get in gear around the last turn, he would get his head over to his right side and bear in. (I was using a headpole on his left side, but it was worn loosely.)

I thought that if I tightened the headpole I could keep How Bout It's head straight around the last turn. However, when I did that and forced him to straighten his head, he wouldn't go like I knew he could. How Bout It had learned to get his head around, and he wanted it that way.

What I finally had to do with How Bout It was put the loose headpole back on him. It gave me the control I wanted, but allowed him to get his head around the way he preferred. A horse trainer doesn't always get to do what he wants!

I am sure that anybody who watched me race How Bout It probably thought the horse could be improved by adding a tough, tight headpole. I had tried that and it didn't work. So I went back to letting him do what he wanted. I just had to be careful with him and what I asked him to do in a race because of this little quirk.

Another key point is that How Bout It never got his head around to one side during his entire training period. He only began to do that when we went to racing, and it was a habit he developed very quickly. This is one reason why a trainer must rely on the catch drivers for information about how a horse acts during a race. Even though I think I might know a colt pretty well by the time he starts racing, there are always things that come up during racing that would never come up in the training miles. It is just a different experience for a horse. A lot of what I decide to do with a horse, in terms of his equipment and overall soundness, comes from information I get from the catch driver.

For example, I related the story from Magical Mike's two-year-old season when Mike Lachance recommended the use of a steering bar on the colt on the eve of the Woodrow Wilson. I have great respect for Mike's judgment; he would make a great horse trainer because he knows horses so well and knows what to do to help them steer better. A number of the better drivers are also very good at helping to diagnose lameness, by telling me where they think a colt might be hurting.

BRIDLE SELECTION AND USE

Another important aspect of training is the proper choice of bridles for each individual horse.

I guess every horse trainer would prefer to race a horse in an open bridle. However, the truth is that most horses cannot race with an open bridle. They see too much.

The four basic types of bridles are: 1) an open bridle, with no obstructions on the cheek pieces; 2) a blind bridle, which is the most used bridle

The blind bridle is the most common used on Standardbreds. The illustration above left shows a blind bridle properly positioned. The center illustration shows how a correctly positioned blind bridle looks from the side. The illustration above right is a blind bridle where the blinds have been squeezed too close to the horse's eyes.

in the industry; 3) a "Kant-See-Bak" bridle which is similar to the blind bridle, but allows a horse to see something directly beside him; and 4) a "peek-a-boo" or telescope bridle, which restricts a horse's vision so that he can only see straight ahead. Choosing the right bridle is a game you have to play with a horse.

An open bridle is just that. It has no obstructions to a horse's vision in any direction. The cheek pieces are simple strands of leather that connect the crown of the bridle to the driving bit. The basic purpose of the bridle is to provide a mechanism for steering and controlling the horse's activities.

One of the major complaints about an open bridle is that the horse wearing one has a tendency to spend a lot of his time looking back at the trainer or driver or the horses behind him, instead of concentrating his attention on what's in front of him.

An open bridle can be useful in certain instances. Horses who will latch on and take a pretty good hold may become less aggressive and will calm down in an open bridle. Many horses, especially those in a closed bridle of some kind, have a tendency to get fired up when another horse comes up behind them. Putting an open bridle on that type of horse may help relax him and make him more manageable.

Magical Mike wore an open bridle the day he won the Little Brown Jug. He was the kind of horse I knew would continue to be aggressive, even if he could see around. The Jug is a race in which you want to be aggressive because the Delaware track favors front-end speed so much. But Magical Mike was a nice, game horse who probably would have raced great for us that day anyway.

The bridle of choice in the Haughton Stable is a conventional blind bridle. The proper adjustment of this bridle is the key to its use. One of the more common mistakes with a blind bridle is having the cheek blinds improperly adjusted. The cheek blinds should be off a horse's eyes enough that the horse does not appear to be pinched in his vision.

To determine this, put a blind bridle on a horse and stand in front of him and look at the way the bridle fits. The cheek blinds should be away from the eyes at such an angle that the horse's vision is diminished only to the side and behind him. You want to avoid pulling the blinds in too tight. This will cause a horse to be very timid. The blinds should hit a horse at the center point of his eye; there should be as much blind above the eye as below it. The cheek pieces are adjustable at both the crown and bit ends of the bridle, so it is easy to adjust the bridle in either direction to ensure the proper fit.

Another way to determine the proper adjustment of the cheek blinds is to look at the horse from the side. If you look at the horse from the side and can see any part of his eye, the blinds are improperly adjusted. A blind that is either too low on the eyes or too high will allow a horse to see some of what you are trying to block him from seeing. A blind that is too low becomes ineffective when the horse is checked up, because the horse can see behind him over the top of the blind.

I talked earlier about proper bit placement, and while we are on the subject of bridle placement, this is a good place to reiterate my position on bit placement. Bits should be placed in a horse's mouth and adjusted carefully. This is done by using the holes punched in the cheek pieces of the bridle, thus allowing the bridle to be shortened or lengthened as need be. If you make an adjustment to one cheek piece, be sure that a similar adjustment is made on the other side of the bridle. Otherwise, the bit will not sit properly in the horse's mouth and result in an uneven pull or a compromised use of that bit. A horse's mouth is a very important part of his overall training. Great care should be taken to see that whatever is done around his mouth is done with the utmost care and attention.

Blind bridles are useful in that they cover a multitude of sins, so to speak. They prevent horses from seeing things that might alarm them, and also give the driver a measure of control not available in an open bridle. Most importantly, the horse does not have his front vision obscured in any way. I have done a lot of experimentation with bridles, and find that the blind bridle is most effective, especially with young horses.

About the only possible drawback to a blind bridle is that a horse's sideways vision is obscured. This can result in some training accidents, especially when a colt shies from another horse or track equipment. If a horse is trained at a facility which has hubrails, this can also create some problems because the horse may not be able to see the rail and will get into it without realizing it beforehand. A good trainer has to take this

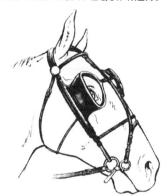

The Kant-See-Bak (left) shown in the correct position relative to a horse's eye. The illustration at right shows a telescope, or "peek-a-boo" blind which the author does not recommend.

into account and stay out of situations where a horse may get spooked.

Conventional theory also dictates that a horse who is lazy in an open bridle can be made more aggressive by using a blind bridle. In most cases, this is true. However, I have seen just the opposite occur. I have had colts who were lazy in a blind bridle, perk up for me when I took it off and replaced it with an open bridle.

Sometimes, as you can see, the reverse of what you expect will occur. Every trainer is encouraged to experiment, because not every horse will respond to bridles in the same way.

Once they begin to learn a little speed and catch on to the training routine, a lot of colts can become pretty aggressive. A trainer needs to watch this carefully and decide what changes are to be made with either the bridle or the type of bit in use.

KANT-SEE-BAKS ARE USEFUL BRIDLES

Another useful bridle is the Kant-See-Bak, which obviously takes its name from the fact that a horse can see in front and to the side, but "can't see back." The bridle is designed much like a blind bridle, in that there is an insert in the cheek piece which restricts the horse's rear vision.

This is a good bridle to use on a horse who needs to be covered up and have his vision somewhat restricted, but who may also have a tendency to run sideways on you if he is spooked. The Kant-See-Bak allows a horse to see what is beside him. Generally speaking, a horse will not run into a fence if he can see it.

As with all bridles, the Kant-See-Bak must be properly fitted and adjusted. The cup on the cheek insert should be adjusted so the eye is at the bottom of the cup when viewed from the side. The Kant-See-Bak

The Murphy blind is a valuable aid in helping a horse to carry his head straight. The illustration on the left shows a Murphy blind positioned on the right cheek piece of the bridle. The illustration on the right shows a Murphy blind with a "window" that would allow the horse to see others behind him.

often provides just the right combination of restricted and available vision; many horses will respond better if they can see a horse coming alongside.

The last of the conventional bridles is the "peek-a-boo" or telescope blinds. The telescope bridle was originally designed for horses who would shy from or spook at objects or other horses on the track, but it may be used on any horse who continually shies from things he sees or that he thinks he sees. I must say I am not partial to this bridle, because I think it obstructs a horse's vision too much.

The telescope bridle is made much like a blind bridle in that it has a cheek piece which restricts the side vision of a horse, but it also has a cup which encircles the entire eye, enabling a horse to see only what is directly in front of him. In my experience, this bridle makes a horse very timid. I just do not think a horse wearing this bridle can see enough to have the kind of confidence he needs to go forward. I have used this bridle, but realistically, I have used it only on bad horses. I know a great many trainers who use it a lot and seem to have good results, but I never have had much luck with it and do not recommend it.

THE MURPHY BLIND—A GREAT INVENTION

The great 1920's horseman Thomas W. Murphy was the inventor of the Murphy blind, and every practicing horseman should pay him homage daily for this invention.

The Murphy blind is a single vision obstructor which can be added to the cheek piece of a bridle on either side. It is very useful in helping a horse to straighten his head and carry it in front of him.

The concept behind the Murphy blind is simple. It is designed for any horse who wants to carry his head off center; that is, a lot of horses learn to go with their heads turned toward the inside or the outside, which, of course, is not desirable.

The Murphy blind is larger than the cheek insert of a blind bridle. In fact, it is nearly twice the overall size of the standard blind on a blind bridle. The Murphy blind affixes to the cheek piece and obscures a horse's vision when he turns his head, so the idea is that the horse will learn to straighten his head in order to have his vision restored.

To illustrate this, let us assume you have a horse who is turning his head to the right. You put the Murphy blind on the opposite eye, the left eye. When the horse turns his head to the right, he will not be able to see out of the left eye. This should cause the horse to learn to carry his head straight in order to see. If the horse carries his head to the left, the Murphy blind goes over the right eye.

Nihilator wore a Murphy blind over his right eye. He learned to go with his head turned slightly to the left, especially when you had to take a good hold of him. To overcome some of that, we used a Murphy on the outside, or right side, to force him to straighten up. It worked just enough to straighten his head enough to suit us. Nihilator also wore a headpole on the inside, or left side.

Another little trick we used with Nihilator was putting on a Murphy blind with a window cut in it to allow him to see just enough on the side to urge him on. Nihilator wound up racing on the front end in a lot of his races, so it was important that he be able to see to the side out of his right eye in the late stages of a race. We did not want him to get caught at the wire by an unseen horse coming fast at the end of the mile.

Napoletano also wore a Murphy blind. His was somewhat different in that it was also on the outside or right eye, but was used in connection with a blind bridle. (If the Murphy blind is used in this way, it is important to put it inside the blind bridle's cheek piece.)

Like all other bridle pieces, the Murphy blind should be adjusted carefully, and should be attached to the bridle in order to stay in place when the horse is in motion. Because it is so large, the Murphy blind should be affixed in a solid way to the bridle. Often it is necessary to use a small strand of wire to affix the top and bottom of the Murphy blind to the overcheck which runs up between the horse's eyes.

Use as much wire as is necessary to allow you to adjust the Murphy into the proper position. Again, you can assess the placement of the Murphy blind by standing in front of the horse and holding his head straight. If the Murphy blind covers the eye, it should be adjusted so it will allow the eye to be seen when the horse's head is straight.

If the Murphy blind is not adjusted properly, the horse will be forced to turn his head in the other direction in order to get full vision from the blocked eye, and you will have defeated your primary objective, which is

Running horse blinkers may be used and their correct position is indicated above left and center. The flyscreen (right) was originally invented for a horse's comfort in the paddocks, but has now proven useful as racing gear for a horse that doesn't like dirt hitting him in the face.

to keep the horse's head straight.

Another piece of equipment used with bridles is the so-called "running-horse blinker," so named because it is generally used on Thoroughbreds. These blinkers have a cloth hood which goes over the horse's head, with holes at the top for the ears and eyes. The hoods come with two adjustable "half-cups" that are designed to fit around the eyes in several different configurations.

By rotating the cups, a trainer can get a variety of different setups. I do not see the advantage of the blinkers over the more traditional blind bridle, or Kant-See-Bak. I think they do virtually the same thing.

Another piece of equipment which has come into use in a number of stables in recent years is the flyscreen. It was originally invented for horses to wear only in paddocks. The idea behind the flyscreen as equipment is that a horse will still have his vision, but flies cannot get onto or into his eyes. The latter problem is a major one for horses who are turned out, especially in the long, hot days of summer.

The flyscreen is a hood, much like the running horse blinker, but it does not go on over a horse's head. I have seen the flyscreen used both on top of and underneath the bridle. I suppose it could work in either fashion, although it certainly looks better under the bridle.

Somebody had the bright idea that a horse could be helped by wearing this flyscreen while he was racing. At first, everyone thought this was a bad idea, because we were not certain how much a horse could see while wearing the screen.

However, as time has gone by, more and more horses seem to be wearing these flyscreens to race. The flyscreen appears to be very good, espe-

The illustrations above left and center show two types of shadow rolls correctly positioned. The illustration above right shows a shadow roll that is too high on a horse's nose and will interfere with his line of sight.

cially on horses who do not like dirt hitting them in the face. It seems to help take the edge off a horse and keep him quiet. I am not opposed to anything which helps keep a horse comfortable and quiet. These are two of the most important things a trainer can do for any horse.

One last item before I leave the subject of bridles: Every bridle should have a nose strap that connects the two cheek pieces. This is important if the cheek pieces are to be kept in the correct position and it makes certain that the cheek pieces do not work their way toward the back when pressure is exerted on the driving lines. The nose strap is just a simple piece of leather that has a very important function: If a nose strap is not used, a bridle can be rendered useless.

SHADOW ROLLS

Before concluding the subject of bridles, I want to talk about shadow rolls. Dad told me a long time ago that nearly every pacer he ever trained needed a shadow roll, but that only the odd trotter would need to wear one. I asked him why this was so, and he said he didn't know why; this was just the way it was. It does seem strange that most pacers need to wear a shadow roll and most trotters do not. However, Dad did use shadow rolls on Green Speed, Cold Comfort and Speedy Count, three of his best trotters.

A lot of it may be psychological. The pacer may be more afraid of making breaks than a trotter, who can make a break without fear of falling or interfering badly.

Whatever the reason, it is clear that most every pacer will have to wear a shadow roll at one time or another. I think a lot more horses could race without them, but horsemen are often reluctant to take equipment off if the horse is performing well.

 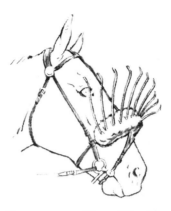

The brush shadow roll (left) shown in its proper position. The illustration above right shows the shadow roll made famous by the pacing mare Shady Daisy. The various straws interrupt the horse's line of sight and provide a distraction from flying dirt or shadows.

As with every other piece of equipment, proper positioning of the shadow roll is very important. The most common shadow roll is covered with sheepskin and is about two to three inches in diameter. It fits across and around the horse's nose below his eyes, and buckles under the jaw. It is important that a properly fitted shadow roll strap be run through the cheek pieces of the bridle so as to not interfere with the tension on the driving lines and to keep the shadow roll in its proper position.

The name "shadow roll" comes from the fact that the piece was invented for horses who were inclined to jump shadows on the track. The shadow roll obstructs the downward vision and prevents the horse from seeing the track directly below him. It is important that the shadow roll not be positioned to obstruct a horse's vision directly in front of him. The properly positioned shadow roll for most horses will lay across their noses at nearly the midpoint between their eyes and nostrils.

Shadow rolls come in varying sizes, from a small, sheepskin covering to the larger diameters. I wore a small sheepskin shadow roll on Magical Mike when he won the Little Brown Jug.

Shadow rolls not only come in different diameters, but they are also available in different lengths. A longer shadow roll is available that completely covers the downward vision of a horse and extends beyond the cheek pieces of the bridle. If you use the longer shadow roll, the strap of the shadow roll will necessarily have to go on the outside of the cheek piece of the bridle. This shadow roll cannot be pulled snugly, because it will interfere with the driving and overcheck bits.

Another type of shadow roll is the brush roll, which has stiff brush fibers inserted in a leather or plastic base and that stick up in front of a horse's eyes. These brush fibers generally are about four inches long and are light enough that they flutter in the wind when the horse moves

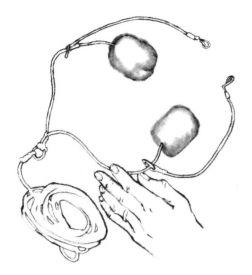

This illustration shows an earplug assembly, complete with foam earplugs which go in either ear.

down the track. The movement of the fibers creates a distraction for the horse and causes him to center his concentration elsewhere. However, I am not fond of the brush shadow roll because I believe it obstructs a horse's vision too much.

A shadow roll that has become fashionable because of the great pacing mare Shady Daisy is what I will call the "pipe cleaner," or "straw" roll. This is a shadow roll similar in design to the brush roll, except that it has single strands of plastic in an upraised position sticking up out of a noseband. These individual strands move in the wind and keep the horse distracted.

I know Shady Daisy absolutely needed this device to race, and I have seen it work on a number of other horses as well. I do not believe that it is currently available for mass purchase, but something like it will no doubt be marketed since it worked on such a great horse as Shady Daisy.

(Another thing to remember with any bridle adjustment is that the angles of sight can be affected by the manner in which the horse is checked. If adjustments are made on the length of the overcheck, either higher or lower, it may be necessary to re-position the cheek pieces of the bridle and any Murphy blinds, shadow rolls, etc. For instance, a shadow roll otherwise properly placed on a horse can become a problem if a horse is checked high and the angles of sight are thereby changed.)

EARPLUGS USEFUL IN KEEPING A HORSE QUIET

A lot of my time in training is invested in keeping horses quiet, and one of the more useful tools for keeping horses quiet is the use of earplugs.

The proper position of the plastic hobble is illustrated here. The two side hangers should be somewhat longer that either the front or rear hangers, allowing the hobbles to "sag" a little in the middle.

In the past, many trainers used cotton to plug a horse's ears, but there was a major drawback to this: The cotton, once it was in place, had to stay there. Now, with the invention by the Swedes of the pull earplugs, the earplug has come into widespread use.

Over the years as the Standardbred has progressed and gotten more naturally aggressive, a trainer has to be concerned with keeping a horse from getting too riled-up and rammy. As I said, earplugs are effective tools in keeping horses quiet.

The newer, pull earplugs are designed with a line which runs from the top of the bridle back to the driver's seat. With this design, the driver can pull the plugs whenever he desires. There is some misunderstanding on the use of earplugs, however. The earplugs are not for making speed with a horse; their primary purpose is to keep horses quiet and relaxed, particularly in warming up for racing and going to the gate. In most cases, by the time a driver pulls the plugs in a race, the horse is going flat out and pulling the plugs has no real benefit.

As with all equipment, make sure the earplugs you use are the right size for the horse in question. A horse will learn to resent something which makes him uncomfortable, and this can develop into a real problem, especially around a horse's head. Great care should be taken when putting in earplugs for the first time, because a horse can be set back in his training if he gets touchy around his head.

HOBBLES—FOR PACERS, AND NOW TROTTERS, TOO

Hobbles have been worn principally by pacers, although some trainers have, for many years, resorted to using crossed hobbles on trotters who make repeated breaks. As with most areas of horse training, the development of lighter, more durable and useful hobbles has made this aspect of training a little easier.

What has also occurred is that the pacer has become a naturally-gaited horse who does not require the kind of manufactured gait that existed just a few decades ago. Most yearlings now hit a pace pretty easily.

Nearly every hobble in use today is plastic, and the average hobble weighs less than a couple of pounds. It is very light and very easy on a horse. The main purpose of a hobble, of course, is to assist a pacer in staying on gait. Each hobble consists of two oval loops that go around the legs and come equipped with an adjustable strap in the center. The adjustable strap allows the hobbles to be sized for each horse. Each hobble also has four upright straps in order to be hung properly.

I like to start out an average-size yearling with a hobble that is just a trifle short; a 54-inch hobble is a good length for the average yearling. A bigger colt might require a 55-inch hobble, and a smaller one might be started out in a 53-inch hobble. The reason I like a hobble to be a little snug the first few times is because I want to be sure a colt hits a pace right away. If a horse is a little mixey-gaited, the hobble will have to be shortened. If his gait is pretty natural, but he appears constricted, I let his hobbles out. The first time, however, I want them a little shorter.

Hobble length is measured from the inside of the front loop to the inside of the back loop. The hobble should also be measured in a stretched position rather than relaxed, because the length of the hobble is important only when the horse is in motion and the hobble is stretched.

The easiest way to do this is to have a simple tape measure with two people stretching the hobble between them. It is important, too, that the hobbles on any horse be the same length on each side.

When placing the hobbles in the correct position, note that the only difference in design is that the larger oval loop is intended to go around the hind leg, and the smaller loop is designed for the forelegs. The height of the hobbles—that is where they ride on the horse's limbs—can be changed by adjusting the buckles on the plastic straps called "hangers." There are four sets of hangers that match up with the four upright straps on each pair of hobbles.

The front hangers are attached to a yoke which goes over the horse's withers. To start off, the front hobble should be hung at the mid-point of the foreleg between a horse's chest and his knees. The hind loop is attached with a little more complex rigging that has a hanger which buckles into the strap on the horse's back and runs back to a point between the horse's hind quarters and the butt of the tail. At this point, the hanger divides, with a single strap running down the back of each leg. This strap buckles into the upright buckle on the top of each larger hobble loop.

Like the front loops, the height of the rear loops can be adjusted. The ideal position for the rear hobble loops is at a point where the hobble rides just below the large, prominent stifle muscles but above the hock joint. This is one of the narrower spots on the hind leg.

The final two hangers are simply straps that are hung from the backstrap of the harness and attach to uprights on the hobbles just behind the foreleg and just ahead of the hind leg on each side.

Like the front hanger and the rear hanger, the height of these side hangers can be adjusted. Ideally, the hobbles should hang a little lower in the middle than either in front or back. When the horse is checked up, but standing still, the hobbles should be noticeably lower in the center. This will allow the hobble to ride correctly on a horse's leg while he is in motion, and cuts down on chafing.

Hobble length is something every trainer has a different idea about. Some trainers prefer to have a very long, loose hobble. Others prefer a tight, constricting hobble. I cannot stress enough that, as in most areas of horse management, this should be an individual judgment. Every horse will tell you what he wants after some experimentation has been done.

With young horses, it is also important to note that a lot of growth occurs during a training and racing season. If a horse is growing rapidly, it may be necessary to let the hobbles out to accommodate the new growth in order to keep a horse "set up" the same way, relative to his size.

Hobbles sometimes are adjusted for a horse's first start and for track size. It is customary in some stables to take a horse's hobbles up the first time he races, because racing conditions are far different from training miles. It is important that colts stay relaxed and confident in their first few starts. If it is necessary for you to take the hobbles up for a start or two, it is better to err in having them too short than too long. As a colt develops confidence and ability, the hobbles can be let out.

It also is sometimes necessary to take the hobbles up for a first-time starter on a half-mile track, but this is not always the case. Sometimes, such a change can produce a poor performance.

When Magical Mike was a three-year-old, I was ready to start him in the Dancer Memorial at Freehold, one of the better and faster half-mile tracks. I had raced Magical Mike earlier in the year in the Adios at The Meadows and he had made a break when he went into the first turn. I thought his hobbles might have been too long, so, prior to the Dancer, I took his hobbles up an inch, added a pair of knee boots for protection in the event he made a break, and added a Raymond leverage overcheck.

Magical Mike warmed up good, but he went kind of flat; it was just an O.K. race. He was not good and free-gaited like I wanted him to be. I was a little panicked that he raced so badly, because his next big race was the Little Brown Jug at Delaware, again on a half-mile track.

I was lucky to have another start for Magical Mike before the Jug, however, and that was the Jug Preview at Scioto Downs near Columbus, Ohio. Before that race, I let Magical Mike's hobbles back out an addi-

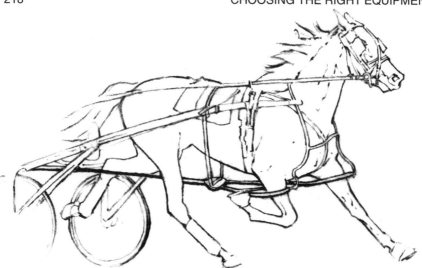

Trotting hobbles were designed for a trotter having difficulty staying on gait. The hobbles have a spring-loaded pulley which hangs under the belly of the horse and attaches to the arch of the sulky to keep it in position.

tional one and one-half inches, took his knee boots off, put a pair of front half-round, half-swedge shoes on, and added a Crit Davis overcheck. Mike Lachance drove Magical Mike in the Jug Preview, won with him, and reported that the horse was perfect, set up this way.

I was still concerned about how Magical Mike would be at Delaware, so on the Friday before the Jug I trained him with the same hobbles and rigging as the Jug Preview. He trained three trips, with the final heat paced easily in 1:59. He was perfect!

It made sense to me that Magical Mike needed a shorter hobble for a half-mile track, but the reality was that the shorter hobbles constricted his gait and changed the way he travelled. And I only took them up an inch! I used to think a horse could not tell the difference in just an inch, but this incident and several others taught me a very valuable lesson.

THE TROTTING HOBBLE—IT WORKS

One of the more interesting recent developments has been the use of trotting hobbles. In the past, if a trainer felt that a trotter needed to wear hobbles, he would simply hang a regular pair of pacing hobbles on the horse, but would cross them underneath its belly. As you might imagine, this would be a cumbersome, tiring rigging for any horse. I do not know of a single horse who ever performed at a high level wearing this rigging.

The modern trotting hobble, however, is a different story.

The trotting hobble in use today consists of two conventional loops

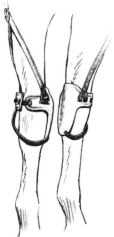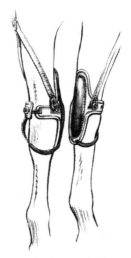

Knee boots offer protection to the horse during training and racing. The knee boots (left) are designed to cover only the knee joint. The knee boots (center) are designed to offer protection of the knee joint and the forearm above the knee. The boot on the right is a knee and arm boot commonly worn on trotters only. Knee boots should always be worn with suspenders.

joined together by a nylon rope that runs through a pulley hung beneath the horse's belly and attaches to the sulky beneath the driver's seat. The pulley is spring-loaded, thereby creating pull in the opposite direction when the horse steps forward.

Trotting hobbles really work in keeping a horse on gait. I think they are most useful with a horse who makes breaks for no apparent reason, although trotters normally make breaks because they are unsound or are interfering. These hobbles appear to steady a horse, particularly behind the gate and for those first few steps out of the gate. They also seem to steady a horse who may be interfering, a common problem with trotters, as I noted earlier.

Having said that, I personally do not like trotting hobbles and the whole idea of a trotter's gait being manufactured and don't think they should be used at all. I think great trotters should be naturally gaited horses and should not have to be helped along by the use of artificial means. I just wish trotters were not allowed to wear them in a race. As a training aid, they might be extremely useful, but I would prefer that a trotter race without this kind of assistance.

KNEE, TENDON AND SHIN BOOTS

Now, let us conclude our discussion of equipment with a description of, and the uses for the various knee, tendon and shin boots worn by trotters and pacers.

First, with respect to knee boots, there are three different types designed to cover all, or part of the knee joint. Let me say right off that I think it is very important that boots of any kind should fit a horse well, and it is important when buying boots that you take great care and patience in selecting boots that are the right size for each horse.

A boot that is too small can pinch a horse. A boot that is too big will have trouble staying in place. Boots do come in several different sizes. The easiest thing to do when boots are necessary for any horse in your stable is to take a number of different sizes and try them until you see which boot fits the best.

Most knee boots are designed to fit the contours of the horse's anatomy. With a little experimentation, you can find a boot which fits snugly over the horse's knee joint and does not stick out at the bottom. A boot which protrudes at the bottom can create more problems than it solves, since the horse may strike the bottom of the boot with an opposite foot.

Most knee boots come with suspenders. There are some boots that a manufacturer or a tack supplier will tell you can be used without suspenders, but this is not recommended. I have used knee boots without suspenders, and generally, it does not work. The boot invariably slides down the leg during training or racing, and ends up around a horse's ankle. Use the suspenders!

Another reason to use a suspender is that any boot designed for use without suspenders has to fit pretty snug on a horse's knee. Putting a boot on too tight can create a situation where a horse could be injured. Use the suspenders, and the boot can be attached snugly, but not too tight.

The three basic types of knee boots are the half-knee boot, the full knee boot, and the knee-and-arm boot. The half-knee boot is necessary for a horse that interferes right on the knee joint.

The most common incidence of knee-knocking occurs with pacers, and has them striking a foreleg with the opposite front hoof. That is, a pacer often strikes his right knee with the hoof of his left foreleg, or vice-versa.

The full knee boot offers protection above and below the knee joint, as well as protecting the knee itself. This is the knee boot that is most widely used in the industry.

The full knee boot is used whenever a horse interferes with different parts of the knee joint. Many horses who start to hit their knees do so over the area the knee boot must cover, and the use of the full boot is a necessity. What happens in this instance is that a horse may brush his knees on the low part of the knee joint when he is going slow, but will strike the knee higher as he trains or races faster.

Knee boots are made using the classic, molded white felt, or the lighter and more practical plastic. However, a horse who learns to hit his knees seems to like the sound of striking his opposite leg. In this instance, the felt boot is recommended because it absorbs a lot of the sound of impact.

The light plastic boot is very useful because it fits so well and is easier to clean and maintain, but it makes a lot of noise when a horse hits it.

However, I firmly believe a horse can get used to that sound.

The other common or basic type of knee boot is the knee-and-arm boot. This boot is more commonly associated with trotters, and is designed for a horse who has a lot of front action and strikes his knee joint at the very top, or interferes with his foreleg above the knee joint. Generally speaking, a trotter will need this boot if it strikes this area of the leg. This boot is very rarely used on a pacer.

Knee boots also can be used on horses who never offer to touch their knees. I do not like to add unnecessary equipment on any horse, but a knee boot can be worn for protection only. If a horse makes a break, or has to be taken up drastically during a race, he may hit himself, even though it appears from the nature of his gait that he does not go anywhere near his knees. It is better to err on the side of protection in most instances.

TENDON BOOTS ALSO PROVIDE PROTECTION

Perhaps a more common problem for pacers is interference in the area of the tendon between the knee joint and the ankle. This interference can come from two sources: The horse may brush his tendons with the hoof of the opposite foreleg, or he may strike himself with a hoof of the hind leg from the opposite side. For instance, a pacer can cut right through a tendon sheath by striking his right foreleg with his left hind hoof. This can be a very serious injury, sometimes career-ending. When the hoof strikes the area, the shoe the horse is wearing can act like a knife and cut the tendon area. Naturally, you want to avoid this. For this reason and many others, I prefer to put tendon boots on most every horse in my stable at a very early point in training. You simply cannot risk a serious injury. Every young horse is going to make a mistake sometime in training, so an ounce of prevention is necessary.

Tendon boots protect not only the inside of the leg, but also the back of the leg in the ankle area. Such boots come in several different designs. The plain tendon boot is very light and offers protection for a horse who does not interfere regularly, but might brush this area of the leg.

Tendon boots are also available with additional plastic or leather protection. These boots are good for a horse who interferes regularly at several different points along the tendon area. Another type of tendon boot is an ankle boot which, as the name implies, only protects the ankle of the horse. This boot is normally used for a horse who interferes in the area of the ankle, and is good because it offers protection on both the side and back of the ankle.

Tendon boots are commonly associated with pacers, but a trotter may need a tendon boot during the early part of his training. Generally, when a trotter starts going faster training miles, he will go up above the tendon area and is not likely to interfere in that area.

 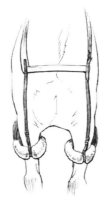 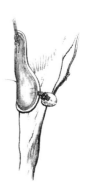

Tendon boots (left) offer protection to the inside and back of the foreleg between the knee and ankle. This illustration shows a tendon boot used with a quarter boot. The quarter boot goes over the coronet band and protects against cross-firing. The center and right illustrations show the elbow boot assembly most commonly worn by trotters. The center illustration shows how to hang the elbow boots from the front, and the illustration (right) shows the side view of the elbow boots properly positioned.

Pacers, however, are liable to hit anywhere up and down the leg due to the nature of their gait. It is not uncommon to see a pacer race with both tendon and knee boots.

ELBOW BOOTS FOR SOME TROTTERS

A source of interference among trotters is the odd horse that goes so high in front he strikes the underneath side of his elbow. Such a horse often will make breaks for no apparent reason, but will not interfere anywhere else. When I have a colt who is making breaks and I cannot find indications of interference anywhere on the hind limbs or knees, I always check the elbow area to see if there is evidence that the elbow joint has been struck. If there is evidence of this, the use of an elbow boot is necessary.

The elbow boot is one of the more clumsy-looking attachments that can be used on a horse, and is very difficult to fit properly. The boot has two suspenders that attach over the neck and withers in a fashion similar to a hobble hanger.

The front suspender attaches to the front of a strap going around the horse's leg and goes up over the neck. This suspender is adjustable at both ends and has a strap, also adjustable, that goes across the horse's chest.

The other suspender is attached to the boot. It goes over the withers and fastens to the hook on the saddle pad. In this way, the boot can be raised or lowered as needed in order to secure the proper fit. The cup of

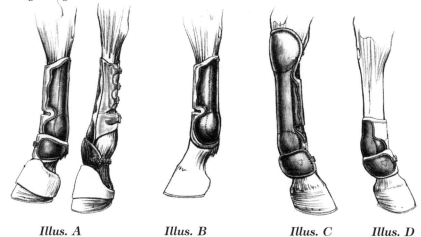

| Illus. A | Illus. B | Illus. C | Illus. D |

Trotters who interfere may wear several different types of hind shin boots. Illustration A is the standard hind shin boot with speedy cut attachment and a low scalper. Illustration B is the standard hind shin boot. Illustration C is a hind shin boot with the speedy cut attachment and the hock protection. Illustration D shows a hind ankle boot with the speedy cut attachment.

the elbow boot should fit right over the elbow joint, but should not be so tight as to restrict movement of the shoulder.

HIND SHIN BOOTS AND THE NATURE OF INTERFERENCE

I know that a number of trainers have been successful in recent years in racing trotters with only a pair of brace bandages on the hind legs, but I have never felt very comfortable about doing this myself. I am always worried about a horse whacking a shin without adequate protection. Personally, I haven't trained many trotters who did not catch a shin at least once in training or racing.

Hind shin boots are made in varying styles and shapes. As with knee boots, the type of shin boots used will depend on the nature of the interference.

While on this subject, let me take a moment to discuss the nature of interference by most trotters. Many people believe that trotters interfere when the foreleg and the hind leg on either side initially come together. They believe, for instance, that the right foreleg may be struck by the right hind leg.

The reality is that the interference in the area of the shin or ankle occurs after the two legs *pass* each other and start back toward full extension. For example, the front hoof doesn't strike the inside of the shin as the two legs come together, but as the hoof starts back forward. The front hoof can strike the inside of the shin with some considerable force, too.

I have a slow-motion videotape of Napoletano's action, and I learned a lot about the nature of his interference. He would often strike the inside of his hind shin and would "bounce" off that leg. The bounce can send a trotter into his knees, which explains why it is so common for a trotter to make breaks when he interferes badly.

The arc of the front hoof is dramatically affected as the hoof is going forward, not when it originally passes the hind leg. A horse can also get into a situation where he begins to change his natural gait behind to avoid the interference. This often results in soreness and gait flaws, such as stabbing or hiking.

There are four basic types of shin boots.

There is a shin boot which covers the shin and ankle areas, but does not offer protection in the area below the ankle. This boot is designed for a horse who only hits on the shin or ankle.

Another type of shin boot has the same design as the ankle and shin boot, but adds what is called a "speedy cut" attachment to offer protection in the area between the ankle and hoof. This boot normally has three small straps, which can be fastened in the area of the shin, and a fourth strap that attaches just above the ankle. The speedy cut attachment also has a strap which fastens below and around the ankle.

Peace Corps wore this type of boot because she would hit all up and down her leg at one time or another. She was a very determined filly, and would trot right through interference.

Peace Corps hit her hind legs mostly in the area between her ankle and her hoof. She would do this a lot going to the gate and in going slow warm up and training miles. In a race, she would most likely hit in the shin and ankle areas.

I will never forget watching her win the Merrie Annabelle at The Meadowlands as a two-year-old. She was coming through the stretch, and you could tell that she was hitting her shins pretty regularly. But she kept right on coming and won. She was an amazing filly in that respect.

I had a lot of trouble shoeing Peace Corps to go cleaner until she hit the dirt tracks out in the midwest. They seemed to hold her just enough so that she could develop some real confidence. After racing at Springfield and Indianapolis at two, she was a much different filly. And by the time we got to Lexington with her, she was going pretty clean (for her). I always raced her in a full shin boot with a speedy cut attachment and scalpers. At three, Peace Corps was so good on the dirt tracks that I raced her barefooted in the World Trotting Derby and she set a world record of 1:52.4!

The third type of shin boot is similar to the full hind shin boot, but has an extension which covers the hock area as well. This boot is designed for a really big-gaited horse who interferes up high on his hind leg above the regular shin boot.

Napoletano wore a full hind shin boot with a hock extension at three

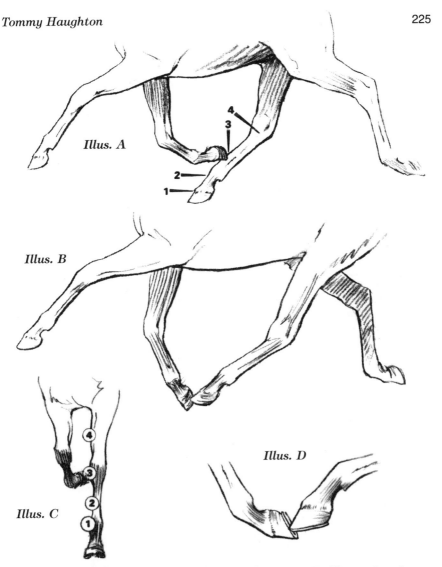

Various types of interference are shown on this page. In illustration A, interference at the trotting gait occurs when the front foot comes in contact with the hind foot on the same side. When it takes place at (1) it is known as scalping; at (2) speedy-cutting; at (3) shin-hitting, as illustrated; and at (4), hock hitting. Among pacers, illustration B, the basic type of interference between front and hind legs occurs when the hind foot on one side interferes with the front foot on the opposite side. This is known as cross-firing. Illustration C indicates the manner in which a horse interferes with one front leg by hitting it with the opposite front leg in passing. This horse is shown hitting the knee (3) but may also hit the ankle (1), shin (2), or forearm (4). Forging, illustration D, is when a trotter's hind foot strikes the bottom of the front foot on the same side.

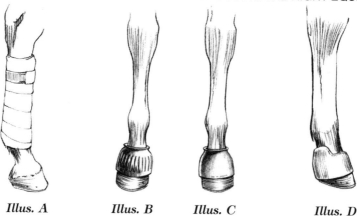

Illus. A   Illus. B   Illus. C   Illus. D

Illustration A shows the use of brace bandages to proved protection for the hind limbs. Illustration B and C are two types of bell boots used for protection. The ribbed bell boot (B) is often worn by trotters as a training aid because of the extra weight. The plain bell boot (C) is more often worn by a pacer. The low scalper (D) is often worn on the hind leg of a pacer to protect from cross-firing.

when he won the Kentucky Futurity. He was a passing-gaited horse who had tremendous reach and extension. He had also learned to trot very fast! It was necessary to wear a hock extension on him because, the week before the Futurity, he had set a stakes record in winning The Transylvania at Lexington and had hit himself just above the shin boot and below the hock.

The fourth kind of hind shin boot is not a shin boot as much as it is an ankle boot. This type of boot offers protection for a horse who only hits his ankle and speedy-cut area.

Any or all of these boots may be worn with or without brace bandages under them. A lot of trainers prefer to wear brace bandages under a boot, especially if a horse is difficult to fit. A small horse, particularly one with small legs, may be difficult to fit and the use of brace bandages may assist in fitting the shin boot to the leg.

However, it should be noted that the use of shin boots with bandages will make the hind leg larger in diameter, and could result in increased interference. In most instances, I have obtained just as good a result with either the bandages or the boots, but seldom found great success with them together.

Brace bandages should never be used without some sort of padding underneath. I prefer a rubber pad which will not absorb water. In the past, cotton pads were used under brace bandages, but the rubber pads do a much more effective job in providing protection.

As with knee boots in front, the hind shin boots should be fitted properly and not be too tight. Some injury can occur if the boots are improperly attached. Great care is therefore recommended in seeing that the boots are fitted properly. This also ensures that the boot will not come down during the course of a race.

One of the things that has helped is the importation of the so-called "Swedish shin boots" which are made of plastic and use VELCRO® attachments. The old, leather shin boots were a real maintenance headache, but these new plastic boots can be submerged in water for cleaning, and don't absorb any moisture. They are much lighter and also seem to cut down on chafing.

BELL BOOTS AND SCALPERS FOR PROTECTION

Other common pieces of equipment are bell boots and scalpers. These are designed for hoof protection. The bell boots are commonly used on the front hooves, while scalpers are designed for use on the hind hooves.

Bell boots are training aids only, and, in my opinion, should never be used in races. A bell boot can be caught easily and can cause a horse to hang up and make a break, or even go down during a race. For that reason, though I often train a colt in bell boots, they come off when we go to race.

Bell boots are also recommended for more than protection. They can help establish the gait of young trotters by adding just enough weight to balance a horse effectively. As with all equipment, bell boots should be sized according to the horse. A bell boot that is too long can be stepped on, so a pair of scissors can be used to trim the boot so it fits.

The properly sized bell boot should cover the entire hoof area without touching the ground while the horse is at rest. If the boot touches or drags on the ground, it is too long!

I like scalpers behind on my trotters in training, but the scalpers, too, come off when I start racing. I have found that scalpers invariably move up during a race and end up dangling around a horse's ankle. I can cut down on this by having a blacksmith turn a nail on the outside of the hoof that I can "hook" the scalper to and assist it in keeping in place during training miles.

Peace Corps always wore scalpers; I left them on her because she had a tendency to scalp badly when she was behind the gate as the gate was just starting to roll.

There are two types of scalpers, the low and high varieties. The low type of scalpers is worn on a horse that tends to interfere right on the coronary band of the hoof. The higher scalper is used on a horse that may brush a little higher between the ankle and hoof in the speedy cut area.

KEEP IT SIMPLE—USE ONLY WHAT YOU NEED

Do not use equipment as a crutch. I do not like to see a horse wear a lot of equipment, especially if it is unnecessary.

A general guideline is that equipment can be used to help a horse with minor problems. It can help him go straighter and be more comfortable.

But equipment never got a horse sound who was lame.

And it never will.

Use only what you need to use, and mix it in with a large dose of "horse sense." Be patient, be willing to experiment, and remember that it may take a while for some piece of equipment to work its magic.

Thomas L. Haughton had mighty big shoes to fill when he suddenly and tragically was thrust into the stead of his father, Hall of Famer Billy Haughton, after the latter's death in 1986 as a result of a racing accident.

The years since have proved that Tom Haughton was a worthy heir to his illustrious father's racing fortunes. The younger Haughton has developed and/or driven such fine performers as Caressable, Napoletano, Farmstead's Fame, Final Score, Golden Greek, and Naughty But Nice. More noteworthy was his victory in the 1982 Hambletonian with Speed Bowl, making him the youngest driver to capture the revered trotting classic.

A couple of other trotters most likely hold an even softer spot in Haughton's heart, though. Under his tutelage the somewhat less-than-beauteous Peace Corps became 1989 Trotter of the Year, set world records of 1:52.4 and 1:56 on mile and half-mile tracks, respectively, and won the Kentucky Futurity and the World Trotting Derby. The incredible mare retired as the richest Standardbred in history, with U.S. and foreign earnings totalling nearly $5 million.

Another Haughton pupil was the "little rat" of a trotting colt named Somatic who stunned the harness racing community with a 1:53 heat win and raceoff triumph in the 1991 World Trotting Derby. That same year, Somatic also captured heats of the Kentucky Futurity, Review Stake, and a division of the Arden Downs stake.

But Tom Haughton was not finished. His pupil Magical Mike attained Two-Year-Old Pacing Colt of the Year Honors in 1993 and became the first horse to win both the Woodrow Wilson and the Governor's Cup. The next year, the electrifying colt brought him at last to the hallowed ground occupied five times as a driver and once as a trainer by his late father: the winner's circle at the Little Brown Jug.

6

TRAINING THE TROTTER

CHARLES SYLVESTER

I have been training horses for more than 35 years and I guess I would say my most valuable asset in training horses is a very poor memory.

I know that might sound as though I'm trying to be funny, but I actually believe that I am a better horse trainer because my memory is so poor. This is an asset because it leaves me open to try almost anything. If there is anything that three and a half decades of training horses has taught me, it is that the opportunity to try almost anything will present itself.

Training horses, particularly trotters, is a very difficult, yet very rewarding way of making a living. I have been extremely fortunate to have developed a few champions using my training methods. My ideas about training and shoeing trotters are neither revolutionary nor dramatic, but I hope these suggestions will offer some assistance to anyone who has ever tried to solve the puzzles of the gaited horse.

It is in the pursuit of solutions, I think, that many horse trainers lack the adequate background or don't leave themselves open enough to trying new ideas, or changing their habits. That is where my poor memory kicks in, because I don't remember what I may have done in any one instance unless I really sit down and think about it. I try to react instinctively.

A lot of the good decisions I have made were intuitive and were based simply on an accumulation of experience through years of trial and error. I remain open to almost any solution. I can say that my ideas about training horses have changed dramatically over the past decade. I have tried almost everything there is to try to improve a horse's performance. I don't think there is anything that I might hear about that I wouldn't be willing to try, at least once!

I think the ability to change is a very valuable asset for any horse trainer. The trainer who has survived the recent changes in the breed is the one who has adapted to new methods and new shoeing techniques. I know that I now train a horse much different from what I did just a few years ago.

A lot of that, generally, has to do with the way horses are trained, and specifically, with the way they are now raced. Particularly with trotters, the way we shoe and rig them has been altered forever by the many good ideas brought over here in the late 1970's and throughout the 1980's by the Scandinavian trainers. I have incorporated some of their techniques into my training arsenal because they worked for me as well. Some of their ideas did not.

Some of their shoeing ideas have been incorporated into my daily routine. For instance, when the great trotter Pine Chip won the Kentucky Futurity and set his 1:51 record, he wore a shoe that was brought to this country from Scandinavia.

I think the influx from Europe has been both good and bad for the trotter. It's been good in the sense of the ideas they brought over here and in the money invested in American breeding stock, but bad in the sense that some of our greatest horses have been exported.

I love the fact that Mack Lobell, a horse I developed, is now standing at stud in this country, because I should get a chance to train some of his offspring. It wasn't possible before to have him at stud here in the U.S. because of his value overseas, but I am delighted to see him come home for the balance of his stud career. I understand he did quite well as a sire with his first few crops in Sweden.

In the text which accompanies and supplements what I have written about here, Per Eriksson describes, in good detail, some of the more "exotic" ideas the Scandinavians have about training trotters. It is recommended reading. What I am doing in this chapter is giving the basics that I have used in developing my good trotters.

These are the ideas and practices that I have developed over the years to produce the good horses that I have been fortunate to be around. These are the practices that produced Mack Lobell, Pine Chip, Armbro Keepsake, Winky's Goal, Whiteland Janice, Britelite Lobell, Diamond Exchange and others along the way. I hope the reader will find something on these pages that can be used in dealing with the everyday, practical problems that come from training trotters.

BREAKING AND GAITING

The first step is the breaking process, and in these early days of development I don't treat my trotting colts and fillies very much differently than the average horse trainer.

I want them handled correctly. I like them to be well-mannered.

I hope to avoid any trouble that might lead to a more serious problem in the coming weeks and months.

I still line-drive yearlings, although I suppose I could do away with that because so many of the colts come to us after being handled for a long time in the sales prep process. They are very much accustomed to human contact. I haven't had any big problems over the years breaking colts. I have had my share of tough ones, but the Standardbred is, on the whole, a docile breed. Most of the colts respond very well to their early training.

I want a colt broken to the harness and broken to drive before I ever get him on the track, because there is no more helpless feeling in the world than trying to drive a colt and not being able to steer him as he heads for trouble on the training track.

In my stable, colts are line-driven a couple of days. If I am satisfied with their progress, I will attempt to hook them. I can usually tell right off if a colt or filly is going to be a problem. Sometimes, you can just sense when a horse will be trouble.

I like to start yearlings in a blind bridle with a latex-covered snaffle bit and plain overcheck or just a chin strap with a very long overcheck. I don't want to put a yearling in a vise right off, because I want it to be free in this early stage of development. I have seen trainers use too-short an overcheck on a yearling, and this can lead to big problems. If a colt is checked too high and it rears, it can go right over backwards pretty easily, and be seriously injured. I would rather have a colt with its head way down so that if it does rear at all, there is no chance of having it go over backwards.

When colts are line-driven, I like them to be escorted by one or two assistants, with long lines attached to the colt's stall halter. This is really a safety precaution in the event the colt gets a bit rambunctious, or gets spooked by something and attempts to run off.

For the same reason, I also like to drive the yearling in the long lines for the first couple of days. It is like an insurance policy against trouble. I will leave the stall halter on under the bridle only as long as I need to attach an extra line. After a few days, I get to the point where I have only one extra line and if everything goes O.K., the third line is no longer used. When the third line is no longer being used, I leave the stall halter where it belongs—in the stall. I dislike seeing a horse jogged in his stall halter. It is very unprofessional to present your horse this way to the public and to your fellow horsemen.

I keep my yearlings barefoot for the initial training. A lot of trainers put shoes on right away, but I prefer to wait. Some of the yearlings come from the sales with a flat, plate shoe on the front hooves. I normally remove that and rasp the foot around the toe to remove any sharp edges. This is done for a couple of reasons.

First, the rasping of the sharp edges is a safety precaution. You don't want a colt cutting himself if he should happen to jump or interfere. Secondly, rasping the sharp edges will keep the hoof from breaking off during this initial breaking period.

I also might slip a pair of ribbed bell boots on a colt for the first few times for protection. This is also useful to get some idea of his gait and habits. I really prefer to have them go as natural as possible. I can tell more about a colt's true gait and action if he is without extra equipment.

I start off jogging yearlings about two miles since most of them are in pretty good condition from the sales. In the old days, you would get colts from the sales who would be fat and slick and out of condition. But now, the breeders understand that horse trainers prefer yearlings who are in good condition. It saves a lot of time in the fall if a colt arrives without a lot of excess fat.

There are still times, of course, when a yearling will be line-driven and jogged in the same day. If I am not happy with the way a yearling is driving and responding to the bit, I will line-drive him a little before I hook him, with special instruction time in turning and responding to bit pressure.

This might also happen if a yearling is a little tough and is giving me trouble on the track. I like yearlings to step right off on the trot and stay at it for a couple of miles.

I can tell more about them when they are fresh and full of themselves. Of course, they also begin to learn when they get a little tired. I am careful to not go too far with a yearling in the first couple of weeks. A yearling who gets tired easily can start knuckling over and/or interfering. I pay special attention to the conditioning aspects during this period of time. I am conscious of assessing and building condition here for the hard work that lies ahead.

Normally, I will jog a colt two miles a day for about a week and then start to go three miles a day thereafter. I go both ways of the track because I don't want him to learn to go just one way. I know a lot of trainers who only jog their colts the wrong way of the track and I think that is a definite mistake. I don't have a set program but I prefer to jog a colt the wrong way of the track the first mile or two and then turn him and go a mile the right way. That routine more nearly duplicates what the colt will do in more serious training in a few months.

I also find that going the right way helps them learn to trot the turns in both directions. This is very important and should not be overlooked right from the start.

If a colt or filly misbehaves at first, I will sometimes come directly out of the stable area and go the right way. This can confuse a colt who might want to fight me a little. I confuse him by altering the routine. Sometimes, this confusion will serve to get him looking at other things. This often helps me get along a little better. It can help to mix up their routine a little and this technique can help you get through a tough jogging session.

THE FIRST PAIR OF SHOES

After about a month of jogging, the colt is ready for his first pair of shoes. In most cases, this will be a pair of half-round shoes, either 9/16 or half-inch, depending on the colt's action in front. There is, however, something that I would like to explain here.

I don't put this first pair of shoes on in the normal fashion.

The shoes are put on backwards, with the open-heeled part of the shoe to the front and the half-round portion covering the horse's heel. The backwards shoe is another innovation from the Scandinavians. I really believe it gets a trotter started the right way.

The backwards shoe acts very much like a bar shoe but without the extra weight. The weight in the heel is very desirable because it produces the same kind of results we used to obtain with weighted heel boots—but without the potentially damaging weight.

The fact that the toe of the shoe is open helps get a colt breaking over nicely. I like this shoe very much. The weight of the shoe, either 5/8, 9/16, or 1/2-inch thick, will depend on the amount of action I want to produce or enhance. If I have a colt who has plenty of natural action, he will get the 1/2-inch half-round, which weighs about five ounces.

If a colt needs some additional action to supplement his natural stroke, I use the 9/16-inch half-round, which weighs seven ounces, or the 5/8-inch half-round, at approximately ten ounces.

PREFERENCE FOR A LOW FRONT ANGLE

I also like my trotting yearlings to have a low angle in front. I have found that most of my good horses, and all the great ones, had low angles in front, so that is what I prefer. I think a low angle gives a horse the right kind of action and avoids problems like quarter cracks later on.

If I am not satisfied with the action after putting the first pair of half-rounds on, I will add a pair of ribbed bell boots. I like the ribbed bell boots better than the lighter brown gum boots because they are a little heavier and help to steady a colt in the early stages of training. The ribbed bell boots also provide more protection than the lighter gum bell boots.

This combination normally gives a yearling the right amount of knee action and extension, and gives me a pretty good idea of what I have to work with.

What am I looking for at this time?

I am looking for several things. I believe it is very important that you do all you can at the very early stages to gait a yearling the right way. I want him to develop the proper stroke in front, one that is evidenced by good knee action and good reach. I want that nice, rolling action in front that horse trainers have preferred for ages. There's no big secret about that.

I have always believed that I could change a colt's action in front and modify his stroke, but can't really do much about the way he handles his hind limbs. I will talk more later in this chapter about possible remedies for horses who handle their hind limbs poorly.

I prefer a horse to carry a low angle in front and I will explain what I mean by a low angle. I do not consider a 50-degree angle a low angle! By a low angle, I want something in the 46-47-48 degree area.

A lot of trainers think a more normal angle for a horse in front is something around 50 degrees, but I have found that I have much better success in keeping horses sound in front—that is with their knees, ankles and feet—if I carry an angle below 50 degrees. I think the low angle produces the kind of action I want and is conducive to producing speed, while preserving soundness.

Nearly every one of the good horses I have trained, including Mack Lobell, Pine Chip, Britelite Lobell, Diamond Exchange, etc., has had low angles in front. And every one of them have been good-gaited, clean-going, and relatively sound horses.

Another of the major advantages of the low angle in front is that it avoids problems with quarter cracks. This a very natural angle for a horse to strike the ground since we know that a horse's heel is the first part of the hoof to strike the track. Nearly every horse I have ever seen with quarter cracks had what I thought was too high an angle in front.

If a trainer is having trouble with a lot of front-end lameness or soreness, I recommend a good long look at how his horses are shod up front.

A higher angle of 49-50 degrees in front also creates problems with a trotting horse because it may slow him down and cause him to interfere with his shins behind.

Most of my yearlings come to me with a higher angle. It may take a number of trips to the blacksmith to get that angle where I want it, but I am convinced that the low angle in front is a necessary, successful component of my training regimen.

PREFERENCE FOR A HIGH ANGLE BEHIND

I also believe that a horse should have a very high angle behind. Again, all of my good trotters have had low angles in front, and relatively high angles behind.

For instance, Mack Lobell carried a 47-degree angle in front but had a 56-degree angle behind. Britelite Lobell, Armbro Keepsake and Armbro Devona had nearly the same setup and they were all about the best-gaited trotters anybody ever trained.

Mack Lobell was an interesting horse to gait. From his very early stages of development, he just missed hitting his elbows, just missed hitting his knees, just missed interfering with his shins. He was like that his entire career. He just missed touching everywhere.

As a two-year-old, Mack Lobell needed a little more weight in front to steady him than I preferred. With a normal, light shoe that I prefer, he was a little unsteady and pacey at times.

The extra weight he needed caused him to go pretty high and near his elbows. I was so concerned about this at two that I eventually raced him in elbow boots. In fact, he wore elbow boots when he set the two-year-old world race record of 1:55.3 at Lexington. At three, however, and thereafter, he didn't need the elbow boots, because as he matured I was able to remove the heavier shoes and eliminate that problem.

After Mack made a break in the World Trotting Derby at Du Quoin at

Mack Lobell, the author's richest pupil, carried nearly 15 ounces of weight in front in order to steady his gait at two. This weight caused him to go high at full speed, and Sylvester was forced to use elbow boots for protection. The colt was set up this way when he set his 1:55.3 world record at Lexington in 1986 for John Campbell.

three, I did use the elbow boots on him in his next starts at Delaware. But he wasn't as good in them as he had been at two and I took them off before his next start in the Kentucky Futurity at Lexington.

He eventually raced at three in an aluminum bar shoe with a toe grab. Mack Lobell always had trouble with his feet and he wore a full pad his entire career.

I was always trying to "steal" as much weight off Mack as possible. I was always concerned about him getting into his elbows. I am convinced that he would have hit his elbows consistently if I had not eventually taken some of the weight off him.

As a two-year-old, with a 5/8-inch, half-round bar shoe, a full pad and a plastic grab boot, Mack Lobell had about 15 ounces of weight on each front hoof. In my estimation, he needed that much weight to be confident and safe.

At age three and beyond, I got Mack down to where he wore an aluminum bar shoe, a full pad and grab boot that together weighed less than nine ounces.

He raced that way when he won the Hambletonian and set the world race record of 1:52.1 at Springfield. He also was shod that way when he won the Elitlopp in Sweden at four.

While horses generally don't come with a high angle behind, it's advisable to move them in that direction with every shoeing. Just ask the blacksmith to remove more toe than heel and the higher angle will result. Don't make this change too dramatic in one shoeing. Every time the horse goes to the shop, just try to get his angle up by taking away the toe and not trimming the heel. After several trips to the blacksmith, I have the angle where I want it.

I find that this helps to gait a colt or filly and keeps them from interfering during the early stages of training. I also think a high angle behind keeps a horse from knuckling over a lot, a common problem with trotters.

TEACH THEM TO "JOG ON"

A lot of interference can develop during the very early stages of training, particularly when I am just jogging along with a yearling going slow. He can begin to interfere behind. This can and does create problems. That is one of the reasons that I like to teach a colt to jog on at a pretty accelerated rate. This serves several purposes.

First, the solid jogging builds great condition and secondly, there is less interference if you teach a colt to jog on a little bit and keep him serious about his work.

I have found over the years that I have a lot less trouble with a colt or filly interfering if I teach them to jog on a little bit. Most interference at this early stage will occur when going slow, when a colt is not paying attention or gawking around.

This is particularly true with a colt or filly who has a predisposition to knuckle over behind. I don't have a lot of trouble with this due to the combination of a couple of factors.

First, the high angles I use behind allows a trotter to hit the ground with a very natural angle. I am told that Billy Haughton, one of the all-time great trotting horse trainers, liked a high angle behind for the same reason.

Secondly, I like to jog a horse with a tendency to knuckle over at about a 4:00-4:30 mile rate to build condition and keep him on his toes. Most knuckling over occurs because a yearling is either tired or bored. Try to keep them in the bit and keep them interested and you should avoid most, if not all, of the knuckling over problems. If the knuckling over problem persists, you may want the veterinarian you use to do an examination of the horse to determine if some kind of chronic weakness or soreness exists. Do not ignore a yearling that knuckles over a lot. Try to find out why he does it. If the knuckling over persists, he can injure a suspensory or even break a bone if he stumbles badly. Most colts will not be as eager to jog that fast, but I have found that it is very valuable both as a conditioning tool, and as a good way to gait a trotter properly before you ever begin to turn him and ask for real speed.

At this time in a young horse's training, I am more concerned with the action in front than I am with what goes on behind and it will be nearly two months into the training period before I put hind shoes on a yearling.

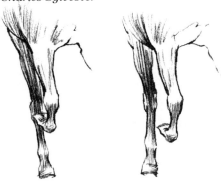

Trotters are either line-gaited or passing-gaited. The line-gaited horse (on the left in this illustration) is often cleaner-gaited and a little more reliable. Mack Lobell was gaited this way. The passing-gaited horse is so named because his limbs pass one another on different planes rather than coming together the way a line-gaited horse does on the same plane.

When I do add shoes behind on a yearling, the shoes will be a half-round, half-swedge shoe with the swedge on the outside.

Traditionally, the full swedge shoe has been the shoe of choice for trotters behind, but I like my trotters in the half-round, half-swedge shoe because I think it widens them out a little behind and allows them to trot a little cleaner. I have had very good results over the years with the half-round, half-swedge and would recommend it to anyone who was dissatisfied with trying to use just a full swedge behind.

I guess most horse trainers would prefer a trotter who is line-gaited. Mack Lobell and Britelite Lobell were line-gaited and had great, clean action.

Diamond Exchange was a passing-gaited horse who had a very wide stroke behind but he was a very powerful going horse who generated tremendous strength from his hind limbs. He had some problems with interference behind and I ended up racing him in a full shin boot with a hock extension because he would interfere very high up on his hind legs.

Mack Lobell was an interesting horse to train because he was a line-gaited horse who had a tremendously efficient way of going. He probably had the most direct action down the track of any horse I ever trained. He came very close to hitting himself in a lot of places, but he never had any serious interference problems.

He would pick up his front feet and throw them straight down the track in front of him. Behind, he had a real straight, piston-like action back and forth. I think this is the reason Mack Lobell was such a fast horse. He had nearly flawless action. He was not a big horse with an impressive stroke and he did not generate enormous power behind. But he had a wonderfully efficient gait and maximized his kind of slight frame to become what many people consider the finest racing trotter in history.

He was a squarely built horse as well. He was 15.3 hands tall at the withers and almost exactly the same length across his back. I actually

Keystone Request was a pupil who required a lot of weight behind in order to learn to trot. She wore heavy "keg" shoes weighing nearly 17 ounces, in order to learn to trot squarely. The Super Bowl filly made the races and got a mark of T1:58. She is shown at Lexington with Joe Marsh, Jr.

prefer a trotter with a little more length over his back. Mack Lobell got away with his short-coupled frame because he was such an efficiently-gaited horse.

As I said earlier, Mack Lobell just missed interfering in lots of places. I know he had more speed and natural ability than any trotter I have trained, either before or since, although his problems came later in his career from his temperament and disposition.

While it is not all-important whether a horse is line-gaited or passing-gaited, I do want both sides of the horse to match. Often, I break a colt or filly and find that they carry their hind quarter off to one side or another and end up trotting sideways, like an automobile that has been wrecked and goes down the road with the rear end out of alignment with the front end.

This is also often called "dog trotting" because it duplicates what a dog does just trotting along.

I once broke a filly owned by Herb Liverman named Keystone Request. She was a nicely-made filly but when I broke her I discovered that she put her left hind leg in underneath her body between her front legs. She placed her right hind leg right where it belonged, but the left hind leg scared me to death. I told Herb she was a real longshot to make the races.

I put a pair of real heavy keg shoes on this filly behind. These shoes are anywhere from 14 to 17 ounces each! They are made for Saddlebred horses and have a light crease that runs the entire length of the shoe.

For the first four or five months of Keystone Request's training, I went very slowly with her, working to get her to even up behind. She learned well and while she never completely got rid of her problem, she made a respectable filly and got a two-year-old time trial mark of 1:58. Had I not taken the time gaiting her, I am quite sure she would not have made it to the races.

The use of the heavy keg shoe can be pretty valuable in situations like hers. The heaviness of the shoe creates a lot of action behind and seeks to change the natural gait of the horse who puts his foot where it does not belong.

Keg shoes can also be very valuable in dealing with trotters who stab a leg. Some trainers prefer to put a keg shoe on only the affected limb, but I prefer keeping a horse's weight distributed evenly. I use kegs on both hind feet, even though a horse may carry the other leg in an acceptable manner. I don't want a horse to be unbalanced.

One important thing to remember is that if you are using the keg shoe to aid in gaiting a horse, you must not attempt to make any speed while the horse is wearing this shoe. What is important is the establishment of gait. Take your time and have some patience. Believe me, it will pay off in the long run.

I also want a colt to carry his hindquarters directly behind the front limbs. He must learn to trot straight. Gaiting straps and gaiting poles, particularly, are effective ways to move a colt's hind quarters one way or the other, and I recommend their use.

Some trainers only think of gaiting poles and gaiting straps for training purposes, but a lot of good can be done with the gaiting straps and poles while a horse is learning and just setting his gait. A horse must be taught to go straight in the shafts.

I also am a real stickler on a colt learning to carry his head straight. Often, I will start using headpoles on the colts who are having trouble getting their heads out in front of them.

A horse who learns to carry his head off to one side or another is never going to amount to much. This is a bad habit I want to correct right away.

A lot of times a colt will carry his head off to one side or the other because he is sore someplace. For years, we have known that headpoles don't cure lameness, but even though you might be treating a colt for lameness or soreness somewhere, he must learn to carry his head straight, even if the lameness or soreness persists.

A colt who learns to carry his head off to one side or another will continue to do that even after you get him sound.

Most of my horses end up racing with two headpoles, so I often add a headpole in the early part of a yearling's training program if he is not carrying his head straight in front of him. I will put an extra ring on the colt's head halter so that the headpole is not tight and does not confine him, but I want him to learn to carry his head straight.

The first time I use a headpole, especially if it is very early in a yearling's training, I will line-drive him with the headpole first to see how he might respond to it.

If the headpole won't straighten him up, I begin to look for a little soreness or lameness that I might have to address.

COVER UP YOUR TROTTING YEARLINGS

Another important concern with trotting colts and fillies is that they be covered up behind for jogging and training purposes. I don't really care if a colt wears stable wraps, brace bandages or shin boots but I want him covered up behind so that if he does interfere, he won't get cut or hurt.

A horse who hits himself—and they all do at some point—can become very reluctant to trot on if he thinks he will interfere. Once into training miles, I always want a colt to wear boots behind.

I prefer the normal shin boot that covers the entire shin area from the bottom of the ankle to up near the hock. If a colt is interfering lower on the ankle, you can add a speedy cut extension on the shin boots.

By covering a colt up behind, I give myself some insurance and protection that even if he does interfere, I lessen the problems that ensue from that. Avoiding interference is important, because a horse will want to get away from the interference, and may develop bad habits, such as stabbing or hiking.

REMEDIES FOR INTERFERENCE

As I said earlier, I am very much concerned with establishing a horse's gait during the early part of his training. I am looking for the right kind of action and stroke.

If a colt is interfering, the first thing I will do is to try to quicken him up a little by adding a little heavier front shoe. If he is wearing a 1/2-inch backwards half-round, I will move him up to a 9/16-inch or even 5/8-inch backwards half-round to try to get him to clear. The extra weight forces the colt to have a little more action and to break over a little better. This is often enough to clean him up and allow him to trot cleanly.

If anything, I want to start a colt off in a shoe heavier than I think he needs, because as the spring progresses, I am going to want to take weight off. Colts just cannot race all year with a lot of weight. I have found that as a colt progresses in the spring, it is possible to start "stealing" some weight off him with each shoeing.

If a colt or filly is still unsteady late into the spring or early summer, and I need to add weight to keep them trotting, that it is more likely a veterinary problem than a shoeing issue. If a colt needs additional weight to stay on the trot in June, he probably is sore somewhere.

If I have added weight and quickened a colt in front and this does not eliminate the interference, my next step is to try blocking his toes in front and/or behind a little. Remember that my yearlings are wearing the backwards half-round with the open toe, so blocking the toe in front is an easy chore for the blacksmith. Blocking their toes behind stops them a little faster and should assist in cleaning up their gait. The terms "blocking"and "squaring" are interchangeable here. They mean the same thing.

Squaring the toe behind also serves to keep that hind angle high, which is a very important part of my shoeing theories. I prefer to block or square a colt's hind toes instead of changing his angle in front. I think, over the long run, a trainer will be better off if he has low front angles and high hind angles on his trotters.

USE OF TOE WEIGHTS

If I have added weight to a horse's front end with a heavier shoe, and either squared his front feet or blocked his toes behind, and the horse still interferes, I am not afraid to use toe weights in front to give a horse a little more action. This extra weight can also help to steady a colt who is having problems with soundness.

I would not put toe weights on a colt with a lot of action because it might send him near his elbows, but certainly it is a consideration with any colt who lacks some fundamental action in front. The toe weights are also useful if a colt trots cleanly but is a little unsteady when you ask him to trot on a little. The extra weight often gives him enough balance to stay on the trot.

Toe weights are available in different sizes. The plate which affixes directly to the colt's outer hoof wall weighs approximately two ounces, and three different size caps are available at one, two and three ounces each.

USE OF THE BAR SHOE

If a colt or filly is mixey-gaited or pacey, as they often are with short toes, and I have tried a heavier shoe and even toe weights without success, my next move would be to try a bar shoe. I like a bar shoe a lot.

A bar shoe serves a dual purpose. It absorbs much of the shock of the hoof striking the track, and it adds weight to the heel of the horse. I actually prefer bar shoes over toe weights. Because my yearlings start off in the backwards half-round shoe, the conversion to a bar shoe is not that dramatic. The bar shoe, however, is a very different shoe.

The major difference is that the bar shoe gives a horse much greater support on the heel, and provides extra traction across the toe at the same time.

The backwards shoe provides support for the heel area but leaves the toe exposed. The bar shoe provides support and traction all around the hoof.

Remember, it is very important that you get a horse going clean before you attempt to advance his training. A colt who hits all over going slow is never going to develop the confidence necessary to learn any speed for you.

LEARN TO WAIT

In many cases, the minor adjustments take a lot of time but I have learned over the years that a lot of patience is required with trotters. I have learned to wait. It seems that almost every time I really wait on a trotter, he ends up being a useful horse.

Don't be afraid to experiment, but don't attempt to advance a yearling into his early training if you have not gaited him the way you want him. A bad-gaited yearling becomes a bad-gaited two-year-old. I have learned this lesson through years of experience and would recommend a disciplined, careful approach with any yearling experiencing gaiting problems. Don't try to go on with him unless you have him where you want him.

EARLY TRAINING LESSONS

Once you get a horse going clean and can brush him with a little confidence, it is time to begin the traditional training process. After the initial breaking and training sessions, I am ready to test the colts a little. My colts are always in company. From the first time I turn them and ask them for a little speed, they are working in sets of two or three.

I don't even carry a watch the first few training miles because I am not concerned with speed as much as I am teaching a colt that I want him to stay on gait, learn to follow and pass a horse, and accelerate in the later stages of the mile.

Horses learn from the repetition of tasks. The earlier you get started teaching, the better off you will be in the long run.

After four to six weeks of three miles per day of jogging, I will add a fourth jog mile and begin to turn the colts twice a week. This is the traditional four days of jogging, two training days per week that has become commonplace throughout the sport.

For example, colts are jogged four miles per day on Monday, Wednesday, Thursday and Saturday and trained on Tuesday and Friday. For the colts that train on Monday and Thursday, the jog days are Tuesday, Wednesday, Friday and Saturday. Sunday is an off day in my stable unless we have missed a lot of time during the week.

If I have missed getting the colts out for two or three days straight, I will jog on Sunday. If they stand in the stall too long they can get awfully tough, or even tie-up, after a period of inactivity.

Carry The Message was a standout two-year-old for the author, although he required a lot of jogging to overcome a kicking habit. The Royal Prestige youngster was a stakes star at two, winning at Lexington in 1:57.1 and earning over $200,000.

I have had a few colts and fillies that I jogged farther than four miles. This normally is done with a colt who is having a little trouble finding his gait, or who misbehaves while he is fresh, but settles down and trots after he gets a little tired.

I have jogged colts as much as five miles or more before they settled down. I recommend this if the extra jogging produces positive results.

JOGGING AS REMEDIAL ACTION

I had a filly named Sharon's Steak who, when I broke her, was one of the most nervous, high-strung horses I had ever been around. I would get her on the jog track and she just would not settle down and begin to trot. She was wild. Everything spooked her. She was afraid of tractors, harrows, water trucks, other horses; you name it, it spooked her.

I tried a number of tricks to get her to relax and come back to me, but I finally decided that she just had a lot of nervous energy and needed to get a little tired. I decided to jog the nervousness out of her, and see if that helped.

I got her to where she was jogging 8-10 miles per day! She really settled down after a period of time and made a respectable filly for me. She was no good with just four or five miles of jogging. She was still too tough. But when I jogged her a long session, she got tired, finally hit a nice, square trot and started to learn what I wanted from her. She eventually made a good filly, got a T2:00.3 mark and I bred her to Diamond Exchange and got a very good filly named Happy Diamonds that I sold overseas.

Another good horse who responded to the extra jogging as a yearling was Carry The Message. He was a great-looking yearling who could really trot in the paddocks at Castleton Farm.

He was a good-feeling, robust colt, and when we broke him he had a real tough streak to him. He would kick whenever he got spooked or the lines or the shaft of the jog cart goosed him a little. He didn't need much of an excuse to kick.

I eventually tied his tail and started jogging him extra miles. He was the kind of colt that you had to jog five or six miles before you really got his attention. After we got him over the habit of kicking (and it cost us a few broken-up jog carts), he was O.K. He is a very good example of extra jogging helping with the breaking process. He went on to trot in 1:57.1 at two and won over $200,000 as a two-year-old.

KICKING STRAPS NOT RECOMMENDED

While I am on this subject, let me say that I do not like, nor do I recommend, the use of kicking straps on yearlings. I know trainers who use them and swear by them, but I have found they cause more trouble than they alleviate. I believe a kicking strap actually contributes to a horse kicking, by goosing him when he raises up to kick.

I have had much better luck teaching a colt to behave by tying his tail, and going farther with him, than by using a kicking strap.

What I am trying to do is to teach the colt or filly that what I want is good behavior and not the bad stuff. When a colt jogs a long way and gets tired, he can learn a lot in a hurry.

The effective use of jog miles in gaiting a horse is often overlooked. Some trainers believe you only teach a horse the proper gait by going the right way of the track and training him.

However, I have found that I can do a lot of work in gaiting and mannering by the use of tough jog miles, especially with the horse who is full of himself, and won't behave until he gets a little tired.

END OF EARLY TRAINING

The early training period, for me, is over when a colt trains in 2:40. This signals the end of the initial segment of the training program, and the beginning of a second phase. Many times, a colt will get to this level without me or any of my assistants carrying a watch. When a colt can train comfortably in 2:40, he is ready to go on with.

If he can't trot in 2:40 comfortably and show me he has a little more trot in him, he will stay at this level until he can demonstrate that he is ready to go on with.

If 2:40 is a bit of a struggle, or he seems unsteady, I hold him at that level until I get his problems straightened out. Some of these colts need time, others need shoeing problems addressed. Still others have veterinary problems which must be treated.

DON'T BE BOUND BY SCHEDULES

Let me make an important distinction here regarding schedules for horses. Every trainer has his own idea about a schedule for his stable.

Schedules are a necessary evil in the horse business because a particular race that we are pointing for may only be conducted at a certain time of the year.

For instance, if I think I have a trotting colt good enough for the Peter Haughton Memorial at The Meadowlands in early summer, I must have him on an advanced training schedule throughout the winter.

These schedules can create artificial pressures in your training regimen that you must resist. A lot of trainers have been undone and, consequently, a lot of good colts have been ruined over the years by trainers trying to adhere to some set schedule of development.

If there is one piece of good advice I can give to horse trainers everywhere, it is that you should not allow yourself or others around you to put pressure on a colt to perform at a set level at a set time. Let the horse seek his own level.

If you do not allow him his own pace of development, this is a recipe for trouble. You will pay the price in rather devastating fashion. Patience is the over-riding virtue of all horse trainers.

BEGINNING TO REPEAT

After the 2:40 threshold has been crossed, the colt is ready to begin repeating workout miles. Up to this time, I have been going single workout miles.

For instance, the first time a colt trains, he might trot in 3:00. The next week, on the one day a week you should ask him to trot on, he will trot in 2:55, then 2:50 the third week, and so on right down to 2:40.

Most yearlings are so naturally equipped anymore that getting to the 2:40 level is really a breeze for them.

When I begin to repeat my trotters, I don't automatically ask them to do more every week. I know there is a certain school of training that says you should ask a colt for a faster mile every week. I am not one of those who believes that is necessarily the right thing to do.

For instance, even with my most advanced set, I might stay at the 2:40 level for some time, but start to ask the colts for a little more speed at the end of the mile. I eventually work a training mile in 2:40, but the last half might be around 1:12 to 1:15. If a colt can trot a mile in 2:40 with a half in 1:15 and a quarter in 35-36 seconds, he is ready to go on with.

And even though a colt has not beaten 2:40, the first time I ask him to trot more than that for the mile, I might end up going in 2:28 or 2:30, or wherever he is comfortable. After a couple of months of conditioning, if a colt can't accept a drop at this level and stay sound, then you are probably in trouble with him anyway.

I know trainers who demand that their stables train by the watch every time out. I suppose in a big stable with lots of assistants, that might be a more organized way to train, but it's only organized for the people's sake.

I also know trainers who go ballistic with their help if a colt was supposed to train in 2:35 and the guy goes a mile in 2:28. I don't believe that training a horse is that exact a science. A few seconds one way or another is not critical at this point.

While I am not overly concerned with seemingly big drops in time while I am going these slow miles, there are concerns.

What concerns me more is how the colt is doing it.

> *Is he good-gaited?
> *Is he staying on the trot?
> *Does he follow other horses willingly?
> *Is he good and straight in the shafts?
> *Does he grab one line?

A very interesting anecdote will serve to tell you what little concern I have for time in these early training miles.

When Mack Lobell was a two-year-old, he nearly always trained good, but he already exhibited some of the same temperamental tendencies that would appear later in his life. To be diplomatic, let's just say there were mornings when he would train better than others!

One morning, I was training another colt in the same set with Mack and I looked over several times during the training miles. I like looking at the other colts in the set because often times I can spot something that will help a colt by looking at him from the side. This often is helpful in determining if a colt's head is set right or needs to be taken up, or let down.

This particular morning with Mack Lobell, it looked to me as though Mack was cheating a little. By this I mean he was not really interested in what was going on, and was a bit reluctant to pick up the pace when urged. I asked the assistant who had been driving him about this, and he said that he thought that Mack was acting lazy and wasn't really interested in his work.

With that in mind, I took Mack out on the track for another training mile all by himself after the others in his set had finished and were being cooled out. At this point in his training, I don't think he had beaten 2:20, but there was every indication that he had a lot of natural ability.

I turned him and let him trot away from the wire. He was going along pretty good, but about the three-eighths, I asked him to pick it up a little. He did not respond. I asked him again. He still did not respond.

This was a good time, I thought, to teach him that when he was called upon, he was supposed to respond. I was carrying a long training whip, and I grabbed the lines in one hand and spoke to him again. When he failed to respond, I lashed him pretty good along his stifle area and under his belly. He took off like a rocket—but he did not make a break! In fact, he trotted the final half in 1:02 without lifting his nose or even offering to run. While the mile was only about 2:20, he trotted a wonderful half without breaking stride. For the next few workouts, he was pretty responsive!

I was not upset or even concerned that he had trotted an extremely fast half-mile because I had put a lot of conditioning into him at that time. This incident led me to think that Mack Lobell could be a special horse if I got him to the races. He had so much wonderful, natural ability. A word of caution here. You must be careful in doing something like this. For instance, I would not recommend this sort of "schooling session" with a horse who had a tendency to be nervous or aggressive. Something such as this should absolutely never be done with a filly. There may be an occasional filly who will take some schooling and improve, but generally, the fillies have to be handled in a much less aggressive manner. The fillies test your patience the most. If you overtrain a filly, she will let you know it pretty quickly.

I would never have done anything like that with Pine Chip because I was always concerned that he might get too aggressive. Pine Chip was never a lazy horse and always responded willingly to what we asked him to do. With a horse bred like Pine Chip—who was by Arndon—I would not do anything that might make him more aggressive.

Knowing your horse, his pedigree and a little family history can help you determine the right course when remedial actions are necessary.

TRAIN ONLY TWO TRIPS

Like most trainers, I used to work colts up to three training miles at the end of their spring training programs and before they raced for the first time.

A couple of years ago, I decided to alter that program and now I ask my colts to only go two training miles. I follow this pattern right up to the time the colts start racing. It's been several years since I worked a colt three trips at the conclusion of his training program.

I think trainers at all levels are realizing that today's horse takes less work to go fast and that we, as trainers, must learn to manage horses better if we are going to succeed.

Horses have so much natural ability now, that your success probably will depend on attention to health and veterinary issues more than on the nuances of shoeing and gaiting.

Having said that, I still may train a colt three trips, but the only time I will is if I am not happy with the way he trained earlier in the day or if I have made some sort of shoeing or equipment change and am anxious to see if it helped him.

After clearing the 2:40 threshold, the colts will be asked to come down gradually in most instances. But again, my program is a little different than most because I might train three times in 2:40 and then one morning, the colts will get going pretty good and we'll let them trot around 2:30. Then, I might hang around 2:30 for awhile. This might include as many as four or five fast workouts.

GETTING THEM USED TO A SULKY EARLY

At the 2:30 stage, I begin working my colts hooked to a sulky. Although it is very uncomfortable for me and my assistants, I am a firm believer in hooking a colt to a sulky at this critical stage in the training. I have seen too many horses helped by this practice to believe otherwise.

In my opinion, a lot of lameness can be attributed to pulling a jog cart at accelerated speeds. I think we would have more sound, young horses if trainers would get out of the jog cart and into a sulky at an early stage in the training. I have had any number of colts who were helped by hitching them to the sulky. A colt has to pull a jog cart, whereas the modified sulkies in use today don't create much drag on a horse at all. Not having the added stress of pulling a jog cart just has to help them learn to go fast.

TRUST YOUR INSTINCTS

The question comes as to when in training you should lower the boom on a colt or filly. That is, when should you ask them to really trot on? This is a matter of instinct.

After the many training miles I have gone, I have developed a feel for this, for lack of a better term.

If a colt can trot in 2:30 and come a half in 1:10 and a quarter in 34-35 seconds, he is ready to go in 2:20. I have had colts that I trained in 2:30 four or five times, and then dropped to 2:18, without any negative effects.

After this sharp drop is made, the horse is held again at that level until he begins to learn more and more. I might stay around 2:18 to 2:20 for a few weeks, then work them in 2:12 or 2:14 one morning. Remember that I am still going three or four jogging miles on the off days and jogging 2 to 2 1/2 miles before the first training trip. These are intuitive decisions based on my judgment of just how far a horse may have progressed.

THE TRAINING ROUTINE

My training routine with a colt looks like this:
  *Jog 2-2 1/2 miles, work a mile in the 2:40-2:45 range.
  *Come back about an hour later, jog one mile, turn a mile in
   whatever time you deem appropriate.
When I work a colt in 2:30, I want the fractions something like :40-

1:20-1:55-2:30. When a colt has done this comfortably, he is ready to go on with.

It is important to make a distinction here. The first time a colt works in 2:30 or makes any dramatic reduction in time, the mile should be pretty evenly rated. With each repetition of the 2:30 effort, I begin to emphasize closing speed a little more. This keeps him fresh and cheerful and assures me that I have made the right decision in asking him to go on. If he cannot handle the reduction in time off an evenly rated mile, he is not ready for any further reductions. I want to keep him around this time level until he gets comfortable, and lets me know that he is ready to come on down further in time.

When I work a colt in 2:20, I want the fractions like this: :37-1:13-1:47-2:20. Again, this is after several repetitions of 2:20 miles, with the first 2:20 mile evenly rated. Whenever you ask a colt to come on down in time for you, you should make the work evenly rated the first time. This will keep his attitude good and fresh, and let you know if he was ready for this assignment. I might work a horse five, six, even seven times in 2:20 before asking him to trot more.

At this point, generally, I am deep into the spring in Florida. I have a goal that I wish to train my best set in 2:10 before I leave Florida around the first of May.

When I get ready to go in 2:10, I might have been no more than 2:20 with a set, but they have shown me a quarter in 32 seconds pretty handily. The first time I aim for 2:10 we might go in just 2:12 or we might end up in 2:09. Again, this doesn't bother me because by this time the colt has been hundreds of jog miles and many training miles.

This method affirms my policy of letting the colt find his own level, within limits. It should be noted that I never ask a colt to fully extend himself at this time. There will be ample opportunity for that later. I am more interested in conditioning than I am speed. If the conditioning is done properly, and a horse either remains sound or gets sound, whatever speed is there will come out. The first time I aim for a 2:10 mile, I will want the fractions to be somewhere around :33-1:06-1:38-2:10. Don't be too concerned if the fractions are a bit off. Of course, you don't want to set out to go in 2:10 and go in 2:05, but don't be too concerned. If the half is reached in 1:07, don't try to compensate by coming the final half in 1:03, unless the horses are comfortable. I like to just aim for a general goal in terms of time, and find it acceptable if we come close.

However, the second time I go in 2:10, I might set it up with fractions of :33-1:07-1:39-2:10. As you can see, this starts to ask for a little more speed at the end of the training mile.

The final time I go in 2:10, the fractions should set up :33-1:07-1:40-2:10. If I can train a two-year-old trotter in 2:10 with a quarter in 30 seconds handily, it is ready to begin the final phase of the training period.

SHIPPING AND REVISING TRAINING SCHEDULES

After I ship north from Florida to my summer base at White Birch Farm, the colts all seem to suffer a bit of a setback. There is normally a big difference in weather between central Florida and New Jersey in the first weeks of May. We leave 80-to 90-degree heat and come into 50-to 60-degree weather with lots of rain.

More significant to the move, however, is that a major transition must take place. All the early training is on a mile, clay track at Spring Garden Ranch, while White Birch Farm is a five-eighths-mile, stone dust track.

I can't tell you how many times this causes a major realignment of talent in my stable.

Some of the colts who trained well all winter over the clay in Florida are lost on the stone dust. Colts that may have struggled all winter in Florida come alive once we get to White Birch. I can't really explain it, and there is no way of predicting which colts will make the transition the best.

After shipping to New Jersey, regardless of how a colt makes the transition, I will back off in the training and allow each colt some time to acclimate.

The first fast training miles in Jersey are in the 2:25 range, and I would recommend this to anyone who makes a shift in track surface at any critical juncture in the colt's season: Don't ask too much of a horse after he has shipped a great distance and changed climates.

I have found that it takes about three to four trainings, a period of some two weeks, before a colt is ready to resume his normal training routine.

This also serves to freshen the colts and gives them a nice break from the constant pressures of training. It's like a little vacation for them, and I nearly always see the colts improve markedly after this little respite.

Even if a trainer does not have shipping considerations to affect his training, giving a two-year-old a respite in training can do wonders for his disposition. It also helps to freshen him for the pressures of finishing the training period, and the starting of racing.

MANAGING SICKNESS

Another setback common to two-year-olds is sickness, and this can be particularly troublesome with a young trotter. For some reason, sickness seems to bother trotting colts more than it does pacers. I don't have an explanation for it, but when a trotter gets sick, I am much more reluctant to return him to active training than I am when the same thing happens to a pacing colt.

Patience is really the key here. If you observe your colt carefully—watch his temperature, attitude and overall fitness—you will make the right judgment.

After a colt is sick, I like to wait one week longer than even my best judgment tells me I should before I go back to training. I believe the temperature should be normal for a few days, and the colt should have his appetite and start playing around before you begin training. A lot of damage can be done if you rush one back into training after sickness.

I have seen trotters completely lose their action after a bout with the virus. Caution should be your byword at this point. I have never heard a horse trainer say he gave a colt too much time off after a bout with the virus, but I have heard lots of them say they came back too soon. Again, patience is the key.

COLTS WILL NOT ALWAYS TRAIN WELL

There is another time when patience is required.

Colts are not always going to train well every time you step onto the track with them. I have found over the years that there are certain mornings, especially if the wind blows hard or if there has been a drastic change in the weather, when colts will not train as well as you would like.

A lot of horses are harmed and set back in their training on mornings like these. A decision has to be made at this point which can be critical to the horse's later development.

I find myself being of two minds about this problem, which every trainer who ever pulled a line over a horse has, or will face. With colts, I find that I can sometimes school them and get them to train better. By this I mean that I can go back and train an extra heat, like the story I related about Mack Lobell. A colt will normally respond to a little discipline.

However, with most fillies, I recommend that you just put them away on that occasional morning when they don't train to suit you. Just forget them until the next training session.

I have seen a number of trainers, including myself, keep a filly on the track trying to make her trot away from the wire or not make a break finishing a mile. I think a lot of fillies are hurt in these schooling sessions, where a colt might improve under similar circumstances.

You simply have to make a decision regarding your plan of attack here. Nothing is really lost if you put them away until the next training date. This is when you will find out just how much patience you really have. Don't be fooled into thinking that you can correct problems like these in one morning. Problems will take time to develop, and solutions may take time as well. Be patient, always.

TRANSITION SHOEING

One of the last major transitions before a colt gets ready to start is likely to occur in the blacksmith shop. Whatever shoes a colt wears on a clay track, he is probably going to need some borium tips added to his shoeing arsenal when he hits a stone dust track.

I haven't had too many colts race without the borium. This is particularly true if you race a colt over an off track. You better have a set of shoes with borium because a trotting colt can get to slipping badly on stone dust. The borium tips give him the traction he needs to keep his feet under him.

Slipping is very bad because it not only causes a horse to go off-stride, it can contribute to soreness and even lameness.

When I add borium, I like to drop four small spots on each front shoe—two on the toe and two on the heel—in a symmetrical pattern. Most of my trotters wear a half-round, half-swedge shoe behind. If I am adding borium on the hind shoes, it is only dropped onto the swedge portion of the shoe.

I do this to help widen a colt out behind. The extra traction provided by the borium can be crucial to allowing a colt to go clean. Remember, even the smallest change can affect a horse greatly.

Although my yearlings all begin their training in the backwards half-round in front, they nearly always make the transition to a more conventional shoe at some point in their training.

This is just a matter of making a judgment about when to make the switch. If I feel a colt or filly is making good progress and shows me some steadiness, I will make the transition from the half-round to the more traditional shoe. There is no time threshold for this, or any other signal other than my judgment concerning the progress of each horse. I have to treat them as individuals.

THE FINAL TRAINING MILES—READY TO START

I want a colt to work comfortably around 2:05 or 2:06 on the five-eighths-mile track at White Birch before I send him to The Meadowlands for his first start. I like the fractions to be around :32-1:05-1:36-2:06. If the colt responds well off those fractions, I begin to think I might have a true stakes colt. In any event, after they have worked that much, they are ready to start.

I "baby race" my colts at The Meadowlands, and I want them to trot around 2:04 the first time they see the gate. Most of them have been behind the gate three to four times at either White Birch or in Florida, and I have very few colts who have trouble at the gate.

I tell my drivers to take the colts right to the gate and let them learn to accept the gate and accelerate gradually. I think it makes for better gate horses, and allows a horse to learn not to be afraid of the gate or of other horses.

John Campbell baby-races my colts whenever possible, and John is wonderful with them because he is very good with a young horse. John knows that when I say I want a colt to trot in 2:04, I don't mean the first half in 1:00!

John knows that I want them taken off the gate, taught to follow along well, and then trot home sharply. And even though John doesn't carry a watch, he generally doesn't miss 2:04 by much.

WARM UP PROCEDURES

There is something very important to remember at this point in time. Keep in mind that I have never been more than two training miles on the same day with most colts. So, the first time I start them at The Meadowlands, I will warm them up by jogging a couple of miles, to get them sweating and to empty their bowels, then turn and go a mile in 2:40-2:45, and then come back in 2:15-2:25 before they race. A good-feeling colt or filly should be warmed up a little more just to take some of the edge off before that first start.

If I have one who I think might be a little rank at the gate, I try and warm up a little quicker to take some of the edge off. I may even jog a mile farther before turning the first time. I want everything just right for the first few starts because it is so important for a young horse. If a two-year-old starts making breaks at the gate in his first few starts, you have a real problem on your hands.

GAP BETWEEN FIRST STARTS

If I am satisfied with my colt's first racing mile, I want him to come right back for the second effort, but I don't want him to come right back too soon. Most trainers still prefer a seven-day gap between races, but I feel a ten-day gap between the first two starts is more acceptable.

For instance, if I start a colt on a Tuesday morning in early June at The Meadowlands, his second start will be on the following Friday instead of the very next Tuesday. This gives me a solid, ten-day interval during which the colt will get a relatively serious workout in 2:20 at the five-day midpoint. Please note here that I do not train a colt twice in that ten-day period.

He is trained only once and then only two trips, with the fast mile in 2:20. I may ask him to trot a good last quarter, in the 31-32 second range, but there is no 2:05 mile between races. He will see enough racetrack before the end of the racing season.

I am more interested in what happens in October and November than I am in what happens in June in the baby races. I train a horse less between races now than ever before, and I would imagine that over the coming years, midweek works with a horse may be eliminated entirely.

These early races are very important to a horse's overall career. They often serve to establish a horse's racing personality that will follow him all his racing life. They also serve to point up problems that need to be addressed.

For instance, Mack Lobell was not a good two-year-old early in his first season at the races. He was giving me fits because he would not finish a mile trotting in a straight line. Bill O'Donnell raced Mack for me one night at The Meadowlands and had the lead coming for home, and Mack started bearing out to the right, looking like he was going to end up on the grandstand apron.

This was particularly perplexing to me because I had worked him a quarter in :26.4 off a slow training mile at The Meadowlands just before this, and he had trotted true and straight for me. I knew he had extreme high speed. I thought he could be a great one, but not if he had trouble staying straight in the stretch.

I have thought a lot about that period in his training and believe that Mack was probably hitting his elbows a little when he got fatigued, and was just trying to get away from that in the stretch. He probably was touching his elbow on the left side, and was running out to try to avoid the interference.

There is an important lesson here for horse trainers. If a horse bears out—that is, he comes out in the stretches—he is probably touching or interfering, or is sore on the left side. A horse always tries to get away from pain or soreness. If he runs in, he is probably having a problem on the right side.

I was very lucky later in the summer with Mack Lobell because, when I went to the midwestern mile tracks with him, I added a pair of elbow boots to his equipment list. He always had gone pretty high in front, but it never occurred to me that he might have been touching all that spring. After I put the elbow boots on him, he was a different horse.

As I indicated earlier, I am not particularly concerned with the progress of a colt or filly early in the spring because I know such things can change dramatically by year's end. My main focus is on the fall of the year.

I had two great fillies in Armbro Devona and Winky's Goal in the past few years, and neither of those fillies was a factor early in her two-year-old season. I never even started Winky's Goal until nearly Labor Day, and yet she became the top filly of her year.

There is a very interesting story involving Winky's Goal. It illustrates how frustrating it can be to train trotters.

Winky's Goal is just about the best-bred trotting filly in the world. Her sire, Armbro Goal, is an impeccably-bred Hambletonian winner. Her mother, Winky's Gill, was a world champion at two and three and is one of the top-bred mares in the world. Winky's Goal cost her Italian owners $210,000 as a yearling.

She is a great looking black filly, but when I got her to Florida, she didn't handle her hind limbs the way I wanted her to. Like Keystone Request, Winky's Goal stuck one of her hind legs between her front legs. She was sticking her left hind between her two front legs. I was sick, because she had looked like such a natural in the paddocks at Castleton,

One of Sylvester's most successful training triumphs was with the royally-bred Winky's Goal. The Armbro Goal filly had trouble finding her gait early in her two-year-old year, but eventually developed into such a reliable trotter that she raced without shoes on her front feet, as shown here in a warm up mile for the author.

and I talked the Italians into buying her, not that it took too much coaxing.

My normal practice is to put a real heavy shoe on a horse like this, and take a lot of time, as I had done with Keystone Request. I added keg shoes to Winky's Goal about two months into her training. I also dropped her out of many of her early stakes engagements, including the Merrie Annabelle. She was going to take some time to develop.

But while Keystone Request had improved dramatically with the keg shoes, they seemed to have little effect on Winky's Goal. She was still putting her left hind leg up between her front legs. Otherwise, she was line-gaited.

One morning, late in the spring in Florida, I decided I would just go on with her. Her training had been set back enough that I would miss most of her early races, but I could still get her ready for some fall stakes.

I trained her and discovered that the faster I asked her to go, the better she handled that leg. I took the heavy shoes off and shod her in a traditional half-round, half-swedge. The faster I went with her, the better I liked her.

As Winky's Goal progressed in her training, she learned to put that foot where it belonged. She eventually became such a good-gaited filly that I could race her barefoot. She never would be a good-gaited horse going slow, but once I put her in gear, she put everything in the right place. She defied all the conventional wisdom of training trotters. Most horses will only get worse as you go faster, but Winky's Goal was an exception to the rule. I think her situation was a combination of the fact that she was growing a lot and just needed time to come around.

Again, don't be afraid to try anything. Had anyone told me that Winky's Goal would have ever raced barefoot, I would have told them they were crazy. She really surprised me.

Armbro Devona was a late comer in her two-year-old year as well. In fact, I came through Lexington in the spring of her two-year-old year and I don't think she could trot in 2:15 at the time.

I sent her home to Michigan and had her turned out during the time I was in Lexington. When I picked her up after getting to New Jersey, she started coming on for me and made a very good filly who won 7 of 11 starts and trotted in 1:58.3 at two. The next year, she earned $445,495, won a heat of the Kentucky Futurity, and was sold for a big price overseas.

I think Armbro Devona needed the time away from the track to mature, and being out in the warm weather and wet grass really freshened her attitude. Attitude is one of the most important variables in horse training, especially with fillies.

Patience is another key, and patience will be rewarded when you are training trotters. Armbro Devona could have been ruined that spring had I continued to train her when she was off. Most trainers would have gone on with her because she was heavily staked and had really trained O.K. up until that time. I just thought that she needed a little time. After six weeks of being turned out, she was a different filly.

Now, let's return to our training and racing schedules.

The second start I like to see them baby-raced again, but this time I want them to trot around 2:01-2:02, if they can do it right. By the third and fourth starts, I pretty much know what I am dealing with, so I can alter a colt's schedule depending upon his own development.

SPOTTING THE RACING OPPORTUNITIES

Through the course of a racing season, I like to spot the racing opportunities as sparsely as possible. I would prefer to race a horse about every two weeks but, of course, the stakes schedules will not allow that. However, you can pick your spots and make decisions about where and how to race your colts.

I raced Mack Lobell a great deal at two—he had 20 starts—but he was a very durable horse his entire career. I do not recommend racing a two-year-old as often as I raced Mack Lobell.

If a colt must race every week, I will adjust his midweek training to a lighter schedule, or I will eliminate the midweek work entirely. This depends on the horse. If I feel the horse is getting enough work and is racing to my satisfaction, I will continue the midweek work for the first five or six starts. Once a horse gets tight, however, the midweek work is eliminated.

I can't imagine racing a two-year-old 20 times now! About 12-15 starts would be ideal. But I can see when we might only start a colt 8-10 times in the coming years. It starts to sound a little more like a Thoroughbred schedule.

The breed is much more natural now, and I think it takes less to get a colt going fast. The successful trainers of the next few decades will be those who are the best managers of horses, not just trainers of horses.

The training always will be important, but the horses with the best careers are those that will be managed carefully. If a colt seems to be coming up a little short when he races, I might add the midweek work back into his training schedule. This is where your instincts take over. If a colt has given you every indication that he will trot on for you, but doesn't, he might be short or he might be over-trained and be dull.

Knowing which way to go at this point is simply a matter of trial and error. If he races below your expectations, you might try to dig into him a little between races. Or you might want to go the other way and skip a midweek work and see how he responds. It's a certainty that no two horses will respond the same way.

The same horse may even respond differently at different times and under diverse circumstances. He may also have a veterinary problem, such as a low blood count that will need to be addressed. I like to monitor blood counts and temperatures as a matter of routine. Often, you will see that a colt's blood count is getting a little low and you can address it before his performance begins to slip. Another reason to monitor temperature and blood counts on a regular basis is to help build a history for each horse which is so important when you have to deal with veterinary issues.

PINE CHIP—LIGHTER WORKS, MORE SPEED

Pine Chip had a great year as a three-year-old in 1993, developing all the way from being a green horse to becoming Trotter of the Year, winning the World Trotting Derby, the Kentucky Futurity, and the Breeders Crown.

He thrived all year on a very light training schedule, and during most of the year, he was worked very sparingly between races. Sometimes, I wouldn't train him at all between starts. He was a sound horse, but I knew he would have to race a lot of heat races, and I wanted him to last.

He also was a horse that I wanted to be very careful with. As I mentioned earlier in this chapter, I was always concerned about his pedigree and did not want to do anything to get him too aggressive. I never trained him fast quarters and never tried to teach him gate speed. Had his pedigree been a little different, I might have "revved him up."

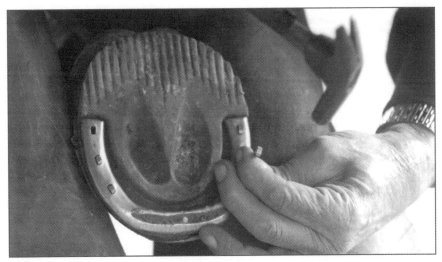

This is a view of the famous "flip-flop" shoe worn by Pine Chip when he won the Kentucky Futurity at three. Developed in Sweden, the shoe does not fully extend to the heels but is used in conjunction with a heel pad that protects the frog of the foot as well. Notice that a crease in the toe of the shoe has been added to help a horse "hold" the track surface.

CHANGE SOMETIMES NECESSARY

In the fall of the year at Lexington, I made a drastic change with Pine Chip because the situation dictated a change in tactics.

The first week of the Lexington meeting he had trotted to a track record of 1:53, beating American Winner in the Transylvania (Bluegrass) Stake, despite being parked the entire mile. It was an unbelievably game and tough performance. Still, I thought he could be better. Many believed it to be one of the greatest races and one of the greatest performances ever witnessed. I still thought he could be better!

So, in between that race and the Kentucky Futurity the following week, I took off the light aluminum shoes Pine Chip had worn for the Transylvania, and replaced them with a lighter, plastic shoe that has a steel insert in the toe.

This is called a "flip-flop shoe" because the steel insert is fastened only at the point of the toe and the shoe can actually be pulled away from the heel.

A lot of people thought I was crazy changing shoes on Pine Chip the week of the Futurity, but my instincts told me he had more trot. But I did more than change shoes.

At midweek, on Tuesday morning, the same morning of the draw for post positions for the Futurity, I worked Pine Chip three trips and really buzzed him the final mile, working him around 2:10, with a final half in 1:00, final quarter in 28 seconds! As good as he had been the week earlier, he was spectacular that morning in his new footgear. It was the first and only time all year I had really dug into him between races.

My reasoning was two-fold. I did not work him that much because he was short. I worked him that way because I was primarily interested to see how he would be in the new shoes. I did not want to wait until Futurity Day to find out! If he had trained poorly, I would have tacked his old shoes back on him for the Futurity.

The secondary reason Pine Chip got the extra work is that a fast training effort like that one, with a good final half and quarter, is a wonderful way to set up a sound horse for an outstanding effort. Pine Chip was better right then than he was at any other point in the season. I felt I could really sharpen him up for something spectacular by using the speed work which horse trainers have used for years to prep a horse for a big race. He trained wonderfully. Had he been an unsound horse, I would never have worked him like that.

As a result, Pine Chip was even better on Futurity Day than I thought he could be. He trotted the two fastest heats in history, winning in 1:52.4, back in 1:52.3, and John Campbell said he never really got off the bit all afternoon!

There is no telling where he might have trotted that afternoon if I had given John the green light to send him. I think he probably could have trotted in 1:50-and-change that day in Lexington. But time was not our goal that afternoon—winning the Futurity was.

I kept the flip-flop shoes on Pine Chip immediately after Lexington, but when I trained him and then qualified him at Pompano before the Breeders Crown, I did not like him as well and I went back to his regular aluminum shoe with borium. He was perfect for the Breeders Crown. On a limestone track such as Pompano, the flip-flop shoe did not provide the traction he needed to get hold of the track.

As a four-year-old, Pine Chip trained well, and I started him at Pompano in the spring in anticipation of a great year. He was as good as he had ever been, and I had high hopes for his 1994 season.

We got an invitation to race him in the Elitlopp at Solvalla, where he would meet most of Europe's top trotters. A problem developed however, in that we were told that Pine Chip could not be raced with two headpoles. This may not seem to be a big problem—and for most horses it would not be—but with Pine Chip this was a problem.

I guess that Swedish racing rules, which are somewhat different from those in North America, state that a horse may not race with two headpoles. This was a problem for Pine Chip because he would get his head around. We decided to race him with the headpole on the inside only. This placed the headpole on the left side and let him go without one on the right.

This also meant that Pine Chip would have to race in a pair of knee and arm boots, which he had not done in more than a year. I often warmed him up in the knee and arm boots just for protection because he would occasionally touch a knee going slow. He never touched anywhere racing, however.

Pine Chip seemed to be getting along well at Solvalla on Elitlopp Day and we were cautious about the way he was handled. We also made a decision which many people criticized later, but it certainly appeared to be the right thing to do at the time.

The situation was like this: We had a choice of post position for the final heat after winning our elimination. We chose the number four position on the gate. We did this for one very good reason. We did not choose the rail because, with only the one headpole, Pine Chip would probably get his head over to the left side a little and might touch a knee or something trying to get out of the gate too quickly. By choosing the number four position on the gate, we thought we could get away and stay close to Copiad for later in the mile.

What we could not have determined was that the straps attaching the knee and arm boot to the elastic support would stretch and let go on him during the second heat. When the boot let go, Pine Chip made a break and was set back out of the money under European rules. None of that ever would have happened if he had been able to race with two headpoles.

When he came back to the U.S., Pine Chip got sick on us and lost a lot of weight. I would guess that during the time he was sick he lost about 150 pounds. He really looked terrible. I could count every rib on his skeleton. I was not at all happy with the way he looked, or was acting.

As a horse trainer, I have always prided myself on the condition of my horses. I was distressed that a horse of Pine Chip's caliber was so thin. But he was so sick he wouldn't eat correctly.

What happened is that I had let him off for a period of a week or two following his return from Sweden, and he was scheduled to start in the American-National. He had a fever of 103 degrees the morning of that race, and had to be scratched. He was slow to react to the antibiotics we gave him to ward off the illness and did not eat well.

I kept Pine Chip in light training during this period because I did not want to blow a chance at the Nat Ray coming up later in the summer at The Meadowlands on Hambletonian Day. He never coughed, he simply lost weight and did not eat as he would normally. I kept him moving, though, by jogging 2-3 miles per day and by turning him out in the afternoon.

What Pine Chip accomplished the rest of the season shows what a remarkable horse he was. I have to say, for history's sake, that Pine Chip was never the same horse after the trip to Sweden, and although he set a world record of 1:52.4 for a four-year-old male on a mile track in winning the Nat Ray, lowered the half-mile mark to 1:54 at Delaware, and the mile time trial record to 1:51 at Lexington, he was not as good at four as he was at the close of his three-year-old season in 1993. John really had to hold Pine Chip together at the end of the Nat Ray, and I really never got to train him like I wanted when he was four. That makes the Delaware and Lexington miles that much more remarkable. He was a special horse with incredible gifts.

WINKY'S GOAL—MORE MANAGEMENT ISSUES

There was another situation at Lexington in the fall of 1993 that demonstrates how interesting training trotting horses can be.

Winky's Goal, as I stated earlier, was a filly that developed into a very clean going trotter at high speed. After she learned to trot, she was shod about as simply as any horse I ever had.

She became line-gaited and wore a very short toe in front with a light, flat aluminum shoe set on a low angle. She went very clean and I thought she would be wonderful at Lexington. She had raced well at two over the clay track and I thought she would be good again. However, I could tell warming her up that she was not acting as free and good-gaited as she had at Delaware a couple of weeks earlier.

I went ahead and raced her in the first heat of the Kentucky Futurity Filly Stake and she was awful, struggling home fifth. She had no trot.

Cat Manzi raced Winky's Goal for me that day and said she seemed to be glued to the track. Clay tracks can stop a trotter. One of the reasons that clay tracks are inherently faster than limestone is because a horse gets very good traction, does little slipping and the clay has excellent bounce to it. The dirt is really alive.

But in this case, it was stopping Winky's Goal too much, robbing her of her natural action and extension. I decided between heats that I would just pull her shoes and race her barefoot.

I suppose of all the horses I ever trained, only about three to five percent of them ever were naturally-gaited enough for me to pull their shoes and race them barefoot. This is something the Swedish trainers pioneered in the U.S.

The first time I saw it done was in 1987 when Berndt Lindstedt pulled Express Ride's shoes and he trotted in 1:53 at Lexington, a world record for four-year-olds.

I pulled all four shoes off Winky's Goal and told Cat to be careful at the gate, to duck her and see what she could get coming for home. She was three-wide and seventh in a field of exceptional fillies at the three-quarters.

But then Cat put her in the middle of the track and she ate them up to win the second heat. She also won the third heat raceoff from in front.

It was a great performance, but I would not recommend racing a trotter barefoot on a regular basis, even one as gifted and great as Winky's Goal became.

As you might imagine, racing without shoes is very hard on the hoof, and I think it would be a problem if you tried to race a horse barefoot very often. The average trotter is not natural enough to race barefooted. Eventually, the foot would shell out and break off and you would be in real trouble.

GENERAL SHOEING PRACTICES

This is a good point in this chapter to talk about shoeing practices. I can use many of the good horses I have been fortunate enough to train to illustrate my shoeing concepts and theories.

To summarize, there are a couple of key areas for me in shoeing trotters:

> *I want them to be as naturally-gaited as possible with short toes, low angles in front, high angles behind with shorter toes, and liberal use of bar shoes and half-rounds.
>
> *I do not recommend the use of full swedge shoes on trotters in front or behind. I believe a swedge denies a horse his natural action.

I have never had good results with full swedge shoes, although it is a shoe I have used with pacers. I have to admit I am not fond of them for a pacer, either.

MACK LOBELL—HISTORY'S FASTEST THREE-YEAR-OLD

Mack Lobell was an unusual horse to shoe because, as I indicated, he needed some weight early in his two-year-old season to get balanced. Mack also had a big, round foot and I could never get his front toes as short as I would have liked them. When he won the Hambletonian, he was carrying about a 3 5/8-inch toe and that is more foot than I normally prefer. But because Mack had such a big foot, that was about as short as I could cut him down.

Mack Lobell carried a 47-degree angle in front and wore an aluminum bar shoe with a full pad because he always had sore feet. I remember how concerned I was the day of the Hambletonian, because the track was really hard and was stinging him.

In fact, in the first heat of the Hambletonian that day, he raced without the full pads. In the second heat, however, I added the pads just to try to give him a little comfort level. He was a very game and courageous horse in winning that day, because the track was stinging him terribly. In fact, he finished both miles by running just past the wire. It was like he went as far as he could to stay trotting, then went to running as soon as he crossed the wire. He was a very smart horse.

Another little nuance to Mack's shoeing was that he wore half-round, half-swedge shoes behind and I always liked him a little better with some borium tips on the swedge part of the shoe. I thought it helped him get a hold of the track and drive forward.

PINE CHIP—FROM GREEN HORSE TO STAR

Pine Chip was shod similarly to Mack Lobell, but he had a little less toe, since he was set up at about 3 1/2-inches in front on a 48-degree angle. He eventually wore an aluminum shoe with grabs and a rim pad except, as I noted earlier, in the Kentucky Futurity.

Pine Chip wore my traditional half-round, half-swedge shoes behind with the same borium tips I found useful with Mack Lobell, and trotted in a 3 1/4-inch toe with a 55-degree angle.

As a two-year-old, he showed me a lot of trot, but had pulled a ligament behind his left knee, which kept him from racing. At three, very early on, he again showed a lot, but I never tried to rev him up. I wanted him to progress naturally. Chris Boring deserves a lot of credit for Pine Chip's development. Chris did a wonderful job with him at Pompano in his early starts of his three-year-old year. Chris never allowed him to be rank, and kept him quiet and relaxed. As Pine Chip matured, the driving duties were turned over to John Campbell, and our patience was rewarded.

In the Hambletonian, Pine Chip was shod a little differently. At that point in his season, he was still wearing a 1/2-inch half-round bar shoe. In the first heat of the Hambletonian, John reported to me that he was not safe enough, and really couldn't ask him to trot on. Between heats, I took the 1/2-inch half-rounds off and had a heavier, 9/16 half-round bar shoe tacked on. He was much better the second heat, although he still could not handle American Winner.

At four, Pine Chip raced most of the year in the flip-flop shoes, except for the Elitlopp, when he wore the aluminum. He also wore the flip-flops when he trotted in 1:54 at Delaware, and in 1:51 at Lexington. That was the ideal shoe for that horse on those tracks.

WINKY'S GOAL—A REAL FOOLER

Winky's Goal was about the most surprising horse I ever trained. The only problem that ever robbed her of her form was physical and was not related to any shoeing problems. She interfered less than any horse I ever trained.

She was shod very plainly in front with a 1/2-inch, half-round aluminum shoe with a 3 1/2-inch toe and 48-degree angle. Behind, I wore a full swedge bar shoe on her with a very short toe at approximately 3 1/8-inches, and a relatively low 54-degree angle. I wore the bar shoe on her behind to give her a little more heel leverage and support, since I prefer a much higher angle behind.

I also thought the bar shoe was a little heavier than the traditional half-round, half-swedge and helped her handle her hind limbs a little better at high speed. The fact that she became a good-gaited filly after

Armbro Keepsake was another of the author's standout fillies. A daughter of the world champion Armbro Fern, the Super Bowl filly had nearly a ten-degree difference between the angle of her front feet (48°) and her hind feet, which were at 57°. This filly also wore the author's trademark sheepskin rolls on her bridle cheek pieces and two headpoles.

starting off with such problems, as I noted earlier in the chapter, is a testament to her real class. She overcame a lot to be a good horse.

BRITELITE LOBELL—MILLIONAIRESS

Britelite Lobell was another of those clean-gaited, naturally-gifted horses who was not difficult to shoe. At two, she wore a 9/16-inch, half-round with borium on the toe only. At three, she raced in a 1/2-inch half-round with borium, a 3 1/4-inch toe on a 48-degree angle in front, while behind she wore a traditional half-round, half-swedge at 3 1/8-inches on a 56-degree angle.

ARMBRO KEEPSAKE—I KNEW HER DAM

Armbro Keepsake was another exceptional filly that won the Breeders Crown at two and four and the 100th Kentucky Futurity. Keepsake was the daughter of a mare that I trained named Armbro Fern, a Speedy Crown filly who trotted in 1:56.4 at two, a world record at the time. Armbro Fern probably had more ability than any horse I ever trained. Fern's problem was that she was lazy, unlike a lot of gifted fillies. She just wouldn't try like I wanted her to. If Armbro Keepsake could have added her mother's speed to her natural determination and grit, I would have had an unbeatable filly.

Whiteland Janice overcame soreness during her three-year-old season when the author suspended her training sessions between races and increased her jogging miles. The Nearly Perfect filly could never be trained extensively, but the long jogging miles set her up to win the World Trotting Derby filly stake and later the 99th renewal of the Kentucky Futurity in 1991.

Armbro Keepsake was shod very simply. She had a 3 1/2-inch toe in front, with a 48-degree angle. I wore a 1/2-inch, half-round shoe on her because I always wanted a little more knee action from her. I also had the blacksmith pound the half-round portion down just a bit, and put a crease in the toe to help her get hold of the track.

I did not use borium on her because the borium tends to slow one down just a bit. Since I was always trying to speed her up, the borium did not suit me in this case. The crease in the toe of the half-round shoe fills with dirt and helps with traction without slowing the natural stroke.

Armbro Keepsake wore a 3 1/4-inch toe behind, and I was able to keep a very high 57-degree angle on her. I was fortunate in this respect, because she was a weak-hocked filly and the high angle helped her action and helped keep her a little sounder.

WHITELAND JANICE—JOGGING KEPT HER GOING

The year before Keepsake won the Kentucky Futurity at Lexington, I won the race for the first time with Whiteland Janice, a Nearly Perfect filly who was destined to be a real star before she injured a stifle and knee.

Whiteland Janice was an exceptionally good-training filly and I always had very high hopes for her. However, after she hurt her left stifle at two and then her left knee at three, she had chronic weaknesses and I could never train her enough to suit me.

What I did with her was address her conditioning by going long jog miles with her. I couldn't train her and hope to have her hold together, so I kept her fit by just jogging her five or six miles a day and either training or racing just one day a week. I only trained her when she wasn't racing. If she was racing, she was only jogged.

Trainers often believe that a horse cannot be fit enough, off jog miles alone, to stay competitive, but I can attest to the fact that it can be done. Horse trainers are often put in situations where serious training has to be compromised if you hope to keep them going.

I am seldom faced with the situation of training a horse where everything is in my favor. Training a horse seems like the ultimate act of compromise. You must walk the tightrope between fitness and soundness, between too much work and too little. Between too much, and not enough racing.

I know if I had left Whiteland Janice on a traditional midweek training program, coupled with the tough racing she had, she would never have won the races she did. She would have been dead lame in a matter of weeks, and her career would have been over.

Whiteland Janice wore a 3 1/2-inch toe on a 47-degree angle, with a heavy 9/16-inch, half-round bar shoe. I used the bar shoe on her because she was a very narrow-heeled filly and the bar shoe did a wonderful job keeping her heels spread.

Behind, Whiteland Janice had a 3 3/8-inch toe with a 55-degree angle to go with her half-round, half-swedge footwear. I was not able to use the borium on her half-swedge shoe because she had stifle problems. Borium would have stopped her too fast and jarred her stifles.

DIAMOND EXCHANGE—HE WAS AFRAID TO TROT

The first really good horse who got me noticed nationally was Diamond Exchange. He won the World Trotting Derby for me when I really needed the money.

Of all the good horses I have had, he probably represented the biggest training and shoeing challenges. All the rest of the good horses I have had have been pretty naturally-gifted horses who required just a little attention now and then to get them straightened out and to keep them going.

Diamond Exchange was a challenge from day one. He was a very bashful horse who would shy from just about anything. He was afraid, seemingly, of everything around him, including both natural and man-made objects. This made him a very difficult horse to train, although he came with a world of ability.

He would get spooked at something, and I finally got totally exasperated with him and put some welder's goggles in a pair of peek-a-boo blinds. These goggles had grey, tinted lenses, and it seemed to take enough of the spooks away from him to allow him to learn some speed.

Sylvester believes the angle of the front feet, as determined by the use of a blacksmith's tool (on the right in the illustration) is more important than the length of the toe.

Diamond Exchange wore a 9/16-inch flat bar shoe with a 3 1/2-inch toe on a 47-degree angle. I was never able to get his angle up to where I wanted it behind. He would beat his heels down behind and therefore, the highest angle I ever got on him was about 53 degrees. He was also the only one of my good horses who was not leveled up all the time when I shod him. Behind, I would ask the blacksmith to make him just a touch lower on the outside. This widened him out behind and allowed him to trot a little cleaner.

KING PINE—PATIENCE WITH A KICKER

I have always believed that patience is one of the best virtues a horseman can have. One horse who really tried my patience was King Pine, the Nearly Perfect colt who is a half-brother to Pine Chip.

King Pine was a slow learner, and was a real problem kicker. He was a colt with a lot of ability, but when he would get afraid of anything, he would kick. If he was afraid of a tractor, he would respond by kicking. If he got spooked by birds, or the wind, or by another horse going by, he would kick. These habits really set his training back.

King Pine was a lot like Carry The Message, whom I talked about earlier in this chapter. He was a colt who needed to see a lot of racetrack before he began to improve. There were days that he would jog seven or eight miles a day. I do not like to jog a colt that far, but with a situation such as this, it is imperative that the colt get over his kicking habits. I had to get King Pine tired before he really began to learn to trot. The long jog miles took the edge away from him, and he began to learn rapidly.

I always knew that he would have ability. He is a bigger colt than Pine Chip was at two, and he had good action. He also needed more foot than Pine Chip. I had to keep about a 3 5/8-inch toe on King Pine in front to keep him trotting safe. I also wore a 5/8-inch half-round shoe on him for most of his two-year-old year. I thought he was better in the heavy shoe.

King Pine started late in the year, but showed me right away that he would be a special colt. Without much experience, he got right into the thick of stakes competition, winning the American-National in Chicago and a stake at Lexington. He also won in 1:56.4 at Garden State, beating Donerail, the champion two-year-old of 1994.

The author prefers to have the front shoes set "full-out." In this way, the horse has additional leverage and support when the hoof strikes the track. The shoe length is extended beyond the line of the heel as much as 1/16 or 1/8 of an inch. This subtle variation of shoeing is also recommended in cases when a bar shoe is used.

NOT CONCERNED WITH TOE LENGTHS

Of the major factors in shoeing, I know a lot of trainers who are meticulous about the length of a horse's toe. I am not nearly as concerned with the length of the toe as I am with the angle.

As I have noted repeatedly in this chapter, I prefer as low an angle in front as I can get away with. I don't really care if a horse has a 3 1/4-inch toe or a 3 1/2-inch toe, as long as the toes are the same length.

I normally do like to get them as short as possible, because the modern trotter does not need the four-inch toes of their ancestors. I remember that trotters wore those long toes years and years ago, but it has been a long time since I had one who needed that much foot to trot.

I see trotters shod with 50-degree angles in front, but it does not work for me and I do not recommend it. Mack Lobell and Pine Chip are two of the fastest trotters in history and both of them had very low angles in front coupled with very high angles behind. I think that is the perfect setup for the modern trotter.

POSITIONING THE SHOE VERY IMPORTANT

There is another pet peeve in shoeing that I want to address in this chapter, and that concerns the position of the front shoes on the horse's foot.

I have seen a number of blacksmiths who will shoe a horse, and set the front shoes squarely on the horse's foot and trim the shoe at the end point of the heel. This looks symmetrical and clean, but what I prefer is for front shoes to be set back on a horse's foot a little and let the iron, or aluminum, or plastic hang over the end of the horse's heel a little.

This is what I call setting a shoe "full-out." I have had arguments with blacksmiths who tell me this will cause the horse to forge and pull these shoes off with his hind limbs, but I have not found that to be true.

The major benefit in setting the shoe "full-out" (by that I mean as much as a 1/16 or 1/8 of an inch beyond the end of the heel) is that the horse gains additional leverage and support for the heel area. This is especially true if the horse wears a bar shoe. And please do not be concerned—he will not catch it and pull it off!

I hate to see a horse shod with his front shoes snubbed off under his heels. To me, it would be like taking a part of the heel of your own shoe and removing it. You simply would not have the same support as you would with a full heel.

OVERCHECK LENGTHS—HEADS UP, OR DOWN?

A lot of trainers have a real obsession with the position of a horse's head. Some trainers like a horse with his head up. Others prefer to have a horse get his head down.

I solve this dilemma pretty much by letting a horse have his head wherever he wants it, as long as his progress suits me.

I haven't had any horses with their heads jacked way up in the air. But I also haven't had any exceptionally low-headed horses who were stars. In the old days, when a lot of horses were manufactured to hit a trot and stay at it, they had to have their heads high to stay on the trot. The breed is much more natural now, and we can race horses with their heads much lower.

Mack Lobell had a fairly natural head-set to him. So did Winky's Goal and Britelite Lobell. About the only horse I ever trained who needed his head in the air was Park Avenue Joe, and that was only because he had a breathing problem. I wore a Crit Davis overcheck bit on him and checked him pretty high and it seemed to help him get his air.

It seems to me that a lot of trainers will fall into traps with things like overcheck lengths. If they have one good horse who is high-headed, pretty soon everything in their stable has their heads jacked up. The converse is true, as well.

There is no system for training horses. Every horse must be treated as an individual.

OPEN BRIDLES PREFERRED

If I have a choice with a horse, I prefer to race him in an open bridle. It seems to me that down through the history of the breed, most of the really good horses raced with open bridles.

In training, I prefer a horse to wear a blind bridle, or even a Kant-See-Bak, or peek-a-boo blinds, but once I get to racing, my preference is to put them into an open bridle.

I also like to put a sheepskin roll on either or both cheek pieces of the bridle. Mack Lobell wore those cheek pieces most of his career here in the U.S. and Winky's Goal wore them, too.

WHY IT'S USEFUL TO HAVE A BAD MEMORY

I said at the beginning of this chapter that one of my assets as a horse trainer was a very bad memory. I don't mean by that to be cute or funny, but what it does mean is that it leaves me open to experiment and keep an open mind on any possible solution to a shoeing or training problem.

A lot of my good horses share common attributes, but every one of them presented challenges to my ability to overcome their idiosyncrasies.

For instance, the week at Solvalla with Mack Lobell before the Elitlopp became a nightmare. Mack didn't want to train, he didn't want to eat, he didn't want to do anything. I would get him out on the track and he would just stop and freeze on me. I couldn't even get him to trot. He would walk a ways and then stop.

He didn't like being on the track by himself. He was a very social horse who liked company but the quarantine restrictions specified that the American horses had to be kept apart from the other horses stabled there. The same thing happens when European horses come to the U.S. I had to get on the track with Mack all alone. Mack did not like that at all.

I finally appealed to the management at Solvalla to let me have some horses to work with and they finally relented. Stig Johansson is one of the top trainers in Sweden and Stig agreed to provide a couple of horses for Mack to train with. Mack Lobell was a horse who needed to train and I finally got him worked with Stig's help.

I also remembered that morning in Florida back when he was a two-year-old. I had to get after him pretty good or "school" him but, of course, I could not treat him that way in full view of the Swedish media and all the people who watched his workouts. Luckily, there is a jogging track up in the hills surrounding the Solvalla track and I was able to slip away one afternoon and have a schooling session out of sight of everyone.

Still, on the day of the Elitlopp, Mack was back to his old tricks, stopping on the track and just looking around. I was at my wit's end!

Luckily, when the field turned to go to the gate, Mack picked it up with the rest of the field and won both heats, although there were other times in his career when he had a lot more trot. All that fooling around and shipping overseas had cost him a little condition.

Had I not had an open mind to all solutions, I don't think Mack would have won the Elitlopp that day. I was the most relieved person on the face of the earth that night after that victory. Mack aged me a lot that week.

The other thing that a bad memory does for me is to allow me to start fresh with every horse. I really have a clean slate for each one of them. When they need help, I don't have a pat answer for all their problems. I experiment. I try different things. I search for solutions when none are apparent. This willingness to not be bound by convention is a useful tool for any horse trainer.

This includes the ability to make changes when necessary. I have developed a reputation over the years as someone willing to change shoes on a horse during the course of a race program. If I warm a colt up and he doesn't act right, I often have another pair of shoes ready to meet the situation. I don't want my horses compromised in any way if I can avoid it, so being ready to change shoes during the course of an afternoon or evening is something I am always prepared to do.

Certainly the most important attribute of any trotting horse trainer is patience. You get rewarded when you wait with a trotter. The wait can be frustrating and perplexing, but the wait is worth the results.

When you are standing on the track at the Meadowlands with that shiny Hambletonian bowl in front of you, or sitting in the floral chair at Lexington after winning the Kentucky Futurity, or receiving Breeders Crown crystal, it can be the most pleasant and rewarding moment in your life. You are glad to have chosen a career with so much reward for a job well-done.

A lthough Charles "Chuck" Sylvester has trained a few above-average pacers in his day, he has reached the elite level in his profession as a "trottin' horse man." In listing the outstanding trotters developed by the Toledo, Ohio, product, the question is not "where do you start," but "where do you stop."

Sylvester's career took off when he developed the invitational trotters Slomen and Sirloin and the stakes standout Diamond Exchange. Since then, the Sylvester Stable has included such performers as the superb fillies Armbro Devona, Britelite Lobell, Whiteland Janice, Armbro Keepsake, and Winky's Goal. On the male side, there are Hambletonian winner Park Avenue Joe, Armbro Iliad, Carry The Message and Incredible Abe.

But all of them pale in comparison to two that are the jewels in Chuck Sylvester's crown. Their names are Mack Lobell and Pine Chip, and they have to rank among the finest trotters harness racing has seen.

Mack Lobell captured nearly every major stake as a three-year-old, including the Colonial, Old Oaken Bucket, Yonkers Trot, and the Hambletonian in 1987 and earned $1.2 million. The highlight of his sophomore campaign was a 1:52.1 world record-smashing victory at Springfield, Illinois.

Five years later, Sylvester added Pine Chip to his arsenal. The son of Arndon was named Trotter of the Year in 1993 and 1994; his 1993 earnings, $1,363,483, were the second-highest single-season total for a sophomore trotter in history. In 1994, Pine Chip set a race record for his age and gait at The Meadowlands in the Nat Ray, and an all-age half-mile track mark of 1:54 in Delaware, Ohio, before time-trialing at The Red Mile in 1:51, making him the fastest trotter of all time.

One key to the success Sylvester has achieved is his skill in making last-minute changes in shoeing and equipment and his willingness to be innovative in a sometimes tradition-bound profession.

7

TRAINING THE TROTTER
An Alternative Method

PER ERIKSSON

First of all, let me say that I think there are a lot of ways to train a good horse. I also believe that there are no methods that will work on bad horses. I have been lucky enough to train a number of prominent stakes-winning trotters who were Hambletonian and Breeders Crown winners, and nearly all of them were good horses to begin with.

Nevertheless, a lot of these horses had problems that needed to be overcome. They all had weaknesses. They all had a sore spot or something that would have robbed them of their abilities had I not tended to it.

In fact, I think the real art in horse training is in learning a horse's weaknesses and then devising a plan to overcome them.

I guess all horse trainers would like to have the ideal trotter who is wonderfully conformed, perfectly balanced, great-gaited and quick off the gate, with the ability to finish as strongly as he started.

The reality of training horses, though, is that you never seem to get the whole package. Every horse, it seems, has a weakness, something that you have to work around in order to keep him going.

I also firmly believe that in order for a horse to achieve, he must have innate courage, that in-born ability to shrug off the aches and pains of racing and still win races for you.

I have been fortunate to have had a number of stakes winners, and every one of them was a courageous horse, able to work through his problems and still achieve.

PRAKAS—A GOOD CASE STUDY

Such a horse was Prakas, with whom I won the Hambletonian, World Trotting Derby and Breeders Crown.

He was by Speedy Crown and from the Star's Pride mare, Prudy Hanover, and right from the start he was a different horse from any I ever trained. He had a lot of natural ability, but he could not take my normal training routine and stay sound.

So, how did Prakas accomplish so much without training?

As a two-year-old, I started out with him like I do with all my horses. He was broken and initially trained on a regular basis, but sored up very early. It was obvious that he was not going to be able to train on a regular basis like the other colts in my stable.

I could train him a couple of trips and he would seem to be all right, but the next time I went to train him, he would be sore all over. As a

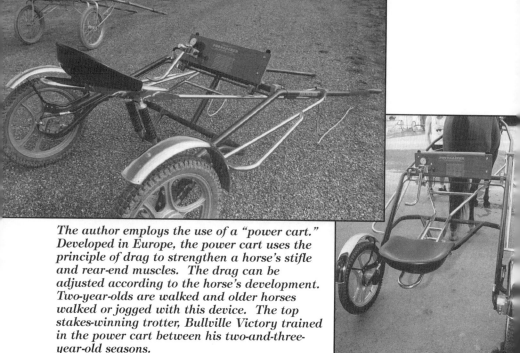

The author employs the use of a "power cart." Developed in Europe, the power cart uses the principle of drag to strengthen a horse's stifle and rear-end muscles. The drag can be adjusted according to the horse's development. Two-year-olds are walked and older horses walked or jogged with this device. The top stakes-winning trotter, Bullville Victory trained in the power cart between his two-and-three-year-old seasons.

result, instead of training every three to four days, he was a colt who trained only about once every 12 days! It is safe to say he had the lightest training schedule of any horse I ever trained who became a good horse.

Prakas had problems with his knees, which came from the fact that he was calf-kneed.

THE POWER CART—THE ANSWER TO A NEED

One of the training tools I make extensive use of is called the "power cart." This is a device that modifies a regular jog cart by adding a mechanism which forces a horse to pull the weight of the jog cart, plus a drag created by using tension generated from a series of gears located on the hub of the wheel. The mechanism can be set to varying degrees of tension. These different settings allow you to increase or decrease the drag you want to use on a horse.

Let me explain the operation of the power cart and the theory behind its use.

First of all, it was originally designed for walking horses as much as an hour at a time. The theory behind its use is that it builds strength and endurance by forcing the horse to use his back muscles, stifles and hocks in such a way as to assist him when he is training and racing. It should make the horse stronger.

Many trotters suffer from weak back and stifle muscles, and I have found over the years that this situation can be helped by employing the power cart. Use of the power cart in the correct way can be very effective in dealing with horses with these kinds of problems.

On my two-and three-year-olds, who are training regularly in the normal pattern, I use the power cart to supplement their training program. The training program is different for the two-year-olds. After the normal training regimen in the morning, I have the groom take the horse back out in the afternoon for about an hour of walking while hitched to the power cart.

It is very important to note here that a two-year-old horse does not jog or train with the power cart. He only walks. I let his head down and let him relax, but he learns to pull the cart and walk. Having his head down forces him to use his back and stifle muscles in such a way as to build strength and endurance. The only horse who cannot be helped with the power cart is one with a very thin hock or whose hock is poorly conformed. The power cart should not be used on a horse with a bad pair of hocks.

I have seen the power cart transform a number of horses from problem trainers to excellent horses. And there is no finer example than Prakas. I used the power cart extensively on Prakas at two and again at three.

I would walk him for an hour in the morning and then repeat the process in the afternoon. He made such good progress on the power cart that I got to the point where I seldom jogged him, and used the cart almost exclusively between training sessions.

I always marvelled at Prakas' ability to thrive on this routine because I was not able to give him much conditioning work, yet he had good wind and seemed not to miss the regular training regimen. I will talk more about the power cart later in this chapter.

One of the advantages I had with Prakas was that he was a natural-gaited, line trotter with very few shoeing problems. As a two-year-old, he wore a 9/16, half-round shoe with a squared toe, and wore a full swedge shoe behind. He had a short toe and a normal 50-51 degree angle in front.

At three, when he was really good, he wore a half-inch, half-round shoe and a full swedge behind. He had a short toe and was pretty easy to keep going as long as I avoided giving him a lot of work.

As a three-year-old, Prakas also was prone to soreness and could not be trained or raced in the normal manner. He had less work and less training than any horse I ever had, or probably ever will have. He was hardly ever trained between races. Yet he thrived and became a truly great racehorse, winning nearly $2 million.

THE IDEAL TROTTER

I guess every horse trainer has his own ideas about the ideal trotter. My own view is that a horse needs to have several different things going for him in order to learn to be an effective trotter.

First and foremost, for me, is the basic conformation.

I want a horse to be at least as long as he is tall. In order to determine this, I measure all the yearlings I buy at auction. I measure them from the ground to their withers and also measure the length of the body from the front to back.

I absolutely prefer a horse to be longer than he is tall. The ideal length would be about 2 centimeters (one inch) in excess of his height. For instance, Prakas was much longer across his back than he was tall. Most of my other good horses have been longer across their back than they were tall. Only one of them, Giant Chill, was squarely built. He was just about as long as he was tall.

My other good ones, including Giant Victory, Alf Palema, Bullville Victory and King Conch were all long-barrelled horses with lots of clearance underneath them.

Another of my prerequisites for a trotter is that he have a nice, clean hock that is neither too big in proportion to the rest of the horse, nor smaller than what is required.

The hock is so important in a trotter because it is the one joint which provides the drive for a horse and ultimately will determine what kind of trotter he will be. A horse with a weak hock will not learn to trot a lot (and stay sound). He will be sore, get to making breaks, start compensating for the hock soreness and either not get to the races or not stay there.

I want the hock area to be clean and straight from the point of the rump down through the hock, the leg and the foot. A good, straight line is very important. I also prefer a horse to have a wide, well-developed rump. This shows me he can have speed. A horse with a good, clean hock may not make the races, because something might go wrong somewhere else, but a horse with a bad hock almost certainly will not race.

The bigger the muscle through the rump and stifle area, the more ability the horse will have. None of my good horses have been light-muscled behind, in proportion to the rest of the body. I don't see how a trotter could get to be a good horse if he did not have a good, solid combination of back, stifle and hock muscles and tendons.

I also want my ideal trotter to have good size. By this, I do not mean a big horse, because I do not like big, heavy horses.

I do like a horse with some size, in terms of having some leg under him, but I do not like a heavy-bodied horse with big bones and heavy musculature. These horses are not quick to learn and are not good athletes.

A tall, light-boned horse can come to his speed naturally and is easier to keep sound. I have to admit that I have had more luck with a horse of average size, say 15.2 or 15.3 hands, and slight of build. For instance, Prakas was a tall, light-boned horse and this helped him deal with his other problems.

I also want a horse with a good eye and a sharp, intelligent head. I do not like a horse whose eyes are very close together and who does not have an intelligent look to him. A common characteristic of good horses is that they are all smart. I never had a dumb horse who became a good horse.

One of the areas of conformation I also pay special attention to with my trotters is how the horse stands in front. A lot of trainers will refuse a trotter who toes out, but I won't. It doesn't bother me, because I have learned that a horse who toes out a little might trot a little cleaner than a horse who squares up good and straight. If he toes out slightly, he will probably never hit his shins.

While I will accept a horse who toes out, I would be careful about recommending a horse who toes in—but only under certain circumstances. These horses are a problem to gait and balance, and should be avoided if you wish to train trotters successfully. I would recommend a trotter who toes in only if his body length far exceeded his height, by as much as five to ten centimeters, or nearly five inches.

A TROTTER NEEDS A LOT OF WORK

One of the main aspects of my program—with the exception of what I have already said about Prakas—is that a trotter should have a lot of work.

I believe a trotter learns a lot through repetition and a level of work that will allow him to develop his natural abilities. A trotter must train harder and more often than a pacer, for instance, because the pacer seems to be manufactured into its speed.

THE EARLY LESSONS

I break my yearlings to drive just like everybody else does, I suppose. I line-drive them a couple of days and if they seem O.K., I put them to a cart and start the breaking process.

Most of the horses have been handled a lot by the time I get them to Florida in the fall, so the breaking process usually goes pretty smoothly.

I start my colts off barefooted. Their first shoes will be half-rounds. I normally tack a pair of shoes on after I have seen what a colt is doing and have made a decision regarding what shoes he will wear. With most of the colts, the shoes will be half-rounds, put on in the normal position. A few of the colts, if they need some action right away, are fitted with the half-rounds turned around and the toes open and squared. This helps them to learn to break over properly and helps establish their gait.

The first few months of training are very important to a trotter because what I do is experiment to find a combination of shoeing and equipment that will properly balance the horse and get him set and square on the trot.

I like to build my colts up quickly by jogging them a couple of miles right off, then adding a mile each week to where they are jogging five or six miles daily after a couple of months. This gets them ready for the work ahead. It builds condition and wind and sets them up for a long season of training and racing.

I also begin to use the power cart on my two-year-olds in February or March. This is about the time their training begins to get serious and problems tend to develop. I do this to build their back and hock muscles and to strengthen the stifles. I have seen a lot of colts get to the races using this combination of training and power cart walking whom I thought would never make it with conventional training only.

TWO-YEAR-OLD TRAINING PROGRAM

After I get a two-year-old broken and gaited, I begin to train him twice a week to condition him for the season that lies ahead.

My regimen for two-year-olds is considered tough by some quarters, but it has worked successfully for me for a number of years. When I break my two-year-olds and get them to jogging on a daily basis, my central focus is on conditioning. I am not interested in speed. I am interested in how a colt behaves, and in his rhythm and gait and his overall attitude.

I do believe a horse has to have a lot of work to prepare him for the upcoming season, so I quickly advance a two-year-old up to five or six miles a day jogging. After a colt has jogged that far in the morning, he may walk an hour on the power cart in the afternoon. If a colt sores up from the jogging, we back off with him and he gets more time on the power cart until he can build himself up.

When I begin to turn colts, I am not too interested in time. I feel that speed in a horse is a natural thing and that if he is shod correctly and conditioned properly, he will learn to go fast. I have never been able to teach speed to a horse without natural ability and have him hold up. A hard-going or bad-going yearling makes a bad-gaited two-year-old and is a longshot to make it to the races. He might learn to go fast, but he won't stay sound.

The jogging that I do is not at a high rate of speed, but rather around a 4-4:30 clip. The two-year-olds begin to go their miles as they are advanced through the early training period down to the 2:25-2:30 rate.

For instance, early in the winter, I might work a colt a couple of slow miles in 2:50-2:40 after jogging three or four miles. For many colts who have a lot of nervous energy, this is a very effective way of getting a horse tired, but without stressing him. I find that a lot of horses don't really begin to learn until they get a little tired. In dealing with young horses at any gait, this is, I feel, an important principle.

With all my two-year-olds, their regular work is supplemented by additional work on a quarter-mile-long straight strip.

THE "STRIP"

The strip is a valuable part of my training program and supplements

The author believes in the use of a training strip, a straight quarter-mile track where the horse is interval-trained a series of quarters. The training strip has turn-arounds at either end. Work on the strip is used to complement training on the main oval track and varies the horse's work, helping to keep him cheerful and willing.

the training on the main track. Whenever the main track is unavailable due to rain, I use the strip to condition the colts and give them work outside of the normal routine.

What I do on the strip amounts to what is popularly called interval training. The strip is an all-weather track slightly more than a quarter-mile in length, with turnaround areas at each end.

Two-year-olds are put through a routine of as many as four to seven quarter-mile workouts in gradually decreasing times, starting in the neighborhood of 45 seconds.

As the training routine progresses, a colt might work up to going three quarter miles in 45 seconds and four in 35. The work I give them on the strip is very effective in freshening a colt or filly and improving their attitudes. They learn the routine pretty quickly and also learn to like it.

The strip is also very effective in getting a struggling colt untracked. I have helped many a trotter find himself on the strip. He learns he can trot fast without interfering, he never gets too tired, and the boredom of the same work pattern on the same track is decreased. Horses actually seem to cheer up and do their work more aggressively after a few sessions on the strip.

One of the questions I am asked about the strip is what factor it plays in teaching a horse to trot the turns. I would not recommend training a horse on a strip exclusively, because it is mainly a conditioning tool and not meant to replace the hard training that must occur on the track, including trotting the turns. The strip can help a horse get sound and in better condition, and his ability to trot the turns then will come. An unsound horse is not going to trot the turns anyway.

I must confess I don't really have a magic formula for this. If I have a colt who is fumbling on the main track and having some trouble keeping up, he will go to the strip until he learns to trot with some speed and confidence.

It doesn't help some of them enough. Realistically, not every horse you train is going to make it to the races.

If left alone, I will keep a colt on the main track working his regular miles, and once every third training day will go to the strip with him to vary his routine. My first day on the strip is normally spent teaching the horse the routine. The second time I come to the strip, I will begin to teach the horse to accelerate quickly and hold his speed throughout the quarter-mile. I am constantly surprised by how quickly the two-year-olds adapt to this program and learn to like it.

If I trained on the strip exclusively, I think I could get a horse ready who had already raced, but I would not recommend it for young horses. They simply have to have the training track regimen as well, or they will not be adaptable enough to racing conditions. The strip is mainly a conditioning tool.

THE IMPORTANCE OF CONDITIONING

I think that horse trainers today can go a lot farther with a horse if they pay more attention to conditioning than to speed. Horses seem to have so much natural ability and speed that the real mission of a trainer is to condition a horse for the racing that lies ahead of him. The repetition of regular workouts and long jog miles builds condition in a horse and sets him up for a long racing season. Not every horse will be like Prakas and thrive with little work. Most of the good ones require work to get them to the races.

I think it is useful at this point to discuss some of the ideas I have concerning training trotters. A lot of people think I give my horses too much work and that I put too much stress on a horse. I understand this critical appraisal. Let me explain my methods.

During the early part of my training period for two-year-olds, I will never ask a colt for high speed. I will ask him to learn to trot the right way and to have good manners, but I don't think my job in training two-year-olds is to teach them speed.

My job is to condition them, to keep them sound, and gait them. If I do that correctly, the speed will come. I have never trained a good horse who had to be taught to go fast. The good ones will learn speed as you improve their conditioning, gait and temperament.

I think a lot of trainers, particularly those who train trotters, are not patient enough. Horses, after all do not fit neatly into categories. They are all individuals. Every horse trainer has his own ideas about these subjects, but I believe the more successful trainers are those who remember that each horse has his own set of problems, advantages and disadvantages.

The one thing that horses have in common is that if you try to produce speed in them too early, you develop problems that you may not be able to contend with.

During the early part of the winter when I am going my training miles with the colts, the training program includes a couple of jog miles, followed by a training mile in 2:50, with pretty even fractions. A mile might have fractions of :43-1:26-2:09-2:52 at this point in training. I am not looking for speed.

I am not concerned at this early point with teaching a horse to accelerate when he is finishing. That will come later. During the early training, I am more concerned with manners, gait and the ability to react to other horses.

I work my colts in sets of two or three at a time and try to match the ability level of colts at all times. I don't want a particularly troubled colt to compete with one who is pretty natural. This can get a colt discouraged and doesn't help him build confidence.

As the training progresses, I try to teach a colt to accelerate during the early part of the mile. I think it is very important for a trotter to learn to leave the gate quickly, since position in a race is so important. This is also the point in a race where most trotters make breaks, so teaching them to leave the gate quickly is a very important part of my program.

It is also important for a horse to learn to finish, but it has been my experience that it is much harder to teach a horse to leave the gate than to teach him to finish strongly. The good horses I have had all had the ability to finish well without being taught. You can take a horse with only average ability and improve his chances of making money if he can leave the gate quickly.

When I work them down to 2:30, for instance, the first quarter might go in :35 or :36 and then each quarter, including the final one, is slower than that. There are a number of reasons for this.

First, a colt is fresher earlier in the mile and can learn to trot away from the gate easier. Secondly, by slowing the rate of each succeeding quarter, you keep a colt from getting too tired late in the mile. This assists you in keeping him on gait and keeping his confidence level up.

There is a lot of psychology involved in training horses and I think it is very important to keep a horse's confidence level high if he is to learn anything. Many trainers overemphasize the importance of finishing strongly. This is where colts can get to making breaks and creating problems that would be minimized if the trainer forgot about finishing well in each and every workout. A good horse learns to go fast soon enough. After all, speed is the real killer with young horses. It should be avoided at all costs. I think a lot of trainers like to ride fast and think it is O.K. for their horses, but speed is a very destructive thing for a young horse.

A HORSE WILL LET YOU KNOW HIS PROGRESS

If a colt is not making as much progress as I like, I will back off and not ask him to go on until I discover what his problem is.

I like a horse to tell me if he is progressing as I would like, and I get him to do that by watching him closely. If he remains cheerful and willing, you can continue to ask him for more. He can begin to tell you that he likes the work, that he is progressing, learning and accepting each new task.

Conversely, a horse will tell you if he is not ready for more. His attitude might change, he might become unwilling. If he is interfering and making breaks, I will have to make changes with him that will free up his gait and allow him to trot cleaner.

GAITING PROBLEMS AND ISSUES

There are not a great many options for a trotter to clean up his gait. You must either quicken his front-end action or slow him down behind. The biggest problem we run into, is finding enough room for the horse to clear himself. The first thing I like to do if they have interference problems is to square the toe in front. If that doesn't help, you may have to take the overcheck up some. I prefer to keep the head normal, but sometimes you have to take it up more than you want to. If that doesn't help, the next step I have had success with is to take a half-inch flat shoe and turn it around to make an open toe shoe. What you are trying to accomplish with that is to make the horse break over faster. I'm not scared to have a real short toe with an open toe shoe. If I have to go a step further, I may try to put on heavy hind shoes and attempt to slow him down behind, but the problem you sometimes run into with the heavier shoes behind is that the horse may get pacey-gaited. You have to understand that it is a very fine line to find the right balance. But you should never be afraid to try because there are no set rules. The important thing is not what you have on their feet but that you find the right rhythm.

KNUCKLING OVER

One of the most common problems for trotting horse trainers is the horse who knuckles over going slow. This is a sign of weakness in a horse and should be addressed by the trainer. I believe that a horse who knuckles over is weak in his stifles.

If I have a horse who is knuckling over a lot, I will do a number of things to help him. First, I will probably square his toes and cut them down as short as possible. I prefer a trotter with a short toe anyway, but for a horse who knuckles over, the shorter, squared toe will help him.

The author does not like to use a jog cart or regular racing sulky to train a horse. He recommends the use of this special type of "training sulky" developed in Finland. This training sulky is lighter than the traditional jog cart and more comfortable for the driver than the regular racing sulky.

If the problem of knuckling over continues, I will have the groom put an external stifle blister on the horse to increase blood flow to that area and strengthen the stifle muscle. With this kind of horse, I will also use the power cart to strengthen his stifle, if possible.

Not every horse can use the power cart. Giant Force, one of my very best horses, could not use the power cart because he would not put his head down while walking. He kept his head up and the power cart made him too sore across his back. A horse must put his head down and really pull with his hind limbs for the power cart to be effective.

MORE TRAINING TIPS

As a two-year-old progresses through the early training, one of the important items for me is to use a training sulky during all work miles. I never train a two-year-old in a jog cart during the winter. I just think it is too hard for them. I jog my colts in a jog cart, but all training is done in a training sulky made specifically for this purpose.

The training sulkies I use are made in Finland and are a cross between a jog cart and a racing sulky. They are heavier than a racing sulky and more comfortable to ride in, but much lighter and easier for the horse to pull than a jog cart.

I think a jog cart is responsible for a lot of lameness in a lot of American-trained horses. There is no question the jog cart is more comfortable for the trainer, but I believe the training sulkies and even race bikes allow the horse to do his work easier and better. As a trainer, my main concern is the horse's comfort and not mine.

THE USE OF GAITING POLES

One of the unique aspects of the Finnish training sulky is the use of gaiting poles, which can be attached to either side of the sulky shafts. These gaiting poles are very useful in teaching a horse to carry his hind limbs in a straight line with his front.

This is a recurring problem with young horses, and a lot of American trotters are taught to wear headpoles and use gaiting straps to accomplish what I can do with the gaiting poles alone.

The poles are a stronger barrier for the horse than plastic-coated gaiting straps and are mounted on a string. This allows them to slide back and forth, with the driver moving them with his leg. For instance, if I have a colt who bears out in the stretches and gets his hind end over to the right, I can use the gaiting pole to keep his hind end squarely behind him. Also, I use the gaiting pole on the left side if a colt has a tendency to get his hind end over to the left in trotting the turns. This is another common problem.

The driver has to learn to handle the horse and use the gaiting poles, but they can be very effective in teaching a young horse how to carry his hind end.

GAITING THE PROBLEM TROTTER

One of the more common problems with trotters is the colt or filly who does not handle his hind limbs as you would prefer. There are all sorts of common problems and one of them is the horse who sticks one of his hind limbs between his two front feet instead of either being line-gaited or passing-gaited.

A line-gaited horse is one whose limbs line up and his action allows him to pass the limbs without interference. The passing-gaited horse normally is aligned with the rear limbs passing outside the front limbs.

I really don't have a preference either way, as long as a horse trots cleanly. I have had good trotters who were line-gaited, such as Prakas and Bullville Victory, and good horses who were passing-gaited, like Alf Palema. I do believe a line-gaited horse will be faster than a passing-gaited horse because he will be much more efficient and expend less energy.

I have trained a number of horses who overcame gaiting troubles in the early part of their training, most notably the Hambletonian winner Giant Victory.

His problem was that he was a very good-gaited horse in front, with a real nice stroke and overall action. He was also line-gaited on his right side. But on the left side, he put his left hind leg in between his two front feet.

Because of this, when combined with some sickness and overall immaturity, he struggled a bit at two. The issue of maturity is something trotting horse trainers should all be aware of, because not every horse is ready to go with at the same time.

I was very careful with Giant Victory at two and it paid off at three because he got to be a very good trotter. I used a heavy shoe on him behind at two to teach him to put the left hind leg where it belonged. I also worked him a lot of slow doubleheaders throughout the winter between his two and three-year-old seasons.

I was fortunate because he was a horse who could stand a lot of work. I worked him really hard throughout that winter and early spring, with a lot of slow miles designed to teach him how to handle himself.

Giant Victory eventually wore an aluminum shoe with a full pad in front and only a light, 1/2-inch full swedge behind. I qualified him in mid-April at The Meadowlands and he improved greatly during the course of the summer.

He went a very good race for me in the Beacon Course just a week before the Hambletonian, and that convinced me he was good enough to enter.

When he won the Hambletonian and went on to become Trotter of the Year, I was very pleased because he had come so far. It takes a good horse to respond to the kind of program he was on. He got a lot of work with a lot of miles and like most of the good ones, he responded and made a fine horse.

THE FINAL PHASES OF TRAINING

When I get to 2:15 with my two-year-olds, they are now ready to enter the final phase of training. I want to work my colts in 2:09 or 2:10 before I leave for New Jersey for the summer. A lot of trainers will tell you they want to work a colt in 2:09, with a final quarter in :30.

My idea of a good 2:09 mile in Florida is one that is evenly rated at :32-1:05-1:37 with the first and last quarter in :32 and the middle half in 1:05. This never puts the horse in a stressful situation. The first quarter is worked in :32, but the first eighth might be in :15 or :15.2. It may be the fastest eighth of the mile.

Again, this is done to teach a colt to leave the gate properly and on stride. This also teaches him to leave sharply, then be taken back and be kind until late in the mile. This process is repeated at three. I do not believe any horse needs to be trained fast in the winter. There is a time for training fast quarters and halves and I will get to that later.

I believe a colt can be dropped two to three seconds a week if all the rest of his progress is acceptable to me. If he is holding his weight, is driving as I would like, has a good attitude and is trotting cleanly, I will continue to drop him according to his ability level.

If I feel he needs to stay at a certain level for a while (this is as much instinct as anything), then I will be patient and give him the chance to develop naturally. After he tells me he is ready to go on, I resume the normal reductions in time.

With my two-year-olds, I am aiming for a first start in early or mid-June. I ship from Sunshine Meadows in Florida to Showplace Farms in New Jersey around the first of May. This gives me time to acclimate the horses to the move and to adjust my training schedules.

A few of the colts will get sick when you ship them that far but that is a normal part of the training process. A two-year-old will be sick some time, so I like to get it out of the way as early as possible. I guess they have to be sick to get their immune systems built up for the rest of the year, so it does serve some useful purpose.

After the move from Florida, I resume working the colts three trips. I hardly ever go more than three training miles in any one session unless I feel a colt needs more work. Normally, by this point, you can tell where the real talent is and can focus your attention on those horses.

I work a colt three trips timed in 2:40-2:15 and a final mile in 2:10 in each session the first time in New Jersey, followed by reductions of about three seconds the next week to 2:07, and then to 2:05, before a colt is started.

It is important to note again that the 2:05 mile is an even-rated effort, with a first and last quarter in :31 and a middle half in 1:03. Again, I want a colt finishing sharply and in the bit.

In making the first start with a colt, I am more concerned with how he handles the starting gate, how he responds to the other horses, and how his overall manners are than I am with how fast he trots.

Quite often, I will train a colt faster before I start him than he will trot the first time I race him. That is because the first race is being used as a schooling event rather than asking him for a maximum effort the first time out.

GIANT CHILL—A TOP TWO-YEAR-OLD

I remember when I baby-raced Giant Chill, the top two-year-old of his year and winner of both the Peter Haughton Memorial and the Breeders Crown, that I had trained him in 2:04, handily, at Showplace Farm.

However, the first time I started him, he trotted in 2:06.1 and was beaten by nearly 15 lengths. This alarmed his owners who thought they had a better colt than that, but I was more concerned with how he raced, rather than how fast. I already knew he was a good horse. I wanted to teach him to be a better one.

The second time Giant Chill raced, I asked Sonny Patterson to drive him, and I trained him differently between races. As I have indicated, I do not believe in fast quarters during the initial and late phases of conditioning. However, I do believe they are necessary to get a horse sharp enough to be competitive.

For instance, I worked Giant Chill midweek between his first two starts three trips in 2:40-2:20 and 2:15. In the 2:20 mile, I let him trot the last eighth right around 15 seconds, and in the 2:15 mile, he trotted the final quarter under 30 seconds. This was the first time I ever asked him for speed.

He responded wonderfully, winning his next baby race in 2:02.2, last quarter in :28.4. I knew right there he was a very good horse and I could expect a lot from him. He took the work so well and responded very naturally.

Giant Chill was a good example of a colt who came very quick at two, but then did not improve enough at three to be competitive at the top level. Of course, we ran up against American Winner and Pine Chip that three-year-old season, and Chill simply could not trot with them. He could out-leave them at the gate, but could not stay with them late into the mile. He was the best gate horse of all of my good horses. Position was never an issue with him. He could grab the track whenever necessary.

GIANT FORCE—TIME IMPROVED HIM

A horse who went through the same training program a year earlier, but who never learned to leave the gate quickly was Giant Force, a son of Meadow Road, who really got good for me as a four-year-old after a solid three-year-old season. He was one of those who "also-started" at three, but at four he blossomed into a genuine top-class horse, winning the Nat Ray at The Meadowlands and the Yonkers International.

Despite my efforts to make him a horse who could leave the gate sharply, he never developed the kind of early speed I would have liked. But boy, could he finish! He could take a lot of abuse and still keep coming.

I always had some trouble with his front feet, and I wore a bar shoe on him sometimes when his feet bothered him. He wore a light, 1/2-inch, half-round shoe most of the time, and I liked him that way.

Giant Force was a horse who did not like to train, so I was always looking for ways to keep him interested and keep him comfortable, happy and fresh. Because he could not use the power cart, he was a horse who jogged five to seven miles per day, and I liked to use the strip with him to lessen the sting of the track on his sore feet.

When his feet hurt him, it would have been a perfect time to use the power cart to condition him. But as I said earlier, he couldn't use it, because he would not put his head down and pull. He kept his head up, and the power cart sored him all over.

THREE-YEAR-OLDS ON THE STRIP

While the two-year-olds were restricted to walking on the power cart, I began to use the power cart on the strip with my three-year-olds in the winter of '93-'94.

This marked a huge departure for me, since I had not used the power cart at all in conjunction with the strip training. My past use of the power cart was restricted to walking a horse in training in conjunction with the regular strip routine.

What I did was lessen the drag variable and use it on the theory that the drag might strengthen a horse behind enough to allow him to overcome a problem there. The horses I use the power cart on in this way seem to be progressing better than under the normal training regime, so I am encouraged.

YOU MUST ANALYZE AND EVALUATE

This illustrates another good point. As a horse trainer, I am constantly analyzing what I am doing and changing my methods. Like most businesses, if you continue to do the same things the same way you will end up losing ground to your competition.

I had never used the strip and the power cart together, because I thought it would be too hard on a horse, but then it occurred to me that the basic principle of the power cart is to strengthen a horse by forcing him to pull some added weight without stress.

When I tried the power cart on the strip, I was amazed at the improvement of some of the weaker-stifled horses. By lessening the drag variable of the power cart significantly, I was able to use it in conjunction with my three-year-old plan.

I had always trained my three-year-olds on the strip and worked them to where they could make nine separate passes on the strip at about a 33-35-second rate for a quarter mile, depending upon their overall ability.

When I first started to use the power cart, I would apply it for only a couple of trips on the strip, then gradually increase its use up to the full nine passes.

However, with the power cart now, I am keeping the quarter times in the :40-:45 area. I believe the combination of the regular fast quarters and the drag of the power cart would tear a horse up behind.

I am already convinced that some version of this plan is a valuable addition to the training program in the winter. To what extent, only time will determine. A horse must have a very clean hock and stifle area before I would try this on him; a horse with conformation problems behind could not be helped by this program. The horses I have used it on seem to do good on it, and it is no problem for them at all once they get hitched to a conventional sulky. After the power cart, the sulky must feel like no weight at all.

BULLVILLE VICTORY BENEFITTED FROM THIS PROGRAM

One of the horses who benefitted greatly from this program was
Bullville Victory. I must admit that this horse surprised me a lot during
the 1994 season because he became a much better horse than I ever
thought he could be.

Entering the 1994 season, I thought Smasher, another son of Valley
Victory, was the better of the two colts. Smasher had raced well for me at
the end of the year, including an impressive showing in the Breeders
Crown when he was second to Wesgate Crown.

Bullville Victory had not been a strong colt at two, and like most of the
Valley Victory offspring, was small. He had a 1:59.1 mark at two and won
only $30,000. I really thought he was just a follower, even though he had
a lot of sickness at two.

During the winter of 1994, I put him on the power cart for some of the
slow training miles, and I do not know if this was the reason for his
drastic improvement later on, but I do think it aided greatly in building
his condition for a hard year of racing.

Bullville Victory did not develop his speed as quickly as I thought he
should have but he was a better horse as the year progressed, and was a
better horse in the second and third heats of his races, due largely to
the fact that he was so well-conditioned. I think the training trips with
the power cart on the strip had a lot to do with this.

I do not think that the power cart, or something similar, should be
used exclusively with any horse, because I think a horse needs to learn
to trot fast. The power cart allows a horse to improve his condition without the stress of the fast works, but he must have the fast work, too, in
order to improve. The use of the power cart was responsible for Bullville
Victory's improvement in 1994, and was also responsible for the toughness he showed in the third heats of the World Trotting Derby and the
Kentucky Futurity.

Bullville Victory was a line-gaited horse who was very easy to shoe. He
wore a flat, aluminum shoe with a Swedish pad, and an open toe. He had
a normal 50-degree angle in front, and I never raced him barefoot. He
wore a very light aluminum, full swedge shoe behind, on a normal 53-54
degree angle.

This horse's improvement throughout the 1994 season was pretty dramatic. He really surprised me. I thought the Yonkers Trot victory was
kind of a fluke, but then he really raced well in the Hambletonian, winning his elimination. I think he could have menaced Victory Dream in
the final heat of the Hambletonian had he not been in tight quarters in
the stretch and made a break.

At Du Quoin, in the World Trotting Derby, Bullville Victory went three
terrific heats and showed us for the first time all year how tough a little
horse he really was. He is a very good example of why Valley Victory has

made the dramatic impact he has. Bullville Victory was a sound, effi-
cient-going horse who was willing and aggressive, yet manageable. He
also was very smart. I have trained quite a few by Valley Victory and find
them to be very easy to work with. They are also a sound group of horses
who trot very cleanly. About the only trouble I ever had with Bullville
Victory was that he would scalp a little behind at slow speeds. Once he
got to going below 2:00, he trotted very cleanly and raced with just a pair
of bandages behind, and a light pair of brown bell boots in front. He also
went with his head down, which is very typical of the Valley Victory offspring.

DOUBLEHEADERS FOR THE THREE-YEAR-OLDS

One of the most valuable tools any horse trainer can utilize is the use
of doubleheaders to condition horses.

I was taught to use them very early in my training career, and I think
doubleheaders are a wonderful way to condition horses for a hard racing
season.

The doubleheader, like the use of the quarter-mile strip, is a variation
on interval training. It is a combination of workout miles compressed
into a shorter time frame which forces the horse's overall condition to
improve without stress.

The doubleheader is an important training tool and has been used
successfully by horse trainers for a number of years. I am certainly not
the first horse trainer to use them and won't be the last.

My main use of doubleheaders is with the three-year-olds between
their two-and three-year-old seasons. As older horses, they will be required to race heats in all of the classic races, and for a horse to do that
in August and September, he must be prepared during the preceding
winter.

I like to turn horses out between the two-and three-year-old seasons,
but if possible, I don't like to keep them out for more than four or five
weeks. I think a horse is easier to condition for his three-year-old season
if he is not let down 100 percent so to speak, at the conclusion of his two-
year-old year.

To keep a horse in good condition and prepare him for the tough three-
year-old season, there is no better tool than the doubleheader. It exerts
a horse without stressing him.

Through the early part of the winter, the doubleheader is used to keep
a horse going. I will give my three-year-olds enough work to keep them
sharp and prepare them for their next season without asking for too much
speed. The doubleheader accomplishes that wonderfully.

DOUBLEHEADERS FOR TWO-YEAR-OLDS

I will also use doubleheaders for my two-year-olds, but only during certain times when they are properly indicated.

If I have a colt or filly who is racing, but I am not happy with their progress, I will often use a doubleheader in the heat of the summer months to improve their fitness. I find it particularly useful if I feel a horse is racing short and I want to improve his strength.

If I am going to do this, I will use the doubleheader instead of training three single miles. If this is done, the doubleheader would be timed in 2:30-2:15, then back again in the identical time. All the work miles would be evenly rated.

This puts four work miles into the horse, instead of the conventional three miles that everyone uses. I have often seen this improve a horse's condition and help him finish his race miles stronger. This, of course, should be done only with a horse who does not have major soundness problems. This much work would harm a horse who had serious problems.

I do not recommend the use of doubleheaders for two-year-olds during the winter of their first season in training. This would put too much stress on their young bones.

ALF PALEMA—THE HEATS MADE HIM A HORSE

I am not a big fan of heat racing. I think it creates great stress for a horse, because almost all of the heat races come in the intense heat of summer. Heats and heat are very hard on a horse.

But the 1992 Hambletonian winner Alf Palema was transformed by heat racing, from being just one of the gang to the best of his year.

Alf Palema was a colt by Speedy Somolli and was a very good-training two-year-old. He took all his work cheerfully and was a very naturally-gaited, gifted colt. But at two and early into his three-year-old season, he acted like he was just a follower.

I had King Conch in my stable that year, and Alf Palema could not handle him at any point during the winter between their two-and three-year-old years. King Conch was a much better horse. The first time these two horses were asked to go heats was in the Founders Gold Cup at Vernon Downs in July, about a month before the Hambletonian. Alf Palema raced better the second heat than he had the first and from that point forward, he was a better horse every week.

He was entered in the Hambletonian and was really improving, but I thought he was still second best to King Conch. Alf Palema, however, had a lot of innate ability. I trained him very hard during the winter between his two-and three-year-old season's and he stood up to it, because he was a very natural-going horse and the extra work was not stressful for him.

As I used the doubleheaders throughout the winter, Alf Palema trained four or five miles twice a week, with the final mile around 2:10-2:15. He and King Conch were not let down after their two-year-old seasons. I kept them going.

The extra work, however, was not good for King Conch. He had some problems with his knees and the extra work I gave him throughout the winter was too much for him. He just could not hold up.

King Conch was the best-gaited horse I ever trained. He was very talented, with enormously quick early speed. He could throw a 28-second quarter at you like it was nothing at all.

He had great conformation, was a very attractive horse and had great body length. He was line-gaited and never touched anywhere.

But Alf Palema held up and King Conch did not.

On Hambletonian Day, when Alf Palema came up the rail to beat King Conch in the stretch, I was the most surprised guy at The Meadowlands. I knew King Conch was the better of the two, but Alf Palema was the sounder of the two and that is what made the difference with him. His soundness allowed him to mature and improve during the course of the season. King Conch could not.

Another thing which made Alf Palema a better horse is that I could race him barefoot. He had a very well-shaped round foot and trotted very naturally with a short toe and a light, aluminum shoe. He was, therefore, a natural for barefoot racing.

He was barefoot the day he won the Hambletonian at The Meadowlands and barefoot again at Du Quoin when he won the World Trotting Derby. I did not start him in the fall of his three-year-old year at Lexington, but if I had, I am sure he would have raced barefooted.

Alf Palema was also a horse whom I trained a little differently during the racing season, in that I did not give him his midweek work between races three or four days away from race date.

I would normally train him in 2:15 two days out from the race and only go two trips. In the 2:15 mile, I would let him trot home good, with a last quarter around :27-28. The speed work really sharpens a horse.

I think a lot of trainers see a horse go a good race after an intense workout between races and they think they should work all of their horses hard between races.

My own idea about this is that intense training between races should be used sparingly, and that you should pick your times to use it. An ideal time is right before a big race, if you wish to sharpen a horse up and make him better. This should only be done with a horse who is relatively sound. A horse with chronic soundness problems should not be trained hard between races, if at all.

Alf Palema's schedule called for him to jog four to five miles daily and use the power cart in the afternoon. This is the schedule he had before the Hambletonian and again before the World Trotting Derby. I would recommend this for any horse who seems to tail off a little after a few starts. I will nearly always attempt to lighten a horse's work between races first, then see how he responds. If that doesn't work, I will try a little more intense workout and if that fails, I will experiment with no training between races.

If what I am doing is not working, I continue to experiment to find the combination that will allow the horse to perform at his maximum level.

AMERICAN WINNER, BJ'S MAC AND SUPER PLEASURE

At some point in their careers, I trained the full brothers American Winner, Super Pleasure and BJ's Mac. I got Super Pleasure as a three-year-old and had American Winner and BJ's Mac as yearlings. They were all about as different as three horses who were full brothers could be.

American Winner was a little horse who was very light-boned and almost feminine-looking. He was very light on his feet, however, and came with a great gait, which is the only thing the three brothers had in common.

Super Pleasure was a big, rugged horse who took after the Super Bowl side of his pedigree. And BJ's Mac was kind of a composite of the other two, since he had a little more size than American Winner, but much less than Super Pleasure.

The thing that undid BJ's Mac was he had a very thin hock behind and his suspensory finally let go. The interesting thing about all three of those horses is that they were all very easy to shoe and had a lot of natural ability. They were good, happy horses with good attitudes.

BJ's Mac and Super Pleasure made good two-year-olds, while American Winner, obviously, was much the better three-year-old.

DELPHI'S LOBELL—A VERY DETERMINED FILLY

While I have talked almost exclusively here about colts, I have had a number of good fillies— and one, in particular, I wanted to write about in this chapter.

That is Delphi's Lobell, a Speedy Crown filly out of the Jurgy Hanover mare Delphi's Delight. She was a beautiful filly, very fine and refined looking. But she was difficult to get going.

I had a real hard time gaiting her and getting her set just right. She was sore a lot at two, but as I wrote in the early paragraphs of this chapter, a horse must have a certain amount of courage to overcome physical shortcomings. No matter what I tried with her, it didn't seem to help her much.

The important thing to remember is that Delphi's Lobell still went forward. She wound up with a mark of 1:56 and won more than a half-million dollars, but I have to admit that she was never as good-gaited as I would have liked, or as sound as I would have liked. But she overcame her problems.

She was a very determined filly, and it seemed like that whatever she encountered, she found a way to overcome it and be a productive horse. If every horse came with this kind of attitude and the courage to race through their physical problems, horse training would be a lot easier.

Another of my horses who had problems and overcame them was Delphi's Daughter, one of 1994's better three-year-old trotting fillies. She had problems with a tendon as a two-year-old, but the use of the power cart for walking made a big difference with her.

I was amazed to see her tendons get tighter and tighter throughout the course of her two-year-old season, and she finally made a very good filly. Another thing I did with her was turn her out for about three weeks following the Zweig filly trot. She was acting a little sour, and had some problems, so I just turned her out. When I brought her back in, she was sounder, had a better attitude, and was freshened by being away from the regular routine of training. Being turned out was a real vacation for her, and she came back strong. She won stakes at Lexington at three, including a rather easy win over Gleam in the Bluegrass Stake.

I cannot overstate the importance of attitude with any horse. Turning Delphi's Daughter out for three weeks improved her attitude, and allowed her to become a multiple stakes-winning filly.

DAVIDIA HANOVER—SHE NEEDED TO BE AWAY FROM THE TRACK

Another filly who brought me a lot of notoriety was Davidia Hanover, a Super Bowl mare who was the best two-year-old of her year, then fell on some hard times in making the transition to a top older mare.

When I got her, she was sound, but her attitude was terrible. She was just sour about being around the racetrack all the time. I think a lot of horses just get tired of the daily routine and are bored. Davidia was tough in the stall and hard on the help. I determined that the only thing I could do was to change her pattern of training and get her away from the track.

I decided to give Davidia to one of my best female grooms, whom I also knew liked to ride horses. I told her not to hitch Davidia, but just jump on her and ride her around anywhere but near the racetrack. At Showplace Farm, there is a park nearby and Davidia loved being ridden around that park.

She began to eat better, her attitude improved, and I gradually started working her on the track just on the day she was to train. On the other days, she would be ridden in the park. I really had her treated like a pleasure horse instead of a racehorse. This improved her attitude to the point where she improved her overall barn demeanor and her racetrack prowess returned as well. She got very good again, raced wonderfully in Europe and returned to the U.S. to claim a world record for aged mares at The Meadowlands.

I would not recommend this program for every horse. However, if you have one who is sound, but has a poor attitude, just completely modify its conditioning program by giving it a lot of time away from the track. This will normally improve the horse's attitude enough to return it to form.

If I could give one piece of advice to anyone training trotters, it would be that I have seen about everything there is with respect to different kinds of shoes, shoeing techniques, training, and exotic programs. And I have tried a lot of these approaches.

However, I believe a trotting horse trainer can succeed if he will keep his shoeing as basic and as simple as possible. Most modern trotters really will be better with a short toe, a light shoe and very little added weight on a fairly natural angle.

As naturally gifted as the trotters have become, thanks to Super Bowl and Speedy Crown and their sons, the breed has really improved to the point where I believe shoeing is less of an issue than management.

The successful trainer is the one who can manage his horses and keep them going through the speeds at which they can and must compete.

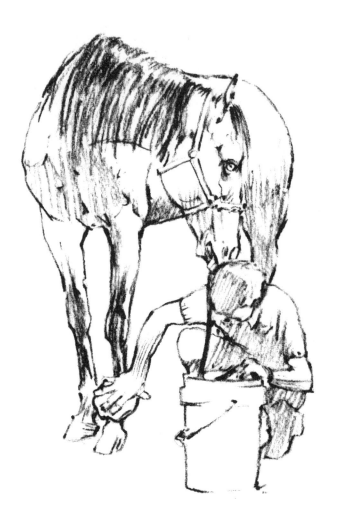

ew trainers have made an impact on the American trotting
scene as quickly or as pro-
foundly as Per Eriksson. A protégé of
the noted father-son trainer duo of
Soren and Jan Nordin, Eriksson opened
his own public stable in the U.S. in 1983 and found immediate success
with the trotters Desert Night, Spirits Supreme, and Socrates Lobell.

The star of his stable the next year was the colt Prakas, who would
propel Eriksson's name recognition to new heights. Prakas was named
1985 Trotter of the Year after winning the Hambletonian, World Trotting
Derby, and Breeders Crown, and became the sport's all-time fastest trotter.

In 1986, Eriksson sent out the crack filly and intercontinental star
Davidia Hanover, who set world records in the U.S. and Europe. For the
next five years, you could count on at least one Eriksson colt or filly challenging for trotting honors.

Then in 1991, Eriksson-trained Giant Victory became the second
Hambletonian victor for the personable Swede. Giant Victory also won
the Breeders Crown and was voted Trotter of the Year.

The following year Eriksson's pupils finished 1-2 in the Hambletonian
final as Alf Palema upset King Conch. In 1994, Eriksson conditioned
Bullville Victory, winner of the Kentucky Futurity, Yonkers Trot, the World
Trotting Derby and an elimination of the Hambletonian.

8

A NUTRITIONAL GUIDE TO PRACTICAL HORSE FEEDING

JOHN LEW, Ph.D.

s with most horse endeavors, regardless of the breed of horse involved, there is a good deal of misunderstanding when it comes to the science and practice of feeding horses who are required to perform athletic feats and to produce other horses capable of speed and productivity.

I have been asked in this chapter to relate the scientific, clinical aspect of equine nutrition to the practical information needed by the everyday horseman. This is a challenging assignment. Some understanding of the science of equine nutrition is important in order for anyone charged with feeding horses to make good decisions on a day-to-day basis.

However, as director of nutrition for a company that does nothing else but produce and sell equine nutrition products, I confront these same problems almost daily in attempting to help horsemen with their horse nutrition questions.

I do believe there are many misconceptions when it comes to the feeding of horses. For instance, horse people generally do not understand where the nutrients they must get to the racehorse originate. They are generally confused about what oats, for example, really supply to a horse's metabolism. Horse people also may not realize that hay can vary a great deal in its value to the horse.

Aside from water, the most important nutrient is energy, and every horseman should concern himself with the proper way to provide his horse with energy. The demand for energy in a racehorse, and the ways chosen to furnish the energy required, are often what separate the everyday horse person from the really successful trainer.

There are many myths, some of them of long-standing, regarding feeding practices for horses. For instance, one of the most common myths is the notion that feeding a horse an abundance of corn will make him "hot" on the inside, or high strung. That is simply not true. There is no scientific basis for that assumption. A horse may react poorly to the large consumption of corn, but the corn is not the culprit. If fed in the proper quantities in a total nutrition program, shelled corn can be a very valuable feed.

Another common misconception is that if a little feed is good for a horse, a lot of feed is even better. This is especially true of feed supplements. This, of course, is not true as well. There are no panaceas available in the feed tub, regardless of what it contains.

A good horse may still perform, even on a marginal diet. For optimum performance, however, a balanced diet integrated into a complete training and management program is indispensable.

WHY DO WE FEED OATS?

Horses have been fed oats since the time of the Roman legions. There is a long, historical record of horses being grained, primarily with oats.

Oats have many good characteristics, which is why they are so desirable as a foodstuff for horses. Oats are a very safe grain, because of their high fiber content, and they supply adequate levels of energy and protein. There is, however, a great variation in the quality of oats. The important thing to remember in buying oats for racehorses is to judge the quality of the oats based on the bushel weight. All else being equal, the heavier the oat — that is, the more pounds to the bushel — the higher in quality the oats should be. It is important that a horseman "know his oats."

For instance, the U.S. Department of Agriculture standard for #1 quality oats is 36 pounds per bushel. However, I believe the USDA standard to be far too low for racehorses. Racehorse oats should weigh somewhere in the neighborhood of 42-45 pounds per bushel. If you are buying oats for racehorses and believe that you are getting first-quality oats by getting USDA #1 oats, you could be mistaken. If the oats are very heavy in the high pounds per bushel area, they could be of high quality. At the low end of the #1 rating, however, the oats could be of a low quality for racehorses. You should feed a much higher quality oat. This is where the term "heavy racehorse oats" originated.

Another item to check is the amount of foreign material (dust, weeds, seeds and cracked grain) contained within a bushel of oats. The presence of foreign material can decrease the energy content. Ideally, there should be no foreign material present, but many people buy oats directly from farmers and elevators. Most of this type of oats will be contaminated to some extent with weeds and dust, and I do not recommend this type of oats for racehorses. They may be adequate for barren broodmares or in the early part of an in-foal mare's pregnancy, but they are not acceptable for growing young horses, any horses in serious training, or pregnant mares in the final trimester of gestation.

Oats are valuable because they are a reasonable source of protein for a horse. High-quality oats may have a crude protein range of about nine to 13 percent. This is within the acceptable ranges for horses. Young horses will need the higher protein oat.

Another of the common misunderstandings about oats occurs when the hull of the oat appears in a horse's feces. This is due to the fact that the horse's digestive system does a poor job of breaking down the hull of the oat. Many horsemen are concerned with this and do not feel that the horse is getting the full benefit of the oats because the oat grain has passed through the horse without being digested. In most instances, this is not the case. Upon examination, it can be determined that the hull remains, but that the encapsuled grain has been at least partially digested. There is very little nutrient content in the hull, and nature has devised a pretty good system of getting rid of something that is of little value.

FEEDING THE RACEHORSE

Having said that energy is the most critical nutrient, aside from water, how do we supply the required energy? And how much energy *is* required? Although I will also address the dietary requirements for young horses, such as weanlings and yearlings, and for older horses such as stallions and broodmares, the racehorse will be the central focus of this chapter. This is proper since the dietary requirements and the manner in which they are delivered may often determine how productive a horse will become.

The amount of grain to be given to a racehorse should depend on the horse's overall diet, body weight, work load and condition. The amount of grain also will be dependent upon the quality of the hay that is fed.

•What are the demands being placed on the horse?
•If it is a young horse, is it still growing?
•If it is being asked to expend a great deal of energy, that energy needs to be replaced, so its system stays in balance. If this balance does not exist, the horse either loses weight or gains it.

It is also important to say here that a racehorse cannot be expected to hold weight and perform at a high level on a diet of hay alone. Hay, even of the highest quality, is not sufficient to meet the necessary energy requirements of a racehorse.

Horses also vary a great deal as to body type, metabolism and different abilities to process their food stuffs. Racehorses are not selected or bred based on their ability to utilize their feed as many domesticated animals, such as cattle, hogs and chickens are. Some selection occurs indirectly, of course, because a horse who is a "poor doer" will often be an underachiever and may not find his/her way to the breeding shed. The variables we use to select horses are almost totally dependent upon performance. They have nothing to do directly with the ability to utilize feed.

As a general guide, though, let us say that a racehorse in training is carrying acceptable weight, is trim and fit, and looks as though it is making good progress as far as its nutrition program is concerned. On the average, a horse like this is probably getting about 15 pounds of oats per day. This is a typical grain allotment.

Many horsemen use a three pound coffee can to "dish up" oats. When measuring your daily oats allotment, however, keep in mind that today's "three pound" coffee can holds less than three pounds of coffee, and that oats weigh more than coffee. How much more, depends on their quality.

Therefore, it is a good idea to take your feeding can, fill it with oats, pour the can's contents into a plastic bag or other ultra-light-weight container, and have the bag and contents weighed on commercial scales.

This will reveal the number of pounds of oats your feeding can actually holds, and that information will be a gauge in determining your horses' daily ration of oats. If you change to a different quality of oats (which could be heavier or lighter than what you're presently feeding), you need to weigh the level can's contents again before continuing with the daily feedings.

If a horse has a rapid metabolism, or is doing poorly and needs to gain weight, he might require as much as 20 pounds of oats per day to begin putting on weight. In the extreme, a horse with a very high rate of metabolism and a poor digestive system could conceivably lose weight on even 20 pounds of oats per day.

If there is a central theme to this work, it is that every horse in training will require a somewhat different feeding plan. No two horses are alike in this regard.

If each racehorse in a stable receives the same ration in the same amount, it is a safe bet that some are receiving an inadequate ration and others are getting too much. Good trainers not only personalize the training regimen of their stable, but also recognize that customized feeding programs are indicated for each and every horse in their care.

For example, a two-year-old colt who is "full of himself" and feeling good, may require a great deal more food than a two-year-old filly who is very quiet around the barn, and on the track.

Every good nutrition program takes into account the activity load and temperament of the horses involved. And it is also important to determine the habits of each horse and how calm, or nervous, each horse may be.

Another important item is the overall quality of the grain. If you feed oats, you want to look for a well-filled kernel of grain. This is important because the quality of the grain will determine how much will have to be fed. A poor-quality grain will have to be fed in larger quantities if the horse is to obtain the same amount of energy.

Using my guide of 15 pounds per day of oats for a racehorse, this regimen would have to be modified one way or the other, depending upon the quality of the grain. The 15-pounds per day requirement assumes that the grain is of high quality and the horse's workload is normal. If the workload is light, especially in the initial phases of training, the requirement can be reduced.

As the workload increases, the amount of the ration will have to increase if the horse is expected to hold his weight. A good starting point would be to feed a youngster eight to ten pounds of grain per day at the beginning of the training and increase the feed as the intensity of the training increases.

The simplest way to determine the quality of the feed and the proper ration is to observe a horse over a period of time. If a horse begins to lose weight, his ration will need to be increased before the weight loss begins to affect his energy level.

An important note at this point: I do not recommend the feeding of more than five pounds (or one-half of one percent of the horse's total body weight) of grain of any type at any one time. If a horse eats too much grain at one time it can lead to colic, and everyone knows that colic in a horse is a very serious matter. It can also contribute to the development of ulcers.

If you have a horse who must eat more, do not increase the intake at any one time. Give smaller portions, but allow a horse to eat more often. Feed four or five times a day, if necessary.

This is particularly important to note, because we must remember that horses in a natural environment will eat almost continuously during their waking hours. Horses are grazers. Left to his own devices, a horse should have free choice to food stuffs, especially hay, at all times. A horse should have many "meals" during the day, because most of the time is passed in grazing activity. This is a very important concept, and the failure to recognize this is often responsible for the high incidence of colic in horses. For instance, many racehorses do not have access to hay during the non-active hours. It is not uncommon to see trainers take away a horse's hay on race day. Then, after the race, the horse is fed a large amount of hay and grain. This is a dangerous practice and can lead to a bout with colic. Quite often we find that racehorses who have developed colic problems may have been fed incorrectly and that the feeding pattern contributed to the onset of colic.

Part of this problem also rests with the fact that a horse's intestines have some peculiarities, in that they are poorly designed to allow the intake of a large volume of food in a single feeding. There are many twists and turns of the intestines and several changes in diameter. Furthermore, the intestines are loosely attached to the body wall and are easily susceptible to movement and subsequent twisting. This creates the well-known problem of twisted intestines and blockages, which prevent the digestive tract from functioning normally and preclude the normal movement of the bowels. Worse yet, it often strangulates the blood vessels, if the problem is not quickly corrected, and that part of the intestine will die from lack of blood supply. The infection which ensues is deadly.

These are some of the reasons that horses are so predisposed to colic. If a horse's intestines are full, they are less likely to be twisted in such a way as to cause a blockage and bring on a bout with colic and all its devastating effects. A horse who has been fed properly will have full intestines and his system will be busy continuously breaking down what he has eaten.

There are other advantages to feeding a horse in this manner. If you keep hay in front of a horse at all times, he will eat when he wants, his intestines will work better, and he will be happier and more content. There are many psychological advantages, therefore, to feeding a horse a continual ration. Many horses who are stall walkers, or who dig up huge holes in the stall, may just be hungry or bored.

There are other factors as well. The average mature racehorse has a stomach volume of about eight quarts maximum, or about 10 pounds of grain stuffs. A smaller horse will have a smaller stomach; thus a bigger horse may be able to consume more feed without a hint of trouble.

An ideal feeding pattern for racehorses in training is to feed grain at certain times, evenly spaced during the day, and with hay available at all times. For example, you might wish to feed grain at 6 a.m., then again at noon, and then at the evening feeding at 4 p.m. However, if a horse con- sumes too much hay when it is available at all times, a little hay should be fed after the morning feed, some after the morning exercise, then again after the mid-day feed, and the major portion of the hay should be fed in the evening. (Please refer to the chart which accompanies this chapter for recommended poundage of hay for horses at different stages of development.)

The importance of routine in the feeding program should not be over- looked. Horses, by reputation and reality, are creatures of habit. They have an internal clock that functions very well on a set routine. A horse normally will do better in any nutrition program which is a matter of routine; that is, when he is fed at the same times of the day and in the same manner.

There is little to be gained by introducing variety to a horse's diet. In fact, it often can be dangerous. Some variety may be necessary if the horse does not eat well on a regular diet, but any horseman should be careful when making dramatic changes in a horse's diet.

A horse could grow to maturity, live out his life to the full term, and be content with the same kind of grain and hay every day of his life — and his productivity might not be affected. It is not necessary for him to have variety. This is a human concept we often attribute to the horse. A horse can be quite productive and happy eating the same thing every day.

That is not to say that a horse will not respond to change. This is particularly true in the case of an animal who is being fed a poor-quality feed, such as a very stemmy hay. If you introduce a high-quality alfalfa or alfalfa/clover hay to his diet, he will eat like he never has. This would also happen if a horse was receiving a ration of poor-quality oats and was suddenly given a high-quality sweet feed. But if you feed high-quality oats and a top-quality hay, a horse can thrive and perform for you without ever needing any variety in his diet.

WHAT TO DO ABOUT THE "POOR DOERS"

From time to time, every horseman is faced with a horse who will not eat. This is particularly true with fillies who have been stressed. It seems that females are more predisposed to have dietary problems than males. The clinical reason for this is not clear, but much of the problem with fillies is attributable to hormonal changes. Many fillies will not eat or perform well, for instance, when they are in a heat cycle.

The question of what to do with horses who eat poorly is really multi-faceted. There are many factors which must be addressed. Among these are:

• The overall quality of the grain being fed. Quite often we find that a poor-quality grain or hay is involved when a horse won't eat.

• Analyzing the vitamin content of feed. For instance, a B-vitamin deficiency often manifests itself in poor appetite.

• A common remedy for a horse who is a poor eater: Add some yeast to the regular ration. This can stimulate the horse's appetite. Brewer's yeast is readily available and can be added to a regular ration in the amount of about one to two ounces per feeding, or about two tablespoons. Brewer's yeast is an excellent source of B vitamins, very important in maintaining a healthy appetite. Another common remedy is to add sliced apples and/or carrots to the grain mixture. The only problem with that is that too many apples or carrots will increase the moisture content of the feed beyond acceptable limits.

• Switching the diet every couple of weeks and experimenting with different types of feed, which may be necessary in some cases. While variety in the diet may not be necessary in normal situations, it may encourage the horse to eat more on odd occasions.

• Remember that the highest quality feed needs to be used for a horse who is a poor eater. In all cases, it is vitally important if a filly will eat only 8-10 pounds daily, to make sure the amount she receives is of the highest quality, with the highest energy density available.

HOW SHOULD THE DAY OFF BE MANAGED?

Most racehorses are on a schedule where they train and/or race six days a week, then are off one day, when they do little except relax in a stall. They can sometimes be turned out in a small paddock and also may be walked and hand-grazed.

Often, their ration is unaffected by the day off. If a racehorse has a day off, I recommend that the grain ration be decreased by almost half. If a horse is getting 12-15 pounds of grain per day, I believe it should receive only half that amount (approximately six to eight pounds) on the off day. The hay ration should be increased on the off day to compensate for the poundage lost due to the reduced grain. Remember, a horse with a full gut will be healthier, happier and more content.

WHAT ABOUT FEEDING ON RACE DAYS?

This is a somewhat controversial question.

Many trainers feed their horses the same amount on race days as they do every other day of the week. This is acceptable if the overall feeding program is a good one. However, the normal feeding pattern is established by horses training in the morning hours. For all of the months leading to racing, the horse is fed on a pattern that includes regular morning workouts.

Once a Standardbred gets to the races, however, this pattern is altered rather dramatically by the fact that most of the racing is at night. This changes the horse's dietary needs, and the hours of ingestion may be dramatically different. Now the horse is required to perform under extreme stress. A change in his dietary program is indicated. But how?

As expected, the time interval between grain feeding and exercise does affect some blood constituents, such as glucose and insulin. What is not clear is how these changes affect performance. The bottom line is, researchers have not determined the optimum time to feed before a race. However, I would suggest feeding grain at least four hours before a race. This gives the horse time to get some benefit from what is ingested. As for hay, the routine should be the same for race day as for non-racing days. I do not recommend taking hay away from a horse on race day.

After the race, there may be an advantage to feeding some grain as soon as the horse has cooled out, or within two hours after it has raced. There is evidence to suggest that a horse may be able to make better use of the feed during this period. Many trainers like to feed a bran mash after their horses race. A handful or two of bran is added to the regular ration, along with some liquid molasses and warm water. This after-racing mixture produces a thick, but rather tasty concoction that many trainers like to use. This practice is acceptable — as long as the ration is in the proper quantity.

The nutrition program of racehorses is one of the greatest variables to performance. A horse's performance may be significantly affected by what he eats and when he eats. I have seen a great many horses leave one stable and go to another, and their performance improves radically, even in a very short period of time. In these instances, I find most often that the horse has gone into the stable of a trainer who has a very good understanding of nutrition and its role in performance.

I believe a good, individual feeding plan for each horse is just as important as the overall conditioning program. I have not seen too many cases of a successful horse being in the stable of a trainer who did not understand the importance of a good feeding program.

A RACEHORSE SHOULD HAVE HAY AT ALL TIMES

If at all possible, a racehorse should have hay available at all times, because this will allow the horse to "graze" as he would in a more natural environment. The availability of free-choice hay for a racehorse can help to remove one of the main causes of colic.

I would caution, however, that access to free-choice hay should only be given if the horse is also consuming his daily ration of grain. A racehorse cannot hold his weight and overall condition on hay alone. He must have the grain to supplement his diet and keep his energy at the required levels. If he eats his hay, but leaves his grain, it may be necessary to cut back on the hay ration until he has cleaned up his grain.

HOW MUCH HAY SHOULD BE FED?

As with grain, the amount of hay to be fed will depend somewhat on the quality. Generally speaking, a horse should be receiving about three percent of his total body weight a day in his total diet.

For instance, a young racehorse who weighs around 1,000 pounds should have a total diet of about 30 pounds of hay and grain daily. This might be reflected in 20 pounds of hay in combination with 10 pounds of grain. As the workload increases, the ratio of hay to grain should decrease. An increased level of grain will be necessary to provide the energy required. As the horse grows and his body weight goes up or down his ration should be changed as needed.

Let me also mention at this time that is very important for a racehorse to receive a good quality hay in order to sustain appropriate calcium levels in his diet. I actually prefer a combination hay of alfalfa and orchard grass for most racehorses. Alfalfa/timothy combinations are also good in some instances, although some alfalfa and timothy varieties have different maturation rates. If the alfalfa is ready to cut, the timothy may not be, and vice versa. This makes it more difficult for the alfalfa and timothy combination hays to be cut where optimum quality can be achieved. Alfalfa and clover hays are generally of the highest quality, because they have the largest levels of protein, energy and calcium. They are also high in vitamin A. However, they may have too high a level of protein and calcium for racehorses.

Grass hays are cheaper, but they are cheaper because they do not provide the same kind of quality nourishment available in the legume (alfalfa and clover) hays. For instance, the calcium level of the average grass hay may only be 20 percent of that of the legume hays in some parts of the country. A combination in the type of hay provided to the racehorse will provide a better-balanced diet.

Generally speaking, hay which is the result of the second and third cuttings of any field will be the highest quality. First-cutting hay can be weedy and fourth-cutting hay generally comes at a time when curing conditions are poor. The second- and third-cutting hays mature and cure at the optimum times. Any horseman should question his vendor with respect to the age and condition of the hay and when it was cut. There is also a strong visual aspect to determining whether you are buying an average hay, or a very high quality hay. A competent horseman will learn to recognize what his horses will eat and what they will leave to be pitched out with the manure.

I firmly believe that horses who are confined to stalls should have free access to hay at all times. These horses will be happier, less bored, and more importantly, will have normal gut function.

The controversial part of this subject concerns the practice of many trainers in taking a horse's hay away from him on race day. The theory behind this is that the horse should race as lean as possible. However, because of the horse's slow digestive rate, this practice will not make much difference in the weight of the horse. Also, as I noted earlier, this can be dangerous with regard to the onset of colic after strenuous exercise.

What is really important is the proper maintenance of weight. A horse trainer must balance the desired ability to have a lighter horse at race time with the desire to have a horse with adequate muscle and energy stores able to meet the demands of racing. I would encourage experimentation in attempting to determine the optimum racing weight of an individual horse, because no two horses are going to react in the same way.

An analogy is often offered in regards to the practice of racing Greyhounds "lean," and the fact that the leaner dog often will outrun one who is not as lean. This analogy is full of troubling comparisons when applied to racehorses.

First of all, dogs are carnivores, and carnivores have always existed on a pattern of gorging after the kill, so to speak, then not eating for days. A racing Greyhound, in fact, may do very well racing "lean" for this reason. Horses, however, are not carnivores. The horse is a herbivore, a domesticated grazer who will do best when he is allowed free choice to his food sources.

CARBOHYDRATE LOADING?

I also am often asked about the adaptability of the practice of carbohydrate loading, which is practiced by human distance runners, to the racehorse diet.

The theory is that human distance runners have found they can improve their overall performance by loading up on carbohydrates for a period of 24 hours preceding competition. Carbohydrates are important in this equation because they increase the energy stores in the muscle. This increase gives the human athlete extra staying power over long distances.

In my opinion, the practice of "carbo-loading" is not applicable to the racehorse. What racehorses do more nearly approximates what human sprinters are asked to do, rather than distance runners, and it has not been demonstrated that carbohydrate loading improves the performance of sprinters. Therefore, it would seem to have little adaptability to the racehorse nutrition issue.

AN OFTEN OVERLOOKED ALTERNATIVE

There is another area, however, that is often overlooked in equine nutrition. And that is the subject of fat in a racehorse's diet.

The normal diet of a racehorse does not contain much fat. Oats, for example, contain less than five percent fat. But fat can be used effectively in a racehorse because fat contains energy. And energy is critical to the performance of any horse.

How do we get fat into a horse's diet?

The best source of fat for horses would be liquid vegetable oils, such as corn or soybean oil. Corn oil is preferred slightly over soy oil by horses. Soybean meal, on the other hand, is not a source of fat, as most of the fat has been extracted. Soybean meal is a good source of protein, but there is very little fat left. Animal fats are less digestible by horses and their use is less preferred.

A horse may enjoy up to 10 percent of his total diet in fats or oils and could probably eat a half-pound of fat (or oil) for every five pounds of feed. We have long known the value of soybean meal and soy oils in making a horse "bloom" and look better, with a healthier coat, but the fat stores of soy oil could also greatly affect performance.

One of the drawbacks to introducing fat or oil into the diet is that some horses will not eat it if it is added to the grain. It will be impossible to feed a lot of fat since the horse simply will not eat it, but a small percentage of fat can be of great help.

An easy test to determine if your racehorse could use some fat in his diet is if he is eating everything you give him, including high-quality hay and grain, and salt and other additives, but is still losing weight. The addition of oil to his diet may be of some benefit. You may also want to assess his overall health, including the possible presence of parasites. Proper worm control is not strictly a nutritional issue, but is certainly a major player in a horse's overall health. If you give more feed to a horse who is wormy, you simply end up feeding the worms and not the horse!

"HAY, OATS AND WATER"

We all have heard this expression.

There are those in the horse business who believe that racehorses should only receive hay, oats and water. They believe there should be no feed additives, minerals, or other dietary aids except for the basic food stuffs.

This is an unrealistic point of view.

It is virtually impossible for a horse to perform at a high level without vitamin and mineral supplementation. Racehorses' requirements for vitamins, particularly vitamins A and E, may not be met by a diet of hay, oats and water. Vitamin A is sufficient in good-quality alfalfa hay, but vitamin E often is not. The B vitamins are also important for a horse, as are many of the trace minerals.

These trace minerals include iron, manganese, zinc, iodine, copper, selenium and cobalt. Racehorses also have definite requirements for the macro-minerals such as calcium, phosphorus, sodium and chloride (salt), magnesium and potassium. (Please refer to the table of nutrient requirements for a guide to levels of the proper minerals.) A horse with a phosphorus deficiency, for example, will manifest this by becoming a wood chewer. Other important minerals for horses that are directly tied to performance are selenium and vitamin E. These are very important for the integrity of muscle tissue.

A vitamin-E deficiency, for example, often manifests itself in repeated episodes of "tying up." A long-term vitamin-E deficiency can cause real problems from which it will take a long time to recover. Nutritional balance is an important component in the overall fitness of the animal.

While many nutrients can be supplied by hay, oats and water, these feed stuffs alone are low in not only some vitamins, but also many of the more important trace minerals, most particularly zinc, iodine, copper and selenium.

HOW CAN WE DETERMINE IF NUTRITION IS IN BALANCE?

The simplest way to determine if a horse's nutrition requirements are being met is to simply assess his performance and his overall physical condition. The chances are very good that if a horse is competing at a very high level, is holding his weight, has a good sheen to his hair coat and a willing attitude, his nutritional requirements are being met. In other words, you can tell by looking!

One of the most common problems with racehorses is the presence of a very loose and watery stool. That is, the feces are eliminated in a watery stream instead of the firm excrement normally associated with healthy horses. This is a certain sign that some kind of nutritional or health problem is troubling a horse.

It could indicate a poorly balanced diet that does not include enough fiber, or that the horse is getting too much grain and not enough hay. Or it may indicate that the hay is very rich in protein. This also can be seen if the horse is allowed to graze in large quantities of grass in very lush pastures.

It could also indicate the presence of some kind of bacterial infection. In that case, the condition will persist and the administration of antibiotics is indicated to remedy the problem. In some serious cases, powerful broad spectrum antibiotics which may be required will also kill off some of the good bacteria present in the horse's gut. If this is the case, recovery time is extended until the good bacteria have a chance to recover in the digestive system.

IS THERE SUCH A THING AS AN IDEAL WEIGHT?

This is another question that troubles horsemen.

Quite often, I am asked the ideal weight for a racehorse. This is a subjective question which cannot be addressed generally. Certain horses will perform well while carrying a good deal of weight. Others may only succeed if they are a lot leaner.

Much of this is breed specific and, more importantly, specific to the individual horse. By that, I mean certain types of horses seem to do better at certain weights. Many offspring of certain stallions seem to do better while carrying a little extra weight. This is true in Standardbreds with a horse such as Abercrombie, for example. His get seem to race better if they carry a lot of flesh.

If a trainer hopes to succeed with one of these horses, he will need to be conscious of the body type of successful horses sired in the same family. This also can be true of the maternal influences. In principle, the ideal weight for a racehorse is when there is enough flesh to allow for good muscle definition, but no appearance of excess fat. I like a horse not to show any rib, but the ribs can be felt just under the skin. A horse who is too thin will have poor muscle development, and good musculature is absolutely imperative for a horse to perform at a high level.

A horse will need a little reserve during the racing season. It may be desirable, therefore, to enter the racing season with a little extra flesh to give the horse something to draw on during the season. It should also be noted that horses with soundness problems should never be too heavy, as this will affect their ability to overcome the unsoundness.

GROWTH PATTERNS OF THE YOUNG HORSE

It is vitally important to understand that there are two ways in which horses grow.

A horse grows by gaining both weight and height. The weight gain is gradual, but more rapid, the younger the horse is. A young horse in his first months of life, for instance, should be gaining weight at an average of about three pounds/day. A yearling, however, should gain only about one pound/day. I have often heard horsemen say that a horse should be fed a pound of grain for each 100 pounds of weight. This can be a problem because, unless a scale or weight tape is used, a horse's weight can be hard to assess.

An easier guide, perhaps, is to use one pound of grain for each month of age. A six-month old weanling should be getting about six pounds a day, for example.

On the other hand, it is important to understand that a horse grows in height sporadically—in quite rapid spurts — and may also grow disproportionately. We have all seen young horses whose hind quarters are higher than their withers. Later on, the horse grows at the withers to catch up. This growth can be dramatic and can be affected by feeding patterns.

Water and energy are still the most important nutrients for a young horse, but protein is more critical for the growing horse than for mature horses. The earlier the stage of development, the more protein is required. In fact, the younger the horse is, the higher the concentrations of all nutrients required. Protein is very important to young horses because it is critical to muscle development. Protein is required to build muscle. As we all know, there is some misconception as to how much protein is sufficient for a young horse.

Excessive protein and energy may contribute to rapid weight gain. This rapid weight gain can, in turn, lead indirectly to skeletal problems with the horse. There are no studies, however, that indicate a direct link between excessive protein levels and skeletal problems, such as OCD lesions.

FEEDING GUIDELINE

	Average Amount of Feed (lb/day)	Crude Protein of Feed (%)	Amount of Hay or Pasture Equivalent (lb/day)
Maintenance	4	10.0	18
Stallion	6	12.0	16
Pregnant Mare	7	14.0	16
Lactating Mare	11	14.0	18
Light work	6	10.0	15
Medium Work	10	10.0	15
Intense Work	14	10.0	15
Weanling, 4 month	5	16.0	9
Weanling, 6 month	7	16.0	9
Yearling, 12 month	8	14.0	12
Yearling, 18 month	8	14.0	14
Two year old	8	12.0	14

*	This Guideline is for Standardbreds, average mature body weight of 1200 lb.
*	The hay in this Guideline is a good quality mixed hay. As the hay quality drops, the amount of feed will need to increase and a higher protein level may also be required. Conversely, better quality hay can reduce the quantity of feed needed and may also allow for a lower protein feed.
*	The feed should be of good quality and fully fortified with proper levels of vitamins and minerals.
*	The amounts of feed in this Guideline are meant as starting point only. Individual horse needs will vary, therefore feeding should be adjusted per individual.
*	The range of feed required is wide. For "easy keepers" on excellent hay or pasture, the amount of feed may be halved. On the other hand, with extremely poor hay or pasture, the amount of feed may need to be doubled.

One of the problems with the study of development of young horses is that there is a great deal of variability in the quality of pasture, hay and grain in the various regions of the country where horses are raised.

A good, well-maintained pasture may contain as much as twice the daily minimum requirement for protein levels. A horse on pasture of this quality will have no need for additional high concentrations of protein in his grain and hay. A poor-quality pasture may be as low as only half the daily requirement of protein. A young horse raised on pasture of this kind will have significant, additional protein demands if he is to grow to the fullest possible development. If the pasture is of poor quality, there is no problem with feeding a higher protein-content grain.

(Please refer to the chart which accompanies this chapter for appropriate protein levels for horses of all ages and workloads.)

Let us look at the issue of protein levels in a little more detail.

The solid portion of mare's milk (milk is about 90 percent water) contains about 20 percent protein, and some clover and alfalfa hay of superior quality can have protein content of as high as 30 percent, although the average for alfalfa hay is probably around 18 percent. Therefore, it is vitally important that you know the protein content of the foodstuffs your horses are being fed.

If a horse is getting a grain with about 12 percent protein, and is also getting a good alfalfa hay with a high protein value, he will probably be getting more protein than his body needs.

In the case of a racehorse or broodmare who is housed in a box stall for any period of time, there is any easy, telltale sign that a horse is getting excessive protein. There should be some ammonia odor in a horse's urine naturally, but if the odor is overpowering when you open up a stall at cleaning time, that horse is getting more protein than necessary.

A final point on feeding a young horse is probably appropriate here. The horsemen who do the best job raising young horses are the ones who realize that feeding according to a chart is appropriate in the case of a "model" horse. However, very few young horses grow exactly according to charts or textbooks. There is no substitute for the daily visual inspection of each horse to determine its progress and to take whatever steps are necessary to ensure the proper growth and development of that animal.

FEEDING THE BROODMARE

I have already addressed the feeding of racehorses and young horses in their early stages of development. Next, I want to address the subject of nutritional requirements of the in-foal broodmare.

The in-foal broodmare has significant nutritional requirements throughout her pregnancy, but the really critical stages of development occur during the last trimester of the pregnancy; that is, during the final three to four months of gestation. During this time, as much as three-fourths of total fetal growth occurs, so the nutritional requirements are significant.

The average in-foal broodmare can be sustained on about seven pounds of 14-percent protein feed daily, combined with good pasture and/or hay. If the pasture or hay is of really high quality, the feed can be lower in both quantity and in protein content. Broodmares, however, require grains of a very high quality supplemented adequately with vitamins and minerals in order to provide the nutrients to themselves and their *in-utero* foals, especially during the critical final trimester.

I recommend to anyone with in-foal broodmares to ascertain the protein levels of grain and to make sure they meet the minimum 14-percent requirement. Optimum foal development *in utero* can only occur in the presence of optimum nutrient levels.

It is also important to note that, before the last trimester of the pregnancy, very little grain should be necessary. Mares in the first two-thirds of the pregnancy should be maintained on good pasture and the use of mineral supplements. This alone can suffice in many cases. Of course, as the availability and/or quality of the forage decreases, additional grain will be necessary.

As winter approaches, and the mare approaches her foaling date, grain, vitamins and trace minerals should be supplemented to her daily diet. And after foaling, a lactating mare will need more feed to sustain herself and the newborn foal. In this instance, as much as 10-12 pounds of feed with 14-percent protein levels is recommended.

PASTURE SHOULD BE WELL-MAINTAINED

If a horse is on pasture primarily during the temperate part of the year, as most broodmares are, the grasses should be well-maintained.

One of the biggest misconceptions regarding nutrition is the picture we all have seen of horses grazing in a pasture with tall, knee-deep grass. This is not the right scenario. Grass pastures should be mowed regularly, because the young, growing grass is where you will find the highest concentrations of protein and other nutrients. The ideal grass height is about eight to ten inches. Grass with long, stemmy shoots is not desirable. Pasture should never be allowed to grow to seed, or to get out of control.

It is vitally important in any situation to know the quality of the foodstuffs a horse receives. If there is any question about this, you can have the grasses, the grains, and the hays analyzed so you know what you are feeding, although a complete analysis of foodstuffs may be cost-prohibitive (about $30 per sample is the going rate at this time for a group of 13 important nutrients and about $20 for each additional nutrient) and probably should only be contemplated in a large horse breeding operation.

For even small operations, however, the group assay on the year's supply of hay will provide the bulk of the important information on the major nutrients.

PELLETED FEEDS—A SOLUTION TO MATTERS OF UNIFORMITY

Because of the great disparity in the quality of oats and the desirability of controlling protein levels consistently, many feed manufacturers have gone to producing pelleted feeds.

Pelleted feeds are very desirable in most cases because they allow for uniformity, the presence of the same nutrient levels in every bite. They generally will not be wasted as readily as regular grain feeds. The more uniform the grain product, the better use that can be made of it. Horses cannot sort through pelleted feed and leave what they do not wish to eat, as they will with sweet feeds and other natural grain mixes. Pelleted feeds are also easier to chew, and this can be a factor in the general health of a horse's teeth. A high-quality pelleted feed can be fed in smaller quantities to achieve the same result, because the horse receives the maximum benefit of what it has been given.

Pelleted feed should be about 1/2-inch in diameter and of the consistency that begins to break down when a little water is added. Such feeds should be large enough to be picked up by a horse easily. The pellets should not be allowed to dry out and harden, because the horse's digestive system will have a difficult time breaking down a hardened, grain-based pellet. There are problems with some pelleted feeds because they are too hard. On the other hand, a pelleted feed which is too soft might arrive at its destination as mostly powder!

In addition, because pellets are created by the introduction of heat and steam, any potentially harmful micro-organisms are killed off. The only caution here is that because the quality of the ingredients are even more difficult to assess than in "sweet feeds," you need to be confident of the manufacturer's integrity and ability to produce a uniform, high-quality pelleted feed.

WHAT ABOUT SWEET FEEDS?

Sweet feeds can be used with racehorses, particularly in instances where some variety in the diet may be necessary to stimulate a horse with poor eating habits.

In the summer, though, sweet feeds can be a problem because of their high molasses content, which can attract flies if the feed is not consumed quickly. In cold weather, the feed may freeze solid.

Having said that, I find no real problem with sweet feed used alone, or in concert with the regular ration of grain. A horseman should be careful not to give too much sweet feed to a horse who is real energetic, real "hyper," or who is really high strung. Sweet feeds are a problem for this type of horse because they provide too much sugar. This extra blood sugar will only make behavioral problems worse.

Sweet feed may be used effectively to stimulate the diet of a horse with poor eating habits, but there are other troublesome problems.

Cribbing or savaging may worsen if you feed molasses, a major component of all sweet feeds. The advice given most commonly is that sweet feeds or molasses should not be used for horses inclined to behavioral problems.

It is particularly important that if a mixture of different kinds of feeds are used, the total weight of ration be monitored closely. For instance, a can of sweet feed will weigh less than a can of racehorse oats or pellets, and a can of corn will be heavier than either oats or pellets. The entire ration will have to be modified to keep the ration at the same poundage.

THE USE OF FIELD CORN

Many horsemen feed field corn on the cob. This is not an inherently unsafe practice, but it does have significant perils.

One of the concerns with field corn is the possible presence of fungal disease, or toxins. If field corn is to be fed, it should be carefully analyzed by a professional to be certain that it is safe to feed. This cannot be accomplished by a simple, visual inspection. Corn may appear normal in color and odor, but possess toxins, some of which are deadly to horses.

Field corn may provide very positive psychological advantages for horses and make them more content, but it is important to use caution in supplementing grain with a lot of corn.

I do not recommend the use of field corn for horses. I believe the risks outweigh the benefits. If the horse needs a lot of grain, oats or pelleted feeds are far safer than field corn. There is less potential for colic. Oats provide relatively high fiber content and contain more protein.

One word of caution is necessary regarding fiber. All other things being equal, the higher the fiber content, the less energy that will be present. However, a fiber content of about eight to ten percent in the total diet is the minimum level for normal gut function. On the other end of the scale, a very stemmy hay is not really good for horses, because it has far too much fiber content. A hay with a good leaf, young stems and immature seed heads is a much more valuable feed.

Hay should also be cured out nicely; that is, it should be dried properly. Properly cured hay is a good source of protein, energy and natural vitamins. Hay that has been rained on can be ruined, because the nutrient content will be less. Worse yet, it may become musty. There is always the potential for toxins to develop in spoiled hay.

There is very little difference in the nutritional quality of hay cubes versus regular field hay. Field hay can be a problem if it is particularly dusty, especially if the horse is having respiratory and allergy problems. If this is the case, the flaked hay should be sprinkled down with water before feeding. Wet hay that is not eaten should be removed from the stall or rack because it will spoil rapidly, especially during hot weather. Cubed hay cuts down on the waste of hay, tends to be less dusty and is a very effective way of keeping a hay ration in front of a horse at all times, the desirability of which I have already discussed.

TRACE MINERALS AND SALTS

One of the great advantages to the feeding of pellets from a reputable manufacturer is that the trace minerals are supplied in a consistent, reliable manner.

The balance of minerals and salts in the total diet is very important. As noted before, a horse needs some of these supplements, but they are not needed in larger quantities than the horse can use. There are certain minimum requirements which should be met, and those are indicated in the table on the next page. Certain trace minerals can be added to feed, but a good deal of attention should be paid to the amounts given in the total ration.

Salt is also vital to a horse's dietary needs, but too much salt added to the ration of grain will restrict the horse's grain consumption. There are a wide range of salts available, from block salt to granular, and from trace mineral salts to plain white.

ACCESS TO GOOD DRINKING WATER IS IMPORTANT

Another important component of horse nutrition is access to plenty of fresh drinking water. This is one of the most overlooked issues in horse nutrition. Water is the most important nutrient.

There are two common sources of drinking water: One is water obtained from wells or from rivers and streams. Well water is available in most rural areas and can be high enough in minerals, such as calcium, to have a significant contribution to the overall diet.

One of the major disadvantages to well water and water from rivers and streams is that it may become contaminated by the runoff of agricultural chemicals or through other ground contaminants. Well water should be tested on a fairly regular basis to determine how safe it is, and to determine its chemical makeup.

The other common source is city water, now also available in most areas and recommended because of the safety factor that is a problem with well water. City water will be fresh, and its overall quality is consistent and easily determined.

There are many areas of the world where the water is of poor quality, and yet good horses can still be raised there. But without water, no horse can be raised.

NUTRIENT CONCENTRATIONS IN TOTAL DIETS FOR HORSES

This table indicates the various stages of development and the minimum nutrient concentrations that are required at those stages. These are nutrient concentrations in the **TOTAL DIET!** This includes grains, feeds, hay, pasture, salt, electrolytes and all other additives.

	Digestible Energy (Mcal/lb)	Crude Protein (%)	Lysine (%)	Calcium (%)	Phosphorus (%)	Magnesium (%)	Potassium (%)	Sodium (%)	Iron (ppm)	Vitamin A (IU/lb)	Vitamin D (IU/lb)	Vitamin E (IU/lb)	Vitamin B1 (ppm)
Maintenance	0.80	7.2	0.25	0.21	0.15	0.08	0.27	0.10	40	750	136	23	3
Stallion	1.00	8.6	0.30	0.26	0.19	0.10	0.33	0.10	40	1080	136	23	3
Pregnant mare	1.00	9.5	0.33	0.41	0.31	0.10	0.35	0.10	50	1510	273	36	3
Lactating Mare	1.10	12.0	0.41	0.47	0.31	0.10	0.38	0.10	50	1240	273	36	3
Light work	1.05	8.8	0.32	0.27	0.19	0.10	0.34	0.30	40	1100	136	36	5
Medium Work	1.10	9.4	0.35	0.28	0.22	0.11	0.36	0.30	40	970	136	36	5
Intense Work	1.20	10.3	0.36	0.31	0.23	0.12	0.39	0.30	40	800	136	36	5
Weanling, 4 month	1.25	13.1	0.55	0.62	0.34	0.07	0.27	0.10	50	650	364	36	3
Weanling, 6 month	1.25	13.1	0.55	0.55	0.30	0.07	0.27	0.10	50	760	364	36	3
Yearling, 12 month	1.15	11.3	0.48	0.40	0.22	0.07	0.27	0.10	50	890	364	36	3
Yearling, 18 month	1.05	10.1	0.43	0.31	0.17	0.07	0.27	0.10	50	930	364	36	3
Two year old	1.00	9.4	0.38	0.28	0.15	0.08	0.27	0.10	50	1080	364	36	3

	Sulfur (%)	Manganese (ppm)	Copper (ppm)	Zinc (ppm)	Selenium (ppm)	Iodine (ppm)	Cobalt (ppm)	Vitamin B2 (ppm)
All Horses	0.15	40	10	40	0.1	0.1	0.1	2

Lysine is an amino acid critical to protein-building.
Mcal/lb = Megacalories per pound.
ppm = parts per million.
IU/lb = International Units per pound.

HOW MUCH WATER SHOULD A HORSE DRINK?

As a general rule, the average Standardbred should consume about ten gallons of water daily. Since the average water bucket is of the five gallon variety, the horse should be drinking the equivalent of two full buckets of water daily. The amount of water required is closely tied to the amount of dry matter consumed by the horse. The rule of thumb is one to two quarts of water for every pound of feedstuff.

Water is vitally important to the horse. He may survive for nearly a month without eating, but he will survive less than a week without water. A horse should, in most cases, have free access to water. There are times when a horse should be denied free access, and most professional horse people are aware of these situations. For example:

A horse should not have free access to water when hot, especially after a period of exertion, such as training and racing. The horse should be "watered out" for a period of roughly one hour with about five to eight swallows of water every 15 minutes or so.

Another situation where free access to water should be denied is after a horse has been without water over a long period of time, such as during a severe winter storm, or after a long ride in a trailer or van. In these instances, a horse may need to be watered out in the manner described in the preceding paragraph.

HAY RACKS, FEED TUBS, WATER PAILS

The types of hay racks, feed tubs and water pails to be used are not as important as the overall nutrition program for horses. However, the racks, tubs and pails can play a role in the efficiency of a horse operation and the overall nutritional condition of the horse.

Hay racks come in all shapes and sizes. Wooden hay racks may contribute to the development of cribbing, even though the major factors in cribbing are boredom, environmental stress and low-fiber diets. There is some evidence that horses who crib have lower baseline endorphin levels, and cribbing releases more endorphins so as to be closer to the levels of non-cribbers. Certainly, the release of endorphins would explain why cribbers become addicted to this activity.

Metal hay racks, therefore, are slightly more desirable and will cut down on the waste of hay products and, perhaps, the incidence of cribbing. Hay bags or hay nets are also acceptable.

Feed tubs should be cleaned on a regular basis and hung at the chest level of the horse. I do not recommend putting feed tubs on the floor of stalls, as this allows a horse to step in the feed and upset the tub, resulting in waste of the feed products. I do not have a preference as to the types of feed tubs. Hard plastic, metal and rubber tubs are a little easier to maintain than wooden ones, and discourage cribbing. Any feed tub should be large enough for the feed to be spread out to discourage ingestion of large quantities in a very short period.

Water pails should be cleaned regularly and hung at chest level as well. It is a good practice to empty out old water from buckets with every watering or, at the very least, once a day. If a horse does not drink enough water over a period of time, he will not eat correctly.

In pastures where automatic electric waterers are used, there can be maintenance issues as well. These waterers should be cleaned on a regular basis. It is also difficult sometimes to determine how much water is being consumed, since the design of the waterer allows it to re-fill after a quantity has been consumed. Situations have also developed where horses would not drink from the waterers because of an electrical short. The automatic waterers bring with them the responsibility of maintenance and cleanliness.

FEEDING IS MORE ART THAN SCIENCE

As with many things associated with the horse business, there is more art than science in the proper feeding of horses.

Almost any horseman can spot a horse whose diet is grossly deficient. A horse who is dropping weight pretty dramatically is not going to perform at a very high level for an extended period of time. If a horse cleans up his feed regularly, is holding his overall condition, and his hair is slick and shiny and his performance is maintained, it is a good bet his nutritional requirements are being met.

The absence of any of these factors might indicate the presence of a problem associated with nutrition. A good horseman continually monitors results and makes mental notes on the overall appearance of every horse in his care.

With all racehorses, broodmares, and even the young horses, the maintenance of a good diet and good physical appearance is very important. Horses who are overweight will not perform well. Horses who are too thin will suffer.

The most important notion to take away from this entire discussion is that each horse is an individual and should have an individual nutrition program. That is not to say that nutrition patterns are not desirable. They are. But the nutrition patterns need to be specific to the individual horse and his needs.

J ohn Lew's selection to author a
chapter on horse nutrition for
this book was a natural, for he
is one of the industry's leading equine
nutritionists.

Professionally, Lew is a director of
nutrition for McCauley Brothers, internationally acclaimed feed manufacturer located in Versailles, KY. McCauley Brothers is one of the few
feed manufacturers to produce nothing but horse feed products.

In his daily duties, Lew is responsible for the formulation of feed products, quality control in the manufacturing process and the choice of ingredients.

Lew earned his PhD in equine nutrition from the University of Kentucky in 1989, and prior to that he served as a research fellow at UK,
centering his studies on animal science and pharmacology.

He also managed the University of Kentucky horse farm for four years.

Lew's professional expertise in equine nutrition is supplemented by
practical, hands on horse experience. He is a certified riding instructor
and donates much of his spare time to a successful riding program for
the handicapped (Central Kentucky Riding for the Handicapped) which
is located at the Kentucky Horse Park. He is a former steeplechase jockey
and has successfully participated in 3-day eventing and show jumping.
While a student at UK, he also worked at many of the horse sales as a
groom and handler of yearlings, weanlings and broodmares.

Lew was born in Hong Kong but grew up in Melbourne, Australia. He
was graduated from the University of Tasmania with an undergraduate
degree in Agricultural Science.

Lew's mission in this chapter was to remove many of the misunderstandings regarding equine feeding problems and patterns, and to offer
practical guidelines in a non-scientific format on the correct way to feed
racehorses, as well as young horses and broodmares.

9

TRAINING THE PACER

GENE RIEGLE

Training the modern pacer has never been easier. At the same time, training the modern pacer has never been more difficult.

There have been dramatic changes in the way horses are trained and raced in just the last decade. I would have to say that the pacing horse is undergoing changes now that could not have been foreseen by me, let alone my father or grandfather when they trained horses years ago.

I know that I manage my own stable remarkably different from the way I did just a few years ago, and I feel that every single thing I have learned in my career has been questioned, analyzed and evaluated over the past decade. In fact, some of my methods have been discarded because they do not apply to the modern horse. I have also added many things to my arsenal, tricks I picked up by observing, reading, and paying attention to other successful trainers.

I have been extremely fortunate to have owners who have been willing to change along with me. In some instances, my owners have been the instrument of change. I feel like I am one of the few trainers of my generation to have made the leap from the way we managed horses 20-30 years ago to the way we train them today. I am very proud to still be developing champions some 50 years after I started training.

I guess if I had to summarize the big changes in the way the pacing horse of today is different from his ancestors, even his recent ancestors, it would be that today's pacing horse is more naturally-equipped to go fast.

After breaking hundreds of colts and fillies, I can tell you that the modern pacing horse is not as difficult to gait, not as difficult to drive, nor as difficult to hang-up as his ancestors.

Today's horse seems to come with built-in abilities, almost like standard equipment on an upscale car. I think this is true at all levels of our industry. Even the guy training colts in the regional stakes programs is dealing with a more naturally-gifted horse now than he was in the past. Horses go faster at all levels.

I marvel constantly at how much our breed has improved over the past two decades. A cheap pacing horse now is capable of a 1:55 mile. That fact would have set me back, to think about it, just a few years ago.

Because of this, today's trainer is more a manager of speed than a creator of speed. In the past, we really had to work to create or find speed in a pacer even when he might not have been naturally-gifted. The colts I am breaking every fall now have a lot more natural ability and much more of a natural inclination to hit the pace.

Today's trainer will tell you that the pacing colt usually comes with speed, and getting him to the races is a matter of managing the speed in such a way as to maximize the horse's potential.

I can also tell you that my horses today go more jog miles and fewer training miles than they did just a few years ago. This is more than a fad and will become more and more the standard operating procedure in the future.

This is especially true for horses who are racing. It used to be that every horse in my stable trained between starts. Now, most of my horses only jog between races. The racing is just too hard on them, at the speeds of today, for them to train hard as well.

For instance, I could never have conceived that I would go only a single warm up mile before starting a horse in the Little Brown Jug. But that is what I did with Life Sign.

On the afternoon he won the Jug, Life Sign warmed up by jogging three miles and then went a single warm up mile in 2:25, before he won the fastest Jug heat in history. I have started a lot of horses in the Jug, but never started one before off a single warm up mile.

To continue my point, Life Sign did not train the week of his Jug victory either. After racing him the previous week at Hazel Park in the Jug prep race, I did not train him again before the Jug. John Campbell raced him for me in Detroit, and told me he was as good then as he had been earlier in the summer.

I only had six days with Life Sign before the Jug, and decided to just jog him into that race. The fact that he went such a remarkable pair of heats to win the Jug is testimony to my point.

Horses formerly needed a lot of work to get sharp and stay that way, but I believe the modern pacer has the speed built into him.

BREAKING THE YEARLINGS

While some of my training methods have changed over the years, my methods and techniques of breaking colts and starting them off has changed very little.

I trained for years at my home in Greenville, Ohio, but I now winter train in Florida. However, the techniques used in breaking and gaiting colts are the same ones I have employed my entire life as a horse trainer.

Let me point out right here that I think the type of groom that you put on a yearling makes a great deal of difference. I want a groom who is easy with a colt, who doesn't slap him or knock him around. I think this is very important. A lot of women make good grooms for these babies, especially the fillies.

During the winter, my grooms usually have two to three horses; maybe more, depending on the ability of each groom. I like a groom to have one or two three-year-olds and a single two-year-old.

This is important in scheduling the work, because a groom with a couple of two-year-olds might cause you a scheduling problem with the rest of your stable roster.

A groom who has an older horse and a two-year-old will not have many conflicts because I schedule the stable work so the older horses train on Monday and Thursday and the two-year-olds train on Tuesday and Friday. Wednesday and Saturday are reserved for bad weather days.

The first thing I do, like most trainers, is to ground break my pacers. This period might last as long as a month, depending upon the progress being made by a particular horse.

When I first break a horse, I like to do it in a paddock or some kind of enclosed, fenced area. That way, if something goes wrong and the horse gets loose, it will be in an enclosed area and will normally avoid injury. It can get pretty hairy in the fall at some of the training centers, as there seems to be a loose horse at least once a day. That is why I prefer an enclosed area for the first few sessions of ground-breaking.

During this time, you're also teaching a colt to turn properly, along with stopping, standing and moving off. A colt needs to learn to turn in both directions comfortably before I go to the racetrack with him.

I am very cautious with a yearling at this stage and conscious of not forcing anything on him. He should be taught to stop and stand, as well as to go forward. This is a lost art with some horse trainers. A truly classy horse should learn to stop and stand quietly in the harness. A colt that has to be hooked to a jog cart or have his head checked on the move eventually is going to be more trouble than you may wish to handle. I like to teach a horse to stand while being hooked, and to stand still after his overcheck is fastened.

It used to be standard procedure for me to keep a colt on a set of long lines for a long period of time, but I have found over the past few years that I am hooking my colts now after only a couple of days on the long lines.

There are still some tough ones that require a little more, especially a colt or filly that has not been through the yearling sales process. I end up breaking a bunch of homebred colts and fillies each year for various clients and myself, and I find I have to take a little longer each fall with them than the colts who have been through the sales process. Sales colts have been handled a lot and are accustomed to people.

There is no real secret to teaching a colt to turn. I like to see a colt respond to light pressure on the bit, and generally, if I take my time with a colt he will respond to the bit pressure after only a couple of sessions. The Standardbred of today is a pretty smart horse. He learns very quickly.

One of the major advantages in teaching yearlings to turn today is that you can get jog carts with the shafts bobbed off at a point just beyond where the harness connects. This so-called "quick-hitch" is a revolution in design that not only saves time, but is user-friendly for the horse. It

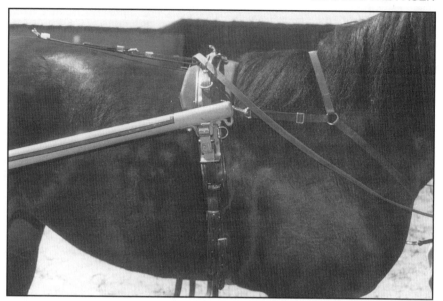

*The author recommends the use of "quick-hitch" harness. The jog cart
shaft simply snaps into position on the harness. This design also lessens
the problems of horses being difficult to turn because of long jog cart shafts.
The "bobbed" shaft is also safer in the event of an accident.*

eliminates the sometimes uneven way a horse used to get tied into a
conventional-shafted jog cart. I don't know who came up with the idea,
but it was a great invention.

If you don't have a jog cart with the shafts cut off at the tips, just
remember to hook a yearling out a little further in the shafts the first few
times you hook him. You do this by simply tying down the harness out
toward the end of the shafts instead of at the normal position.

By doing this, the shafts will not dig into a colt's neck and will not
offer any resistance when he tries to turn. This should lessen the problems you have in teaching him to turn.

Some of the tougher yearlings, particularly those that won't move once
you get to the track, have to be towed behind a truck or jeep vehicle. I
don't like doing this because there is a real risk of injury to the horse.
Sometimes, however, you use up all your other options and it simply makes
sense to pull a yearling behind a truck.

There is, of course, a right and a wrong way to do this. Be careful to tie
the horse to the vehicle in such a way that you will not injure him should
he get down. You also want to guard against him getting loose from the
truck.

To ensure against both of these problems, I like to tie a colt to the
truck with a rope running from his stall halter, but I also like to loop a

second rope around the horse's neck that will prevent him from getting loose should he break the primary rope leading from his stall halter.

One such case was the well-bred filly Bashful Angel. In plain words, she was a hellcat. She wanted to hurt her groom, her trainer, or anyone around her. She also was one of the worst I've ever had for kicking. I had a pickup truck with a starting gate on it at Greenville, Ohio, where I trained then, and if I hadn't used that with her, I never would have been able to break her.

I would put the harness and hobbles on her, hook her to the arm of that makeshift gate and simply let her fight that, instead of fighting her trainer. She lasted about 30 to 40 days behind that truck.

Bashful Angel was a real fooler, because you could jog her five or six miles a day behind the truck and think that you had taken the fire out of her. But then the minute you'd touch her, she would squeal and start kicking.

It was a long time behind the truck for her, but it paid off. She eventually became a good filly, got a 1:55.3 mark as a three-year-old and earned over $173,000. She also has made quite a good broodmare. One of her foals, a Tyler B colt named Gamma Ray, was good enough to win an elimination of the Little Brown Jug.

BLIND BRIDLES A MUST

I always break my yearlings in a blind bridle. I have had good results over the years with the blind bridle and heartily recommend its use in the early stages of training. I like a blind bridle on yearlings because they can see enough ahead of them to avoid trouble, but can't see behind them. It helps to keep their concentration focused.

After the harness and bridle have been on for a few days, it is a good idea to put the equipment on a yearling, and leave him loose in his stall for a short period of time with his head checked.

I am careful at this point to not have the overcheck too short. Make sure the colt can get his head down to a normal, alert position. Don't have the check so long that he can get his head down below his shoulder, but don't have him checked too high, either. If you attempt to get a colt's head too high to start with, you can create all kinds of problems. Just let him have his head at a normal position.

Using blind bridles also helps you with the annual war that must be staged between a trainer, a colt, and draw gates. Colts that don't wear blind bridles are going to find out where home is pretty quick, and they will test you to see if they can run out draw gates.

Wearing a blind bridle on a colt aids the trainer in this annual battle. Colts seem to carry their heads a little straighter, look down the racetrack more, and tend to their business a little better while wearing a blind bridle.

A colt who starts to jog pretty aggressively in a blind bridle can be a problem because I don't want to teach him to latch on to me. So, with a colt like that, I will either go to a Kant-See-Bak bridle or an open bridle.

In Florida, my training barn sits adjacent to the mile track I use for training, so this is an area of particular concern for me. To avoid having colts running off the track near the training barn, I take advantage of an inside cinder jog track. I use that to bring the colts off the track first, then cross the main track and come to the barn.

In the early training period, all the yearlings leave the track to the inside. None of them come directly off the track and to the barn. If you do not have an inside track like this, I recommend that you always drive a colt by a draw gate, then circle him back, and let him walk out the gate. I do not recommend driving a colt down the outside of the track, then turning out the draw gate. This can lead pretty quickly to a colt wanting to run out. It is also useful to teach a colt that as long as he is jogging he will not come off the track. If you teach him that the only time he will come off is when he is walking, it will go a long way toward solving the draw gate problem.

My trainers and I drive everything ourselves the first time. As a matter of fact, I don't ever have a groom jog a two-year-old until we get to the races. It is very important for the head trainer and his assistants to jog a two-year-old each morning.

If the only time you see a colt is on the day he trains, I don't see how you can judge his development, his gait and his overall attitude.

This surprises people, but it's the way I have always managed my stable. I remember back when I didn't have much help, and I did things this way. I would ride behind 15 or 16 horses each day.

The reason I did this is I believed that colts might get bad habits from being jogged by grooms. Bad habits can become a real problem and can be hard, if not impossible, to break.

The yearlings might start turning their heads, or get on one line with a groom, who may not be alert enough to pick that up. Sometimes a horse can get away with being lazy with a groom, but a trainer won't tolerate that and will make the colt step right along. This is a very critical stage of training. I am getting a colt mannered and putting a mouth on him, and I don't want my young horses in the hands of an untrained groom.

START THEM OFF BAREFOOTED

After the colts are broken and I'm ready to start the ritual of getting them to the races, I start my pacers off barefooted in front, but with a heavy half-round, half-swedge shoe on their rear feet. If your training track has a good cushion, their front feet won't break up. If a yearling has sharp edges on his front feet after you remove his front shoes, just rasp down the edges a little with a conventional hoof file. Rounding their feet off should prevent any significant problem from a hoof breaking off. I

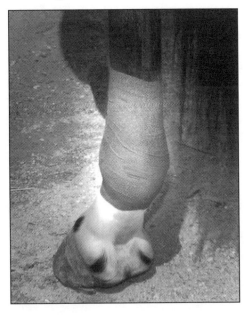

One of the common problems for pacers is the tendency of a low-heeled horse to hit the track with the back of the ankle joint. This can be detected by the presence of dirt on the ankle at the conclusion of racing or a training session. For such horses, a run-down bandage can be used to lessen the irritation caused by the contact with the track.

don't put front shoes on until I am ready to hang a pair of hobbles on my pacers.

As a general rule, my pacers are shod about once a month while in training, and about every two weeks after they get to the races. I don't make a trip to the blacksmith with every horse, but I certainly go with any colt or filly who is having foot problems, or who has a shoeing problem that needs to be addressed.

For most yearlings, the blacksmith keeps a card with that horse's shoe type, toe length and angles. With a colt who is on the road during the racing season, the groom keeps a shoeing card with the colt's records, such as eligibility papers, Coggins test and any other health papers.

Like most horse trainers, I prefer my horses to have low angles on their front feet and higher angles behind. I would say that every horse in my barn will have a front angle in the 48 to 50 degree range and carry a higher angle of about 53 to 55 degrees behind.

Life Sign, for instance, had a low, 47-degree angle in front and a 53-degree angle behind. I would have liked to have a little higher angle behind on him, but he beat his heels down a little and I could never get his angle up where I wanted it. This is why he wore a set of run-down bandages, to protect his hind ankles.

He was always showing me a little dusting of dirt on the underneath side of his hind ankles where his hind foot struck the track. If I could have gotten a higher angle on him behind, he would not have needed the run-down bandages.

I LIKE ALUMINUM SHOES

I am a big believer in aluminum shoes for racing a horse. Life Sign, Artsplace, Western Hanover and Leah Almahurst each won over $1 million while wearing aluminum shoes, and that's enough proof for me!

I also am a big believer in borium tips for shoes, regardless of whether you are training in a warm or cold climate. In a cold climate, you will probably need the borium just to get back and forth from the track on slick roads.

In a warmer climate, you may not want to use the borium. Whatever way you shoe a colt, you want to avoid allowing him to slip as he tries to pull himself down the track.

A lot of people don't understand the nature of a horse's gait. It is just as important for a horse to get a hold of the track in front as it is for him to get a hold behind. A horse must get a hold behind because that is where a great deal of the push comes from as the horse moves down the track.

But a horse also is pulling with his front end, and traction for the front feet is very important, too. A horse who slips when he attempts to pull forward is going to develop some muscle soreness or a problem with his knees, ankles or suspensories.

If I use borium tips, I like to apply two points, or spots of borium on the toe of the shoe, and one each on either side of the heel. I have to admit that over the past few years, I have gotten away from using borium as much as I used to. My colts training in Florida on a clay track wear a flat, training plate shoe with a crease in the toe. I would not recommend the use of borium tips for young horses training on dirt tracks. It will stop them too quickly, and would provide too much stress for their young bones.

The clay track I train on has great tackiness to it, and the flat plate shoe is very compatible with that surface. Your choice of shoes will really depend on what type of surface you train over.

For instance, if you train on limestone, a flat plate shoe probably would not work. You would probably have to go to a full swedge shoe or an aluminum shoe with borium or a grab, or both. With a plate shoe on limestone, a colt would probably get to skating around on you and slipping, which could create real problems.

SHADOW ROLLS & HEADPOLES—STANDARD EQUIPMENT

Most of my pacing colts end up wearing a shadow roll at some time in their lives and it's best to get them used to it at a very early stage in training. I like a shadow roll because a colt doesn't learn to jump things, both real and imagined, if he wears a shadow roll. A colt who learns to jump tire tracks can be a real adventure to drive. I put a shadow roll on early and avoid that problem. Not every pacing horse needs one, of course,

The author believes that a shadow roll is a necessary part of a pacer's every-day equipment. The illustration at the left shows a shadow roll that does not allow a horse to see things directly in front of him on a low sight line. The illustration at the right shows the same shadow roll but from a side view. Both views of the shadow roll show it to be positioned incorrectly. The shadow roll is setting too high on the nose and this restricts the forward vision.

but it is an insurance policy against trouble.

I like to break colts to a shadow roll in the stall. I use old shadow rolls fixed to the stall halter first to get a colt used to the roll. Just let him wear it in the stall for a couple of days. The important thing to remember about using a shadow roll the first time is to not put it too high on the horse's nose and restrict his vision too much.

Most of the problems that develop with shadow rolls come from the fact that trainers put them up too high on the nose and a colt can't see over them properly. When just starting out, put the shadow roll just above the horse's nostrils and then move it up gradually until it produces the desired results.

Most of my horses will wear two headpoles—one on either side. I think this comes with our Meadow Skipper blood today. I think every Meadow Skipper-line horse I ever trained eventually wore two headpoles. I much prefer headpoles to the use of severe driving bits. I like to teach a colt to carry his head straight. Two headpoles do a much more effective job of that than some kind of side-reining bit or other combination of driving and overcheck bits.

A Murphy blind is also useful in keeping a horse's head straight, because the Murphy blind restricts a horse's vision and forces him to have his head straight to see. If a colt wearing a Murphy blind turns his head, he won't be able to see. The colt doesn't like this, of course, and turns his

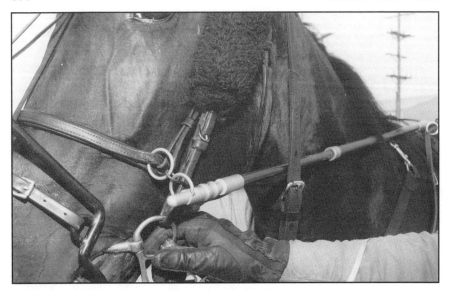

Headpoles are also standard equipment in the author's stable. The headpole should be attached in this manner. Note that the rings are ahead of the bridle cheek piece in order to avoid interference with the bridle's function. This is a so-called "loose" headpole in that it is fastened to a double ring. The headpole can also be attached to the ring directly tied to the head halter to provide more resistance.

head back in order to see again.

You want to use the Murphy blind on the opposite side of the problem. If a colt is carrying his head off to the right side, for instance, you put the Murphy blind over his left eye, which causes him to turn his head back to the left in order to see.

The Murphy blind also can be particularly useful in helping a horse get by draw gates. You may find the Murphy blind is not useful in straightening a horse's head, because not every horse responds the same way to these tricks. But even if the Murphy blind does not help a colt straighten his head, it will block his vision to the outside of the track and he will be unable to see a draw gate.

Generally speaking, however, it's been my policy to break my pacers to two headpoles, and that usually eliminates the need for Murphy blinds and /or severe bits.

When breaking a colt to a headpole, I put the headpole on in the stall the first time. The headpole is never attached too tight, to begin with. What I do is attach an additional small ring to the ring which comes on the head halter, and clip the headpole to the smaller ring. This puts enough pressure on the neck to teach a horse to carry his head straight without putting him into too tight a situation. If a colt feels too confined, he may come to resent the headpole and give you a lot of trouble.

START OFF WITH LEATHER BITS

The colts in my stable start off with leather bits. I learned about leather bits from John Simpson, Sr., one of the greatest horse trainers in history.

The leather-covered bit is a little kinder and easier on a colt's mouth during the early part of training and really helps to develop a good mouth on most horses.

Some trainers prefer to use a snaffle bit with a latex covering, but I don't feel the latex works the same as a leather bit. The latex can get real sticky and grab the skin on a horse's mouth. This can create sores or act as an irritant. The leather bit, properly cared for, stays nice and supple, and will move more freely in a colt's mouth.

Of course, one secret to using a leather bit is caring for it properly. It cannot be dipped in a water bucket to rinse it off the way a steel bit can, and it cannot be treated with a leather conditioner, either. Like anything else that is leather, dipping the bit in water will eventually dry it out and crack it. To avoid this, clean a leather bit by simply wiping off the bit with a damp cloth. With good care, a leather bit can last up to two years.

I normally use a leather bit on a young horse until I start to "baby-race" him. When a colt responds to racing and starts to get a little more aggressive, I will start using a Swedish snaffle bit, which gives me more control.

Although I start my colts out using a plain overcheck, most of them end up wearing a Crit Davis overcheck bit before too long. The Crit Davis overcheck bit is a nice cross between mild and severe. If a colt sets his head nicely and doesn't hog down into the Crit Davis, he won't feel anything. But if he does, the Crit Davis overcheck will remind him to keep his head up.

I know there is a lot of discussion these days about horses being able to get their heads down, but I firmly believe that horses train and race better for me, are better-balanced and better-mouthed, with their heads up in the air.

I have always believed that a colt will develop back problems if you don't do something to get his head up. When a colt starts to hog down into an overcheck, he is also exerting pressure on the crupper, and pretty soon he may have problems with back soreness.

HOBBLES—WHEN AND HOW?

I won't put hobbles on all my pacers right away. In fact, I generally hitch them a time or two before deciding. If a colt keeps switching back and forth between pacing and trotting, I like to get the hobbles on as quickly as possible. If a colt is naturally a free-legged pacer, I will wait a couple of days before putting the hobbles on, but, believe me, the hobbles are going on. They are a basic, fundamental part of a pacer's equipment. Let him get used to them as soon as possible.

In most cases when the hobbles go on for the first time, the colt is line-driven in them even if he has been hitched for some time. You cannot assume that a colt who behaves nicely without the hobbles will behave nicely once the hobbles are added. Usually, I like to get the first pair of hobbles on a colt within the first two weeks of his initial training.

Putting the hobbles on a colt for the first time and heading straight to the track can sometimes end up in a pretty serious problem. Particularly with fillies, the hobbles can frighten a horse the first time it really stretches them. This can lead to a run-away, or serious kicking problem, or both. A little caution here can go a long way.

Most colts these days hit the pace pretty naturally, but occasionally you have a yearling that is racky-going or mixey-gaited, and the hobbles seem to be of little assistance. These are the ones that need a little help.

It is rare these days, but it used to be common practice to have to help a colt hit the pace. The most common aids to helping a colt find his pacing gait are (1) shorten his hobbles; (2) use a heavy shoe behind, say a 9-10 ounce keg shoe that forces more action and allows the horse to hit the pace; (3) use an old-fashioned, sideweight shoe where the thicker part of the shoe is weighted to the outside of the foot; and (4) go to a leather hobble.

Some horses just need time to find themselves. If I have exhausted the above remedies and a colt still has not hit the pace, he is telling me that he needs some time or possibly has a veterinary problem that might need immediate attention.

This can run the gamut from back soreness to problems with stifles, development of the testicles, or even a problem involving the horse's central nervous system. This is where your experience and instincts as a horse trainer must take over. Patience is normally the best course of action. I have seen a lot of colts that had trouble finding themselves in November become good horses by July, so don't be too panicked if your yearling doesn't hit the pace right away. Trust me, if he is meant to be a good horse, he will be—unless you make a careless mistake with him.

I remember, particularly, when Bilateral was a yearling, I had a very difficult time getting him to hit a smooth pace. I had tried the heavy shoes, and had shortened his hobbles, but he still didn't really suit me. I finally found a remedy.

I still have a couple of pairs of leather hobbles hanging in the equipment room. I don't know anybody who still uses leather hobbles to a great degree, but I find them useful in this kind of situation. The leather hobble is heavier than a plastic hobble, and the leather won't "give" as much as the plastic. Leather hobbles also ride on a horse very nicely and there is much less whip. If a hobble is too long, it can get to slapping against a colt's legs and spook him. You want to avoid this. The leather hobbles provide a little more support for a colt feeling his way along.

I put leather hobbles on Bilateral and it helped him find his gait. After that, getting him going was not a problem, and I eventually got him into a pair of plastic hobbles. But every trainer should have a pair of leather hobbles around, because they really will help certain horses.

As for fitting the hobble to the horse, this is something I judge pretty much by my eye. I watch the colt or filly jog and see how it handles the hobbles. If a colt is fumbling along and his hobbles look long, they need to be taken up. If he is on the pace and looks good, he may want a little more hobble.

One thing I want to avoid is having the hobbles so long that a colt can trot with them on. Again, you have to trust your instincts and observations. A too-tight hobble can start to burn or chafe a horse a little, and if he has a low pain threshold, this can become a problem.

Other than Bilateral, I don't have a story to tell about a real good horse who was a problem to gait. The truth is that all the real stars I have had were pretty much naturally-gaited horses.

THE EARLY TRAINING PERIOD

I don't like to put boots on pacing yearlings at the start, either. By this, I mean I don't like bell boots or quarter boots on a yearling. I might use the light, brown gum bell boots for protection, but not much else. A big, heavy bell boot is going to affect a pacer's gait in front, and you must be careful not to get him going too high.

I also don't like to use the low-cut quarter boots, because they fly off too easily. The opaque, brown gum bell boots are a nice match of form and function, if you will.

Like everybody else, I start off jogging my colts a mile or two, depending upon their condition or attitude. Within a month, I want them built up to where they are jogging four miles a day.

I like jogging four miles a day because it builds a lot of stamina and endurance without overworking the yearling. My normal practice is to use the four miles per day jogging routine until I begin to turn the colts against time.

During the early months of training, the colts jog four miles a day, six days a week, for about ten weeks. That puts between 250 and 300 jog miles in them before I start going timed miles.

This is the same plan I have used for years. I have always prided myself on having well-conditioned horses, and, to achieve that, there are no substitutes for good, tough jog miles.

Ideally, I would like a colt to jog at about a 4:30 mile rate. An older horse should jog at a faster 4:00 rate. You are jogging for condition, and nothing is gained by those lazy, slow jog miles that are friendly to a groom, but do nothing for the horse. After a horse gets to the races, the jog miles as conditioners are less important. But in this early stage of development, the jog miles serve as the foundation for you to build on later. They build wind, put legs under a horse, and increase his lung capacity. All those things equal speed.

AVOID THE TEMPTATIONS

The temptation to start brushing colts along at this stage is overpowering. You always have a colt or two who is a real fast learner. He acts like he wants the work and wants you to cluck to him in order to go fast. This is a temptation that must be avoided. There is nothing to be gained from buzzing a colt along in late winter or early spring. The payoff comes later. Patience is the key.

Another factor at this early stage is that some critical decisions must be made regarding the staking plans for each horse. The first two-year-old payments come due mid-February or mid-March, and while I might have a pretty good idea about what colts are not going to make it by that point, I really have no idea about who the stars will be.

I remember Artsplace very well at two. He was not a real glib training colt. In fact, he was only in my second or third set all winter in Florida. He was lazy, like most of the good Abercrombie colts, and really didn't show me too much. Going slow, he was kind of a sloppy-gaited colt. In fact, I wore a pair of heavy half-round, half-swedge shoes on him behind all winter.

But as Artsplace got nearer and nearer to the races, his gait really improved. I could tell as we cleared 2:10 that he was improving a lot, because he was better-gaited the faster he went. It wasn't until he had started a couple of times that first summer that he really busted loose and made such a great colt.

The two best miles he went that year were his heat of the Fox Stake and, of course, the miracle effort at Pompano Park in the Breeders Crown.

Jeff Fout drove Artsplace for us in the Fox Stake and he drew in the second tier. Artsplace was parked the whole mile and finished in the middle of the track, but he paced around 1:52 in what was then a world record effort by the winner, Deal Direct.

The mile Artsplace went at Pompano in the Breeders Crown really surprised me. I knew he was a sensational colt, and he had already won the Metro for us, but I was not prepared for what he did in that race.

The wind was blowing hard, gusting up to 30-40 miles per hour, and I thought that 1:55 would be enough to win the race under those conditions. John Campbell drove Artsplace for us that night and John put him in high gear, parked everybody, and the colt just kept right on going, setting a world record of 1:51.1f that still stands.

Prior to Life Sign's win in the Little Brown Jug in 1993, I thought Artsplace's race at Pompano was the greatest mile by any horse I ever trained.

Artsplace was a little peculiar in that he liked the front end a lot. He never lost a heat for me or for Bob McIntosh, who trained the horse at four, when he was on top at the half. In his whole career, no horse ever passed him from the half on if he was in front at that point.

My primary owner, George Segal, keeps a record of what I say about the colts throughout the spring. George and I agree that speed kills. We long ago decided not to stake any two-year olds to the early, major stakes. For instance, George hasn't paid a colt into the Woodrow Wilson in many years. It is hard to pass up that kind of money, but George believes a horse will last longer if he is not subjected to that kind of punishment. We have started horses in that race and have come close to winning it, but we felt the strain of the race was too much, too soon, and, therefore, we do not prep for that race any more. None of our stars, including Artsplace, Western Hanover, or Life Sign, has started in the Wilson.

George and I agree that the payoff down the road is a better aim than the early two-year-old money, because you pay such a high price to get a horse to a race like the Wilson.

JOG AND WORK IN COMPANY IF YOU CAN

I like to jog and train my colts in sets. I think it helps them establish the right attitude, and helps to stoke the competitive fires that are bred into our racehorses. I like to jog horses both directions of the track, and I like to jog them all over the track width. I don't just jog the wrong way on the outside. I like to turn a set and jog them the right way along the inside of the track, as well as jog them in the middle of the track going the right way.

It is a great thing for our business that most racetracks have removed their hubrails. I think every training center should also remove it's inner rail. I think it improves the appearance of the facilities and it is much, much safer. Anyone who has ever driven a colt while he is going sideways and heading for the inner hubrail knows what I mean. Without the inner rail, a horse going sideways simply goes right into the infield grass, avoiding possible injury.

Jogging a horse the right way of the track gets it used to making left turns, and lets it learn to relax, which is very important. Think about it: If the only time you turn around and go the right way is when you train a horse fast, he gets the idea that is what you want. This is the beginning of a puller. The horse needs to learn to relax and wait for you to tell him when it is time to pick up the pace.

TURN THEM LOOSE AFTER JOGGING

I now train in a warm climate in central Florida, but even when I trained at Greenville, Ohio, I liked to turn a colt loose in the stall after jogging.

I know a lot of trainers prefer to cover a colt up with a blanket and cross-tie him, or tie him to a hay rack, but I prefer to just cut him loose, and let him roll in the stall.

I learned this from Curly Smart, one of the truly great all-around horsemen our business has produced. The only problem with this plan would be if your barn was drafty and a lot of cold air was moving across the colt's body. If this was the case, I would recommend that you cover him with a blanket until he is cooled out.

I don't mean a cold barn; I mean a drafty barn where a lot of air is moving. A cold barn is not a problem, as long as there is no draft. A horse can cool out fine in the coldest weather without a blanket.

A lot of people want to clip horses, too, but I do not recommend it. I have grooms who complain about a horse's long hair because it makes him tough to clean up after he has rolled in his stall, and dried out. But I think you hurt a horse's overall coat when you clip him.

Once the weather starts warming up in the spring, a horse will start to shed naturally, and his coat will be easier to maintain. This is where the real work begins anyway, so have a little patience and work a little harder in the winter. The rewards will be there come springtime.

FEEDING PRACTICES

Like most horse trainers, I want my horses to eat well. I like high-quality feed, and for many years I have fed a combination of oats, sweet feed, vitamin supplements, corn and high-quality hay.

Unlike some trainers, I don't feed my horses any grain at the noon hour. My horses get fed very early in the morning (around 4:30) by the night watchman, and have grain again in the early evening, around 4 o'clock.

Feeding a horse should be a matter of observation, trial and experimentation. This is where a good groom will help you make decisions regarding a horse's ration. A good groom will notice if a horse is cleaning up his feed or leaving some.

I tell my grooms to watch for any change in a horse's eating habits. If a horse is eating good, but then starts to get off his feed, I want to know about it immediately. If I see that a colt is starting to lose weight, I ask the groom if the colt is eating all right. Many times, we can increase a horse's ration if he is cleaning his feed tub. I like a horse in good condition, so keeping him eating is very important.

Hay is fed pretty much on a free-choice basis. I like to keep some hay with a horse all the time, if the hay is of high quality. I like a combination alfalfa-timothy grass mix. The alfalfa is high in natural nutrients and the timothy provides great fiber for a horse's diet.

For years I have used "the eyeball method" of judging how much to feed my horses, and it's a pretty good plan. Just look at your horse. If he looks fit, his feed ration is about right. If he is thin, or is starting to tuck up on you, add some feed to his daily ration. You must be vigilant here, because you are seeing these colts every day, and it is sometimes difficult to notice a horse's condition beginning to deteriorate.

I also can tell a lot about a horse's condition just by looking at his coat of hair. A fit horse will have a shiny, glossy look to him, and he will have a good, willing attitude.

Every trainer has horses, however, that won't eat right. This is particularly true with fillies. For some reason, they seem to be more particular about their feed than colts. I have tried many remedies over the years, including injections that are available to stimulate appetite. Consult your veterinarian about any horse who has an eating problem. Beyond science, however, there are some other avenues to pursue if a horse won't eat properly.

Sometimes, you can trick a horse into eating. What I have found with a lot of fillies is that you can cut back on the ration they get, but feed them a little more often. You might try giving a filly only a half-ration, but give it to her in the morning, again at noon, then again in the evening, and maybe even late into the night. Like on the training track, don't be afraid to experiment. A horse must eat well to train and race well, so good eating habits are a priority. If you have to feed a filly six times a day to get her to eat properly, so be it.

I also like giving a horse a bran mash after a tough race or serious workout. The combination of oats, sweet feed, bran and molasses is a reward for a good effort, and my horses have liked it since I was a very young horse trainer. Just combine the grain and molasses with a little warm water.

A horse who eats poorly may also be troubled with bad teeth. Have their teeth examined to see if everything is alright inside the horse's mouth. He may have a wolf tooth that needs to come out, or a sharp edge on a tooth that needs to be filed down by an equine dentist.

Another problem is that the condition of a horse's teeth might also affect the way he drives, since a horse with wolf teeth that need to be extracted can not only be a problem-eater, but can get to grabbing one line during training.

Again, pay attention to your horse. The signs of problems are always there. If you ignore these signs of possible problems, more problems will develop later on. In most cases, you can head off trouble before it develops into real problems.

THE IMPORTANCE OF CONDITIONING

Once all my colts are broken and moving regularly, I start to develop a set program for each group of colts. One of the vital components of this program is the importance of conditioning.

Speed is there in our horses today; it is inherent to the breed. What we have to do as horse trainers is to put a foundation in a horse that allows him to achieve his potential, his natural level of talent. This foundation cannot be built if a horse stands in his stall.

A horse absolutely has to have regular work. I don't care if you train in Florida or in a cold climate, it's important to get out every day you can. Often, this means you won't get your stable out until the afternoon. People think because I train in Florida that I don't miss any days. They forget it rains a lot in Florida, and there are mornings when we simply can't train. Often times, however, the track dries out in the afternoon, and we get out then.

When I winter-trained in the north, I had to settle for afternoon workouts a lot because it simply would be too cold in the morning to train.

A lot of the time we got out late, but we did get out!

The important thing, wherever you train is to use good horse practices and try to manage your stable so that the colts get regular work. It builds condition, stamina and soundness. If your training plan calls for six days a week, like most horse trainers, that might also mean you work on a Sunday if you have missed a few extra days during the week.

Even if your track surface is in poor condition, you can still jog horses. You don't have to train them to build condition. A good stiff jogging session does a lot for a horse. Just get them moved.

THE BEGINNING OF FORMAL TRAINING

After the basic fundamentals of gait, attitude and shoeing have been addressed, it is time to start training in a serious way. For me, this is along about the first week in February. Up to this time, my colts have been jogged and maybe turned a few times with miles in 3:00, but no serious training has taken place.

However, now it's time to start reducing the training times.

One way in which I am different from a lot of horse trainers is that I don't have a "fast day" and a "slow day" for my horses. That is, I don't alternate one fast workout with a slow workout.

My schedule for a colt calls for him to go more every training session, although the increments are never major drops in time. At the beginning of training, it comprises about two seconds. For instance, during the first workout in early February, the colts are only asked to pace around 3:00, but by the first of March, I want to be in 2:40, with drops of two or three seconds each workout.

With most of the colts, I am aiming for a June 1 starting date. My training program leading up to the first race has been pretty much the same for many years now.

This program, of course, will depend on each horse. I remember when Western Hanover was two that he was a small colt. I decided that Western should not be on the regular program that aims for a June 1 start. I put him on a less accelerated program, and aimed for mid-July with him. He trained great, like a good horse, and I could have hurried him along like all the others. I had a great group of colts that year, including Caprock and Gamma Ray, two very fast horses, and Western Hanover never trained with that number-one group, only because he was not on the same training calendar. He always could go as much as any of them.

I finally started him in mid-July at The Meadowlands and he paced in 1:57-and-change the first time he saw the gate. I remember I told John Campbell that I thought Western could be a good colt. John had already seen Caprock and Gamma Ray race. After he qualified Western Hanover the very first time, John told me Western Hanover was the best colt I had. I guess John was right. Western Hanover ended up winning two legs of the Triple Crown, and just missed winning the Little Brown Jug by a nose.

USE THE HOBBLES EVERY DAY

There is another little item about my plans for two-year-olds that I want to explain. I said earlier that I like to sit behind the two-year-olds each morning, or have one of my assistant trainers do the driving. This includes the jog miles.

I also would like to mention that I like to jog my two-year-olds in the hobbles every day. I know a lot of trainers will tell you that a colt should jog free-legged, and only wear the hobbles when he trains, but I like the daily routine of wearing the hobbles. This includes the entire pre-racing period of training. This is a problem for some grooms, of course, who don't want to take care of all that equipment, but if you work in my stable, you will have to contend with it. I want the colts to learn to wear the hobbles. I think it helps them to pay attention. They are better-conditioned and more alert if they wear their hobbles.

When I begin repeating colts, they are trained in sets of at least three, and sometimes four horses, depending on ability levels and their overall progress.

In the training miles, it is important to vary the roles of your two-year-olds. Let one colt cut the first mile, then let him set behind the next trip. And make sure you teach a horse to sit on the outside, too. These days a horse simply has to be ready to race outside for a long way in order to stay in a position to win a race.

I believe in mixing things up with colts. Sometimes, we will vary the speed of jog miles; sometimes we jog the right way of the track and sometimes the wrong way. The colts will be called upon to do a lot of different things once they get to the races, so we do these things with them in their training.

I also want to teach horses to finish their training miles alertly. I don't mean I want them tiptoed every time I train, because that can develop soreness and/or a sour attitude. I always want to work colts so they are within themselves. I want them to finish "in the bit." What I mean by this is that they take their work willingly and learn to grab the bit and go forward, finishing their training miles strong.

You'd be surprised how fast a colt learns this, once you ask him for a little speed at the end of his training miles. He is bred to race. He likes the speed and the competitiveness, so try and keep him cheerful about his work.

That is not to say that I want to see the colts brushed a lot. I don't believe in that. I do believe that a colt should learn to manage his speed. This means that you will want to teach him to pace away from the gate as well as learn to finish. That is why, in some training sessions, our first quarter may be the fastest quarter in the mile. This teaches the colt that he cannot relax until late in the mile. He has to be ready for anything on the racetrack, so he might as well learn to be alert at any point in the mile.

For instance, in a 2:40 mile, I wouldn't want to see a colt brushed any faster than a first or final quarter in 37-38 seconds. In a 2:30 mile, a quarter in 35-36 seconds is adequate. When we get to 2:20, a fast quarter around 32-33 seconds is acceptable.

As I drop the colts each training session, I am looking for problems that need to be addressed. I used to see problems develop a lot sooner with colts, but it seems to me that, as the breed has developed, we have to go a lot farther now before the problems surface. It used to be that I could tell a lot about my stable at the 2:20 level. Now, it seems that I have to go a good ways beyond 2:20 before I can really begin to assess the talent. About the only clue you get at 2:20 is that you can determine which colts are not going to make it!

I have had great horses who were automatic. For instance, I could tell, after no more than 30 days, that Three Diamonds was going to be an exceptional filly. She had gait, attitude and class from the first time I put the harness on her.

Then there are the foolers, such as Artsplace, who need time to develop. I think sometimes this is specific to whatever line of horse you have. Most of the good Albatross offspring I've had were pretty natural horses. The Abercrombies I have trained have been late comers, with the notable exception of Life Sign, who was much like his dam Three Diamonds. Life Sign was a great, fluid-moving colt right from the start, and trained in my top set all winter as a two-year-old.

Troublemaker was a big, strapping Most Happy Fella colt and he did his work right. He was a little on the lazy side, too, and I like that in a colt. I think the lazy ones last a little longer than an aggressive-minded colt.

Western Hanover was also a natural, with just the right combination of aggressiveness and class. He was a super-gaited, slick-going colt, and made it to the races without ever doing anything wrong. He would take a nice hold of you, and was ready to give you his "pop" when asked.

Artsplace became a better training horse as he matured. In fact, I was able to train him in 1:53 and change at Scioto as a three-year-old before I started him. All you had to do with him at that point was just put him in gear, let him know what you wanted, and then just ride along with him.

Sometimes, you have colts who show the necessary ability, but just are not quite right. These are the ones you look to change some part of their equipment—you need to check hobble lengths, inspect their shoeing, or perhaps add a headpole to straighten them out.

Moonrock, a Storm Damage colt from the same family that produced Silk Stockings, is a good case study. He was a colt that I liked a lot early, but then he seemed to hit the wall in training. Late in the spring, I was not happy with his development. Finally, I just decided to back off on him and wait.

It took Moonrock all summer to find himself, but at Lexington in the fall he finally broke through and made a good pacer. He just needed the time.

Leah Almahurst, an Abercrombie filly who won a Breeders Crown and more than $1 million, was another filly who took her time making a good horse. She was a very quiet filly, and was slow coming around. Leah did not train or race early like a real exceptional filly, but at Springfield as a two-year-old, after three or four starts, she broke loose and went a good race. From that point on, she never went a bad race for me.

If a pacing colt is making breaks, it is generally due to something physical. Perhaps he is not balanced correctly. Maybe he has a physical problem, such as a hairline fracture in an ankle or knee. Pacing colts should not make repeated breaks. If you feel that their hobbles are at the correct length, that their shoeing is correct, and you have their heads set where they are comfortable, pacing colts should not be making breaks with you.

I have seen trainers who are very hard on a pacing colt who makes breaks. The truth is that the colt is probably trying his best to perform for them, but cannot, because of something being wrong. Training a horse can be a frustrating exercise, but you shouldn't overlook the fact that the horse is trying to give his best performance, but often cannot because he is in pain. If you can solve a colt's problems, his performance will improve dramatically.

If a colt makes breaks, or his performance is sub-par, it is time for an overall veterinary physical to see if he is working on a fracture or chip somewhere. I have seen colts go a few good training sessions, then one day jump it off for no apparent reason. This is the time where your management of a colt will become critical.

A colt who is making breaks is asking for help. Don't try to advance this colt's training until you find out what his trouble is. He may have a serious problem, or he may be telling you that he is a little stressed with

Final training miles should be completed to a racing sulky. In this way, the trainer can better gauge a horse's performance since the conditions more nearly duplicate actual racing and the work is easier on a horse than pulling a heavy jog cart.

what you are asking him to do. He may be a colt you will want to back up with, and then go forward later in the spring or early summer.

USE THE SULKY FOR FAST MILES

One aspect of my training program has changed over the past few years, and that is the point at which I begin hooking my colts to a sulky for the first time.

Years ago, I wouldn't hook a colt to a sulky until he was nearly ready to race. Now, I start hooking them to a sulky when I reach the 2:20 level, which is some six to eight weeks before they begin to race. I think this is wise, because working them to a sulky is much easier than pulling a jog cart. I think the stress to colts from pulling a jog cart was not understood for many years.

This is something I learned from the Scandinavians. I saw them training their colts to sulkies from a very early point in the training—and they had great success. So I incorporated some of their techniques into my program. Going a fast mile to a sulky simply has to be less stressful on a horse than training to a jog cart.

WATCH FOR SIGNS OF STRESS

As I begin to make speed with my two-year-olds, I am as much an observer as a horse trainer. I must always be alert for signs that a colt or filly needs a little help, or is getting sour. When I tie into a colt and ask him for speed, and he may begin acting a little sore the next morning or in the next workout, that is a pretty clear signal that he wants a little more time to develop.

I am going to back off this kind of colt, and maybe set him back about a month or so in his training. I am also going to have the vet examine him to ascertain if he has some kind of lameness.

I think it is very important that you let a colt or filly seek their own level. I know a lot of horse trainers "talk the talk" on this subject, but you really have to practice this.

The surest route to trouble is trying to put a colt or filly on a schedule that does not suit their own development. I have had a number of colts who just needed a little time, then came forward nicely for me and made productive horses.

The 2:20 level is where the first signs of stress begin to show up. I might notice that a colt has lost a little weight or condition, or one of the grooms will mention that a colt has a filled leg or has popped a curb.

We are going to find more and more problems these days with ankles and knees in our colts. I think it is a combination of the way horses are bred, along with the fact that we are going faster with them than ever before. Whatever the problems, you have to stay right on top of them, to ensure that the horse has the time to recover from an acute injury.

Knee injuries are really common because the knee joint absorbs a lot of the shock of hitting the racetrack. Just as knees are problems for human athletes, they are also trouble for racehorses.

You can detect a colt who has a knee problem by watching him walk off the racetrack. He will take his foot and toe it out, instead of coming down square and straight. He may try to move his foot by swinging his shoulder, instead of stepping forwardly naturally. You want to watch a colt like that, because he is trying to get away from the pressure on his knees.

Skeletal problems such as knee injuries are treatable if they are not too severe. For years, horse trainers have painted knees on the outside with iodine-based remedies. The problem with these "paints" was that they could not penetrate to the joint where a large percentage of the trouble is found.

THE USE OF ACID

These days, horse trainers have the use of hyaluronic acid for skeletal problems such as in knee and ankle joints. Let's stop right here for a moment and talk a little about the proper choices for colts.

If a colt is hurting, it is important to get the colt examined by a qualified veterinarian and determine the scope of the problem. I do not recommend the use of acid for a colt's joints early in his training program. If you have to inject a colt in his knees when you reach 2:20, you are probably not going to get him to the races. But injecting him in his knees after a couple of tough races, and particularly before a tough race, is a choice you will have to contemplate during the course of a season.

If a colt has a severe knee problem, such as a chip or hairline fracture, I recommend quitting with him. If he simply has weak knees or lacks a little flexibility due to some chronic soreness, you can probably help him with acid.

For instance, I used acid on both Artsplace and Life Sign. The important distinction with those horses is that the acid was used during the racing season. Any horse who races the speeds at which the top colts now are going, is likely to develop problems. Incidentally, I never used acid on Artsplace and Life Sign in their winter training in Florida.

A horse trainer in these times simply must learn to use what is available to him, and the acid injections work. Artsplace needed his feet and ankles injected on a pretty regular basis,(about once every three to four weeks). Ideally, I would like to use the acid about ten days out from a big race. If the Meadowlands Pace, for instance, was going to be raced on a Friday night in mid-July, I would want to inject acid about the first of the month, or certainly within the first week of the month.

Putting acid in a joint is something like putting oil in your car. I think it really helps a horse who may have some soreness, but does not have serious skeletal problems. Do not use the acid to overcome skeletal problems. The only things that overcome a skeletal problem are surgery or rest, or both.

Other common types of trouble are stifle soreness and filling in soft tissues such as tendons, suspensories and check ligaments. You can attack these areas of soreness with either topical applications of leg paint, or internal injections of McKay's or any of a number of products on the market that your veterinarian has available.

I have used a leg paint developed by the late Dr. John Jackman, and have had excellent results over the years. Dr. Ken Seeber writes about Standardbred lameness in another chapter of this book, so I will not spend any more time on that particular aspect of training.

DEALING WITH THE COLT VIRUS

There is another medical problem, however, that all colts seem to get at one time or another—the colt virus. Usually it's not just one colt who will get the virus, it comes in bunches. A lot of colts will get exposed to it at the same time.

The virus is most common when you first get a colt home from the sales. It also comes on in the spring when you ship north, or if you train where a number of other colts ship in from another location. The colt virus often appears in the summer during the first really hot spell, after you have stressed a colt for the first time.

There is really only one piece of advice to relate about the virus: Don't be panicked by it. Most colts will overcome it with a good dose of antibiotics for a few days. Monitor their temperatures and restrict their activity while they are sick. And don't be in a hurry to rush them back into training after they have been sick. Give them a good period of time until they start eating regularly, and start feeling good again. After a little time off, they will start to get their appetite back, and can be trained again without fear.

THE FINAL SIX WEEKS

Remember, in most cases, we are pointing for a June 1 starting date. In reality, not many colts will make it exactly the first week of June because of some setback along the way.

In mid-April, I hope to have worked a colt in 2:18-2:20 and I am now ready to finish him off and give him the balance of his foundation before he is ready to start.

Up to this time, my colts have been only two trips in any one training session. At this point, however, we add a third mile and start getting serious about the work.

While going two trips, I try to avoid beating 2:18-2:20. But the first time I go three trips, I will ask a colt to pace in 2:12 for me. The final mile should have fractions in the neighborhood of :33-1:07-1:40, with a final quarter in 32 seconds. This training session will be in the early part of the week, and three days later the colt will come back and go an identical session with miles in 2:45-2:25 and 2:12.

During the first week of May, he will train twice, with the third trip in 2:15 early in the week and in 2:08 at the end of the week. The next week he'll work twice again, the third trip in 2:15 at the start of the week and in 2:06 at the end. The following week, he gets a 2:18 mile and a 2:05 mile, with good final quarters in the 30-second area.

This is not the traditional slow work/fast work routine that a lot of trainers use, but I've had great success in prepping my colts using this plan; however, I think this plan will change every ten years.

Where my training methods have changed significantly is in what happens when a colt gets to the races. I will talk more about that when I discuss some of the issues related to speed management a little later in this chapter.

After a couple of 2:05 miles, I like to work a colt around 2:02 before starting him. I used to start them off the 2:05 miles, because I could be assured that their first baby races would only go around 2:03 or 2:04. But that is not the case anymore.

At some tracks, a colt will probably be required to pace around 2:00 the first time he sees the gate, so he better be ready to go there. I am not concerned about any colt I have deemed ready to start. If I have made that decision, it means that I am satisfied with his prep, his conditioning and his overall health and development.

THE FIRST FEW STARTS

The first time a colt starts, I want him raced strictly by the clock. That is, I want him to pace wherever I think he is comfortable, hopefully around 2:01-2:02. I want him taken off the gate, allowed to sit in nicely, then sprint home in the final quarter.

After a colt has raced for the first time, I skip a week with him to see how the first race has affected him. That one race will normally change a colt's attitude. I remember that Artsplace felt like a different horse after he had raced just the one time. After a couple of starts, he was a totally changed horse.

During the off-week, I will give a colt a couple of workouts, with fast miles in the 2:06 or 2:07 range. The miles will be pretty even with the exception that we might ask him to zip a little on the end and carry his finish right through the wire and into the turn. I like training a colt "through the wire," and would recommend it for any trainer at any level. What I mean is do not allow a colt to pull himself up at the wire. It is always a good rule of thumb to make him pace right on past the wire and carry his speed on into the turn.

Another thing I want to avoid is racing a colt in a stakes race after only a start or two. I think this is very unwise and unfair to the colt. I think a horse ought to have four or five starts, if possible, before you drop him into a stakes race. Ideally, I would like to baby-race him a couple of times, then drop him in a maiden event or two before asking him to take on stakes competition.

As far as I'm concerned, the only real education a colt gets in a baby race is being behind the gate. He's been trained for six months now, so he should know most of the rest, since we do jog and train in sets. I never have a colt behind the gate until his first baby race, unless he is a real toughie. I don't intend to leave much with a colt anyway in his first few races.

I want my two-year-olds headed for the inside, and to be taught to race out of a hole. After you do that with a colt a couple of times, you will find you can do just about anything with him.

MANAGING A COLT THE REST OF THE SEASON

The major difference in my horse training now, as opposed to just a few years ago, is that my horses get less work between races.

Like I said earlier in this chapter, I did not train Life Sign the week before he won the Little Brown Jug. That was the first time I ever started a horse in the Jug without training him the week of the race. If a colt is required to race every week at the speeds we go now, I don't see how you can logically expect him to withstand training all year long as well. I know a lot of other trainers have told me the same thing.

That doesn't mean that I won't train a colt between starts, however.

Knowing when and how much to work a horse is vitally important. Life Sign is such an example. The author gave him more work at the mid-point of his 2-year-old season, and backed him off in the middle of his sophomore year. In both instances, the horse's performance improved dramatically.

When Life Sign was a two-year-old, I was very high on him and thought he could be a real top horse. I baby-raced him and he raced very good for me. I sent him to The Meadows for a stake on Adios Day and thought he would pace in 1:55 easily.

John Campbell drove Life Sign for us there and had to use him pretty hard getting the lead going to the half. Life Sign then got immediate pressure the rest of the mile. At the head of the stretch, he just stopped. I was very disappointed with his performance.

I shipped Life Sign back to Scioto, and decided I would give him a week or two off before his next start. But he didn't lie around.

Let me explain.

I determined that Life Sign was a horse who needed work at this point. This is a decision that comes from years of experience. I have determined that horses go bad races because (1) they are overworked, or (2) they need more work, and are unfit.

Determining which way to go with a colt is a matter of judgment. More times than not, I choose to work a colt a little more and I have rarely seen it fail. A good horse, who is otherwise fit, will respond to the work.

Having decided that Life Sign needed more work, I drilled him pretty good before I sent him to Indianapolis for his next stake. He worked twice in 1:58 during the week preceding Indianapolis. He was a better horse at Indianapolis, acted like the colt I thought he was meant to be, and won in 1:56.

I also made another decision with him regarding the Indianapolis stake. He was eligible to start in either the Hoosier Futurity or the Fox Stake. I had originally planned to start him in the Fox, because I thought he was that kind of colt. But I chose the Hoosier Futurity, instead, because if he was going to race poorly I didn't want it to be in a race where he could get his head handed to him. I wanted to race him where he could get his confidence back. He won the Hoosier handily and got his confidence back.

By the fall of the year, Life Sign had won a parked-out mile in 1:52 and change at Lexington from the nine-hole! That mile at Lexington really showed me what kind of horse he was, because he took some real punishment and was still alive at the finish.

PLAN A REALISTIC SCHEDULE

I don't like laying out an every-week schedule of races for my colts. If I can, a couple of starts per month is enough for them. Artsplace, for instance, had only 15 starts at two, and I think that is about the ideal amount. He started early in June and raced through the Breeders Crown in late November, but made only 15 starts!

Western Hanover raced 14 times as a two-year-old. Life Sign started only 13 times at two. Years ago, young horses like those would have started a minimum of 20 times. In the coming years, I think we'll see the top colts make only 10 or 12 starts at two, particularly since we are finally getting away from racing two-year-olds in heat races.

I have been an outspoken critic of heat racing for two-year-olds, although I have no real problem with it for three-year-olds. I have never had a good horse who couldn't go heats. In fact, most of the good three-year-olds I have had have been better horses in heat races. I know Life Sign was better the second heat of his races than he was the first.

Life Sign is a good case study, because there were several instances in his career when his management made a world of difference in the final outcome of his season.

I have already talked about his two-year-old season where I gave him a couple of weeks off, but drilled him pretty good before a stakes start at Indianapolis.

However, Life Sign was a very different horse at three. He was more mature. He started off good for us at Scioto and progressed well through his season. I thought he should have won the North America Cup at Greenwood, but he bled there, and raced the rest of the year on Lasix.

After going on medication, Life Sign got good again and, by midsummer was able to come first-over against Presidential Ball and beat him in the Rooney Memorial at Yonkers. He also was about to win the Meadowlands Pace for us, but for some reason he bore in on Presidential Ball in the stretch, lost his momentum and lost the race.

He also went an incredible race in the Cane Pace from the second tier.

I had hoped to win the Triple Crown with him, because I thought he was the best, but after losing the Cane Pace due to his poor post position, I made a key decision with him.

Life Sign had six straight races over half-mile tracks at one point in his season, and I knew he would need a break somewhere before the Little Brown Jug. However, in looking at his schedule, there was no hole for him to take a week off.

He had a number of rich stakes preceding the Jug, including the Dancer Memorial, the Messenger, the MacFarlane Memorial, etc. Finally, the horse answered the question for me.

I started Life Sign in the Dancer Memorial at Freehold and he went a poor race. It was a race I thought he should have won. Cat Manzi drove him for us there and drove him well, but the horse just didn't have the same zip finishing he had earlier in the summer.

The Jug was only a couple of weeks away now, and the horse was scheduled to go to Rosecroft for the Messenger, where I knew there would be a light field.

I called George Segal and told him I thought Life Sign needed a week off. George and I talked about it and he finally told me to do whatever I felt was best for the horse. I decided to skip the Messenger. Giving up a shot at the Messenger was a tough choice, but the Jug was really our priority.

I brought Life Sign back to Scioto, and decided to let him have a week away from the races. I did train him on a Thursday, two weeks before the Jug. He went three trips, the final one in 2:00, with a quarter in :28.

You might think that a 2:00 training mile would stress a horse, but you have to remember that a horse like Life Sign, who can pace in 1:52 any time and every time out, can go a 2:00 mile with a fast last quarter like an ordinary 2:00 horse trains in 2:10.

A workout in 2:00 gave Life Sign enough work to keep him sharp, but did not provide the stress of another start. These moves produced the desired results.

I sent Life Sign to Detroit for the MacFarlane Memorial, and he responded like the horse he had been at midsummer. I went into the Jug the following week with a fresh horse.

I don't believe I would have won the Jug with Life Sign if he had not taken a week off before going to Detroit. I also did not want him to have a week off immediately prior to the Jug because I didn't like the idea of sending him to Delaware without a prep race.

It was a difficult decision to miss the big money in the Messenger, but Life Sign vindicated us all with his miracle win in the Little Brown Jug. It was a very satisfying moment for me and George Segal. We have been trying to win that race for some time, and had near misses with Troublemaker and Western Hanover. Artsplace might have won his Jug, too, but he didn't get to start because of illness. To finally win with Life Sign was a real pleasure.

The point I would like to emphasize, however, is that proper management of a horse can produce far better results than just taking your races one week at a time. Try to look down the road with a horse and decide what is best for him.

Missing the big money in the Messenger was not easy for us, but winning the Jug made missing the Messenger pale by comparison. Being from Ohio, I wouldn't trade my one Jug for ten Messengers!

OTHER MANAGEMENT ISSUES

I think it should be obvious to anyone at this point that management of a horse is really the key difference in the way horses are trained nowadays.

If a horse is racing every week, like most of our raceway horses are, I don't believe he needs to be trained midweek. I know a lot of trainers who still train at midweek, but with the speed horses have to go these days, I just don't think a racehorse will stand serious training in the middle of the week.

If you don't like the idea of not giving a horse any work between races, jog him a little further than normal on the day before the race. You might even turn him the day before he races and go a slow mile around 2:40 with a little brush for an eighth just to sharpen him a little. This is what many people call a "blowout," a term borrowed from the Thoroughbred world.

I think horses in the past needed that much work to stay good, but the breed has really improved and progressed. Even in the claiming ranks, the horses have more ability and can go faster with less work. I still think a horse has to be trained tough to get to the races, but I don't believe you can continually drill one between races and hope to have him hold up a full season.

That just about sums up what I have to say on the topic of training the pacer of today.

There is no question the pacing horse of the late 20th century is a far better animal than his ancestors. As we progress through the next twenty years, the breed will change even more. I don't believe we are through with the evolution of speed. I don't know where it will stop.

However, I do know this for certain: A horse trainer must realize that if horses are going to race faster than ever before, we are going to have to continually analyze what we do with them between races, how we space the races and how much we train them. I think it's obvious that horses are going to have to get away from a seven-day cycle of racing if they are going to last an entire season.

I also think the time will come when a horse will only be able to start every other week, and not train a great deal between races. This will cause all of us to change the way we do things. The ability to change with the times will determine our success.

A harness racing season is hardly complete if there isn't one pacer trained by Gene Riegle making headlines on the Grand Circuit and in the major juvenile stakes. And usually there are several pacers from the Riegle Stable making headlines.

Artsplace, Life Sign, Western Hanover, Leah Almahurst, Three Diamonds, Jay Time, Troublemaker, Fundamentalist, Tucson Hanover, Kit Hanover—these are among the best-known sidewheelers to graduate from the Riegle School for young pacers. They are also among the best-known pacers to race in recent decades.

Riegle has teamed with Chicago owner George Segal to send out a string of ambitious young pacers year after year, making this combination one of the most powerful in the sport. Riegle's pacers are well-trained and well-managed, enabling them to hold their form in the rigorous competition at the top of the sport.

Although he is known primarily for his pacers, Riegle has trained many outstanding trotters, including Arnie Almahurst, Worldly Woman, Cami Almahurst, Op Art, and Mr. Saunders.

Riegle is particularly respected for his insight in yearling selection. It is an ability that he has honed over a lifetime in harness racing.

Riegle was born in the Darke County, OH, community of Greenville, a town with a long-standing tradition of support for harness racing. His father, Roy Riegle, was a trainer, and Gene's sons Alan and Bruce have proven to be valuable assistants over the years.

10
TRAINING THE FILLY

BRUCE NICKELLS

I have been fortunate to have developed a number of champion pacing fillies over the past few years and have been asked to relate my ideas pertaining to managing the careers of those fillies.

The fact that my career has taken this turn is very interesting, because all of my life I was given advice from other horse trainers centered on the fact that you cannot build a successful career by training a lot of fillies.

FILLIES—THE QUICKEST WAY TO GO BROKE!

Years and years ago, my grandfather told me that the quickest way to go broke in the horse business was to train a barn full of fillies!

Throughout my career, which now spans more than 40 years, I have always had good horses. I was lucky to have worked for a number of excellent men when I was young, including Del Cameron and Edgar Leonard. I learned a lot from quality horsemen like them and have acquired experience on my own that I apply to my everyday training routine and practices.

I think that a horse trainer acquires something from every horse he draws a line over. I think you acquire experience. You acquire knowledge. You begin to know how a horse thinks and acts. You begin to know what will happen in a certain circumstance. I also think you begin to know how to avoid trouble, and to create an environment in which a horse can do well.

A lot of journalists have asked me to explain my successes with fillies such as Miss Easy, Follow My Star, Central Park West, Immortality, Freedoms Friend and Efishnc. I am hard-pressed to come up with an easy answer.

I think more than anything is the fact that over the years I have acquired the experience necessary to make the right judgments at the right times about how to handle a horse in a lot of different situations.

A GOOD HORSE PSYCHOLOGIST

I think it is vitally important that if you wish to become a successful horse trainer, whether it be with colts and/or fillies, you will have to be a good horse psychologist. You will have to know how to get along with a horse, and get it to relax.

I have watched all of the great trainers of my era, and the only common characteristic of that entire group is that they were all good, day-today horsemen in managing a stable and in treating a horse in such a way as to allow it to excel.

One of the attributes of the great trainers is the ability to get a horse to relax and not be afraid of anything. For instance, one of the problems with young horses, particularly fillies, is the fear of water trucks and tractors. I have seen a lot of trainers attempt to contend with this problem over the years—with any number of solutions.

My solution is simply to not worry about it. A horse will never have to contend with a tractor or water truck in a racing situation. You don't race a horse against a tractor or even race one at the same time when the tractor is on the track.

So, what do I do when I have one who is scared of track equipment?

I try to anticipate the problem and attempt to put myself in a situation where I can contend with the trouble. If I can turn my yearlings or two-year-olds in front of a tractor or water truck and avoid having to go around it during a training mile, that is what I'll do.

If I know a filly will be tough when she encounters a tractor or water truck while she is jogging, I try to put another horse between her and the tractor. Or, I try to stay as far away from the track equipment as possible.

Trainers can get in trouble with a horse when that horse spooks from something. I have come to realize over the years that a lot of equipment has been torn up and a lot of jog carts have been reduced to splinters unnecessarily. I think you can reduce the problems you have if you simply anticipate the trouble and then respond to it in a very careful way.

For instance, if I know I am driving a filly who is afraid of a tractor, I will not force her into a situation where she must confront that fear. If she sees a tractor and wants to run sideways and get away from it, I try and slow her to a walk as she approaches the tractor.

I will keep a hold of her and steer her, but not attempt to restrain her too much.

KICKING—A COMMON PROBLEM

One of the most common problems a horse trainer faces is the horse who will kick. Let me say right off that I do not believe in the use of kicking straps across a horse's back. I think kicking straps actually contribute to the problem, because a horse can raise up and kind of hump his back and the kicking strap actually will "goose" him and cause him to kick.

Horses kick for a number of reasons. The playful kicker—and this is normally where colts will be a problem—is just a horse who feels good and is not a malicious kicker. Every horse will try you at some point, like a teenager who wants to see what the folks will let him get away with.

The problem kicker, or the malicious kicker, more likely will be a filly. For some reason, a kicking filly can be a lot more trouble than any colt. I

One of the author's champion fillies, Bruce's Lady, was a bad kicker during her early training. The author employed a stiff-tailed crupper on this filly and also tied her tail to the crossbar of the jog cart or race bike. The author believes that a filly who cannot swish her tail will not kick, as a rule.

have had my share of kickers; the most notable, probably, was the good filly, Bruce's Lady.

She had a mind of her own right from the first day we hooked her. By the way, I don't line-drive any of my yearlings. I do use a bitting rig for a couple of days in the stall to get them used to a bit in their mouth, but I have not line-driven a horse in many years.

Bruce's Lady was a kicker, and she wanted to find an excuse to kick every morning. What I finally did with her was put a stiff-tailed crupper on the harness and tie her tail to the crossbar of the jog cart.

This helped her, it seemed, because she could not swish her tail, and the stiff-tailed crupper did not allow her to hump up and goose herself. I also have had success with removing the crupper from the backpad on a horse who kicks a lot.

If you are on the track and a horse kicks, or is about to, the best remedy is to try to turn its head while it is getting ready to kick. If you steer a horse and make contact with the bit, you will divert its attention for just a second, and take its mind off kicking.

If a horse is a constant kicker and won't respond to the normal solutions, I put it behind the starting gate for a while. I find that this changes what the horse is thinking about. I also have found that a horse who kicks has a lot of energy and that getting it tired and keeping it tired solves a lot of the kicking problems. I think a horse will stop kicking when it learns that the more it kicks, the more work it will be required to do. A horse can learn a lot when it gets tired.

WORK AROUND A HORSE'S WEAKNESS

I modify my training habits with that horse to conform to its weaknesses. I really think the successful horse trainer is one who can lessen the importance of a horse's weaknesses. Every horse has problems. Every horse has a weakness or bad habit.

Learning what to do, and when to do it, will get a lot of horses who have weaknesses to the races. Everyone wants a horse to behave and have class, so learning to work around behaviors that might cause trouble are the keys to successful horse training.

SUCCESS WITH DIFFERENT TYPES

One of the things of which I am most proud with these good fillies I have had is that they have been remarkably different type horses. None of them was the same kind of filly as the others.

Miss Easy, for instance, was a big, handsome filly with a great, long gait. She was a line-gaited pacer and could carry her speed over a very long distance. But throughout her career Miss Easy had a problem with being on one line. She would be on the right line and bear in, and I had to learn to live with it and work around it.

Follow My Star was a small mare, with a light, daisy-cutting action in front. She was a top filly, but she had very bad feet all her racing days and I had to work around that problem. I was constantly looking for ways to reduce the pounding effects of the racetrack and allow her to become the kind of mare I knew she could be.

Central Park West was a strapping, handsome filly with a long, easy, loose stroke and action. She strained a suspensory at three, when she got run into in a qualifying race, and was never the same filly after that.

Immortality was a little filly with tremendous reach and extension, but I couldn't train her much because she was so small. I didn't think she could hold up all season if I drilled her regularly.

Freedoms Friend at two was a big filly with a slick gait and a great mouth, but she had a rough set of hocks on her. I constantly had to work around that. The challenge was to combine enough work to keep her sharp and let her have the time off to grow into herself. On top of that, Freedoms Friend also had an infected stifle at the midpoint of her two-year-old season.

Efishnc (pronounced Ee-fish-en-cee) was a good training filly who missed her baby races, but got ready in a hurry after that, and won the Sweetheart with very little experience.

As I noted earlier, these fillies did not resemble one another in any way, except that they were all champions.

Each filly wore different shoes.

Each filly wore a different size hobble.

Each filly wore a different bridle.

Follow My Star was a champion two-year-old and aged mare despite some nagging training problems. She was a bad-footed mare her entire career and her training had to be adjusted to overcome this problem.

Each filly was trained differently.

Each filly presented different problems and each had weaknesses that had to be overcome to allow them to become champions.

Although I have a reputation for developing top fillies, I previously developed a number of good colts—such as Kentucky, Batman, Combat Time, Fast Clip, and Lola's Express—over the years before all these good fillies came along.

Kentucky, a son of Tar Heel, was probably the best of that group. Kentucky and I had some memorable battles with Stanley Dancer and Albatross.

Combat Time and Fast Clip, a couple of Good Time colts, were excellent horses. I won a heat of the Little Brown Jug with Combat Time in 1964, the year the race was won by Vicar Hanover and Billy Haughton. Fast Clip won a number of big races, but had to butt heads with Strike Out at both two and three in the early 1970's.

FOLLOW MY STAR—THE TURNING POINT

In the fall of 1984, Follow My Star was sent to me among a group of fillies owned by Ridgedale Farms of California. I didn't pick her out, but I do remember looking at her at the sale. She was a little filly and not particularly attractive.

She did come from a great family—Castleton Farm's very successful group that included Race Time, Warm Breeze and Storm Damage. Follow My Star was bred by Kentuckiana Farms and was a daughter of Governor Skipper from Circle Home, a Steady Star mare whose dam, Charming Time, is a full sister to Race Time.

I broke Follow My Star and liked her, but I honestly thought she was too small to ever make a good horse. She wore only a 57-inch hobble, which is very short even for a small filly like her, and her feet stung her almost from the first day I trained her.

I started Follow My Star in a very loose hobble and right away she showed that she had some grit and speed. She was a very determined little filly who would fight like hell. She didn't like another horse passing her; she wanted to be the leader.

Because she had so little action in front, I put a pair of light 1/2-inch, half-round shoes on her to help her break over easier and have a little more action. I also squared her toes for the same reason. The half-rounds did the trick. This improved her action enough that she made a wonderfully gaited filly. It allowed her to find her gait and then progress from there.

Follow My Star had other problems associated with her front feet, though. She had bad feet and carried a very low natural angle. I was never able to get her angle up much beyond 47 degrees in front. Most of the time, the angle was at 46 degrees.

She landed hard on her heels and kept them pounded down, so she kept her angle very low. I prefer a much higher angle, something in the 51-52 degree area, for most of my pacers, but Follow My Star just would not allow me to shoe her that way.

I eventually raced her in a light, aluminum bar shoe with a leather rim pad. Also, because the soles of her feet were often very sore, I would extend a portion of the pad over those areas where she was most sore. I did not use a full pad on her, but I did like her with a pad over the sorest portion of her foot.

A bar shoe is really your only defense in a situation like this. It is good because it relieves some of the pressure off the sole of the foot.

Follow My Star wore a light full swedge shoe behind with a squared toe. The bar shoe in front helped me contend with her bad feet and low angle.

At three, much of Follow My Star's season was lost to her bad feet, but she came back at four and won the Breeders Crown at Lexington. She ended her career as the richest pacing filly or mare in history, with over $1.5 million earned. There is no telling what she might have done if she had healthy feet under her.

A FUNDAMENTAL TRAINING DILEMMA

Follow My Star's foot problems not only robbed her of her form on occasion, but also presented me with a very fundamental training dilemma. Because her foot trouble was chronic, the kind that wasn't going to go away without rest, it became a weakness I had to work around.

Her foot problems were not as severe in the winter in Florida, where the track's combination of sand and clay is generally very soft and kind to a horse. But in the summer when I shipped to The Meadowlands, the track there was quite often hard, like most raceways, and Follow My Star never was as good when the track got really hard and stung her. She would naturally back off.

This meant that if the track was hard on the days she was to train, I had to make a decision: How could I work her like I wanted to, like I thought I needed to work her to keep her fit, and still find a way to keep her sound?

USE JOG MILES TO RETAIN CONDITION

The remedy was just some stiff jogging on the back track at The Meadowlands, which is generally a lot softer than the main racing surface which, of course, must be all-weather. And that translates to it being hard, so that rain will not soak into it.

What I would do with Follow My Star was take her to the back track and jog her three or four miles, then take her to the barn, and then come back an hour later and jog her another three to four miles. The idea was to give her enough work to keep her sharp without the pounding of actual training. She was racing on an every-week schedule, and I believe there was no way that she would have made it through the whole summer if I had not managed her in this way.

Trainers should realize that you can carry a horse a long way during the racing season with just jogging, but it is also important that you lay the proper foundation in a horse in the off season. That is why regular conditioning is so important. Regardless of where anyone trains, if all the work done throughout the winter and early spring is not done properly, you cannot have the luxury of managing a horse this way with these kinds of problems come summer.

I got along well with Follow My Star throughout her two-year-old season and managed to work around her foot problems. She won 13 of her 14 starts that year. Her biggest win was in the $1 million Sweetheart at The Meadowlands. The only disappointment of her two-year-old season was that I had to scratch her from the Breeders Crown when she came up sick.

At three, though, the foot problems with Follow My Star got a lot more serious.

I qualified her in mid-April at The Meadowlands, and she acted O.K., but I knew we were in trouble. I started her in the Miller Memorial and Buddy Gilmour drove her for me. She won her elimination and took the final, but she was sore on those bad feet.

I gave her a couple of weeks off and then qualified her back on May 20, but I could tell she was not as good as before. I put her in to go the following week, but she warmed up so badly, I scratched her. She would not race again for three months!

During the time off, I kept her up and jogging, but had to stay away from the main track at The Meadowlands. Her problem was that she would get sore in the sole of her foot, because the sole was right on the ground, almost like a horse that was foundered. That was just the way her foot was made. I had to put double leather pads on her during the period of recuperation. Each of these pads were about a quarter of an inch thick, and this allowed me to build her foot up and get her to a point where her sole would not strike the ground. The part of the pad next to the sole of her foot was cut out to allow us to get iodine and hoof treatment into the affected area.

To counter the soreness in the sole, I would pour iodine onto the sole almost weekly to toughen it up. When you do this, you have to be careful not to tub a horse too much as that can soften up the foot too much and make it even more tender. What you are looking to do is get the sole to the point where it is free from soreness. By building Follow My Star's foot up and using the iodine and an occasional DMSO wrap around the coronet band to stimulate growth, we were able to overcome her problems and get her back to the races.

I finally got Follow My Star re-qualified just before Labor Day at Garden State Park and she made her first start back on September 11. She finished second after a first-over trip to the good filly Walkin On Air. I shipped her on to Delaware for the Jugette, even though I knew she would have to go heats.

I didn't think she would be too short, since she was not a filly who required a great deal of work, but I was concerned about her lack of experience against fillies who had raced all year.

I drove Follow My Star myself, and she was second in the first Jugette heat out of the six hole, finishing behind Bonniebell Hanover in 1:56.2. The second heat, I got off to the lead with her, but then she got tired and wound up sixth in the final, won by Anniecrombie. I didn't get to race Follow My Star at Lexington that fall, but I did work her there near the end of the meeting before shipping her back to Garden State for a stakes engagement.

She liked The Red Mile a lot. It was a good surface for her sore feet, and she was very good during the two weeks of the fall Grand Circuit meeting. In fact, I worked her there one morning in 1:54.4. Lou Guida saw her train and eventually bought her from Ridgedale Farms that fall.

Follow My Star ended her three-year-old year by finishing third in the Breeders Crown at Garden State behind Glow Softly and Lavish Laura. I was already looking forward to 1987 because I thought the extra year of maturity would help her a lot. She had won $1 million during her two- and three-year-old seasons, but I knew she was even more filly than that.

She had a great winter in Florida between her three- and four-year-old seasons, and I was very optimistic about her chances to have a very good year for her new owners.

When I sent Follow My Star north in March she was as sound as she would ever be in her life, but when I hit The Meadowlands with her, the foot problems returned. She raced creditably, but she lacked the real punch I knew she had and that everyone associated with her knew she had. She didn't really show us the true Follow My Star until the ninth race of her season, winning in 1:53.2 for Bill O'Donnell on May 29.

She had only three wins in her first ten starts that year, and I must confess that I was happy to see The Meadowlands meet end and get her onto a different surface. This is not meant in any way to be critical of The Meadowlands, but I knew Follow My Star would be better on tracks that might have a little more cushion.

I shipped her to Canada and she won twice at Greenwood in filly-and-mare company. She liked the deep cushion of that track, and was really starting to come around.

Next up was the American-National Open at Sportsman's Park where I dropped her in against mixed company. She raced very well, finishing fourth to Anniecrombie and Hothead after a very tough mile. I drove her myself that night and we got away poorly, but she raced very well, so I sent her immediately to Lexington to The Red Mile to prepare for the upcoming Breeders Crown.

I had a couple of weeks and Follow My Star just thrived on the clay track at Lexington. With every work, she was getting better and better. I had high hopes for her in the Breeders Crown.

She was so good coming into the race that I re-united her with John Campbell. I told John she was sharp and back to her two-year-old form. She drew the 11-hole in a field of 12 starters that included Anniecrombie, Glenn's Superstar, Turola Hanover and Enroute. It was a sensational group of mares.

Like any race with a big field, there was a very fast quarter and half. John got away seventh on the outside from the second tier. Follow My Star was out the entire mile, but rallied through the stretch to win in 1:53.4.

She was getting along so well at Lexington, I decided to leave her there after the Grand Circuit meeting started and race her in a filly and mare overnight event for a $2,500 purse. A lot of the other Breeders Crown mares had stayed at Lexington and we put on one hell of a race. Follow My Star won again in 1:53.3, closing up in :26.3.

The following week, she took a time-trial record for Campbell of 1:52.3. She paced the first three-quarters in exactly 1:24 with every quarter in 28 seconds. She got home in :28.3 for her new mark.

After Lexington, Follow My Star was significantly more fit than before. Throughout the early part of the year at the Meadowlands, I had not been able to give her enough work to get her really sharp, but being on a soft track allowed me to both train her like she needed to be trained, and race her. She got real sharp.

I shipped her back to Garden State where she was second to Tautitaw Bluegrass in 1:56.2 and then won in 1:55.4 for Ray Remmen on October 30. From there, it was on to Yonkers for the Clare Series. She was second the first week in 1:58.1 to Anniecrombie, then turned the tables the following week, winning in 1:57.1 over Enroute and Saccharum.

In the Clare final, she went a really remarkable mile, coming from eighth at the half for Joe Marsh, Jr. to win in 1:58 over Anniecrombie and Enroute. She came three-wide from fifth in the final quarter and just flew by both those other mares.

As winner of the Clare Series, she was eligible to drop in the Haughton Memorial Open EC the following week, and finished third from the rail to Armbro Emerson and Play The Palace.

Follow My Star won over $400,000 as a four-year old and proved herself one of the great mares in history.

I have always thought that if Follow My Star had been a good-footed filly, and I had been able to train her and"rev her up" for her big races, she would never have been beaten in any of those races.

But I was just never able to "zip" her along any fast quarters or really set her up for the big races. She was never a real sound horse.

Follow My Star was so little that even as an aged mare, she still wore only a 57-inch hobble as she had when she was two. She was a very quick mare and a real pleasure to drive. She had a great mouth and wore an open bridle with a shadow roll most of her career. She was a real Cadillac!

MISS EASY—BIG, STRONG, POWERFUL

The filly who broke Follow My Star's earnings record was a completely different type of horse. Her name was Miss Easy.

Whereas Follow My Star was a little, quick, determined filly, Miss Easy was a huge filly. Lou Guida picked her out of the Stoner Creek Stud consignment to Tattersalls and paid $47,000 for her. She was a big, dark bay filly with a lot of polish. She had a real speed look to her.

When I broke Miss Easy, I was impressed with her action. A lot of pacers are not line-gaited and spend a lot of time going sideways. Some pacers also make a wide, circular stroke with their hind legs, which is very inefficient and contributes to a lot of unsoundness.

LINE-GAITED, LIKE A TROTTER

Although a pacer, Miss Easy was line-gaited, like a good trotter, especially behind. She had absolutely the most efficient way of going of any of my good horses. Her action was straight forward and straight back on all four corners. She generated tremendous power and drive behind, but also had wonderful shoulder action in front. She had a very strong front end and got tremendous pull and action from her front legs.

The problem I had with Miss Easy throughout the spring of her two-year-old year and through the final phases of her career was that she would grab one line. She was always bearing in on the turns.

Because of this habit, I actually did not think she would develop into much of a filly. In training, she acted like she would get hot, so I made her stay in behind the other horses in her set and I never let her know she could go fast.

At two, Miss Easy's knees seemed to bother her. I thought that was what was making her get on one line and bear in. About a month before I shipped her north to The Meadowlands, I turned her out for three weeks at a farm near Ocala, Florida.

I like to do that with all my two-year-olds at some point in the spring. Giving them some time off is very important. I don't have a set schedule of when this break occurs. Some of my yearlings will have just been broken when I send them off for some "R & R" if I think they need some time to grow and fill out before the real training begins.

Others, like Miss Easy, need a break before I really dig into them in the final month or six weeks of training.

I picked Miss Easy back up after her "spring break" and she acted a little better, but she was still on the right line some. She was a funny filly in that respect.

You would think the more you went with her the more unmanageable she would become because of her bearing in so badly. But horse training is an imprecise art, and what happened with Miss Easy was just the opposite of what I expected. She got better the faster she went!

I never really knew what kind of speed Miss Easy had until I turned her loose the final couple of training miles at The Meadowlands before her first race. I found that she could really put it in gear and go!

I used a full swedge shoe on her in front at two, with a full pad packed with Reducine hoof pack because I thought her feet were stinging her. She had a natural 50-51 degree angle in front at both two and three. However, when Miss Easy was three, I used an aluminum shoe with a rim pad. By that time, I had concluded that her front feet were not the culprit. She always wore a full swedge behind, with a squared toe on a 54-degree angle.

The fact that Miss Easy grabbed one line her whole life and still earned over $1.7 million is remarkable testimony to her innate ability to overcome her problems. It wasn't until late in her three-year-old season that we finally figured out that she was sore in her right hind foot and was running in to get away from that pain.

Looking back at the winter before Miss Easy's two-year-old year, I could not have told you that she would become the biggest money-winning pacing mare in history in just two seasons at the races. While I was impressed with her action, I honestly did not know if she had the class to become a really good horse. I have not yet devised a system to know how much heart, desire, and courage a horse has.

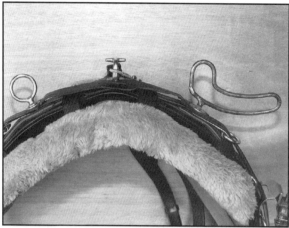
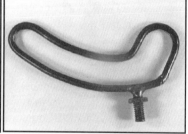

The author developed a device he calls "WINGS" in order to compensate for a horse who grabbed one line. This invention allows you to avoid the use of a side-reining bit but keeps the pressure on the lines equal. The "wing" simply screws into the turret socket and replaces the standard turret. The world champion Miss Easy wore a wing like this one throughout her entire career.

INVENTION OF "WINGS"

A horse trainer often must become an inventor, coming up with a piece of equipment that can help him contend with a horse's weakness. As I said, Miss Easy was on the right line all the time. The standard response from a horse trainer would be to add a side-reining bit or some other exotic device to get her to straighten up on the bit.

I had an idea one day, and asked the blacksmith to make me a new piece of equipment for Miss Easy. I do not like a side-reining bit, and drivers don't like them either, especially during a race.

The new piece of equipment I envisioned would let Miss Easy turn her head, but would retain the same bit pressure and allow her to be driven safely. What I came up with is something I call "wings."

What I did was remove the regular, round turrets from the harness backpad and replace them with a long, pepper-shaped turret that would do some of the same things as the side-reining bit, but without the severity.

The "wings" have a metal loop that allows the line to slide back and forth, from side to side, changing the angle of the line in relation to the bit, producing a different angle of pull. This allowed Miss Easy to drive a little straighter.

Right from the start, I asked John Campbell to race her for me. John is terrific with a young horse. He will do what you tell him and he is very good at getting a horse to relax both before and during a race. He has great hands and is easily the most gifted driver I have ever seen.

John raced Miss Easy the first time for me on May 19 at The Meadowlands. I asked him to take her away easy and see how she would be on the one line. She had the eight-hole that day, and John did what I told him. He backed her off the gate, then put her in the flow of the race as soon as the opportunity developed. She was sixth and out at the half in 1:02.1, which meant she was probably over to the half around 1:03.3 or 1:03.4.

John just sat with her until the stretch, when he put her in gear and she just exploded past the other fillies, winning in 2:03.1. She paced the final quarter in :27.4! John was impressed with her and said she was O.K. on the one line, even at high speed.

Miss Easy missed her next start due to sickness, but came right back on June 2 in another $500 baby-race, which she won easily, on the engine in 1:59.4, with an effortless final quarter in :28.3. I was amazed, and John was convinced that she could be a superior filly.

After she missed some training due to bad weather, we came back with her, but she was a trifle short, and lost in 1:58.4 by a neck. It would be nearly three months before she would lose another heat.

Miss Easy made her first stakes start near the end of June in the Historic Series at The Meadowlands. John got away sixth at the quarter, but he put her in gear going to the half, and cleared to the lead in :57.4. From there, she cruised in 1:56.3.

She then won three legs and the final of the New Jersey Sires Stakes in succession, taking the final in 1:55.1. She then won a division of the Countess Adios in 1:54, during Hambletonian week at The Meadowlands.

During this time, John developed a pattern with Miss Easy where he would take her away slowly, then put her in gear going to the half. In this way, her chronic problem of being on one line was less of an issue because she would never be in traffic late in a race. By the time the half was reached, Miss Easy was generally in front. The Meadowlands still had a hubrail at that time and she would invariably rub a little paint off the arch of the sulky by coming in around the final turn. Miss Easy got her first real stern test in the elimination for the Sweetheart. She drew sixth, and John was seventh with her and apparently in the flow going to the half. But then the outside flow stalled and Miss Easy was caught outside past the half, lying sixth.

John knew he had the best horse, and finally sent her three wide in the last turn. She circled the field, took the lead early in the stretch, and won handily in 1:54.1.

In the Sweetheart Final, John did not take any chances. Drawing the five-hole, he left strongly with her, took the lead past the quarter and just sent her down the road, winning in 1:52.3. The remarkable thing about that mile was that she was just cruising and could have gone more.

From there, I sent Miss Easy to Rosecroft for a couple of stakes. These were her first starts on anything but a mile track, and although she won both races, she was not as good in the turns as I would have liked. Her

Miss Easy roars through the stretch at The Red Mile for John Campbell as a two-year-old in 1:51.2 in 1990, setting a world record. Miss Easy was a line-gaited pacer whose action was all directed down the track.

problem of being on one line was accentuated by the tighter turns of a five-eighths-mile track.

From there, Miss Easy's schedule called for her to go to Lexington during the first week of the Grand Circuit meeting at The Red Mile. She had more than two weeks between the Rosecroft miles and Lexington, so I trained her three trips a couple of times, the final miles in the 2:10-2:12 area, with a couple of good last quarters.

Miss Easy was a peculiar filly in that it did not much matter what kind of work she got, she always raced good. I tried working her a little harder. I also tried backing off of her and training her a little lighter. It seemed to not make too much difference, although with less work she did have the chance to stay sounder. She was a very high-strung, nervous filly and kept herself tight most of the time.

What I finally wound up doing with Miss Easy when she was three was work her three trips between races, but I would work her in the second- or third-horse position away from the rail and train her 1 1/4 miles at about a 2:15 rate.

She loved this and acted like she could have gone two miles at that pace. When Miss Easy got rolling—and she could really roll— she felt like the most powerful pacing machine imaginable. She could really carry her speed a long distance.

AT THE RED MILE, A MAJOR WORLD RECORD

At Lexington in 1990, it was opening day of the Grand Circuit meeting and the weather came up good.

I already had some discussion with Lou Guida about sending Miss Easy after the world record for two-year-old fillies. The Amity Chef syndicate had offered a $250,000 bonus to the breeders of any son or daughter of Amity Chef who set a world record. When the weather came up sunny and warm with no wind, I decided to go for the record with her.

That was the year The Red Mile opened Paddock Park, and this was the first day it was used for the Grand Circuit horses. I thought that sending a world champion out the very first day would be a good way to inaugurate such a wonderful improvement to the track's physical plant. Going onto the track, I told John Campbell to get over to the quarter pretty good, and if she seemed O.K., to send her after the record.

Off a first quarter in :27.2, Miss Easy paced down to the half in :54.2 and the three-quarters in 1:22.3. Leading by some 15 lengths through the stretch, John never really chased her and she hit the wire in 1:51.2! It was exhilarating!

After the world-record mile, I sent Miss Easy to Garden State Park as an undefeated world champion. Her assignment was an elimination for the Three Diamonds. There, she met a field of good fillies. I think she was a little tired after the world record at Lexington and I hadn't really trained her much.

She also endured a very long truck ride from Kentucky to New Jersey. As a consequence, she was short for the elimination and finished a tired third behind Yankee Co-Ed and Cam's Exotic.

Between the elimination and final, I trained her three trips, with the last mile in 2:10, final half in 1:02. It sharpened her back into condition, and she destroyed the fillies in the Three Diamonds final, winning by nearly ten lengths in 1:55.3 over an off track.

Miss Easy always was a robust filly, with the ability that all great horses have to bounce back from all sorts of setbacks. I took the responsibility for her being a little short for the Three Diamonds elimination, and she vindicated me in the final with a very strong performance.

After the Three Diamonds, we had more than a month before the season-ending Breeders Crown at Pompano Park in Florida. I sent Miss Easy home and rested her. Then, John qualified her in 1:57 two weeks before the Breeders Crown and said she was O.K., but that she was not very good in the turns.

Wanting everything to be right, I put her back in to qualify just one week before the Breeders Crown, and John came down to drive her again. She had the two hole in the qualifier and John left out of there with her, and another horse left with him. The other horse squeezed down on them a bit going into the first turn and John had to take Miss Easy up pretty good. She caught and pulled a shoe and made a break.

UNCERTAINTY BEFORE THE BREEDERS CROWN

Coming on the eve of the Breeders Crown, this break caused a lot of commotion. Suddenly, my phone was hot with the media. There was speculation among the writers that something was wrong with Miss Easy. I also had some concerns that she would not be able to start in the Breeders Crown after making the break in the qualifier.

However, the judges ruled that since she was already entered at the time of the qualifier, and had a clean line in the qualifier one week earlier, she could start in the Breeders Crown.

Because of the break going into the first turn in that qualifier, John was not anxious to send Miss Easy sailing right out of the gate. He left cautiously and was sixth and outside at the quarter in :27.2. She did not clear to the lead until past the half, but was pretty safe the rest of the way, winning by a length in 1:54f.

Miss Easy finished her two-year-old season with 15 wins, one second and one third in 17 starts, with earnings of $1,128,956, a record total for a freshman filly.

Miss Easy was not a difficult filly to gait or hang up. She was shod pretty simply. As a two-year-old, she wore a full swedge shoe in front with a full pad. She had a nice foot under her, about 3 1/2 inches of toe and a 51-degree angle.

At three, Miss Easy was converted to an aluminum shoe with just a rim pad, and had the same length toe and angle as at two. In both her two- and three-year-old form, she wore a light, full-swedge shoe, with a squared toe, and a 54-degree angle behind. Her knees bothered her a little all the time, and she did not wear a very long hobble for such a big filly, being fitted with a 59-inch hobble both years. A normal filly of her size would wear a 60-61 inch hobble. A hobble length of 59 inches is about average for most horses.

At three, when I trained Miss Easy back, I tried letting her hobbles out a bit, but I didn't think she was as good that way, so I left them alone. Horse trainers often try to do something with a horse because they think a good horse should go a certain way or should wear a certain piece of equipment. I always let the horse try and tell me what it wants. In most cases, you are better off accommodating the horse than trying to please yourself.

MISS EASY LIKED SOME EXTRA WORK

One of the things I discovered in training her back at three was that she liked to work a little extra distance, so I would jog her up to five miles daily. When I trained her, I would work her up to a full mile and a quarter. When I followed this routine, it seemed to keep her relaxed and keep the nervous edge off her. With the extra jogging and distance work, she learned to relax.

THE VALUE OF LEARNING TO WALK

Miss Easy also loved to walk, and her groom, Laurie Voris, who has cared for all my good fillies, would take off on long, afternoon walks where the filly could graze and soak up some sunshine. Miss Easy was a very social filly who liked being out of her stall and having someone pay attention to her and her needs.

While it is important to have a horse walked during the off hours, I believe it is also important to the overall training effort to teach a horse to walk on the track. This is one of the chief ways that I teach a horse to relax. From a very early time in training, I want a horse to walk when it first comes on the track. I want them to always walk off the track after jogging or training.

I do not like to see a trainer or groom go out to jog a horse and start slapping it on the hind end to get going as soon as he hits the track. I want to see a horse walked to the track on a loose line and then walked a good ways on the track until it is ready to jog off.

At the end of every training trip, a horse walks after being pulled up and walks all the way back to the barn. I never ask a horse to jog back to the barn after working, even if I am dissatisfied with the work.

Walking can also be a valuable tool on the track. For instance, when I am first breaking yearlings to the hobbles, I don't like to ask them to just start off and hit the pace, nor do I expect all of them to take to the hobbles all at once.

What I like to do the first couple of days after the hobbles are added is let a yearling walk a little and then ask it to begin jogging off at a slow gait. If there is some resistance, or if the yearling is a bit frightened by the hobbles, I just slow down and let it walk a little.

Then, when the yearling is comfortable, I ask it to pick it up again, trying to increase the distance each time that a horse moves before slowing to a walk. I have conquered a lot of yearlings who were "hobble shy" with this method, and would recommend it especially for fillies. It keeps them quiet and avoids trouble. Don't be afraid to let a horse walk on the track.

KEEP A FILLY QUIET IN THE BARN

One recommendation that I would make to anyone is to put your quietest help on your fillies. A groom who slaps a horse around or yells a lot is not well-matched with a filly. The average filly will respond to a quiet groom who makes very few loud noises and never gets upset.

The quickest way to undo a lot of positive work is to have a filly mishandled in the barn. A lot of times, a mistreated filly will carry her displeasure to the racetrack. A filly cannot prosper if she is afraid. She must feel relaxed and comfortable.

Another thing about fillies is that they must never be trained lame. A colt can be trained a little when he's sore, but you can undo a lot of work in a hurry if you persist in training a filly while she is hurting.

WATCH HOW A FILLY EATS

If you want to learn something about a filly, watch how she eats. A common problem for all horse trainers is the filly who won't eat when you start digging into her a little. One recommendation I have regarding a temperamental filly is rather than cut back on how much they are fed, feed them more often. In other words, feed them the same amount, but in smaller quantities.

It is also vitally important that a horse have access to plenty of fresh water. I recommend putting two buckets of fresh water in every horse's stall, particularly in hot weather. Access to fresh water is a vital ingredient in a successful feeding program.

I have always thought the way we feed horses is really contrary to nature, anyway. Horses are grazers by nature, and I think we would be better off if we fed our horses a little closer to nature's ways. If you have to feed a horse six times a day in smaller rations to get him to eat, what is the problem with that?

I also tell my grooms to keep some hay in front of my horses at all times. I want the horses to be able to "graze" if they so choose. I use pelleted hay because I think the horses clean it up a little better. I believe you don't get as much waste as with leaf hay.

SHOULD MISS EASY TRY THE COLTS?

Getting back to Miss Easy, she prepped back at three like a champion, and I probably gave her more work than any of my champion fillies just because she got along so well on that schedule. I buzzed her along pretty good before I left Florida, working her below 2:00 on a couple of occasions.

John Campbell re-qualified her in 1991, and she made her first start in a New Jersey Sires Stakes. She won the very first time out in 1:52.3. It was so ridiculously easy that it defied description. She won without being asked to go on.

That is when the chatter began in the press about Miss Easy taking on the boys in the Meadowlands Pace. I was opposed to the idea from the start, but the talk persisted as the filly rampaged through her early starts.

On June 4, in a $100,000 New Jersey Sires Stakes final, she won right back in 1:52.2, on the rim the final half, over Cam's Secretary and Perfect Together. A week later, she won an elimination for the Miss New Jersey final in 1:53.1, complete with a :27.2 final quarter.

She then won the Miss New Jersey Final despite the fact that she drew the 10-hole, was parked the entire mile, and drew off to win in

1:52.3 by 1 1/2 lengths. She was again three wide off the three-quarters and just buried the field in one of the most impressive miles ever seen at The Meadowlands.

This effort did nothing to diminish the speculation about Miss Easy starting in the Meadowlands Pace. Before that, however, she had a stake during Historic week at The Meadowlands, which she also won, this time in 1:52.2 by six lengths. This brought us to the decision whether to start her in the eliminations for the Meadowlands Pace. This was the crop of Precious Bunny, Artsplace, Die Laughing, Cambest and Easy Goer, certainly one of the finest group of three-year-olds in the sport's history.

As I indicated, I was opposed to the idea of racing Miss Easy against the colts, but her owners wanted to see her try it. I was opposed to racing against the colts because I think it takes a lot out of a filly to go against colts. I have seen a few that could do it, but they were exceptions. Billy Haughton raced Belle Acton against the colts on even terms, but that was primarily when she was an aged mare.

Haughton also had some success with Handle With Care against males, but, again, this was as an aged mare. Had Miss Easy raced another year and retained her form as a four-year-old, I would have liked a shot at Artsplace. Racing a three-year-old filly against three-year-old colts in the summer is not something I thought was a good idea then, and I don't think it is a good idea now. Even if you have some success, it takes a lot out of them. Most fillies are just not the same horses after severe stress like that.

John Campbell could not drive Miss Easy in the Meadowlands Pace eliminations because he had committed to drive Artsplace. I asked Mike Lachance to drive her.

Miss Easy drew in with Precious Bunny, Easy Goer and Nuclear Legacy and to show the high regard the public had of her chances, she was sent off at just above even money. This made sense because, up to that time, she had raced 22 times and had 20 wins!

As luck would have it, Miss Easy made a break leaving the gate. It was the only time during her career that she broke in an actual race, other than at two in that infamous Pompano qualifier. I still don't know what caused her to go offstride at the start of that race. Mike said he had a nice hold of her going away from the gate and then he just lost her. Maybe it was my fault that she made a break, because I had told Mike about so many things to watch out for. Mike is a champion driver and I should have sent him out without any instructions.

It is interesting to note that Miss Easy came right back the following week and won the Meadowlands Pace consolation, with Campbell back driving, beating Cambest and Mantese, two of the better colts of that year. I will never know how she might have fared against Precious Bunny in the final.

During Hambletonian week, Miss Easy had another major race, the Tarport Hap, and won that one, too, in 1:52.3. Next up were the eliminations for the Mistletoe Shalee. She took her elimination in 1:52.1 with one of her now-overpowering backstretch moves.

THE MANY BATTLES WITH SHADY DAISY

Then, in the Mistletoe Shalee final, we met up for the first of many duels as three-year-olds with the great filly Shady Daisy. It was clear that Shady Daisy had improved a lot at three and was a much better filly at the midpoint of her three-year-old season.

In the Mistletoe Shalee final, Miss Easy had the two-hole and John sent her winging off the :26.3 quarter. She cleared to the lead after the quarter. The half was in :54.1 and three-quarters in 1:22.4. Shady Daisy came charging at Miss Easy in the stretch, but the challenge was repulsed and Miss Easy reached the wire in a stakes and world record 1:51.1.

Miss Easy was not staked at any of the Midwestern mile tracks and was not eligible to the Jugette at Delaware because the half-mile track would not have been to her liking. She had problems in the turns and not even Delaware's soup-bowl half-mile could have helped her enough.

Besides, it was not Miss Easy's custom to bust out of the gate like horses who do well at Delaware. It did not fit her racing style and we stayed home.

After nearly a month off, Miss Easy returned to qualify at Garden State Park in mid-September, and did so in 1:54.4 for Campbell. John thought she acted fine. She had two stakes engagements within the next couple of weeks, one at Garden State and the other at Lexington near the end of the month.

On September 21, I started her at Garden State in the Nadia Lobell. She was rough-gaited leaving the gate, getting away tenth from the two-hole. She still came an incredible mile, finishing third, out all the way after being almost dead last at the half. She was beaten one and a half lengths by Celebrity Girl and Yankee Co-Ed.

TROUBLE IN LEXINGTON

From there, it was on to Lexington to meet Shady Daisy again, this time in the Cuddy Farms (Bluegrass Stake) at The Red Mile. Drawing the 11-hole, Miss Easy was in for another rough journey. She was extended to get the lead at the half, reached in :54.4. From her back tier starting post, she had to be down to the half individually around :54 flat!

Shady Daisy went on to win that afternoon, with Miss Easy finishing third, beaten some eight-and-a half lengths. I had her scoped after the race and discovered that she had a bad throat infection. I had her treated and turned her out in between races at Peninsula Farm.

She acted fine, so I brought her in and trained her a little two days before her next start. I had dropped her in an overnight event for fillies and mares and, lo and behold, there was Shady Daisy in the box with us as well.

Miss Easy warmed up O.K., but did not have her usual pace, and John reported that she acted as though she could not get her air past the half where she was on top in :54.1. She struggled home some 16 1/2 lengths behind Shady Daisy's world record 1:51 mile.

This was really the only poor race she had ever gone in her life and I was extremely disappointed, to say the least. I had one major objective with her for the balance of her three-year-old season. That was the Breeders Crown, set for October 25 at Pompano Park. I hoped there would be enough time to attend to her throat problems and get her sharp enough to be competitive.

I shipped Miss Easy to the training center in Florida and had her treated once again for the throat infection which involved the administration of antibiotics since her throat was red and inflamed. She and Laurie also returned to her afternoon schedule of long, slow walks. Like most good horses, she responded to the treatment and began to return to form. I let Miss Easy lie around for a week and a half before I trained her back. She acted O.K., but I was concerned about her lack of work going into the Breeders Crown. I did not want to take her back to Pompano and qualify her, because I feared something might go wrong as it had with her under similar circumstances at two.

I had Dr. John Cummins from Lexington go over her from stem to stern about ten days before the Breeders Crown, and I had her hind feet injected. A lot of vets had looked at her during her two-year-old season and again at three, trying to determine why she was always running in. Whatever the reason, after the injections to her hind feet, she was perfect and straight and actually better than at any other time in her life.

CONCERNED ABOUT HER FITNESS

Miss Easy quit coughing, got her appetite back, and, as always, showed her amazing recuperative abilities. Frankly, I was very concerned about her condition going into the Breeders Crown. I decided I had to do something about it.

Let me set the scene:She last raced in Lexington on October 4 and her next start was the Breeders Crown on October 25. Because she had been sick during the Lexington meeting, I hadn't done much with her. Then, here was another three-week interval without any serious work. She had not had any real work in that entire period, which was more than six weeks. To complicate matters, she had been off prior to that period, as well, which meant that in the last ten weeks, she had virtually no serious training.

One of the author's most exceptional fillies was the Big Towner lass,
Central Park West, shown with the author's son Sep. Central Park West
was, by the author's admission, a perfect filly from the start.

I TRAINED HER FIVE TRIPS!

So, a full week before the Breeders Crown, I worked Miss Easy on the mile track at Sunshine Meadows five training miles, with the last two trips around 1:55!

I worked her in the second-horse position out from the rail, and she just cruised. It was the only time I ever drove her when she drove absolutely true and straight. I think she enjoyed the day about as much as I did.

Follow My Star is the only other horse I ever worked that much in my life. This was the only work Miss Easy would get before the Breeders Crown, and I did not want her to go into that race short. But I do admit that I told the press that I trained her in 2:12, but what I neglected to add was the 2:12 mile was her third heat, and that two 1:55 miles had followed that!

I was convinced from that work that Miss Easy had regained her form and that she would win another Breeders Crown.

She did win the Breeders Crown, pacing in 1:52.2, establishing a world record. This was the third world record of her memorable career.

She had one more engagement three weeks later in the Matron Stakes at Pompano, which was the final start of her career. I drove her myself for the first and only time in a competitive race, and she was beaten by Sunraycer in 1:53.4.

Miss Easy retired at the conclusion of her three-year-old season with a lifetime record of 32 starts—with 25 wins, three seconds and three thirds, and a new filly or mare earnings record of $1,777,656.

She was an exceptional filly, and I always marvelled at how far she could carry her speed. I have had quicker horses, but none faster over a long distance. Miss Easy was a truly marvelous, gifted filly. What she might have accomplished if she had driven straight just boggles the mind. I am sure she would have set time records and money earnings marks that might never have been beaten.

CENTRAL PARK WEST—"PINK CENTER CANDY"

For size, gait and temperament, the best of all my fillies to date has to be Central Park West, who came along in between the time I had Follow My Star and Miss Easy.

Right from the start, Central Park West was a special filly. She had great size and substance for a two-year-old early in her career and she broke like a good horse. She was long-barrelled and had that big, wide rear-end. Unlike Follow My Star and Miss Easy, Central Park West trained perfectly at two, without a single problem of any consequence.

She was what we call in our stable "pink center candy."

This is an expression we developed to mean a horse is really perfect, like finding a piece of pink center candy in a box of chocolates. It is a real surprise and a real treat when you find one of those perfect "pink center" horses in your shed row.

After I got her broke, Central Park West started training down, and every time I asked her to do a little extra, she responded willingly and with just the right temperament. She would take a nice hold training, but not too much. She was a quiet filly around the barn, she ate good, was sound and took her work cheerfully. She was just a perfect filly.

Even as a two-year-old, Central Park West was such a big-gaited filly that I wore a 61-inch hobble on her. She had tremendous reach and a ground-devouring stride. She impressed me from the start.

I had very high hopes for her when I left winter training in Florida. I don't like to really dig into my two-year-olds, especially the fillies, any earlier than necessary. I normally leave Florida the first week of May and hope to work them around 2:10 a couple of times before shipping.

I shipped Central Park West directly to The Meadowlands and thought she was ready to go along anywhere. But I was so high on her, I wanted to be very careful. Again, I asked John Campbell to race her the first couple of starts. I told John to be very careful, stay out of trouble, and just race her along.

I wanted her backed off the gate and raced out of a hole the first couple of times, regardless of what anybody else was doing.

I started Central Park West for the first time on May 14, which is pretty early on the calendar. In fact, it was a full week before I like to start, but I thought she was ready to race. I was conscious of the fact that it was early and I wanted to be very careful.She had the six hole, and

John got away eighth and stayed there until the stretch, where he let her pace home freely in :27.3 to finish fifth. She closed some ten lengths from the half on with a final half paced around a minute flat.

DO YOUR "BRUSHING" IN THE STALL

The fact that Central Park West showed so much finishing kick is pretty interesting because I do not believe that two-year-olds should be brushed sharply in training. One of my major philosophies in training is that the only place a horse should be brushed is in the stall—by the groom!

I do not believe in working fast quarters or eighths. When I am finishing off a colt or filly in the final weeks of training, I will come a quarter around 30 seconds if they are comfortable there, but there is no way I would buzz one along at a 27 second clip in a training mile. If the speed is there, it will come.

Central Park West went into her first baby race never having been brushed a real hot quarter, yet she got home in :27.3 the first time she was asked.

I was very pleased with her performance, and she came out of it good and sharp. Every horse trainer will tell you that horses train differently after you start racing. It seems to mature them a lot. The good ones really respond to the competition. They seem more alert on the track. They seem more willing to work. They seem more aggressive.

I could tell in training Central Park West between starts, that the first race had helped her. She was coming along perfectly. Ten days after her first start, I came back with her. This is a nice interval. Although I was anxious to start her again, I am always conscious of where I am headed with a two-year-old.

TRAIN SIX MONTHS AHEAD

I like to think that I am six months ahead of myself with a two-year-old. I continually ask myself,"what is my game plan?" "Where am I headed?" "Am I on schedule for the season-ending races I want to win?"

I don't think enough trainers try to look well ahead with two-year-olds. It is more of a week-to-week thing with them. I learned a long time ago that you better be planning ahead with your stable all of the time, or the time will catch up to you. This is where a trainer can learn to manage both the horse and the calendar to produce the desired results.

In her second start, Central Park West set second early, got shuffled back along the rail to fifth at the half, and closed strongly to just miss getting her maiden win in 2:01.3, final quarter in :28.4.She had closed strongly once again, and I was very pleased with her first two races. Now, it was time to find out what we really had.

For Central Park West's next start on May 31, I told Ray Remmen to drive her a little more aggressively, because I needed to start honing her down a little if I hoped to be a contender for the Sweetheart at The Meadowlands in about 60 days.

Ray got away second with her, then put her in gear going to the half, got the lead and eased up through three-quarters in 1:33.3 before she zipped home in :27 flat to win in 2:00.3. I knew then that this, indeed, was an exceptional filly.

BE CAREFUL IN THE MUD

The track came up muddy for her next start on June 11 and I scratched her rather than taking a chance of racing her on an off track. This was a cautious move, but I would make the same decision again.

Racing a two-year-old over an off track is a risky proposition. They are just really finding themselves and learning. A muddy track, which often means either a hard track beaten down by the rain or a sloppy surface with lots of water on it, can be very damaging to a potential star. I would urge any trainer to be very careful and look at track surfaces when racing two-year-olds. If it is a big stake for a lot of money, you don't have much choice. If the track comes up bad, you have to go anyway. But if it is a $500 baby race, you have all the choice in the world.

If the track doesn't suit you in these circumstances, be patient and careful. Don't be intimidated into thinking you have to race when the track is bad. It might be all right to go ahead and race, but why take the chance if the track is awful? To err on the side of caution is a choice I can live with.

I was very happy with Central Park West's development at this time, so missing this one start did not bother me too much. I worked her in midweek as I always did throughout her two-year-old season. She thrived on that schedule. Usually, I would work her three trips in 2:40-2:20-2:12, evenly rated except for the final mile, which might include a good last eighth around 15 seconds, but no more.

On June 18, I came back in another baby race with her and I got John Campbell back in the sulky. Now, it was time to get a little more serious about our work.

She drew the eight-hole, but I told John that she was ready to go wherever she had to and for him to not be real conservative. I wanted her involved in the race to see how she would respond.

John got away sixth on the outside, but caught the flow and was fourth, in the second-over spot, turning for home. From there, he pulled her and she rocketed home in :27.3 to win in 1:58.3. I knew right there we had one whale of a filly on our hands.

Next up was Central Park West's first official start in a betting race, on June 27 at The Meadowlands. This was during Historic week and she drew the five-hole in a 10-horse field. John got away ninth from her mid-pack position on the gate, but was much more aggressive with her this time, reaching third on the outside past a :58.3 half.

At that point, I was a little concerned about her because she had never been that kind of half before. John finally cleared to the lead with her and coasted home in :29 to win in 1:57. She got a little tired, but that race set her up perfectly for the next start at The Meadows in a Pennsylvania Sires Stake.

Central Park West went wire-to-wire in that one, drawing away with no urging to win in 1:56.4f, complete with a :28.2 final quarter. From there, I went back to The Meadowlands with her, winning a $7,500 two-year-old overnight in 1:56.3, final quarter in :27.3.

I thought the latter race was a perfect setup for the eliminations for the Sweetheart, a race for which she was now the favorite. She drew the rail for her elimination. I could foresee no trouble with that spot since I was training her over the track every day and she was going her miles without any trouble.

Looking back, I should have trained her down next to the fence before that race. I like to train most of my horses away from the rail in the second-horse position. I find most of the time that the footing is a little better, and I think it is good to train a horse a little farther than a mile all the time. Sitting in the second horse position, a horse has to go a little farther, and I think that is good.

Coming to the starting line in the Sweetheart elimination, Central Park West shied from the light and finish poles down near the wire, and made a sideways break just as the word "go" was given. She lost all chance of winning.

I was convinced that she "laid over" those fillies and would have won her elimination, because they ended up pacing in 1:57.1 that night. I think she was ready to go in 1:55 if necessary.

We lost our chance to win the Sweetheart with that break at the gate, but I came back to train her and she was all right, showing no ill effects from her costly break.

After a start at The Meadowlands, I sent her out west to the Grand Circuit meeting at the Illinois State Fairgrounds at Springfield. She had the rail again, and this time went sailing out of there without any trouble and went wire-to-wire for John in 1:53.4, with a final quarter in :27.4.

I wanted to come back another heat with her, but her owner, Susan Laden, thought better of it and we scratched her. I don't really think that heats can hurt a horse who is properly prepared and who has a good foundation. I know that I thought then—and still believe—that Central Park West could have beaten 1:52 that afternoon. She was scary fast and sound at that time.

At Indianapolis, she went one heat again, winning on the engine with Campbell in 1:56.2, final quarter in :28.1.

Then it was back east to Freestate Raceway for the Lady Baltimore Stake. Central Park West was bet down to be the heavy favorite and won by four lengths, pacing in 1:57.

I had no race scheduled for her for the next few weeks and sent her to Lexington to prep for her Grand Circuit appearances at The Red Mile. I trained her there, and on September 21, I qualified her in 1:55.3.

Central Park West was really maturing and coming to herself. Of all my great fillies, I would have to say that she was the most trouble-free at two. She had a great gait, a good mouth, was fast and durable, and loved to go.

The first week at Lexington, she took her elimination of the K.D. Owen in 1:54.4 after being rimmed to the half in :55 flat. She was the safest kind of winner, and John did not chase her much, knowing that she would have to go heats for the first time that afternoon.

She came right back and took the final, too, with John moving her off the first quarter to take command at the half in :56.2. John was able to give her a breather to three-quarters in 1:27.1 and then she scooted home in :28.3 to win in 1:55.4.

At that point in time, I thought Central Park West was just about the finest filly pacer I had ever seen. She was certainly the finest I had ever been around personally. She was just flawless.

The second week at Lexington, she came right back in the International Stallion Stakes to win with another gigantic trip that showed her real grit. She had the seven-hole and was parked fourth past the half in :56.3. She finally got to the top coming out of the last turn and opened up with a terrific final quarter in :27.3 after never seeing the rail, winning in 1:54.3.

After Lexington, I was convinced there was no other pacing filly on earth who could beat Central Park West. She had almost a month off before her final appearances of the year in the Breeders Crown at Pompano Park.

I shipped her to Florida and let her lie around for a week or two and then finally "revved her up" for the Breeders Crown appearance. I trained her three trips a couple of times the second week in October.

I started her in an overnight at Pompano just to make sure that everything was O.K. She needed the race. I did not want to go into the eliminations for the Breeders Crown and have her come up short.

I raced her myself, and she circled the field after the half, winning in 1:57.2 after being nearly last at the half-mile pole.

At that time, the Breeders Crown elimination races were one week before the final. Central Park West won her elimination, in 1:56, with a last quarter in :28.1. I didn't see how she could lose the final, but I took no chances.

I trained her three trips before the final, as I had throughout her two-year-old season, with the final mile in 2:12. She really thrived on that schedule.

For the Breeders Crown final, she was better than ever. She had the rail, and for one of the few times all year, John Campbell had her involved pretty early in the race. She was on top, but parked at the 56-second opening half. But then John opened her up and she sailed by the three-quarters in 1:25.3. In the stretch, John asked her for more and she responded with a :28 final quarter to set a world record of 1:53.3f.

Central Park West's two-year-old season ended with 18 starts, 15 wins and one second and earnings of $527,183. After her break at the start of the Sweetheart eliminations, she won her last 12 races in a row. She was never really seriously threatened in any of those races.

Her average margin of victory in those last dozen starts was something like three lengths, and most of the time she was never driven out.

Therefore, I had tremendous high hopes for her three-year-old season. She trained back perfectly, too, and I sent her north for the summer to re-qualify, knowing that she had matured into a wonderful filly. Up to this time, she had never taken an unsound step.

DISASTER STRUCK IN QUALIFYING RACE

Central Park West qualified twice around the middle of May and seemed like her old self, winning both qualifiers in 1:57. Then, in the third qualifier, disaster struck.

She had the two-hole and a horse beside her made a break and came right down into her while the field was still on the gate. John and the filly were pushed sideways and nearly went down.

The next morning, Central Park West had a front leg as big as a stove pipe, and she was visibly lame. I had her examined and it was thought she had pulled a suspensory. I gave her some time off, blistered the leg and brought her along slowly, hoping to recoup as much of the season as we could.

She came back in what I would describe as just "racehorse soundness" and was, at least to my eye, not nearly the same filly she had been at two. I had John re-qualify her on July 15 and she won in 1:57.3, but that was mostly on heart. She was hurting pretty bad.

I finally started her for the first time as a three-year-old on July 22 in an elimination for the Mistletoe Shalee at The Meadowlands. She was sitting fifth at the half when John tried to put her in gear and get her going to get into the race, but she was in too much pain. She made a break and finished seventh. Her leg looked pretty good after this race, though, and I put her back in to qualify at The Meadowlands on July 29. Just to show you what heart she had, she won the qualifier in 1:56.3, pacing the final quarter in :27.4. I was encouraged by her effort, but she was still far from the filly that I had trained a year earlier.

Good horses come in all sizes. One of the smaller champions developed by the author was the $1 million winning Immortality. The No Nukes filly was an instant training star for the author as a baby, but her training was always a little less than some of her stablemates because of her small size.

I started Central Park West for the final time on August 12 in a division of the Adioo Volo at The Meadows. She raced credibly for a filly in a lot of pain and just missed winning in 1:57, but that effort told me she deserved a better fate. I recommended quitting with her, since to race her would only cheapen her reputation.

Central Park West never raced again. She wound up with two record starts at three, and won only $7,680, but there is no telling what she might have accomplished if she had not been injured.

My own belief is that she would have established records that future generations would have had to shoot at. She was a perfect racehorse before her injury. She was bigger than Follow My Star and easier to drive than Miss Easy. She had no soundness problems at all before she was run into.

IMMORTALITY—ANOTHER $1 MILLION FILLY

At the conclusion of Miss Easy's three-year-old season, Lou Guida handed me the sales slip on a No Nukes yearling filly named Immortality, whom he had purchased for $97,000 at the annual Harrisburg sale.

I shipped her to Florida and began the breaking process. She was a very small filly. But, from the first time I got her between the shafts, she showed me that she was something extra special. She had such a willing attitude and grittiness to her.

I was always concerned about her size, because the saying in the horse business is that a little horse is O.K. until you run up against a big horse. Immortality didn't know she was little. She just learned how to go.

She was a natural-gaited pacer for her size, and had terrific reach and extension. She really got over the ground good. I thought she could be a real good filly. I had no idea she would make one of the greatest two-year-old fillies in the history of the breed.

One problem Immortality had at two was that she was a light eater. She didn't eat like I wanted her to, and I think that eventually caught up with her toward the end of her two-year-old season. A lot of fillies are very poor eaters and I suppose that Immortality could have become a problem eater, but I watched her pretty carefully and monitored her eating habits.

In training, Immortality was always my best filly that season. She came right down for me, dropping with ease every time I asked her. I like to drop a horse two to three seconds per week if they can do it easily and take the work cheerfully. Immortality was always ready to do more. She was, it seems, poised for a little extra.

TRAINING CONCESSIONS DUE TO SIZE

I did make some concessions to Immortality because of her size. I put her on the same schedule as the rest of the horses, but I was careful not to overdo it with her. I was always conscious of cutting back a little on her work to make sure she lasted. It stands to reason that a small horse has to work harder to accomplish the same things a filly such as Miss Easy, for instance, could do.

Like most good, small horses, Immortality was quick. She was cat quick. She could have learned to zip along pretty good all winter, but I was very patient with her. I do not like to rush a two-year-old, even when they take their work very easily like she did.

I like to train the miles that build foundation and provide the toughness necessary to stand up to a season of knocks and bumps that inevitably come from racing. Immortality finished her prep like a good filly, working in 2:10 a couple of times before shipping north.

After arriving at The Meadowlands, she worked in 2:08 one week and 2:05 the next, and zipped home around 30 seconds in each of those workouts.

SHOEING EXPERIMENTS

About the only other problem I had with Immortality at two was her shoeing. It seemed as though I was in a constant state of change with her shoes. I had started her out in a half-round shoe, but didn't really like her that way. I experimented and tried her in aluminum shoes. I didn't like her in those either. Finally, I tried a pair of full swedges. She still did not suit me.

One morning at The Meadowlands, I took Immortality to the blacksmith and was explaining my frustration to the farrier. We talked about her situation and he asked me to look at a pair of shoes hanging on the wall he had taken off a Swedish-trained trotter.

They were steel shoes like the traditional American shoe, but the rim of the shoe looked like the teeth of a chain saw. There were interruptions in the metal, and open places in between. I held the shoes up, and they looked as though they would fit Immortality, so I had the blacksmith tack them on her.

When I trained her in these new shoes, she was perfect. She was better in these light, hard steel shoes than with anything else I had tried. Immortality was very light on her feet and did not wear her shoes down much anyway. With most horses, you need a new set of shoes every month. Immortality wore these funny-looking shoes throughout her two-year-old season. During the summer, all I did was just reset them. The steel was so hard she never wore them out. I have those shoes mounted and hanging on the wall in my home.

For her hind shoes, Immortality wore a conventional full swedge with a 54-degree angle. In front, those exotic shoes I found in the blacksmith shop were set on 3 1/2-inch toes at a 51-degree angle.

Because Immortality was so small, I did not try to train her much before I started her. I also did not want much done to her in her first couple of starts. I thought she was a sensational filly and I told John Campbell not to show her much racetrack the first couple of starts.

She started first on May 23 in a $500 baby race at The Meadowlands. John got her off in front in a :30.1 quarter, but then he was covered. He sat in with her until very late. He asked her to pace a little in the lane and she got home in 28 seconds to pace around 2:00.2.

I came right back with her one week later and she was second again after a first-over trip, pacing in 2:01.2. I was happy with these efforts, but John was not convinced that she was the kind of filly that I had raved about.

What John did not know was that I had not yet cranked her up. I have trained enough horses to know when I have something between the shafts and Immortality felt wonderful. She had such a reach and feel to her. When she really put it in gear, she was a big-gaited small horse. That is what allowed her to overcome her size. She had the gait and reach of a much bigger filly.

SHARPEN THEM UP WHEN THE TIME IS RIGHT

In between the May 30 baby race and her first real money start in a New Jersey Sire Stakes on June 17, I trained Immortality in 1:57.3, complete with a final quarter better than 28 seconds. This was more than the normal training routine for most fillies, but I already had figured out that Immortality was anything but normal.

I told John she would be much better that night, and that this would be the easiest race she would ever have. The extra work had really sharpened her. She bounded home by a widening length in 1:57.1, final quarter in 28 seconds.

The following week, she was right back in 1:55.3, winning by six lengths! She had already earned enough points in the two preliminary races to make the $100,000 New Jersey Sires final, so I shipped her over to Yonkers for the La Paloma Stake.

Immortality was the perfect half-mile track horse. She was both quick and fast. Although I had never even trained her on a half-mile track, I knew she would be O.K. at Yonkers.

The La Paloma elimination was conducted on July 4 and was a non-betting affair. Immortality got away fifth, and was fourth and on the move at the half in :59.2. From there, John eased her up alongside the leaders and wore them down from the first-over spot, drawing away to win by nearly two lengths in 1:58.4h.

SPOT PROBLEM AHEAD OF TIME—CHANGE ROUTINE

I was happy with her performance, but she was beginning to lose a little more weight than I preferred. This is something you should look for in any stable, regardless of whether you are training colts or fillies. When a two-year-old starts to lose weight, it may be time for you to change that horse's routine.

I thought that Immortality might be getting a little more work than she wanted between races, so I made a shift in her training schedule. I eliminated her midweek works.

My normal training routine, like that of most Standardbred horse trainers, is to work a horse two or three trips at midweek if I am racing on a normal seven-day cycle. With Immortality, however, I decided this was too much work for her.

I cut back her training routine. I added an extra jog mile to her daily routine, but only trained her a single, light blowout mile in 2:30 two days before she raced. The normal three trips at midweek were eliminated.

A horse trainer has to be careful with these adjustments, however, because you still must pay attention to a horse's overall condition. While I eliminated the midweek work, I had to find a way for Immortality to hold her sharpness and fitness.

USE WARM UP MILES EFFECTIVELY

Every horse warms up to race. The significance and importance of the warm up mile as a conditioning tool when a horse races is often overlooked by trainers.

From the time she started racing, I was warming up Immortality around 2:25 or 2:30 the final trip. I would just start her up and let her amble along wherever she felt comfortable.

But after the midweek work was discontinued, I had to find a way, whenever it was necessary, to get some additional work into her. What I did was use the warm up miles to replace the abandoned midweek work for conditioning. Instead of a 2:25 to 2:30 mile, I would warm her up in 2:12-2:15.

I did not do this every week, as I didn't think Immortality would stand it since she was so small. However, the warm up miles can be used in this way to provide important conditioning work.

A big, strong filly like Miss Easy warmed up around 2:10 or 2:12 all the time because she liked it that way. But Immortality would not have lasted if I had used a fast warm up mile for her throughout her two-year-old season.

For important races, however, when you want to "rev one up" for a sharp effort, try using a little faster warm up mile for a couple of weeks before the big race and you will come into the race as sharp as possible, even without serious midweek works. I think a lot of trainers overlook the potential benefits of the warm up miles to their overall conditioning program.

Getting back to the La Paloma, Immortality had the two-hole and got away fifth, but was out and on the move past the half in :57.3. Campbell had her really winging when they hit the backstretch the final time and she swooped the field, winning in a season's record 1:56.2. That was one of her finest performances of the season.

As I said earlier, Immortality was already qualified for the New Jersey Sires Stakes final, a $100,000 race. That race, however, was scheduled for only four days after the La Paloma final. I entered her, but then thought better of it and scratched her. I did not want to race her back on only a three-day rest after such a remarkable effort at Yonkers. I thought it might be too much for her.

She was off until Hambletonian week at The Meadowlands where her next start was a $106,000 division of the Countess Adios. Even though she had not raced in 18 days, Immortality was extra sharp, winning in 1:54.2 with a breathtaking move down the backstretch when she moved from fifth to first in what seemed like a single heartbeat.

She repeated that performance on August 6 in an elimination for the Sweetheart at The Meadowlands, making another dramatic move down the backstretch to take command and win in an identical 1:54.2.

In the Sweetheart Final, she was 2-5 in the odds and raced like it. From the seven-hole, she took command past the half in :55.3 and reported home nearly two lengths up to win in 1:53, which became her two-year-old mark.

After the Sweetheart, Immortality had nearly a month off before her next start, in the Lady Baltimore at Rosecroft Raceway. On September 5, she won again in 1:55.4 after taking command past the half, which by now had developed into her racing style.

On September 12, she won again, taking the Kentucky Standardbred Sales Co. Pace in one of her most impressive efforts of the season. She had drawn the nine-hole and was in for a very tough trip. She was sixth and outside at the quarter in :28 and had advanced to fourth at the half in :57. After the half, Campbell put her in gear. She rolled into contention, but was still out at the three-quarters in 1:26.1. She found still more juice and got home on top in 1:55.2.

For a little filly, this kind of mile seemed improbable. She had such great courage, however, and simply would not be denied.

That race was tough on her, so I decided not to send her to Lexington the first week of the Grand Circuit meeting. I had wanted to race her in Lexington, but I thought she needed the week off before the eliminations for the Three Diamonds stake at Garden State Park.

Going into the Three Diamonds, she had won nine races in a row, the only blemishes on her card being the two baby races where we had kept her under wraps.

The Three Diamonds elimination and final were nearly carbon copy races. She had the five-hole for both events and in each, was taken off the gate and then sent for the lead going to the half. The elimination victory was in 1:54.4 by a length and three-quarters, with the final annexed in 1:54.1 by the same margin.

Late in October, I started her in the $300,000 Breeders Crown at Pompano Park, and this turned out to be one of the easiest races of her year. For the first time in her life, John put her in control of the race and went wire-to-wire in 1:54.4f, pacing the final quarter in :28.2 and completing an unprecedented sweep of the LaPaloma, Sweetheart and Breeders Crown.

A SEASON-ENDING MISTAKE

Immortality had one final start planned in her 1992 season. This was for the Matron Stakes at the end of the first week of November, also at Pompano.

Looking back at that race, I probably should not have raced her that night. She had gotten a little sick and had not eaten well coming up to the race.

I had not trained her, and thought she might be a little short, but we were all anxious to put her over the $1 million mark in earnings in her two-year-old season.

The race turned out to be a very difficult mile for her. She was away fourth from the four-hole and was still fourth at the half in :55.3. Campbell then asked her for pace in the final half and she came three-wide to the three-quarters in 1:24.2 before gutting out a very tough 1:54.3 win. It was her slowest final quarter of the season, and it was a race that I think took a lot out of her. I personally never thought she was the same filly after this.

If I had it to do over, I would have limited her to about 12 starts at two, instead of the 15 she had. A big filly like Miss Easy or a dominant

A big filly with a long gait and easy disposition, Freedoms Friend was a champion two-year-old despite some persistent hock troubles. For a filly with this kind of size and substance, the author recommends the use of additional jog miles.

filly like Central Park West could stand a number of tough races, but Immortality was too small. I think we overdid it with her at two. I think that is one of the things that contributed to the problems she had in returning to form at three.

FREEDOMS FRIEND—MANAGEMENT WAS KEY

The last of the champion fillies I want to talk about in detail is Freedoms Friend, a Matt's Scooter filly who was bred and owned by Bob Hamather of Ontario, Canada.

I got Freedoms Friend in the fall of her yearling year after I got home from the Harrisburg sale. She was a tall, gangly filly. She looked thin because she had grown very tall and the rest of her body hadn't kept up with her height.

I immediately began pouring the feed to her and double de-wormed her every 30 days for a couple of months. I got her broke without any problems. She began to fill out and do better. I put her in one of my better sets from the beginning, because I thought she had real natural ability. From the start, she had a great, soft mouth on her. She was a very kind filly on the track, very easy on herself.

Early in her development, I thought Freedoms Friend would make a nice filly if I could keep her together. She was such a big filly that I didn't know if she would stay sound. Her knees bothered her early in her two-year-old year, and I spent a good deal of time keeping them injected with acid about every three weeks.

The amazing thing about Freedoms Friend is that she absolutely thrived on the work. The farther I went with her the better she looked, and the better she liked it.

Freedoms Friend is a good study for a lot of trainers, because a lot of times trainers get these big fillies and don't give them the kind of work they need in order to prosper. This is the opposite of the problem that I faced with Immortality throughout her two-year-old year, when she was so small I felt I could not afford to give her a lot of work.

Freedoms Friend, however, was a filly who thrived on the work. I would recommend that if you are training a big, growthy filly, you give her plenty of solid conditioning work. For instance, I would recommend jogging four miles instead of three with a big filly like this.

She was a filly who was easy to get pacing. I put a pair of half-inch, half-round shoes on her to get started and to get her gaited properly. For such a big filly, she had a nice foot under her, and she carried a natural 3 1/2-inch toe set at about a 50-degree angle. Behind, I put a pair of flat shoes on her to get started and squared her toes. She was a low-angled filly behind, so I put a pair of flat shoes with trailers on her because I wanted her to have a little more support back there.

Freedoms Friend came along pretty quickly once I started repeating her. I like to start repeating my horses after only a couple of weeks. This does not mean, however, that I want to start training right away, but I do a lot of "repeat jogging" with my two-year-olds. I think this does a lot to manner a horse and teach it what you want it to do. This also keeps a horse from getting so tired in any one jogging session, which can lead to knuckling over.

I like to take a filly out and jog her a couple of miles, then come in and let her rest for a half-hour or so, then go back out and jog her another couple of miles. The second time, I might vary my routine by going the right way of the track.

I also find repeating to be very useful when you first put the hobbles on a filly. I might jog her the first couple of miles free-legged, then come in and hang a set of hobbles on her and go right back out while she is still a little tired. There is a lot less resistance when they get a little tired. I don't want to overdo this, because too much stress can cause them to pop curbs and splints and develop all kinds of problems. I just try and judge every horse to see what kind of tolerance level they have, and stay within their limits of endurance. Too much work can get them track sour. Then you have a whole new set of problems.

DON'T PUT HOBBLES ON TOO TIGHT

One thing to avoid with two-year-olds who are wearing hobbles for the first time is having the hobbles too tight to begin with. If I make an error at this point, I want the problem to be that the hobbles are too long. I also recommend that you put the hobbles on your two-year-olds every day, without fail. This is very important. A tight hobble can begin to burn a horse. Naturally, they will not like this, and can get into some bad habits. A good, loose fitting hobble gets a colt or filly used to the slap of the hobbles and won't burn their legs as badly. As a general rule of thumb, you should be able to pull the hobbles a couple of inches ahead of a horse's foreleg while the horse is standing at rest. This should be your guide. From there, you can shorten up or lengthen the hobbles as you feel necessary.

Freedoms Friend did not have any of these problems. She was on the pace pretty easily and showed me right away that she had a lot of class. I am always impressed by any horse with a real soft mouth, and Freedoms Friend was that way. She would take the lightest little hold of me early in her training and she stayed with that. A horse with a good mouth will outdo a bad-mouthed horse every time. The ability to relax on the bit is a real asset for any horse.

Freedoms Friend also was a very good-gaited, slick-going filly right from the start. She wore a 59-inch hobble and was solid and on the pace from day one. She was right on schedule leaving my winter base in Florida.

I got her started a little later than some of my other good fillies. I did not baby race her until nearly June 1, which is about two weeks later than I prefer.

As is my custom, the first few baby races are for experience and maturity. I am not interested in winning these races. I am interested in teaching a young horse gate manners, teaching it to sit in the hole and follow horses and stay on gait. I also am interested to see if it can flash some speed finishing the mile.

Freedoms Friend made her debut the last week of May at The Meadowlands, and although I was very high on her, I had not worked her as much as some of my other good fillies before starting. She had trained a little lighter than Immortality and Miss Easy, because she was a filly who was growing a lot. I was conscious of giving her enough time to develop at her own pace, yet still getting her ready to race.

She finished fifth in her first baby race, but zipped home in :28.2 and paced her mile in 2:02.4. She held her position good in a final half paced around a minute flat. I was happy with her effort.

A MAJOR SHOEING CHANGE

Before her next start, I decided to tune her up a little and worked her a mile in 2:05, with the final quarter in 30 seconds. I put this training into her after a visit to the blacksmith shop for a few changes. I added a plastic rim pad under her half-round shoe and extended the pad across her heel.

I also did something with Freedoms Friend that I thought helped her a lot behind—I put a full pad under her hind shoes. I thought this would take some of the sting away from her and soften the jolt on her hind joints.

The next start came in mid-June in another baby race and, this time, John Campbell put her on the lead and was beaten about three lengths in a 2:00.4 mile. She paced home in :28 again after cutting the mile. I was quite pleased with this effort. She was really beginning to get the idea.

Just six days after that effort, I dropped her into a New Jersey Sires Stake and John sent her right down the road after taking the lead at the half in :59.1. She sailed to a win in 1:57, with a final quarter eased up in :28.2.

This victory earned Freedoms Friend a start in the $100,000 Debutante, which she also won in 1:55.1 after a particularly tough trip.

In that race, she was three deep in the final turn after John ran up onto stalled cover and was forced outside with her. This was an impressive mile and showed me that she was, indeed, as good a filly as any of my former good ones.

Early in July, Freedoms Friend was beginning to show some stifle soreness and that was reflected in a so-so effort the first week of July in a New Jersey Sires Stakes event. She got shuffled to third in that race, came late and was beaten about three-quarters of a length in 1:55.1 by Terrie Letsgo.

In the $100,000 New Jersey Sires Stakes final on July 21, however, she bounced right back to win in 1:54.3, taking command with a devastating brush down the backstretch.

Freedoms Friend drew the rail for the eliminations of the Sweetheart at The Meadowlands the following week, and I had visions of Central Park West's break that had cost her a chance at the Sweetheart final. So, I trained Freedoms Friend at midweek and was careful to work her along the rail at The Meadowlands to give her a look at all the lights and poles.

She acted perfect for Campbell going away in her elimination, and went down the road, but could not stall off the late charge of Lotus Spur in a 1:54.2 mile.

I was concerned that Freedoms Friend was going into the Sweetheart final a little compromised, because her stifles were really bothering her. The night of the Sweetheart final she warmed up poorly. I told John that he would have to be at his best that night because the filly was not.

John was cautious leaving the gate. He did not wish to repeat the wire-to-wire performance that had gotten her beaten the previous week. She was fourth and on the move at the half-mile pole, and got to the lead at the three-quarters in 1:24. At that point, she and John opened a five-length lead and just cruised home to win by two and a half-lengths over a hard-charging World Order.

Because Freedoms Friend was so sore heading into this race, and won simply on class and courage, I gave her a good deal of time off in order to determine what was best for her.

I sent her to one of the better equine clinics in Lexington, Kentucky, and had her examined by Dr. Larry Bramlage from head to toe. He determined that her stifle joint was bothering her and recommended some rest for her. Since she was already in Lexington, I turned her out at Peninsula Farm. She was there for the better part of two and a half weeks.

I qualified her at The Red Mile during the Grand Circuit meeting so she would have a race in her going into the eliminations for the Three Diamonds at Garden State Park. I wanted to test her soundness and how fit she might be after her layoff.

I drove Freedoms Friend myself in the qualifying mile at Lexington and was very concerned about her lack of conditioning. As she paced down the backstretch in that qualifying race, I thought about pulling her and seeing how fit she was, but that brief thought was overruled quickly when I admitted to myself that the mile was more important to her as far as conditioning was concerned. I let her follow the field and never pulled her. She finished third, and was well within herself.

She had won the Sweetheart on August 11 at The Meadowlands and the Three Diamonds eliminations were set for October 2, which meant that the two races were nearly two months apart. During that period, I didn't train her and she qualified off no work miles. That was all she had, going into the Three Diamonds.

Freedoms Friend's long winter of conditioning and her own racing courage paid off. Although she was short, she was still better than the other fillies she faced. In the elimination, she was out the entire mile, moved first-over after the half, and was a winner in 1:54.2. She was all out finishing and got home on empty.

Coming right back for the Three Diamonds final on October 9, Freedoms Friend had the rail, and John got away fourth. But then, he moved her and took over going to the half, only to get immediate pressure from Lotus Spur, who had defeated Freedoms Friend earlier in the year in the Sweetheart eliminations.

John decided he had to park Lotus Spur, and they sailed like a team past a :54.4 half. This is a situation that will tell you what kind of filly you really have. With only a couple of light workouts, a qualifier and one race in just over two months, Freedoms Friend was really being tested now. She put away Lotus Spur in the final turn past three-quarters in 1:23.4 before she got very tired. In the late stages, John was after her, and she just lasted for the victory in 1:54.1 over Hardie Hanover, with the final quarter in :30.2.

I started Freedoms Friend one final time at two in the Breeders Crown at Freehold, but she made a break in the first turn and lost all chance. I

One of the author's Sweetheart Pace winners was the No Nukes filly, Efishnc. Prior to her big win in the Sweetheart, the author trained her very tough, setting her up nicely for the important stake. The author does not recommend the use of heavy training between races for fillies, but does acknowledge and recommend the use of serious training to sharpen a filly for a big effort.

had only worked her a couple of times on a half-mile track and her chronic stifle problems added to our troubles.

She followed my other champion fillies by being named the top two-year-old filly of 1993. I think Freedoms Friend was as good a filly as some of my other champions. She did more with some real problems than any of them.

Central Park West never had any soreness until her accident and was probably the most trouble-free of any of these fillies at two. Miss Easy raced with some chronic problems, but never won a race when she was in as bad a shape as Freedom's Friend was in the Sweetheart and Three Diamonds finals.

Immortality was always a sound filly at two. Sickness cost her a little in her last start, but I never had the kind of soundness issues to deal with that Freedoms Friend lived and raced with.

Freedoms Friend wound up 1993 with 11 starts, six wins and three thirds and won $600,412. She was the fourth one of my fillies to win the Sweetheart and the third Three Diamonds winner in the five-year history of that race. These fillies also won five Breeders Crowns!

EFISHNC—ANOTHER SWEETHEART WINNER

At the Harrisburg yearling sale in the fall of 1993, I spotted a No Nukes filly in the Perretti Farms consignment that I really liked. Her name was No Sputnik. I bought her for $18,000 and took her to Florida. She started off like a good one and had a very uneventful winter. She had a wonderful attitude from the start, and she got over the ground good. She trained down with my best set of fillies, and I put Laurie Voris, my top groom, on her.

I honestly felt she could be a good filly, but I didn't know just how good. She did not have the size or presence of a Miss Easy or a Central Park West, but her mechanics were very solid, and she was very willing. I thought it would be a question of how far and how much she could do. I had decided to change her name before racing her. I requested the name Efishnc and did get approval.

Efishnc was very light on her feet and was rigged about as simply as a horse could be. She wore a 59 1/2-inch hobble and a pair of light knee boots. I broke her in a 1/2-inch half-round shoe in front, with a full swedge behind, and trained her down to the races shod like that. After I had raced her a time or two, I put a pair of aluminum shoes on her, with the grab filed down about halfway. I wore a pair of full swedges on her behind.

After a couple of starts, she started to get on one line, and I looked her over pretty good and couldn't find anything seriously wrong. I thought, however, that because she was such a good, line-gaited pacer that maybe the swedge shoes behind were a little too severe. On a hunch, I took the full swedges off and replaced them with a light, flat shoe. In a couple of weeks, Efishnc squared up again in the bit, and never took a lame step.

Even though she had only the single qualifier before her first stakes start, I was confident Efishnc would go a good race. In schooling, she had shown me that she would bust right off the gate any time you needed. John Campbell drove her for me and he left with her, let a couple of horses go, then rolled out in the stretch and won with her in 1:55.3. I was surprised that she won, and I was surprised at how she had done it, because she had no experience.

She continued to improve and, after a break in a Sires Stakes, was either first or second in her next nine starts, racing against the best fillies in the country. John Campbell continued to drive her, but then John had other commitments, and I asked Ron Waples to take her the rest of the way. Ron drove her for me for the first time in the $100,000 New Jersey Sires Stakes final, where she was second to CR Daniella in 1:53.3.

I never varied Efishnc's training much during the year, and even when I did, it did not seem to make much difference. She was not a strong-finishing filly, and I thought she might be a bit short. I was training her lightly a couple of trips around 2:20 between races, so I decided that leading up to the Sweetheart later in the summer I would train her a little harder to set her up for a big effort. I worked her three trips in between races for a couple of starts, with the final mile in 2:05, last half in 1:00. I also warmed her up before racing, with a mile around 2:07 and a good last quarter around 30 seconds.

I think it served to set Efishnc up for a big effort in the Sweetheart, although I must admit I don't think it moved her up all that much. It may have made her a bit stronger, but I cannot say I thought that the extra training was the reason she won the Sweetheart, although that certainly could have had something to do with it.

Efishnc was a very strong filly off the gate, which was her major attribute. There was never any question about getting a good position with her. She had tremendous gate speed. Had she been able to carry it over the full mile, she would have won $1 million at two instead of the $503,000 she did win. She simply was not strong enough to finish the mile. If she could have learned to carry her speed over the distance, she would have been a very tough filly to beat. Late in her two-year-old year, she tapered off a little, and was not the same filly that she showed us earlier. She was, honestly, not of the same caliber as Miss Easy, Central Park West, or Immortality, but damned few are. But Efishnc was a smart filly and we had fun with her.

I have a lot of admiration for all these good fillies because they all showed me tremendous courage and grit when a lesser horse would have given up the chase. These fillies liked to race, wanted to win and had tremendous wills to go forward. When you get speed and courage in a racehorse, you are almost assured of having a winner.

BEING ENERGIZED

In training horses, there is nothing like a good horse to energize you. It keeps you going. It keeps you young and anxious to come to work in the morning. I look forward to walking under the shed row and pulling a line over a good horse.

With my age and experience, I truly appreciate the qualities of greatness inherent in fillies like these. I was brought up around horses. I was brought up to understand their faults, to get to know how a horse thinks and to avoid ever getting angry with a horse.

The toughest thing a horse trainer has to overcome is the temptations that are inherent in this business. One of the most common problems with young trainers is that they like to ride fast. They like to train a horse a fast quarter. That is why the careers of so many good horses are left on the winter training tracks. A good trainer has to resist those temptations. There are no purse payoffs at the end of training miles.

There are two things which should occur if a trainer is to succeed in training harness horses.

First, the horse must have a certain amount of natural talent. The "manufactured" horse is a vestige of the past at this point. A horse simply must have inherent abilities.

Secondly, a horse trainer has to resist the temptation to train all his horses alike, to shoe them all alike, to rig them all with the same equipment. A horse trainer has to learn to adjust his own thinking to fit the horse.

I have a special joy in that I get to work with my son, Sep, and my daughter, Brooke. They both help me, and I get a chill when we sit down to talk about training. I feel that both Sep and Brooke are good trainers and, with a chance, could do what I have done on their own.

Horse trainers also must never forget to communicate with their owners. You must stay in close contact with an owner on all phases of training and racing. Let them know what you did and why. An owner needs to hear what is happening with his horse, good or bad. I sometimes talk to an owner two or three times a day and if I can't reach him, I will send him a fax to make sure he knows what I am doing. This allows me to be more relaxed in what I do, because I know that an owner knows what is happening. If there is a problem, it can and must be addressed.

There are also hundreds of little things that go into training horses. Being a horseman is an everyday experience. In my opinion, a good horse trainer needs to be on the job and pull a line over his stock before he knows what is really happening. Every one of the champion fillies discussed in this chapter required a different set of circumstances for them to achieve stardom. They were all different. The ability to adjust my thinking and apply that to their training and management had a lot to do with making them the great fillies they were.

Bruce Nickells has a way with pacing fillies. His success in developing starlets such as Miss Easy, Central Park West, Bruce's Lady, Efishnc, Follow My Star, Hazelton Kay, and others proves that.

The accomplishments of these fillies is a testimony to his ability to develop and race members of the fairer sex, but it would be wrong to think that Bruce Nickells has not trained outstanding colts too. The pacers Combat Time, Batman, Kentucky, and Fast Clip and the trotter Lola's Express were among the top colts on the Grand Circuit in the 1960s and early 1970s and they were all members of the Bruce Nickells Stable.

While his greatest fame has come with pacing fillies, Nickells also trained the trotting filly Park Avenue Kathy, winner of the Hambletonian Oaks in 1989.

Horses from his stable made so many headlines in the late 1980s and early 1990s that some people might think that Bruce Nickells is an overnight success as a trainer. That is hardly true. A native of Illinois, Bruce Nickells has been training and driving since the late 1940s and first drove in the Hambletonian and Little Brown Jug in 1964.

Bruce and his wife Joanne developed a pretty good filly of their own in daughter Brooke, who groomed Park Avenue Kathy and who rode Preferential to a world record for trotters under saddle in 1994. Brooke also holds a trainer/driver license. Their son Sep is also a trainer/driver and is with the Nickells Stable.

11

THE ROLE OF THE CARETAKER

GARY LEWIS

I t is a great honor to have been invited to write a chapter on the role of the caretaker. I hope my offering will make a genuine contribution to the understanding of the care of the horse.

If you love horses and you find the environment of the racetrack to your liking, then I think that working as a groom in harness racing would be tremendously rewarding and exciting and would give you a chance to experience thrills and success that you simply wouldn't find in most other jobs.

If you don't have a love of horses and a love of the lifestyle involved in racing, I could think of few other jobs that would be worse. The pay for grooms isn't spectacular, there is no limit to the number of hours you might be required to work, and the living conditions are often abysmal.

A true dedication to the horse is certainly the primary qualification needed to succeed as a groom. You don't necessarily need to know how to fit a harness or a wrap a bandage correctly when you start; those things can be learned.

Traditionally, working as a groom has been the first step in the career path of young men and women who aspire to be trainers and drivers. That is how I began, and how virtually every top horseman got his start. Although many things in harness racing have changed drastically in recent decades, the importance of first mastering the skills of grooming has remained constant.

There is no stereotype for being a top groom. Young or old, male or female—those factors make no difference. In fact, you will often see people whose personal appearance and habits leave much to be desired. You tend to assume that this person certainly wouldn't take proper care of a horse if he doesn't take care of himself. That's not always true.

I personally prefer to hire grooms with track experience; however, the character of the groom can be every bit as important as experience.

I recall a young man who came seeking work and, frankly, I didn't judge him to be too sincere. I agreed to talk to him after I got back from jogging a horse. When I returned, the horse's groom was busy in a stall and this applicant stepped right up and began unhooking the horse.

I'm not even sure that a job was open at that time, but I was so impressed by his attitude that we hired him.

When I was a young man just learning the horse business, I worked for a master horseman named Larry Powers. He was a horseman's horseman, who taught me a great deal. I remember him saying, "If a man shows up looking for work with his hands or a race program in his pockets, you don't want to hire him." He felt that hands in the pockets were a tip-off that the man was lazy, and the racing program meant he was a gambler. Larry's advice probably hits the mark more often than not.

One situation that cannot be ignored today is that some grooms have drug and/or alcohol problems. I would never hire someone with such a problem and, if I learned that one of the grooms already working for me had such problems, I would try to get help for him or her. I could not allow that groom to continue working for me, not only for the sake of the horse, but also for the tremendous investment of the owner.

In truth, I seldom have to ask a groom with a drug or alcohol problem to leave, because they simply can't maintain consistently good work habits.

Once a groom begins to work, I think that a veteran trainer can quickly tell how he or she will work out. You might hire a passive, quiet girl and give her a yearling filly to groom, and pretty soon you'll hear shouting and fighting coming from that filly's stall. In that case, you'd better rescue the filly and send the groom packing. I've found that if a person doesn't possess the temperament to work with horses, especially young ones, he or she seldom acquires that temperament.

Patience is perhaps the most important virtue you can have as a groom.

For example, let's say that I'm having problems with a young trotter and I've trained the colt three trips and had several different sets of shoes or boots on him in an effort to get him hung up and balanced properly. When I come back to the barn, and his groom says, "I hope you're not going to go another trip," I know that he or she doesn't have the kind of patience and dedication I need in a groom.

The ideal groom will be willing to put in the hours and do whatever is necessary to help a horse's progress. That dedication is not often found, but there are grooms who are willing to put their horse's needs above their own.

You will often find that certain grooms work better with certain horses and that a groom might not get along with a particular horse. Let's say you've got a well-bred yearling colt, and one of your grooms is quite anxious to care for him. You can certainly pair the groom with that colt, but you need to be sure that the groom and horse are compatible. If you see that they aren't getting along, for whatever reason, even if the groom is otherwise capable, then you'd better put another groom on your colt. In human terms, we'd call that a "personality conflict." Sure, the groom might be upset, but, again, your first responsibility is to the horse and to the owner of that horse.

Speaking of owners, I should point out that many misunderstandings are caused by grooms being questioned by owners, so I make it a general rule that communication with owners should be handled by me or by one of my assistant trainers. That might sound harsh, but a groom is not paid to break bad news to an owner. The groom might not fully understand what is being done with his horse or why. So if an owner calls and a groom happens to answer the phone, he should merely take the owner's name and number.

This presumes, of course, that the grooms have respect for the trainer. I think that is essential to a sound, working relationship. A trainer can't have a groom second-guessing and questioning his methods. The groom must respect the trainer's knowledge and experience. If a groom really thinks he knows more than his boss, he probably should start his own stable and find out for himself.

Now let's go through what might be a typical day for a groom in my stable, although I hasten to add that each day is a little different and that is one of the enjoyable aspects of working with horses.

I expect all of my grooms to be at the barn by 6 a.m. Some of them live at the track and will arrive earlier and that's not a problem. We don't work by a time clock in the horse business.

The horses in my stable are fed by a night watchman at 5:30 a.m., so they should have cleaned up their feed by the time the groom arrives to begin work.

Most of the grooms in my stable take care of two horses. However, some of my more talented, dedicated grooms take care of three horses upon occasion and, of course, they are compensated extra for that work.

Although my grooms are given a great deal of latitude, I do expect them to adhere to a system of work, because I think an established regimen is essential in a public stable. There are no exceptions to the system in my stable.

The first thing that a groom does upon arriving in the morning is clean the stalls of all of his horses and wash out their water buckets and feed tubs. Let's say that one of those horses raced the previous night and will just be walked that day. His stall is still cleaned and the water bucket and feed tub done before the jogging and training of other horses gets started. In that way, he's not penalized for what is being done with the groom's other horses.

Before I go any further, let me add that my stable uses a water-purification system which goes with us wherever we're stabled. Water today is so full of chemicals and minerals detrimental to a horse that we use our own purifiers. Before water is ever given to a horse, it is first put through a filter—and that makes an enormous difference.

I'm not saying that a thirsty horse won't drink water with impurities in it. When a horse or a human needs water badly enough, he'll drink. When the water is purified, the horses will drink far more water.

In fact, we find that our horses like the purified water so much, that we keep two buckets in many of our horses' stalls.

I use the heavy, plastic feed tubs and water buckets instead of the metal ones which were used years ago. A groom can clean these out using a stiff brush, warm water, and detergent.

After that is done, the groom should set out the noon feeding for all of his horses. I would rather have this done first thing in the morning, so that feed cans are not being rattled for some horses and not for others. We have covers for the feed tubs which keep the dust off the feed and prevent flies from getting to it.

If a groom is taking care of two horses, I naturally try to schedule our work so that both horses aren't training on the same day. That's not always possible, but it usually is. If a groom has one horse who is scheduled to jog and the other one scheduled to train, he will usually work on his "jogger" first and get him put away before starting on the "trainer."

I say "usually," because you can't make any hard-and-fast rules here. Let's say that you have a horse who is very nervous and he's scheduled to jog. You might find the horse is more relaxed and manageable later in the morning when things have calmed down a bit on the track. So you may wish to have the groom of that nervous horse start in on the horse to be trained first, and save the other horse to jog later on.

One thing that complicates my training schedule a bit is that I try very earnestly not to do any training on Mondays. I know that is a bit unusual, but I think that you encounter so many cases of tying-up on Monday that it's a good idea to limit your Monday work to jogging alone.

When the groom goes into the stall, the first thing he usually does is put a halter on the horse. I do not believe that a horse should wear a halter in the stall. I know there are good horsemen who would disagree. They feel that if there is a barn fire and someone has to grab a horse quickly, it helps to have a halter to control the horse. I believe, however, that wearing a halter gives the horse too many opportunities to snag it on something in his stall. It might be a nail that no one noticed, or it might be a snap on his water bucket. I've seen horses nearly tear their eyes out because their halter was caught on something, so I leave them off.

(Each horse in my stable has a nylon work halter, plus a leather dress halter which is usually kept in the trunk. I know that it looks nice to have the leather halter displayed on the stall door, but my belief is that a trainer should not advertise which horse is in which stall. If someone wanted to get at a horse to impair its racing ability, having its halter outside the stall would be like a neon sign. The leather halter is excellent for shipping.)

Most of the time I feel that our horses are protected by the track security and our own night watchman, but I have seen many incidents at tracks where the stall door is opened and the horse gets out and gets hurt. Or things even worse. And whatever happens is ultimately the trainer's responsibility.

So the groom in my barn will use a nylon work halter when he puts the horse into the crossties. I feel that a groom should put his horse in both crossties, or not use the crossties at all. I'm totally against using just one crosstie, although you see it all the time.

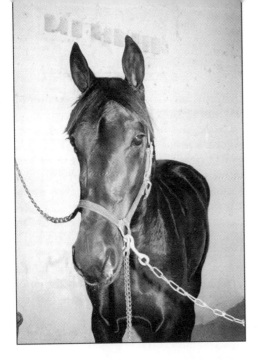

A horse should not be "vised" into crossties where it has no freedom of movement. Crossties should secure the horse so that the caretaker can do his work, but should not be too tight.

In many cases, if a groom gets to know a horse and the horse has commendable deportment in the stall, you can often handle the initial grooming chores without even putting the horse in the crossties. Of course, that doesn't work with young horses or with fidgety horses, but it's a good practice with horses who have learned the routine and can be trusted.

When you do use crossties, I think the rubber crossties that have some "give" are excellent, or even the ones with the plastic coating are good. And remember that a horse should not be "vised" into the crossties where he has no freedom of movement. He's got to have some flexibility or he'll quickly come to resent the time he spends in the ties. The crossties also shouldn't be so loose that he can chew on a blanket or get down and roll.

Let's assume you're working with a young horse and you've put him in the ties. The next step is to take the horse's temperature. You need to know if a horse is running a temperature first thing in the morning. (Often an observant groom will sense if a horse isn't feeling just right. An almost certain tip-off would be if the horse has not cleaned up his morning feed, especially if the horse is usually a good doer or eater.)

It must be noted that a horse's temperature is always taken rectally, with a conventional thermometer (mercury). Vaseline makes an excellent lubrication to facilitate insertion. A thin string put through the hole at the end of the thermometer attached to a clothespin insures that there is no chance of losing the thermometer in the rectum or, if a horse defecates, in the straw.

I have begun using a digital thermometer which is hand-held. After about a minute, a beep indicates completion. It is accurate, fast, and safe.

The normal temperature of a horse is 100 degrees Fahrenheit. There are, however, individual variations from that norm. Some horses might normally carry a temperature of 99.6 and it's important to know that.

Any time a horse carries close to a degree higher than normal, it is reason to be concerned and the groom should immediately notify the trainer. Even a mild temperature would be an indication that a horse is harboring an infection or that something is not right with him.

My grooms record temperatures on a daily basis, and this gives me a good record of what temperature a horse normally carries.

After taking the horse's temperature, the next step is to clean the horse's stall. Perhaps it's appropriate here to discuss the various forms of bedding.

Bedding serves two purposes: First, it affords something softer than a hard stall floor and, second, it serves as insulation. My horses are bedded on wood (pine, when available) shavings in Florida, and straw when we ship north to race.

I love to see a stall fully bedded with straw because a horse looks so comfortable and happy in it. Straw is expensive, so it is essential that the groom not remove any more straw than necessary. When I was younger, I would even see horsemen take wet straw out and dry it in the sunlight and use it over again. That's a little extreme and no one does that today.

If a horse is bedded on straw, when the groom cleans the stall, I like to see the straw banked around the walls so that the center section of the stall can be raked and swept out and allowed to dry.

If you're bedding your horse on shavings, you must make certain that you keep the shavings moist—to keep the dust controlled and to help keep moisture in the horse's feet. You can simply take a hose and spray down the stall periodically.

Occasionally, we will use peat moss as a bedding. It is indicated if you have a horse with sore feet. You don't have to worry about packing feet if you're bedding on peat moss. It's expensive, however, and will make the grooms unhappy because peat moss ruins the appearance of bandages and equipment.

There is quite a technique to cleaning a stall properly. The manure is picked up first, keeping the fork close to the straw, and dumping only the manure. (A groom should never work between a horse's legs with a sharp instrument, for obvious safety reasons.) Out of habit, a horse generally urinates in the same location. The wet straw is picked up next and that area is raked, swept, and limed. The straw should be shaken out in one pile. Leave no straw under feed or water areas, as horses spill their water or mash or grain and it is never a resting place for them.

When starting to groom a horse, you use a soft brush and start on the horse's head. Always brush in the direction that the hair is growing. Then you work back over the neck and body with a currycomb to loosen the dirt, and use the brush to remove the dirt from the coat.

To watch a skilled groom use a currycomb and brush in tandem is truly a sight to behold, but you don't see it much any more. It's like watching a shoeshine man make his rag pop when giving you a shine. You always use your currycomb in a circular motion, but the hair should be brushed in the direction it is growing.

A plastic currycomb works well on manes, providing a groom isn't in a hurry and doesn't tear the hair.

The mane is usually trained to fall on the right side of the horse's neck. When I was grooming horses, I always liked to bring the mane to the left side of the neck and make certain I curried and brushed the right side of the neck, which was usually covered by the mane. That stimulates the neck and picks up much of the dirt under the mane. At the same time, I brushed the mane the wrong way, swung it back, and brushed it the right way.

When you brush out the tail, the best way is to hold the base of the tailbone in one hand, lift the tail, taking small portions of hair, and gently comb out the tail in sections from underneath.

It's also a very good idea to brush off the horse's legs, or towel them off. That not only helps the horse's appearance, but it also gives you a chance to study the horse's legs up close and to check for any filling which may have appeared overnight. Or you might notice some white paint from the walls of the stall on his hocks. That will prompt you to check for capped hocks or any problems that may have resulted from the horse being cast in the stall.

(Let me say here that a groom should never hesitate to bring any problem or irregularity to a trainer's attention. No matter how insignificant the problem might be, it is better for the trainer to know about it and investigate, than to find out about it too late. A trainer should always be willing to listen if a groom thinks something is amiss.)

When you are done brushing the horse, you can go over him with a clean towel or cloth and, if you really want the horse to look sharp, you might put a little mineral oil or glycerine on the towel and clean out his nostrils.

In my stable, I do not believe in cutting a horse's foretop because I think it was meant to be there and it affords the horse some protection from flies, wind, and dirt. I also think it adds to the attractiveness of a horse's face. The foretop, however, should be dampened and braided or at least secured at the end with a rubber band so that it can be pulled out of the way when the bridle is put on.

Your job of grooming the horse isn't done until you have cleaned his feet. If you're bedding your horses on straw, the mud used for packing feet will stay in the foot and needs to be cleaned out. Even if you're bedding on shavings, sometimes they will get pressed into a horse's feet.

When you pick out a horse's feet, you should have a manure basket handy so that the clay or shavings picked from the horse's feet are not assimilated back into the stall.

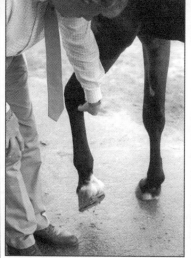

Getting a horse to pick up his feet does not necessarily require strength. The author demonstrates how you can place your hand on the back of the tendon just below the knee and the horse will usually cooperate by lifting his leg voluntarily.

One of the most enlightening insights I can think of is the infallible method of picking up a horse's leg. This applies especially to working with colts. If you're examining a yearling at a sale, for instance, and he's stubborn or tired of being scrutinized, it's virtually impossible to pick up his foot. But if you run your hand down the back of his knee where the bone protrudes, and gently (no unnecessary force) squeeze both sides of that bone with your fingernails, you touch a nerve and instantly you're examining a foot. It also becomes a reflex response, and after a couple of experiences a horse will pick up his foot when you simply run your fingers down the back of his knee.

Now you are ready to begin to put the harness on the horse, and this is where being patient and gentle can pay major dividends. Even if you're harnessing an aged performer who has been through this routine a thousand times, a harness should never be slapped on a horse's back. If you do that, the horse will be frightened and will begin to resent the harness routine, and that's not a very pleasant way for the horse or the groom to begin the day.

When you put the harness on a horse, you should set it midway on the horse's back so that the crupper extends far enough back to get it under his tail. The tail should be lifted gently and moved to the side, and the crupper should be slipped under the tail. You must make certain that no hairs are under the crupper.

I've seen many grooms (and trainers) just forcefully lift a tail straight up and put the crupper beneath it. The tailbone is very delicate, and I don't think you want to be bending or flexing it too vigorously.

Once the crupper is in place, the harness should be pulled forward to where the saddle sits just at the base of the withers. Now you must fasten the girth—and I use the word "fasten" instead of "tighten" because I like the girth as loose as possible initially. The girth should be just tight enough to keep the harness from flopping over.

After the crupper is in place, the harness should be lifted, brought forward, and gently placed into position on the saddle pad. The girth can then be fastened.

After the harness has been put in place, you then put on either the Buxton martingale or breast collar, depending upon the preference of the trainer. Years ago, every horse wore a leather breast collar with the long traces, but now the short breast collar is used and the Buxton martingale is also quite popular.

I prefer the Buxton martingale (leather or nylon). It is very easy to put on the horse, as it snaps around the base of the neck and then is looped through the girth underneath the belly.

The next step would be to put on whatever boots or bandages the horse normally wears, but if the horse is merely jogging I think you should use as little equipment as possible. A horse is an athlete and should be able to jog in a relaxed fashion so that he doesn't need boots or bandages, because he's not going that fast and consequently shouldn't be hitting anywhere.

As with all aspects of training horses, there are, of course, exceptions. For example, if I had a horse who was such a good feeler that he would normally run and buck when he first went on the track, it might be wise to slip a pair of bell boots and tendon boots on him. So if he happens to grab a quarter while playing, he has some protection.

The proper fitting of boots is crucial to grooming and, ultimately, successful racing.

A quarter boot or scalper must fit snugly, yet be large enough to cover the heel and quarter or coronary band. If too large, of course, it will either come off or slip up onto the pastern offering no protection against cross-firing.

A knee boot must fit the individual knee in size and then be strapped

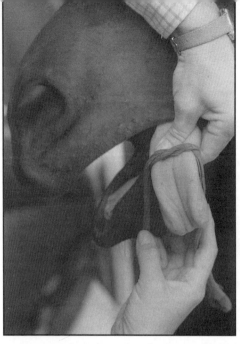

Tongue ties are used on many horses and they should not be applied too tightly as they can cut off circulation. A tongue tie should also be far enough back on the tongue so that it is secure.

snug enough not to slip down, and loose enough not to shut off the circulation, possibly "cording" a horse. A trotting shin boot should be fastened like a knee boot, but starting with the ankle strap of the trotting boot and working up. When putting on a tendon boot, you start with the center strap.

After the boots are on, the next step is to put the bridle on. Most of my horses have two bridles: a barn bridle for jogging and a separate one for training and racing.

The barn bridle is simply an open bridle with a plain snaffle bit; there is no overcheck used.

I like to use this bridle when jogging because I think a horse will be more relaxed if not covered up with a lot of equipment. The more you trust a horse, the more comfortable he will be on the track.

Just think of all the equipment and contrivances that man puts on a horse to lock him into place, to make certain he won't kick, won't fall down, won't knuckle over. Most of that is unnecessary. The racehorse is an athlete.

Some horsemen feel that jogging a horse without an overcheck is an invitation to disaster, as they believe that a horse not wearing an overcheck can get his head down and become difficult to control. That simply hasn't proven to be the case in my experience, and I would say that 99 percent of my horses can jog comfortably in a simple barn bridle.

One piece of equipment that most of my horses do wear while jogging is a tongue tie. I find that a horse often plays with his tongue and switches it under and over the bit. A horse can't possibly be comfortable in that situation, so I like to use a tongue tie.

I prefer a piece of nylon or cotton to a leather tongue tie, but, whatever, it must be applied far enough back—not twisting the tongue or tying it too tight—to prevent discomfort or again cording it.

When putting on a bridle, just as with a harness, you must be careful, gentle, and patient. Take the crown of the bridle in your right hand and approach the left side of the horse's head. You can then take the fingers of your left hand and slide them into the horse's mouth until you find a soft spot, and the horse will almost automatically open his mouth. You can then guide the bit (or bits, if you're using an overcheck) into the horse's mouth.

Once you get the bit in, you need to work with your right hand to slip the bridle over the horse's ears. My personal preference, because I'm left-handed, is to slide the crown of the bridle first over the left ear. Then you should pull the foretop clear to one side and then bend the right ear down and slip the bridle over that ear.

You should be careful at every stage of this process that the horse doesn't begin to fight you. You must be especially careful if the horse has warts in his ears or is sensitive. Patience pays dividends. There is seldom any need to become abusive or to resort to tactics, such as using a twitch, if you've approached the horse patiently from the beginning.

After buckling the throat latch, making certain that it is not too tight, the groom should buckle the ends of the lines into the rings of the bit. This sounds simple enough, and it is simple, but every trainer has had a groom who has forgotten to buckle the lines or who has mistakenly buckled them into the rings of the head halter. Good trainers just check those things before taking a horse to the track. That is similar to a final tightening of the girth to make sure the harness is secure.

Since many trainers will use an overcheck on a horse, a groom should know how to "check" a horse properly. A horse learns very quickly that when his overcheck is fastened, it's time for him to get on with his work. Fastening the overcheck is the last thing a groom does before sending the horse to the track. The period of relaxation is over, and now the horse gets psyched up.

(In most stables, grooms do most of the jogging while trainers concentrate on taking the horses during their faster work miles. That is certainly the case in my stable most of the time, although both my assistant trainers and I also jog horses regularly. Certainly we would not permit an inexperienced groom to jog a horse. We usually allow a groom to get at least a month's experience working with a horse before we allow him to jog for the first time. Even then we would select an experienced, passive horse and take him to the track at a time when things aren't so hectic.)

Because the horse will take on a different attitude when his overcheck is fastened, it's important that the trainer be seated in the jog cart when the horse is checked. Many horses will move suddenly when checked and the driver better be in position. If the groom is jogging the horse and must check the horse himself, then he should make certain that he has a firm grasp of the lines when he fastens the overcheck.

Once on the jog cart, you shouldn't shake the lines or slap the horse's hind quarters with them. You should just speak calmly to the horse in a natural voice and the horse will understand that he's supposed to move forward toward the track.

When the horse gets to the track, I think it is important that he be allowed to walk prior to going off on a jog. I think that's all part of the relaxation and stretching process. I absolutely do not like to have the horse jogging when he goes to the track and then step out at a fast clip immediately. If such is the case, you are allowing your horse to dictate the schedule and speed, and there is no respect for you in simple daily exercise. How could you expect any special effort in a horse race?

I tell my grooms to let a horse walk as much as a quarter to a half mile once he reaches the track. That way the horse can look around and relax and accept the other horses jogging around him without becoming unnerved.

Once the horse does begin to jog, I think he should remain fully relaxed. Today I see some horses jogging so fast that they are practically going a training mile. Jogging is simply a stretching and conditioning exercise and there is no need or benefit in stressing the horse. I think that most horses are jogged too fast.

If a trainer feels that a horse needs more conditioning work from his jog miles, then he should jog *more* miles instead of faster ones. In other words, if the horse is jogging three miles each day and the trainer wants to give him more work, try extending his jog miles to four, five, or six miles each day, but still allow the horse to be comfortable.When a trainer or groom wants the horse to jog faster, you often see him tapping the horse repeatedly with the whip. I don't think the horse enjoys that constant goading and it sets up an attitude problem down the road when a whip is used for racing.

I do not think that the rate of speed at which a horse is jogged is important. I think it's like asking which weighs more: a pound of feathers or a pound of gold? Obviously, they both weigh the same. I don't think jogging three miles at a 4:00-per-mile clip accomplishes any more than jogging three miles at a 6:00-per-mile clip. I know, however, that many trainers will disagree.

While jogging a horse, the groom must remain alert at all times. You can't permit yourself to daydream. A horse can shy at something in a fraction of a second and, if the groom isn't alert, you can instantly be involved in an accident or get dumped from the jog cart. This, of course, includes keeping your feet in the stirrups at all times.

Horses often have a tendency to run out draw gates because they'd prefer being back in the barn to being out on the track. It's just a mischievous prank with some of them. You should always be watchful for that, but a horse is particularly apt to duck toward a gate if you're jogging him some extra distance.

Let's say that you train on a half-mile track and you normally jog your horse three miles, and you decide to go four miles one morning. Horses can be pretty good at counting when it comes to their morning jog routine. That horse will know his work is over when he's gone around the track six times, and when you start that fourth mile he's very likely to head back to the barn. To avoid that, I would suggest that you jog him a little farther toward the inside of the track than normal. If you're too close to the outside of the track, that makes it too tempting for him to duck out the gate.

A blind bridle is also helpful in preventing a horse from ducking out the draw gate. That keeps a horse's attention focused on the track in front of him instead of permitting him to see all the distractions or exits.

(This is a good point at which to interject that I have no objection to having a groom use hand holds on his lines if he feels more comfortable and more secure. Some trainers feel that hand holds make pullers out of horses, but I don't think that's necessarily true.)

Grooms will invariably encounter water trucks and harrows on the track, and you must be careful with young horses who are naturally frightened of these mechanical monsters. The important thing is to anticipate any situation and perhaps talk to the horse to take his mind off the water truck or harrow. And a groom should not tense up and take a snug hold on the lines. That would just encourage the horse to react negatively.

Another way to steer a fractious horse around hazards on the track is by using indirect pressure on a line. By that, I mean that you maintain even pressure on the direct line while releasing the other line.

Let me give you an example. You're jogging a horse on the outside of the track and a harrow is coming to the inside of you. The normal tendency would be for the horse to shy away to the left, and the driver would pull firmly on the right line while releasing the left line. Instead, I suggest that you simply maintain an even pressure on the right line and loosen your grasp on the left line.

It's amazing how horses will straighten themselves up when you do this. They think that they're actually going in the direction they want to go instead of the direction you're guiding them.

One of the horsemen who taught me a great deal was Vern Devlin. He believed that a horse only needed to be jogged enough miles to empty out well. Most horses will defecate during their jog miles and that, too, can create a safety hazard on the track that a groom must watch for.

When a horse empties out, his natural tendency is to pull himself up, and that is just like a driver suddenly slamming on the brakes of his car on a crowded expressway. Jog carts, however, don't have brake lights, so it's not unusual for another groom to unwittingly jog right up on top of the other horse.

Grooms shouldn't let a horse stop in the midst of a crowded track. I would insist that discipline be taken on this horse to teach him to con-

tinue jogging while he empties out, by gently tapping him with a whip as
he tries to slow up.

Let's assume that your jog miles are done and you're bringing the horse
back to the barn. You allow him to walk off the track. This is a let-down
period for him. With all the problems today with tying up, the build-up of
lactic acid is significantly reduced by post-jogging walk and exercise.

Most of our horses can be hooked and unhooked by one person after
they learn our routine. Once the horse is unhooked from the jog cart, he
goes back to his stall. Occasionally you will find a horse who refuses to go
back into his stall with all of his harness and equipment on. I don't argue
with him in such cases. I do not feel that anything is accomplished by
winning every argument with a horse. Sometimes you're better served to
give in to him and remove a shadow roll or bridle rather than fight him.
Again, patience is essential, and if you don't force the situation, the horse
will eventually go into his stall willingly with the same equipment he
previously rebelled against.

After you get the lines and throat latch unfastened, the bridle can
come off, and I think the horse should be given a drink right away, even
before the halter is put on. Often you will find that a horse will take a few
swallows then, but might refuse a drink once his halter is on and he's in
the crossties. The horse should be covered with a cooler right away.

While the horse is relaxing under a cooler, the groom should prepare
its bath water. It should be approximately the same temperature as a
person would bathe in. Warm, but not hot. I like to put a body brace such
as Tuttles or BAL in the bath water; we might use about four ounces in a
bucket of bath water. That, however, is never added to bath water until
the horse's face has been washed first, because a body brace with any
kind of strong astringent could get into a horse's eyes and cause burning.

If you are bedding your horses on shavings, a horse can often be bathed
right in the stall. The moisture of the bath water will be soaked up by the
shavings and keep down the dust. Most of the time, of course, the horse
is bathed outside in the shedrow.

You should always bathe a horse's head first. Your bathwater is the
cleanest then. I take a sponge full of water, right dead-center between
the horse's ears at the poll, and squeeze it and let it run down his face.

As you wash the top of the horse's head, you should bring the ears
down forward and gently squeeze them together so no water gets into
the ears. It's also important to wash under the jowls, because horses
often itch there from accumulated dirt and it's an easily-overlooked area
that they cannot reach.

Then you simply work down the neck and chest and along the back of
the horse. You should always lift the tail and take the sponge down between the horse's hind legs and back up again. Then you finish off by
doing the horse's legs.

In bathing a horse, your work is not done until you have washed the horse's feet. To me this is one of the keys to keeping a horse sound.

Over the years I have heard numerous trainers complain that the track surfaces were so hard their horses were popping quarter cracks and gravels and that they had to start using pads on their horses because the track was so hard.

Most of that reasoning, I think, is misdirected. I believe that many problems stem from neglecting the care of the hoof. The hoof wall contains pores which allow it to breathe and release toxins. The stonedust on track surfaces today clogs those pores, as does the lanolin-based hoof dressing. They prevent the hoof wall from breathing.

In cooling out a horse after training or racing, I have been very pleased with the results of my special cold-water bandages. I first apply a regular stable bandage that's been saturated in cold water. I follow up with a dry stable bandage over the wet one. My experience has been that when you remove the outer (dry) bandage, the under (wet) bandage is warm and the leg is cold; without the dry wrap, the wet bandage is cold and the leg remains warm.

The subject of cooling out a horse brings up that subjective and common-sense aspect of understanding the particular needs of the individual animal.

Obviously, if a horse has had a hard workout, if the weather is unbearably hot and humid and he's blowing excessively, good grooming doesn't call for throwing him in his stall with hay and a full bucket of water.

But, on the other hand, if a horse jogs four miles, the morning breeze makes him feel like a million, and if he hasn't turned a wet hair, I see no reason to insist that he be walked for the sake of routine.

Training trotters primarily, I am more inclined to begin my cooling-out process on the racetrack. After completing my training mile, I jog one mile (usually with the horse unchecked) to let the horse relax. I have found that instead of the horse being "hyper" or blowing hard after this procedure, the cooling-out process is simplified and accelerated.

Walking or not walking a horse is a decision in which common sense is foremost.

Wind must be a determining factor against walking a horse. Horses can founder in the wind. On a very windy day, I would opt not to walk a horse. However, that doesn't mean he has to be turned loose in his stall. He can be put in crossties and watered out every ten minutes (about 12 swallows) and rubbed with towels under his blankets until his body temperature cools. Usually, after 30 to 40 minutes, he can eat some hay and will be ready to be put away.

When you are ready to put away a horse for the day, you bring in a small bucket of warm water and a hoof pick. Use the hoof pick to loosen any chunks of dirt that have become trapped in the foot, then wash the foot (hoof wall and sole) thoroughly in the water. You're eliminating all the stonedust and other impurities that may have accumulated during the horse's time on the track and you're allowing the foot to breathe for the next 24 hours.

I believe in the positive effect of packing feet, but not indiscriminately. If the sole is hard (usually when fever is present) Forshner's or good California Mud or White Roue can be used daily until the foot becomes supple. A well-thought-out maintenance program should follow once you are comfortable with the condition of the foot.

When you bathe a horse and wash its feet, invariably some water is going to get into its heels. It's very important that you dry the horse's heels before you turn him loose. Use a soft towel to dry them gently; there is no need to scrub vigorously back and forth in the heel area. Sometimes I will recommend that a groom use a little talcum powder in the heels or a heel salve or aloe product. You often can find salves in health food stores which are cheaper than the products sold in tack shops, and usually they're just as good and often even better. Never clip the hair in the heels or the fetlock.

If you wish to use a hoof dressing, use it only at the coronet band, not over the entire wall of the foot. It softens the new growth of the foot which comes from the coronary band. Apply the dressing while the hoof is still damp in order to retain the moisture.

I have had good luck using Reducine mixed with liquid DMSO (ratio of four parts Reducine to one part DMSO) as a hoof dressing to encourage the growth of a foot and relieve soreness. As I previously mentioned, this would be applied only to the coronet band which you could clip first. The hoof dressing will run, if not applied carefully.

Years ago, it took a master groom to poultice a foot. The burlap grain sacks that we used aren't available any more. However, 3M Company came along and introduced the horse world to "Vetrap" which makes a wonderful covering—flexible, coherent, and neat—for retaining poultice and allowing a horse comfort.

In our system, feet should be done first before you bandage a leg, because if you have to pick up the foot all the time while you're working on the feet, then the bandage will come loose. After the feet are done, the groom should then brush off the horse—body, mane, and tail.

If a horse is easy on himself and doesn't have any significant leg problems, then you need not necessarily put bandages on him. A horse does not need bandages on his legs all the time, but that is a decision the trainer, not the groom, should make.

The time will come, however, when a horse will incur leg problems or some stress that will be eased by bandaging his legs. Unless a horse shows a specific leg problem, I think that alcohol is adequate as a mild leg brace.

If the problems become more severe, a light iodine paint on the horse's knees or hocks to increase the flow of blood to that area might be indicated. Or it may be necessary to use a liniment and bandages on the horse's legs. I should emphasize that the groom should always act under the direction of a trainer in this matter. No groom should take it upon himself to apply these products. Each trainer has a preference in leg paints.

What the groom should know, however, is the proper method of applying a leg liniment and a bandage. We use plastic bottles which have tip applicators. The groom can take the bottle in one hand, cup the other hand near the inside of the leg, and squeeze the liniment onto the hand and then use the hand to apply the liniment.

You want to saturate the tendon, the pastern bone, and the back of the ankle where the sesamoid bones are located, but you don't want the liniment to run down into the heel.

You also want to massage the liniment in gently. You do not need to rub hard. Your initial rubbing can be done in the direction the hair is growing, but there are times when you want to raise the hair and massage a specific area gently.

The massage helps the liniment penetrate the hair and reach the skin where it will do the horse some good. You need not massage the leg more than a minute or two unless the horse has a more serious leg problem.

After the liniment has been worked in on all four legs and allowed to dry, you are ready to apply a cotton bandage. Over the years I have made my own cottons, as most horsemen have done. We also used a bandage that would either be pinned or tied in order to fasten them, but now I prefer to use a synthetic sheepskin bandage with a bandage that fastens with Velcro®.

I prefer to use white bandages in my stable because I think they give a nice antiseptic look. Grooms will often complain because those white bandages must be washed regularly, but I think it helps the appearance of the horse. Each groom should have several sets.

A cotton or quilt is placed just under the knee and extends to cover the ankle joint. After positioning the cotton on the leg, you begin to wrap a bandage to secure it in place.

You should start at the width of one wrap from the ankle. Most wraps are about four inches wide, so you should leave about a four-inch gap. Start the wrap on the inside of the leg. It is a good idea to tuck the end underneath the cotton. Then you take one wrap down and you're at the bottom of the quilt.

Then you start the wrap back up the sheepskin, each time covering about half of the previous wrap. You should encircle the cotton on a horizontal basis. The bandage is secured with VELCRO® at the top.

Although you don't often see this these days, when I worked for Larry Powers he would always have grooms reset bandages in the afternoon because they do have a tendency to become loose and slip down around a horse's ankles. A good groom will always watch for that and reset his

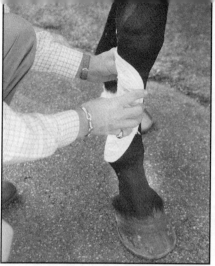
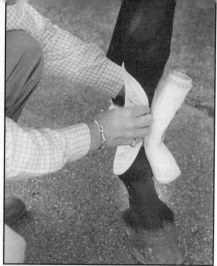

The author demonstrates proper application of a stall bandage. Since even the best bandage can become loose or undone, it is wise to check a horse's bandages and reset them if necessary.

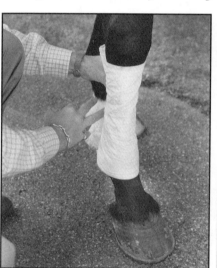
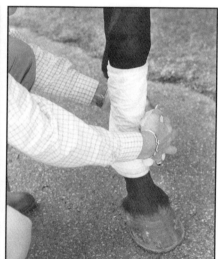
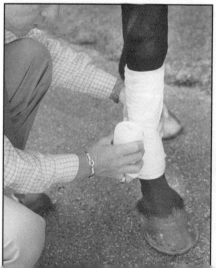
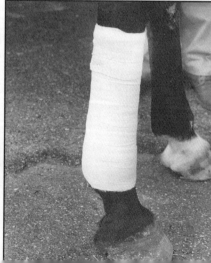

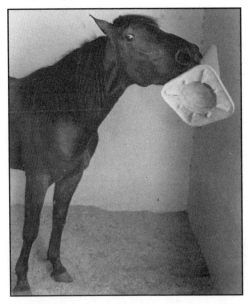

The author feels that toys, such as this rubber traffic cone, can be good for horses and help relieve the boredom of many hours in the stall. He stresses that care should be taken to make certain the horse cannot injure itself on toys or anything else in the stall.

bandages as necessary.

When you look at a properly-applied bandage from the side, it should be slightly lower on the back of the ankle than it is on the front. (This is especially true when using brace bandages.)

When you have bandaged the horse's legs, you can turn him loose. There is no need to keep him in the crossties all day and prevent him from relaxing. I hate to see a horse "swinging on the ties," as the old timers would say. In fact, the crossties should be removed from the stall after you are done with the horse. When bored, horses look for ways to amuse themselves, and they can get hurt badly on a crosstie.

I have no objection, however, to putting certain toys in a stall for a horse. Ask yourself how bored you'd be if you stood in a 10-by-10 stall for 23 1/2 hours each day!

You see many horses with rubber pylons or traffic cones in their stalls and I think those are fine. Soccer balls or medicine balls are okay to put in stalls, too.

When you do put a toy in a horse's stall, you must consider what a horse might do with that toy. Could it get stuck in his throat? Could he hurt himself on it? You frequently see vitamin or milk jugs hanging on a string or chain in a horse's stall, and I'm always very suspicious of those because a horse could literally hang himself from the string when playing with that jug.

After turning the horse loose, the groom must clean the harness. I prefer to use leather harness because I think that leather fits a horse much better than synthetic harness. I have used various synthetic harness, but the nylon gets stiff in cold weather and tends to crack.

The leather used in harness today is treated. There are new and effective cleaners on the market specifically for them. A harness need not be taken apart each day to be cleaned, but the dirt should be removed.

Periodically, it is essential that a groom take apart his entire harness and clean it, because dirt can accumulate beneath buckles and in areas that don't get cleaned daily. Hand holds are a problem, because the lines will tend to crack where the hand holds are set. They must be removed to clean the lines.

Now, I would like to depart from describing the daily routine of a groom and touch on problems which a groom must be able to recognize and know how to respond to. In many cases, grooms are on the road with horses worth hundreds of thousands of dollars and, thus, the groom has a terrific responsibility. He practically has to be a lay veterinarian.

Because so much is expected of a groom when a horse is on the road, some stables assign the best, most experienced grooms. I don't think that's necessarily the best thing for the horse, as I think the horse would benefit more by having consistency of care from the same groom. And you would not want a groom to be doing a terrific job with a horse good enough to send on the Grand Circuit and then suddenly switch. That's not fair. And I don't think you want to break the bond between the horse and the person if that combination is working.

The first part of sending a horse on the road is, of course, loading the horse. He can't go very far unless you can get him on a truck, and some horses are very particular about getting on a van or loading in a trailer.

Force is used only as a last resort. Using force in loading makes matters worse almost 99 percent of the time. You want the horse to think he's doing what he wants to do.

Contrary to common practice, putting the chain section of a lead shank over the horse's nose isn't mandatory. You've got to be patient and you've got to let the horse know you're not going to hurt him.

If patience eventually fails, I will put the chain over his nose or his upper lip to get his attention. But don't make a big fuss about it. Just give a gentle tug on the shank and he'll understand that the situation is different now. Don't raise your voice and don't start knocking the horse around, and you'll find he usually cooperates.

As a last resort, you can blindfold him or have two people link hands behind him to assist him into the van. I find it seldom comes to that.

One note regarding a lead shank: The button on the snap must point out. If turned around, it can press painfully into a horse's face, or in some cases cause the snap to come open.

Colic, of course, is a common problem with horses. It is analogous to a stomach ache in humans, but it can become much more serious in a horse. He could be suffering from an intestinal blockage, and he might twist a part of his intestine and die.

Most often, when a horse has colic he wants to get down and roll in his stall. Every horse will do that periodically, but if a horse is rolling more than usual and seems to be in distress, the groom should immediately get the horse on his feet and start walking him. Rolling is the worst thing for a horse with colic, because the thrashing about can aggravate the twisting of his intestine.

The trainer should be summoned immediately, but if he is not available, the groom should not hesitate to then call for veterinary assistance, particularly if the horse is breathing rapidly and looking back at his sides. If there is any doubt in the groom's mind whether a veterinarian should be summoned, it is best to be on the side of safety.

The important thing with a horse who's suffering colic is to keep him walking until you get some assistance. You might have to walk him several hours, but keep at it.

The groom may wish to administer a full-dosal syringe of glycerine or mineral oil to the horse, with an oral syringe to help loosen up the blockage. That might help, and it certainly can't hurt.

Tying up is a problem that you see in horses, often when there has been a significant change in the horse's routine. You often see horses tied up on Monday because they didn't get jogged on a Sunday. And sometimes if you decide not to train a horse one week, that will be enough to cause a horse to tie up.

The tying up syndrome won't become evident until a horse has been jogged and comes out of the stall to be bathed. Then you'll see the telltale stiffness that is a sure indicator. Another indication is when a horse will back up to the stall wall and rub its tail or try unsuccessfully to urinate. It is quite rare for a horse to actually tie up on the track, although Garland Garnsey had a mare named Marcon Neva who would tie up so badly during her jog miles that he would have to stop and have her treated right on the track in order to make her fit enough to get back to the barn..

Tying up is often called "Monday morning sickness," and it's one of the reasons we don't train on Mondays in my stable. Once you see a horse exhibiting signs of tying up, don't move him. Keep him warm. You don't want to risk causing further muscle damage. You must be very gentle and considerate of an animal in the process of tying up. Again, summon the trainer or veterinarian as soon as possible. Although vets will give you clinical explanations for the problem and solutions to keep it under control, it is impossible to pinpoint the cause of or cure for tying up in each horse.

It used to be that tying up was strictly a mare's disease, but now we are seeing more and more colts suffer from it, too. Milk of magnesia, baking soda, Buchu leaves, copper coil, vitamin E and selenium, Horse-Aid, light morning feed, and free paddock exercise before stress have all been considered as ways to prevent tying up. There is no panacea.

Dehydration is another problem that a groom must recognize, and it is most likely to occur when the weather is terribly hot and humid. The classic test for dehydration is to pinch the horse's skin and, if it doesn't bounce back quickly but instead hangs there, chances are your horse is dehydrated and will need fluids soon.

Again, the groom should notify the trainer first. And then a veterinarian, if necessary.

Founder has plagued horsemen for centuries, and a groom should be aware of how founder develops, too. It originates from a shock to the horse's system. Let's assume a horse comes off a van after a long ride with a temperature of 106°. It's in the middle of the night and there is certainly no veterinarian around. What is the groom to do?

First, the groom should administer some aspirin or bute paste to the horse to help reduce the fever. Then he should apply cold swabs around the coronet band or, better yet, stand the horse in a tub or manure basket full of ice.

Founder can arise from a severe rise in temperature, and that's why it is imperative for a groom to take the horse's temperature after the horse completes a long ship—and every half-hour thereafter, for about two hours. You never know when a horse might have a normal temperature after he gets off the truck and then have a 104° temperature an hour later. Founder, however, also can result from the trauma of overfeeding (feed founder), giving the horse too much water after stress (water founder), standing in the wind after a workout (wind founder), etc.

Another area of horsemanship where a groom should have a basic understanding is in selecting feeds, because a groom on the road often must purchase his own feed. A groom should be taught to know the smell of quality hay and to know the smell of moldy, musty hay.

We have portable units that crimp oats and they go on the road with our horses. The nutritional value of the oat lies in the meat, and by crimping the oat you allow the horse to get at that meat much easier. Some feed companies will deliver crimped oats, but you never really know how long ago they were crimped. If the oats are stale, they lose much of their nutritional value.

Sooner or later, every groom is going to encounter a horse who is a picky eater. One of the tried-and-proven remedies when a horse is not eating is to introduce a goat into its stall. Often the horse is lonesome, and just the companionship will brighten his attitude and start him eating again.

You may wish to turn out a horse that hasn't been eating well. Or you may wish to vary its feed. Or the horse may have a tooth problem which is impairing its chewing ability. I have even found that some horses won't eat if the feed tub is in the stall, but will eat if the tub is snapped on the outside of the stall screen. When you have a picky eater, you simply must be resourceful and keep trying until your find a solution that works for your horse.

I once got a horse from another trainer, and he told me that she didn't eat anything but hay. Well, I tried all the remedies I could possibly imagine to induce her to eat her grain. After quite some time, I just gave up and threw her feed on the floor of her stall and walked out in a fit of frustration. You would've thought I'd turned a wolf loose. She ate ravenously. And thereafter she would always eat if her grain was put on the floor!

Whenever you ship into a new track, you should be wary of turning a horse loose in a stall. Ideally, the stall should be clean when you arrive, but, if not, it should be cleaned immediately. You never know if a sick horse has been in that stall just before your horse arrived. We make it a practice to spray the walls with creolin, a disinfectant. It comes in concentrate form, and we dilute it and use it in a spray bottle to treat the stall.

A groom should always check the walls for nails or anything that could injure the horse. You should also make certain that the stall isn't drafty and, if it is, do whatever you can do reduce the draft on your horse. Drafts are very dangerous.

(This reminds me that I hate to see the bottom half of a swinging stall door placed behind the tack trunk. Sure, I know it makes for a neat shedrow and I'm particular about appearance, but I'm more particular about my horse's health. That bottom door should always be accessible so you can close it if a sudden storm or strong breeze picks up. You've got to be able to protect your horse from drafts and you can't do that if the bottom half of your stall door is wedged in behind the trunk.)

The danger of drafts is one reason why you must be very careful when using a fan in the barn. Some nights when the air is moist and heavy, the fan can cool off the barn and get the air moving, but you should never direct the fan on a horse, and make certain that a horse can't reach the fan cord and electrocute himself. I have found that putting a fan high up in the barn and letting it circulate the air is the best procedure.

I have touched on many different areas of a groom's responsibility, but by no means has this been an exhaustive chapter on the subject. There are so many details and fine points of being a topnotch groom that it would take a thick book to discuss them all.

Much like a trainer, a good groom will be learning all the time. Never take the attitude that you know it all, because there is always something new to learn in the horse business. So a groom should keep his eyes and ears open, be patient, keep his devotion to the horse foremost, and he will find his work very rewarding indeed.

G|ary Lewis knows that horses respond to good care; they respond with good performances on the track. Lewis is fond of saying, "Good waiters get good tips." Like all knowledgeable horsemen, he knows that having good grooms can make a world of difference to a trainer's success.

A native of Utica, NY, Lewis learned his basic skills from various Empire State horsemen before opening his own stable. Although he has never trained a large stable, he sent out such standouts as Davidia Hanover, the champion freshman filly of 1984, and other good trotters such as Graf Zepplin, Hot Blooded, Lady GB Coaltown, and Perfect Cyd.

As impressive as their racing records are, the horses trained by Gary Lewis are also noted for their manners and their first-class appearance on the track. These attributes are the direct result of outstanding work by Lewis and his assistants.

Lewis has come to be known as a specialist with trotters and especially with trotting fillies, who seem to delight in his patient training program. Although he often drove over 200 times a year earlier in his career, Lewis drives sparingly now and often uses catch drivers.

12

CONDITIONING & TRAINING

BOB McINTOSH

I have been fortunate in my lifetime to have trained a number of outstanding horses and have developed a reputation for being a good conditioner of raceway horses and stakes colts and fillies. If I have a specialty, it is in the art of bringing a horse back to the races after a previous, successful campaign.

This is a difficult task for most trainers and has been a problem for horse trainers since the beginning of harness racing history. How quickly do I bring him back? How much work is necessary? How far should he be jogged? How many training miles should it take to get him back to the point where he was at the conclusion of his previous season?

These are certainly difficult issues, and my system for training horses has developed over the years and has served me well. Like any other horse trainer, what I have done includes many stories of success and failure. Anybody who has trained horses will tell you that training horses is a very difficult, yet rewarding profession.

I grew up in a horse environment. My father, Jack McIntosh, was a good horseman and we always had horses. Dad concentrated on colts, so I grew up learning on young horses. My brother, Doug McIntosh, who is ten years older than I, and had a stable before I did, also concentrated from the start on young horses.

When I got started, however, I had no capital and therefore had to enter the business by claiming horses. Fortunately, I've come to a point in my career where I can now concentrate on young horses.

**My dad was a good feeder and conditioner of horses and I really learned all the basics of training and conditioning horses from him. He is basically my hero. I am the horse trainer I am today because of him. I have taken the basic understanding of horses he imparted to me and have enjoyed a very successful career as a horse trainer.

I owe a lot to him and my brother, Doug, whom I also worked for and from whom I learned the art of stable management—how to manage help, using good people to perform important tasks and how to run a big business like training a stable of horses. A lot of guys are good horse trainers, but lousy business people. They can train a horse, but cannot handle the business aspects of training horses, communicating with owners, dealing with help that doesn't show up to feed, and so forth.

When I worked for Doug, he gave me a lot of responsibility, and I am indebted to him as well for allowing me to take on as much responsibility as I could, because I learned a great deal from that period of my life.

I have been asked in this chapter to impart what I know about the training and conditioning of horses. As a general topic, that is very broad, and I suppose an entire book could be devoted to that topic alone. It is, however, a very basic and simple thing to do once you understand horses, understand their habits and how they think, understand their desires, understand their personalities and what it takes to get them to respond in a positive way.

If there is one overriding philosophy I have about training horses, it's that my horses are taught to relax, have fun on the track and take their work cheerfully. I want to be training happy, relaxed horses. I do not believe a horse can flourish and go forward for you if he is depressed. That is, if a horse is not happy about his work, not happy with his environment, not happy with the people around him, not happy with his equipment and just generally is not satisfied with his program, it will be very difficult for him to race successfully.

When I got started in the business, I had no capital to get going with and, therefore, as I said earlier, I had to start by claiming horses. Everybody has done this, and it's a very good way into the business. It's a good way because you learn a lot.

As John Campbell writes in his chapter on race driving strategy, a race driver is better if he learns the art of driving by learning to race lower-class horses. The same can be said for a trainer. When you can make a living training horses with little ability, you can make it in a big way because by being around horses with problems (and that's what cheap horses are) you begin to understand a horse and understand horse psychology and, most importantly, you get a large dose of understanding about lameness, its causes and its cures.

CLAIMING "DEPRESSED" HORSES

The normal claiming route is to claim horses who are winning races. The most oft-claimed horse is the one who maybe has gotten good and is on a two- or three-race winning streak. I never claimed these horses. I didn't think there was room for improvement. When I claimed horses, I looked for what I called "depressed" horses.

What do I mean by a depressed horse? Generally speaking, a depressed horse is one who shows no desire to go forward, is racing poorly and doesn't show a great deal of desire. He looks depressed on the track. His ears never come up and he may be grabbing on pretty good because of soreness or lameness. I also looked for a horse who may have been, at one time, a class horse with real ability, but had somehow fallen through the ranks.

A lot of times I claimed horses from trainers who I knew trained their horses very tough between races or had horses I thought looked uncomfortably rigged up. By reducing their training schedules and simplifying the rigging, I was able to improve their performance.

I had a great deal of success using this route, although people would often say to me, "Why in the world would you claim that horse?" I claimed them because I thought I could improve them!

I improved them, generally, on a number of fronts. Most of the horses claimed were stabled at the track and only got out to work, jog or race. The only time they were out of their little box stalls was to work. I think this is a big reason for horses who generally do not want to race. How would you like it if all you did was stand around in one square, little room all day and night and, when you did get out, you had to go to work? I don't believe you would like it. I don't think a horse does, either. That is why one of the prime elements in my training system is the ability to get a horse out in the paddock, even if it's just for a couple of hours a day.

Training off a farm is a much better environment, and I believe anyone can be more successful as a horse trainer if you get away from the racetrack and have paddocks where you can get your horses out every day.

This is a critical part of my program, and I believe that I could not be as effective a horse trainer if I had to stay at the raceway with my stable. There is more work and certainly more expense involved in maintaining a training track of your own, but I believe it can pay for itself by the success you will enjoy.

I also claimed horses who were being driven poorly on a regular basis. My dad taught me very early in my life as a horse trainer to leave my ego at home. Dad was a very big believer in using the guys listed in the back of the program (the leading drivers) to race his horses. He was really one of the pioneers in this in Canada because, as in the U.S., most horse trainers wanted to race their own horses.

USE A PROFESSIONAL DRIVER

I drove some horses and I will still qualify a horse once in a while, particularly if he is a difficult horse to drive or I want to see how he is. But generally speaking, I don't drive. I leave it to the professionals. I believe that a lot of horse trainers deny themselves success by insisting on racing their own horses against the guys who are driving every night and maybe even every race. I think young people should decide if they want to train a horse or drive it, because very few horsemen I know are able to do both extremely well.

I know if I have to drive against a guy like Steve Condren or Bill Gale in Canada; John Campbell or Bill O'Donnell at The Meadowlands; or Dave Magee in Chicago, I will starve. But when I go to those places, that's who gets first call on my horses. I want the best driver I can get. I am a better horse trainer because I use better drivers.

USING THE "HAPPY BRIDLE"

If a better driver will help a horse who is racing poorly or who is—as I described—just depressed, a horse can also be helped by analysis of his problems. These kinds of horses can have a number of problems.

The first thing I did with the cheap horses back when I got started training is the first thing I do today when I am sent a horse. I don't get horses normally who have performed well. People send me horses who, for the most part, are having trouble. The diagnosis and treatment of their trouble is the key to success with these horses.

One of the first things I will do with a horse when I get him is to strip him of all the equipment he wears. I firmly believe that most horses are way over-rigged and they just wear entirely too much equipment. When I get horses from other barns and they have an extensive equipment card that might include severe driving and overcheck bits, headpoles, blinds, burrs and the like, I basically ignore that card

I will hook that horse after I have put a plain, open bridle on him with a plain, snaffle driving bit and no overcheck. If I do use an overcheck, I use only a chin strap and don't actually put an overcheck bit in a horse's mouth. This is particularly true if the horse comes with a very short check and has been training and racing with his head high. I know this sounds extreme, but it is a very good way for me to determine whether his problems lie with unsoundness, attitude, poor shoeing, rigging or some combination of all those areas.

I have a real aversion to high-headed horses and have had a great deal of success in training by letting a horse tell me where he wants his head, rather than me telling him where he should carry it.

The next thing I do with these depressed horses is teach them to try and relax on the track.

This is difficult because a lot of these horses are pullers, or have been for their previous trainers. They are often sore, out of condition, and ill-tempered. I want to teach them to relax, and my chief tool in doing that is to teach them to walk on the training track. You might think this was a very easy thing to do, but it's a lost art with horse trainers. Over the years, I have cured more horses of their pulling habits by teaching them to walk on the training track than by any other single aspect of my training regimen.

When a horse comes out to jog or train, the first thing I want him to do is to walk to the track under a loose line and then walk on the track for at least a quarter of a mile.

When a horse does begin to jog, I want him to jog slowly. I don't want him to jog right off at a three-minute clip. I want him to jog off slowly and at a very leisurely pace which is often no more than a fast walk. People have watched me jog horses, or watched my help jog them, and they marvel at how I like a horse to be jogged.

It offends me greatly to see a horse jogged at a very high rate of speed. I think a lot of grooms are responsible for this because they want to get their work done. They are in a big hurry with a horse and actually teach them to grab on and jog fast.

Anyone caught jogging a horse for me at a very high rate of speed will find himself back in the barn rather quickly. I want my horses to jog slowly and at an even pace. But I also want them to jog a long distance. I like a horse jogged anywhere from four to six miles daily, because my basic belief is that the average Standardbred is under-jogged and over-trained. What I mean by this is that I believe most trainers train their horses too hard and don't jog them far enough. I also want to get a horse out of the barn and into the paddock for a couple of hours daily. You would be surprised what immediate impact it can have on a depressed horse to get him out of the barn, if even for a brief period. It's like a mini-vacation. It serves to freshen him and reward him for doing what you want him to do.

I have found over the years that a number of horses are helped in this way, particularly fillies and mares. A number of the good fillies and mares I have had over the years spent a great deal of time in the paddocks. It seems to keep their attitudes perked up and keeps them in their feed tubs.

LEARN TO DIAGNOSE LAMENESS

By learning as I did on cheap horses, one of the most valuable lessons is the ability to diagnose lameness and learn what to do about it. I know that a chapter of this book is being devoted to lameness in the Standardbred by Dr. Ken Seeber.

While I do not wish to cover the same ground as Ken, I think a lot of horse trainers lack a real understanding of lameness, its causes, cures and prevention. I believe it critical for anyone who wants a career training horses to spend as much time as he can learning about lameness. It is the most frustrating part of the business because lameness is often very difficult to diagnose. I have been very fortunate in my career to have been around a lot of good vets who had a real understanding of what goes wrong with a horse, whether it be skeletal or soft-tissue problems.

I would advise anybody who wanted to train horses for a living, to learn as much about lameness as possible. Spend some time with your veterinarian. I was fortunate, in my early days as a horse trainer, to become acquainted with a vet, Dr. Joe Johnson, of Windsor, Ontario. Dr. Johnson taught me a lot about diagnosing lameness. He was uncanny about finding splints on a young horse by simply palpating the area below the knee with his fingers. He also taught me to see lameness developing on the track.

For example, I learned that a horse who went abnormally wide in front, or who started to go that way, probably had a check ligament problem. He also taught me that a horse who crossfired probably was suffering from some kind of hock soreness, and that a horse who started going real high behind was probably suffering from some kind of stifle ailment. These were very important things for me to learn as a young horse trainer.

Horses are not going to go forward with you until you can diagnose their lameness problems and then do something about it. This is often a function of trial and error, and any horse trainer will tell you the hardest part of the business is just finding out where a horse is off. Treatment is normally not a problem once you have found the problem, but finding it can be an extremely frustrating experience.

Any horse has to learn to race with the lumps and bumps that come with the territory, but no horse with serious lameness is going to race for you.

I faced a difficult situation in the spring of 1993 when the wonderful filly Immortality came into my stable. She had been the top two-year-old pacing filly in North America the previous season and was expected to return to that form in 1993.

Bruce Nickells had her at two and did a wonderful job managing her season. But she did not train back as good as she had been at two. She came into my stable after a couple of starts where she was dull and did not have the pace she had shown a year earlier.

The pressure with this kind of situation is enormous, and I was very anxious to determine what was wrong with Immortality and see if I could resurrect her season. Several vets and I went over her and we finally determined she had two problems.

First, she was sore in her whirlbone area. We also determined that she was sore in a high check ligament behind. We attacked the two problem areas by injecting her whirlbone and blistering the check ligament on the left hind leg.

I had an idea that her whirlbone area had become sore because she was over-compensating for the problems with her check ligament. While working on her, I just kept her going with light training only one day per week, as I will describe later, and long, slow jog miles. She gradually came around and got sounder.

I spun her into racing shape and she raced very well, equalling the world record at Lexington and winning the Breeders Crown. Successes like these are the rewarding part of horse training, and she was a great enough filly to respond to what we did with her. A great deal of credit should go to her groom, Lorie Clark who did a wonderful job with this filly.

Another important area for any horse trainer is a basic understanding of nutrition. A horse will only be as good as the feed you put into him.

My dad was a good feeder of horses and always told me that I should always be proud to show my horses to anybody and that I should want them in good condition—their coats shiny and clean, their girths rounded and firm, their feet healthy and packed on a regular basis.

I take great pride in this aspect of the business and think it is responsible for a large part of the success I have enjoyed through the years.

I want a horse to eat and I want him to eat a lot. My horses eat four times daily. I feed all of my horses in virtually the same way, at least with regard to what they eat. I might alter the amount fed, but most of my horses are on the same diet.

I also have spent a great deal of time and attention on the subject of horse nutrition, and it is an area that I feel strongly about. I think its importance is overlooked in the general practice of training horses and, like lameness, nutrition is something every horse trainer should know something about.

I feed a combination of rolled oats and cracked corn blended with soybean meal and molasses. I also add a feed supplement twice a day that I helped develop, and which I have just recently begun to market to other trainers. The feed supplement is an important part of my feeding program and is being used by other trainers with good results.

My horses are fed first early in the morning around 6 a.m. and then fed again at noon after the regular training period. The evening feeding is at about 4:30 p.m. and then I like to throw some ear corn to a horse at about 8 p.m.

The use of ear corn is something a lot of trainers overlook, but I like it because it is a very good source of carbohydrates and the horse likes the corn and likes getting it off the cob. I think it is also good for his teeth and helps build condition all the way around. When I say I throw some corn to a horse, I mean he gets anywhere from six to eight ears of cob corn, depending upon the size of the ears and the quality of the corn.

I have often been told that my horses gain weight during a racing season, and I can receive no higher compliment.

I don't know if Artsplace did gain weight or if Staying Together added bulk during the seasons they were both named Harness Horse of the Year. But I will always believe that their conditioning, including my feeding program played an important role in the career of both horses.

I am very proud of these horses and also very proud of the fact that both horses finished their Horse of the Year seasons in outstanding condition. They were as fresh and fit at the end of the season as they were in their first few starts. This is another case where a top groom who was vitally interested in the welfare of the horse played an important role in the season of both horses. Jim Stocker was responsible for both Artsplace and Staying Together during their Horse of the Year seasons. A good groom like Jim, who can travel with a horse and who has a genuine interest in the day-to-day welfare of the horse, is absolutely essential. A good groom can add races and productivity for any horse. Any horse trainer who shorts himself on the quality of his employees is only going to be taking money out of his own pocket. There is no substitute for good help.

The author believes that older, experienced horses should be jogged without an overcheck whenever possible. The theory is that horses will be more relaxed and cheerful without an overcheck.

Each of these horses was a different type, because Artsplace was an unwilling trainer who needed company and Staying Together was a horse who was pretty aggressive and needed a little refinement on how to relax and enjoy himself.

I also like to feed good hay, and I am fortunate in Canada to get a good hay supply from parts of western Ontario. I like to feed a combination of timothy and alfalfa.

Earlier in my career, when I trained those cheap horses, I often saw a dramatic improvement in their attitudes due to the combination of a relaxed training environment and a good feeding program.

A lot of these horses would be pretty thin but once we got them to relax, they would get back into their feed, start gaining some weight and then start to come forward in their training program. It stands to reason that if you get a horse sound, get him to eat, and teach him to relax and enjoy his work, he is going to improve.

As I said earlier, I don't know if Artsplace and Staying Together actually gained weight during the racing season. It may be that they just retained their weight during the season and didn't tuck up as badly as some of the competition.

USE OF OVERCHECK BITS

There is an element to my training program that I want to relate to you that is a very critical part of what I do with horses. This relates to the use of overcheck bits.

I often train about 70 head of horses at my Ontario training center, and during the course of the morning, only about ten of these horses will be wearing an overcheck, let alone an overcheck bit. Most of the ones that are using an overcheck will have just a chin strap. There actually won't be an overcheck bit in their mouths. This is by design. I think a lot of trainers have their horses' heads too high. This is something I learned from Jack Kopas a long time ago. Years and years ago, I noticed that Jack, a top horseman in Canada for a long time, checked his horses on a long, loose check. This convinced me that horses do not need to have their heads in the air to get to be good horses or to stay good horses.

Even my two-year-olds go to the track without overchecks after they are broken. Sure, they play and kick and fuss with their heads while jogging, but by the time we are gearing them up and going training miles, they set their heads where they are comfortable.

I believe this to be an important part of my system and think it goes a long way in helping a horse relax while he's on the track. I don't see how a horse could be expected to relax if his head is kept unnaturally high.

Thoroughbreds go a lot faster than we do and their heads aren't checked, so why should a harness horse need a check? I think it's a holdover from the horse and buggy days.

I will race a horse in a check, but it's only a concession to convention for me. I don't like to use them training, and won't unless I am having trouble gaiting a horse. But once I get him where I like him, the check is coming off while he trains.

A lot of people have asked me about this and asked me to tell them how I deal with horses who get their heads way down and hog. When a horse "hogs," he lays in the overcheck and is unresponsive or seems to lean into the overcheck bit. To be perfectly honest, I don't have that problem. A horse can only hog into an overcheck if he is wearing one. If there is no overcheck, he can't hog into it. I really think if a horse is hogging down into an overcheck for a trainer, he is trying to tell you he wants his head down.

A lot of trainers use overchecks simply because they think their horse looks better and is better balanced with his head in the air. I don't really care how he looks as long as he is balanced and going straight for me. I have found that just the opposite is true for me. I think a horse will be balanced better with his head in a more natural position.

Most horses require an overcheck to race, and if I feel they do, I am not hesitant to use one. In fact, nearly all of my racehorses do wear them to race, but I am sure they wouldn't necessarily have to except that a horse might be able to get under the starting gate if he were not checked.

Here is the typical setup for a McIntosh-trained pacer, this the world champion Artsplace, shown at Delaware, Ohio as a 4-year-old. The horse wore a leverage overcheck, two headpoles on an extra ring, a Kant-See-Bak bridle, and a long, loose hobble. Please also note the low position of the head, which caused the headpoles to point down from the saddle pad.

LONGER HOBBLES AND SHOEING ISSUES

When I got Artsplace and Staying Together, about the only changes I made on both horses were to let their heads down and let their hobbles out. In both cases, they both had their hobbles let out about an inch, and this goes hand in hand with the head-down theories I have.

I believe by letting a horse's head down, it actually allows him to extend better, and if he is going to extend, he will use a longer hobble. I think in the case of Staying Together, for instance, I let his hobbles out about an inch the first week I got him, and he went right down to the Meadowlands and paced in 1:50 for us.

He might have gone in 1:50 anyway, but I think he did it easier and with more pace at the end by rigging him this way.

Artsplace also carried his head a lot lower at four than he had previously, and I think this contributed to his improvement into a horse who had an undefeated season and paced to a world record mile.

Another thing I did which was critically important with both of these horses was they wore shoes in front that allowed them to get hold of the track. I believe if horses are going to pace this fast and have a quick step to them, they have to be able to get hold of the racing surface. If they are skating around out there, you can bet they are not going to be able to give you a maximum effort.

Most of this has to do with the fact that we have to race over all-weather tracks which, to a large degree, are pretty hard. In Canada, we also have a lot more cushion on our tracks, but they are still pretty hard underneath. Therefore, a horse needs a lot of help in getting his feet under him.

Artsplace and Staying Together both wore full swedge shoes in front. Artsplace wore a bar shoe, while Staying Together had borium tips all the way around. They were pretty easy horses to shoe and, as I have related earlier, both of them could give you a 1:50 mile about any time you asked them to. They were amazing horses, and I am extremely proud of each of them.

I will also use an aluminum shoe with a toe grab, but I actually prefer the full swedge with borium. I think the toe grab is a little severe, although I have worn it on some horses with success. Bill Robinson, another very successful Canadian trainer, uses the aluminum shoe with a toe grab almost exclusively and he has had wonderful results as well. I really don't think there is a whole lot of difference. If it works for you, use it.

TRAINING ON A HALF-MILE TRACK

My training center in Ontario has a narrow half-mile track. The track surface is limestone chip, and I use the quarter-inch limestone. I have used the finer stuff, but find in the winter that the fine-granule limestone will knit together and get hard and be difficult to work. The larger grain limestone is easier to break up with the hydraulic harrow, and unless I have ice, I am going to be on the track most days.

I try not to miss any training with my horses. I want them moving six days a week. However, I do something a little bit differently with my stable. Monday is my day off. Every horse works on a Tuesday through Sunday schedule, with Monday off. I do this because I am both racing and training horses and that is the racing schedule in Ontario. Therefore, I have adopted it as my training center schedule as well.

I really don't like the idea of working on Sunday, but it's a reality of the business, so I have adopted the schedule. If I hadn't, I would have work to do every day of the week. This way, at least one day of the week is reserved for errands and spending some time with my family, catching up with business matters or making a plan for the coming week.

I am absolutely religious about getting a horse out in all kinds of weather. Most trainers won't get out with their stable when it rains. I just figure that horses will have to race in the rain so they might as well train in it as well. As my Dad used to say, "Good horsehide don't leak, get out there."

My other trainers and the rest of my employees think I am a bit crazy when it comes to this aspect of my system, but it is critical for me to get a horse out and give him his jog miles and training miles. He is going to get ready for you and be fitter if his work is taken on a regular schedule. Proper conditioning requires regular work.

CARRYING A HORSE FROM ONE SEASON TO ANOTHER

I am asked often about what I do that is so effective in getting horses from one racing season to another. I have tried a lot of different programs, and the system I have developed really centers on whether the horse is let down and turned out at the conclusion of his racing season or is kept up until the start of the next racing year.

I will first relate my program for horses that are being carried over from one season to the next and then explain the program for horses who are turned out briefly and then brought back.

I don't really have a preference; it really depends on the horse and his condition. If a horse finished the season and was really tired and rundown, I would recommend he be turned out, unless his unfitness had to do with unsoundness. If he is unsound, I want to know why he is hurting, where he is hurting, and I want to do something about it. Just turning a sore horse out won't get him sound. When he comes back in and starts working again, he is going to develop lameness all over again, probably in the same spot.

A horse can also develop other lameness because he is trying to get away from some other problem. A horse can get lame behind because he has splints bothering him in front. Or he can get off in front because he has some curbs pinching him behind. Again, these lameness issues are being dealt with in another chapter of this book, but they are keys for me in determining whether a horse ought to go out for a while or should stay up.

Let's say I have a horse who is two or three and is being carried over to the next racing season and aimed at a relatively early start the following season. He is not going to be turned out.

If this horse is relatively sound and in general good health and fitness, I will follow a fairly regular pattern. That horse will jog every day at least four miles a day, with most of the jogging the right way of the track.

I actually prefer to jog a horse the right way of the track because I see it as critical to getting the horse to relax. You can jog a horse the wrong way every day if you like, but I like to jog them for at least four miles at a very slow, deliberate pace. I feel this builds condition. A lot of trainers I know jog a horse only two or three miles a day at the most. I feel as though a horse who has jogged only a couple miles a day is going to be short for you, because he simply hasn't had enough work to sharpen him.

The jogging pattern includes about a quarter-mile walk to begin the jogging, which is also done the right way of the track. Then I start them jogging for about three miles, then turn them and let them walk another quarter of a mile before jogging them a mile the wrong way. Before they come off the track, they are slowed to a walk once again and walked to the draw gate in order to come off. A horse never leaves the track at anything but a walk. Any trainer or groom who jogs a horse for me and leaves the track at anything but a slow, relaxed walk is in big trouble. I have very little trouble with horses running out draw gates, even though my barns are very close to the track, because the horses learn that they cannot come off the track at anything but a walk.

I also want a horse to jog on a loose line, and this is where I think having the horse's head free aids that desire. My horses also jog in company, if possible, because I think they enjoy being with other horses. Horses are very social creatures, and anyone who has spent time with them knows they like to be with other horses.

However, a horse who is a puller will not be jogged in company unless he is making real progress at relaxing on the track. The horse who is an aggressive jogger will go out very early by himself, while nobody else is on the track, until he learns that I want him to relax. When I say early, I mean early! Such a horse might go out before sun-up and jog in the darkness just before dawn. This takes some real patience, because the horse may have years of training to undo in order to get him to relax. But I have had good results with this program and think it is central to the success I have enjoyed.

The four miles-per-day jogging routine continues for five of the six-day work week for the horse being carried over to the next racing season. On the sixth day, however, the horse is trained in the following manner:

I will jog the horse two and a half miles the right way, then gear him up and go a slow mile around 2:50. Then he walks about a quarter of a mile, jogs back around and goes a second mile timed in around 2:30 to 2:35, which is pretty even rated, except for a final eighth around 16 seconds.

This is what is commonly known as a doubleheader, and I am a very strong believer in the doubleheader as a tool in conditioning horses. I use the doubleheader on my entire stable and use it in all kinds of weather, including the heat of summer. My two-year-olds will go doubleheaders down to about 2:25.

This means that if you take a horse out and jog him two and a half miles, then go a doubleheader with him, with another mile jogged in between, you are going to be out with him about 45 minutes. The doubleheader saves time, and I find it a lot more useful in terms of conditioning because the alternative is to take the horse back to the barn after the first mile, let him stand for an hour and then come back for the 2:35 mile. By going the doubleheader with him, you build condition, heart, and lung capacity. My stable has thrived on the use of doubleheaders for a long time.

A horse who is being carried over, I will return the barn, let him stand for the conventional 45 minutes or so and then come back and work him in 2:20, with a final half in 1:08, final quarter in 33 seconds, final eighth around 15-16 seconds.

Remember, this work is done only once a week, but is repeated throughout the carry-over period until about a month before I plan to start this horse in a qualifier.

Another critical element of my program is that the day before a horse works the doubleheader followed by a single, he will be jogged six miles. I feel this, too, helps a horse's overall condition, helps empty his bowels for his work the following day and puts the miles into him. As I said, I feel most Standardbreds are under-jogged and over-trained.

Add this up and you will find that the horse jogs four miles five days a week, jogs six miles one day a week the day before he is trained, and then jogs three miles and goes three training miles the day of his work. This gives the horse a total of 32 miles of work a week, with 29 of the miles jogging and three work miles.

This heavy jogging load and once-a-week training, with a doubleheader followed by a single mile in 2:20, is the schedule I used on Immortality during her period of convalescence. When it was time to spin her into racing shape, she hadn't lost any ground and was ready to train again.

The doubleheader is the old-fashioned term for what amounts to, in the popular parlance, interval training. It is now known that athletes prosper under interval training programs that include long, slow works coupled with speed trials over a shorter distance and work at the regular competing distance.

I remember years ago that my dad could get a horse ready to race without even getting him on a racetrack. Dad used to get them ready on the roads around home by jogging them great distances and giving them short, little brushes over the best footing he could find on the road. I have seen him get many a horse ready to race in this way and I always marvelled at that, but what he was doing basically was interval training.

This routine of long, slow jog miles and one work day per week continues up until about a month before I wish to qualify.

Let me summarize the once-a-week training schedule:

   *Monday - Off

   *Tuesday - Jog four miles

   *Wednesday - Jog four miles

   *Thursday - Jog four miles

   *Friday - Jog six miles.

   *Saturday - Jog three miles, followed by a doubleheader in 2:55-2:35, one hour rest and then a single mile in 2:20, half in 1:08, final quarter in 33 seconds.

   *Sunday - Jog four miles.

"SPINNING" INTO RACE SHAPE

Let's say a horse who has been carried over is about a month from starting in a qualifier. What I want to do now is what I call "spinning" into racing condition.

This process might seem a little quick, but I find that if I have used the right formula described in the preceding paragraphs, I can send my horses to the races fit and full of themselves.

I repeat the same jogging pattern of four miles a day, with three miles at a slow rate the right way of the track and one mile the wrong way separated by walking intervals of about a quarter of a mile. On the day before training, the horse is jogged six miles. But because his racing debut is only a month away, his training is stepped up to the twice-a-week schedule everyone is familiar with. However, you may not be familiar with the way I do it.

A month before the qualifier, the training regimen gets serious. Remember, the horse has not been worked a mile faster than 2:20 for a period as long as three, four or five months. I have used that program for as long as six months on horses and they seem to thrive on it, so I recommend it heartily. They have gotten some speed work, but only little, short bursts at the end of training miles, normally the 2:20 effort.

With only a month until racing, the first serious work is in a similar program that includes the doubleheader, but the fast mile is 2:12, evenly rated, say, on Tuesday. On Friday, the horse is trained another doubleheader and worked another single in 2:12, again evenly rated.

To summarize the first week of the intensified period, it would go as follows:

> *Monday - Off
> *Tuesday - Jog three miles, followed by a doubleheader in 2:50-2:30 and a single in 2:12, final quarter in :32.
> *Wednesday - Jog four miles.
> *Thursday - Jog six miles.
> *Friday - Jog three miles, followed by a doubleheader in 2:50-2:30 and a single trip in 2:12, final quarter in 32 seconds.
> *Saturday - Jog four miles.
> *Sunday - Jog four miles.

The third training session begins the second week of intensified training and on that Tuesday, the training will be a doubleheader with a 2:08 single mile following.

If the horse handles this drop well, and most of them are pretty willing at this point, the next training is a doubleheader on a Friday or Saturday in 2:50-2:30 with no third mile.

Here is the summary for the second week:

> *Monday - Off
> *Tuesday - Jog three miles, doubleheader in 2:50-2:30, final mile in 2:08, final half in 1:02-03, final quarter in 31 seconds.

*Wednesday - Jog four miles.

*Thursday - Jog six miles.

*Friday - Jog three miles, doubleheader in 2:50-2:30.

*Saturday - Jog four miles.

*Sunday - Jog four miles.

The start of the following week, that horse trains a doubleheader, followed by a mile in 2:05, final half in 1:01, quarter in 30 seconds. Again, every day before he trains, he is jogged six miles at a slow rate. There are no fast jogging or blowout miles.

The following training session, the horse works a doubleheader with miles in 2:50-2:35 and then comes back for his last serious workout before qualifying.

To summarize the third week's work, it would look like this:

*Monday - Off.

*Tuesday - Jog three miles, doubleheader in 2:50-2:30, final mile in 2:05, final half in 1:01, quarter in 30 seconds.

*Wednesday - Jog four miles.

*Thursday - Jog six miles.

*Friday - Jog three miles, doubleheader in 2:50-2:30.

*Saturday - Jog four miles.

*Sunday - Jog four miles.

The horse is now ready for his final works before re-qualifying.

Depending upon his ability, I like this mile to be around 2:00 with a final half in :59, quarter in :29 on my farm track. I have found that if a horse can do this, and do it pretty comfortably, he is ready to return to the races.

The final week look likes this then:

*Monday - Off.

*Tuesday - Jog three miles, doubleheader in 2:50-2:30, final mile in 2:00, final half in :59, final quarter 29 seconds.

*Wednesday - Jog four miles.

*Thursday - Jog six miles.

*Friday - Jog three miles, doubleheader in 2:50-2:30.

*Saturday - Jog four miles.

*Sunday - Jog four miles.

I like them to qualify twice just to get them set and to see if their equipment is right and if I like their attitude, soundness and condition.

This may seem, as I indicated, a pretty radical reduction for a horse, but it is a program I have used for many years. I think it is very successful because the doubleheader combined with repetitive miles in 2:20 for an extended period really puts a solid foundation in a horse.

I have found that by training the doubleheaders, using the long, slow jog miles and using the 2:20 singles to keep their edge, they get enough work to maintain their form and keep them cheerful at the same time. If a horse can't stand one day a week of serious training, he probably will not survive a racing season.

I have developed this program over a number of years, and most of my raceway horses are on it, except for minor variations due to sickness or soreness.

I like this program, though, because it works and I have found that I can spin a horse into racing shape in just a month and he will come to the races fresh and willing.

TRAINING ON A HARD OR FROZEN TRACK

I train in southwestern Ontario and my training center is located in an area of Canada that doesn't get the kind of severe weather that most people associate with the northern climes.

Therefore, we get a lot of cold weather, but we don't get a lot of the snow that the people east of us get. Our track condition remains pretty good most of the time, but we are in Canada and for most of the winter our ground is frozen hard.

I am asked a lot about training over frozen ground, since people know that my horses get out every day and I am religious about going with them despite poor conditions.

I guess everyone assumes that, in my system, I train over a bad track. Yes, I will get a horse out on a bad track, but I will not train over my track unless I can break it up with the hydraulic harrow and put some cushion on it. That is why I like the larger limestone chips. They don't break down as much and I can normally dig up a cushion that I feel is safe enough to train over. This means during the winter that we might often work the track with our hydraulic harrow most of the night to keep it from freezing deeply. When we work it all night, the track is usually pretty good and certainly good enough to train over.

I trained Artsplace for his four-year-old campaign at my farm and sometimes we trained with the thermometer way below freezing and the conditions not anywhere near perfect. But I was able to get a respectable cushion. Artsplace must have been able to get ready because he did not lose a race that year!

The tracks a horse must race over during the course of a season are generally hard anyway, especially if they are scraped or a hard rain washes away the cushion. If a horse can't stand a hard-track training, he is going to be in a bad way when he has to go to race over one. I feel like my training track on its worst day sometimes is better than some of the tracks I have to race on.

What you have to do with respect to training a horse is to use good judgment in this area, because a lot of damage can be done if the track is too hard and doesn't have any cushion.

My training center is pretty close to Windsor Raceway and while Windsor is open I will van my horses over there to train a fast mile if I am not satisfied with the condition of my track. This is only done for the serious kind of work, say the training where I am setting up a horse for his 2:00 mile before starting. Otherwise, the work can be done at my farm.

My older horses don't get any gate schooling unless we have a horse that we know is a problem at the gate. I have a gate that fits on a pickup truck and we use it, particularly on our two-year-olds, but most of the time the gate is used only if we are trying to work on an older horse's gate manners.

TRAINING BACK AFTER A LAYOFF

The training program I described earlier refers to the horse who stays up after the racing season and is not turned out, and that program relies on the basic philosophy of the doubleheader and 2:20 mile once a week to keep a horse sharp.

But what about the horse who is let down, turned out for a couple of months, and then returns to training?

This is an entirely different program which I will describe by saying it is a much more conventional route to getting a horse back to the races than the carry-over program described in the preceding paragraphs.

I like to take five months getting a horse back to the races. I know that a lot of trainers say they can get a horse back quicker than that, and I know it can be done as well, but this program is what I recommend when there is no pressure from owners to get a horse back real fast after being turned out.

I know a horse can get ready for one race in a hurry, but if your goal is to prepare him for a season, you best not hurry with him. To train a horse back quickly who has been turned out invites problems. I know a lot of times a horse will train back sharply and even go a few good races for you after a short prep, but I think it often shows up after a couple of starts if the foundation isn't there.

A horse can also develop lameness with the short prep because you ask him to extend himself without having the proper foundation. As I indicated, I have prepped horses quicker, but I do not recommend it since the five-month program has been so successful for me.

THE FIRST MONTH BACK

The first month back for any horse is an important time. I really like this time because it's a chance to either get re-acquainted with an old friend or to get acquainted with a new horse.

Whenever a new horse arrives at our facility, I like to look him over and assess his overall condition. Is he fat? Did he lose weight or gain it while out? Does he look hard and trim or did he come in with a grass belly?

If a horse looks pretty fit and relaxed, he will just be jogged six days a week about three miles a day for the first two weeks of his return program. This jogging is the same, slow jogging routine the rest of the horses are on. A horse in my stable is never jogged fast.

Of course, I don't want a horse to knuckle over either, and a lot of horses will knuckle over jogging slow so I will step them along a little bit. But no horse in my stable jogs fast. If a horse has loose stifles, I will get after him with an iodine injection in his stifles and try to tighten him up. I also keep a high angle, like 55 degrees, on a horse behind and that helps with the knuckling over issue.

After two weeks of jogging six days a week three miles per day, I add an additional mile in the third week so a horse will be jogging four miles a day. In the fourth week of the first month, I will add a fifth mile to the jogging routine, particularly if I am trying to get some weight off a horse who I feel is not really fit enough to begin his comeback training program.

A lot of trainers will tell you that this month of jogging can be accelerated by jogging a horse the same distance, but going out with him twice a day, by jogging him, say, three miles, then returning in an hour or so and jogging an additional three miles. The only time I might do this is if a horse is pretty aggressive and fights me and needs the extra jogging to get tired and calmed down, but I do not recommend it. In many cases, this much work with a horse who is unfit will result in some lameness the horse might never have had before.

After a month of jogging, the horse is ready to turn.

If a horse comes to me in very good condition, I start right out jogging him four miles a day and just stay with that until the month has elapsed. This is particularly true if the horse has not been out long and still has his wind and legs under him when we start jogging back.

For instance, when Artsplace came to us after his three-year-old season, he had not been turned out too long and we started right in jogging him four miles a day. He was a horse who carried a bit of weight and yet he was sound and ready to go on with, so I just started right in with him at four miles a day for the first four weeks. Some work had been done on his feet in the off season after his three-year-old year, but he came to me absolutely sound, so I set right into him with the four-mile jogging program. Like most good Abercrombie offspring, he thrived on the work.

Let's summarize the first month back:

*Week one - Three jogging miles per day, six days/week.

*Week two - Three jogging miles per day, six days/week

*Week three - Four jogging miles per day, six days/week.

*Week four - Five jogging miles per day, six days/week.

THE SECOND MONTH—BACK TO TRAINING

The first week of the second month, I will jog a horse four miles on Tuesday (remember that Monday is an off day in my stable) then jog him four miles on Wednesday and turn him a single mile in 3:00. On Thursday, he will jog four miles and on Friday, another four miles with a single training mile in 2:55.

On Saturday, he will again jog four miles and on Sunday, he will jog four and train a single in 2:50, completing his first week of training with every-other-day training sessions. This serves quite a few purposes.

First, it allows me to assess a horse's condition. By that I mean I can see how sound he is and how he handles the work, particularly his wind. If he appears a little short, we will lengthen the jog miles he gets for the next month or so.

The second week of the second month back starts out just like the return month. The horse has been off on Monday and on Tuesday, he will jog four miles and go a single in 2:45, followed by a jog of four miles on Wednesday.

On Thursday, he goes the first of many doubleheaders, jogging two and a half miles and then working a doubleheader in 2:50-2:40 with a half-mile of walking and jogging in between the training miles. But on Friday, after the first doubleheader, the jogging is reduced to three miles. This is done because I am now ready to transfer him to the twice-a-week training schedule.

On Saturday, he will jog six miles and on Sunday, go the two and a half jog miles, followed by a doubleheader in 2:50-2:40. This completes the first two weeks of the program to return him to the races.

For the balance of his training period coming back to the races, he will jog and train on the same routine. He will jog three miles on the day after training and six miles the day before every training. As I explained earlier in this chapter, I think the long, slow jog miles really build a foundation in a horse by increasing his heart and lung capacity.

The third week, the first doubleheader of that week is 2:50-2:35, followed by a workout in the same times the last part of the week. The fourth week, the twice-a-week doubleheaders are in 2:50-2:30 pretty evenly rated.

A horse doesn't normally need any speed work at this point, although I am not adverse to "revving one up" a little at the very end of his training miles and letting him zip on around the first turn at the end of his training trip.

I think a lot of trainers could make good use of training a horse a little farther than just the mile. I think you build condition and attitude with a horse by letting him go on around the turn after you finish a training mile. It's a regular part of our training program with all horses, and they are all eager and willing. A horse learns soon enough where the end of the mile is and, therefore, most of my horses train at least a mile and an eighth.

Let's summarize the second month:

> *Week one - Jogging four miles/day on a six-day week with miles in 2:50 every other day.
> *Week two - Monday off.
> *Tuesday - Jog four miles, train in 2:45.
> *Wednesday - Jog four miles.
> *Thursday - Jog three miles with doubleheader in 2:50-2:40.
> *Friday - Jog three miles.
> *Saturday - Jog six miles.
> *Sunday - Jog three miles with doubleheader in 2:50-2:40.

The third week of the second month continues as follows:

> *Monday - Off.
> *Tuesday - Jog four miles.
> *Wednesday - Jog six miles.
> *Thursday - Jog three miles, doubleheader in 2:50-2:35.
> *Friday - Jog three miles.
> *Saturday - Jog six miles.
> *Sunday - Jog three miles, doubleheader in 2:50-2:35.

The final week of the second month can be summarized in this way:

> *Monday - Off.
> *Tuesday - Jog three miles.
> *Wednesday - Jog six miles.
> *Thursday - Jog three miles, doubleheader in 2:50-2:30.
> *Friday - Jog three miles.
> *Saturday - Jog six miles.
> *Sunday - Jog three miles, doubleheader in 2:50-2:30.

THE THIRD MONTH—ADDING A THIRD TRIP

The third month begins with a little more variety by adding a single training mile to each set of doubleheaders coupled with the three-miles-per-day jogging routine after work and six miles a day jogging on the day before work.

The doubleheader is 2:50-2:35, followed by a single in 2:25. The end of the week, we go a doubleheader in 2:50-2:35, but there is no single the end of the week.

This program of three training miles-one training day and two training miles-one training day continues throughout the third month. The second week of the third month, we train a doubleheader in 2:50-2:35, followed by a single in 2:20. The third week of the month, the fast work is a doubleheader followed by a single in 2:20 once again.

At this point, an assessment is made; I try to determine if a horse is making adequate progress. If he is, I will continue training him down. If not, I will address whatever problems he may be having. A horse may be showing some unsoundness by beginning to grab or hang on a line. He may not be extending his gait like I want him to so I will back off until I determine where and what the problems are. A horse cannot talk, but he has ways of telling you that something is wrong. If he is not straight in the shafts of the cart or is beginning to drive a little crooked, these are warning signs that something is wrong.

The final week of the third month back, I train the fast mile in 2:18 after a 2:50-2:35 doubleheader.

Let's summarize the third month:

The first week of the third month begins on:

*Monday - Off.

*Tuesday - Jog three miles.

*Wednesday - Jog six miles.

*Thursday - Jog 2 1/2; doubleheader 2:50-2:35, single in 2:25.

*Friday - Jog three miles.

*Saturday - Jog six miles.

*Sunday - Jog 2 1/2; doubleheader in 2:50-2:35.

Week two of the third month is as follows:

*Monday - Off.

*Tuesday - Jog three miles.

*Wednesday - Jog six miles.

*Thursday - Jog 2 1/2; doubleheader 2:50-2:35, single in 2:20.

*Friday - Jog three miles.

*Saturday - Jog six miles.

*Sunday - Jog 2 1/2; doubleheader in 2:50-2:30.

The third week of month three is a repeat of the second week. The final week of the third month repeats the same pattern of jogging and training, but the fast work on Thursday is 2:18.

THE FOURTH MONTH—FINE TUNING

The fourth month continues the same regimen, with the first fast mile of that month in 2:15 following the 2:50-2:35 doubleheader. At midweek, the horse works a doubleheader in 2:50-2:35 and gets the three miles a day jogging after work and the six miles jogging the day before training.

The following week the fast mile is in 2:12, half in 1:04, quarter in 31 seconds. I might let a horse step off a good last eighth if he is pretty willing and can do it well within himself.

The slow work still is just a doubleheader in 2:50-2:35.

It is in this week, however, that I do something a little different. In this week, I will give the horse back-to-back fast works. This really serves to let me know if the horse is ready to really finish off or has some more work to do to get ready to qualify.

What I like to do is to come back on the regular interval in 2:12 again, but the very next workout, I will go a doubleheader followed by a mile in

2:08 with a half in 1:02, quarter in 30 seconds. This is followed in week four of the fourth month by the regular 2:50-2:35 doubleheader.

THE FINAL MONTH BEFORE STARTING

Now, I am ready to finish off a horse and send him back to the races. This is a critical period, as well, because I am making my final adjustments, assessing condition, addressing a horse's overall fitness and just getting a feel for his readiness.

Part of the art of horse training is making intuitive judgments about your horses. Knowing when to go on and when to back off with a horse is the real test of a horseman's ability. I lay awake a lot of nights worrying about a horse or a group of horses and I often make critical adjustments in their training routines after thinking about it for a while.

Sometimes I just hold up on a certain horse because I feel like he needs a little more time. Other times, I will feel that a horse needs more work to get ready, so I will dig into him a little more. It's a judgment thing, and I really can't tell somebody how to make those judgments. Horses are all different and what works with one won't work with another.

Learn to trust your instincts, however. The times I have gotten in trouble with a horse are when I didn't trust my instincts. In the final month of training, I will concentrate the first week on getting a horse in 2:05 for the first time. He will get two 2:05 miles a week apart, with a slow doubleheader between them, and that is followed in week three of this last month by a mile in 2:02, final half in 1:00, quarter in 29 seconds for the fast work.

In the final week of the month, the horse is trained his fast mile in 2:00, final half in :59, quarter in at least 29 seconds. If a horse wants to finish more aggressively, I will let him, provided he is within himself. If he wants to close up in 28 seconds and can do it sharply, I will let him. This shows me his fitness for starting.

With that completed, the horse is ready to qualify.

On the day he qualifies, he will warm up two singles in 2:50-2:25 and I will buzz him the last eighth just to get him into his work, show him that I am serious about today's task and get his mind on his business. A little speed work goes a long way.

A lot of trainers work their horses, particularly the good ones, a lot faster mile than 2:00 before racing, but I am preparing a horse for the last race of his season and not his first. I do not see an advantage over the course of a long season in working a horse a 1:57 mile before he starts.

If he is going to last all year, I have to leave a certain amount of gas in the can. The way horses must race now, a horse will not hold up for you if you dig into him too much. The secret is in giving him enough work to get him sharp without overdoing it. If I knew the formula for this, something that would work with each horse, I could be a very rich man. But the truth is, the formula is different for each horse.

An important element in the training program I just laid out is the fact that a horse gets only one serious workout a week with three training miles, except for the one time I put back-to-back serious works in him.

On his slow training days, I only go a doubleheader in 2:50-2:35. I feel this is sufficient, and it not only helps to build condition in a horse, but it keeps him cheerful, relaxed and eager.

Most horses are not good training horses and need the work to get sharp. You are looking to strike a balance between fitness and the length of the racing season.

With a horse like Artsplace, for instance, I wanted him good at the end of the season for the Breeders Crown. That race was more important to me and his owners, George Segal and Brian Monieson. Had there been an important race like that early in the year, I might have spun Artsplace into top form a little earlier.

Remember what I said earlier about horses being under-jogged and over-trained? That is why it is central to my program for a horse to get plenty of long, slow jog miles coupled with the repetition of double-headers—with a sprinkling of reduced fast work.

ONCE BACK TO THE RACES—HOW MUCH WORK?

I am often asked by other trainers and owners how much work I give a horse between races, and that is a very difficult question to answer because every horse is different and it is impossible to prescribe a program that will suit everyone's needs.

I can tell you that the horses in my stable now get a lot less work than they used to, for example, ten years ago. I have really backed off in this area from what I used to do and from what I learned many years ago. The old-time trainers used to give their horses a lot of work between races, but a horse simply cannot stand that now because of the speeds at which they race and the tracks they race over.

As a general rule of thumb, I never train a horse a fast mile between races. I may train him a fast quarter or eighth off a mile in 2:30 or even 2:40, but there are no 2:05 or 2:00 trips in between races, even when a horse might miss a race.

For instance, with horses like Staying Together and Artsplace, two of the fastest racing pacers in history, I found they stayed in better shape by just going a 2:45 mile the day before they raced, with a 30-second quarter and a final eighth around 14 seconds.

Both horses also got two days off after racing. For instance, if they raced on a Saturday, I would ship them home on Sunday and then also give them Monday off. On Tuesday and Wednesday, they would jog four miles a day and then jog six miles on Thursday, followed by the training mile in 2:45 on Friday, before racing again.

I really abandoned the midweek work for horses racing every week several years ago when it became apparent to me that horses were starting to tail off on me at the conclusion of the season. They simply were getting too much work. What I decided was that I would just back off the training but add a jog mile to each day's routine. This has worked wonderfully for me with most horses.

About the only time I will work a horse a fast mile between races is if he is just not racing as I think he should. A lot of horses will respond to this procedure because work improves a horse most of the time, but you have to remember that you want the horse good all season and not just good the next week.

If I have a horse who I am a little dissatisfied with, I might train him at midweek between races in 2:50-2:35-2:10, with a half in 1:00 just to see if it helps him. But this is not a procedure I will repeat all season.

I am almost to the point where this, too, is a relic of the past. I can't recall the last time I did this with a horse, and I really don't recommend it unless you are at wit's end with a horse who is racing poorly. Most of the time now, I have found that a horse only races poorly if he is sick or is developing some soreness or lameness. It only makes sense that if those are the reasons for him to race poorly, more work is only going to hurt him, rather than help him.

Another area where I now have a little different idea than in the past is the decision regarding training when a horse fails to get in every week or, in the case of a stakes horse, doesn't have a race every week of the season. The best way to look at this would be to show you how I handled Artsplace when he had two weeks between races.

After his races, he got two days off and if he had raced on Saturday, he would resume jogging four miles a day on Tuesday, Wednesday and Thursday. On Friday, he would jog four miles and on Saturday a week after his race and a week before the next one, he would train a doubleheader in 2:50-2:35 evenly rated.

He would have Sunday off, and on Monday he would jog three miles. On Tuesday, he would work a doubleheader in 2:50-2:35, followed by a mile in 2:05, half in 1:00. On Wednesday, he would have the day off for shipping, then jog six miles on Thursday, be blown out a single mile in 2:45 on Friday, and then raced again on Saturday.

I know this might not sound like enough work for a horse, but I have found this schedule really allows a horse to keep his speed, keep his condition, keep his attitude and soundness and allow him to do those things over the course of what is, for most horses, a very demanding schedule these days. If a horse is going to be whittling around 1:50 every week, you simply will kill him off after a while with fast training efforts between races.

One of the author's training successes was the exceptionally fast Camluck p,T1:48.4, a horse that thrived on the long, slow jog miles employed in the McIntosh training system. The author believes the added jog miles are necessary to replace heavy training between races, which is not possible when horses have demanding races each week.

I would recommend more jogging for a horse before I would recommend more training. Even if you jog him farther than you should, he will be better off than if he is over-trained.

I also used this kind of program for horses such as Camluck and Odds Against and found that they responded throughout the course of the season, held their weight and kept their form.

I had a claiming mare years and years ago named Brilliant Bonnie who is a case in point. She was racing poorly for me because she was a mare who grabbed on pretty good. She was running off down to the half each week and then stopping.

One week, we got a snowstorm and I wasn't able to get her out for, what was at that time, her regular, midweek work. Well, she raced much better for me in her next start and I never trained her again mid-week. I just jogged her a little farther, and she jumped up a couple of classes for me and raced a lot better.

For years now, I have been training my fillies and mares a lot less, with very good results. If your stable is not racing as you would like, I would recommend fewer training miles and more jog miles.

I would also recommend putting a horse into a situation where he can get out of his stall for some reason other than just jogging and training.

For instance, I never dug into Camluck the week before he paced in 1:48.4 at Lexington in a time trial and I never set up Artsplace or Staying Together for any of their sub-1:50 miles by training them hard before or between races.

The old trainers used to really step them along the week before a big race, but I think that practice is really outdated now. The successful trainers are the ones who can modify their training programs with the times. Horses simply are asked to do so much these days that their training between races is less important than it ever has been in the history of the breed.

I am sure that as the breed progresses, further changes will be needed and trainers will be forced to modify their programs to an even greater degree.

WARM UP MILES

Another area where I have modified what I do involves how much I warm up a horse the night of the race. Years ago, I would warm up a horse with miles in 2:40-2:15 and let him ramble pretty good the last half. I came to feel this was too much work before the race for the same reasons as I have already talked about—due to the length of the racing season and the demands placed on a horse.

My pre-race routine now is to jog a horse two or three miles until he is broken out with sweat and empties out his bowels, then I turn him and go an evenly rated 2:50 mile. In actuality, time does not often permit you to both jog and turn the horse the first mile between races, so you jog the three miles before a race and then come back immediately after the next race and go your 2:50 mile.

About three races later, I come back and go a mile around 2:25 and ask a horse to step the final eighth just to see if he is good, to thaw him out a little, to see if the hobbles look right, his head is where he is comfortable and he is ready to race. While an assistant trainer might go the first mile, I like to go this last warm up mile myself.

I know a lot of trainers prefer to be in the clubhouse and watch their horses race from there, but I am more comfortable in the paddock warming up my own horses.

I could watch my horses warm up from the clubhouse and tell if they are fit enough to race good, but I just like being in the paddock and going the last mile myself. Since I always use catch drivers, I want to be able to tell the driver how he is for certain, rather than have a second trainer talk with my driver.

These warm up miles are also an extension of the training period, and because of my schedule, they are the only real training miles a horse will get if he is racing every week, except for the blowout mile in 2:45 the day before a race.

Therefore, these warm up miles serve an important purpose in maintaining a horse's condition and building his heart and lungs. I want to warm up a horse enough to get him involved, but leave all the energy I can for the race mile itself.

DEALING WITH THE "TALENT-TESTER"

Every horse trainer has had those horses who have a world of ability but have a personality trait, a soundness issue or a racing pattern that may compromise their true ability and never allow them to realize their potential.

I would like to relate a couple of stories to you that will emphasize the importance of conditioning and training decisions on the career of certain horses.

The first horse I want to discuss is Lustra's Big Guy, a Big Towner gelding I bought privately at the beginning of his three-year-old season. He was a horse with a lot of ability, but he was a real talent tester because he was not a sensible jogger. He was a fast, great, game little horse, but he was too hard on himself.

I had two goals for him when I got him.

1) I thought he could be an open pacer, and;

2) I thought he could only do this if I could get him to relax between races. His racing personality was pretty well set, but if I could get him to relax between races he would last longer and race better.

I worked with him for many long hours on the track, trying to get him to relax. He jogged a lot of mornings before dawn by himself. He finally got to the point where he would jog more sensibly. I also trained him ever so lightly and jogged him those long, slow miles I prefer.

He did become an open pacer and made nearly a million dollars. He was a lot of fun because I owned him with my cousin Al McIntosh and Al has always said that Lustra's Big Guy was one of his favorite horses.

Another real talent tester was the wonderful filly So Fresh. She was by Laag, and like that fast horse, she had a mind of her own right from the start. She had a world of ability, but she was temperamental and headstrong.

I always thought she was just a careless head slap away from becoming a cheap horse because we always sort of walked the line with her. If a groom had abused her or knocked her around a bit, it might have ruined her forever.

Good grooms don't often get the kind of credit they deserve. I was very fortunate to have a groom, Lorie Clark, on So Fresh who really was largely responsible for this filly's ultimate successes on the racetrack. Lorie was very quiet around her. As Bruce Nickells points out in his chapter on training fillies, being quiet around the barn is an absolute must for fillies.

I had to try to out-think So Fresh. She was the kind of filly that could have been spoiled if she had not been handled properly. I want a horse to be fiddle-string tight, but So Fresh was the kind who came tightly wound.

The author also has a light touch with fillies, as exemplified with his handling of the top pacing lass, So Fresh. Nervous and high strung, So Fresh was always treated gingerly by the author, his training assistants, and caretakers. The Laag filly developed into a Breeders Crown champion and was the top sophomore lass of the 1992 season.

She was very high-strung and always acted like she was looking for an excuse to misbehave. She tried running out draw gates. I finally put a Murphy blind on her which helped alleviate that problem. As a three-year-old, I also raced her in an open bridle because she tended to get pretty fired-up in a closed bridle. I always was conscious of telling the guys to be very careful around her. She ended up racing very good for me, winning the Breeders Crown, and was named the top filly of her year, but she was never a kid's horse and never would have been.

While So Fresh and Lustra's Big Guy were testers in the area of attitude and personality, the top filly Instant Rebate was a tester in another area. I got her when she was coming three and she, too, was extremely high strung. But, I found her problems were associated with soreness rather than a personality trait.

Instant Rebate had a poor set of knees under her. She was arthritic in her right knee. And that filly just wouldn't perform with any pain! I became aware of this because, right after we injected her knees, she would train good. But then as the injection wore off, she would revert to her old ways.

Getting her to the races was a combination of veterinary attention and slacking off in the training regimen. She came to me with a knee problem and an unwillingness to go forward and left my training center with a mark of 1:54.2f and earnings of more than $400,000. She was very high-strung and a lot like trying to hook up a Thoroughbred every morning. She was tough!

I also have to give driver Bill Gale a lot of the credit for Instant Rebate's success because he figured out her habits behind the gate. Bill was having trouble with her at the gate and he finally suggested that we school her behind the gate.

We took her over to Windsor Raceway and Bill tried just taking her right to the gate and turning her head loose. She liked that and from there on, she was a better post horse as long as you let her get to the gate.

CONDITIONING ISSUES RELATED TO BARN MANAGEMENT

Since this chapter is devoted to issues relating to training and conditioning, I want to talk about a few other areas associated with training that concern the way my stable is managed with regard to the use of coolers and stable sheets, because I believe this directly impacts the condition of all my horses.

Even though I train in the north, my horses do not wear stable sheets in the barn. I know I wouldn't like it if I wore a coat inside and then had to go outside and perform without one—and I don't think the horse does either. I think it can lead to sickness, and sickness leads to lost training time and lost conditioning.

After I get my horses out for jogging and training, they are turned loose in their stalls after being rubbed down good and thrown some hay. They also get immediate access to water. I don't think a horse likes standing in the crossties for a long period of time or likes being tied to a hay rack with a cooler on.

I prefer that my horses be stripped, rubbed down and turned loose. Normally, they get right down and roll a couple of times and then go to eating hay and then we clean them up after they are cooled out.

An important element in this program is that a horse must not stand in a draft while he is hot, but I firmly believe that a cooler is not necessary in the barn for a horse to cool out properly. A lot of people using coolers also want to clip a horse's coat, but I haven't done that in years and do not recommend it.

THE TRAITS OF A GOOD HORSE TRAINER

To boil all of this down, I think a horse trainer needs to have several things going for him. First and foremost, I think he must like horses. I see horse trainers who must not like their horses very well because of some of the things I see them do. I never understand this because, like children, horses respond to a positive environment.

If a horse is being jerked around, pulled on severely, whipped or mistreated, he is not going to perform at a maximum level. There are a few horses who will "take a licking and keep on ticking," but not many of them will.

The whole basis of my program is relaxation through patience and kindness. I will ask a horse for a great deal, but I also want to put him into the kind of environment that allows him to respond to the fullest extent possible.

Another valuable asset is good judgment. Knowing *what* to do is only half the battle. Knowing *when* to do it is the operative half.

I also think horse trainers have to be good observers. I mean by this, not only watch your stable, but watch other successful operations and the way they do things. I want to pay attention to the way other horses are rigged and gaited.

A horse trainer who is a good observer will also save himself a lot of time and money because he will spot something in a horse that he will see going wrong. I train all of my horses in sets and I encourage all of my assistants to spend a good deal of time looking at the other horses in their sets. Often, we can find a problem developing with a horse before it becomes serious.

The final qualities of a good horse trainer are to have common sense and patience. I suppose of all the abilities or qualities that a horse trainer should have, these are the most important, because training horses is a subjective project. No two horses are alike. No two horses will respond the same way. No two horses will give you the same effort.

The exercise of patience is one aspect of my own personality that I think has helped me become a success. I think I can out-wit and out-wait a horse. But there is not a day that goes by that I don't learn something new about being a horse trainer.

But the pursuit of that goal is more fun than I could ever have imagined.

**I would like to dedicate this chapter to my late father, Jack McIntosh. Without his wisdom I wouldn't be the horseman I am today.*

Bob McIntosh has accomplished something that no other trainer has ever done: He has sent forth two different horses to win successive Horse of the Year titles.

Those two horses were the pacers Artsplace and Staying Together. Artsplace ripped through a dream season in 1992, winning all 16 of his starts and pacing the fastest race mile in history when he won in 1:49.2.

The following year McIntosh guided the destiny of the gelding Staying Together, a winner of 21 of 26 starts. Staying Together blistered The Meadowlands' surface in June of that year with a 1:48.2 mile, dethroning Artsplace as the fastest racing Standardbred ever.

Keeping these horses in peak form over such a long and grueling season of competition at the very highest levels of the sport is a testimony to McIntosh's conditioning ability.

McIntosh learned his horsemanship from his father Jack and his older brother Doug, both good trainers in their own right. The Ontario native has specialized in pacers, but knows how to hang up a trotter, too, as he proved when Armbro Officer won the Cadillac Breeders Crown in 1995.

McIntosh has conditioned such other standouts as Camluck, Delinquent Account, Immortality, Odds Against, So Fresh, Vine Street, Water Tower, Electric Slide, and Lustra's Big Guy.

McIntosh's reputation as an expert conditioner is well-known. And he has taken his interest in conditioning beyond the subjects of lameness and training schedules. Along with his cousin, John McIntosh, he has developed a feed supplement which is now marketed throughout North America.

13
STABLE MANAGEMENT

RAY REMMEN

school teacher once told me that teaching would be a wonderful profession if she didn't have to put up with the students. And I'm sure some horsemen feel that training horses would be a wonderful profession if you didn't have to put up with the owners.

However, such an attitude simply isn't acceptable in a horse trainer today. A trainer must learn to accommodate his owners and he must communicate to them and be absolutely honest in his dealings. After all, the owner is the trainer's customer, and no business, whether it's a racing stable or a restaurant, can survive if the customer isn't treated properly.

Communication and honesty are good practices in any business, but I think they are more important than ever for horse trainers today. Certainly the new breed of owners in our business represents one of the biggest changes I've seen in harness racing in my career, and your relationship with owners is a cornerstone of successful stable management.

Years ago, many owners were sportsmen who understood racing, loved the horse as an animal, and seldom, if ever, questioned the trainer's procedures. That type of owner is virtually a dinosaur. Today's owners want—and deserve—open lines of communication and often a hand in the decisions involving their horses.

The sooner that we as horse trainers recognize how times have changed and learn to relate to the new breed of owners, the better off we will be.

Perhaps I should first explain that I operate a stable based at The Meadowlands in New Jersey and my two assistants are my brothers Larry and Gord. While we compete primarily at The Meadowlands, naturally we also race at tracks all over North America, particularly in Grand Circuit stakes with our young horses. Larry supervises the raceway division of the stable while Gord's primary responsibility is with the colts that are broken and developed at Gaitway Farm in New Jersey.

Larry and I share a lot of responsibilities at The Meadowlands, but there are specific areas of stable management that he supervises. He is the person to whom the grooms report, and he deals with most of their day-to-day problems. Larry also is in charge of scheduling blacksmith appointments and seeing that equipment is repaired. It's my responsibility to work with the race secretary to see that horses are entered properly at The Meadowlands, while Larry handles getting them entered if they're racing out of town.

Having explained how the stable is structured, let me address my philosophy of stable management.

The most important word in stable management is honesty.

It is certainly the most appropriate word in all of your relations with owners, but it should also characterize your dealings with employees, veterinarians, blacksmiths, and everyone else.

Of course, honesty is the best policy in all phases of life, but it is doubly important in managing a stable because there is so much room for misunderstanding and disagreement caused when things don't go well or when a trainer is less than honest.

Sometimes honesty involves telling a person something he doesn't particularly enjoy hearing. For example, no owner likes to hear that his high-priced yearling is badly lame, and yet if that is the case, that owner should know all the details.

Realism is also a necessity and it goes hand-in-hand with honesty in running a stable. Sometimes a trainer can be honest with an owner and yet not be realistic.

For example, a trainer might tell a new owner about Beach Towel, who was purchased for $22,000 and who has earned over $2.5 million.

"You could buy a yearling for $22,000 and wind up owning a horse just like Beach Towel," a trainer might tell an unsuspecting owner.

Is the trainer being honest? Technically, yes he is. Those rags-to-riches stories happen all the time in the horse business.

But is the trainer being realistic? Not exactly. The chances of any owner getting a horse of that caliber are almost one in a million.

So a trainer must be realistic with an owner and be forthright about the realities of the horse business.

I've been accused of being too realistic with owners over the years and, if a man must be accused of something, I don't mind pleading guilty to that charge. For example, when a new person wants to get into the harness horse business, my brothers and I will tell him the costs involved and also tell him that there is a very good chance he will not make money owning horses.

That might discourage some owners before they get into the business, but, if so, those owners would probably get discouraged sooner or later anyway. It's much better to level with a new owner completely so there are no surprises waiting for him when the bills and inevitable disappointments roll around.

I know that all trainers don't handle things that way. Some of them can paint a very rosy picture of harness horse ownership and, indeed, owning horses can be both profitable and pleasurable. But it isn't always that way. If owning harness horses were an easy road to riches, why would trainers need to bother with owners? We'd own and train our own horses and just let the money roll in.

As I said, owners are the customers. If a trainer doesn't have owners, he's out of business, unless he's confident he can make enough money training and racing his own stock.

Please don't think that I try to discourage people from owning horses. To the contrary, my business is training and racing horses and I naturally would like to have more people involved. There is absolutely nothing wrong with an owner being optimistic about his chances of having a champion like Beach Towel, but he should also be realistic about those chances and I feel it's the trainer's responsibility to make certain the owner is fully informed about the dollars-and-cents aspects of the business.

How does an owner become involved in the horse business? I guess every owner has a little different story to tell about how he got started, but most of them were racing fans who simply decided to make the jump from fan to owner.

Anything that the tracks or breeders associations can do to encourage new owners is wonderful, because I am certain there are people sitting in the grandstand or clubhouse who would love to own a harness horse and who have the capital to afford it, yet they simply don't know how to take the first step.

My advice would be to read the program at your local track and see who the leading trainers are. The trainer standings are usually listed in the program. Or maybe an owner might notice that a certain trainer sends out very competitive horses even though his stable is small and he's not among the leading trainers. You can usually contact trainers by placing a call to the race secretary's office or simply by writing a letter to the trainer in care of the track.

If a prospective owner happens to know veteran owners, it's not a bad idea to ask the experienced owners for their suggestions. Just about every owner will tell about his experiences—good and bad—with various trainers. Keep in mind, however, that it is your decision about who will handle your horses. What works for one owner won't necessarily work for you. An owner-trainer relationship is a little bit like a marriage; some are perfect from the very beginning and last for decades, while others seem doomed from the start and don't even last a year.

Another time-honored way of finding a trainer is by contacting the race secretary or horsemen's association at your local track. They are usually able to give you the names of several trainers who are interested in taking on new owners, I know that I have had owners referred to me by a race secretary.

No matter how an owner gets the name of a trainer, he should sit down and have a very candid discussion with him about why he wants to own a horse. How much money can the owner afford to invest to purchase a horse? Can he afford the monthly bills? Does he fully understand all the charges he'll be required to pay? Would he be interested in entering into a partnership?

Ideally, a prospective owner should meet with several trainers and ask them all the same general questions. Then he must decide with which trainer he feels the most comfortable. An owner should beware of any trainer who promises the sky. It's easy to promise that; it's much harder to deliver.

I have never solicited owners for my stable, as that's just not in my nature, but I realize that will have to change. I see nothing wrong with a trainer soliciting owners and I think you'll find such practice occurring more frequently, just as lawyers and doctors are advertising now. For example, I see nothing wrong with a trainer putting an ad in a magazine or newspaper indicating that he's accepting colts to break or that he's available to look at horses in an upcoming sale. That's just good business.

I should point out, however, that a trainer should never become so preoccupied with courting new owners that he neglects to communicate with existing owners. They must have first priority.

A new owner must decide not only how much he can invest, but also what type of horse he wants. Generally, it is best for a new owner to buy a horse who is racing because the owner can see that horse compete regularly and get a feel for horse ownership. Also, the horse should be earning money to defray the training costs.

Buying a racehorse is preferable to buying a yearling because you never know if the yearling will make it to the races or not. And with every yearling there is a period of six to nine months from the time he is broken until the time he begins to race. A new owner might get a bit discouraged with all the ups and downs that go along with owning young horses.

With a new owner, a trainer may wish to look for a promising horse in a claiming race. Most states have done away with the rules that limited claiming to owners who had horses racing at that meet. So a trainer or a new owner can spot a claimer who looks as if he might be entered at a fair price and enter a claim.

In this fashion, a new owner could claim a horse on a Wednesday night, move him into his trainer's barn, and probably get to see that horse race under his name the next Wednesday night. A new owner must realize that if he enters his horse back in a claimer, there is always a chance that someone else might claim him the very first time he races. It doesn't happen often, but it is something to remember.

Over the years, a "buddy system" has often prevailed at tracks where trainers are reluctant to claim from their friends. That shouldn't be the situation, but it does occur. Whenever you put a horse in a claiming race, he's fair game for anyone to claim and you'd better reconcile yourself to that.

Claiming races exist for two purposes: (1) as a system of classifying horses and (2) a system of buying and selling horses.

It's very effective in both situations, but some trainers and owners enter a horse in a claimer and never give much consideration to the fact that they might lose the horse. No trainer likes to lose a horse; a horse represents income for the stable. And some trainers are quite offended when a friend claims one of their horses. It was just understood that you didn't claim a horse from a friend.

Harness racing is a business, however, and no trainer should take it personally when a horse is claimed. Frankly, I think it is tough to find a claimer that is worth the claiming price. There is a great demand for quality racing stock today. If a claimer wins a couple starts at a $30,000 price tag, you'd better jump him up to a higher class of claimers or you won't have him very long.

The most important thing I look for when I consider a claiming a horse is soundness. I want to watch that horse race and watch him warm up and be assured that he's sound enough to race on a regular basis.

Not everyone interested in claiming a horse bothers to watch a horse race or warm-up. It amazes me, but I have trained horses who were not all that sound, so I dropped them down a notch in claiming price, thinking that the horse would do better in a lower class and that no one would dare claim the horse if they watched him go.

Then someone will claim that horse. It surprises me, but some trainers or owners claim strictly off paper. They never bother to watch the horse move to make certain he is sound. I sure wouldn't recommend that anyone try that, but it has worked in some cases.

I also think it's important that a claiming horse be finishing his miles strong and not quitting at the end of his races.

Human nature is such that a trainer or owner is always looking for that $30,000 claimer who looks as if he might have the potential to go with the $50,000 claimers.

To me, those people usually have stars in their eyes and they won't be able to magically transform a $30,000 claimer into a $50,000 claimer very often. They would be much better advised to look for a $30,000 claimer who fits in that class.

It's also human nature to think that you're a competent trainer and that if you claim a horse from an inexperienced or relatively unknown trainer, your superior horsemanship will move that horse up a few notches.

Don't count on it. In western Canada, we always said, "The dumbest farmers grow the biggest potatoes," and that saying can also apply to claimers. I sure haven't had much luck claiming horses from trainers who weren't supposed to know what they were doing.

Another consideration in claiming a horse is how many starts the horse has had without a layoff. If you see a horse who has had only four or five starts since a layoff, he's probably a better claim than a horse in the same class who has raced 20 times since his last vacation.

That logic can backfire on you occasionally. It's not easy to find a sound claimer whom you really like at a certain price, so sometimes you might have to ignore how many starts the horse has had. Some of these horses are tough enough to keep racing competitively in a class month after month. All things being equal, I would, of course, give an edge to a fresher claimer.

Occasionally a new owner will choose to go the yearling route, but a trainer should explain the percentages that apply with yearlings. We all know that many yearlings won't make it to the races and fewer yet will become top horses. The trainer should tell a new owner that. As I said before, you must be realistic. Sure, the rewards of owning a top stakes colt or filly are enormous, but the odds against that happening are also enormous.

Because I do not solicit owners, we seldom get owners who are entirely new to the business. We usually get owners who have been in other stables and who come to us after being unhappy with previous trainers.

Many of these experienced owners don't even bother to ask about training costs, but it's still a good idea to review what costs they can expect each month so there are no misunderstandings later.

Like most trainers, I bill my owners once a month for charges incurred in the previous month. Although my brother Larry's wife Doreen once handled this for our stable, I now use Sheldon Golus who operates the Standardbred Bookkeeping and Tax Services, Inc. in Bellmore, New York. Mr. Golus handles this function for a number of stables, and I pay him a fee to handle my bookkeeping and accounting.

I would urge other trainers to consider using a professional accounting or bookkeeping service. Very few horsemen are comfortable in the area of accounting, and using an outside service takes much of the worry away from the horseman, leaving him to do what he does best: train horses.

On my bills, I choose to use a standard daily rate for training. In 1995, that rate is $46 per day, although that rate will surely increase in future years as my costs increase.

That daily rate includes the cost of professional training, feed, the groom's services, insurance, and payroll taxes.

In a month with 31 days, the base training cost will be $1426.00.

From that $46 daily fee, I must pay myself and my second trainers in addition to the groom and the feed. In 1995, I calculate that it will cost $10 per day to feed a horse.

The payroll taxes must be paid by any employer, of course. These include Social Security taxes, disability, and state and federal unemployment taxes.

An employer must also carry Worker's Compensation. This is mandatory in each state, but the laws vary from state to state, as do the costs. If one of your grooms gets hurt on the job, Worker's Compensation will cover his medical costs. If the employee is permanently injured, he will receive additional benefits.

The cost of Worker's Compensation coverage will vary according to your location and according to your claims history. Let's say that it is $10

```
BOOKKEEPING SERVICES                      BARN: (201) 939-6465
(516) 938-5588



                         REMMEN STABLE INC.
                             P.O. BOX 812
                         BELLMORE, N.Y. 11710



  JOHN SMITH                              DATE:   AUGUST 31, 1995
  750 MICHIGAN AVENUE
  COLUMBUS, OH 43215-1191                 HORSE:  NIATROSS


TRAINING, FEED, GROOM, PAYROLL TAXES & INSURANCE   31 DAYS @ 46.00    1426.00
PADDOCKS (INCLUDING TAXES & INSURANCE)        4 @ 52.00                208.00
5% OF EARNINGS                                                       1807.10

        DATE      TRACK    PURSE   FIN    EARNED      5%
      08/04/95    M        26000    1    13000.00
      08/11/95    M        22000    1    11000.00
      08/19/95    RCR      11121    2     2780.00    139.00
      08/26/95    RCR     133448    2    33362.00   1668.10


SHOEING-----------------------------------------------------------    131.18
TRANSPORTATION OF HORSES ------------------------------------------    600.00
STAKE PAYMENTS & STARTING FEES ------------------------------------
TURNOUT OR OUTSIDE TRAINING ---------------------------------------
VETERINARY EXPENSES -----------------------------------------------    525.00
STALL & PADDOCK RENTAL - FARM -------------------------------------    135.00
HARNESS AND OTHER SUPPLIES: DIRECT CHARGES -----------------------    134.20
                         : PRO-RATED SUPPLIES --------------------     10.54



MISCELLANEOUS -----------------------------------------------------



GROOM AND SECOND TRAINERS BONUS --------------- 2 % X 60142. ------   1202.84



                                                                    ----------
                                   TOTAL FOR MONTH                    6179.86
                                   OWNER'S INTEREST                      100%
                                   TOTAL FOR MONTH                    6179.86
                                   PREVIOUSLY BILLED

                                                                    ----------
                                   TOTAL TO DATE                     6179.86
                                                                    ==========

HORSES RACED, TRAINED AND BOARDED AT OWNER'S RISK
```

This is a sample invoice produced by Remmen's accounting firm.

per $100 pay. That means that if your payroll is $10,000 per month, then you will be paying the company which carries your Worker's Compensation coverage $1,000 each month, or $12,000 per year.

At the end of the policy period, the insurance company usually sends an auditor to review your payroll records. The auditor will determine the amount of payroll subject to audit. Because the rates and the maximum subject to audit for each job classification varies, we usually classify our payroll into three categories: (1) grooms' wages, (2) office salaries, and (3) officer salaries.

Although the rates are set by statute, the Worker's Compensation Board for each state offers a reward for few accidents and claims. This reward is called an experience modification and sometimes could result in a 10 to 15 percent reduction in premium.

At the end of each year, your account will be reviewed by your insurance carrier to see if the premium is too high or too low with respect to your claims coverage. If the stable has had few accidents and few claims on Worker's Compensation, the chances are that your premium would be judged to be too high and you would be issued a refund premium.

Of course, if you've had several employees who have had injuries, and thus your stable has had costly claims against Worker's Comp, then your premium could be raised. But that seldom occurs.

(I should point out that many horsemen's associations provide major medical coverage for all grooms working at a track, so if a groom gets sick, his hospital expenses will be paid. That would even cover one of my grooms if he were working at a training center and caring for a horse racing at The Meadowlands.)

Unlike payroll taxes and Worker's Compensation insurance, liability insurance coverage is optional, but I would strongly urge that a trainer carry it. At the very least, a trainer should meet with a reputable insurance agent to discuss what liability coverage is available and what the costs are.

What would happen, for example, if a groom left a rake lying in the aisleway and an owner walked into your barn and stepped on the rake and was injured? You could wind up facing a rather serious lawsuit.

Or what would happen if a horse got away from one of your grooms and ran into a car parked in the stable area? This has happened at many tracks. Once again, you could be liable.

Let's take a worst possible case scenario in which a veterinarian gives a horse an injection and the horse reacts adversely and dies. The owner may want to sue to recoup his loss, and he'll probably try to sue both his trainer and the veterinarian. The trainer might claim that it was the veterinarian's negligence that caused the horse's death, but the trainer still might be named as a party to the lawsuit.

In all of those hypothetical cases, liability coverage would protect you. In the latter example, if you were sued, under many policies the insurance company would pay for the trainer's legal defense. We carry what is called a comprehensive general policy, but coverage is so varied and so important that I would suggest that you discuss the specific provisions of the policies with your insurance agent.

In general, a trainer can figure that he must pay 30 percent of a groom's wages in payroll taxes and insurance coverage. That is, if your payroll for grooms is $10,000 each month, you will be paying approximately $3,000 on a monthly basis in payroll taxes and insurance.

Both Worker's Comp coverage and liability coverage can be purchased from insurance agents, and some carriers won't sell one without the other.

While on the subject of insurance, many of the horsemen's associations will provide insurance coverage for a sulky if it is damaged during a race, but this coverage does not extend to sulkies or jog carts or any equipment damaged during training. It would also not cover this equipment if it is stolen, so it is imperative that your grooms take precautions to keep accidents from happening. It is not unknown, for example, to have a car drive over the shafts of a jog cart.

It's sad but true that theft can also be a problem at some tracks, so you should be careful to protect your equipment. Many trainers lock equipment in a tackroom, but that is not always practical with harnesses, jog carts, and sulkies. The best protection is to have someone around the barn all the time, if possible.

Getting back to the monthly bill to the owner, note that we also bill him $52 for the "paddock fee" for each time the horse races. The groom receives $40 for the paddock fee. Since we incur payroll taxes and insurance, we have to bill the owner $12 in addition to the $40 (30 percent of $40 is $12).

Then, of course, we bill the owner for the customary five percent of the horse's earnings, as that is the standard "percentage" or "commission" paid to the trainer in the industry. That rewards the trainer when a horse does well and, of course, gives the trainer extra incentive to develop horses that earn lots of money. You will find that the five percent paid to the trainer is standard among trainers, while drivers are also paid five percent of their earnings. Most tracks now pay that directly to the driver.

Then, on the bill we list the horse's starts within the past month so the owner can have a recap of when the horse raced, the track, purse, finish, and earnings.

There are many other items which are not included in the $46 daily training rate, and those items must be listed separately.

They would be such items as shoeing, transportation, stakes payments and starting fees (when the stable, not the owner, has paid these), turnout costs or outside training fees, veterinary expenses, stall and paddock rental, and harness and other supplies.

Most of those are self-explanatory, but allow me to comment on a few items.

If a horse requires veterinary care, new shoes, or a new piece of equipment, or anything from an outside supplier, those bills are sent to us and we, in turn, bill the owner.

It is not handled this way in many stables. Some trainers prefer not to be bothered trying to collect money for the blacksmith or veterinarian and ask that these suppliers bill the owners directly. I have found that owners do not want to get many different bills each month. They would prefer to get one bill from the trainer, but they naturally want to see the charges itemized.

For example, if the horse has required veterinary work, I will photocopy the veterinarian's bill so the owner knows that he's paying the exact amount for which our stable was billed. And your bill should always contain an explanation of major charges such as an unusually large veterinary bill.

For example, if the horse has incurred $310 in vet work that month, you'd better make certain the owner knows that work was done. He might not have any objection whatsoever to the bill if he knows what was done, but he can't be blamed for questioning a bill if he doesn't know what services he got for his $310.

By being billed directly by the veterinarian, blacksmith, or harness shop, I can make certain that they are paid promptly, and that goes a long way to establishing the rapport I consider so important. Prompt payment isn't always the code of the backstretch, and those people appreciate a trainer who pays promptly. I can assure you that you'll get better service from them if you are prompt in paying them.

(Interestingly, I had an accountant—not Mr. Golus—tell me once that I paid my bills too quickly. He said I didn't need to pay so fast. I told him that at a racetrack it simply makes sense to get those bills paid right away.)

Whenever I must travel to race a horse, the costs of that travel are billed to the owner of the horse. Those costs are generally airfare, rental car, and lodging. I do not bill food costs because I figure that I've got to eat no matter where I am, but many trainers do bill for meals and I really see no problem with that.

If I am traveling away from my base at The Meadowlands and racing several horses at Lexington, for example, the total costs of my travel will be divided pro-rata among the horses I raced while in Lexington.

While I am based at The Meadowlands, I do not charge an owner for traveling to either Yonkers or Freehold. I think that since we operate a New Jersey-based stable, it is isn't fair to bill owners for those costs. Of course, if a horse must be shipped to race at any one of those tracks, there will be shipping costs for the horse.

The turnout cost or outside training might be a factor if you send a horse to another track and turn his training over to another horseman. For example, if I sent a horse to Sportsman's Park for a week and had a trainer there supervise his care, that trainer would bill me. I would pass those costs along to the horse's owner. Of course, I would not charge the owner myself for those days when someone else was training the horse.

In the expenses on harness and other supplies, there are certain costs that are directly attributable to a particular horse. A new pair of knee boots or a new overcheck, for instance, would be charged directly to that horse. There are, however, certain supplies (such as rakes, training whips, brooms, etc.) we buy that are used by the entire stable and thus those costs are pro-rated over all the horses, rather than being billed directly to one horse's account.

Then there are other costs which may fall into the miscellaneous category, such as an eligibility certificate from the USTA.

Each month we also bill for two percent of the horse's earnings for a bonus pool for grooms and second trainers. I will come back to my philosophy on paying bonuses later.

You will note that on each bill I have stated that horses are raced, trained, and boarded at the owner's risk. There is always a risk of injury in the horse business and it is helpful for a trainer to reinforce this fact on each monthly statement sent to an owner. If a horse should get injured for whatever reason, this would help protect the trainer in case the owner or someone else should wish to sue him.

On the bill, I have listed the phone numbers for Sheldon Golus the bookkeeper, and both my home number and the barn number. It's very important that if an owner has a question on a bill, he be able to pick up the phone and call either Mr. Golus or myself and get an explanation.

Explaining costs is particularly important to a new owner, because he often doesn't understand what charges the stables assumes and what charges are billed on to the owner.

I remember that I once had a relatively new owner who had a horse entered in a stake several hours' drive from our base at The Meadowlands. One of my assistants drove down to warm up the colt and we got a top driver at that track to race him. Because there was only a little gas money involved, my assistant didn't put in for expenses, and the stable, in turn, did not bill the owner for the assistant's travel costs.

Later, this same horse was in a stake out of the state and the owner wanted me to drive him, so I got a seat on a charter flight with some other horsemen going to the race. Because I was able to save the cost of renting a car and overnight accommodations, I billed the owner only for my share of the charter flight costs.

The owner called me and said he didn't understand why he was being billed for that expense. I told him that was a customary practice since I had incurred costs to race his horse. He was very understanding about the situation and paid the bill, but I feel as if I must shoulder the blame for some of the misunderstanding.

A veteran owner would have known that the travel costs are billed to the owner, but this man was new and simply didn't realize that. Besides, when his horse had shipped out of town and my assistant went to warm him up, there was no charge and I thus assume he expected there would be no charge when I flew out of state, too.

Some of this could have been solved if we had billed him a minimal amount for the first trip, or even if we had listed the assistant trainer's travel and put an "N/C" on the bill to indicate "no charge."

That incident illustrates how it is helpful to explain your billing procedures fully to a new owner. And it's not such a bad practice with experienced owners, too.

It's helpful for a new owner to understand about harness racing, and to that end I would encourage him to subscribe to the trade periodicals and to feel free to ask questions in an effort to learn about the business.

I do not think, however, it is in the best interests of the owner to try to second-guess the trainer or to interject himself into the day-to-day supervision of the horse. That's the trainer's job. The owner should certainly be consulted on racing schedules and major decisions, but when an owner starts to question how a horse is trained or rigged, then he is usually on thin ice.

If the owner is not satisfied with the job that the trainer is doing, then he should talk to the trainer and, if the problem can't be resolved, he should find another trainer.

The trainer is a professional in his field and usually knows best about the welfare of the horse. If I have a legal problem, I consult with my attorney and rely upon his judgment to act in my best interest. I might have some suggestions and I might even know a little about the law, but I'm a horse trainer, not a lawyer, and I'm better off leaving the legal decisions to him.

That is not to say that I discourage owners from taking an active interest in stable operations. They're always free to come visit the stable, and I like to have an owner interested enough to jog or perhaps even train his horse once in a while.

You certainly don't want an owner to climb on a jog cart for the first time some morning and take a horse to the track at The Meadowlands. It's simply too congested out there for a novice to be handling a horse. So you should try to teach an owner (or even an inexperienced groom) to handle a horse on an uncongested track.

If an owner wishes to put in the time to learn how to handle a horse, I think it is great if he can go training miles with his horses. And if he really wants to work at it and become very adept at handling a horse in all situations, then he may wish to drive in some amateur races. This is great and it's one of the big advantages that we have over Thoroughbreds. An owner, virtually regardless of his age or size, can climb on the jog cart and jog or train his horses. That's something that very few owners could ever do with a Thoroughbred.

As they become more experienced handling horses, owners will realize that horses don't necessarily steer like sports cars. Often a horse will get on one line or become foul-gaited and there is very little that the man sitting behind him can do. I think those owners who have spent some time in a jog cart are far less apt to criticize the way you drive in a race because they know the driver is often the victim of circumstances. Sometimes the horse wants to run over horses when you want to stay in a hole, and then you may have to pull him simply for safety's sake.

While I'm on the subject of owners criticizing drivers, I should caution owners that it's never a good idea to confront a driver immediately after a race and criticize his drive as the drivers are dismounting.

That not only embarrasses him in front of his peers, but it can lead to some arguments. In most cases, the driver realizes he has driven badly even when the owner doesn't. If the owner is unhappy with a drive, it's best to wait until the next day to talk about it when everyone is likely to be more rational.

With so many owners busy operating their own businesses, they don't always have time to follow their horses, and I think the responsibility of communication rests with the trainer.

An owner simply can't get enough communication from his trainer. I've never known an owner who has said, "Gee, I sure wish my trainer would quit calling me to tell me how my horses are doing."

When I am stabled at The Meadowlands, most of our communication is done by telephone. That is because most of our owners are in the New York metropolitan area and that's the most expedient way to handle things.

We also make extensive use of the fax machine. Whenever an owner has a horse in to race, we fax him the overnight sheet as soon as it is available from the race office. We'll also fax a copy of the program page if the owner wishes. Fax machines are in almost universal use now in offices and homes and they can be a handy tool for communicating with your owners.

Often owners come to the races and see their horses race, so they know what happened. Or they read the trade papers and know what happened. In many cases, however, the owners will call me, and I make it clear that I never hesitate to talk to an owner.

I would prefer, of course, that the owner call late in the morning, usually after 11 a.m. when we're winding down the training work. Most of the owners understand that, but if an owner calls at any time, a trainer should be ready to talk.

In some cases, you might have to talk to several owners about the same horses. For example, if you have a horse owned by a partnership, several of the owners might call and ask you how the horse trained or raced.

That can be time-consuming in that you have to repeat the same thing several times, but that's all part of communication. I would add, however, that it is best in a partnership to have one person responsible for checking with the trainer.

By all means, if there is a problem with a certain horse, don't wait for the owner to call you to inform him. Call him and keep calling him to keep him posted. If a horse is seriously sick or lame, that owner should know about the problem and what you're doing to solve the problem.

If you are winter training in the South or if you're racing at a track away from where most of your owners live, then it is doubly important to communicate with them. They don't have the chance to see their horses race or train regularly.

Most trainers will send out a fax with a brief message on how a horse is doing. I think that's a great idea. Even if the message is simply, "This colt is continuing to train sound and good-gaited. Mile today in 2:18, last quarter in 32 seconds." The owner likes to know those things and, in fact, has a right to know what his horse is doing.

Even though we use modern technology such as the fax machine regularly, the Remmen Stable is not computerized. It may sound funny in the 1990s to say that you're operating a business and that you're not computerized, but we have not found it to be necessary.

I know that some stables do maintain billing and medical records on a computer and that's fine if it works for them, but our accounting is done by an outside firm and our stable isn't so big that we can't maintain our records in the traditional ways. Back in the 1980s, many trainers had huge stables, and I can see where a computer might have been essential, but I haven't found it so.

Perhaps part of the reason that we're not computerized is that my brothers and I are horsemen, not computer whizzes. Some trainers, however, are familiar with computers and the software available and they really enjoy working with computers. In those cases, a trainer should use a computer.

I know of one stable that pays to have a crew come to the track and videotape horses in training. Copies are then made of the videotapes and they are sent to the owner. That's a terrific idea to keep owners posted and I'm certain those owners watch those videotapes over and over. Of course, I must add that the owner is paying for that videotape in his monthly training bill, but he is probably happy to do so.

While stressing the importance of communication, I must add that you should never forget your horses. The owner wants results with his horses, so they should take priority. A trainer with a large stable could easily become a "telephone trainer" and spend all day talking to owners on the phone, but his horses would suffer.

One of the areas where communication is most critical with owners is when it comes time for making stakes payments. One of the major costs associated with owning a young horse in today's racing environment is staking costs. The money that a top horse can win has skyrocketed in recent years, but so have the costs of playing in the stakes games. Since the owners are often racing for their own money, the stakes payments are very expensive.

For example, before an owner purchases a yearling, he should remember to budget for the stakes payments that he might have to make on that colt. They can add up real quickly. If you're going to stake a colt to the hilt, it can easily add $20,000 to the cost of owning that horse. Of course, if you're racing in a Sires Stakes program it won't be nearly that expensive, but any owner should be well aware of the cost of stakes payments.

After you purchase a yearling, it's a good idea to verify the stakes engagements for that yearling. They are usually listed right on the catalog page with the yearling's pedigree, but mistakes do occur and occasionally a colt will be listed as being eligible to a certain stake when, in fact, he really isn't eligible.

This is where the *Stakes Guide,* which is available for purchase from the U.S. Trotting Association early each year, can be invaluable. It lists the names and addresses of all the stakes sponsors and you can verify your yearling's eligibility.

It's a good idea for every owner and trainer to get a copy of the *Stakes Guide.* It's literally the "Bible" when it comes to staking and will prove to be invaluable throughout the year.

Staking is an area where communication between the owner and trainer is essential. It is very difficult to know in February or March exactly how good a two-year-old will ultimately be. Every top horseman has been fooled by colts. We can all tell tales about a colt who couldn't get out of his own way in February who later developed into a top stakes star.

Actually, the reverse situation is more often true. Often you will have so many colts who train down wonderfully and show great promise until they hit the 2:05 stage and then they just seem to hang while others keep dropping.

There is a temptation to stake a colt to just about everything, but when you begin to add up the payments, that gets extremely expensive for the owner. I mentioned earlier that there is nothing wrong with an owner and trainer being optimistic, as long as they are realistic, too—and that advice certainly applies in the area of stakes payments.

I tend to be conservative with my stakes payments. I will try to assess what potential a colt or filly has shown and, based upon that, I will advise an owner how extensively I think that horse should be staked. Again, I tend to be conservative. If the owner wishes to put the horse in additional stakes, that is fine with me.

Some trainers might actually encourage an owner to overstake a colt because the trainer makes a percentage of the horse's earnings and thus the trainer stands to make more if the horse is eligible to all the big stakes. Besides, the trainer might reason, the money is coming out of the owner's pockets.

That might sound good, but unless a trainer is honest about a colt's ability and realistic about the costs of staking, he is doing a disservice to the owner. Those stakes payments are a major cost factor in training a horse, and the owner is undoubtedly going to add up his costs at the end of the year and balance his costs against his earnings. If an owner consistently loses money using one trainer, chances are that owner will be shopping around for a new trainer soon.

In my stable, the owners make the nominating and sustaining payments themselves and I would prefer that they make the starting payments, too. Those starting payments can involve some hefty amounts and that is too much for a stable to pay up front.

That isn't always practical, of course, but since you know when a horse will be starting in a race and you also know the entry fee, it's best if the owner makes the check payable directly to the track. I have made those payments for owners in the past if the payments involve only a few hundred dollars, but if you're talking about entering a horse in the Hambletonian ($15,000) or in another major stake, that is more money than a trainer can afford to pay out.

If we do pay a couple minor starting fees for an owner, those are billed to him on the monthly statement.

In staking their horses, most owners use a stakes service which has complete information on the dates and payments on virtually every stake. Stakes services can provide excellent computer-generated printouts of a horse's stakes engagements, and I personally feel that it is well worth the cost to use a stakes service.

While I think that stakes services can be invaluable, you don't need one if you're willing to do the work yourself and if you have only a few horses to stake. In these situations, the *Stakes Guide* becomes even more essential to your operation.

Despite the costs involved, many owners are all too happy to make stakes payments. In reality, they are buying a dream. They want to be able to dream of having a horse in the Hambletonian or Little Brown Jug, so they'll make that payment.

Far more horses are overstaked than understaked. It's just the nature of our business for the owner and often the trainer to be optimistic and stake a horse extensively.

I would urge a trainer and owner to use caution and good judgment in staking, or those costs can escalate quickly. Remember, even if your horse is "understaked" he still can make money. People talk about how lightly staked Jate Lobell was, and it's true that he was not eligible to the

Woodrow Wilson or Breeders Crown at two and not eligible to the Jug as a three-year-old. However, that didn't prevent Jate Lobell from winning over $2.2 million in two seasons.

Another reason why a horse can make money despite being "understaked" is that many major events are now early closers and some of the major stakes allow supplemental entry payments.

I have no problems with paying supplemental payments or advising an owner to supplement a top colt to a major stake, but the stakes sponsors should make those supplemental payments stiff enough so they discourage horses from supplementing on a whim. That isn't right and it isn't fair to the owners who have made the nominating and sustaining payments.

I do think, for the good of harness racing, that our major stars should be in the major races and should not be excluded by ineligibility.

I know that Yonkers Raceway was certainly happy that it provided for supplemental payments to its Triple Crown events earlier in this decade. In 1982, Cam Fella was not eligible for the Cane Pace, yet he was supplemented to the race and won. Two years later, the same situation existed with On The Road Again. He also won the Cane. In 1983, the three-year-old trotter making headlines early in the year was Joie De Vie, and Yonkers was able to showcase him in the Yonkers Trot only because his owner made a supplemental payment. Joie De Vie won that race.

Another example involving supplemental payments hits closer to home for me.

In 1990, Jake And Elwood was one of the best three-year-old pacing colts in North America. I knew how good Jake was because I had to face him on a regular basis with Beach Towel. The owners of Jake And Elwood supplemented him to both the Cane Pace and Messenger Stake and he won both of those legs of the Triple Crown.

Jake And Elwood was not eligible to the Little Brown Jug, the third leg of the Triple Crown for pacers. That was bad news for the horse and his connections because he lost his shot at winning the Triple Crown since the Jug does not allow supplements. That was certainly good news for me and for Beach Towel and his owners, because not having Jake And Elwood in the Jug made it a lot easier for us to win.

You can say that's one situation where I am glad they didn't allow supplemental payments.

You must remember, however, that a supplemental payment is like betting on a race. You're not guaranteed you're going to get your money back. George Segal, one of the smartest and most successful owners in harness racing today, found that out in 1991 when he paid $68,928 to supplement Artsplace to the Messenger Stake and watched in dismay as Artsplace drew post position nine and finished out of the money.

So supplemental payments enable the public to see our finest stars, but I think they should be costly enough to make an owner really think long and hard before entering a horse. In reality, only the very wealthy owners can take the gamble of making a steep supplemental payment.

Another consideration in staking a horse is the impact it has on his value if you wish to sell him.

Let's say you are selling a green or lightly raced three-year old pacer early in the year. If you can tell prospective buyers that this colt is eligible for a host of major stakes, you can be assured that colt is going to sell for appreciably more money than a lightly staked colt.

The reasons for this are two-fold. The first is obvious: A horse who is extensively staked has the potential to win more money, so that makes him worth more.

The second reason is less tangible and gets into buyer psychology. It's only natural that a prospective buyer will be impressed if he reads that a pacing colt is eligible to the Meadowland Pace, Jug, Breeders Crown, etc. He will naturally assume that the owner and trainer must have thought highly of the colt to make those payments and he, therefore, might be more willing to bid on that colt.

Stakes payments can have a negative impact on a colt's training, too, and I think every trainer has seen colts suffer because they were pushed to be ready for a major stakes when, in fact, they weren't physically ready.

Remember that when an owner makes those stakes payments back in the late winter and spring, he is counting on the trainer having the horse ready to race in those events. So often something will come up to interrupt a colt's schedule. Maybe he gets sick, maybe he gets a little sore. The trainer feels pressure to have that colt ready because, after all, the owner has already invested a lot of money in stakes payments. Some of that pressure is self-imposed and some of it comes from the owner who frequently calls asking if the colt will be ready to race in time.

That's where the trainer must use his judgment in determining what is best for the long-term good of the horse. A young horse will suffer when pushed to meet a schedule beyond his current capacity. So you can run the risk of ruining a potentially good horse just to race in one event. That's not good management of that horse.

Just as owners are essential to the success of the stable, so are the grooms you employ to care for your owners' horses. In years past, we had many career grooms who knew how to rub a horse and took pride in their horse's condition and performance. Sad to say, there aren't many grooms like that left.

When you hire a groom, it's important to know who that groom has worked for in the past. If he has worked for a top horseman from another stable, chances are he will be able to handle just about any horse or assignment you give him.

There is a downside to having experienced grooms, too, in that they've been around long enough to know the shortcuts and how to do as little as possible to get by.

Getting grooms and keeping them working is a problem that every trainer must face. There are times when you're short of help. Then everyone must pitch in and help out, including the trainers.

At any track it seems as if there are always grooms who are stopping by the barn asking a trainer if he needs any help. And the network in the backstretch is such that a trainer might say, "No, I've got enough help right now, but I hear that John Doe in Barn 9 is looking for grooms."

Often you don't find the best grooms wandering around looking for work, but if you're really desperate, you might have to hire someone like this just to get the work done. One approach in this situation is to have the new groom just clean stalls or other less important work and ask your better grooms to handle the jogging and harnessing.

If you're at a remote training center instead of at a pari-mutuel track, you simply don't get grooms coming through the barn area looking for jobs. Then you might have to place an advertisement in a local newspaper or contact the local job placement office to see if you can find any help that way. It's important, however, that you specify that the applicants should have some experience with horses.

I've tried this approach in the past without much success, but a trainer must do whatever he can to find help. Finding and keeping good help is a constant problem for any trainer.

We try not to hire grooms with no experience whatsoever, because you have to spend so much time teaching them the fundamentals it detracts from the time you can spend on other areas of stable management.

We absolutely would not let a rookie groom jog a horse. That's just asking for trouble. Putting a valuable horse in the hands of an inexperienced groom on the track can be dangerous to both the groom and the horse and to others on the track, too. Some stables put rookie grooms out on the track with horses, and I'm surprised that there aren't more accidents at a track like The Meadowlands with so many neophytes on the track each morning.

If we do hire a green hand as a groom, it will be several months before we feel that person can be ready to jog a horse. That means that another groom or one of the trainers must jog a horse and that, of course, adds to the work load.

In the case of yearlings being broken or two-year-olds early in the winter, the grooms seldom, if ever, jog these horses. The young horses are at such a critical stage of training that it's important to have an experienced horseman sitting behind them.

As a two-year-old progresses, learns manners and becomes acclimated to what happens on the racetrack, a groom might start to jog him. That decision depends upon the ability of the groom and the manners of the two-year-old involved. Like so many things in training horses, it is an individual decision.

You can usually tell right away how knowledgeable a groom is when he comes to work for you. Some of them will try to mislead you about their work background, but their shortcomings become readily apparent when they start to work.

The reality of stable management today is that you must overlook faults in many of your grooms. They're not all perfect, and if you insist on having perfect grooms you'll be cleaning a lot of stalls and harnessing a lot of horses yourself.

Some grooms require almost constant supervision, while others can be trusted to do their work professionally and to inform the trainer if anything is amiss with a horse. Some grooms must be handled with kid gloves or they'll sulk, while others need a stern word or two periodically.

Some grooms are better at feeding picky eaters than others. Some grooms do a great job cleaning the horse and equipment, while others don't. I recall one groom who frequently didn't do the best job brushing up his horses before they were harnessed, but his horses all raced well and it is, after all, the performance on the track that counts.

Some grooms just seem to fit some horses better than others. For example, if you have a filly who is a little high-strung and flighty, it might be wise to put an older person on her. The older person might work a little slower and not upset this filly. Sometimes a woman will get along better with a horse than a man will, and a trainer should be aware of the interaction between groom and horse.

The way our stable operates is that the groom rubs three horses, and we pay $100 per head. It's difficult for a groom to get by on less than $300 per week these days. Plus, we pay $40 each time the horse races (this is known as a "paddock fee"), so a groom can make an extra $160 per month if his horse is racing each week.

Most stables have grooms who have been with them for a number of years and are top-notch in every respect. Those grooms should be assigned to your best horses whenever that is possible.

The groom of a top horse has a great deal of responsibility and I frankly don't want to entrust an exceptional horse to a rookie groom. If you're in the final game of the NBA playoffs and you're down one point with 15 seconds left in the game, you want to get the ball to a veteran who won't wilt under the pressure. Much the same thing is true with a groom on a top colt. That groom will probably be required to travel and assume responsibility for a very valuable horse.

If a groom is on the road with a horse, it's impossible for him to take care of three horses, so usually a groom going on the Grand Circuit has one or two horses, at the most. We will try to adjust the wages per horse so the groom will still make about $300 per week. The owner, of course, will have to be billed to make up the additional amount.

A groom on the road has a great deal of responsibility since the trainer is seldom there on a day-to-day basis to oversee things. Therefore, you should make certain that you have a capable groom on a horse when you send a horse away from your base of operations. A groom must be trusted with making certain that the horse is properly jogged, cooled out, and fed each day.

The groom's responsibility does not, however, extend to training the horse. I have seen grooms going training miles with Grand Circuit-caliber horses when the trainer wasn't around. To me, that is unacceptable. The groom might be capable of going a training mile, but that isn't the right way to handle that task.

If our stable has a horse at Vernon Downs, for example, and one of my assistants or I can't be there to train him, it is our responsibility to contact a trainer at Vernon that we trust, and ask him to work our colt. Usually you will find a trainer is willing to accommodate you, because we all get caught in this bind sometimes. Next week, that same trainer might be asking me to go a few trips with one of his horses at The Meadowlands. It's just a courtesy that trainers extend to one another.

Once the trainer has made the arrangements to have the horse trained, it's important to tell the groom. Don't leave the groom in the dark.

If our stable has more than one or two horses on the road at a particular track, we will usually send one of our trainers to make certain that they get trained properly. The travel costs for that trainer will get billed back to the owners.

At The Meadowlands, most of our grooms will rub three horses. We feel that a good groom can care for three horses and still do justice to each horse. In fact, you will find that a good groom could care for five horses and they'd probably all get good care, while a poor groom can't adequately care for one horse.

By keeping the cost for a caretaker to $100 per week, per horse, we feel we are trying to keep the owners' bills down.

Taking care of three horses means that a groom must get to work around 6:30 a.m. and work steadily until about noon, but he should be able to have the afternoons free on most days.

That schedule does not permit time for much horseplay in the barn. I prefer to have the groom stay at the barn and do his work while the horse is on the track being trained. My assistants and I will drive the horse back to the barn instead of handing it over to the groom at the draw gate. That not only enables the groom to get work done at the barn while we're on the track, but it also makes certain that the trainers are in the barn frequently, checking to see how things are going.

I should point out that this system is contingent upon your barn being close to the track where it doesn't take the trainer long to go from the track back to the barn. And our system also requires that a trainer jump in every once in a while to help out a groom by jogging a horse.

That is not to say that there is anything wrong with the system used by trainers who have the grooms bring the horses to them at the draw gate.

If your barn is not close to the track, that is probably the only practical system. Plus, by standing at the track, the trainer gets to see some of his horses jogged by the grooms and he might be able to detect a little soreness or the need for an equipment change that he might otherwise not have noticed.

Our system allows us to put a groom on three horses, but it takes teamwork to make this happen. We feel, however, that the groom can use his time better at the barn than he can standing by the draw gate watching his horse train.

As with so many things, however, you must make exceptions. It used to make me mad to see a groom come to the track to see his horse go a training mile. I thought that the groom could better use his time cleaning a stall and tending to other chores.

However, it's difficult to get angry with a groom for showing that much interest in his horse's performance. Maybe he wants to see if the horse has overcome a breaking problem or maybe he just wants to see how the horse does in a set. A trainer should never discourage that kind of interest in a horse.

In fact, if you have some experienced grooms who know how to handle a horse, it's not such a bad idea to let them go a slow training mile once in a while. They get a thrill out of it and I have found that they will dig in and work a little harder if given that chance. It makes them feel more a part of the stable. I should emphasize, however, that only experienced grooms should go training miles, and preferably when the track is not too congested.

Many stables pay a year-end bonus to a groom based upon a certain percentage of what his horses earn. I think that the idea of a bonus has merit, but I have found that a percentage based upon the horse's earnings is not the fairest way to distribute bonuses.

Each month I bill an owner for two percent of a horse's earnings. This goes into a common fund for the year-end bonuses. At the end of the year I will divide that money up, according to which individuals I feel are most deserving. Usually 1 1/2 percent goes to the grooms and 1/2 percent will be divided among my assistant trainers.

I have often found that your hardest-working groom might be taking care of a horse who has had various problems and who has earned only $20,000. Yet that groom might be working faithfully to help that horse overcome lameness problems. Another groom might have "lucked" into rubbing a stakes colt who earns over $100,000 and who is always sound and healthy.

Is it fair for one groom to get a bonus which is five times larger than the other groom who may, in fact, have worked harder? I don't think so. I think my method is fairer because I can divide up the money according to individual merit of the groom.

In addition to owners and grooms, a trainer must frequently deal with veterinarians. Today veterinarians play an important role at any racetrack. Horsemen want to have the quick fix for a horse's sickness or lameness problems. We all know that many of the sick or lame horses would get well on their own eventually, but the cost of keeping a horse in training is so high today that we want to solve the problems quickly.

In our stable, we try not to overuse the veterinarian. A good veterinarian can be a handy crutch for a trainer, but a good horseman should be competent enough to resist the temptation to turn to the veterinarian every time he has a problem. Remember, all those veterinary charges are ultimately going to be passed along to the owner and increase his bill. It's the trainer's responsibility to use a veterinarian only when necessary and to handle minor problems himself.

At any track, there are often numerous veterinarians and most of them are quite adept in their profession. It is my belief that a trainer will do better if he selects one person as his primary veterinarian and stays with that person long enough to develop the rapport so necessary between trainer and veterinarian.

You might, of course, have to send a horse to a specialist in surgery or another area, but a good veterinarian can handle most of your everyday problems and he should be willing to refer you to a specialist when the problem is beyond his expertise.

Developing a rapport with a veterinarian is important because the trainer must be able to communicate to the veterinarian. The vet can't do you much good if you're not telling him everything about the horse, nor will the veterinarian's remedies do the horse any good unless the trainer makes certain that the veterinarian's instructions are followed religiously.

In our stable, my brother Larry works closely with the veterinarian. He and I will discuss what medication or treatment each horse will need, but Larry is often the one communicating directly with the veterinarian. So it's his responsibility to know exactly what each horse is being given in the way of medication.

This leads me into a discussion of the "trainer responsibility" rule. That rule makes the trainer ultimately responsible if, for example, one of his horses comes up with a positive post-race test. The rule is enforced even if the trainer did not authorize the medication given to the horse. It doesn't matter if the trainer is totally innocent; he is also totally responsible, and he'll have to face the consequences of that positive test.

I don't particularly like the trainer responsibility rule, but I recognize that it is necessary. No matter how well you try to protect your horses with a night watchman or whatever other measures you take, it's still possible for an outside party to gain access to your horses and administer an illegal substance. So the horse races and tests positive. The trainer knows nothing about the illegal substance, yet it shows up clearly on the post-race test. Who is responsible? Obviously, it has to be the trainer of the horse.

Medication is a fact of life in racing today, and I don't think that is all bad. It simply depends upon what type of medication you are giving and when you are giving it.

For example, I tend to treat my horses after a race rather than before a race. That is, I will often give a horse a small dose of phenylbutazone (usually called "bute"), a pain killer, to help the horse get over whatever aches and pains he may have incurred in a race.

We use cortisone and sometimes hyaluronic acid to inject a horse's joints. We subject horses to a great deal of stress today, and injecting joints is often necessary if you're going to keep a horse racing week after week. It's true that if you had plenty of time, nature would heal many of these injuries, but if trainers didn't use some therapeutic medications, the track wouldn't have enough horses to fill a racing card.

Many trainers have used anabolic steroids on horses in hopes of getting better performance from them, but I question how much good these products do a horse. I have used anabolic steroids without much to show for it. Research has pretty well established that anabolic steroids can have detrimental impact on a horse, but I'm not certain that the advantages of anabolic steroids have been fully established.

Invariably, on any backstretch you will hear rumors that "so-and-so in barn 3 has some juice that'll make horses go faster." Everyone is looking for the edge, and a lot of trainers fall for any new product that comes along. Most of these stories are myths, of course, and I've been around long enough to know that the trainers who supposedly have some magic potion don't last very long in the business.

Owners have every right to know what kind of medication their horses are receiving and they get a copy of the veterinary bill each month, so the treatments and charges are all listed right on that bill. And certainly if he has any questions, an owner shouldn't hesitate to call a trainer to inquire about medication.

Occasionally you will get an owner who will want to specify that his horses not be treated with a commonly used product, such as cortisone. There are many negative studies out now about the effects of cortisone, but we have used it quite successfully without any negative results. In those cases, we will talk to the owner about how we use cortisone, why we use it, and how it benefits a horse. Again, this is an area where the owner must rely upon the professionalism of his trainer.

Veterinary medicine is an essential adjunct of stable management today, but the less you use a veterinarian, the better off you will be. When you use a veterinarian, make certain that you have full confidence in him and that you fully understand what treatments he is giving your horses.

Another important part of stable management is the blacksmith you use. I admit that our stable is a bit unusual is this respect. For many years we practically had our own shoer who was with us from the time we moved our stable to The Meadowlands from Windsor Raceway in the mid-1970s. That arrangement wasn't practical after we reduced the size of our stable, so in recent years, we have been using Tom Gambino at The Meadowlands.

The working relationship that we have developed with the men who shoe for us has helped us immensely in our shoeing needs. Every trainer would like to have the time to accompany each horse to the blacksmith's shop, but that simply isn't practical. That's why having a steady relationship with one shoer can be very important.

So my assistants and I will make out a card indicating how we want a horse shod and send it along to the shop with the horse. Because of our relationship, Tom Gambino understands exactly what we want done with our horses. If there is any question, of course, and we're not there, he can simply pick up the phone and call us.

Tom also is very good at alerting us to any little problem with a horse's hoof. For example, if he sees a quarter crack starting, he lets us know right away. If he notices that a horse's feet have become unusually hard and brittle, then he tells us that the groom might not be packing the horse's feet. He knows shoeing and foot care better than we do, and we trust him implicitly.

It's important that you select a good blacksmith and stick with him. It's much like developing a working rapport with a veterinarian.

Of course, a trainer must work on a daily basis with the race secretary at each track to make sure that his horses are entered in the easiest possible class for them. This means that you must be familiar with your horse's earnings and recent performance. At The Meadowlands, most race conditions are written based upon the horse's last seven starts, so our stable keeps a file of past programs so we know for certain how much our horses have earned. Even if you don't have the programs on file, you have the opportunity to go to the race secretary's office to look at the eligibility papers to see how much a horse has earned in his last seven starts.

In entering a horse in an overnight race, I always try to find the softest spot for him. Many times a horse's earnings might make him eligible to a couple different races, but I always try to pick the easiest race for him. Even if he's eligible to one race with a $14,000 purse and another with a $12,000 purse, if that $14,000 race looks to attract tougher horses (and it usually will, because purses are tied closely to the quality of horse), I would enter my horse in the $12,000 race. The purse is not the primary consideration.

Why not race for the higher purse? Because you're much better off winning a $12,000 race than finishing second, third, or fourth in a $14,000 race. That's the financial reason.

A more important consideration is that you never want to get a horse in "over his head" so that he gets discouraged about racing. And, believe me, nothing will discourage a horse faster than racing his heart out against tougher horses and getting beat week after week. You are much better off to race your horse for a slightly lower purse and keep him winning. That builds his confidence. The purse is secondary; if the horse is good enough, he'll earn himself out of the lower classes and step up the ladder so he is racing for those better purses.

In today's racing environment, where many trainers do not drive their own horses, it is important that a trainer also develop a good working rapport with a number of catch drivers.

Ten years ago, I would have said I could put more money on a horse's card in a year by training and driving him instead of just training him and turning the lines over to a catch driver. I guess I proved that in 1990 when Beach Towel was the leading money-winning horse in the sport with over $2 million.

Today, however, racing has changed, at least it has on the New Jersey circuit where I race. Today's owners do not want a trainer who drives. They want to be able to use the best catch drivers at a given track and then have the luxury of changing drivers if the horse doesn't race well. The trainer-driver is going the way of the dinosaur.

The new owners who have come into the sport in recent years have forced a big change in the way harness racing is conducted. They are paying the bills and want to take an active role in the management of their horses, especially where catch drivers are concerned. An owner isn't too likely to question a trainer's decision on shoeing or the length of a horse's hobbles, because he isn't familiar with how those will affect a horse's performance. But he definitely can see what happens on the track when a catch driver is in the sulky.

The catch drivers are well aware that they're just hired hands who are only as good as their last race. They're under tremendous pressure to get every ounce of performance out of the horse they're driving. If they don't, they probably won't be driving that horse again next week.

This has resulted in the aggressive style of racing we have now. Some drivers move horses earlier in the mile than is necessary because they feel the pressure to get their horse in the thick of battle. They have to race the horse as aggressively as possible or risk losing the mount behind that horse the next time he races.

The horses we race, the tracks that we race over, the equipment we use, and many other elements in racing today are conducive to front-end speed. Front-end speed holds up much better than it did years ago. Even on mile tracks with long stretches, the come-from-behind horse is at a severe disadvantage in today's style of racing. That's why catch drivers feel the need to be so aggressive in each race. Races are won today by horses involved on the front end.

I certainly don't question the right of the owner to make decisions relative to his horses, but I don't think that switching drivers after every bad performance is the answer. I think that a horse would fare better over an entire season if the owner and trainer were to select a top catch driver and assure him that he'll have the mount behind that horse all year long. They need to assure him that he won't be fired if he happens to get locked in during an important race. With that assurance, I think the catch driver can drive the horse better.

Owners should always consider what's best for the horse over the course of an entire season. Some owners might pressure a trainer to use whatever catch driver has the hot hand that month, so a horse gets driven by several different catch drivers over the season. Owners should be looking for consistency of performance on the track. It doesn't do an owner's bottom line much good for a horse to go one big mile, if that results in the horse being "gutted" for the remainder of the season.

There is no question that horses don't last as long at The Meadowlands because the pace of the races is so wearing here. There isn't much chance for a horse to get a breather, and some horses just can't stand that stress for much more than a year.

If you are using a catch driver, I would urge you to try to communicate well with him, too. At The Meadowlands, a lot of catch drivers help trainers hang up a horse properly by saying, "His hobbles are too tight. Let them out about two inches." Or, "He was pretty sore behind tonight. You might try injecting his hocks."

In many cases, problems with rigging or soundness only show up when a horse is subjected to the stress of racing, so the catch driver might be seeing problems the trainer doesn't encounter in the horse's work miles. It's wise to pay attention to what a catch driver has to say after a race.

There are many trainers today who stable their stock at farm tracks or at training centers and ship in to the raceways to race. There is a widespread belief that horses will relax more and hold their form longer if they are in a farm environment away from the sterile backstretch environment of a racetrack.

I agree with that contention up to a certain point. I think that the advantage a farm or training center environment offers is the opportunity to turn a horse out. Many such facilities have paddocks where you can turn out a horse for a couple hours a day, and that will do more than anything else to keep the horse's attitude fresh.

If you cannot turn your horse out on a regular basis, such as during the winter at training centers in the north, then I see little advantage to training on a farm or training center facility. A stall at a training center is no different than a stall at a racetrack. Horses aren't that smart.

Besides, you must remember that there are costs associated with using a training center or farm facility that will increase the overhead of your stable. Stalls are provided to horses at racetracks without charge, but there are substantial costs involved in renting a stall at a training center or operating your own farm facility.

Since you must ship in from a training center or farm to the track itself, you must figure in your shipping costs. That will have to be passed along to the owner. And every time you put a horse on a truck or van, there is always the chance that the horse will be hurt in shipping.

I do think there is merit to using a farm training facility, however, and when we ship our horses in from the farm to race at the track, I generally try to get them into our barn about noon on race day. It also is a good idea to have a person riding with the horses in the van or trailer, because that can help you avoid the many injuries horses can incur while shipping.

I make it a practice to put shipping bandages and bell boots on a horse when he ships into the track. That can help reduce the severity of some injuries that occur. Most injuries occur when the horse is being loaded or unloaded, and the only answer to properly loading a horse is plenty of patience. Don't let a groom or driver rush a horse in or out of a van.

Horses can get hurt on the truck, too, as sometimes they will get crowded, get kicked, or lose their balance and go down in the van. That's why having a person ride with them is important.

Incidentally, not every horse is a good shipper. We have had horses who would have raced better off a farm facility, but they got so upset during the shipping process that it simply wasn't worth it to try to ship them back and forth. Those horses were stabled at the track.

We have a fortunate situation because we have horses both on and off the track. If your entire stable is stabled at a farm facility, then a horse will have to go into a ship-in barn when he arrives at the track. Many horses, however, arrive just shortly before they are scheduled to go their first warm up mile, so they come right off the truck and go into the paddock.

How far in advance of the race you need to arrive at the track is governed by personal preference and by the length of the ship. If your horse will be on the truck only an hour or so, he can probably go right into the paddock and begin his warm ups without significant fatigue.

If your horse is shipping two hours or more, then I think it is wise to get your horse to the track at least several hours in advance of his first warm up trip. It's simply not fair to ask a horse to stand on a truck that length of time, then harness him and go to the track without giving him some chance to relax and lie down.

Of course, it is always wise to allow yourself plenty of leeway in shipping to a track. Better to be there too early than too late. You never know when you might encounter engine trouble, a flat tire, or a traffic jam.

Besides training off a farm track, I have also trained in Florida, and southern training has obviously become popular because it is a horseman's paradise. I'm not convinced it's any better for the horses, but it surely is for the people involved, and you can't discount the human factor.

For example, I know there is a tendency to get your work done as quickly as possible up north when it's so bitter cold. You want to get that horse out on the track and get him back in the barn as quickly as possible. In the south, with that warm sun on your back, you might be a little more inclined to spend more time with a problem horse and help work through his problems.

The same goes for grooms. I know that a groom will be more willing to stay in a horse's stall and tend to his legs if the temperature is 70 degrees than he will if it is 10 degrees.

Of course, that can work against you, too. Sometimes the horses actually don't need all the leg attention a trainer or groom might be giving them. There are probably more horses who are overtrained in the south. Sometimes you can overdo your efforts in training a horse.

There is no question that I encountered more sickness in the south when I trained there. Trainers who have been there for many years just accept that. I didn't have problems shipping our horses from Florida back north, but when they go from the cool weather in the north to the warmth, they do seem to get sick.

Many owners are under the misconception that training is so much more expensive in Florida. That's not necessarily true. Sure, you must pay stall rent, but you'll have to pay stall rent at any training facility. And the cost of shipping a horse back and forth to Florida is not that significant when considered in the overall costs of training a horse for a year.

Some horsemen have felt that the warm weather in Florida enables them to test their young horses earlier and, therefore, they can determine which ones are worthy of stakes payments and which ones can be lightly staked.

Most trainers like to ask a little something extra of their two-year-olds just before the first stakes payments are due in February and March. However, I think it's very difficult to tell which young horses are going to make it as stakes horses. There is a tendency for most of them to look good when they're going in 2:30; often how a colt handles that 2:30 mile is no real indication of how he'll do when he gets in a few baby races and has to go in 2:00. It's often only in the heat of battle that you find out how much desire and ability a horse really has.

Training in the south has its advantages, but good horses can be trained anywhere. Just remember that the climate never made a horse good.

Part of any trainer's job is to keep replenishing his stock, because the grueling pace wears out horses so much more quickly than in the past.

In recent years, there has been a tremendous market for horses ready to race. If you have a horse who has been racing well and who can be dropped in the box the following week, he will often command a premium price.

Most horsemen would like to try to buy horses privately, but that option isn't always available. Thus, you must look at the horses entered in mixed stock sales to find a racehorse.

When appraising horses in such a sale, it's important to keep in mind that the horse is in the sale for a reason. He might be slightly sore, tired, or bad-mannered. Or the horse might simply be racing better than ever and the owner knows he can get top dollar for him.

The most important thing is that a horse show race lines right up to the date of the sale. That will tell you so much about his ability. It's great if you can see a horse race, but those race lines will give you valuable information, too.

You shouldn't be hesitant to ask around about the horse. Maybe another horseman might know him. But you may not always get the entire truth, because if another horseman thought the horse was a possible bargain, he wouldn't be telling you about him.

It would be great if you could train a horse before bidding on him in a mixed sale, but that opportunity is seldom available. I know that I did train Bree's Brief, a Big Towner mare who sold for $505,000 back in 1986. Many times a trainer will be glad to let another trainer go a trip with a potentially high-priced horse.

Sometimes, however, the trainer will not want you to do so, and he'll say, "No, you just have to buy him as he is." That should alert you to a possible problem, so it is essential to go over a horse very carefully physically before bidding on him.

It's tough to get a bargain at a mixed sale when there is such a strong demand for racehorses, but sometimes you can buy a reasonably priced horse if you're willing to lay that horse up for a few months. For example, you might notice that a horse has raced without interruption for a long period of time and his form is starting to tail off a little. The trainer and owners who want a horse they can drop right in the box will probably pass on him. But if an owner is willing to buy a horse and rest him after the sale, you might be able to get a better value for the money you invested.

What is a racehorse worth? For many years the rule of thumb was that a horse was worth what he could earn in a given year. That is, if a horse could earn $25,000, that's what he was worth.

That's still a good general rule, but the cost of keeping a horse in training today is so high that you need to factor that into your price. For example, it might cost $25,000 to train a horse at The Meadowlands in any given year, so if he only earned $25,000, he'd just cover his expenses.

Therefore, I think you'd be better advised to build that training cost into your price estimation. I'm not saying that you should figure a horse who can win $50,000 is worth only $25,000 because he'll accrue another $25,000 in expenses. Perhaps you need to assume that the horse will have a longer payback period.

If you are buying or claiming a lower-priced horse and you intend to race that horse in claimers, make certain that you leave yourself some leeway if the horse isn't as good as you think he might be.

For example, if your track's minimum claimer is $5,000, it's not always a good idea to claim or buy a horse for $5,000. What happens if he loses his form and can't race with the $5,000 claimers at your track? You have no options. You're already at the bottom of the ladder at that track.

In that situation, you would be better off to buy or claim a $7,500 claimer and hope that he's good enough to compete in $7,000-$8,000 claimers. If you're wrong and his form does deteriorate a little, you can always drop him down to the $6,000 claimers or even the $5,000 claimers and still get starts for him.

We operate a stable in which we have a certain percentage of raceway horses and we also break and develop young horses. So that means part of our time each fall will be spent going to yearling sales to pick out colts and fillies.

Many trainers take comfort in having an owner along with them at a sale because the owner will authorize the trainer to spend a certain amount for a yearling. And if the owner really wants a yearling and gets involved in a bidding duel, it's not uncommon for the owner to exceed his pre-set bidding limit.

I have had my best results, however, when I go to a yearling sale on my own and sort through the available yearlings without having an owner there to influence me. Billy Haughton certainly was successful that way for many years. I find that an owner might unconsciously steer me toward yearlings by a particular sire or from a particular breeder when I think I am better off with freedom to shop around.

When I buy a colt at a sale, I then get on the phone to some of my owners and ascertain who might be interested in assuming full or partial ownership of the yearling.

I try to tell the owner straight out what I think of a yearling. Obviously, if I didn't like the colt and didn't think he was worth a certain price, I wouldn't have bought him. There is always a chance that I won't be able to find an owner for the colt, so I might just have to take full ownership myself.

That seldom happens, as I am usually able to find an owner for my yearlings, but I often will take a partial interest in the yearling myself.

A trainer should always know if one of his owners is having an unusually good or unusually bad year. Maybe an owner bought some nice yearlings and they just didn't earn much as two-year-olds because they encountered some sickness or soreness problems. You might suggest that the owner back off at the yearling sales the next year and wait until his other horses turn three and begin to generate some income. You don't want an owner to get snowed under by the bills. I simply think that's a consideration a trainer should show an owner.

It is, of course, an owner's prerogative to plunge right back into the yearling market. Most of your better owners are quite game. How much money an owner spends is his decision, and I don't ever want to pressure an owner to spend more than he can comfortably afford.

I've known owners who have bought one yearling after another and simply haven't had much luck, yet they're always there at the sales raising their hands. I've asked them, "How can you do this?" One owner told me, "Sooner or later, I'm bound to come up with a good one." Owners with that kind of positive attitude are few and far between, and it's great if they can afford to do that. But I'll never lobby an owner to spend so lavishly.

Now let's turn to the subject of selling a horse. Let me emphasize that is another area where honesty is of the utmost importance. I don't think a trainer should ever misrepresent a horse to a potential buyer. The truth will "out" in the long run and it will hurt your reputation.

By the same token, a trainer is certainly not obligated to point out a horse's shortcomings. Emphasize the horse's attributes honestly, but don't point out his curbs or the fact that the horse has a habit of stopping badly in a race. A smart buyer will pick those things up by himself.

One time when honesty and communication are important is when a horse you're training is being sold by one of your owners to another one of your owners. Such a transaction is just fraught with the possibility for misunderstandings, and you're better off to have everyone informed up front. Let me give you an example:

Let's say that one of your owners bought a well-bred trotting colt with hopes that he'd be the kind of colt he could race in the Hambletonian and Grand Circuit stakes.

You train the colt along at two, and he doesn't show you that he has the makings of a top Grand Circuit star, so you dutifully inform the owner of your opinion. The man then says he doesn't want a mediocre colt and advises you that he intends to sell the horse.

Now let's say that you have another owner who doesn't have quite the same ambitions as Owner #1. He just wants a nice trotting colt to race in the Sires Stakes or in overnights. The colt would probably fit his purposes nicely, so Owner #2 purchases the colt from Owner #1. It doesn't really matter if the sale is private or at public auction; there are traps inherent in such a situation for the trainer.

Let's say that the colt stays in your barn and surprises you with the progress he shows. By the time he's three years old, he blossoms into a legitimate Grand Circuit-type trotter and you race him in the Hambletonian and he picks up a big check. Owner #2 is certainly going to be pleasantly surprised, but how will Owner #1 react?

He probably couldn't be blamed if he thought you had misled him on the colt's ability when, in fact, you were probably as surprised as anyone else. Some horses are just slower to come to their ability, particularly trotters, and this colt just benefitted from the maturity. But that won't be much consolation to Owner #1, who will probably be pretty upset—and I don't blame him.

Now let's reverse the situation and suppose that the colt goes to Owner #2. Instead of improving, however, the colt races poorly even in cheaper trots and eventually goes lame. Owner #1 might be happy he agreed to sell this colt, but Owner #2 might think you gave him a bum steer. He might think that you overestimated this colt's ability just to help one of your wealthy patrons unload an unsound horse.

The bad thing is that if I put myself in the place of either owner in these situations, I can empathize with their perspective. So this is almost a "no-win" situation for the trainer when a horse is switching owners in your barn. The only solution that I know is to be scrupulously honest with both parties. Give them your honest opinion of a horse's potential, but make certain they understand that horses have fooled a lot of top trainers over the years.

Another aspect of owner-trainer relations which leads to many misunderstandings is the payment of commission on the sale of horses. Frankly, I think that if a trainer works hard to make a horse extremely valuable and the horse is sold for a handsome profit, then the trainer deserves a bonus or commission. I think that five percent is adequate.

Having said that, let me add that I think the subject of commission should be discussed and resolved long before the horse is put up for sale.

Let's say that I buy some yearlings for an owner and I will be putting hard work and long hours into breaking and training them. I tell that owner, "If we should happen to get lucky and one of these horses sells for a big price, I feel I'm entitled to a commission on that sale."

It has been my experience that no owner will balk at paying the trainer a bonus or commission if it has been discussed in advance. You do, of course, need to discuss the details.

Why is a trainer entitled to a commission? Look at it from his perspective. Let's say an owner buys a $25,000 yearling and it races several times and shows that it has the potential to be any kind of horse. His earning potential is virtually unlimited. Your owner senses that he has a chance to make a good profit on this colt, so he sells him for $200,000.

Suppose the new owner and trainer take that colt who has been developed from an unbroken yearling into a star, and let's say he earns $200,000 the remainder of the season. The original trainer has now lost all the earnings the colt could have generated for the stable. In fact, all the trainer would have to show for his efforts in developing this colt would be an empty stall in his barn. Shouldn't he share in the profit to some small degree?

I think so. And I think that five percent is an adequate commission on most sales. Now if the owner tells the trainer that he wants to sell a horse and the trainer is the one making the phone calls and contacts to look for buyers, then the trainer is entitled to 10 percent in such transactions. There are many details involved in the sale of a horse, and the trainer should be compensated for his time and effort.

What if an owner absolutely refuses to pay a commission? That would have to be handled on an individual basis, but I know that I'd be willing to overlook that if the $200,000 were invested in another horse (or horses) in my stable. That way, you still are keeping your stalls filled and you have another chance to make some money.

Let's hope that all of our colts turn out to be good enough to justify $200,000 price tags! That would be a horseman's (and owner's) dream.

In this chapter, I have touched on many aspects of stable management. Much of it, frankly, is just good common sense. I don't pretend to have all the answers and I don't claim that my way is the only way.

If you remember nothing else, just keep in mind that you should always be honest and realistic with your owners. If you're in the horse business long enough, you'll endure plenty of ups and downs, and if you maintain your honesty through the good times and bad, you will probably find most of your owners to be quite loyal. If you treat your owners fairly, you'll probably find that they treat you fairly, too. That's a good basis for stable management at any track.

R|ay Remmen is a complete horseman. He can train and drive with the best in the business, and he can also select yearlings and manage a stable.

Remmen has proven that ability year after year as his stable has been among the best at The Meadowlands, the highest level of competition in the United States.

A native of Saskatchewan, Remmen once said, "The only way to get out of western Canada was harness racing or playing hockey." He chose harness racing and it has proven to be his ticket to stardom.

When the first Hambletonian was contested at The Meadowlands in 1981, it was Ray Remmen who splashed through the slop in the raceoff with Shiaway St. Pat to win the sport's biggest prize. In 1990, Remmen guided the fortunes of Beach Towel as that powerful colt swept to Horse of the Year honors, winning such classics as the Little Brown Jug and Meadowlands Pace.

Although he has curtailed his driving in recent years, Remmen has won the Woodrow Wilson with Grade One and the Peter Haughton Memorial with Keyser Lobell.

In the management and operation of the Remmen Stable, Ray is assisted by his brothers Larry and Gord.

14
RACE DRIVING STRATEGY

JOHN D. CAMPBELL

From the time I was five years old, when I pretended that I was driving a horse hitched to an old pump stand, all I ever wanted to do was to drive harness horses.

My father and grandfather were both professional horse-men, so I have been around horses my entire life. There were many valuable lessons taught to me in those early days by my family, and by what I observed from other horsemen.

My grandfather and father taught me a number of very valuable lessons concerning horses. First, horses are unique animals. They are all different. What will work for some won't work for others. The same can be said of training methods. Some that may seem unorthodox to many people can prove to be very successful for others.

As the years go by and my own experience piles up, what my family taught me about horses is made clearer than ever before. Although there may be certain similarities with some horses, no two of them are ever absolutely the same. What works with one horse with a certain set of problems may be of absolutely no use to you whatsoever in dealing with another who has the same set of problems.

I want to make it very clear that what I am about to relate deals in generalities. As with horses, every race and every racing situation is different. Many times, a decision made in a race may be the exact opposite of what I have said here.

This chapter will deal with the strategy of driving horses in competitive races. Let me say right off that I think the biggest failing of many race drivers is that they fall into a routine, or develop habits that become predictable to your competition.

You must be conscious of the strengths and weaknesses of the horse you are driving. You must not force your style or driving habits on the horse.

The only good habit is winning, and that comes about due to hard work, perseverance, patience and adaptability to situations that you will face on the track.

It is also very clear to me that we are driving a different breed of horse from the one our parents and grandparents raced. We are even driving a much better horse in the mid-1990's than we were just a few years ago. The Standardbred of today is a faster horse, a tougher horse, equipped with more speed and the ability to carry it farther than his ancestors did.

THE IMPORTANCE OF POSITION

Because of this improvement of the breed, particularly the ability to carry speed farther into a race, the race driver must be conscious that if he expects to win his share of the races, position in a race is paramount to his success.

My general philosophy about racing horses is that I always want to be in a position to win races. What that means, I hope to be able to explain to you in the following text.

But basically, it means in general terms that if you are sitting last in a field of horses coming to the three-quarter pole and your horse will have to pace a 25-second final quarter to get to the wire first, you were not in a position to win!

Simply stated, being in the right position means that I must drive a horse and put him in a position where I will win the race if the horse delivers his effort in the stretch drive. As a professional driver, I performed my job well if I set that horse up to win. He may not win the race, but at least I have put him in a position to perform well.

Understanding the importance of position will put me into the winner's circle more often than counting on receiving a maximum effort from the horse I am driving. Many horses get to the winner's circle based on the driver's ability and strategy, and the positioning factor is not lost on today's successful driver.

Races can be won from way behind, even classic events, but, generally speaking, the successful race driver of today is more aggressive than ever. Races are therefore won mostly from near the front end of the field.

This is so because of the evolution of the breed into a more speed-favoring style of racing. I want to be careful here to explain what I mean by racing a horse aggressively. It does not mean that I want to race every horse I drive on the front end, or leave with every horse. I can be aggressive, but still stay in the pocket. I can be aggressive by conceding the lead when it is appropriate, but not giving it up when it is not. By being aggressive, I mean I want to be forwardly-placed in the mile.

One of my favorite sayings is "I would rather be going than whoaing." This means I want my horse to be involved in the race, to be a player in the outcome, to be an integral part of the action. I can't do that by being passive and waiting for the other guy to make a mistake.

I want to make things happen and not wait for them to happen. I want to force my driving opponent into a mistake, to put him in a situation where he doesn't want to be, to make him go on when he'd rather take back. And conversely, to make him take back when he'd rather go on.

As a race driver I also think it is very important that everyone should understand the absolute need to be forwardly placed at the critical junctures in a race. When it is time to move, I want to be in a position that is forward enough for me to get there if I get the kind of effort I expect. I will talk more later in this chapter about the winning positions on the different size tracks and how to find them and use them to your advantage.

I always remember, too, that the public has bet on me and they deserve my best shot. If I am driving a horse who has gotten a lot of support from the public at the windows, I have an obligation to myself, to the horse's trainer, his owner, and to the betting public to race him as aggressively as I can within the scope and character of the race.

GET SOME EXPERIENCE

One of the most valuable teaching arenas for anybody who wants to race horses is with lower-class horses at the smaller racetracks. I believe that the experience factor in these situations is invaluable. A young driver will have a much better chance to pick up drives in this situation and get the experience required to move his career forward.

Only when I drove lower-class horses did I begin to understand what it takes to win races; where the drive can be the difference between winning and losing. I made real progress as a race driver when I began to think instinctively and realize instantly what it takes to win a race as a situation develops during the course of that race.

I started out driving all kinds of horses, and with the instruction from my family, I received a good basic understanding of horses. I don't know of a single driver whom I consider to be a top competitor that didn't learn by driving lower-class horses at the smaller tracks.

We all want to drive a horse as courageous as Life Sign, as fast as Mack Lobell, as determined as Peace Corps, as strong as Artsplace or as quick as Immortality. It is only when you understand how to drive a lesser horse that you can really appreciate the superstar.

Good horses are infinitely easier to race than bad ones. There is more pressure, certainly, with better horses because the stakes are much higher. But good horses are also more adaptable in their racing styles.

With lower-class horses, you are often in a trap and feel that you must race a horse a certain way in order for him to get there. You may be working around unsoundness or that horse just might be a little overclassed. Some horses need an absolutely perfect trip to win.

I have been fortunate to win a lot of big races, but I still get a charge out of winning a race at any level when my strategy and positioning have worked perfectly and I feel that's the only way my horse could have won the race.

MAKE MISTAKES AND LEARN

I make mistakes driving horses, and I think anyone who drives a horse or who hopes to, must understand that you will make mistakes. The key, of course, is to learn from the mistakes.

I might anticipate that a driver will make a certain move, but then he doesn't. I might think I can get to the front and clear to the lead, but then a longshot hangs me and leaves me out for a long trip.

I might think a guy will be easy on me and let me go past a tough half, only to look over and see his whip is raised and he's driving on. These are mistakes we have all made, and they can be very costly.

There are two keys after you have made an error in judgment during a race. The first is to try and develop a different strategy or position to give yourself some chance of winning. The other is to make sure you do not take your frustration out on the horse. Abusing a tired horse does not help anything.

What I will try to do with this chapter on race driving is to prescribe ways to avoid these mistakes, or to assist in the development of a different strategy as the race unfolds. I will describe in detail a little later several instances where my strategy developed during the course of the race.

When I make mistakes, they are usually because I drove a horse too aggressively. I prefer this to driving too passively. If I did what I thought was the right thing in the race, got my horse involved in the flow of the event and he just didn't reach, I don't mind losing so much—although the idea of losing any race does not appeal to me.

One thing I detest more than anything is to drive a horse and have him closing strongly and run out of racetrack. I don't mind getting caught right at the wire as much as I hate to have a big rally going with a horse and just miss.

This bothers me so much because it means I was out of position or that I underestimated the ability of another horse or driver.

If the margin of victory was less than a length and I just missed, that means I probably gave away too much ground at some point in the race. It may be something as simple as just being the second horse to move instead of the first. It has always amazed me to watch races and notice that a lot of races are won by the first horse to make a move. This is because that driver was the first to put his horse into position to win. That driver *made* things happen, rather than *waiting* for something to happen.

I like to err on the side of aggressiveness for several other reasons. I am driving a horse for several different interests. The horse has an owner. The horse has a trainer. Both have a vested interest in the outcome of the race.

But the betting public also has a vested interest in the outcome as well, and as a race driver I always remember that. Race drivers have a big responsibility to the bettors and to the parties with a big investment, because everybody has money riding on the outcome. Both bettors and owners are needed to keep harness racing flourishing and neither is more important than the other.

If I do make a mistake I want it to be that I was too aggressive and not that I was too passive and the horse had no chance to win.

KNOW YOUR COMPETITION

Another area that is critical for anyone wanting to become a successful race driver at any level is to know the competition. I must know the other horses. I must know their habits and abilities, their speed and where each horse might be during the course of the race.

I will need to make as objective a judgment as possible about where my horse realistically fits in that race. This is a difficult area because human nature enters into it. I might have an unrealistic opinion about my horse or the ability of the other horses in the race. This is an area that separates the good and great drivers.

I am always working on honing my appraisal skills. Results from the track will tell you how you are doing. I simply must be able to assess the class of my horse relative to the field he will be competing against. Later in this chapter, I will talk about actual races where the outcome was affected by pre-race determinations.

I must also know the other drivers. This is very important. All drivers have certain habits and characteristics. Some drivers tend to be aggressive. Others may be timid and slow to react. Some are totally unpredictable. If I don't know much about the horses and drivers I will be competing against, I am really driving at a disadvantage because the information about my competition is so critical to the development of my pre-race strategy.

LEARN TO READ THE PROGRAM

The most valuable asset for assessing my competition is the racing program. The program does not lie. Learning to look at the program objectively is a real valuable asset for any driver. You can learn an awful lot about a horse by seeing how he was raced before; who drove him; how fast he is; can he close?

This information is valuable. I have also learned to rate horses from other tracks shipping into my track. Over time, I have studied the performance of ship-ins from other parts of North America to see how it translates to the style of racing at my home track, The Meadowlands.

KNOW THE TRAINERS

I have also developed a working knowledge of the trainers involved with each horse. Certain trainers, like drivers, are more capable than others. Some guys have a reputation for sending fit horses to the track. Some have a feeling for where to classify their horses. This is another necessary part of the equation.

For instance, if I am in a race with no definitive early speed, yet there is a horse shipping in from another track who has been winning on the front end and he's from a barn noted for sending out winners, that is not a horse I will want to pull on too early. He will park me, as he probably will not want to change a winning strategy just because the track changed.

Just like a professional athlete studies his competition from game films to learn the habits of his opponents, a successful race driver must learn to observe, study and note the habits of his competition. If I am going to be at a disadvantage, it is not going to be because I didn't work, study or observe as much as my competitors.

I have had situations where I was going to drive a horse and tried to visualize in my mind the way the race would be driven. Sometimes, particularly if I am on a hot streak, a race will actually unfold just the way I planned. When this happens, racing a horse is easy. As in other sports, it is called being "in the zone."

Everything seems very easy. Everything I plan works out just right. I have had some streaks where I drove a number of good horses and won with nearly all of them. I'm sure any athlete can tell you about these times. This is when the work becomes fun.

But there are the other times, too, when nothing goes right. I have had those streaks as well when it seems I couldn't win a walkover. What works for me is that I try not to get too upset when the losing streaks come, nor too high when I am on a winning streak. I know both will pass and I simply ride them out.

The only times I do get upset are when I have several horses that figure to do well on a particular card and I don't come close with any of them. I don't mind a losing streak too much if none of the horses figured, but I feel I have not done my job if I am driving competitive horses and cannot hit the board all night.

There is one thing to remember when you are on a good or bad streak. The great driver Herve Filion says it best: "The drivers get too much credit when they win and too much blame when they lose."

USING OBSERVATIONS TO DEVELOP RACE STRATEGIES

To explain the use of observations in developing strategy, I want to refer to two separate races that will serve to illustrate how important objective observations are to the development of a successful pre-race strategy.

In the first example, I will talk about a pre-race strategy that was abandoned at the start of the race. In the second example, I will tell you about a race where I stuck with my pre-race strategy even when other conditions dictated I shouldn't.

It is important to note here that I won both races, but these are opposite examples of the same premise.

In 1982, I got named to drive Hilarion in the Meadowlands Pace, certainly one of the most important races of the year and a big thrill for any driver. It was my first Meadowlands Pace win and a race I will remember for a long time.

This was a field that included No Nukes, McKinzie Almahurst, Elitist and a bunch of top horses. In assessing my chances with Hilarion before the race, I really did not think I could win the race. I had the outside 10 post, and not many classic races are won at The Meadowlands or anywhere from post 10. Hilarion was clearly not the best horse.

The pre-race strategy that I developed was to try and get away moderately with Hilarion, find the flow in the race and get dragged into the money. I was hoping to get a big check, but really had no idea that the race could be won.

However, as the gate folded, I made a quick check of the inside horses and nobody was leaving. Everyone seemed reluctant to leave at the start.

I made an instant decision to trash the conservative race plan I had developed and sent Hilarion for the lead, making it rather easily for this caliber of horse. I immediately got covered by Elitist and was sitting in the pocket after three-eighths of a mile with a strong, front-running horse and driver ahead of me.

Going to the half, No Nukes made his expected charge toward the front end, but failed to clear to the lead as Elitist parked him to the half and past it. In the final turn nearing the three-quarters, No Nukes finally inched past Elitist and was clearing to the lead and I was able to get out and follow him into the lane. This is where knowing my horse was very important.

Hilarion was a good horse with a very high turn of speed for a short ways. I had already stung him pretty good off the gate, but he still had pace, and I figured my only shot would be to stay behind No Nukes as long as I dared and then try to get by him late in the mile.

I followed No Nukes for as long as possible, then I spoke to Hilarion, got some momentum coming out of the hole and got up to win the race. Had I not abandoned my pre-race strategy and instead just ducked him like I had planned, I might not have gotten a check, because everyone behind us was held up by horses clogged in the outside tier.

This race also clearly demonstrates the importance of another factor that all the preparation and strategy cannot account for, the factor of luck. I was fortunate that the horse following No Nukes could not keep up around the last turn. This allowed me to get out on No Nukes' back and was something that could not have been anticipated.

The other example of retaining a pre-race strategy took place in the 1981 Mistletoe Shalee final at The Meadowlands when I was driving JEF's Eternity. She was a little filly, like her famed daughter Immortality, but she could not carry her speed like Immortality. I simply could not use her hard early and have any horse in the drive to the wire. The major problem that JEF's Eternity and I faced in this race was a filly named Fan Hanover.

I studied this race a great deal and came up with a relatively simple plan. I would try to find Fan Hanover coming off the gate, get as close to her as possible and follow her as far as I could and then try her in the stretch, utilizing my filly's one quick burst of speed.

The problem that I faced, however, was that everybody else was leaving hard and Fan Hanover got away poorly. I had an inside post and did something that I normally do not like to do.

I actually backed my filly off much farther back in the field than is my normal custom. I had to do this in order to hook up with Fan Hanover.

I had made another observation about this field in developing my strategy. I had determined that Fan Hanover was far and away the best filly in the field. I decided if I beat her, I would probably win the race.

I was not going to be distracted by what the other horses did, and I put my filly on Glen Garnsey's back and followed Fan Hanover deep into the stretch and then eked out a narrow win. To beat a good horse is a thrill, but this one was special because I trained JEF's Eternity as well.

The key to victory in both races lay in the pre-race assessment and knowing what to do when opportunity (and luck) presented itself.

This illustrates how adaptable a race driver must be to racing situations. It is important to know all the different scenarios that might develop and what to do in response to them.

WATCHING EVERY RACE

I never make written notes about the horses I drive nor do I believe that is necessary, but I certainly think it is a good idea to make mental notes about the horses I drive and those I will be competing against.

I also watch every race that concerns a horse or horses I might drive, or drive against. I try to watch the replays because they are a very valuable source of information. I already know what happened to my horse in a race and the way I drove him, but I may not know what happened to somebody else during the race.

I have a mental checklist for watching these races that includes some of the following:

- What happened to a beaten favorite?
- What horses appear to be rounding into form?
- What horses are tailing off?
- Was anybody alive, but blocked in the stretch drive?

This information is so valuable because it can help me determine my strategy for the next encounters. If a horse is coming into form and yet is dropping in class the following week, he is a horse I must keep track of during the next race.

If a driver has raced a horse aggressively for a number of weeks, and he has raced poorly, he might have a tendency to be more conservative the next time out.

If a driver is winning with a horse on the front end, I can expect that he will stay with that idea and, therefore, he is not someone I wish to pull on too early in the mile. He probably is not going to let me go if he thinks his horse will stay strong.

As I come to race night, I go over the racing program once again and see how many drives I have. I review each race and ask myself several key questions.

The first, and probably most important matter for me is to make an objective determination as to where my horse fits in this race. I do this by using another mental checklist.

Among the items I run through in my mind are:

- Will he be the favorite?
- Is he really the best?
- Should I leave with him?
- Will he need a trip to win?
- Who are the other contenders?
- Who is driving them?
- How will the race likely develop?
- What will the fractions be?
- Can I be first-over with this horse?
- How much can my horse close?

This pre-race self-examination continues into the paddock area. I am beginning to develop a strategy, but I want more information. The trainer keeps you up to date on the physical status of the horse:

- How did the horse warm up?
- Is he better tonight?
- Has he been shod recently; are there any shoeing changes?
- Has this horse been sick?
- How did he train?
- If he missed a training, is he likely to be short tonight?
- If he missed a week, how will he be off the layoff?

All this information is vital and has to be factored into the development of my pre-race thoughts. This is a matter of routine with me now and is accomplished in a matter of minutes. I take the information I receive and use it to develop my pre-race strategy.

Most trainers have a very good opinion about their horses. However, some don't. All of this needs to be taken into account as well.

OBSERVATIONS MADE DURING SCORING

Regardless of the opinions I have developed during the pre-race analysis, all that might change once I swing in behind the horse and get on the track.

The horse might not respond as I had thought he would in scoring. He might seem a little off. He might be better than I thought. He might seem more aggressive than usual. If this happens, I have to consciously reconsider my strategy, taking this new direct information into account.

The horse is the best source of information, and there have been many occasions when my plans for a race changed dramatically because of the way the horse scored down. Another thing I like and want to do during scoring is to look at the other horses.

What are they doing? I want to find my main competition on the track and assess his status for the race. Is he warming up good, or does he look a little sore? This is all valuable information that I use in determining my strategy.

I race a lot of horses through the course of a year and have occasion to drive a number of sore horses. These horses are not a safety threat, but are what we call in the business "racehorse sound." They can race, but they have a number of aches and pains.

My experience with some of these horses over the years has taught me that these horses are often better the farther you get into a race. They are often rough-gaited behind the gate and then flatten out later as the race develops.

If this situation presents itself, and the horse is not a puller, I like to score that horse down a little more than normal in an attempt to thaw him out. I have found that with these kinds of horses, I am better off to warm them up more and get their kinks out before we go to the gate. I can then use this horse earlier in the mile without the worry of him being rough-gaited.

Any driver will tell you that a driver change on any horse can produce dramatic results. This is another of my key areas in assessing the possible outcome of a race.

Why does a driver change affect some horses greatly? That is a relatively easy question to answer. The first and most obvious answer is that some drivers are better than others, and the better driver will put the horse into contention at a key point in the race.

But there is another, more subtle reason for it. Drivers are human and subject to habits. Many drivers get in a situation with a certain horse where they think he must be raced in a certain way. They are either always leaving or always taking back; or always coming first over or always setting in too long.

The reason a horse will respond to a driver change is that the new driver does not come into the race with any preconceived notion about how that horse will be raced. I know that if I get named on a horse who has not raced well using a specific, similar plan of attack, I will try and shake that horse up psychologically by using a totally different plan. This often wakes a horse up and he will go a good race.

CAN THE HORSE READ THE RACING PROGRAM?

There is an old saying in racing that certain horses can read the program. I do believe that horses have definite competitive instincts, like any athlete, about the caliber of competition they will face. I played a lot of hockey when I was young and it was usually pretty clear to me after only a few minutes on the ice who the good skaters were. I could spot them, and more importantly, I knew instinctively if I could skate with them.

I think a horse knows the same thing.

Many horses can tell once they get into a race, if they are in tough competition. When a horse is at his best, he is right on the bit scoring and going to the gate and will normally race very competitively.

On the other hand, if he has been raced over his head, he will have lost his desire and confidence. He will be sluggish in the parade and scoring, and will be nonchalant going to the gate. Some people outside the horse world think this idea is crazy, but I have seen enough to know it is true. What can be done by a driver in this situation?

What I try to do with a horse who is a bit sulky or unwilling is wake him up during the parade and scoring down. He might just need a little confidence, and if I can transmit some interest to him, often times he will get into the bit and race pretty good. I may also shake him up by scoring him right beside another horse and try to shake up his competitive instincts by laying the whip on his rump and speaking to him. I want to let him know that I expect a good effort. I have seen this work, and have seen horses who were sulky go a good race and get a nice check.

DEALING WITH THE AGGRESSIVE GATE HORSE

The opposite of the horse who is unwilling and lazy is the aggressive post horse who is difficult to handle parading, scoring and going to the gate.

This kind of horse requires a totally different approach, because the last thing I want is to get into a wrestling match that I cannot win. Fighting with a horse only wears out both of us before the start and serves two very harmful purposes. It robs you of the level of concentration required to race this horse successfully and it robs the horse of his own strength.

With a horse who has aggressive tendencies, I try to get him away from the field and get him to relax. Often, I find I can take a horse like this to the backside of the track, get him near the outside fence, turn his head in the direction of the fence or just let him walk. Sometimes just walking in a circle will keep a horse calmer than anything else you might try.

Getting a horse to relax before the start is paramount, especially with young horses who are just learning to race. If I am driving a young horse who exhibits aggressive tendencies, the trainer and I often discuss what we want to do about it.

Such a horse was Pine Chip during the early part of his three-year-old season at The Meadowlands. I had raced him a few times, and he was beginning to show us that he could be an exceptional trotter. He had a very good flight of speed.

I have driven a number of horses who simply never realized their potential because their racing personalities were too aggressive and they became unmanageable. It is very important that a driver realize that one of his main jobs, especially with young horses, is to get them to relax. A horse who is too aggressive will never realize his potential. I did not want that to happen to Pine Chip if it could be avoided.

One night at The Meadowlands, Pine Chip acted a little tough in the post parade like he wanted to get aggressive. I just took him up the stretch to the gate that leads to the regular paddock. I aimed him right for the gate, and he slowed to a walk. I just tricked him into thinking he was coming off. Instead, I walked him right past the gate and just let him walk on around the turn until the starter called the field. He relaxed, came right back to me and I never had any trouble again with him throughout the remainder of his season, which was quite extraordinary for a green trotter. With young horses, you often set their racing personalities early, so be careful to always keep them as relaxed as possible. Teaching them to relax can affect them their whole career.

Some of the old, veteran horses are pullers, and every driver deals with them a little differently. My own feelings about pullers are pretty simple. If a horse wants to raise me right up in the stirrups parading and scoring, I just take that horse directly to the outrider. A competent outrider simply takes hold of the horse's bridle and restrains him, and this lets me relax and, more importantly, it lets the horse relax as well. The last thing I want is to have a wrestling match with a horse.

If there is no outrider, and the horse is particularly tough, just take him to the paddock and let him stand until the field is called. He'll last longer, race better and have a lot less wear and tear if you can do this with him.

BE CONSCIOUS OF THE TOTE BOARD

One of the last things I do during the scoring period of the race is look at the tote board in the infield. I am very conscious of the tote board for a number of reasons. First, I want to know if the horse I am driving is the betting favorite. I want to know this because, as the betting favorite, I have an extra responsibility to race this horse as aggressively as possible.

If a situation arises in a race where this horse should be moved, there can be no delay in my actions. The favorite has to be driven like the favorite because of the responsibility to ensure the bettors the best trip for their money. The last thing I want to hear as a race driver is that I drove a favorite and got him locked in.

The author recommends that a raceway driver check out the tote board during the last score, or on the way to the gate. The tote board is, in the author's opinion, a valuable tool for the driver to assess the competition and to see if the public agrees with his pre-race evaluation.

Bettors are always going to be critical of the way horses are driven when they don't win, but I am satisfied with my effort when I give the favorite every chance to win. Every driver needs to be mindful of this responsibility.

If I am 3-5 in the odds and don't pull a horse at the right time or don't race him aggressively, I am doing myself and the betting public an injustice.

One thing the public doesn't readily understand is that a favorite, a real favorite, is often beaten not because that horse didn't race well.

A favorite is often beaten because some other driver drove an exceptional race, by putting his horse in a more favorable position to win the race.

But regardless of what somebody else does, if I have the favorite I can assure you I won't be locked in late running over horses, if that situation can be avoided. That is not always possible, however.

The other reason to be conscious of the tote board is to test my objectivity about the level of competition. Is there a horse in the field that I overlooked? The fans are very good handicappers, often better than most race drivers, and I can and have learned a lot by seeing which horses are getting some support at the windows.

GOING TO THE STARTING GATE

My ideal gate horse is one that will go directly to the gate relaxed, put his nose right on the iron, and then let me pick him up once the gate gets rolling and make my decisions about how he is to be raced.

This is the ideal. There are certain horses that are finicky, however, about the gate and who will never get away if I take them right to it. I

Mack Lobell's quick gate speed was one of the reasons for his development into one of history's best trotters. The author recommends keeping a horse as relaxed as possible at the gate and advises against quick bursts of speed which will rob a horse of his speed later in the mile. Steady acceleration will allow a horse to go farther into the mile. This photo is the start of the 1987 Hambletonian. Note that Campbell is leaving strongly with #2 Mack Lobell, but still has a good, snug hold of the horse.

have raced a lot of veteran racehorses and some of them are gate shy their entire careers. I simply have to avoid hitting the gate with them.

Most of the really good horses I have driven are excellent gate horses. Mack Lobell was a terrific gate horse because he was so safe and was ready for you to pull the trigger as soon as the gate shut. Peace Corps on the other hand was safe enough, but she did not have the quick step out of there that Mack possessed.

After an eighth or so, you could start her up and send her with full confidence, but she just never developed that super-quick gate speed.

There is one aspect of starting horses that I do not like, and that is the practice that many drivers have of coming in late to the gate from five or six lengths out by making a big charge right before the word "go" is given.

These drivers are trying to get a flying start on the field and gain an early advantage. Actually, I think a driver who does this compromises his horse, because if he is coming in late he is at a disadvantage from a strategic point of view. He is committed to sending his horse, regardless of what happens. This takes away his ability to be adaptable to conditions that might arise, and is not a recommended practice.

It also drains a horse of some energy because he actually races more than a mile. I always try and conserve as much energy as possible before the start, and a dramatic move like this robs most horses of their edge late in the mile.

I will come in late with a horse myself sometimes, particularly if that horse is gate shy, but when I come in late I am coming in from only a length or two off the gate. Even then, I am not charging into position. I am trying to time the gate, but by coming in steadily and still having all my options open. There is also much less wear and tear on a horse over the course of a season if he is handled this way at the gate.

The last thing I want is to have to take a strong hold of my horse and double him up during the final moments before the start. This is what can cause the horse to hit himself and you ultimately could find a horse making a break.

When another driver comes in late and is charging, it can also excite the horses on either side of him and create problems for everyone.

If I know another driver will come in late dramatically with a horse, I try to stay away from the gate myself to give me some room for error. This is particularly true if that horse who is coming late is beside me and I know this move will excite my horse and make him aggressive. I have to leave some margin for error. This again is an area where knowing the horses and the drivers and their habits is extremely useful.

I said earlier that an aggressive horse is a problem parading and scoring and, certainly, that same horse is a real problem at the gate as well. I feel that you are still better off as a driver if you take that puller directly to the gate. With some of them, you can put their nose right on the gate and just let them hit the gate, if you know they will tolerate this action.

Often, a horse who is a puller or who is extremely nervous will be a little kinder at the gate because he learns that he really cannot go anywhere as long as the gate is there.

However, in some instances I want to stay away from the gate with a horse who pulls. It serves no purpose to get yanked right up out of the stirrups behind the gate; you and the horse are expending valuable energy.

What I like to do with a puller, or a horse who is just difficult to restrain, is turn a little late and come to the gate at a controlled rate of speed that will get me there about the time the gate really gets rolling good.

I can come in steady and at an even speed, and if the horse is still controllable, he will be less likely to get doubled up and get in trouble.

STARTING ON HALF & FIVE-EIGHTHS TRACKS

The previous discussion in this chapter regarding starting gate strategy dealt with mile track racing. I want to take this opportunity to talk about the different situations I encounter as a driver in starting on half and five-eighths-mile tracks.

There are three different areas behind the gate on the smaller tracks and each presents advantages and disadvantages.

If I have one of the three inside positions, particularly on a half-mile track, I want to be careful to get away as strongly as I can to take advantage of this position. The last thing I want to do is have trouble at the gate on a smaller track and surrender inside position. Most of the races on the smaller tracks are won from the inside, so learn to get away good in these situations.

The inside positions, however, can be a problem, particularly if you do not have a real safe gate horse. The chief problem comes from the fact that the gate must swing around a turn just before the start and I do not get the long carry behind a smoothly accelerating gate that I receive on a mile track.

If my horse in an inside position is not a horse who will accept the gate hitting him as it pivots out of the turn before the start, I have to stay away from the gate until it is out of the turn. This is particularly true of the horse at the rail because he can nearly get stopped, and then in just a few steps has to be in high gear.

What I try to do with a half or five-eighths track is leave myself some room by staying about a length or two away from the gate as it rolls around the turn, then try to anticipate the acceleration down toward the start.

If you school a horse correctly and he becomes a good horse, he learns it too and will be easier to manage. This is again a function of knowing the habits of your horse and what he will tolerate.

The second area of concern on the smaller tracks deals with post positions four through six. These are the easiest positions from the horse and driver standpoint, because they are in the middle of the track and the gate acceleration problem is diminished. However, they can be lousy positions as far as the race goes, particularly on a half-mile track.

The middle post positions get a lot of horses parked on half-mile tracks because drivers overestimate the ability of their horse to leave and find themselves taking a lot of air.

The outside positions on the smaller tracks have just the opposite problem that the inside horses face. The outside horses, particularly the horse with the eight or nine hole have to catch the gate going at a high rate of speed. That horse races farther than anybody because he has to be in high gear when the gate swings around the turn or he will be left behind.

Because of this I don't like to put a horse right to the gate if I have an outside post on a smaller track. What I like to do if the horses inside of me are right up to the gate is hang back following them in the middle third of the track, then slide over into position after the gate has come out of the turn. This saves a lot of energy and valuable ground.

MAKING DECISIONS AS THE FIELD IS TURNED LOOSE

I already addressed the issue of the importance of good decisions at the gate earlier in this chapter with my comments about Hilarion's Meadowlands Pace win and JEF's Eternity's Mistletoe Shalee victory. While these are good illustrations of the importance of gate decisions, there are several other points I wish to discuss about decisions that are made behind the gate.

I come to the gate with several different strategies in mind, depending upon what occurs. I might have a priority plan that is my favorite, but I don't come to the gate with just a single thought as to how I am going to race a horse. This is a sure-fire recipe for problems to develop. I work on a couple of different ideas about what I am going to do, based on the actions of the other horses and drivers.

- Am I leaving? If so, am I leaving hard, or am I floating away from the gate hunting the flow?
- Is there a strong inside horse who may park me?
- If I'm taking back, whom would I prefer to follow?
- Who is likely to get me into the race in the late stages if I decide to follow him?
- What other horses do I need to account for?
- Where is the favorite?
- What other horses looked good in the parade and scoring, and might be altering what I thought they were going to do?

All of these decisions must be made instantaneously, and that is why the professional driver has such a big edge over the others he competes against. A good driver is able to see a situation develop and instantly take advantage of any opportunity that might present itself.

It is impossible for me to relate any general rule of thumb about what you should do at the gate, but the key is in preparation. I want to have several different plans in mind and I want to be quick to seize opportunities that present themselves. An opportunity might only present itself for a brief moment and then is lost, so a good race driver must be ready to seize the moment when it comes. And remember, if I do err, I want to err on the side of aggressiveness.

This does not mean, of course, that you are leaving hard with every horse you drive. That is foolish. And even if you do, most horses need to be held onto going away from the gate.

A lot of breaks are made in the first few steps after the gate folds and often it is because a driver has simply turned a horse's head loose, or the horse has interfered or just over-paced himself and he runs.

A good general rule of thumb employed by every successful driver I know is to hang onto your horse going out of there unless you are very familiar with the horse and he is an exceptional, safe leaver.

This is the start of the final heat of the 1993 Little Brown Jug, where the author, up behind #2 Life Sign, attempts to get the jump on the rail horse, Riyadh, driven by Jim Morrill, Jr. Again note that Campbell believes a horse should retain bit contact with the driver even in these instances where he is driven hard for the lead.

I can relate a rather famous race to illustrate my points about decisions made behind the gate, and then being adaptable to race circumstances.

This was the 1993 Little Brown Jug final with Life Sign. In winning that race, Life Sign went one of the most incredible miles in the history of the breed.

This is a race that I won, but my gate strategy failed. However, I believe the race was won because the horse and I were adaptable to the circumstances before I ruined my chance.

To set the stage, Life Sign had drawn the two hole for the final heat. I was sandwiched between the entry of Riyadh, who had the rail, and Presidential Ball, who had post three. A third horse from the same stable, Ready To Rumble, was in post four.

My strategy for the final heat was simple: I wanted the lead, and I thought the only way for Life Sign to win the Jug that afternoon was to get the lead coming off the gate.

Riyadh did not get away well in his elimination heat, and I thought I might be able to beat him out of there in the final if that pattern repeated itself. A few steps from the start, Riyadh was right tight on the gate and was obviously going to leave much better than he had in his elimination.

I still wanted to test Riyadh as much as I could. We went sailing into the turn about as fast as horses can pace, but it was clear that my strat-

At the half of the famous 1993 Little Brown Jug, Campbell has Life Sign in the first-over position, racing third on the outside behind the pace-setting Riyadh and next to Presidential Ball. The author does not recommend putting pressure on the lead horse if caught in this position. Rather, he attempts to maintain his position for a challenge later in the mile.

egy of grabbing the lead was going to fail. I had a slight advantage of about half a length after the eighth pole, but I could not clear to the lead.

I had to come up with another plan pretty quickly.

Since Riyadh and Life Sign went head and head to the eighth, that gave Jack Moiseyev, driving Presidential Ball, and Joe Pavia, Jr., on Ready To Rumble, time to close the holes behind Riyadh and deny me the pocket. I can tell you, after just an eighth of a mile, I would not have given much for our chances of winning the Little Brown Jug that afternoon.

But another part of my pre-race plan took over. I had already determined something that I was not going to do. I was not going to engage Riyadh all the way to the quarter. All you accomplish is running your horse down. A horse cannot survive on the outside for an extended period while being driven hard.

Therefore, I grabbed Life Sign and started taking him back. He was revved up pretty good and I had to take a strong hold of him to collar his speed. But he did come back to me, and I glanced over my shoulder and saw an opening in fourth along the rail.

This is not a conventional move and I don't recommend anyone doing this on a regular basis, but I thought if I could get in for just a few steps, Life Sign would get the little rest he needed.

It worked, because I was able to get Life Sign in just before the quarter and he was able to catch a short breather and be at the rail through the second turn.

This was very important for the horse psychologically as well. I knew we would be first over the rest of the mile, and when I did come right back out, Life Sign swelled right up and was ready to go again.

The point I wish to make is that by abandoning the early strategy of going for the lead well before the eighth, I actually had extended Life Sign for only that brief period off the gate, and after his brief rest I was able to regain my spot on the outside during the slowest quarter of the race.

From there, Life Sign just dug in and went a remarkably game and splendid mile.

There is another drive during the 1993 racing season that will serve to illustrate another nuance of race driving concerning the start of a race.

This was the Woodrow Wilson final with Magical Mike. I liked Magical Mike's chances to get a big piece of this race and thought I had a good chance of winning if the race broke just right. It did.

I had an outside post position, and the Wilson is a race in which you can almost be assured of a fast early pace. In the past few years, the Wilson has been won by the horse getting the best trip and not necessarily the best horse.

I had handicapped the race, and my ideal position would be to get a good position off the gate without being anywhere near the lead. I had been parked with Bonnie And Clyde in the Wilson in 1992 down to a suicidal half from the outside, and I wasn't about to repeat that.

Leaving the gate, I was able to pick out Armbro Mackintosh, a colt who I respected as one of the favorites and who was being driven by Ron Waples, one of our sport's very best drivers.

The key to victory in the Wilson with Magical Mike, however, did not rest with choosing the right horse to follow, although that certainly played a role. The key was that both Waples and I left pretty strongly with our horses, while some of the other guys were looking to duck and take back. This is the nuance I want to explain.

From an outside post position, you are naturally going to have to concede position to inside horses because they generally are not going to allow you to loop them going away from the gate.

Because of this natural concession of ground that occurs, you can actually leave a little harder from the outside when you have this much early speed inside of you. Waples and I, by leaving pretty strongly, saved a good piece of ground.

If you take back in a 27-second first quarter and head for the back of the field, you will give away far too much ground that will be difficult to recover. So, although I got away near the back of the field, in terms of lengths I was not that far from the front pack.

Advancing down the backstretch, the outside flow was active and I was able to follow Waples right into the race. At the three-quarters, Magical Mike had some pace and I followed Waples as long as I could into the lane, then my colt had the courage to carry his rally down to the wire and win the race. I won by the scantiest of margins, but I would never have been in a position to reach had I conceded even a half-length more ground at the start.

DRIVING ON THE LEAD

Another area of importance in race driving is how to rate a horse on the lead.

The key is to discourage an aggressive first-over challenge. This is because you want to have your own way on the lead as long as possible. In this way, it is your race, your fractions which dictate all the race's strategy. This is the ideal. There are many ways to accomplish being left alone on the lead.

I like what I call the "cruise control" approach. I call it that because, just like setting the cruise control on your car, a horse on the front end of a race, on the lead, will go farther, carry his speed deeper into the race and be more courageous in the stretch drive if you rate him through fractions as even as possible.

If you go the first quarter in 28 seconds, grab him for the second quarter in :30, then extend him again through the three quarters because of a first-over challenge, it is my belief that horse will not be as game on the lead as a horse who gets to the half off two even :29 second quarters. The even rating discourages the strong first-over challenge.

If I am driving a horse on the lead, I want him to go as evenly as possible. That does not mean, however, that I don't want to steal a fraction with him if possible. I would be nuts not to want to get as cheap a half as possible. But how do I steal a fraction when I have to keep the fractions fast enough to deter someone from attacking?

The key is when you choose to steal it.

Many drivers have a good sense of pace and will react instantly to another driver attempting to back off the pace. Others, however, will only react to the posted quarter times at the quarter and the half.

Let's say I have made the lead just past the eighth and the pace is a little faster than I would like. I anticipate the quarter is going to be around :27.4 or :28, and I would prefer a half in the range of :56.4 or :57.

The key is to realize that you need to back your horse off—and do it as gradually as possible. If you slow the pace too quickly, you are inviting someone to attack you. After you have slowed the pace, go on a little just before the quarter flashes. The other drivers see the quarter time and they can feel you go on, so they will be less likely to move at this point. You can then rest your horse as gradually as possible.

The key, if you want to race in front, and I cannot stress this enough, is going at a fast enough pace to avoid someone making a hard first-over move against you. But please do not forget you are racing a mile. You must save something for the stretch.

If I am driving what I feel is the best horse, I am going to attempt to put him in control of the race by driving aggressively for the front end. If I feel a horse is much the best, as Mack Lobell was for most of his career, I think the front is the place to be.

When I am in front, I am determining the pace of the race and setting the fractions, and if I have a manageable horse I am setting them to my satisfaction.

An aggressive horse can be a problem on the front end. Some of these horses are actually more manageable following cover. They pull more or try to run off on the front end and do all their racing the first three-quarters.

These horses are generally much better to race conservatively the first part of the mile. Even if you come first-over, the more you throttle their speed, the more they will give you later in the mile.

SHOULD I LET HIM GO?

One of the most common errors that race drivers make, and I am as guilty of it as anybody, is that we don't let enough horses go, past the half. Race drivers are taught from a very early age that you should not let anybody go after the half in a race, but I believe this thinking, like most hard and fast axioms, is a little flawed.

This is a very difficult issue for most race drivers, but the importance of good decisions on the lead was brought home to me in the 1992 Breeders Crown two-year-old colt pace at Pompano Park. I was driving Bonnie And Clyde, one of the choices, and the field included such colts as Presidential Ball, Life Sign and Village Jiffy.

I made the lead early in this race and steamed past the quarter in :27, and almost immediately I had pressure from Presidential Ball and Jack Moiseyev after three-eighths of a mile.

I might have been inclined to let Jack go at this point, but it was clear to me that Presidential Ball did not have his usual step and was not at his best.

I drove on, then past the half Presidential Ball found a spot behind me and Life Sign came first over to attack me. Considering that Bonnie And Clyde had been extended to the quarter in :27 and urged to a sub-:54 half, I should have let Life Sign go at that point. But the old training dies hard.

I drove on and eventually cost myself not only the race but also a chance at a bigger check, because Bonnie And Clyde got very tired. Had I let Life Sign go, Bonnie And Clyde might have had enough class to hang on for a better check. As it was, I got a lot of criticism. The criticism was deserved, because under those conditions I drove a very poor race.

Let me add at this point that I still believe it is poor policy to let somebody go past the half, because you are conceding position at a key point in the race.

Generally speaking, you should let somebody go past the half only if your horse has been forced to really extend himself in either making the lead or in retaining it. If I am on the front end and my horse is full of pace and has not been driven hard, you will find me very difficult to pass.

Another key to this might be the identity of the horse who is attacking first-over. If he is a horse I respect as one of the contenders, I may want his cover into the stretch if I feel he is the kind of horse who will not quit in front of me.

However, you should not let a longshot by you past the half, because most of the time he will not carry his drive to the wire and you will end up being locked in behind him in the late stages of the race. Another factor which might enter into this decision is whether or not you are racing with a passing lane in the stretch where the fear of being locked in is somewhat reduced.

PUT A LAZY HORSE IN FRONT

Another thing I want to mention is that I like driving a horse who is a bit lazy on the front end. I think it serves to get him more involved. Most lazy horses don't have a big brush, but can carry their speed a long time.

Two such horses were Run The Table and Dexter Nukes. Both of those horses were extremely lazy and needed a good bit of prompting to get involved in a race. But both horses were very strong and enjoyed great success racing on the lead. If I had a lazy horse who didn't want to try coming from behind, I think I would try and "rev him up" and go for the lead early in the mile. It often creates a much improved performance.

One thing you have to be careful about with a lazy horse on the front end is keeping track of everybody behind you, because your horse lacks the quick response to meet a dynamic drive from another horse. When I drove Run The Table and Dexter Nukes, I was always checking out the field behind me because I knew I would have to get them "revved up" before a horse got to us.

CHARACTERISTICS OF THE FIRST-OVER DRIVE

No driver likes being first-over in a race. It is normally the death seat, particularly in a field of well-classified, conditioned horses. The first-over horse in most cases will not win races, unless we are talking about certain instances in half-mile track racing. A first-over horse on a half-mile track is in one of the three key positions in the race that I will talk more about later.

I really have only two choices when I am forced to come first-over with any horse.
1) I must either attack the horse on the front end with a strong surge, hoping I can clear to the lead; or,
2) I attempt to advance steadily and force the pace while attempting to conserve my horse for the stretch drive.

This latter option is essentially the position I referred to earlier in this chapter when talking about Life Sign's Little Brown Jug. After I came back at Riyadh going to the half, I was a passive, first-over contender who hoped to wear down the leader and win.

Again, it is impossible to give you a rule that you can apply in racing first-over horses. Much of what you will do will depend upon the horse on the front end. How hard has he been used? Is he still fresh? Will he let you go? The quickest way to answer these questions is to just look over at him as you come alongside. Visual observations are really a key here.

Let's say the pace has been moderate and you are forced into a first-over move. I like to get a good look and immediately ascertain how tough the horse on the lead is. There are a number of ways to determine how tough the horse in front is going to be. If you look over at him and he is full of pace and looks strong, you will have a tough horse to contend with.

On the other hand, your observation might tell you that the horse on the front end is already off the bit or has even pinned his ears. This is a certain sign of fatigue.

In a conditioned race, the leader will probably be pretty tough. However, in a stakes race, particularly with two-year-olds, the leader may be vulnerable to an aggressive attack.

This is especially true if that horse has been driven hard to make the front. I will nearly always attack strongly in these situations, hoping to clear to the lead, because I much prefer trying to hang onto a race from the front end rather than being first-over and trying to stall off rallies from behind me.

The exception to this is if one of the horses to beat is locked in behind a tired leader. In this instance, rather than brushing to the lead, I would choose to wait on the outside and keep the fresh horse locked in. I then don't have to ask my horse to pace until the rest of the field starts fanning out behind me.

The only time I would not wait on the outside is if the track we were racing over had a passing lane. In that instance, I would almost always choose to go on past the tired horse and make the other horse who was locked in wait for the passing lane.

SUCCESSFUL FIRST-OVER MOVES

Let me describe two different races in which I made first-over moves that were totally different, but each produced victory in an important race. One of these moves was very aggressive, the other was confidently passive.

The first was Armbro Keepsake's win in the 1992 Kentucky Futurity, the 100th renewal of that great, classic race.

Armbro Keepsake was a very good filly, and in assessing her chances in the Futurity I thought she could win, but she far from laid over the field.

She had won her filly stakes race the week before. But, now she faced the colts. That is a whole different ballgame.

She won her elimination on Futurity Day very convincingly and I drew the rail for the final. Armbro Keepsake was a good, safe post horse and I could roll her out of there pretty good. I thought, however, that she did not lay over the field for this final, which included good horses such as Giant Force, Herschel Walker and Baltic Striker. I did not think she could go wire-to-wire and win.

I considered Baltic Striker to be the horse to beat, and going away from the gate, both Giant Force and Herschel Walker went head to head for the lead. The first eighth was pretty quick, and Keepsake and I got away third. Baltic Striker got away fourth right behind us, and I was concerned about him following me. I finally let Herschel Walker in front of me before the quarter. Both he and Giant Force had trotted a fast first quarter.

Heading down the backstretch, I looked over my shoulder and saw that, indeed, Baltic Striker was right behind me. With two horses in front of me, it looked as if Keepsake was going to be forced to come first-over past the half.

Mike Lachance, driving Baltic Striker, had his horse in the perfect spot, because I am certain he wanted to track me. The problem I had was that I wanted to avoid the first-over move with Keepsake because that would mean that Baltic Striker would get a perfect second-over trip following me on the rim. I had to figure out a way to take away the advantage that Lachance had at this point.

One of Armbro Keepsake's attributes was that she had a very good brush and could get in gear very quickly. I quickly decided that I would pull her, and instead of advancing steadily on the rim, I attempted to scoot past Giant Force, thinking that Sonny Patterson might let me go because his horse (Giant Force) had been stung going to the quarter.

I pulled Keepsake and spoke to her and she shot past the front two horses in just a few steps. By making this move, I had forced Baltic Striker to be the first-over horse and, now, there were two horses between him and me. Now, I had the advantage.

The filly made the lead and managed to hang on, although the margin was dwindling at the wire as Baltic Striker came flying late. I am positive that had I stayed in and took the conventional route by coming first-over, Keepsake would not have won that Futurity.

Another first-over drive I want to talk about came with Peace Corps in the 1989 Futurity. As I indicated, Peace Corps was not a superior gate horse. However, after an eighth or so she could go anywhere that any trotter who ever lived could go. She was awesome and very determined. In fact, I am certain that she is the most determined horse I have ever driven. I recall several times with her when I would get in trouble in traffic and she would get all doubled up and hit herself on the shins, or even knuckle over behind. I was certain I would lose her, but she would come right up trotting. She was a great, great filly.

In this Futurity, I thought she was much the best, and even though I had the rail in the final heat, I could not grab the track like I preferred and just force everybody to tuck.

Peace Corps got away third, then past the quarter Park Avenue Joe came and grabbed the lead. This made us fourth along the rail. It was obvious that a first-over trip was in the offing.

I was supremely confident of Peace Corps in this field, so I just sat there and let the natural first-over trip develop with her. I was not at all concerned about her ability to put this field away, as long as I did not use her too hard in the middle half.

I came out just at the half and came to the leaders, but not aggressively. Instead, I advanced steadily on the rim and just tried to pressure Park Avenue Joe enough to make him go on a bit.

In the stretch, I spoke to Peace Corps and lifted the lines with a light hold and she just opened up and drew off to win handily.

Using Peace Corps as an example might not be fair, but what is important here is that the strategies employed in these races are applicable and relevant to any first-over drive.

If you feel your horse is the best, and the situation dictates a first-over move, these are your options.

AN UNSUCCESSFUL FIRST-OVER MOVE

Now, a not-so-pleasant first-over story.

This involved Run The Table's Meadowlands Pace and, in this event, I drove a very indecisive race and let another driver affect my game plan.

This was one of the best Meadowlands Pace fields of all time that included not only Run The Table, but the fast gray Laag, Jate Lobell and Frugal Gourmet. This was one I have driven over and over in my head many times, but I was not as aggressive as I should have been in getting my horse involved in the race at an earlier point.

Getting away from the gate, I found myself nowhere near the early lead, but that was O.K. since I had a poor post and only looked to get in the flow and then come charging late.

Run The Table, as noted earlier, was a much better front-end horse, but the situation to make the front here did not present itself, because I thought there was too much early speed and I would get run down trying to make the top.

As it was, my strategy was flawed. Everybody else was fearful of the front-end speed, so there wasn't any. I wound up on the outside entering the backstretch, with Laag and Jate Lobell following me. Frugal Gour-

One of the best situations for a driver is to have his horse in a position to win. Here the author is in the "second-over" position in the last turn of a stake at Lexington's Red Mile. The author feels that nearly every harness horse will race better with a second-over trip. The "second-over" spot is on the outside, following the horse attacking the leader.

met, meanwhile, was sailing along on an uncontested, soft lead.

I started to advance early on the backstretch, and a horse looked like he was going to come out ahead of me from mid-pack. I waited for him to come because his cover would have been O.K. When I paused, this other horse went partly back to the rail. I came forward again, but then he was half-in, half-out and never did advance.

At the start, I should have been much more aggressive and forced the issue and taken the race to Frugal Gourmet, who got lazy fractions and stole the race. Run The Table raced extremely well and wound up third in this race, but I am certain he would have won or been second had I been more aggressive with him at the start.

CHARACTERISTICS OF THE SECOND-OVER DRIVE

A few years ago at The Meadowlands, the second-over spot was the preferred position. It was the spot from which most of the races were being won. This was because it was very difficult to go wire-to-wire. Lead horses just did not win that often. Over the last few years, however, as front-end speed got to be longer-lasting, the second-over and even third-over trips are not as desirable as they once were.

Still, if you can get a second-over trip, I recommend it — all things being equal. The second-over trip allows your horse to follow cover into the race, and almost every horse is better off with cover. It allows them to advance without cutting their own air and is both a decidedly real and psychological advantage.

You can be aggressive from the second-over spot, too. I like to stay pretty tight on a horse I am following in the second-over spot if I have confidence that the horse in front of me is going to carry me to or into the lead at some point.

If I am not so confident of the horse in front of me, I will leave myself some room to avoid being jammed if the horse I am following backs into me. It also gives me some room to maneuver if someone behind me starts three wide.

A driver often receives some criticism for "gapping his cover." What this means is that a driver following another horse on the rim does not stay tight on the horse he is following. He is gapped a half-length or more, and thus is said to be gapping his cover.

When a driver does this, there are really two reasons for it. First, it is a consideration for safety. If I am following a horse around the last turn and he suddenly stops or is rough-gaited in front of me, it can jam things up pretty badly. I want to avoid this. I stay really tight only if I am following a horse who I think will take me a long way.

Secondly, the driver has a desire for forward momentum. If I lay off a horse I am following, it gives me some room for error. If I feel a horse I am following might stop suddenly in front of me, I can leave some room to go three wide and not stop my momentum. If I am tight on a horse who stops, I can lose my momentum and lose all chance of winning.

The best way to work out the second-over trip is to leave moderately and try to get away in the middle of the pack. After a quarter or three-eighths, you can take out, and that move will normally flush somebody to give you cover. Often times it ends up being the horse to beat, because he cannot afford to stay at the rail if you are advancing on the rim. He will be caught in if he stays at the rail.

How long I can follow cover depends not only on the horse I am following, but also the horse in front. How fresh or tired does he appear to be? What kind of fractions has he posted?

If the horse you are following has stalled, you still need not tip three wide if the horse in front is also tired. However, if the horse in front is fresh and waiting on the field to come before he sprints home, I want to be moving on him and attacking. I want to be aggressive in this situation.

AVOID THE THREE-WIDE MOVE

There is another aspect to the second-over trip that I want to address, and that is the temptation to make the big, sweeping three-wide move with your horse in the last turn on a mile track. On a half or five-eighths-mile track, this is not so much of a problem because it is hard to avoid not moving three deep in the last turn. I am as guilty as the next guy when it comes to this move, because I consider it to be very aggressive and, therefore, it falls into my accepted choices. However, being three wide in the last turn on a mile track rarely produces victory, because it takes a lot out of your horse.

It can also take you right out of a race. You often do not have a choice, because the horses behind you are forcing the issue—and you cannot afford to follow a horse whose drive has stalled in front of you. I would recommend heartily that the three-wide move be avoided from second-over, if possible.

I can be three-wide if I am driving the best horse. I had Freedoms Friend, the two-year-old filly champion of 1993, three-deep a couple of times during her freshman season at The Meadowlands and it didn't cost me, because she was much the best.

But I don't like to use the three-wide move in a close field of conditioned horses unless the guy I am following is quite dead and will back me through the field if I stay behind him. Then I have no choice, I have to tip three-wide.

SAFETY CONCERNS

This is as good a time as any to talk about a couple of safety concerns in driving horses. I believe this is an area that race drivers, particularly young and/or inexperienced ones, don't often face until they are actually in competition.

This concerns horses who grab a line badly or who "lug," in racetrack parlance. These horses can be safe and will still drive in a straight line most of the time.

The great world champion filly Miss Easy, whom I raced almost exclusively, was a filly who grabbed one line her entire career, but she was never a problem and never caused any trouble for other horses.

But every driver, particularly anyone who grew up with lower-class horses, has driven the horse who literally locks on a line and runs in with you around the turns or runs out in the stretches.

The only feeling more helpless than driving the lugger is having a broken line, which I will talk about again in my closing paragraphs.

Every driver has a responsibility for his own safety and for the safety of his fellow competitors, both horses and drivers. The horse who is lugging badly on one line creates a significant safety hazard. When I say that a horse locks on a line, that is exactly what I mean. The horse is totally unresponsive to the pressure on that line. It is as if the line was attached to an immovable object.

I recommend that any driver who finds himself in the midst of competition with a horse who is lugging badly, or is very rough-gaited, forget about winning the race. If your horse is on a line that badly, you are not going to win anyway.

Your first priority should be safety and getting back in one piece. There are other races and other nights, and all of you can live to fight again.

If faced with that previous situation, all inexperienced drivers should try and collect the horse and get him back in one piece. I have seen the inexperienced drivers who will attempt to drive on even though a horse might be lugging in and it usually results in at least a minor problem in the form of locked wheels.

It is also vitally important that drivers learn to communicate with other drivers during the course of the race, particularly if they are faced with safety problems.

Let the other drivers know what is happening. Everybody wants to be safe.

BEST PLACES TO MOVE TO CREATE WINNING POSITIONS

There are several key areas on all different-size tracks where winning moves are made in horse races. The first, as we have discussed in detail, is the start. If you desire the front-end trip, you need to be forwardly placed, not necessarily on the front end at the quarter or the eighth, but near the front.

After that, there are several key areas on any size track that you need to be acquainted with as far as gaining position in a race.

On a mile track, the first of these other key points is the first quarter pole. Ask yourself at this point if you are happy with your position, and see if the race is unfolding in front of you as you planned. Are the main competitors where you thought they would be? Are the horses you are following going to take you into contention?

If you are sitting third or fourth, the quarter move is a very effective way of getting control of a race during what it is often the slowest quarter in the mile. The rate of the first quarter, who is on the lead, and how quick your horse can brush, are factors in determining if this is the right move.

The next key point is the three-eighths pole. If you have not made a move at the quarter from any of the two, three or four positions, making it now is a poor move unless you want a first-over, parked-out trip. However, if you are farther back in the field at this point, the three-eighths pole is an excellent spot to move out with some momentum and hopefully force cover.

As I said earlier, the first horse to move often ends up winning or getting a big chunk of the race. That is simply a function of good position.

While driving on a five-eighths track, the author recommends putting a horse into position during the second quarter of the race. Here, the author hustles Cam's Card Shark past Roger Hammer and Keystone Luther in a heat of the 1994 Adios. The second quarter advance on a five-eighths can be very effective because this is often the slowest quarter of the race.

The last point on a mile track for a key move is the half-mile pole because, by this time the action generally has begun to heat up and there is both an inside and outside stack of horses—usually four or five in, and the same number in the outside flow. At this point, strategy becomes less important than how much horse you have between the shafts.

On a five-eighths track, the key points are much the same, except that the quarter move can be more effective than the mile track quarter move, because you can advance in a quarter that is slower and also over a straight part of the track. You also have the second turn to rest your horse going to the half if you make the lead.

If you wait until the three-eighths on a five-eighths-mile track, this means your move will come the first time past the stands at the finish line. I do not recommend this because you are attempting to advance into a quarter around a turn. Always attempt to move where the price of advancing is not as high.

When moving from far back on all size tracks, how and where you advance depends on the pace of the race and what horses ahead you would like to follow. If the pace is very fast, delay your move until it slows.

Trying to advance into a fast second quarter is bad strategy. If the pace has slowed, however, and the horse you would prefer to follow is ahead of you, move early and move quickly. You want to try and keep the horses between you and desired cover at the rail, then slow your horse and wait for the horse you want to follow to make his move. If you are already following desired cover, wait until he moves in front of you, unless forced to move from behind. That way, you are saving your horse as much as possible.

On a half-mile track, the key points at which to move are off the gate and off the five-eighths entering the backstretch the final time. Position is more critical on a half-mile track than on any other size track, and a driver's choices are severely limited. On a half-mile track, you have to find a way to get near the front if you hope to win.

Any other moves on half-mile tracks, Life Sign notwithstanding, are not going to produce consistently good results for any driver.

BE READY TO MOVE ALERTLY

It is also vitally important that when you make any move with a horse (to advance in a race) that you have some momentum built before you attempt this move. I have seen many inexperienced drivers make the right move in a race, only to have their horse stall in the outside lane or take awhile to get going. This is because the horse has no momentum for his move coming out of the hole.

To advance, a horse must be going faster than the horses he is attempting to either engage or overtake, and it is vitally important that the driver build some momentum before the move is made.

There are ways to accomplish this. The best rule of thumb is to attempt to anticipate your move and have the horse ready when you are. This can be done by simply speaking to him, raising the lines a little, or laying the whip on his rump while you are still in the hole.

It is my signal to him that I am going to ask for something a little different. Some horses, particularly those with a lot of racing class, are like sports cars coming out of a hole. All I need to do with them is just touch the right line and they know what to do. They fire out of the hole and attack.

This also allows me to come out of the hole going forward and lets me get into the flow without asking my horse for a quick burst of speed. These quick bursts are dramatic, but the steady, forward advance on the rim is always more productive because the quick moves take too much out of a horse, unless he is a high-caliber stakes horse.

It is also important to be conscious of the pace of the race. If you have it in your mind to pull—off the three-eighths, or at any other point in the race—take notice of the pace of the race.

If the leaders are steaming along up front, I will want to delay my move until the pace slacks off a bit. Trying to advance into a wicked quarter will not produce a good result.

The bigger the track the more options I have as a race driver. My options are really limited on five-eighths and half-mile tracks. The half-mile track usually eliminates horses with outside post positions, unless one of these lays over the field.

A REVIEW OF THE WINNING POSITIONS

To summarize this portion of the chapter, let's take a brief look at a review of the winning positions on each size track. These are the spots I want to be in at the critical point in each race which, for this purpose, I will say is the half-mile mark.

On a half-mile track, I want to be in front or in the pocket. First- or second-over is O.K. if the fractions have been fast. I know that sounds like a limited number of winning positions, but I feel those are the only spots from which I am going to win races on half-mile and five-eighths tracks. Most of our racing is in conditioned races, and most fields are well-matched enough that horses just can't reach from beyond these positions on the smaller tracks.

If the fractions have been fast, I don't mind being first-over. You can rest your horse around the third turn (second on a five-eighths) then try to sprint by the leader and clear to the rail before the last turn, often opening up a lead. The same strategy works if a horse ahead of you has been used hard and is now parked. You can follow him second-over around the turn and sprint down the backstretch.

The key to both these moves is that you have to clear the horses you are trying to pass, before the last turn. If you do not clear to the lead, you have used your horse hard and you will be giving ground away on the last turn.

The methodical, wear-them-down advancement is more effective if you don't believe you can out sprint your opponents before the last turn. This is a judgment the driver has to make, and no one makes the right decision every time.

On a five-eighths or mile track, the key positions for winning at the half-mile pole are somewhat expanded, but not greatly. If you are going to win, you must be forwardly placed at the half.

KEEPING A HORSE ALIVE IN THE STRETCH

Any driver will tell you that the stretch drive is the most demanding part of the race because this is where the payoff occurs. This is where all my strategy and all my pre-race observations are tested in the final, dramatic moments of the race. People who have watched me drive tell me that I am not a driver who uses a lot of whip on a horse. I know that perception is out there and it may be accurate in the sense that I do not think there are many horses whose performance is enhanced by the use of the whip.

This is an area of some controversy and I believe the dialogue is healthy, because there are some drivers who hit a horse way too often.

I will use the whip on a horse who is actually contending for the win, or for any of the first three pari-mutuel placings. I will normally not use a whip to any great degree on a horse who is finishing back of third.

I still drive very aggressively to try and maintain a check, but generally I will only use a whip on a horse who I think might be cheating me a little.

There are some horses who will not race well unless they are stung with the whip, but they are few, and this is where the driver's judgment comes into play. There are very successful, competent drivers who can hit a horse hard and often and get him to respond. It does not work for me, however, and it does not work for the average driver.

I also won't whip a horse whom I believe has given me a maximum effort. For instance, I did not sting Life Sign in the final stages of the 1993 Little Brown Jug because the horse was giving me everything he had. I also don't like it when I see a driver abuse a horse after that horse has gone a very big mile. Particularly with a young horse, this can turn its attitude bad quicker than anything. I also don't like to see a driver take out his frustration over a bad racing decision by hitting his horse with the whip.

"MAKING SPEED"

I am often asked by young drivers how to make speed with a horse. This is a question I cannot answer. I don't know how to tell anyone how to make speed with a horse. I believe it is a God-given talent that allows me to communicate with the horse and give him confidence and allow him to dig down deep into his background to give me his best effort.

I suppose any athlete would have a hard time telling you how he can do anything. I know I have heard baseball players say that they can hit a curve ball, but cannot explain to someone how to hit a curve ball. Making speed is the same kind of thing, I suppose, that just cannot be explained in words.

I do think the term "making speed" is often misused. To me, it means more than getting a horse to go fast. It also means getting a horse to go fast without him realizing it, giving him confidence, having him alert and being able to carry him in the late stages of the race when fatigue starts to overtake him.

My own driving style, as I have said many times in this chapter, is to be aggressive with a horse—and the Standardbred of today responds wonderfully to this kind of racing.

In the late stages of the race, I like to keep a horse busy and keep the bit in his mouth by leaning backwards in the sulky, trying to get a forward surge, but keeping a light hold of him. At the same time, I am popping the wheel disk with the whip or hitting the saddle pad or laying

The author does not recommend losing contact with a horse in the late stages of a race. Note here that he is asking the horse, in this case In The Pocket in the 1990 Adios, for a maximum effort but has kept bit contact with the horse by not allowing any slack in the lines. He has laid the whip on the horse's back and kept a light hold on the lines.

the whip on a horse's rump and speaking to him. I might try giving a horse a shot with the whip to see what response I get.

Another important thing to remember is that if you hit a horse and there is no response, there is little reason to continue to hit him in the same fashion.

If a horse doesn't go on after you have touched him or hit him with the whip, don't keep hitting him. Most horses will respond immediately if they have anything left.

As I get down to the wire, I will attempt to reach up and touch the horse's rump or wrap the lines around his stifles and literally push him. This is a trick we all learned from Buddy Gilmour, and it is very effective with some horses.

Some drivers, on the other hand, prefer a very aggressive lifting motion where they actually will attempt to lift the horse's head with the lines, then release them, and then repeat the motion. Anybody is encouraged to try anything that works.

Another trick that is very valuable in the late stages of a race is the ability to hit a horse on the left side. There have been a number of successful left-handed drivers, most notably the late Lew Williams and, currently, Eddie Davis.

Lew Williams, particularly, was very good at rallying a horse in the lane, and I think his hitting a horse on the left side was something new and different to most horses.

Hitting a horse on the left side is also useful if that horse is running in during the stretch drive. Hitting him on the left side if he is running in toward the rail can be effective in straightening him out. All drivers should learn to use a whip in both hands for the stretch drive if at all possible.

YOU MAY HAVE TO "SIT AND HOPE"

There is another aspect of stretch driving I want to discuss because I believe it to be an important part of driving.

Every driver, regardless of his or her experience level, has driven horses who are unsteady finishing the race. This is the kind you simply cannot turn loose in the stretch drive.

This most often happens with young and/or sore trotters. You find yourself deep into the race. In the stretch, your horse is getting tired and losing his gait and action. This is a tough time because the heat is on and if your horse is still in contention, the temptation is to keep driving and hope that he will stay together and carry his drive to the wire.

This is not likely to happen, however, since most of these horses end up making breaks in the late stages if you continue to urge them on. The important thing for a driver to remember is that even though your first obligation is to win the race, your secondary goal is to get as much out of the race as possible. I see a lot of drivers who make critical mistakes in the deep stretch because they are still trying to win after they have already lost that opportunity. They forfeit a check by continuing to drive.

Many drivers caught up in driving their horses forget about the horse's gait in the deep stretch. You can't win in a tight field if you are offstride at the wire, and the safety factor at this stage of the race cannot be overstated.

When this situation of an unsteady horse in the stretch happens, I employ what I call my "sit and hope" technique. I will take a hold of the horse and attempt to steady him and keep him on gait with either minimal or no urging.

This is very hard to do when I see horses coming to me or going past me, but I have found that I end up getting a check with a horse who otherwise would have made a break and lost all chance. When I have lost the chance to win, I still want to get as much as possible and I don't do that by continuing to drive a horse aggressively who might make a break.

PROPER USE OF THE PASSING LANE

One of the newer developments which is an outgrowth of removing hub rails from our tracks is the use of passing lanes in the stretch drives.

The passing lanes are an interesting addition to a driver's equation and they have succeeded in changing some key strategy elements in driving on tracks equipped with these lanes.

In the past, particularly on half-mile tracks, a horse in the pocket could simply be taken out of a race if the first-over horse maintained his drive deep into the stretch.

Now, with the advent of the passing lanes, the pocket-sitting horse, or any horse sitting along the rail, can still find a way to win a race with a big rally.

I have a couple of observations about the passing lanes.

First, all horses should be taught by trainers to pass a horse on the inside. I have found that some horses are reluctant, even when they have pace, to pass a horse on the inside. I think this comes about largely due to the fact that they are not trained to do this. Any driver who plans to use the passing lane, had better know if his horse can pass on the inside. It can be pretty embarrassing if you leave the pocket, only to find your horse won't come up inside another horse.

My second observation about the passing lanes is that they are a very short piece of ground to make up a significant amount of position late in a race. If I am going to attempt to use the passing lane, the most effective method is to build some real momentum with the horse before I swing him to the inside, because he really has to be alert and ready to go to get up in those short lanes.

If my horse is not a real quick horse with a good brush, use of the passing lane may help me hold a position, but will probably not be very effective as far as winning goes.

I don't know of a single race driver who is not overjoyed now that most of the tracks we race over have removed their hub rails. It is one of the most innovative moves ever made. It has taken away much of the danger of racing horses, simply by giving all of us an additional escape route in the event of trouble.

WHAT TO DO WHEN A LINE BREAKS

Every driver's nightmare is the broken line, or the broken bit.

A driver faced with this situation has two options. He can either stay with the horse or he can bail out. I think what you do depends on the situation. Generally speaking, I want to stay with the horse if I can, but that can also be just the wrong thing to do.

If I am in the middle of the field when the problem develops, I am going to communicate my dilemma to the other drivers and let them know I have a problem. Secondly, I am going to assess my chances for staying with the horse. This decision will depend on how much control, if any, I have with the one remaining line or the nose band of the bridle. If I have some measure of control and response from the horse and think he can be easily caught by the outrider, I might stay with him.

I might also decide to bail out.

If I do decide to bail out, there is a right way and a wrong way. If I am going to bail out, I try to swing my legs free to the outside of the sulky, that is the side nearest the outside of the track. From there, I will drop the lines, grab a hold of the sulky at a point just above the wheel arch, and attempt to let myself down onto the track gradually.

The last thing I want to do is just roll off the side of the sulky. That is like stepping out of a car going 30 miles an hour.

The secret here is to let your feet drag on the track before you let go, and then slide and roll when you hit the track. I have done this and it still hurts to hit the track, but I feel I have a much better chance of minimizing my injuries by using this technique.

THE IMPORTANCE OF REPRESENTING OUR INDUSTRY

I wish to close this chapter with a few remarks addressed to the young drivers out there who wish to follow a career with the horses. I can think of no more rewarding way to make a living than by being paid well for something you love.

But along with the opportunity to race horses comes the obligation to represent our business in a positive way. Every driver should be conscious of his appearance on the racetrack. He should choose colors that are bright, easy-to-see and easily identifiable. These colors should be clean, and the driver should be neatly groomed.

All drivers should wear boots to race a horse. I see guys race a horse in soft-soled sneakers and I just cringe. This not only looks unprofessional, it is very unsafe. Be aware that you represent our industry and you should want to represent it in a very positive way.

You should learn to communicate and speak well. You should be gracious and patient with the media. You should explain our craft, allowing the media to question you about what you did, and why, in a professional way.

I have never forgotten how fortunate I am to be racing horses. To dream about driving horses as a youngster, and then have a career that exceeded my wildest imagination is something for which I am very thankful.

If harness racing is to survive and be healthy into the next decades, all of us must do our part to make racing as professional as possible and free of even a hint of impropriety.

It is our solemn obligation and we should do no less.

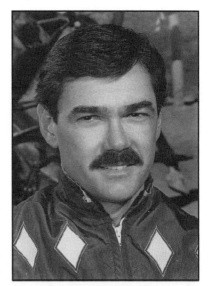

J ohn Campbell is harness racing's brightest star.

Campbell vaulted into national prominence in the early 1980s and has maintained his position at the top of the sport's active drivers since then. The top trainers in the sport recognized long ago that John Campbell was blessed with a special brand of magic when it comes to driving horses.

Of equal importance to his driving ability is Campbell's role as a first-rate spokesman for the sport. He has given willingly of his time and talents to help promote harness racing in countless ways.

Campbell's dominance among drivers made him the first person in the sport's history to win $100 million in purses, a mark he passed in late 1991.

In 1988, Campbell went to Sweden to drive the vaunted Mack Lobell against the best in Europe in the Elitlopp, and the team of Campbell and Mack dazzled the appreciative European audience.

The list of great horses Campbell has driven would fill pages of this book. You can start with the trotters Mack Lobell, Peace Corps, and Pine Chip, and continue with other trotting stars such as Armbro Goal, Harmonious, Tagliabue, Armbro Keepsake, Britelite Lobell, Joie De Vie, Davidia Hanover, Wesgate Crown, and Donerail.

The list of exceptional pacers Campbell has steered includes Artsplace, Life Sign, Merger, Miss Easy, Dexter Nukes, Cheery Hello, Direct Flight, Cam's Card Shark, Amity Chef, Follow My Star, Immortality, In The Pocket, So Cozy, Jake And Elwood, So Fresh, Arrive At Five, and Run The Table .

15

THE ALL-AROUND HORSEMAN

RON WAPLES

I have been asked in this chapter to address many different issues relating to general horsemanship and the racing of Standardbreds. This is a difficult subject to cover in comprehensive fashion. A book could be written on each of the subjects I will discuss here. I am sure that my friends who wrote other chapters of this work have addressed many of the same issues.

I am also sure that some of them have different points of view about certain ideas relating to horsemanship. But that is one of the things that makes this business what it is. Almost everybody has a different idea about how to train, rig and drive a horse. Everybody has a different notion about what kind of horse they like. Everybody sees a horse a little differently. Everybody sees a race from the perspective of their own prejudices, likes and dislikes.

This chapter will contain my opinions regarding the general subject of horsemanship, and I want to emphasize that these are just that—my opinions. I do not have all the answers, nor do I insist that everyone should do what I say. I have, however, made a living doing this, and have had the opportunity to train and/or drive many a good horse. I have learned a lot from the very first day I grabbed a lead shank for the first time.

I continue to learn. The day I quit learning is when I will walk away from the business.

A COMPLETE REVERSAL

One of the most valuable things a horseman can learn is to adapt and change with the times. I have seen many a noted horseman swallowed up by change because he was not willing to adapt his practices and techniques. I have noticed that others have been willing to alter the way they handle their horses and have succeeded, even though they may have been brought up to do things a certain way.

From my own point of view, I know that the way I train and race horses today amounts to almost a complete reversal of the techniques and practices I first learned from my cousin Keith Waples, one of the great all-time horsemen of any generation.

When I first learned the business, and especially when I first learned to drive, horses were sprinted away from the gate, raced Indian-file to the three-quarters, then were asked to sprint home the final part of the mile.

Today, horses are sprinted away from the wire and generally are asked

to carry their speed over the entire mile distance. Our races have constant movement, and a successful driver is the one who continues to advance his horse and keep him in a position to win. Position has always
been important in a horse race, because the average horse needs a good
trip to win a race. But it is much more important today than it was 30
years ago, mainly because of the speeds they go.

The way I am expected to drive today bears no resemblance to the way
I was taught to drive. Today's driver must be more aggressive and be
willing to subject his horse to two or even three moves in a race. This of
course, is much tougher on horseflesh than ever before. This is why our
horses do not race as often, do not race as long, and are not as productive
over a career as they once were.

I have a horse in my stable, an Abercrombie horse named Cimarron,
who has raced for me for the past seven years since I bought him as a
three-year-old. He has made a lot of money for me and has raced a long,
long time, competing mostly at The Meadowlands and along the East
Coast. He is a throwback to the tough, old, hard-hitting racehorses of
the past. But he is also somewhat of a dinosaur. Horses like him are very
rare anymore.

HORSES JUST DON'T LAST THE WAY THEY USED TO

I have not seen any published statistics on this, but I would hazard a
guess that the average racehorse of today makes far fewer starts in a
career than the horse of, say, 20 years ago. I used to have horses in my
stable who annually made 30-35 starts from the beginning of the racing
season until the snow flew in the late fall. Now, I am fortunate to get 20-
25 starts out of a horse. This is a huge drop-off when you consider that
purses continue to shrink and, therefore, the average horse has less
chance to earn his way now than ever before.

This puts a lot more pressure on trainers and drivers, because we realize more than ever that "the iron must be struck while it is hot" and that
all opportunities have to be seized while a horse is able to compete. I see
this occurring at all levels of the sport.

I do think there has been a general and drastic improvement of the
breed that begins at a very early point. Broodmares are better managed
than before, with attention given to their nutritional requirements. Foals
are fed better and grow stronger. The breed has improved greatly at all
levels. We know more about training techniques. The professional horseman of today has the advantage of professional veterinary care, and the
racetracks we compete over are faster and safer than some of the
"bullrings" I raced on as a youngster. I also believe there have been many
advances in training techniques, and that the professional driver of today gives a good horse the ultimate chance to succeed.

That is not to say that today's horse is better than the horses of the
past. Today's horse is faster, but not better, in my opinion. And because

he is faster, today's horse has to be managed differently than the average racehorse of 1960, for example.

The horse of today also has more natural speed, versus the manufactured speed of the past.

Today's pacer, for instance, comes to his gait and speed more naturally than the pacer of the past did. Trotting colts and fillies do not interfere like the ones of the past. A lot of the horses I had early in my career were manufactured: They wore short hobbles, were checked high, and had to be shod in just the right way.

One of the first trainers I ever saw who made the transition to a new style of training was Jack Kopas in Canada. Jack developed pacers who went with low heads and a very long hobble. He had a great deal of success hanging his horses up this way, and was years ahead of his time. The same techniques are used today by some of our most successful trainers, including Bill Robinson, Bob McIntosh and others. Robinson has changed the equation even further by adding the aluminum shoes he uses almost exclusively. Bill's use of aluminum shoes with a full grab is somewhat controversial, but you certainly cannot argue with the results.

The old timers would say that the aluminum shoes are too tough on a horse, and stop him too much and contribute to front-end lameness. That may have been true on the dirt tracks of the past, but I think the aluminum shoes with a grab are very useful on the hard, limestone tracks we race over today. Traction is a very important issue which the aluminum shoe addresses quite nicely.

Most of the horses of the past trained a lot more miles to get ready to race. They trained a lot harder between races with more trips. Today's horses often compete off shorter training preps, make fewer starts and get less training between races. In the past it was common to train four or five trips while today we only go two or three.

I can give you a good example of what I mean. I had a horse in my stable some years back named J.D's Buck. He was a tough, hard-hitting racehorse who competed a long time for me. However, he never would have lasted as long as he did if I had not understood that he was a horse who did not want to be trained between races.

J.D's Buck was not an average horse, by any means. He was a tough, free-for-all type horse who could go with the best of them. He became this type of horse only when I discovered that he did not want any work between races. I would go six to eight weeks at a time and never train the horse. If I had J.D's Buck in my stable when I first broke into the business, and was taught to train a horse hard between races in order to keep him sharp, I am certain that J.D's Buck would never have developed into the kind of useful horse he became.

There is a dilemma that many horsemen face in racing today. There are horses who still require a lot of work between races to stay sharp. But even that has changed.

Four or five training miles between races might have amounted to a lot of work for a horseman 30 years ago. I remember times when, before a big race, I would see a horse trained five trips, with the last two trips anywhere from 2:05 to 2:10 with fast last halves.

I had a pacer named Love That Fella, a Most Happy Fella horse who I had to "drill" between races. He was a high-class conditioned horse and could go pretty good, but he had to be trained hard every week. I had to work him in 2:03 to 2:05 at midweek, or he was no good at all. I tried working him less, but he did not have his "step" when I was kind to him.

I don't know anybody today who would even consider training a horse like this. Today, a "lot of work" between races might consist of three trips, with a final mile around 2:10 with a fast last quarter. The trainer of the past aimed for endurance, but today's trainer is forced to aim for speed. A horse can still be primed for one start, especially before a big race, but generally speaking, today's horse gets less work between races than the horse of 20 years ago. Most of my better horses need very little work between races to maintain their sharpness, and a horse will always be better off if you keep him as cool and calm as possible between races.

Another reason for training horses lighter is the fact that the Standardbred of today is a far more aggressive horse than the horses of just a decade ago. If you wound up these horses every time you trained them, you would be in a world of trouble. These horses would get so keyed up you wouldn't be able to manage them. The breed has changed a lot in this respect. I like to keep a horse as cool as I can now. The cooler he is around the barn, on the track and in training, the easier he is to manage on race night. He will also last longer for me.

I travel a lot and get to see a lot of racing in all parts of North America. One of the things I notice is the proliferation of talent among the average horse population at almost every racetrack I visit. Even the bottom-rung of claimers often has horses with good pedigrees and past racing glories to their credit. I see pacers by Cam Fella, Albatross, and all of our leading sires racing at these tracks in classes all the way from the respective Open divisions to the bottom class of claimers.

The other thing I have noticed is that younger and younger horses all the time are spread through these classes. I remember when I broke into the business that Windsor Raceway used to race to the end of the calendar year, and one of the highlights of the year's-end was a retirement race for 14-year-olds. Windsor's racing office would assemble all the old campaigners together for one last hurrah, and it was a good promotion for the track.

Well, I don't think you could find a competitive field of 14-year-olds in this day and age if you canvassed the entire racing population of North America! Now, I see five-year-olds who are "used-up," winding down their short careers by competing in cheap claimers.

MAJOR CHANGES IN PRACTICE OF SHOEING

Another area where I see a drastic change is in the practice of shoeing horses. The horsemen of the past—at least the ones I grew up with—had pretty rigid ideas about how a horse should be shod. Generally, the two front hooves had to be as similar as possible, with the same angles and toe lengths and with the same kinds of shoes. The hind shoes—and hooves—as well, had to be as identical as possible. Pacers were all shod the same way with full swedge shoes in front and half-round, half-swedges behind, with trailers and caulks turned on the outside of the shoe.

Today, I try and shoe a horse the way his foot is. This is something I learned from the Swedish blacksmiths who have followed many of the Scandinavian trainers to North America. The Swedes, I feel, are way ahead of us in the theory and practice of shoeing horses. These blacksmiths shoe a horse to his individual needs. This might mean that the two front hooves are on different angles, and have different toe lengths. They also tend to shoe a horse toward his natural angles.

This allows a horse to develop his true potential a lot better than forcing him to wear what I prefer as his trainer, and at an angle I am comfortable with. I have learned that a horse wants what is natural for him. Today, most of my pacers wear swedges all around and are levelled up. I never turn trailers or caulks on a pacer now. They don't need this severe shoeing. I think this is an important practice horsemen of today should consider.

Human nature being what it is, every trainer has a system he likes to employ. We like to do, and we learn to do, what has worked for us in the past. Unfortunately, horses are very much individuals and often require us to step outside of our traditional training methods. The most valuable thing I have learned in the past few years is that my horses require a lot of individual attention and thought about what is best for them. I don't think you can train a stable of horses "by the book" anymore. You will need to experiment, to try new things, new techniques, and be receptive to fresh ideas and concepts. A horseman cannot be stubborn or bullheaded with today's horse, unless that horse is the kind who can flourish in that system.

Every so often, I see a trainer come out with a good horse, and I notice the horse seems to conform to the type that particular trainer prefers. A lot of trainers, for instance, like a big horse. Others prefer the smaller, less-muscled, more feminine type. Each of these trainers is capable of success, it seems, but only with a certain type horse. The really successful trainer is the one who can adapt his training style to the kind of horse he has. A good trainer should find different ways to succeed with many different types of horses. It would be a much easier business if every horse could be shod, rigged and trained the same way but, of course, they cannot.

Sportsmaster was a major driving success for the author. The pair scored their biggest win in the famed Woodrow Wilson at The Meadowlands, when the author worked out a perfect pocket-sitting trip. Sportsmaster, a son of Abercrombie, is shown here before a winning effort at Lexington's Red Mile.

EACH HORSE HAS TO BE DRIVEN DIFFERENTLY

Horses nowadays need to be driven differently, according to their own most productive styles. The successful driver must assess the individual capabilities of his horse and how his horse shapes up against the competition of that night. At most of the raceways, the fields of horses assembled are pretty competitive. There may not be much separating the best horse in the field from the worst. Some, or all the horses, have a chance, it seems, in today's races.

My own driving style is that of a position driver. If every horse, or nearly every horse, has a chance to win a race, the most likely winner is the horse who has the best trip. It is my job to get him that trip, and I try to get a good trip for my horse by having him in the right position.

John Campbell describes this very well in his chapter on Race Driving Strategy elsewhere in this book, and I will not attempt to improve on what John has written. But I will say that what I have learned comes from a combination of many hard years of experience.

Race driving has become a combination of aggressiveness and conservatism. I have been very lucky to have driven a number of good horses, but if I am not on the favorite, I have to be more conservative in my approach to the race. I cannot, however, allow this to keep my horse out of the race. What it does mean is that I have to be aggressive enough to

The Triple Crown champion Ralph Hanover was Meadow Skipper's leading money-winner, and the author enjoyed great success with the easy-to-drive colt. Here, Ralph Hanover hustles home to victory in the famed Little Brown Jug.

be ready to seize any opportunities that might come my way. I must drive for the situation.

I try to single out the key horses in the race and stay close to the ones to beat. Quite often, I hit the board with a longshot simply because I worked out the very best trip for him.

A good example was the night I won the 1991 Woodrow Wilson with Sportsmaster. He was not the best colt in that race, but everything broke perfectly for me. I had a good post position and got to sit close to a wicked early pace set by Big Brat. I never had to make a move until we turned for home. Big Brat had pressure from Shore Patrol through the middle half, and when it came time for me to go, I had the fresh horse.

I would like to be able to say that I never have a plan going to the gate with a horse, that I am such an excellent driver I simply wait for the word "go" and then develop my strategy. In reality, it is much too late by then to make any decisions. Race driving needs to be instinctive, but you should have a plan, and you had better have considered an alternative plan as well. However, you want to avoid coming up with a plan and going ahead with it, despite what happens during a race.

For instance, I may think that my horse belongs in front. And if I think he is the best, I want him to be in front, because I want to control the race fractions. If I can be in control, I have a huge influence over the outcome of the race. However, I must not allow this desire to be in front force me to do something that I shouldn't do. The key word here is control. If I have to set suicidal fractions to control the pace, I am not in control. The guy who forced me to the fast fractions is the one in control.

I have to have a sense of pace and the ability to let a guy go if the circumstances dictate that I should.

I remember in Ralph Hanover's Triple Crown year of 1983 that somebody was always ready to take a shot against Ralph trying to beat him. The great thing about him, however, was that he was so handy and such a good horse that I could do anything. Ralph was kind enough to let a horse go and had the class to come right back and re-take it for me if I wanted. Or he might lay in the hole without tightening the lines until it was time to go. When I spoke to him, he would take off for me and generally win. Driving a horse like that is a real joy.

I had a similar experience in 1993, a full decade later, when I got to catch drive Presidential Ball for trainer Bill Robinson. Jack Moiseyev had the drive on the horse, but Jack was injured in a racing accident right before the North America Cup. I don't ever remember a situation where I had more confidence in a horse winning a race. I could not conceive of a way that Presidential Ball could have lost that race. He is the best horse I have ever driven. He had very useable speed, was very manageable, and could be raced anyway you chose. He was just a handy, do-anything type of horse.

In the North America Cup, I got away near the back of the pack, but I was never concerned about the outcome of the race. I knew Presidential Ball would win unless I made a bad mistake. I just laid back with him until I felt the field was beginning to back up, then I put him in gear going through the last turn and he rallied to win the race.

I know a lot of people thought I raced Presidential Ball too conservatively that night, but I knew he was the best. Even when we were three-deep through the last turn, I never really had an anxious moment. Presidential Ball was so handy through the turns that he was eating them up with every step. I knew he would get there, and he did.

A lot of race drivers concede too much if they feel the horse is out of a race beforehand. One of the earliest lessons I got about driving was that if you routinely back up out of the eight-hole, you are beaten before you start. If every driver could simply remember to single out the key horses in a race, and stay as close to them as possible, he would find himself dragged into the money a lot more often.

I had occasion to use this principle in 1988 when I had a very good trotter named Huggie Hanover. He was a nice colt who had a good turn of speed for a ways, but he did not possess the kind of racing courage to carry the speed over a long distance, or to slug it out with a horse from the first-over spot.

In the Kentucky Futurity that year, Huggie got two perfect trips and was able to come up the rail both times to win. I got position with him, never left the rail in either heat, and the race opened up for me late. The key is that I had Huggie in the right position at the right time to win.

The fact that the rail opened up twice for Huggie Hanover in the same

Sometimes a driver has to be lucky to be in the right place at the right time. The author's superb sense of position in a race was never better showcased than in the handling of Huggie Hanover. By choosing the right horse in a race and staying close to the chief opposition, victory can often be achieved when the luck breaks in your favor. The author used these tactics to produce an upset victory for Huggie Hanover in the 1988 Kentucky Futurity.

day in such a big race is quite amazing, but the point is that I put him in a spot where he could win if everything went our way. He really should not have won the race, and would not have, had I been forced away from the fence. He probably went two of the shortest miles in the history of that great race.

IDENTIFY YOUR HORSE'S STRENGTHS

Huggie Hanover's Futurity win is also illustrative of using a horse's strengths to get him to the wire first. Playing a waiting game with a horse with a good brush is a useful way to get a lot of checks.

I catch drove Dream Maker at The Meadowlands in the Driscoll Series final when he was a six-year-old in 1979 for his trainer, Bill Robinson. Dream Maker was by Race Time and was very fast—but only for a short piece. He could brush by anybody for a sixteenth of a mile, but that was about the extent of it.

Dream Maker had the rail in the Driscoll against such horses as Abercrombie, Rambling Willie, Le Baron Rouge and Battling Brad. I thought I could win if I could just follow everybody to the stretch without using my horse. I crept along against the rail in a short field of seven and put Dream Maker on Rambling Willie's back early in the race. We got

The author thinks that Sugarcane Hanover is the best trotter he ever raced. A late-developing horse with little gate speed, Waples helped the horse mature into a stretch-charging terror.

shuffled back during the race because there was plenty of movement. We were third at the quarter, but were shuffled to fifth at the half, with Battling Brad cutting the mile. Abercrombie came first-over and cleared past the half and Le Baron Rouge followed him, but was hung and unable to gain ground.

I really didn't mind getting shuffled back, because Dream Maker did not like any air and I knew I would get a bigger piece of it if I just stayed at the rail. Into the stretch, I still had no place to go, although a gap opened about halfway to the wire. Le Baron Rouge put away Abercrombie and I got through between them. Finally, at the sixteenth pole, I maneuvered Dream Maker sideways and unleashed his brush. He won the race by sprinting past the field at the wire. These are the kinds of races you remember. Dream Maker had no right to win the race that night; he was just lucky to get there with the kind of trip he needed to win.

SOMETIMES YOU DON'T WORRY ABOUT POSITION

There are times I never worried about position, such as whenever I drove Sugarcane Hanover for trainer Jimmy Simpson. Sugarcane was a very pleasurable horse to drive because he could respond like a hobbled pacer out of a hole. His only drawback was that he never learned to leave the gate and get position early.

This bothered me a little when I first started to drive Sugarcane as a three-year-old, but then I developed so much confidence in him that I

One of the author's famed catch drives came in the 1992 Little Brown Jug with Fake Left. A fast and aggressive horse, Fake Left won the Jug because the author used the horse's speed and aggressiveness to take control of the race. The win denied Western Hanover the Triple Crown.

could concede all kinds of ground and still win with him. Most of the time when we raced, I never took my hands out of the hand-holds. He was just a terror in the final quarter.

The only time I even lifted the lines on him was in the Breeders Crown at Garden State Park. I thought I had misjudged Royal Prestige that night, and that he was going to beat me, but Sugarcane came flying late to get the job done. I actually had to hit Sugarcane that night for the first time, and he nearly jumped out of his hide and made a break.

Another time I never really worried about position was when I catch drove Fake Left in the 1992 Little Brown Jug for trainer George Sholty. I knew Fake Left was a very fast horse and a very aggressive horse. I had seen him race all summer at the midwestern fairs and he was a strong, front-running type.

His style was a very good match for the Little Brown Jug because the track at Delaware favors front-end speed. Fake Left's style fit the track, and that race in particular.

I asked Mickey McNichol about Fake Left because Mickey had driven him a few times, and Mickey's only advice was to "not get locked in," because the horse was impossible to rate. Mickey, in fact, was down to drive the horse in the Jug. I only got the drive because Mickey got hurt in an accident earlier on Jug Day. It was a real catch drive!

I decided to let Fake Left go his race and see what happened. I had to do this because I remembered that I tried to take him off the gate in the first heat and he just lowered his head and bulled me. I was really just a passenger.

In the first heat, I was parked going to the quarter, but the horse was going to have no part of taking a hole so I had to go on with him. Bill Fahy was driving Western Hanover, who had already won two legs of the Triple Crown. Bill let me go near the first quarter and then attempted to re-take the lead. I would have preferred at that point to let Bill go back to the front because the first quarter had been pretty hard and it is always a good idea to try to follow the favorite.

But Fake Left would have none of that and refused to be rated. Bill was pretty frustrated that I would not let him go back to the lead, but I had no choice. I don't think there's a driver who could have stopped Fake Left on the lead that day. Besides, any driver that would have been strong enough to back Fake Left off would have choked the horse down and lost all chance of winning.

I ended up winning the heat, while Bill was parked all the way, then Fake Left prevailed in the raceoff as well, after Western Hanover had gutted it out and beat us from the first-over spot in the second heat.

The point is that Fake Left was put into a position to win the race, and did. Had he been raced conservatively, I am sure he would not have even hit the money that day. There is a lot of common sense to racing a horse. And the common sense that day said to do what I needed to do to win the race.

DRIVERS OFTEN CRITICIZED

A lot of people criticize drivers for the decisions we make in racing horses. A lot of this results from the fact that many members of the media do not understand what we are trying to accomplish. They some-times accuse us of having a "gentlemen's driving club," almost a clique where we exchange favors to each other on the track.

While I am sure that some of that criticism is justified, I would not agree with the criticism aimed at drivers who compete at a very high level. For instance, I got a lot of criticism for driving Fake Left the way I did in the Jug. Everybody thought I should have let Bill Fahy go with Western Hanover. As I indicated, I wanted to let him go back to the lead because he was the horse to beat. It is always a good strategy to follow the favorite. However, I had no choice. Fake Left was not letting anybody go.

On the other hand, I often face a situation where the pace of the race dictates the strategy and my decision about who I will let go and who I won't. Let's say I am driving a longshot and I get off the gate and make the lead early then just at the quarter, the favorite comes alongside.

At this point, I normally am going to concede the lead to the favorite and hope to follow him the rest of the way. If I am on the favorite at the quarter, however, and a longshot comes alongside, I might decide to park the longshot because I cannot allow him to go and leave me to be caught behind a dead horse later in the mile. If no one is following the longshot, I might let him go if I feel I can re take the lead quickly.

Another racing situation that might develop is where a longshot comes alongside at the half and I want to get him out of my way. Many times, I simply allow that horse a hole behind me, or even in front of me. It is very useful strategy sometimes to simply let a horse in front of you in order to have clear sailing when it is time to go. I think you will find that most professional drivers are never going to concede position to anyone unless they feel they are helping themselves by doing it. I certainly do not let someone go in order to help him. I do it to help me!

RACING THE LAZY HORSE

There are horses whose racing personalities are not as aggressive as we would like.

These horses like to "cheat" a little, it seems and they must be driven accordingly. A very effective thing with a lazy horse is to shake him up a little, maybe by busting him out of the gate and getting him involved early. A lot of horses are raced with specific patterns, and you can often improve a horse just by changing his pattern.

If I catch drive a horse who looks to have been raced previously with a specific pattern in mind, I will ask the trainer if he cares if I modify the way the horse is to be raced. If the horse has been taken back, for instance, in most of his races, I just might fire him up and race him very aggressively. A horse often responds to this by going a very good race.

Ralph Hanover was a very lazy colt as a two-year-old, and one night in Canada, Doug Brown raced him for us. Doug knew Ralph was a little lazy, so he just chased him off the gate and Ralph went a big mile. It really served to bust Ralph loose. He was a different horse after that. He was more aggressive.

MEDICATION HAS MADE RACING DIFFERENT

Another way in which racing is much different today from when I first broke in is that medications are allowed to be used on horses on race day.

I have two points to make with regards to the issue of medication: I think that Lasix is a great drug, and I cannot see it as being a problem, if used correctly. A lot of horses bleed, and Lasix can help control that. However, you have to watch for dehydration in a horse on Lasix, particularly in very warm weather.

Conversely, I do not like butazolidin or any other analgesic type of

The author believes that 2-year-olds are asked to do too much too early. By always racing a 2-year-old within himself, you always leave a little bit in him. Every attempt should be made to prevent a 2-year-old from knowing that he can get tired. The author is shown here with the precocious colt pacer, Sands A Flyin.

drug, because what we are doing essentially with these types of drugs is allowing unfit horses to race. This is not fair to the betting public, and certainly is not good for the horse.

LESS RACING IS THE ANSWER

I do think that as the breed continues to progress we are going to see horses raced less and less. A number of prominent two-year-olds in the past few years have had very few starts, but still had a high degree of speed and versatility.

I raced a colt, Sands A Flyin, in 1994, from the first crop of Beach Towel, who could really fly from the very first time I raced him. He was a natural and had a lot of useable speed. I raced him quite a few times early in the season, and even won in 1:52.1 with him in the New Jersey Sires Stake final, and I never took my hands out of the hand-holds with him. He was just naturally gifted with terrific ability.

There is, however, a down side to this. A great many of our better two-year-olds do not improve much during their three-year-old seasons. Billy Haughton and Delvin Miller both predicted years ago that two-year-olds would have all the world records someday and I think they were absolutely right.

However, in the future, I think the best two-year-olds may not improve much for the rest of their careers. I have had horses in my stable who could do more at two than at any time in their careers. This is the price paid for two-year-old speed.

For this reason, I try to be as conservative as I can with my two-year-olds. I try to go as far with them as possible before I let them know that they can get tired. I am very careful in the first few baby races, for instance, not to ask a colt to do too much and cause him to get tired. I want my colts to think they can't get tired. I want them fresh and with good attitudes. The average horse will learn to get tired soon enough.

However, there also are horses who do improve greatly between their two- and three-year-old seasons. Ralph Hanover was one such horse. He was not the dominant two-year-old of his year, but by the mid-point of his three-year-old season, he won not only the Triple Crown, but captured the Meadowlands Pace, the Burlington and Queen City Stakes, and the Tattersalls Pace. He won only half his starts at two, but was 20 for 25 as a three-year-old, winning more than $1 million.

When Ralph Hanover got good, it would have been tough for him to lose against that crop of colts. My only concern was in staying out of trouble with him. I knew if I stayed out of trouble, he would have a good shot to win.

I want a colt to learn to go right to the gate, and to relax. The relaxation is very important, because, as with anything in life, you cannot perform if you are too keyed up. A horse is no different.

I try to jog my colts behind the gate during the late winter and early spring to allow them to be comfortable at the gate. I want them to put their nose right on the iron and then pick up speed gradually as the gate rolls away.

The importance of relaxation cannot be overstated.

I had a horse named Kick Up A Storm, who I raced in the New York Sires Stakes and on the Grand Circuit. He won more than $600,000 and got a 1:54 mark racing for me and was a very productive horse, but he was so keyed up and aggressive that he was never the horse he was meant to be. I tried everything to calm him down, but he had me right up in the stirrups almost every start.

His full brother Ramblin Storm won over $1 million, but he was a very manageable and, therefore, durable horse. Kick Up A Storm had as much ability as Ramblin Storm, I believe, but never got to fulfill his potential. Kick Up A Storm would leave a lot of his race on the track before we ever got to the gate. He would wash out and refuse to calm down. I tried everything with him to get him to relax. I tried different bridles, different bits, different training methods, but nothing worked. I finally just let him have his way and worked around his habits.

A lot of horses get keyed up, of course, and all drivers have learned ways to tone down an otherwise aggressive horse. One of the most effec-

The author conceded that sometimes a horse is so strong-willed that he cannot be tamed, but he can still be a viable racehorse. Such a case was the good pacer Kick Up A Storm, trained by the author, and a real handful to race because he was so aggressive. A lifetime winner of more than $600,000, the horse became useful only when the author decided to use his aggressiveness to his best advantage.

tive tricks with a tough post horse is to take him away from the field, maybe to the backstretch of the track, and try to get him to walk and relax before going to the gate.

I think we have a bigger problem with this now than ever before because a horse must be raced so aggressively, and the breed is more naturally aggressive, because of the breeding.

One of the remedies for this would be to race our older horses a greater distance. I think, for instance, that the Breeders Crown races for older horses or the Senior Jug could be raced at distances greater than a mile. The Senior Jug at Delaware could be raced at mile and a quarter, or even at a mile and a half, and I think it would be a much better race. A lot of horses who cannot win at a mile might find a whole new life racing a longer distance.

We could also have better fields and have a better betting race if we adopted some of the characteristics of European racing, namely the distance factors. I think it would also prolong the careers of some of these horses. It is my belief that distance racing at 1 1/2 miles at a mile rate of 1:56 or 1:57 would be easier on a horse than racing a mile in 1:52.

And what good is it if all the races are at a mile, and all the races go in

1:52? On a Saturday night in the summer at The Meadowlands, every race goes about as fast as the others. Every race seems to go in 1:52! The only separation is the class of the horses and their ability to get the final sixteenth of a mile. I do not think the betting public is really all that interested in time, and I don't think we should be either. We spend too much time publicizing the time aspect of our business when it really has become relatively unimportant in comparison to really beating someone.

Distance racing would be a good solution to many problems. I know, for one, that I would not be opposed to racing my older horses at a distance, rather than "sprinting" them all season long. Racing greater distances would help horses last longer, because drivers would have to be more conservative. We would get just as much movement in a race, which the public likes, but the pace would be less taxing and a horse would not wear out as quickly. This would provide some variety in comparison to the constant mile races, and I think the betting public would support these longer-distance races after form is established.

CHANGES IN EQUIPMENT

There have been several changes in equipment over the past few years, many of them brought from Scandinavia. Developments such as the sliding gaiting poles, earplugs and pull-down blinds, were brought to North America by the Swedes and Norwegians, who have used these techniques for quite some time.

The sliding gaiting poles are really a novel idea, one which helps a pacer as much as a trotter, I think. They were, of course, developed for trotters since the trotter is king overseas in Sweden, Norway and Finland. But the truth is, I have found the gaiting poles just as valuable to me in straightening up a pacer as a trotter.

EARPLUGS ARE MISUNDERSTOOD

There is a misconception about earplugs.

I do not think the public, or even many harness writers, understands what earplugs really do for a horse. It is my experience that earplugs are most valuable in keeping a horse calm and manageable during the early part of the race, but are of little value late in the race when a horse is commonly asked to accelerate.

The average racing fan thinks the driver will pull the earplugs when he is asking for maximum effort from the horse. In most cases, pulling the earplugs makes very little difference. Most horses do not respond to the plugs being pulled. Usually, the driver pulls the plugs and feels no response.

What is evident to me is that the earplugs do assist in keeping a horse quiet and manageable in the post parade, and when he swings in behind the gate. I have seen many a difficult post horse calmed down by the use of earplugs. In short, the earplugs are more effective in getting horses to

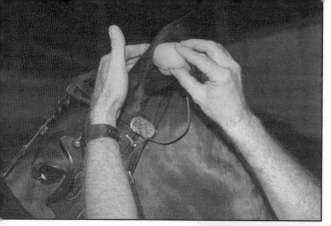

The proper way to insert an earplug is shown at left.

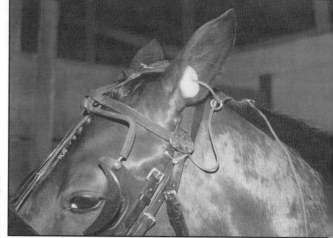

The earplug should not be shoved down into the ear, but placed firmly and clearly visible as shown here at right.

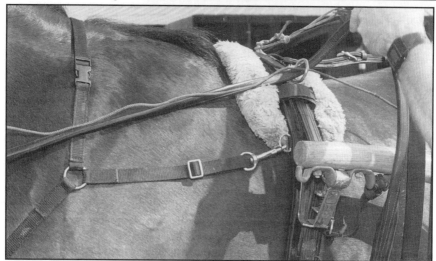

The line leading from the earplugs to the driver should be run back through the same turrets as the driving lines.

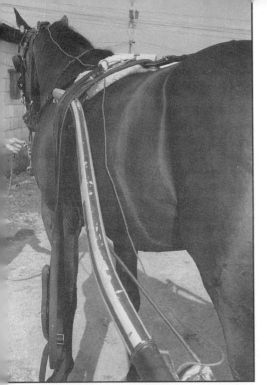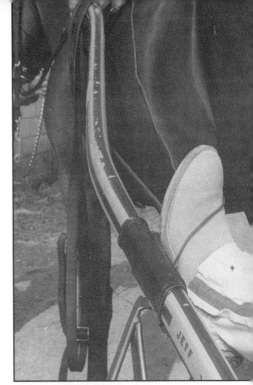

The line leading to the driver should come back to the driver on whatever side of the horse the driver is most comfortable with. This shows the line coming back on the horse's left side.
In order to pull the earplugs, the driver must wrap the line leading from the plugs around his foot. When the time has come to pull the plugs, the driver simply lifts his foot and pulls, removing the earplugs from the ears.

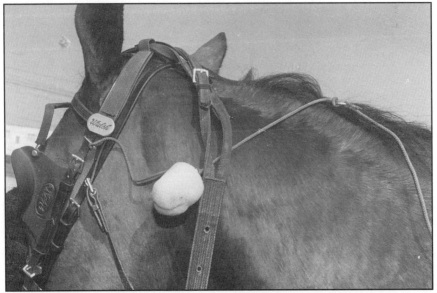

The line should be taunt enough that the earplug leaves the ear canal completely when pulled. An earplug that had been correctly pulled is shown here.

relax than they are to making speed.

One horse who did respond to the earplugs however, was Towner's Big Guy, a horse I catch drove for Dick Williams a few times. He was a horse who would really accelerate when the earplugs came out. The first time I raced Towner's Big Guy, Dick warned me not to pull the earplugs unless I had clearance. I made the mistake of not listening, since it was my experience that most horses did not respond to the plugs being pulled. But when I did pull his plugs, Towner's Big Guy really took off and we nearly climbed into the sulky ahead of us!

THE CARETAKER IS STILL VERY IMPORTANT

One thing that has not changed in our business is the role of the caretaker. The caretaker is just as important today as he or she has always been. The caretaker is still the hub of the wheel, the only person really responsible for the day-to-day maintenance of any horse.

A caretaker is very important to the success of the horse, and this is never more clearly illustrated than in the case where a caretaker and a horse do not get along in the barn. In most of these cases, the horse will carry this behavior to the track.

Everybody needs to be happy. If a horse is not happy with the people around it, it is a safe bet that the horse will not be training and/or racing well. I think it is important for every trainer to understand this and to know that he must carefully observe all his caretakers to see how they relate to, and care for their horses. If you have a mismatch between horse and groom, you need to resolve it as soon as possible.

Caretakers are a vital ingredient in the success of any stable, and they always have been. There is no better judge of soundness than a good groom. The groom can be the first to notice when the horse backs out of his feed tub, an early indication that something might be wrong. The groom is with that horse more than anyone, and a good groom will learn to spot trouble and report it before it can become a real problem.

There is one area in which this equation has changed a little. When I broke into the business, I was taught to take a lot of pride in the way my horse and my equipment looked. These days, a lot of grooms do not take that same kind of pride in their work. They can't wait to get out of the barn, it seems to me. I encourage all my help to take pride in themselves, and in their horses. Things always go a little smoother when everyone understands what is expected of them.

HORSES DO NOT NEED TO BE WALKED AS MUCH

One of the areas where we have changed a great deal involves the subject of how much horses should be walked after training and racing. This has been a controversial subject because there are trainers who have had a great deal of success and who walked their horses for more than an hour after racing. And there have been successful trainers who have never walked a horse.

I firmly believe that a properly conditioned horse does not need to be walked after he races. A lot of this will depend on what he is used to, of course. If a trainer has his horses walked after serious training and/or racing and then suddenly stops doing it, he could encounter some problems. It all depends on what the horse is used to having done with him.

I know a great many trainers who simply towel a horse off and turn him loose in the stall after racing. In cold weather, particularly, it is very rare that a horse will be walked after he races. In most instances, a cold weather race is followed by a bath and a good toweling, then a blanket is placed on the horse until his respiration returns to normal.

In hot weather, it is much more common to walk a horse, and I recommend it if a horse is in some respiratory distress following a race in very tough conditions. If a horse is blowing a lot, I will definitely want to see him walked until he is out of distress. It is important in either case to ensure that the horse is watered properly during the cooling-out period. I do not think there is a right way, or a wrong way to cool out a horse with or without a blanket, or walked or not walked, but there are definite problems with watering horses after exertion. A horse should get only about five to eight swallows of water every five minutes or so until he is watered out, regardless of whether he is walking or standing in the stall.

SHOULD A HORSE BE TURNED OUT?

As with many horse management issues, the answer to this question lies with the individual horse. I do not think it is a good idea, for instance, to turn out a horse who is big-boned and heavy-bodied, for an extended period of time, because he will probably pick up some weight while turned out and might break down while attempting to return to racing condition. Frank Ervin never turned Bret Hanover out at all for this very reason. Bret was a big, heavy-bodied horse and Ervin was concerned that Bret would pick up too much weight if turned out between racing seasons.

Another type of horse who shouldn't be turned out for an extended period of time is a real aggressive, hyperactive horse. He may be prone to hurting himself because he will spend a great deal of his day running the fences and chasing horses in adjoining paddocks or in just expending nervous energy.

I generally am in favor of turning a horse out for short periods of time, but it is not always the right thing to do. This is where your acquired judgment as a horseman will come into play. I know of a great many horses who flourish while turned out. I have also seen a number of horses who come in from the pasture more fit than when they went out.

But I have also seen a good number of horses injured in a paddock during a turnout period that was supposed to help them. As with most training decisions, an individual judgment needs to be made with respect to the overall temperament and attitude of the horse involved.

Turning out a filly seems to help her more than her male counterpart. I know of several top fillies who raced out of paddocks and who maintained their fitness and condition doing it. They would not have fared as well racing out of a box stall. I do not know why this is so; it just is. A good turnout period seems to help fillies and mares and keeps their attitude better and their appetites a little stronger; if it works, do it.

THE AGE OF SPECIALIZATION

There is more and more specialization in the business now. Much of this is due to the fact that the public wants the best drivers in every race. The public wants to see specialization.

I still train a stable, race a lot of horses myself and also get a lot of catch drives. But the whole industry is moving toward specialization. There will be trainers who never race a horse in their entire careers. There will be drivers developed who have never trained, or managed a stable.

These are not necessarily positive developments for the industry, because a guy who just trains horses will have a tough time making a living unless he is lucky enough to get a string of very good horses. The average trainer is going to work very hard, get up early in the morning, and work late into the night and still not make a very productive living. A trainer cannot charge enough to make a good income because there is always the other guy who will undercut you on price. An average trainer who has payrolls to meet, workmen's compensation and hay and feed bills to pay, will not find much income left over at the end of the year.

However, I would hope there will always be room for the guy who can break a yearling, train him, shoe him and then race him. If we get away from the basic fundamentals of horsemanship at all levels, I think we could be in for real trouble.

The best horseman, in my mind, is a person who understands the business and everything that goes into producing a good, productive horse. A lot of the trainers we have now started out as fans of the game, but never spent a lot of time on the end of a pitchfork. That is why I think most of the good drivers are guys who grew up in the business, who understand and like horses and practice good horsemanship.

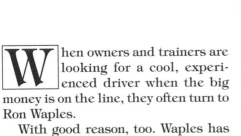

W|hen owners and trainers are looking for a cool, experienced driver when the big money is on the line, they often turn to Ron Waples.

With good reason, too. Waples has proven his ability to handle the pressure of driving in big-money events, often steering longshots to victory. He has won virtually every major stake in the sport, some of them several times.

He swept the Triple Crown of pacing in 1983 behind Ralph Hanover and won the Hambletonian in 1989 when he steered Park Avenue Joe to a dead-heat in the raceoff with Probe. In 1992, he was a last-minute catch driver for Fake Left in the Little Brown Jug and Waples managed to pull off a major upset and win the Delaware classic.

He drove Sugarcane Hanover to many of his biggest triumphs in North America and also won the 1993 North America Cup with Presidential Ball.

Ron Waples, of course, is not the first Waples to enjoy international acclaim for his accomplishments on the track. His cousin Keith Waples is acknowledged as one of the craftiest men ever to sit in a sulky, and Ron learned much of his basic horsemanship while working for Keith.

His superior all-around horsemanship is one of the assets that has made Ron Waples so successful as a catch driver. He drove No Sex Please, who was owned and trained by his son, Ron Jr., to two victories in the Breeders Crown, trained and drove Kentucky Futurity winner Huggie Hanover, and scored memorable victories with the top pacers Dream Maker and Armbro Dallas.

16
VETERINARY ISSUES - DIAGNOSIS AND TREATMENT

DR. KENNETH P. SEEBER

I have been asked to follow in the footsteps of Dr. Edwin A. Churchill, who wrote the corresponding chapter on lameness and other veterinary issues in the original *Care and Training of the Trotter and Pacer.* Dr. Churchill was my distinguished mentor, and as a former student and colleague of his, I am pleased to address some of the same issues as they apply to the modern Standardbred horse.

The competitive Standardbred horse racing today is a far different animal from the one analyzed by Dr. Churchill in the 1960s. Dr. Churchill was quite prophetic in saying back then that the breed was heading towards becoming more like the Thoroughbred; indeed, today this process is almost complete.

The Standardbred of the past was a heavy-bodied horse with an unattractive head, heavy bone structure, and coarse physique.

Today's Standardbred is sleek, leggy, athletic, and streamlined, more closely resembling his Thoroughbred cousin and nearly able to duplicate his speed.

Cambest, in his world record mile in 1993, paced a quarter in less than 26 seconds. The difference between the current Thoroughbred world record over a mile, which is approximately 1:32, and the Standardbred world record, which is 1:46.1, is only 14 seconds. I am sure that the next major world record reduction will get the Standardbred mark under 1:45. From there, it's only about three seconds in each quarter away from the Thoroughbred mark, and I am convinced that one day the Standardbred will go as fast as Thoroughbreds do.

As a useful analogy, the Standardbred of today is more like a sports car compared to the Standardbred of Dr. Churchill's day which was like a pickup truck. The rapid evolution of such a speed machine is the result of concentrated selective breeding as well as great advances in equipment and race bike design, plus improved racetrack engineering.

Improvements such as the quick-hitch harness, lift race bike, and track design with banked, super elevated turns have all contributed to the phenomenal increase in speed at which the modern Standardbred travels. However, records are still broken regularly on tracks that have not been vastly improved, so the sheer ability of the modern horse to go fast has been bred into it.

When I see horses as quick and good gaited as the likes of Presidential Ball, Life Sign, American Winner, and Pine Chip, I know that these are horses our ancestors just would not have believed. Such horses are aggressive and competitive from an early age because they come from long lines of fast horses.

This evolution towards speed, however, is natural and to be expected. At this time there is no substitute for speed in the formula for success in harness racing. The use of artificial insemination has brought about even more rapid change and allowed the spread of "speed" genes to all corners of the industry.

In some respects, this has brought positive characteristics of good horses to the hinterlands, but, in some ways, it has also narrowed the gene pool by allowing the dominance of certain male lines. The primary focus in breeding has been, "How fast did the sire go and how fast did the dam go?"

In my opinion, not enough attention has been paid to whether the sire and dam were sound in legs and wind. If a certain cross works, people continue to use it, and the effects of this are now being observed in the occurrence of congenital conformational, physiological and other defects in some dominant families.

I will at the outset deal with what I feel to be the predisposing causes of lameness in the Standardbred racehorse, followed by a discussion of how I diagnose and treat lameness. Always keep in mind that like human medicine, veterinary medicine is not an exact science and there are many ways to both diagnose and treat a particular problem, depending on the circumstances surrounding each particular case and the veterinary practitioner who is handling the case.

PREDISPOSING CAUSES OF LAMENESS

1) SPEED:

From a veterinary point of view, the intense emphasis on speed over the last 20 years by the Standardbred industry has major implications on the predisposing causes of lameness. In my opinion, there is too much emphasis on speed in the Standardbred industry today. There is nowhere near the same obsession with it in the Thoroughbred racing sport where patrons are more interested in who their horse beats and whether he won a Grade 1 or Grade 2 stakes race.

Whether you are talking about automobiles or horses, speed kills. The faster a horse goes, the more stress on the musculo-skeletal system. The muscles, tendons and ligaments are asked to do things that nature never really intended. This is the old physical equation of "the force on a horse's leg is directly equal to the weight of the horse times the speed he is traveling." When you increase the speed, you increase the force.

The concept is very well understood in the auto racing world. Racing cars have to be specially reinforced and strengthened to withstand high speeds. Great attention is paid to wear and tear on the chassis and suspension, knowing that if it is not strong enough, it disintegrates.

I like to use the race car analogy on the horse. The skeleton and muscles, ligaments and tendons of the horse can be thought of as analogous to the chassis and suspension of the racing machine. In some cases, due to breeding an unsound mare to an unsound stallion, the framework of the racing machine is defective before training and competition even starts.

Unfortunately, some of the dominant families that pass on conformational weaknesses in their feet and legs make the future job of keeping their offspring sound enough for racing very difficult.

As we have created this more handsome, fine-boned, Thoroughbred-type individual without the "jug" head and with a longer neck and slender throat, we are making a sacrifice in the quest for speed. Not only are we seeing more lower-leg lameness problems now, but also a great many more mechanical respiratory problems, such as upward displacement of the soft palate.

When Dr. Churchill wrote his chapter in 1968 I had just graduated from veterinary college. I can remember when a two-minute horse was a champion. Today, on any Saturday night at The Meadowlands, a good horse easily goes in 1:51. Over 28 years, this is a phenomenal increase in speed.

Speed certainly costs the industry dearly. The price is paid by owners and trainers struggling to keep their horses sound and competitive over longer racing seasons. Not only are we asking horses to race faster than they ever have, we have also extended the racing season into an all-year-round endeavor.

To maintain the racetracks all year in rain, ice and snow, racing surfaces have become harder, which also takes its toll. Nobody at this time is going to stand up and tell the industry to slow down, so the limiting factor must ultimately be the durability of the horses, or racing them less frequently.

2) FATIGUE:

In motor sports, race car drivers are very concerned with how the suspension of the race car feels at high speeds in the turns.

Using the analogy of the horse's skeleton to the race car chassis, and the muscles, tendons and ligaments to the suspension, we have the situation in horse racing where the suspension gets tired. When fatigue sets in over the last quarter of the race, the resiliency and elastic, shock-absorbing qualities of the suspension are gone and the smashing onto the skeleton begins. Most bowed tendons, torn suspensory ligaments, and fractures occur between the three-quarter pole and the wire.

It is extremely important that the horses be conditioned so they do not experience extreme fatigue during a race. I remember when Nihilator went in 1:49.3, someone asked Bill O'Donnell, "Could you have gone faster?"

Bill's reply was, "I don't know and I hope I never have to find out."

Good drivers do not like to push their horses to the very edge where banging and smashing on the skeleton could mean the destruction of the horse. They prefer to finish with something left.

Over-training as well as under-training can result in the horse becoming fatigued. In the interest of the Standardbred industry, we must realistically consider the limiting factors on the horse, be prepared to change training schedules to suit the modern breed, and change the way horses are being campaigned.

As it is, horses today do not make as many starts as in the past. I remember when Nevele Pride was a two-year-old in 1967. He started 29 times! We would not think of racing a two-year-old that many times today. Perhaps 12 to 15 starts is considered ideal.

Whether in training or in racing, when the vital tendons and ligaments of the leg become tired, they no longer act as shock absorbers and the entire weight of the horse is impacting the bone structure of the leg with every stride. Correct conditioning cannot be emphasized enough.

Year-round racing has also contributed to fatigue in racehorses. The every-day raceway horse is asked to start as many as 25-30 times a year on a seven-day cycle. Racing schedules and stake schedules are all geared to weekly races, but, unfortunately, the horses are not strong enough to compete on these weekly schedules at the speeds they are racing.

As it becomes harder and harder to keep the horses sound, there will be fewer horses to fill the race cards, as we are now seeing. At some time the Standardbred industry will have to adopt the Thoroughbred industry format where a horse only races every 2-1/2 to 3 weeks.

Every driver and trainer in the Standardbred industry has a desire to race or train a fast horse. The natural speed and aggressive competitiveness we have bred into the horses necessitates intelligent management. Horses should be asked for their speed only under the best circumstances, and never when they are compromised physically.

Unfortunately, this frequently is part of the business today and will not change until owners and patrons realize that horses are not prospering on weekly, year-round racing schedules and must be conditioned and campaigned carefully.

3) IMMATURITY:

When an owner purchases a young horse, they are naturally looking for a rapid return on their investment; so there is great anticipation and expectation to get that horse to the races.

The staking program of two and three-year-olds asks a lot of young horses. These young horses may be able to go very fast, but still don't mature completely until they are at least five years old. However, the economics of the business are such that there are large rewards for the fastest juveniles.

I do not propose that we abandon two-year-old racing or drastically change the racing format, but there needs to be an increasing awareness

One of the biggest improvements in Standardbred racing over the past two decades is banking of racetrack turns and stretches. This has allowed horses to race faster and safer because the track elevation attempts to keep horses perpendicular to the racing surface.

of the high price of speed on the future racing careers of these young athletes.

To have developed a good two-year-old colt and be within two weeks of a major race such as the $750,000 Woodrow Wilson is thrilling. To have him come out of a preliminary race and be unsound the next day, is anything but thrilling. If an examination shows that he has sore knees or similar joint soreness elsewhere, the owner is put in the position of choosing between resting the colt for a while or possibly injecting the joint that is sore.

The owners may have the purchase price of the colt, along with a possible $16,000 or $17,000 in staking fees, and $25,000 in training fees invested at that time. It is a very competitive business. Given the choice of turning the colt out or injecting its joints to make him sound again for a bit longer, most people want to try injecting one time to see how it works, and force Mother Nature to vary her course.

4) RACETRACK DESIGN AND SURFACES:

The banking of track turns is a beneficial development because it allows horses to go faster and yet reduces the stress of racing at such high speeds. Banking, as much as 10 percent on half-mile tracks, creates speed because it keeps the horse more perpendicular to the track surface. This allows the horse to "corner" without a dramatic weight shift to the outside limbs.

In this respect, Standardbred racing has been more progressive than

Thoroughbred racing. Thoroughbred racetracks have been slow to implement the idea of banking racetracks, which is certainly a contributing factor to the large number of breakdowns in that business. In spite of the fact they do it easier, speed is still the limiting factor when it comes to keeping a horse sound.

All-weather racetracks have very hard surfaces, by comparison, which is necessary to make them resilient to rain, ice and snow, and most are maintained to promote speed. These hard surfaces create a great deal of musculo-skeletal stress in young and old horses alike, and are a major predisposing cause of lameness.

The ideal track is one with some cushion and spring so that the horse's legs do not have to be the sole source of shock absorption. On a hard track there is no "give," and the punishment to the horse becomes even greater when he is fatigued. Horses who are trained and raced only on hard tracks become bruised and sore in their feet, and will alter their gait. As soon as the horse starts changing the symmetry of its gait there will be excessive strain on other structures of the leg.

A track that is too soft or breaks away under the horse's feet can also cause lameness. If a horse cannot get a good hold of the track, or if the track breaks out from under him, this causes him to slip.

In my opinion, the very fastest horses of the breed pull as much with their front limbs as they push with their hind limbs. I am convinced that one of the greatest causes of lameness in any performance horse is slipping.

Track conditions can exacerbate certain lameness problems. On hard tracks with little cushion, horses will develop a lot of foot and ankle problems. If the track is loose and "cuppy," horses will tend to develop hock and knee problems. It is very hard on horses to switch from a hard-"or good"-surfaced track to a deep-surfaced track, because the muscles will not be conditioned to that type of going.

However, a horse transferring from a deep track to a hard track has developed a greater amount of muscular ability and is more apt to race to his true form. The ideal racetrack is one with a cushion that is not too deep and a surface that is well knit together by the generous application of water.

There are many other reasons why a horse can become unsound in addition to what I have discussed above. When I was training a stable of horses, I used to tell the caretakers that one minute of negligence can ruin a whole year of work or more.

Jogging horses, bandaging legs, loading and unloading a truck or van, turning out in a paddock, losing your patience are all situations where career-ending injuries to a horse can take place. Unfortunately, most of the injuries that take place in these situations are to soft tissue structures of the horse such as tendons and ligaments. This type of injury can many times be as difficult to deal with and in some cases more difficult that a broken bone. I have said in conversation many times that a horse's greatest enemy can be man.

Two additional factors that can be important predisposing causes of lameness in the performance horse are conformation and shoeing which are discussed at length in other chapters of this book.

VETERINARY ISSUES:

DIAGNOSIS OF LAMENESS:

The practice of veterinary medicine is different from human medicine because the patient cannot speak to us. The successful diagnosis of lameness depends largely on your ability to observe what the horse is communicating.

The most obvious communication is when the horse is visibly lame, but the truth of the matter as to the source of the problem and how best to manage it lies in your ability to interpret the lameness in the context of the horse's nature, his performance history and, most importantly, your findings from a thorough physical examination.

First, it is important to keep in mind the nature of the horse. The Standardbred horse is bred to be a top athlete and, generally, knows his job and likes it. The horse can be his own worst enemy because he is programmed by his breeding to race at speed, when asked, and will often continue to perform with pain.

Lameness in many of the exceptional performers can be very difficult to diagnose, because the horses are so courageous they will ignore their soreness in striving to do what is asked, and the only indication of a problem may be an uncharacteristically poor performance.

Temperaments and abilities vary, and some horses have a higher tolerance for pain than others. A collection of horses can be likened to a group of football players, be they high school or professional, in that some of them with tremendous talent don't put out because their mental attitude compromises effort. These are the underachievers with raw talent who never live up to expectations. Then there are those who have such low tolerance to pain that they let small injuries get the better of them and refuse to perform. Others go out and give a tremendous effort and shrug off both small and large injuries. Invariably, the great racehorses are the ones who want to go out and "do it," no matter what.

The successful diagnosis of lameness is basically a combination of common sense and a commitment to not overlook the obvious. Probably 85-90 percent of unsoundness problems are quite straightforward, such as sore feet, ankles, knees or hocks, with secondary implications of shoulder, back, and stifle soreness.

The other 10-15 percent of problems may be more complicated, and in many cases of lameness in Standardbreds there may be combinations of primary and secondary areas of soreness. Sometimes, the obviously visible swelling or lameness may be secondary in nature, and treatment

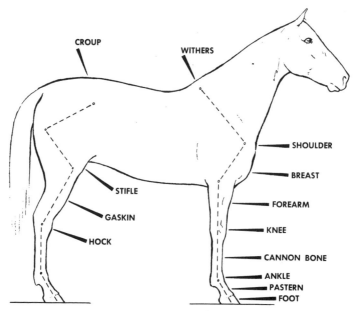

This profile identifies the main areas of external anatomy referred to in this chapter.

directed at this problem will be largely unsuccessful in restoring soundness.

For example, the horse may have filling in the left fetlock with joint distention and tendon-sheath swelling, which will not respond to treatment for any length of time. The trainer indicates that, at high speeds, the horse is on the right line, and further examination shows that it is sore in its right knee, thus throwing its weight to the left front. Treatment of the right knee will relieve the pressure on the left front, and the swelling and soreness there will subside. Similarly, a great deal of hind leg lameness is secondary to primary soreness in the front legs. In trying to protect sore front legs or feet, the horse throws more weight onto his hind quarters with every stride. This is the result of the gait peculiar to the Standardbred and the fact that the Standardbred is pulling a sulky and driver.

A Thoroughbred at full gallop projects all his forward-going weight over a single foreleg in each stride, whereas a Standardbred, fully extended, lands on a front leg and a hind leg simultaneously. Consequently, rear leg lameness in the Standardbred is more common than in the Thoroughbred and is frequently the result of the horse compensating for soreness in front.

Another factor in the process of determining which is the primary problem and which is secondary is the consideration that most of a

Standardbred's fast work miles are in a counter-clockwise direction. Many primary points of soreness are on the right-hand side and secondary points of soreness are on the left-hand side because the centrifugal forces of traveling in that direction throw the horse's weight to the outside, or right side. Consequently, as it lands harder and pushes off quicker from its right side, this part of the body suffers from over-use. Hence, if speeds were equal, a horse would stay sounder on a larger track; i.e., a five-eighths or mile track, than on a half-mile track.

One of the important first steps in investigating lameness is to take a careful history, compiling as much information as possible from the trainer, driver, and caretaker. Everyone who has contact with the horse has observations which may be of potential help in this investigation. It is impossible to make a correct diagnosis without combining a comprehensive history with a careful physical examination of the horse.

In this section I will discuss how I conduct a physical examination of the horse, and what can be some of the specific causes of lameness. I will then discuss some of the clinical techniques available today to assist diagnosis. Treatment and other factors that can affect performance will be discussed later in this chapter.

VISUAL EXAMINATION FOR LAMENESS

PHYSICAL EXAM AT REST:

My personal preference is to first examine the horse when its muscles and joints are cold prior to its being exercised or moved. A lot of soft-tissue soreness and swelling will change if the horse is moved, and when it is hot after being jogged or trained you will not find the same things as when it is cold.

I like to see the horse unbandaged in its stall, and feel the legs for thickness and intensity of digital pulse. I watch the horse's attitude, and whether it looks as though it has any apparent soreness in the first few steps out of the stall. I will ask that the horse be walked a short distance away from me, turned, and then brought back towards me. I look to see how it moves, and to see if there are any outward signs that might give me a clue as to where to look for problems.

I also take note of its general outlook and sense of well-being by the expression of its eye: Does it have a cheerful, pleasant look in its eye, or is it sullen and depressed?

As the horse stands before me, I am also, at this time, assessing its conformation. How does it stand? Is it back or over at the knees? Does it have well-shaped feet that are in proportion to the size of its body? A horse will tell you a lot through these simple, initial visual observations.

Having made mental notes of my first impressions, I then systematically begin a careful examination of the horse from head to tail. I generally start on the left-hand side, because horses are most used to having humans approach from that side. I am always aware of allowing the horse a comfort level and keeping him at ease, because many horses can sense a veterinarian and will not be willing patients.

It is a good idea to try and position yourself where you can watch the horse's head at all times while you carry out the examination, so you can see how the horse reacts to your every move.

Horses often try to guard the area that is painful, or will become nervous or wary as you approach the place where the soreness is. If you try to keep the horse relaxed from the start, you can make the horse "talk" to you by watching how it responds to your examination.

I usually run my hands under the jaw and check for any abnormalities there while inquiring about how the horse drives. I inspect the mouth and teeth for the presence of wolf teeth, caps, or sharp teeth which may be making the horse pull on one line or the other and be confused with a lameness problem.

EXAMINATION OF THE FORELIMB:
After checking the head, I run my hands down the horse's throat area and neck, observing its conformation and the width of the throat, plus feeling for any swelling which could indicate the presence of mechanical respiratory problems. I continue to run my hands down its shoulder and left foreleg to the hoof, to which I pay particular attention.

The old axiom of "no foot, no horse" is one with which I absolutely concur. A horse may be blessed with great speed, but it will have difficulty achieving such speed if it has bad feet. Thin walls, flat soles that bruise easily, or small feet in proportion to the size of the body may all predispose a horse to a lifetime of nagging foot problems. The ideal foot corresponds to body size and bone structure and is nice and round with a concave sole, wide frog, and broad heel.

I will check for heat in the hoof and the intensity of the digital pulse, then pick the foot up and observe the condition of the hoof wall and sole and the shoeing. I pay particular attention to how well the feet are taken care of and how the horse is shod.

The extent to which improper shoeing creates or aggravates lameness problems cannot be stressed enough, with insufficient traction being perhaps the most serious source of aggravation. In addition, failure to correctly balance the foot causes stresses and strains around the joints of the limb and alters the flight path of the leg during movement, and the degree of damage worsens with time and miles.

A good blacksmith will generally shoe to the natural conformation of the horse's foot and ensure that the ground surface of the foot is level and that the horse is landing on its wall and not its sole.

At this time, I will also check for any signs of gait interference around the coronet and apply manual pressure to the bulbs of the heels to see if they are tender. Using hoof testers, pressure can be systematically applied all around the perimeter of the foot and across the heels, checking

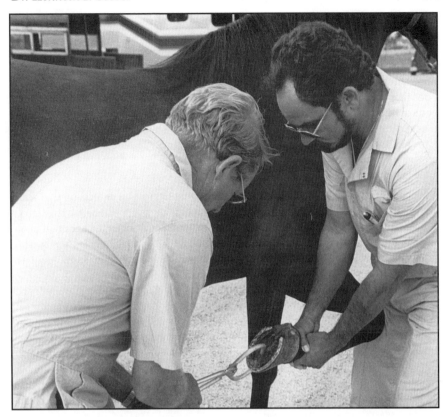

The use of a hoof tester can be very beneficial in determining if soreness exists in the internal structure of the hoof. When pressure is applied with a tester, the horse will flinch with pain if a sore spot is found. This process is especially helpful in finding corns in the hoof.

for any signs of flinching by the horse that indicates pain in the internal structures of the hoof.

SPECIFIC AREAS OF LAMENESS IN THE FOOT

BRUISES:

Sole bruises result when the foot lands heavily on a hard, irregular surface, and this causes immediate lameness. Severe lameness may be present for only a few strides after the injury, but some degree of soreness may last for several weeks as the bruise subsides. Particularly at risk are horses with thin, soft soles and horses with flat feet. Typically, the bruised area can be seen as a red mark, indicating leakage of blood into the horny layers of the hoof wall or sole, and the hoof itself may also be carrying some heat due to the increased blood supply to the area.

When the bruise is deep, the red discoloration may not be seen on the surface for several days.

However, with bruising there always will be some reaction by the horse to the pressure applied to the area by hoof testers. If uncomplicated by infection, bruises will resolve themselves, providing the horse is kept on smooth ground. Horses who are regularly worked on rough or hard surfaces will gradually harden their soles and develop increased resistance to bruising. The use of full pads will protect the sole, but does not allow this toughening process to occur.

CORNS:

Corns are chronic, severe bruises that occur in the angle of the foot between the hoof wall and the bar on either or both sides of the frog, although they most commonly occur on the insides of the front feet. Corns usually result from poor foot conformation, with flat soles, too long or too short toes, and under-run heels predisposing to excess pressure on the heel region.

Improper shoeing puts the horse at risk of developing a corn where the sole, instead of the adjacent hoof wall, is taking the brunt of the weight-bearing at the heel. Corns produce varying degrees of lameness. Some horses will merely stride short when worked on hard ground.

Hoof-tester examination will usually reveal tenderness in the heel area, and the corn can be seen easily when the superficial horn of the sole is pared away with a hoof knife. Corns are not serious, if present in a well-conformed hoof and caused by a singular event, such as poor foot trimming or overdue shoeing.

However, if they are persistent in a poorly conformed, flat-footed horse who is to be worked on hard surfaces, they can cause a lifetime of trouble. Heredity can also be important since horses with bad feet, like flat and thin soles, will gradually pass them on to their progeny.

Many of the fast horses that I have been fortunate enough to be involved with have low or underslung heels and may have not been born that way. It is my opinion that most horses land heel first and then drop the toe to pull forward in their stride. Buying a young horse or any horse with this condition requires careful attention to the heel area when it is shod so that excessive bruising and corns do not occur.

GRAVEL AND FOOT ABSCESSES:

Penetrating wounds of the foot can develop into a pocket of infection and cause sub-solar abscesses, which can vary from an acute problem that responds promptly to treatment to chronic, complicated problems with deep-seated infection inside the hoof.

The term "gravel" is an old-fashioned term for what was supposedly the migration of a piece of gravel up the white line between the hoof wall

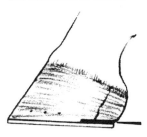

A quarter crack can begin at the coronary band or from the bottom of the hoof. A common procedure to relieve pressure on the hoof wall is to rasp away the wall of the hoof back to the heel and let the bar shoe extend for support.

and the sensitive internal layers, eventually bursting out at the coronary band.

What actually occurs is this: A penetrating wound permits infection to enter, which then follows the white line upward, as it is the line of least resistance. Because there is no area behind the hoof wall for drainage, the infection emerges and bursts out at the coronary band.

Infections may also enter the foot through the sole via a severe bruise due to a hole made by a sharp stone or object. It is the formation of a pocket of inflammation and pus that creates the lameness, as there is no room for any swelling inside the hoof. Sometimes it takes a few days of slowly progressive soreness before it builds up, and at other times the horse can go from being sound to non-weight bearing in a matter of hours.

It is the intense pain from the build-up of pressure inside the hoof that at times can cause a lameness so dramatic the only differential diagnosis is a fracture. The horse gets instant relief when the abscess breaks out in a discharging wound at the coronary band, or drainage is established with a hoof knife in the sole area. Further infection and swelling may spread up the leg, depending on the severity. The nature of this type of lameness is usually acute, and responds readily to treatment.

QUARTER CRACKS:

Cracks in the hoof wall can occur at the toe, quarters, or heels. They are a result of either abnormal stresses on the hoof capsule, caused by unbalanced foot trimming or due to poor-quality hoof wall in a horse who has shelly, brittle feet. Interference of gait, such as cross-firing, can also cause quarter cracks. The problem always will be exacerbated by training and racing horses on tracks that have little cushion, especially during the winter.

Quarter cracks may start at the bottom of the foot and work up, or they sometimes begin at the top and work down. In the early stages, the crack may not be readily visible to the naked eye, but as it develops, it becomes obvious and always reacts to hoof testers. The more unstable and deep the crack is, the greater the pain and lameness.

There is a genetic predisposition for quarter cracks, in that the quality of the hoof wall is a hereditary trait. Dry, brittle feet with thin walls will crack more easily under the pressure of training. However, the problem

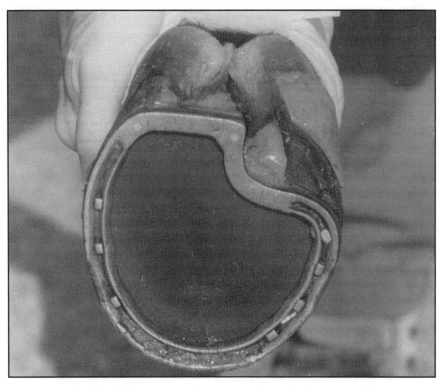

The shoe worn by Nihilator as a two-year-old on his right front foot was specially fitted in order to deal with a troublesome quarter crack. The quarter crack, which occurred in the heel was cut out and the horse was fitted with a special shoe which took the pressure off the area.

can be minimized by keeping the foot level so that it impacts the ground evenly when the horse lands on it.

A good blacksmith with an eye for proper foot balance will not allow the toe to become too long, which can cause leverage at the quarters as the foot breaks over. Neither will he allow the ground surface to be unlevel so that extra pressure is exerted on one area of the wall.

I remember an example of this: The great pacer, Nihilator, had problems with quarter cracks as a two-year-old. One side of his foot grew faster than the other and his foot became unlevel over the course of a shoeing period. Once the foot was kept level, the quarter-crack problem disappeared and never returned.

NAVICULAR DISEASE:

The small, oblong, navicular bone is a deep internal structure of the foot that acts as a pulley for the deep digital flexor tendon where it attaches to the bone of the foot (commonly called the coffin bone). As such, it plays a critical role in every step the horse takes and is subject to great punishment if the forces acting on the leg are compromised in any way by poor conformation or improper shoeing.

The most delicate factor about this bone is its blood supply, because it is so easily disturbed by the interactions of the surrounding tissues, particularly the coffin and pastern bones and the associated actions of the tendons that attach there.

Long upright pasterns predispose to concussion on the navicular bone, as do long toes and low heels. Poor circulation causes deterioration of the bone over time, and lameness may be insidious in onset and wear off with exercise, but then slowly progress until the horse is lame in front. A primary cause of poor circulation in the foot is insufficient frog pressure to expand and contract the blood vessels in the foot.

The horse may show pain when hoof testers are applied over the center of the frog or across the heels, but the assistance of clinical techniques such as X-rays and nerve blocks is usually required to confirm the diagnosis. Navicular disease is usually found more frequently in older horses, but occasionally is seen in young horses.

LAMINITIS:

Laminitis has probably been the most widely researched lameness involving the horse's foot, and it has so many causes and clinical manifestations that an entire book could be devoted to the subject. However, I will discuss it briefly here, simply because it is so devastating that horse trainers need to be aware of it and alert to the dangers.

Laminitis or "founder" is an inflammation of the sensitive layers (laminae) which intermesh between the internal soft structures of the hoof and the external and hard hoof wall. It results from a circulatory disturbance to the blood supply of the foot, which can be secondary to metabolic processes associated with overeating, grazing lush pastures, obesity, or serious internal organ problems such as colic. It also can be secondary to running a high fever for a long period of time, or associated with some severe diseases such as Potomac horse fever.

Affected horses show reluctance to move and adopt a typical "sawhorse" stance with the forelimbs held well out in front of the body. The onset is acute, and is accompanied by many of the signs associated with pain due to colic, such as sweating and lying down for long periods. In severe cases, the coffin bone will detach from the hoof wall and rotate down through the sole of the foot. There are varying grades of severity, but it should be understood that laminitis is potentially fatal and should be treated as an emergency.

After a thorough examination of the foot, I then move on to examine the joints of the pastern area. I will rotate and manipulate these joints to

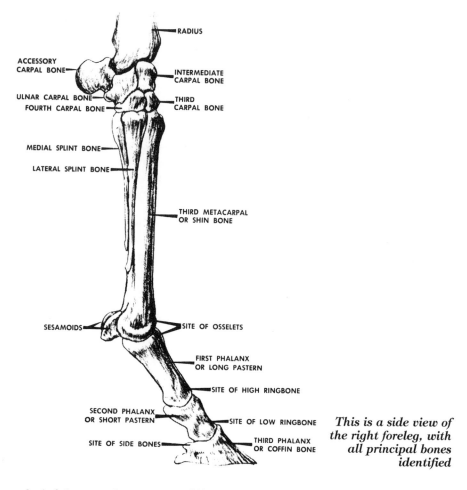

This is a side view of the right foreleg, with all principal bones identified

feel if there is distention or filling in the joint capsule or any decrease in range of motion.

Continuing the examination of the left front foreleg, I will then take the foot in one hand and the knee in the other and flex the ankle or fetlock joint to assess its range of motion and the condition of the joint. I am looking for any thickening or swelling around the ankle or distention of the joint capsule, and I am feeling for the presence of heat—a sure sign of inflammation and subsequent pain. Whenever there is injury or damage to the body, extra blood flow to the area is triggered and may lead to a build-up of fluid and heat.

It should be kept in mind that ankle problems in the Standardbred rarely are primary lameness problems. They are almost always secondary to problems in one or more feet. Close examination of the feet and assessment of the shoeing cannot be emphasized enough.

Lameness in ankles will commonly result when a horse alters its gait to compensate for soreness in the feet. The horse will change the way it is putting its foot down; for example, landing on its toe instead of its heel. This creates undue torque on the ankle because the horse's gait suddenly is no longer symmetrical. As the symmetry of the gait is lost, the mechanical forces of the leg are changed and the lameness becomes more complicated, involving other structures of the leg, starting with the ankle.

I pay particular attention to the sesamoid bones, which are the two distinct bones found at the back of the ankle. Sesamoids are a vital part of the lower leg anatomy because they are points of attachment of the suspensory ligament which, as its name suggests, has a major role in the suspension of the limb during the weight-bearing phase of the stride.

There sometimes is confusion among horsemen about the difference between a ligament and a tendon. A tendon connects bone to muscle and a ligament connects bone to bone. In this case, the large suspensory ligament is one of the major structures of the horse's limb, having its origin on the back of the shin or cannon bone, behind the knee and splitting above the back of the ankle to form a Y-shaped sling to cradle the fetlock.

The two sesamoid bones are nature's way of strengthening the ligament at the points of greatest stress, and they are part of a ligament "pulley" system that supports the weight of the horse. During my examination I very carefully palpate the sesamoids and their associated ligaments, along with the suspensory ligament which lies deep along the bone at the back of the cannon, because these are structures that are often injured when a horse is engaged in fast work.

SPECIFIC CAUSES OF LAMENESS IN THE FETLOCK AND PASTERN:

RINGBONE:

Ringbone derives its name from the fact that, in advanced cases, new bone growth developing in response to trauma will go completely around the circumference of the pastern at the level of the joint. It is called high ringbone if the bony changes are in the upper pastern joint, halfway between the coronary band and the ankle. It is called low ringbone if it is in the lower pastern joint just above the hoof itself.

Ringbone is most common in the front limbs and may or may not be associated with the joint surfaces. It is usually the result of trauma and may often be associated with upright pastern conformation. There is a varying amount of swelling and lameness and there may not even be a lot of pain upon flexion and palpation of the joint.

However, if the problem involves the joint, chronic lameness will result as the joint stiffens and the horse will lose the proper action of the limb. Fortunately, this condition is not seen very often in Standardbreds. It is much more common in jumpers and polo ponies.

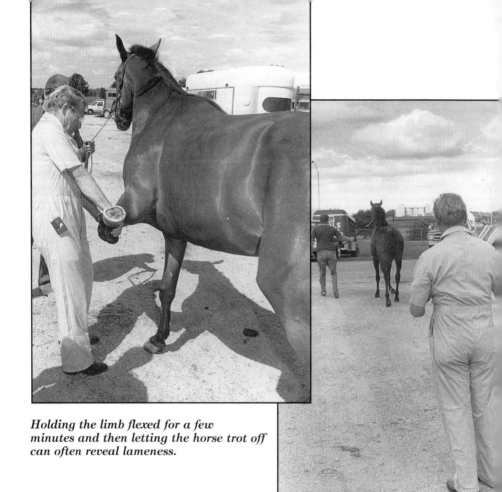

Holding the limb flexed for a few minutes and then letting the horse trot off can often reveal lameness.

OSSELETS:

This is a term used to describe traumatic arthritis of the fetlock joint, which is evident when there are prominent swellings on the front of the ankle. It is a common wear-and-tear injury in racing horses and begins with fibrous thickening of the joint capsule on the front of the fetlock. In a continuous cycle of trauma inflicted by racing and training and the accompanying cartilage degeneration, the joint gradually becomes stiffer and loses its range of motion.

As the horse continues to train and race, lameness becomes evident and can be aggravated by holding the fetlock flexed for a few minutes, then letting the horse trot off. X-rays are useful in determining the stage of degeneration and extent of involvement of the joint and in ascertaining whether chips of bone are present in the joint.

Horses who have very upright pasterns are particularly prone to develop osselets. Many racehorses can maintain successful careers despite these prominent protrusions on the front of their ankles. For example, the Triple Crown champion Ralph Hanover had prominent osselets which never gave him any serious problems.

SESAMOIDITIS/SESAMOID FRACTURES:
Similar to the navicular bone in that they are surrounded by tendons and ligaments, the two vital little bones called sesamoids have a very fragile blood supply. Any inflammation resulting from damage to the sesamoid area can impair the circulation, which in turn contributes to the degeneration of these bones.

Sesamoid problems are serious in any horse and have the potential to end a promising career. Sesamoids are frequently injured during fast exercise when great stress is placed on this area due to the action of the suspensory ligament. A young horse may often break and injure a sesamoid if he hits himself while interfering with another limb, such as occurs in cross-firing.

The worst injury is a fracture of the sesamoid bone due to over-extension of the fetlock joint. This is very serious, especially if it occurs at the base of the bone adjacent to the attachment of many ligaments. If the fracture occurs in the middle of the bone, it may be surgically repaired with a guarded prognosis. And, if it occurs at the top of the bone, it will heal with rest or can be easily removed.

Although the surgical repair of a fracture of the apex or top of the sesamoid is not difficult, the problem is that a portion of the suspensory ligament has to be cut to do the surgery. How well the suspensory heals is what usually determines how successful the surgery will be in returning the horse to racing. Diagnosis is not difficult because there usually is some heat and swelling around the ankle, and X-rays can verify the presence of a fracture.

Next, I examine the tendons of the leg, starting with the extensor tendon on the front and working around to the deep and superficial flexor tendons at the back of the leg. The extensor tendon runs down the front of the leg and pulls the leg out straight, and the superficial and deep flexor tendons run together up the back of the leg and flex the leg up at the end of the stride. It is the superficial flexor tendon that is the most frequently damaged and referred to as a "bowed tendon."

Tendon damage is usually easy to see and feel, because at the point where the tendon is torn, it protrudes from the normal clean line of the horse's leg. Part of the tendons are housed in a tendon sheath, which is like a sleeve containing natural lubricants that allow the tendon to slide up and down with the movement of the leg. It is important to understand the difference between damage to the tendon itself and to the tendon sheath. They may occur together (in a bowed tendon, for example), but often the tendon sheath is inflamed and swollen even when there is no damage to the structure of the tendon itself.

With the leg flexed, I feel up and down the length of the tendons, from

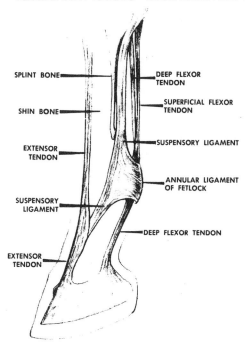

SPLINT BONE

SHIN BONE

EXTENSOR
TENDON

SUSPENSORY
LIGAMENT

EXTENSOR
TENDON

DEEP FLEXOR
TENDON

SUPERFICIAL FLEXOR
TENDON

SUSPENSORY LIGAMENT

ANNULAR LIGAMENT
OF FETLOCK

DEEP FLEXOR TENDON

The principal tendons and ligaments of the foreleg are identified in this illustration. Remember that tendons connect bone to muscle, while ligaments connect bone to bone.

the sesamoids to the knee, and palpate the suspensory ligament near the bone, also feeling the splint bones on each side of the leg below the knee. The splint bones are the anatomical remnants of the two outside toes of the small, deer-like ancestral horse who ran on a three-toed foot. By touch, I search for any irregularity in the shape of these structures or any pain on pressure. I then put the leg down and check to see if the superficial and deep digital flexors are nice and straight and tight when weight-bearing occurs.

SPECIFIC CAUSES OF LAMENESS IN THE CANNON OR SHIN AREA

SUSPENSORY LIGAMENT DAMAGE:

The suspensory ligament is the shock absorber and suspension of the foreleg. Tears or strain to the suspensory ligament can be very serious and need to be treated very carefully. A horse who has had too much work at too high a speed, or is compensating for some other problem, can develop a tear or pull in the suspensory ligament anywhere between the knee and the ankle. High tears are serious because the integrity of the ligament's attachment to the bone is damaged.

Further down the leg, in the area of the splint bones, tears can occur

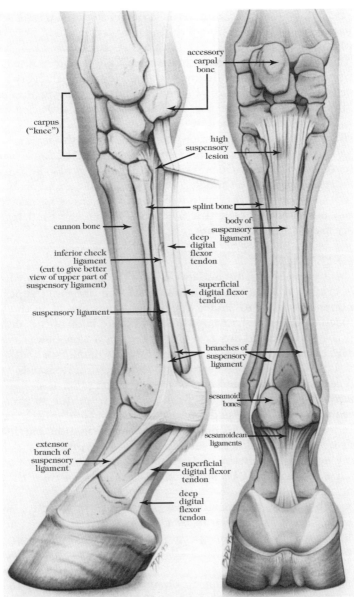

accessory carpal bone

carpus ("knee")

high suspensory lesion

splint bone

cannon bone

body of suspensory ligament

deep digital flexor tendon

inferior check ligament (cut to give better view of upper part of suspensory ligament)

superficial digital flexor tendon

suspensory ligament

branches of suspensory ligament

sesamoid bones

sesamoidean ligaments

extensor branch of suspensory ligament

superficial digital flexor tendon

deep digital flexor tendon

This illustration combines the internal skeletal structures of the foreleg with the location of the tendons and ligaments. This clearly shows how many different locations for trouble there are in the anatomy of a horse. It is also important to understand the size and significance of the suspensory ligament which clearly encases most of the ankle joint and gives that area the support and strength to absorb repeated pounding on the track.

where the splint bone protrudes away from the cannon bone, and such tears can be painful and irritating. This is not as common nor as serious as tears at the site of the division of the suspensory ligament or in one of the branches around the ankle. In such cases, the sesamoid bones often are involved, and the area is very slow to heal due to the compromised blood supply and the constant flexing of the ankle joint with every stride.

Slow healing of the suspensory ligament is further complicated by the fact that the elastic-tissue properties of the ligaments and tendons are lost during healing and replaced by scar tissue. The healed tissue never has the same resilience and elasticity as it did before the injury.

The high suspensory area where it attaches behind the knee can be a very difficult area to deal with as the check ligament is also in this area. This is a very important area and sometimes can cause a real problem in separating this area from the knee itself when lameness is involved. I will go into more detail about this when discussing the hind leg high suspensory area later in this chapter.

BOWED TENDONS:

There is obvious heat, pain and swelling of the affected area which is easily discernible when a tendon bows. Both the deep and superficial flexor tendons are prone to injury due to the forces acting on the leg at greater speeds. They can tear anywhere along the back of the shin. Accordingly, they are termed either a "high bow" or a "low bow."

A low bow occurs near the ankle and a high bow manifests itself below the knee. Both involve serious structural damage that demands immediate and careful attention and can be career-ending injuries.

Tendon damage usually results from severe strain due to excessive loading or over-stretching. Inadequate conditioning and muscle fatigue contribute to over-loading. Horses with poor conformation, particularly those who are back at the knees, suffer a lot of tendon problems. A horse with a very light leg but heavy body can also be predisposed to tendon trouble since his legs will be subjected to more stress than they can handle.

Horses with long, sloping pasterns are favored by prospective owners because such horses are known to be fast. However, a long pastern is also conducive to bowed tendons because of the extra stress-loading on the long pastern area. This is especially true if the horse's toes are kept long.

In my opinion, a lot of tendon problems are also secondary to hock soreness. A horse with tendon trouble in the right front leg should also have its left hock examined, as a sore hock causes the horse to push off of the hock quickly and land very hard on the opposite foreleg.

Tendon injuries are serious and difficult to manage because the horse uses the tendons whenever he moves. Any swelling or change in the appearance of the tendons needs to be addressed quickly, because the

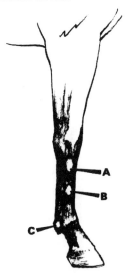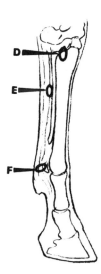

The drawing (left) shows an external look at the leg and has indicated where two splints (A & B) are present. These splints are on the front of the shin bone and are not likely to cause problems. The drawing on the right represents locations of splints in definite trouble areas. D is a knee splint and will interfere with the action of the knee joint. E is located on the back side of the shin bone and will rub and aggravate the suspensory ligament. Sesamoid trouble is indicated by a bulge at the rear of the ankle (left, C and right, F). This is almost a certain sign of sesamoid and/or suspensory damage.

damage is irreparable and the horse will have compromised his ability to a large degree.

There are some horses who return to racing after having bowed tendons, but these cases are rare and you will nearly always find that the horse has bowed both front legs. A horse playing on the track or in a stall can also hit a tendon with another foot and ultimately end up with a bowed tendon. This type of injury to the tendon will usually respond to treatment better than those tendon injuries caused by stress.

SPLINTS:

The term "splint" is used to described a localized swelling due to new bone production on the medial side (inside part) or, less frequently, the lateral (outside part) of the cannon bone or upper splint bone area. The condition is primarily seen in young horses, and the cause in many cases is the conformation of the legs, particularly in respect to the relationship between the cannon bone and the knee.

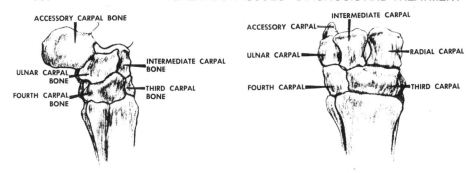

The complicated structure of the knee joint is shown in these two illustra-
tions. The drawing on the left is the side view of the knee and on the right,
is the front view. Knee joint lameness is often recognized by the presence of
swelling and heat from increased blood flow, due to inflamation in this
area.

When conformation is closely tied to genetics, splints may be common
to some lines. For example, the offspring of Super Bowl—one of the top
trotting sires in history—have splints as a standard part of their anatomy
when they are yearlings. I have also heard that splints can occur when
young horses stomp the hard summer ground during fly season.

Diagnosing of splint trouble is usually easy due to the splints being
actually visible, and there may be little or no lameness. The most obvious sign is localized swelling on the medial side of the foreleg below the
knee. Splints may sometimes occur on the hind limbs, but since most of
the weight and stress is on the forelimbs, the latter are more frequently
the sites of the problem.

Once new bone formation has occurred and settled down, splints seldom cause the horse any problems apart from their being a cosmetic
blemish.

EXAMINATION FOR LAMENESS IN THE KNEE AND SHOULDER AREAS

KNEES:

Next to be examined are the knees, and I first run my hands over the
front of the knees to feel for heat and or swelling in the joints. The knee
is the easiest joint in which to feel the presence of heat. Any heat or
distention of the knee joints are an obvious indication of inflammation.
To determine how much the joint is bothering the horse, I apply pressure to the medial splint bone under the knee, more or less pulling it
away from the cannon bone. If you gently pull the top of the inside splint
bone, with the leg off the ground and flexed, and it is painful to the
horse, this consistently indicates soreness in the knee joint.

The theory behind this test is that when a horse has knee soreness,
he won't break over straight and will move with a rolling gait, bringing
the limb in an arc to the outside to avoid bending the knee joint. This

causes the horse to land on the inside of his foot, which soon jars all the structures on the inside of his foot and lower leg. Such concussion causes soreness in the ligament or attachment between the inside splint bone and the cannon bone.

I will also bend the knee up and feel the range of motion, and see how the horse resists to having the joint flexed.

The knee joint is a major cause of lameness in racehorses, because it is prone to over-and hyper-extension during fast exercise. For this reason, it is important that a horse not have "back at the knee" conformation, because that further predisposes it to knee soreness.

Knee lameness is almost always progressive, beginning with minor irritation and swelling. X-rays are important to determine the extent of the problem. A large percentage of sore knees in young horses is due to bruised articular cartilage that is still soft due to immaturity.

SHOULDER:
Going up the foreleg, the next area likely to cause problems is the shoulder. Shoulder lameness, however, is invariably a secondary lameness. The shoulder muscles become sore and over-used because the horse is trying to compensate for a primary lameness elsewhere—either a primary lameness in the foot or knee in front, or a primary lameness behind on the same or opposite side as the shoulder problem. With shoulder soreness the muscles of the area will feel tight and painful and the horse's gait is often quite restricted. While shoulder soreness may be secondary, it still must be addressed as it will not clear up quickly if left alone. Most importantly, however, the primary source of the problem must be identified and dealt with.

EXAMINATION FOR LAMENESS IN THE BACK, RUMP, HIPS, WHIRLBONE, AND CROUP AREAS:
I then check the withers and girth area to determine if there is any soreness caused by the horse's equipment before going to the right foreleg and then repeating the examination process described above.

When examining the back I pay attention to the mid-back, lumbar and sacral areas. I am of the opinion that soreness over the mid-back area—revealed by applying gentle pressure to the area which causes the horse to squat—is associated with sore front feet.

Many horses are quite sensitive over this region and you need to be sure you are not getting a false impression by "goosing" the horse. I usually massage the back a little to desensitize the horse. Then if he still shows pain in response to firm, gentle pressure, I conclude he is possibly sore in his front feet.

In this part of the examination it is important that the horse is comfortable with you; otherwise, the response will not be accurate.

It seems that mid-back soreness is related to front feet soreness as a

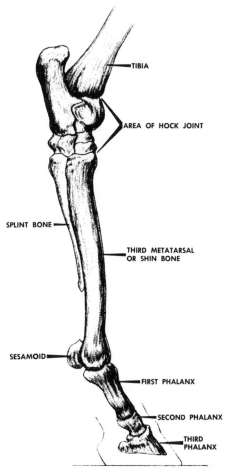

TIBIA

AREA OF HOCK JOINT

SPLINT BONE

THIRD METATARSAL
OR SHIN BONE

SESAMOID

FIRST PHALANX

SECOND PHALANX

THIRD
PHALANX

This illustration depicts and identifies the skeletal structure of the hind leg.

result of the horse trying to get its hind feet up underneath itself to take the weight off its front feet. This strains and over-uses the long muscles along each side of the backbone.

I then move to an examination of the large muscles over the rump and points of the hips. These are the gluteals, the powerful driving muscles of the hindquarters.

Interestingly, I believe Dr. Churchill was the first one to point out that strains and tears can occur in the gluteal region and may be very painful and cause lameness. This problem is seen frequently and sometimes can be difficult to diagnose.

Lameness involving the hind limbs in the Standardbred occurs with as much frequency and is just as important and sometimes more important than lameness involving the front limbs. Generally, all the problems discussed relative to the foot, pastern, ankle, suspensory ligament, and tendons also can occur in the hind limbs because the anatomy of the lower leg is the same in all four legs.

The hindquarters are a critical area for any racehorse since the large groups of muscles over the back, in conjunction with the stifle and hock, provide the horse's propulsion. Going back to the automobile analogy, the horse's heart may be thought of as the equivalent of the motor, while the hindquarters are the drive-shaft giving the power to push the horse forward down the track.

I examine the hindquarters by careful palpation to find evidence of soreness. This takes experience because there is a right way and a wrong way to elicit a pain response from a sensitive patient, and it is important to keep the horse relaxed and not overly reactive. I also will stand behind the horse to check to see if one hip is lower than the other and if both large muscle masses over the rump are even.

Dr. Churchill was of the opinion, with which I wholeheartedly agree, that if a horse has soreness in certain areas of the rump, hip and whirlbone areas, it is often secondary to soreness originating in the lower part of the hind leg. The horse will use its muscles differently if it is trying to protect another area. If I find soreness in the gluteal or large rump muscles, I must also be suspicious of the hock on the opposite side.

When the hock is sore, the horse does not like to flex it, and will shorten its stride on the sore side. In doing so, he takes a longer, deeper stride on his good side and consequently strains and stretches the gluteal (rump) muscle, ultimately damaging its deep, tendinous attachments.

I have also found that when the rump muscles over the point of the hips are sore, many times it can be associated with stifle lameness due to the horse carrying the limb differently. The bony area behind the hip is commonly referred to as the whirlbone, but is not a joint and simply serves as a point where muscles attach. Soreness in this area is often associated with hock lameness.

While checking the muscles over the croup and back I also will feel how much strength and resistance is in the tail. I take the head of the tail into my hand and gently feel the tail's muscle tone by pushing it through its range of motion. I have recently seen a marked increase in the incidence of equine protozoal myeloencephalitis [EPM] which is a slowly progressive and very debilitating disease involving the spinal cord. EPM may not be recognized initially for what it is, and could be confused with hind-leg lameness. When all else checks out normally, a decrease in tail tone seems to be a finding fairly consistent with EPM, but the disease may only be conclusively diagnosed by testing the blood and the spinal fluid.

EXAMINATION FOR LAMENESS IN THE HIND LIMB:
As I progress with the physical examination of the hind limbs, I start

first with the left hind leg, then move to the right hind leg.

One of the most overlooked areas in hind-limb lameness is the hind feet. Trainers often overlook the fact that hind feet are just as susceptible to problems as front feet. They can become bruised, have quarter cracks, corns, or gravel. Having assessed this area, I then check the shoeing and general health of the hoof and look for any signs of interference from gait around the coronet and pastern.

I also apply pressure to the bulbs of the heels and pay attention to how the coffin joint feels when I rotate it. At this time I also closely examine the pastern and fetlock joints, looking for any signs of thickening of the joint capsule, or filling in the joint itself.

In recent times, much more attention has been given to looking for problems in the hind fetlocks, and treating them. Certainly, problems can exist there and, whether the problems are secondary to foot problems or from catching weight due to front leg problems, the horses— especially trotters— seem to improve with treatment.

SPECIFIC CAUSES OF LAMENESS IN THE HIND LIMB
BRUISED SHINS:

This problem is observed most frequently in trotters when they hit their hind shins with their front feet. It is rarely a problem with pacers because pacers are laterally gaited. When the condition occurs, it may be due to the horse being poorly gaited or most likely because it is favoring one leg and striding long and deep with the other.

With an asymmetrical long stride on one side, either due to front-leg or rear-leg soreness, the horse hits its hind shin with the front leg. Since the bone has no covering other than skin in this area, such trauma and bruising cause considerable pain as a consequence.

Therefore, as soon as a horse starts hitting its shins, prompt measures should be taken to investigate and correct the cause of the problem.

CHECK LIGAMENT - HIGH SUSPENSORY:

The area just below the hock, as the area just below the knee as I stated earlier, is probably in my opinion, one of, if not the most difficult areas to determine why a horse is lame and what to do about it. This is because these areas have the upper portion of the suspensory and the check ligament located here.

When a tear occurs in the high suspensory area and/or check ligament, many times there is no swelling or heat in the area. The horse appears to be lame in the knee or hock because he does not flex the joint. Careful examination and diagnostic nerve blocks, plus the now widespread use of diagnostic ultrasound in veterinary medicine, is necessary to make an accurate diagnosis.

Many times there is some heat and swelling in the knee or hock and

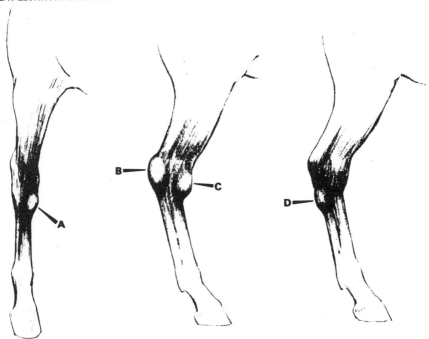

This series of illustrations of a hind limb depicts several different types of skeletal problems associated with rear leg lameness. Drawing A shows the presence of a bone spavin. The middle drawing depicts the presence of a capped hock (B) at the top of the hock joint, and a bog spavin (C) at the bottom and front of the joint. The drawing on the right shows the presence of a curb (D) just below and at the rear of the hock joint.

because of the way the horse travels, it is very easy to diagnose as a knee or hock lameness. When you block the lower joint of the knee or hock the horse will usually become sound because the drug used to block or freeze the joint will penetrate the joint capsule and also desensitizes the surrounding tissues—in this case, the high suspensory or the check ligament areas. This can obviously be misleading when the patient becomes sound by blocking the affected joint. The next thing to do is to radiograph or X-ray the area. With problems in the high suspensory area the X-rays of the knee will be clear. Thus you have the horse becoming sound when you block the joint, you have X-rays that are clean so the next step, many times is either inject the joint or paint the joint with a counterirritant. In both cases, you will get virtually no response and can become quite frustrated. Unfortunately, with always looking to keep a racehorse on schedule, this is one lameness diagnosis that ends up, many times, being done by the process of elimination. Once you analyze your mistaken knee or hock diagnosis, you start over and block the high suspen-

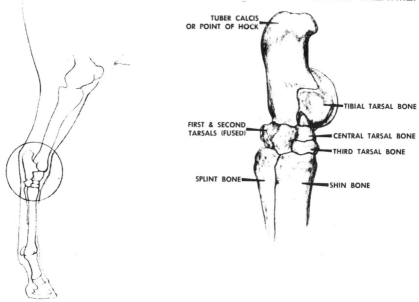

These drawings show an enlarged skeletal view of the hock joint. Note the complex nature of the hock joint, a troublesome area for a horse whose gait requires significant push and drive from the rear legs.

sory area without going into the joint. If the horse travels sound you can usually confirm the tear in the high suspensory area with an ultrasound examination.

This is a serious injury and many times can be the result of overloading one side by making a break at high speeds, getting a leg caught in a feed tub or water bucket or traveling over a rough and rolling surface.

CURBS:

The term curb is used to describe the tearing or rupture of the large ligament that stabilizes the back of the hock joint, and is situated at the level of the chestnut on the back of the hock. Diagnosis is easy, as the bulging and swelling in this area is prominent. A curb is a significant injury and source of pain. Frequently seen in two- and three-year-olds in hard training, a curb will make them bear out or away from the pain.

Weak conformation behind also can cause excessive strain on this area, particularly with horses who have sickle hocks and cow hocks. Curbs also can result from a horse rearing up and slipping, as well as from kicking a stall wall.

In my opinion, when curbs occur in young horses, they often are the result of the knees being sore, causing the horse to get underneath himself to protect the front-end soreness.

Depending on the degree of damage to this ligament, it may or may not be a long-term problem as it relates to the overall soundness of the horse. Many times swelling in the curb area will subside by correcting the forelimb soreness.

HOCK LAMENESS:

Other than the feet, the hock is probably the most important structure in the racehorse. It is a complex joint, comparable to the ankle of a human, and is an area of enormous torque in a horse traveling at full speed. The hock is the pivotal part of the hindquarters that propels the horse forward at speed and, as such, is a point where the power of the huge muscles of the rump is transferred down the leg to drive it forward from the track.

Therefore, it is a great disadvantage for a horse to be poorly conformed or to have soreness in the hock.

SPAVIN:

The hock joint itself is complex and involves two rows of bones above the cannon bone. There is little movement between these bones that are all bound together by ligaments. However, the individual joints between the bones are subject to damage from stress and degenerative joint disease.

Most commonly, bone spavin affects the bottom two joints of the hock and is seen as a bony proliferation on the inside of the leg just below the chestnut where the splint bone attaches to the bottom of the hock. This area, in my opinion, causes the most soreness in the Standardbred racehorse.

A bog spavin is the term used to describe distention of the joint capsule and is evidenced by a prominent swelling on the front of the hock. A jack spavin is the most chronic condition progressing from a bone spavin, where the joints on the inside of the hock actually fuse, with obvious bony enlargement on the inside of the joint. At this stage, there may be less pain, but sharply reduced mobility of the joint.

Spavins have an insidious onset, and initially lameness may be intermittent and disappear with rest.

Similar in a way to the process for determining knee soreness in front, there usually is pain upon palpation of the medial splint bone inside and below the hock joint.

When a horse is troubled by a sore hock, he will bring the hock inwards in an arc to avoid flexing it and will land more heavily on the toe and inside of his hind foot. This jams and jars the medial splint, pulling the interosseous ligament that joins the splint bone to the cannon bone. When the horse is relaxed, a draw-forward pressure on the splint bone will cause the horse to pick up its leg in a pain reflex, a classical indication of hock soreness.

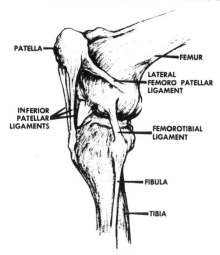

This drawing illustrates the main ligaments of the rear leg, showing how the bones of the hind limbs are connected by fibrous ligaments.

Due to the complexity of the joint and variance in degrees of lameness, the hock usually requires clinical assessment, as it is a primary source of lameness in the Standardbred and a main area of concern. A horse with hock problems will suffer impaired performance, and compensatory soreness in the large back and hind-quarter muscles and the whirlbone area.

OCD (Osteochondritis Dissecans):
This is a medical term for a condition affecting young, growing horses that involves a disturbance in the maturing of the cartilage layers. It occurs most commonly in the hocks, but is also seen in the stifle, shoulder and fetlock joints. There usually is swelling of the affected joint and varying in degree of lameness from none to obvious. Major factors that seem to predispose an animal to OCD include rapid growth and nutritional excesses. There also is a genetic tendency in some pedigrees.

STIFLE LAMENESS:
The stifle joint is one of the largest joints, having a large area of articular surface and numerous ligaments, some of which are very long. As a result, ligament problems are the principal sources of difficulty when lameness occurs.
The stifle is equivalent to the human knee. It has a patella, or knee-cap, which slides up and down in a deep groove in the femur and allows the large muscles above to extend the leg, thus participating in the pow-

One of the most effective ways to reduce rear-end lameness in the muscles is to strengthen the physique by the use of a "power cart" as seen here. First developed in Scandinavia, the power cart employs the principle of light drag and resistance to strengthen rear-end muscles.

erful thrust that produces forward propulsion.

The patella is stabilized in its groove by three large patellar ligaments. These form part of a locking system that also enables the horse to remain standing with a minimum of muscular effort while resting the other hind leg.

However, in certain situations where the horse is poorly conformed in the stifles, or is immature and unfit, the medial patella ligament may cause the stifle joint to lock in extension, a condition called "upward fixation of the patella."

This is seen quite commonly in young Standardbreds, and may occur in one or both hind limbs. It may be rectified by conditioning and strengthening the stifle ligaments. If not, surgery is the treatment of choice.

Except on its front surface, the stifle joint is surrounded by heavy muscle and its strength and efficiency is directly related to the state of these muscles. Certainly, the greatest cause of stifle lameness is inadequate conditioning, because the design of the joint alone makes it very susceptible to partially torn or strained ligaments.

To build up the stifle muscles adequately the horse needs to be exercised using enough pull and drag on the hind leg to really work the muscles. This can be achieved by work on soft ground, up hills, or by the use of a "power cart," first developed in Scandinavia, which creates resistance against the horse pulling it. All are beneficial in helping to build up stifles.

Strains on the stifle ligaments can also be induced by the horse slipping on a track that is breaking away, or when the horse's foot stops too quickly after impact. A horse with stifle lameness will swing his leg in an unnatural, outward arc to avoid flexing the sore joint. And, since it is easier for a horse to trot rather than pace with a sore stifle, the horse may be difficult to gait.

I usually check for filling in the joint, but a helpful diagnostic symptom of stifle soreness is associated soreness in the rump muscles between the point of the hip and the backbone. This is due to the horse's compensating for the joint soreness by carrying its back in a very stiff, rigid position. It is a secondary result of the primary problem—a recurring theme in all lameness, as we have discussed previously.

After completion of the entire physical examination with the horse at rest, the next step is to harness the horse up, take him out on the track and observe how he travels in his work.

EXAMINATION OF THE HORSE WORKING ON THE RACETRACK:

The observation of the horse in motion is an important part of the diagnostic process because it can be used to confirm or disprove the findings of the physical examination done with the horse at rest. During the physical examination, I often find myself feeling that a problem is developing in a certain area, but then determine that the primary trouble may lie in a different area after seeing the horse in motion.

The correct diagnosis of lameness in the Standardbred is often complex and difficult, and it is not always possible—even for someone with considerable experience—to determine the exact trouble spot at first glance. An acutely lame horse, "carrying" a leg or nodding badly, is an easy one to diagnose. The diagnostic difficulties begin when the horse is sore, but not visibly lame.

A lot of horses warm out of their soreness in the early stages of the problem. A horse may jog stiffly at first, but become sounder after going a few miles. This usually is a sign of a degenerative kind of soreness, such as knee and/or hock trouble. The trainer may find that, as training progresses, the distance required to "thaw out the horse" becomes greater and greater as the soreness becomes more advanced.

Another part of the difficulty with visual diagnosis is the willing nature of the Standardbred horse. A great many high-level horses are very game and will not show you where they hurt. They just race with diminished capacity.

I recall when Merger was a three-year-old and not racing well at the midpoint of the season, despite being a world champion two-year-old. His driver, John Campbell, became frustrated trying to figure out what was wrong, because the horse drove straight on the bit and gave no indication of any lameness, other than his performance was unusually poor.

After Merger began making breaks, we finally determined that perhaps his hocks were bothering him. I injected his hocks a few weeks before the Little Brown Jug. Merger was his old self again and went on to win the Jug convincingly. This incident is a good example of the courage of the Standardbred horse and how it will continue to perform with pain.

On the track, I usually like to see the horse work with a minimum of equipment so I can watch how he travels. Horses, like humans, don't enjoy pain and try to get away from it. As the painful side hits the ground, a horse will usually try to throw its body away from that side. A horse hurting on the left side will usually bear to the right, or out, and vice versa.

Initially, I try to take in the general picture the horse is presenting and what its feelings are in relation to what it is doing. Is it aggravated, or anxious about its work, or does it act as though it doesn't care? I notice how the horse prefers to carry its head, whether its back is stiff and how it holds its tail. Normally, if a horse carries its tail either cocked or raised during exercise, this is a good clue that there is some soreness in the hindquarters.

How the horse prefers to carry its head also is a reliable indicator of where it is trying to direct its body and, therefore, where it might be experiencing pain. When a horse tries to carry its head down, and tightens its overcheck in doing so, it is usually sore somewhere in the hindquarters. When a horse travels with its head turned in toward the rail and pulls on the inside or the left line, it is having difficulty extending its inside or left side. If it is bearing in, with its head turned out and pulling on the right line, it is trying to get off its right side. A general rule of thumb is that a horse will always run away from pain.

Similarly, how the horse places itself in the shafts will tell you which hind leg it is trying to avoid using. For example, if it is over on the right shaft, it is trying to protect its left hind leg, and vice versa. Never forget that a horse may be lame in the back and front legs at the same time.

After noting the general picture, I concentrate on looking at the front legs and hind legs, without attempting to look at the entire horse at once. I observe the front legs from the shoulder down, and the back legs from the stifles down. I carefully evaluate stride length, the way each leg moves in stride and how the foot impacts the ground.

Horses can be gaited differently depending on their natural way of going. Some horses hit the ground very hard, heel first, and others hit flat and slide. You can tell by watching the good leg, and by being familiar with the horse, what is normal for that horse and what is not.

Generally, it is not normal for a horse to hit the ground toe first. This abnormality is easy to spot on a dirt track because the foot kicks up a spray of dirt in front as it strikes. If the horse is hitting toe first, he is trying to guard the back of his leg or the heel area.

Heel pain has a number of causes, and pain in the back of the leg could be from anywhere—from the pastern and sesamoids up through the suspensory and tendons. Also, the foot will land toe first if the horse is having trouble extending the leg due to a painful knee or shoulder.

A horse with a sore knee also has a rather characteristic rolling, or "swimmy" gait as it attempts to bring the knee forward without bending it properly. It carries the affected leg away from its body, swinging the leg in an outward arc as though trying to straddle something. In the initial stages of knee lameness this action may be obvious only when the horse first steps out of the stall. But as the lameness advances, the horse is slower to warm out of it until the lameness eventually shows in all of its training miles.

Similarly, the horse with a sore hock will be hitting the ground toe first and carrying the leg in an unusual arc. Once again, this is due to the horse trying to guard its sore hock by not bending it as the horse strides. The foot flight usually arcs inward and the horse will try to carry its hindquarters towards the shaft on the opposite side from the sore hock.

It is possible, if you watch closely, to differentiate between hock lameness and stifle lameness. With hock lameness, the horse swings the affected leg inwards; with stifle lameness, it will swing the leg outwards. When a horse is trying to avoid flexing the stifle it carries the leg stiffly and away from its body and does not land on the toe.

Any doubt as to how a horse is using its legs can be confirmed by closely watching how the horse wears its shoes. This information is evidence as to how the foot is being used and will correlate with other problems further up the leg.

Horses are always communicating to the astute trainer when they are not right. Soreness and gait irregularities long precede mechanical breakdown. Many times, if the sore area is diagnosed and treated in the early stages, a promising racing career can be preserved. Once the visual physical examination has been completed with the horse at rest and then at work, there are a number of clinical techniques available to further assess and confirm the diagnosis.

CLINICAL TESTS FOR LAMENESS DIAGNOSIS:
Diagnosing lameness in the racing Standardbred is a bit like putting together a jigsaw puzzle. What we can see and feel in the horse is an important part of the picture, and the other part is what we can confirm by various clinical tests.

Since Dr. Churchill's day there have been substantial improvements in technology, and we have diagnostic tools today with enormous capabilities. Such sophisticated tools as ultrasound and nuclear scintigraphy are regularly being used to make a diagnosis or confirm one made after a thorough physical examination. In the not too distant future magnetic resonance imaging (MRI) will be another important diagnostic tool available to the veterinary profession. Considering the economics of racing horses today, the question is not always just where the horse is lame or sore, but how do we correct it.

I personally feel that some of the advances that have been made in the diagnosis of lameness only amplifies the need for additional research into methods of treatment for the various conditions that cause lameness. However, before we go on to the important issue of treatment, I will describe the various techniques for clinical testing of lameness that we have available today.

FLEXION TESTS:
I personally do not use flexion tests. However, many veterinarians and horse trainers do use them and have proven the use of the test to be beneficial.

Basically, a flexion test involves flexing or bending a joint for a period of time, then letting the horse step off at a trot. The response is graded on a score of 1-5 as to how lame the horse goes in those first few steps.

DIAGNOSTIC NERVE BLOCKS:
These can be a useful tool for confirming a diagnosis made after a physical examination. The procedure involves infiltrating local anesthetic around specific points along the nerve to prevent the flow of nerve impulses to the area below the blocking. Since pain is perceived in the brain via nerve impulses, numbing or freezing of the area should allow the horse to move more comfortably—and the site of the lameness is localized.

The level of the nerve block starts at the lowest point in the nerve supply to the limb. For example, a mid-pastern block is usually carried out to desensitize the heel of the hoof and, if the horse trots out sound, this may confirm a diagnosis of navicular disease or one of the other causes of heel pain. A block behind the sesamoids abolishes the sensation to the hoof and front of the pastern. A mid-cannon block localizes fetlock and sesamoid injuries. There is a similar block for the knees and hocks.

A series of nerve blocks can provide conclusive evidence of the source of pain. I must caution, however, that a horse should not be allowed to go fast when blocked, as it is very easy to fracture a weakened bone that is suddenly free of pain.

X-RAYS(RADIOGRAPHS):
The use of X-rays is most valuable in assessing the condition of internal bone changes, such as the condition of joints and the presence of chips and fractures. In my opinion, X-rays are not, in themselves, a diagnostic tool. They may yield nothing in the way of diagnostic information other than a range of things that may be potential causes. Therefore, it is very important that X-rays are interpreted only in the context of a thorough physical exam, along with the horse's racing history. A set of radiographs on its own is virtually meaningless, as is the other approach of "Let's X-ray the whole leg and see what's wrong." I think it is quite

impossible to make a judgement on the soundness or unsoundness of a horse based on a set of X-rays alone, short of an obvious fracture.

Sometimes a horse will have certain structural problems or damage that he has learned to live with and is racing with. A study of this horse's last few races in relation to his whole performance history, plus the findings of the physical exam, may prove that the particular defect is not bothering him.

One of the stories which I repeatedly tell is about Mack Lobell. As a two-year-old, Mack Lobell would get on the left line and bear out, and no one was sure if it was due to mental resistance or pain because he was a little dilatory. At age two, Mack was subjected to a pre-purchase examination, which he passed with flying colors. However, the vet at that time did not X-ray Mack's hind ankles because there appeared to be no indication of a need for this.

The horse had a brilliant two-year-old career and an equally brilliant three-year-old career, winning two consecutive Breeders Crowns and the Hambletonian. In May of his four-year-old season he was shipped to Stockholm, Sweden, to compete in the Elitlopp, one of the premier trotting events in Scandinavia.

Concurrently, a sale of Mack Lobell to Swedish interests was being negotiated. As part of the examination for sale and for entry into the Swedish Stud Registry, radiographs of all four fetlocks were required. I happened to be present at the time this was done and was shocked to see—on the radiographs of the left hind fetlock— a large, old, chip fracture or OCD of the long pastern bone, easily as big as my thumb!

Had this chip been discovered when the horse was a two-year-old, every time something went wrong on the left side we would have blamed that fracture or would have operated to remove it. Since no one knew it was there, no one worried about it and, for history's sake, the horse went on to win all those important races and is considered by many to be the best trotter that ever raced.

Bill Haughton used to tell me, "Never X-ray a horse unless he is lame, because you are going to see things on the X-rays that will prejudice your feeling about how the horse is performing." When you see spurs and chips you may develop a mental block about them while watching the horse. Yet they may never actually correlate with an effect on the horse's performance or function.

Horses have different levels of pain tolerance, and what may stop one horse from trying may not affect another one. If you have a preconceived idea based on what was on an X-ray, you may overlook other problems that are truly significant. I do not think, therefore, that X-raying the whole leg to see what is wrong is prudent veterinary medicine.

ADVANCED DIAGNOSTIC TECHNOLOGY ULTRASOUND:
Ultrasonic scanning is becoming widely used to assess tendon, sus-

pensory-ligament and other soft-tissue injuries. It provides an internal image of the tissue structure and the extent of the damaged fibers. The damage is seen on the scan as a "black-hole" where the tissue is inflamed and the internal fibers are torn. An individual assessment, treatment, and management schedule can be planned from the results of the scans.

Sometimes the degree of swelling and lameness does not correlate with the amount of actual tissue damage. An ultrasound scan is a good tool with which to assess the time required for the horse to return to racing.

Experience is needed on the part of the operator to make accurate predictions on the findings of an ultrasound scan. It is a specialized piece of equipment and, usually, only as effective as the skill of the person using it.

NUCLEAR SCINTIGRAPHY (BONE SCANNING):

This technique is new, somewhat expensive, and limited at present to a few clinics because it is so specialized. It has been developed from human nuclear medical diagnostic imaging. It involves injecting a safe radioactive isotope intravenously and then measuring how much of the isotope is taken up by the bones and tissues.

Because the radioactive isotope is in the blood, it will be deposited more intensely in areas with increased blood supply or inflammation, or in areas of the bone where there is high bone turnover, indicating a lot of stress.

The suspected area is scanned at specific time intervals after the injection of the radioactive indicator. If it can be justified, the use of scintigraphy can be an advantage over the use of X-rays and ultrasound because it will give information on stress fractures in bones which normally do not show up with other equipment. Scintigraphy is also beneficial when there are several problem areas and it is hard to determine which area is causing the most pain. However, as in X-rays, interpretation of the results is the key.

MAGNETIC RESONANCE IMAGING (MRI):

This is an extremely advanced and expensive technique borrowed from human sports medicine and seen only in a few privileged university clinics. The technique relies on the properties of the cells, after magnetic excitation, to return a detection signal which is imaged by this specialized equipment. Thus, it allows an image to be formed of all the soft-tissue layers in cross section and is, therefore, perhaps the superior diagnostic tool.

MRI enables perfect visualization of all the anatomical structures and their associated pathology, along with the differences in circulation and degree of abnormality. As this piece of equipment makes its presence felt in the veterinary profession, it is sure to shed some new light on how various lamenesses develop.

TREATMENT OF LAMENESS:

Before beginning the discussion on treatment, I would stress that the best way to treat lameness is to prevent it in the first place. Soreness will be present long before there is mechanical breakdown. A vigilant trainer in the habit of feeling his horse's legs all of the time will immediately detect the abnormality. Every morning before exercise, the legs should be checked for heat or filling and the feet should be inspected. The trainer must get to know each horse, how he goes, and where he may have potential trouble, being alert to anything indicating undue stress on one part of the body. If the problem is detected early, it may be attended to and corrected and not allowed to get out of hand and cause eventual lameness.

A team approach to training horses should take advantage of all the information available from all who have contact with the horse, including the trainer, caretaker, driver, veterinarian, and blacksmith. An observant caretaker can alert the trainer to any subtle changes in the horse and, even when the legs feel good and all seems normal, the driver may say, "Up until this week he always drove straight, but this week he's on one line a little." A close examination may reveal early symptoms of a problem that can be addressed before the damage is irreversible.

However, we are still faced with the difficulty that diagnosis of the problem is one thing, but treatment and management to keep the horse a viable racing prospect may be difficult. Obviously, since Dr. Churchill's day, we have more treatment options just as we have more sophisticated diagnostic tools. Not everything is new, however. Some of the treatment regimens still in use, such as blistering and firing, have been around for a century or more, and others, such as acupuncture, are being revived from ancient history.

In my opinion, some new directions in treatment are going to evolve, because with fewer horses being bred and registered, there will be more pressure on them to have longer racing careers.

In determining a treatment program the veterinarian must consider the best interests of the horse, as well as confer with the owner and trainer. Obviously, time and rest are always safe options and, with some injuries such as fractures, the horse himself will determine the time frame after either surgery or stall rest. However, the fine art of treatment is knowing what is necessary to keep the equine athlete going from week to week and race to race without compromising his overall racing career.

Everyone understands that fractures and serious soft-tissue injuries, such as those involving tendons and suspensories, need prolonged rest periods. This is very straightforward. What is not so straightforward is the management of these injuries when the horse returns to racing, and the management of the myriad of lesser injuries that can affect the horse and cause poor performance. Since the costs of training a good performer are the same as the costs of training a poor performer, it is in the interests of the business efficiency of the racing industry that our techniques of treatment produce results. Therefore, in this section, I would like to focus on treatment programs that keep in mind the best interests of the horse and keep him racing.

SHOEING AND TREATING FOOT PROBLEMS:

Care of the feet and good shoeing are a major contribution to preserving the soundness of the horse and should be considered an absolute priority by every horse trainer. As all humans can appreciate, when your feet are sore you often feel sore all over. Especially when horses are racing on hard surfaces, such as rain-affected, scraped tracks, they may be very sore in the front feet the day after the race. Sore front feet can create sore ankles and sore hocks, so as a preventative approach to preserving the hocks, the front feet should be kept in good shape.

If you think this through from your own experience you know that if the outside or inside of your foot hurts, you don't like to land on it, so you start to put pressure on other parts of the leg and your ankle becomes sore. The same thing occurs in the horse, but the greatest amount of his body weight is carried over the forelegs, so if the feet do not land flat, the ankles will become sore very quickly. When this occurs, the gait symmetry changes as the horse tries to carry more weight over his back legs to keep weight off his forelegs, and the soreness transfers up the leg to the knees and hocks.

A good blacksmith is the key to preventing foot problems. If the foot is kept level, the sole kept concave, and the shoeing is balanced to the natural conformation of the horse's foot, the horse will land evenly on the hoof wall and not the sole. This will go a long way toward preventing bruises, corns, quarter cracks and contracted heels.

Maintaining frog pressure is another important aspect of good shoeing. When too much frog is trimmed out, there will be no frog pressure when the foot hits the ground, either in the stall or on the racetrack. In the majority of training situations the horse is only out of his stall for one hour each day, so how he stands on his feet in his stall for the other 23 hours is going to have a major influence on his body.

Frog pressure is essential to good circulation of all the internal structures of the foot, in particular, the fragile navicular bone. When the blood is pumped from the heart and down the leg, frog pressure is an important aid to venous pressure in maintaining circulation back up the leg and to the heart. If the system is sluggish due to decreased frog pressure, blood "pools" in the foot and the circulation is impaired. If the foot is subjected to any insults, such as concussion from a hard track, the

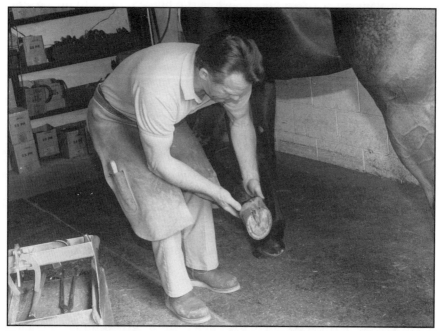

Experienced blacksmiths and horsemen can see if a horse has been trimmed level. If the foot is level, the sole kept concave and the shoeing balanced to the natural conformation of the horse, it will go a long way towards preventing foot problems such as bruises, corns, quarter cracks, and contracted heels.

defective circulation is unable to clear up the inflammation and cellular damage.

Very often, in this situation, the feet will feel cold, leading the trainer to think that the feet could not be hurting because they do not feel hot. In my opinion, cold feet with a barely detectable digital pulse are a definite indication of poor circulation, and the resulting soreness can be more pronounced than from "hot" feet.

If the track surfaces are known to be hard or the horse has shown signs of foot soreness, immediate attention to the feet after the race is beneficial; this attention can include tubbing with ice and/or "doing the feet up" in poultice. Further tubbing with warm water on subsequent days can be helpful to dilate the blood vessels and increase the circulation inside the foot. If cold water is used at this stage it only serves to constrict the blood vessels. It is also important not to neglect the hind feet as they too are subject to jarring on variable and hard surfaces, and the resultant bruises, corns, and gravel.

When the foot is affected with gravel, or a foot abscess, tubbing in hot water with a strong Epsom salts solution is an excellent method to draw out the infection. The foot should be soaked in the hot water solution for one-half hour to one hour, and once the gravel bursts, often near the coronary band, the area should be cleaned carefully and poulticed, and the lameness will subside rapidly.

This type of treatment, especially with hot and cold tubbing, is also an excellent remedy for bruises and corns, because it serves to not only increase blood supply, but also to induce healing and promote healthy growth of horn tissue.

The blacksmith should always trim out the damaged horn of the hoof and, if necessary, apply a supportive shoe or pads. Foot bruises and corns require constant attention and examination to keep them from worsening. There is a great range of products on the market now in the way of pads, dressings and remedial shoes with which professional blacksmiths will be familiar.

Before discussing treatment approaches for various joint and soft-tissue injuries, I would like to give the reader some background on the different treatment techniques available. As this is not intended to be a scientific paper, I will only discuss treatments that I have used and that have withstood the test of time, as well as some of the new, promising techniques. All veterinarians and trainers have their own favorite methods, and what is presented here is strictly my opinion and is based on my personal experience as both a trainer and a veterinarian.

HOT AND COLD TOPICAL TREATMENTS-LINIMENTS AND ICE PACKS:

Liniments contain substances that produce redness and heat by increasing circulation, and cold application—by ice packs or ice water—does the opposite by constricting the blood vessels and numbing the pain in the area. These are both useful, and there are a great range of products available on the market.

The principle to abide by in use of these products is, "When it's hot - go cold; when it's cold - go hot." For example, when the affected area, such as a troublesome joint, tendon or suspensory injury stays hot, cold application with ice boots or ice wraps is ideal for the first 24 - 48 hours. For the injury that is "cold," such as strained back and rump muscles, you want to introduce heat and "steam" to the muscles to increase circulation, which will relieve the stiffness and soreness.

Cold application, therefore, is useful only in the acute period of cooling off after the race or work-out.

The treatment period with the ice should not be too long (about 20 minutes is sufficient); otherwise, the tissues may be damaged by the cold. Wrapping the affected area firmly with supportive bandages after the treatment is also helpful to limit the amount of swelling that may result.

Heat-producing liniments have their effect by dilating the blood vessels to the area and increasing the blood flow. Their effects are enhanced by being massaged in, then covered in many cases. As the blood flow to the area is increased, it flushes out the enzymes and damaged cells that are the by-products of the inflammatory process. Heat also has the very important quality of providing comfort to the injury by reducing stiffness in the joints and muscle spasms in the soft tissues. This helps the horse regain normal range of motion and move more freely.

There are a number of substances that are combined in various formulas to make useful liniments. Camphor, oil of wintergreen (methyl salicylate), turpentine, menthol, rosemary oil, eucalyptus oil and alcohol are a few of these. Today many trainers combine them with DMSO, which helps the substance penetrate deeper in the tissue.

Wrapping the leg after massaging with the liniment is a common practice which must be carried out carefully in accordance with the nature of the liniment being applied, because some liniments can be very irritating to the skin, if covered. Most of these agents do not have a very sustained effect and need to be applied once or twice daily. The massaging and supportive bandaging can also enhance the results.

COUNTER-IRRITATION—LEG PAINTS, BLISTERS AND FIRING:

The practice of counter-irritation, either by applying paints that have a blistering effect or by firing with heat or liquid nitrogen (freeze-firing) to produce inflammation of the skin and subcutaneous tissues, relies on the principle of stimulating the inflammatory process. In a situation where there is a low-grade, inflammatory process occurring over a period of time, healing is delayed. The chronic inflammation simmers along, producing nagging discomfort, and occasionally flares-up with obvious swelling and lameness, depending on how hard the horse is training.

The action of counter-irritation turns this chronic inflammatory process into an acute one, which will subside more rapidly than a chronic one. Once the acute process has subsided, healing is usually completed with the formation of scar tissue. Due to the huge blood supply created in the area by the intense inflammation, the by-products of the chronic, low-grade irritation are flushed away and the tissue becomes firm as it heals by scarring.

Although these practices have successfully withstood the test of time and have been part of the experience of many long-time horse trainers, they have become controversial in modern times. Very few proper studies have ever been carried out to investigate the effectiveness of these practices, and most claim that it is the enforced time-off that cures the horse.

However, it has been my experience and my opinion that these methods, if properly applied, can be very valuable treatments.

Blisters may be applied either in a paint-on form or as a paste. Sometimes they are injected into muscles and soft tissues to produce an internal blistering effect, resulting in a greatly increased blood supply. Most blistering agents contain mercury and iodine and need to be handled carefully. They should be applied as directed onto the affected area, which should first be prepared by clipping off the hair and bordered by a protective coating of petroleum jelly. Care must be taken so the horse cannot lick or chew the area while the blistering agent is taking effect. Blisters are most useful for chronic joint and tendon problems and should never be placed near open wounds.

Firing, either with an electric hot iron or a freeze-branding iron, is a more severe form of counter-irritation than blistering. It produces intense inflammation, and the end result for that area is the formation of scar tissue.

MEDICATIONS—INTRA-ARTICULAR AND SYSTEMIC:

If the topical therapy alone is unsuccessful, then I will move on to incorporate the use of anti-inflammatory drugs, either intra-articularly or systemically. The use of these drugs is well established, both in human and in veterinary medicine, and is regulated by strict guidelines in the racing industry.

There are basically two main groups of anti-inflammatory drugs: the short-and long-acting corticosteroids (cortisone) and the nonsteroids.

The corticosteroids, which have cortisone as their primary agent, are powerful anti-inflammatory substances that decrease pain and swelling. Both the corticosteroids and the nonsteroids (NSAIDs) take effect on a cellular level by directly affecting the mechanisms of the inflammatory process.

All of these drugs have their purpose in treating soreness and other unsoundness conditions affecting a racehorse. But, like all drugs, their precise application should be selected carefully and incorporated into a well-planned strategy to manage the horse's racing program.

Anti-inflammatory agents may be given systemically, either by the oral route or by intramuscular or intravenous injection, or may be placed directly into the joint (intra-articular) or affected area. There are short-acting agents and long-acting agents, but a discussion of the large range of different anti-inflammatory drugs is outside the realm of this chapter.

The success of intra-articular therapy, one of the most favored treatments to keep horses racing, depends on the product being put in the correct place inside the joint capsule. With this procedure there is always the risk of introducing infection into the joint by a plug of hair or dirt being pushed in with the needle, especially if the operator is working in dusty or windy conditions. However, most veterinarians with experience in intra-articular injections develop a technique that incorporates good preparation and sterile equipment, and the risks are minimal.

Different practitioners will have their preference for combinations of drugs, which usually consist of either a straight, long-acting steroid, or in combination with hyaluronic acid. Hyaluronic acid is one of the newer developments in veterinary medicine over the last decade and is a component of the joint fluid which contributes to joint lubrication. Just as engine oil eases the frictional wear and tear on the moving parts of the piston engine, so hyaluronic acid "oils" stiff joints in the hard-working racehorse.

Hyaluronic acid preparations may be put directly into the joint, though some are given in a course of systemic injections either intravenously or intramuscularly. The substances circulate in the blood and are deposited where there is active inflammation. There are also some forms of a substance similar to hyaluronic acids, called glycosaminoglycans, which are made in a preparation that can be fed on a daily basis in the horse's feed. This is a particularly good product to feed to young racing horses as it helps their joint cartilage.

One of the primary causes of soreness in young horses is bruising of the joint cartilage due to the horse being immature. Often, young horses are asked to do far too much before their cartilage is mature and firm, as it would be in an older horse. Rest is obviously the most helpful solution; but, due to the purses offered for two- and three-year-olds, we do not often have time to rest them.

These oral supplements for cartilage strength are very popular and useful to help this situation. If there is a more severe problem with the joint I will choose to inject it with a hyaluronic acid preparation as well.

For intra-articular injections I often use a combination of hyaluronic acid with a small amount of corticosteroid. I feel that it is necessary to decrease the inflammation in the joint in order for the hyaluronic acid to work properly. Some types of products may cause transitory reaction swelling. My choice of drugs is made on the basis of the best interests of the horse on a long-term basis, and how long the injection will last in relation to the plans for the horse.

Many people are critical of corticosteroids being injected into joints. Some years ago, the general attitude was that they were taboo because they shortened the racing life of the horse. This line of thinking was prevalent at a time when most horses raced until they were nine or ten years old. Today, most Standardbreds have finished racing by the time they are six or seven years old, and the average age is actually about four years old.

My thoughts about corticosteroids are that they are still the very best anti-inflammatory agents available in medicine today. They are used widely by the medical profession as the primary intra-articular injection for humans and, when they are used properly, I don't think that they are detrimental to the joint of the horse.

I find the hyaluronic acid preparations work best in young horses with minimal calcification and stiffening of their joints; usually, those with articular cartilage damage. Older horses with lots of bony changes get better relief from corticosteroid injections.

It is prudent to evaluate troublesome joints with a good set of X-rays prior to commencing intra-articular therapy.

TREATING JOINT INJURIES:
As many trainers have seen, the joint of the horse can appear sore and the X-rays will be fine, or the X-rays will show some problem and the horse is not sore.

Most troublesome joints, such as knees and hocks, respond well to leg paints and blisters. However, if this type of therapy is not successful, the next step is to X-ray the joints and decide on an intra-articular injection or, perhaps, surgery, if there is a serious chip or fracture. I have seen many cases where horses with chips or sandy-type calcium deposits in their joints respond very well to having the joint flushed with saline solution prior to being injected. It is not a commonly used procedure, but it can be kept in mind for a horse with a bad joint that is stubborn and not responding well to intra-articular injections.

TREATING SOFT-TISSUE INJURIES:
Joint problems and most skeletal problems, such as fractures, have many treatment options in modern medicine. However, soft-tissue problems, such as those involving suspensories, tendons, and check ligaments, are all very hard to fix and very unpredictable to manage. This is because they heal slowly and the original elasticity is replaced by inelastic scar tissue that is never as resilient as the tissue was before the injury. Therefore, to continue a horse's racing career after such an injury, the trainer will have to be very careful how the horse is trained and raced. Although the horse may be able to go as fast as he did before, it may not be wise to race him at that level in case he over-extends himself. The healed ligaments and tendons are not as elastic.

In the initial stages of the soft-tissue soreness and swelling, the use of ice therapy and cold water after work is useful.

I have seen excellent results on curbs, splints, and some suspensory injuries with the use of freeze-firing. It seems that the liquid nitrogen, when it freezes the tissue, induces a star-burst effect of scar tissue. This not only interrupts the topical nerve supply, but the scar tissue fills in the tears in the original tissue.

Once there has been a major rupture of a tendon or ligament, diagnostic ultrasound is invaluable in assessing the extent of the damage and the prognosis for a return to the racetrack. There have been many techniques over the years, such as carbon fiber implants and tendon splitting, which attempt to repair ruptured tendons. Most have been unsuccessful because of the great difficulty in immobilizing the area on a horse's leg for the long period of time necessary for healing to occur. Every step the horse takes moves these vital supportive structures in the legs, and these types of injuries are really the ones that it pays to avoid by a dedicated preventative program rather than by trying to repair them after they have occurred. If a tendon, suspensory ligament or check ligament is torn, I like to markedly lower the angle of the foot while the injury is healing. By doing this, you are stretching the tendon or ligament as it is healing, so that when the horse is returned to training and/or racing, the soft tissue has some "give" to it when the angle of the foot is returned to normal.

TREATING MUSCLE SORENESS:
The muscle mass of the horse is the largest part of its body weight, and optimal muscle function is vital to every athletic endeavor. Secondary muscle soreness may be related to other primary problems and may form part of the overall picture of stiffness and lameness. However, some types of muscle soreness are related to muscle fatigue and, when serious, can lead to the development of the condition known as "tying up" syndrome.

This is most commonly seen in young, anxious fillies after a day or so of rest with full feed, and is closely associated with carbohydrate overload of the muscles. Electrolytes and hormonal imbalances, as well as genetic predisposition, are known to be other contributing factors in this complicated and difficult-to-manage condition. More exercise, muscle relaxants, mild tranquilizers and attention to diet and electrolyte supplementation are the main management strategies.

Uncomplicated muscle soreness can be relieved by the application of liniments and massage when the horse is hot after working. If the problem is persistent, sometimes the muscles—particularly back and rump muscles—respond to internal blistering with injections of iodine or steroids. Many of the physical therapies discussed in the next section are also very useful to relieve muscle soreness.

OTHER METHODS OF PHYSICAL THERAPY:
Physical therapy and rehabilitation of sports injuries in horses is a rapidly developing area, but it has been neglected previously compared to human sports medicine. Large sums of money often are spent on surgery for equine athletes and then followed up by very poor rehabilitation programs. A number of techniques are becoming more widely available that can assist with the recovery after injury and with the prevention of injury and improvement of well-being in the racehorse.

ACUPUNCTURE:
Acupuncture is a very old, very complex, and sometimes very effective system of medicine that was originally practiced in the Orient nearly 5000 years ago. It has an extremely well-documented history in the treatment of humans and horses. Horses in the ancient Orient were highly revered and carefully tended because of their value as work and war

vehicles, so the practice of equine acupuncture, indeed, has a long history compared to some other veterinary practices.

In modern times, acupuncture is becoming widely accepted in the horse business, mostly for its success in the treatment of back pain, but certainly not limited to that. Acupuncture can be very effective for a wide range of musculo-skeletal problems, particularly of a chronic nature, and also for allergies, hormonal problems and in behavior modification.

The treatment involves the insertion of fine needles at precise points in the body and may include the injection of B12 or saline at these sites, or additional treatment by laser stimulation or moxibustion (burning a special heating herb over the needle points, which provides great comfort for many arthritic conditions).

It is a very deep and complex system of treatment that is normally the domain of a veterinarian with a special interest in the subject, since results from "cookbook" procedures tend to be inferior. Acupuncture often is combined with chiropractic treatment, as the two modalities are complementary in horses.

CHIROPRACTIC:
Chiropractic techniques for horses have been adapted from human chiropractic methods and consist of a range of manipulation of the spinal joints to relieve nerve interference and allow all joints of the body to function throughout their full range of motion. Recent research has shown that as little pressure as that exerted by the weight of a U.S. dime can cause a serious disturbance to nerve function. The principles of chiropractic treatment rely on maintaining the integrity of the spinal nerves as they exit the spinal column. By preserving the mobility of each and every spinal joint, this ensures that no such pressure is inflicted upon these delicate nerves.

Chiropractic is a controversial subject in equine sports medicine, just as it is in the field of human sports medicine. However, positive results in the field at this time, and from very early and preliminary research, indicate that there could be an important role for this treatment modality in the racing industry. It is frequently combined with acupuncture treatments and should be carried out by a well-trained professional, either a qualified chiropractor or suitably trained veterinarian.

LASER THERAPY:
Various laser modalities have been available for years and are one of the most useful treatments because they also can be used to stimulate the acupuncture points without using needles. Laser therapy increases blood flow by dilating the blood vessels to the area and also provides profound pain relief. Cold medical lasers are especially designed now for use with animals and play a role in assisting with the healing of soft

tissue injuries, such as tendon and suspensories which have a compromised blood supply.

Laser therapy is often also used to aid the healing of wounds. It's use must be carefully supervised as it can cause damage to tissue if used incorrectly.

ELECTRO-MAGNETIC FIELD THERAPY (MAGNETS):

Once again, this is a therapy technique that relies on increasing the blood supply and circulation in order to have its effect. All healing processes are enhanced by an increased blood supply, and the advantage of some of these types of techniques over the old-fashioned leg paints and blisters is that they can be used time and time again without damaging the skin.

The electro-magnetic fields of these various pieces of equipment have a dramatic effect on increasing the blood flow to the area. There are a great range of these products available—some being pulsed with variations in strength, frequency and duration, and others being static devices with patterns of magnets producing a field over the area to be treated.

The ions in blood and cells interact with the magnets to create the flow at a cellular level. Therefore, they have a wide application in sports medicine, from being a general training aid to assisting in the healing of fractures and torn tendons.

There is a great range of products produced especially for horses at this time and I have seen some very favorable results from the use of these products.

HYDROTHERAPY: SWIMMING

Besides the use of hot and cold hosing to promote blood flow through the injured area, swimming is a form of hydrotherapy that has been very popular with trainers for a long time. It is a heavy athletic form of exercise which requires a horse to exercise its limbs and cardiovascular system without the pounding forces exerted by training on the track. It may have a tremendous psychological benefit for some bored horses who need a change of scenery from the track and a change of attitude towards their work.

However, swimming, as such, is not a natural exercise for a horse, and some horses are very stressed by it. Some horses actually cannot swim at all and others never do it very well.

A much more effective approach to hydrotherapy is to combine a whirlpool jacuzzi with an underwater treadmill. This creates all the benefits of controlled treadmill exercise with the added bonus of massaging the legs with water jets (the horse has to work against the resistance of the water at a steady balanced walk).

Such a method is the ideal rehabilitation method for an injured horse because the leg injuries do not receive full concussive force, yet are still

One of the best ways to return a horse to training and racing without the continual pounding on the racetrack is hydrotherapy, or swimming. This form of therapy is very valuable because it requires a horse to exercise and to stress the cardiovascular system. A more advanced regimen combines swimming with an underwater treadmill and thermal jacuzzi. The latter should be used for those horses who are not particularly good swimmers. Swimming and other hydrotherapies have been used quite successfully to return many horses to racing condition after serious injuries.

stressed in the appropriate direction so healing will be with maximum strength.

Treatment of the racehorse is aimed at making him feel good. In our training we are trying to instill in him the attitude to go hard, but to do this he must feel good about what he does. If a horse is in pain, we cannot expect him to give an all-out, tremendous effort, although some of the best racehorses will.

Great horses are the ones who are serious about their jobs; they will overcome some discomfort to do their jobs no matter what. Any treatment can be enhanced by such a patient. There are few, if any, horses racing without some degree of discomfort somewhere, simply because of the rigors of their task. However, most horses, through their courage and willingness, work through this and are a tribute to a long line of breeding for extreme athletic ability.

OTHER VETERINARY ISSUES AFFECTING PERFORMANCE:

When I hear someone state that the horse had "no pace" or had a lot of trot or pace until the three-quarter pole and then virtually started to slow down, I am usually inclined to be more concerned about a respiratory obstruction or infection or more recently I have seen this type of performance be due to tying up, which has become a real problem with the modern day Standardbred.

RESPIRATORY PROBLEMS:

Probably one of the major causes of economic loss to the owner in the Standardbred business today is the high incidence of respiratory problems. These problems may be infectious, allergic, or mechanical in origin, and there is no doubt in my mind that their occurrence is far more frequent than it was in the days of Dr. Churchill's practice. There are various theories that can be kicked around as to why this may be happening, none of which are proven, but I have noticed that, many times, respiratory problems can be very pedigree-specific. Susceptibility to infections, and allergies all seem to be related to a less-than-vigorous immune system, which may have a close connection to the narrowing gene pool.

ALLERGIES:

One of the commonly seen respiratory ailments is the presence of allergies. Most racehorses live in closed complexes and much of the racing competition occurs in urban areas where air quality may be poor. Horses are susceptible to common allergies from dust, pollen and other environmental factors, and the presence of allergies should not be overlooked in determining causes of poor performance. If a horse has an irritation of the respiratory system, he can have trouble with the exchange of oxygen in the lungs and the overall functioning of the respiratory system.

Dust allergy is one of the biggest problems in areas of intensive stabling, such as racetracks. Horses may be allergic to hay, straw, and pollen dusts. Consequently, there are a number of non-allergenic bedding and feed formulations coming on the market. Allowing plenty of fresh air to circulate through the stables is very important. Dust can also be minimized by dampening down with sprinklers and moistening the hay and feeds with a little water before feeding.

Some young horses will spontaneously grow out of their allergies as do children. For example, Beach Towel was plagued by respiratory allergies when he was a two-year-old, but grew out of them as a three-year-old.

INFECTIONS:

There are a great many viruses that affect the respiratory system; new ones appear every year. Racetracks are a place where many horses of different ages and immune status gather, some after being shipped all over the country or from overseas. All fit racing animals are under physical stress and, in the intensive stabling situation at the racetracks, are constantly exposed to a great many viruses. Some horses will get sick and some won't.

If the respiratory system is already compromised by chronic allergies or bleeding, the horse will be more susceptible to developing infections and the severity of the symptoms will depend on his individual immune status. Some horses will manifest a temperature, cough, and runny nose, and others may show only a slight nasal discharge, while others may have no clinical signs at all. I have heard trainers say, and I tend to agree with them, that top horses do not seem to get sick with these kinds of infections.

I remember when I first heard this, it was said at that time by Doug Ackerman, a very respected trainer. I was discussing with him one of his best young pacing colts who had a temperature of 104° F, and Doug shook his head and said, "And I thought he was a good horse!"

I couldn't understand how a trainer could judge a horse's lack of merit by the mere fact he had a temperature. However, Doug was adamant that he'd never had a good horse that got sick.

Over the years of being associated with some very great horses, I have noticed that they may ship all over and race hard, but they handle stress well. Mack Lobell, Nihilator, and Jake And Elwood, for example, all seemed to have superior immune systems. They went through the rigors of tough, two-and three-year-old campaigns, including lots of shipping, but never had any major respiratory problems.

Respiratory infections are nearly always complex and involve more than one kind of virus, as well as bacteria. The severity of the illness and the degree of secondary infection depend on the amount of virus the horse is exposed to and the competence of its immune system. The viruses are airborne and are inhaled into the upper airways. If there has been recent infection or damaged and inflamed tissue, the natural defense mechanisms of the lungs cannot prevent penetration of the virus or fight off secondary infection. In the characteristic coughing that results from infected horses, large numbers of the virus are exploded into the air.

In the closely populated environment of a racetrack, it is impossible to prevent young horses from being exposed to infection. Clinical signs usually begin rapidly, with the onset of an elevated temperature, coughing and nasal discharge. Most mild infections without secondary problems will subside in about a week. For horses that get really sick, careful nursing and systematic veterinary treatment is essential. Transporting the horse should definitely be avoided, as recent studies have confirmed the adverse effects of such stress on the immune system.

A condition that I see a lot of and hear a lot about is worth noting at this time. Many times a horse is exposed to a respiratory virus and is able to fight off the infection or has very mild sub-clinical signs such as a low grade fever for 12-24 hours or shows nothing at all.

Then however, it races and goes a poor race. As is done routinely now, the trainer has the horse scoped after the race due to the poor perfor- mance. The veterinarian observes a thick white "cottage cheese" type substance in the trachea or windpipe which is coming up from the lungs due to the physical exertion. This is why it is very important to scope the horse when it is hot or you might never see this material which is basi- cally a mixture of mucous and pus.

What makes this condition so hard to recognize is that prior to the race the horse appears to be fine. His temperature is normal, appetite good and most of the time his blood profile is normal.

The condition results from a horse being exposed to a virus and though it has no outward signs, a secondary bacterial infection has taken hold deep in the lungs.

There will be no indication of a problem until the horse is under the extreme stress at the end of the race when the trachea, or windpipe, will be showered with chunks of the purulent discharge as the exertion causes the horse to breathe very deeply. This causes mechanical occlusion of the air passages and the horse runs out of oxygen and slows up dramati- cally. If left undetected or untreated, such an infection may progress to a low-grade fungal infection which will make the lung tissue very fragile. Such long-standing infections account for many horses that bleed, and are more common than trainers realize. The situation creates large eco- nomic losses for owners because no one knows the problem is there un- less the horse is scoped and examined at the track after a fast workout.

BLEEDERS:

The problem of some horses bleeding from the lungs and/or nose fol- lowing exercise and racing has been around throughout the history of horse racing. There are descriptions of it that date back to the 16th century. In more recent times, extensive surveys have been done in North America of both Standardbred and Thoroughbred horses where hundreds of horses were examined with an endoscope ("scoped") within two hours of racing for evidence of blood in the respiratory tract.

The results of these surveys indicated that almost 50 percent of horses had varying degrees of blood in their windpipe after fast work. Most of these horses had no obvious outward signs of bleeding and were not sus- pected of being "bleeders" by their trainers. Older horses showed a greater tendency to have episodes of bleeding into the lungs, which indi- cated the presence of an underlying problem and the inability of the lung to repair itself in the face of continued training.

Long-standing, low-grade infections of the respiratory tract make the lung tissue very fragile, and this undoubtedly accounts for a certain per- centage of horses that bleed. However, other mechanical breathing problems, such as the upward displacement of the soft palate which results in an actual shutting off of the air flow, create enormous pressure in the lungs, leading to the rupture of blood vessels.

Some horses who tuck their nose or grab on create a very steep angle between the windpipe and the jawbone. This head carriage functionally restricts the air flow. When the air flow is severely restricted something has to give. Usually, the bleeding occurs as the horse's performance is deteriorating and he is being asked by the driver to push on. Equipment changes to prevent this tucking of the head and neck by an overcheck bit of the leverage type, such as a Raymond overcheck or bar bit, may help the horse carry its head better.

There is no doubt that bleeding from the lungs contributes to poor performance and should be considered when examining horses that finish very poorly. The easiest way to confirm the problem is to have the horse scoped within two hours of racing. Besides chronic poor performance, other suspicious symptoms are the horse that cools out slowly and is slightly distressed or anxious after the race, with coughing and frequent swallowing. I have also seen some horses reluctant to drink water if they have bled. It is important to diagnose this problem immediately and give the horse time to allow the blood vessels in the lungs to heal. Continual training prolongs the insult to the lungs and results in reduced lung capacity, which will always compromise performance.

I have observed in my experience that the incidence of bleeders and other mechanical respiratory problems are very common in certain pedigrees. These problems are the cause of great economic loss to the racing industry at the present time. Methods of prevention must be addressed by breeders, trainers, and the veterinary profession. I might also note at this time, that often a horse suffers from having his wind shut off or from bleeding. I think that many horses become frightened by this and even after the problem is corrected may not return to peak performance until they regain their confidence that this problem is not going to reoccur.

OBSTRUCTIONS TO AIR FLOW:
The upper respiratory system consists of the nasal passages, larynx, and pharynx (throat area), and the windpipe which leads down to the lungs, or lower respiratory tract in the chest cavity. The function of the upper respiratory tract is to provide air flow from the environment to the areas of oxygen exchange in the lungs. In the horse, the system is uniquely designed to channel the air flow freely, and any change in the dimensions of the air passages results in disturbance to this air flow and decreased availability of oxygen in the lungs.

The horse can breathe only through the nose and cannot resort to mouth breathing, like many other species, if there is any resistance to air flow in the upper respiratory tract. This is because the soft palate (the division between the nasal cavity and the mouth) is very long in the

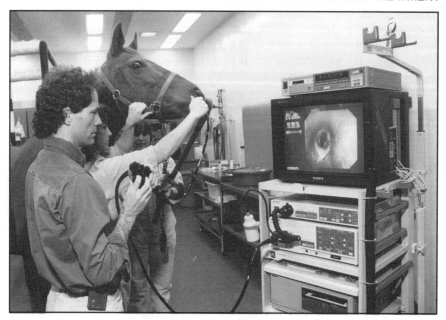

A common practice with racehorses is the use of an endoscope to take a closed-circuit television picture of the horse's respiratory tract. "Scoping" is most valuable soon after a horse has been trained or raced, since functional obstructions of the upper respiratory tract have no visible symptoms while the horse is at rest. In this photo, the technician has inserted the endoscope into the horse's nostril and is looking at a picture of the respiratory tract on the monitor. Obstructions such as an entrapped epiglottis and respiratory bleeding can be detected by scoping.

horse and normally forms an airtight seal between the mouth and air passages to allow efficient movement of air into the windpipe during exercise.

Any deformity in the shape of the air passage causes a tremendous increase in resistance to air flow; this situation is greatly exacerbated by fast exercise. If there is such an increase in resistance to air flow, the horse must do more work with its respiratory muscles to keep breathing. In the racing situation this leads to early fatigue, and the horse stops in the race with a dramatic reduction in speed.

Most functional obstructions of the upper respiratory tract have no symptoms when the horse is at rest, but they become readily apparent when the horse is exercising, either because there is abnormal respiratory noise, or because the horse shows exercise intolerance. The two most common conditions of this nature are the entrapment of the epiglottis by tissue from underneath the epiglottis, and upward displacement of the soft palate.

UPWARD DISPLACEMENT OF THE SOFT PALATE : "FLIPPING OF THE PALATE"

As I have described it, the soft palate of the horse is very long and forms an airtight seal to close off the oral cavity from the nose when the horse is breathing. Normally, the epiglottis, which is the cap over the windpipe that stops food from going in when the horse swallows, lies over the top of the soft palate and helps form the airtight seal for the air flow to pass straight into the windpipe. When the soft palate is displaced, it flips upwards and gets caught on top of the epiglottis. This has a dramatic effect on air flow because the soft palate suddenly is flapping in the middle of the air flow through the larynx. Not only does it decrease the horse's performance, there is also a lot of stress on the blood vessels in the lungs, and this certainly contributes to respiratory bleeding.

My experience is that if this condition is understood it can be dealt with by making management and equipment changes and only after these fail should surgery be considered.

First of all it is important to keep the horse relaxed when jogging and training as pulling or "grabbing on" causes the nose to pull towards the neck and shut a horse's air off. In the process of shutting the air off, a negative pressure occurs within the upper airway and the soft palate flips up over the epiglottis.

Obviously, in a racing situation when a horse is behind the gate or gets "caught in" this situation can occur. When it occurs frequently the back or caudal edge of the soft palate become thickened and many times an area of redness and irritation is seen from where it continues to ride on top of the epiglottis. The only way for a horse to get it off is to swallow. When his head is checked or he is pulling, it is very hard to swallow. If the palate is caught, it stays there. The thicker the palate gets, the easier it is to get caught when it gets on top of the epiglottis when the horse is under the stress. CKS was a horse that I trained and he would cough whenever he ate or got up from lying down and swallowed. He won several stake races and over $950,000 and never had surgery. Whenever he jogged, trained or raced his tongue was tied in such a way that it hung out the side of his mouth. By doing this, the back of the tongue which is very long and thick in a horse puts pressure on or holds down the back of the soft palate. He also wore a Crit Davis overcheck bit so he could not tuck his nose. As long as he was "rigged" this way, he would be fine.

Another case in point was Magical Mike. When he was a two-year-old, he had won the Woodrow Wilson and was racing in the Presidential when a recall occurred. He got "fired up" and apparently "flipped" his palate and finished a disappointing fifth.

His trainer, Tom Haughton started tying his tongue double and put a Crit Davis overcheck bit on him and he came back to easily win the Governor's Cup and had a brilliant three-year-old career.

If these management and equipment changes do not work, then surgery is indicated.

A surgical technique has been developed by Dr. Hugh Llewellyn and involves surgical re-section of the muscles that displace the larynx, particularly the sternothyrohyoideus muscle, and also re-shaping of the soft palate. This allows the larynx to remain flat, so it is less likely the soft palate can displace. It also repairs the soft palate where it is frequently ulcerated and damaged due to its rubbing up and over on the epiglottis.

ENTRAPPED EPIGLOTTIS: CAUSED BY THE ARY-EPIGLOTTIC FOLDS:

The epiglottis covers the windpipe when the horse swallows and must be fully open to allow air to flow freely into the windpipe when the horse breathes. There are two folds of tissue underneath the epiglottis called the ary-epiglottic folds. When this tissue is inflamed or irritated, it curls around the epiglottis and prevents it from functioning properly and thereby obstructing air flow. In some cases, structural deformity of the epiglottis is a predisposing cause of the problem and, in other cases, it may occur concurrently with a flipped palate.

Symptoms of poor performance and exercise intolerance are also a feature of this condition. It is diagnosed by endoscopic examination and surgical correction is usually necessary because it cannot go back by itself. This tissue frequently becomes ulcerated where it rides up and over the epiglottis.

ROARING (LARYNGEAL HEMIPLEGIA):

This condition may be hereditary and affects the left side of the larynx and is most common in large male horses. When the condition is present the nerves that supply the muscles of the larynx do not function properly, especially on the left side. This results in obstruction of the air passage and the horse makes a characteristic "roaring" or whistling sound when exercising. Classically, the condition manifests itself when the horse is between two and three years of age.

There are a number of surgical techniques that have been developed to correct the problem.

I have also seen this condition occur when there is a problem with the left jugular vein which is the primary location used for taking pre-and post-race blood samples for testing and giving medications intravenously. Hence care should be taken when using this vein.

PARASITE CONTROL:

As we are dealing with a finely tuned athlete, bred and conditioned to be a racehorse, it is the responsibility of the trainer to make sure that even if the horse looks and feels good the level of parasites in the system are kept to a minimum. All herbivorous animals have a certain level of parasites normally, and it is probably impossible to get rid of all of them.

However, if parasites are not controlled by a regular de-worming program, in the intensive situation they may become numerous enough to drop the blood count and interfere with digestion. Migrating worm larvae can cause severe colic, which may be life-threatening at worst, or interrupt a horse's racing program.

BLOOD COUNTS:

Blood counts have long been used by racetrack veterinarians in an attempt to correlate performance with fitness. Due to the vital role of the red blood cells in carrying the oxygen to the muscles, it was thought that information relating to stages of fitness could be evaluated from blood counts. However, after many years of research into how training affects changes in the blood, there are still considerable differences of opinion as to the significance of a blood count taken from the horse at rest and its correlation to performance and fitness.

In my opinion, having a series of individual blood counts for each horse is very important. Ideally, the sequence should be obtained for the horse during each entire training and racing campaign. An individual horse will have blood parameters that will stay within a narrow range within normal limits. Small changes for an individual horse can be detected by serial blood counts that would otherwise be obscured by the isolated blood count which merely indicated the horse was in normal range compared to an average of many horses.

The main parameters that are looked at in the blood count are hemoglobin levels and packed cell volume of the red blood cells, and whether there is an increase or decrease in the white blood cells. To get an accurate reading on the red blood cells, the horse must be very calm when the blood sample is collected; otherwise, large numbers of red blood cells can be mobilized from the spleen under the influence of an increased heart rate and fear or excitement.

If there is infection somewhere in the body the white blood cells will be elevated, or if the horse is suffering from a viral infection the level of white blood cells will be lowered. The blood can also be analyzed to assess the state of the internal organs and to ascertain whether or not there has been muscle damage, both of which are very useful in assessing conditions such as tying up syndrome and liver function.

NUTRITION:

As the quest for more scientific sophistication overtakes the racing industry, there has been an explosion of processed feeds and feed additives in the last 10 years or so. The choices are enormous, and I think the tendency has been to make the issues of nutrition more complicated than they need to be. The horse, unfortunately, cannot order what he wants off the menu; what he gets is at the discretion of the trainer. Balanced rations, however, are not as involved as some people like to make them out to be, and I think the more basic the ration the better.

Horses, if given the choice, always prefer oats far and above the most palatable grain. Good-quality oats and a mixture of good-quality alfalfa and timothy hay will provide most of the energy requirements of a balanced ration, and most of the vitamins and minerals as well. Increased energy can be added by the substitution of corn or barley as sources of grain. Grain supplementation allows the ingestion of a greater amount of energy in less volume, minimizing the effect of gut fill on suppressing appetite before energy requirements for a heavy racing program are satisfied.

The greatest hazard with increasing grain intake is balancing the calcium:phosphorus ratio, as all grains have a higher level of phosphorus. Other than this, most vitamin and mineral supplements are not warranted if the diet contains sufficient good-quality hay.

There are, however, occasions when supplements may be beneficial. In some situations, when the blood count is low and the horse may be slightly anemic, an iron supplement is useful. Some of the new supplements containing chondroitin sulphate are beneficial for developing and strengthening cartilage in young horses. Salt should always be provided free-choice, as some horses want more salt than others.

Salt and trace-elements blocks can be placed in the stall to provide the horse with convenient free-choice supplementation. Electrolyte supplements may be needed in summer, when the horse has been training in humid conditions and sweating excessively. Generally, however, if the quality of the diet is good, the feeding of fancy supplements is wasteful and of dubious value to the horse.

In recent years, much more attention has been given to the quality of water given to horses. We live in times when water pollution has become a fact of life. When the quality of the water is poor or contains high levels of dissolved salts, such as ground water and bore water on some properties, the horses will not want to drink as much as they should. In this situation, especially in summer, horses may end up being dehydrated and having electrolyte imbalances.

Good, clean, clear water is very important and is often an overlooked component of a good diet. Many large stables in North America have installed water filters that remove impurities from the water. Monitoring water intake in racing horses is very important and it is preferable to provide the water in buckets rather than automatic watering systems so these observations can be made.

Proper nutritional management and stable care is fundamental to producing maximum performance by the equine athlete. Nonetheless, performance reflects the innate abilities of the horse itself and must be brought out by intelligent conditioning programs and racing management. Nutrition is not a performance-enhancing drug, and resorting to complicated supplements and additives cannot create athletic talent. Good nutrition, however, is the cornerstone of health maintenance and allows the horse's genetic potential to be realized by training.

What a horse gets, either from his food or from supplements and oral medication, is being found to be of greater concern as many horses are being found to have gastric ulcers. As in humans, there is certainly some correlation to stress caused by long periods of stall confinement, increasingly high strung temperaments and the stress of vigorous and frequent racing. Anyone who spends a lot of time around a racehorse sees this fluctuation in temperament and with time, I think nutritional programs will be developed that include a consideration for keeping the stomach lining coated so as to help decrease the amount of ulceration. It has also recently been discovered, in human medicine, that many gastric ulcers are the direct result of a certain bacterial infection.

IN SUMMARY:

The state of veterinary medicine today is no more an exact science than it was a quarter of a century ago. However, we certainly do have more technology available to us and we understand the physiology of the performance horse a little better.

The practice of veterinary medicine should be applied in such a way as to prolong the useful life of the horses bred to race. This is the reason we breed them and train them, and this is where veterinary medicine has an important role to contribute. We should never use our knowledge of science to allow a horse to risk permanent injury or endanger his life or the lives of other race participants.

Many of the advancements of modern veterinary medicine have allowed horses to compete, who 20 years ago might never have made it to the races. This has a wonderful economic impact on the industry and increases the productivity of the horses. Continual advancement in veterinary medicine is necessary for the industry to continue to supply horses for year-round racing.

What we must seek in the immediate future is the intelligent use of medication, combined with the scientific concepts of correct conditioning, and develop the concept of a team effort between trainer, owner, veterinarian, drivers, caretakers, and farriers. We are all seeking to improve the industry. We all want fast, safe, sound, and productive horses.

Dr. Kenneth P. Seeber has an excellent perspective from which to comment on veterinary care of the racing Standardbred. He has been a well respected practicing veterinarian for several decades, and has also trained and managed a stable of high-class horses.

A native of Glens Falls, NY, Dr. Seeber graduated from the New York State Veterinary College at Cornell University. While still in veterinary school he worked two summers for Dr. Edwin A. Churchill, who wrote the chapter on lameness in the original *Care and Training of the Trotter and Pacer*. After graduation, Dr. Seeber spent four years as an associate in Dr. Churchill's veterinary practice.

After two years as the general manager of Lana Lobell Farms, Dr. Seeber resumed his veterinary practice at The Meadowlands. However, that was short lived as four years later Dr. Seeber decided to put some of his beliefs about training Standardbreds into practical application and opened a state-of-the-art training center in upstate New York.

In a relatively short period, he developed such pacing stars as Cole Muffler, Bonnie And Clyde, and W R H. He also trained the $2 million winner Jake And Elwood, In The Pocket, Sandman Hanover, and C K S. His best trotter was the 1990 Hambletonian Oaks winner, Working Gal.

Back at The Meadowlands now, Dr. Seeber has a flourishing veterinary practice.

17

FARM MANAGEMENT
Care & Maintenance of Broodmares and Their Foals

CARTER H. DUER

I have been asked in this chapter to outline the basics involved in the breeding and management of mares and their foals. Like many of the other subjects in this book, several chapters of a technical nature could be written on this issue alone. What I am doing with this particular chapter is relating, in non-scientific language, the basics of broodmare and foal management.

I would venture to guess that in my more than 35 years in the horse business I have bred and foaled more mares than I could ever remember. During some of the years that I was farm manager at Castleton, we were breeding more than a thousand mares a year at the main farm, so it seems like I have been doing this for a long, long time.

I believe that too much reliance is being placed on the technological side of breeding and raising horses and not enough time and personal attention is given to the animals themselves. I have always believed that nature's system works pretty well and is still much better than most things prescribed by man. I try to stay as close to nature as possible and I believe that is where the basics of successful management lies.

Horse care and management can be and has been bettered by technology and I realize that there will always be useful advances. It is necessary to be open to new ideas and there are some things that we do now that are very advantageous that had not even been heard of five years ago. I also think that there are some other things that come along that are a detriment to our operation.

PROGRESS—NATURE CAME FIRST

I am in favor of progress but I am not going to jump on the band wagon just because some new technique or treatment has come along. Part of the problem with some new techniques and treatments is that it may save time and effort on the human end, but the long term effect on the horses is not considered. There are basic things you do with raising and breeding horses that just can't be improved on.

I send mares all over the country to be bred and I think some farms have a tendency to go overboard in the use of hormones in breeding mares. We are dealing with mares whose foals may have a lot of potential value, so, often the quick route is taken as a means to get a mare in foal. Being from the "old school," I still prefer sticking with the "old ways" as much as possible — I still think nature knows best.

I don't believe in "pushing a mare's buttons" with shots. I don't want to bring her in heat with one shot and take her out with another just for the sake of quickly getting her in foal. I would much rather go with nature whenever possible. Of course, there are exceptions to everything and you will occasionally run into some situations where you have to make adjustments. When I get a mare in to be bred and have resorted to all the normal means with no results, I may try the hormone route as a last resort. But again, try nature's way first.

Many farms today do not have a teaser. To me, a good teaser is the most integral part of a successful breeding operation. A breeding operation should have a good teasing program in conjunction with a good veterinarian. I base the work I have my veterinarian do on what I have observed while out in the field teasing the mares. I do not rely solely on what the veterinarian says regarding the breeding of a mare but instead use that information as a supplement to my field observations.

Breeding mares, foaling them, and raising the foals, requires a combination of good animal practices and common sense. I think you need about an equal amount of both. And as far as the science of it is concerned, it is inexact, because it seems every mare is a little different. If every mare showed in heat to the teaser, if every mare carried her foal to term, got ready to foal, and just laid down and spit the foal out, this would be a much easier business for everyone. However, it just doesn't work that way. Like many other aspects of the horse business, the breeding side is not for the faint of heart.

RECORDS ARE IMPORTANT

It is vitally important to record the breeding history of each and every mare, and we have developed a form for this. There are computer programs available to record this data, but I still use a system that I used at Castleton many years ago. I keep a record for each mare in a ringed binder. I can look at every mare's record and tell when her cycles came, when she produced a follicle, and when she was bred. This gives me a history on every mare and will help in future years to determine the best course of action. Samples of these forms may be found at the end of this chapter.

MAIDEN MARES

One of the most common situations I am confronted with is preparing a maiden mare for her first breeding.

Ideally, I would like a maiden mare to arrive at my farm a couple of months before the breeding season begins. This time allows me to assess the mare's overall condition, the status of her reproductive tract, and to find out something about her history.

I am not a big proponent of breeding two-year-olds, unless the filly is very mature. I would also prefer to breed her late in the spring, say after May 15. The best heat periods are those that occur in May. I think this gives a filly time to grow up. I see a great many young females who conceive, but then lose a foal early in the course of the pregnancy. This is simply nature's way of telling us that this mare is not yet ready to have a foal.

EFFECTS OF RACETRACK MEDICATIONS

There is some debate about the effects of racetrack medications on racemares subsequently affecting their ability to conceive once their racing days are over. I had felt in the past that this was a problem but it is now my opinion that the conception rate of most mares seems unaffected by racetrack medications. I do believe, however, that a male horse can be permanently affected by racetrack medications, particularly by steroids. But I don't see any significant correlation between track medications and the future ability to conceive in racemares.

Although a racemare's ability to conceive may not be affected, racetrack medications do seem to have a lingering effect on the reproductive "attitude" of certain mares for some months after the drugs have been stopped. By this I mean that the mare may not come in heat, she may not respond to the teaser or she may even play the part of the teaser to the other mares in her field. Generally though, once drugs have been out of her system for several months, nature will take its course and the mare will begin to cycle and respond normally.

BREEDING CHARACTERISTICS—A FAMILY TRADITION

Many of the fillies who come to me are descendants of mares that I might have known for some time. This is important information, because breeding tendencies are often passed down from generation to generation.

One of the problems in dealing with racehorses is that we do not choose our broodmares based on their reproductive abilities as nature would do. We choose them because of their pedigree and performance. Therefore, many different families with breeding problems have been perpetuated.

In many cases, not showing heat can be a trait passed on from one generation to the next. We have whole families of mares who will not show you that they are in heat. When I was at Castleton Farm, many of the Good Time mares were notorious for that problem. That trait was difficult to deal with at that time because we did not have today's technology such as ultrasound and hormone therapy to help us get the mares in foal. Details about dealing with this type of mare are discussed later in this chapter.

WAIT ON MAIDENS UNTIL FIRST SIGNS OF SPRING

A great many breeders with maiden mares want to get started breeding their mares as quickly as possible. They want you to start teasing their mares in the dead of winter. This is often a waste of time and energy, because the maiden will not begin regular periods of heat until her body is ready to do so.

I won't begin to tease a maiden mare until I see the first signs of spring, which to me are seeing the first robins and the sight of buds appearing on the trees. I have that luxury because I don't have a thousand mares to breed. If I did have that many mares, I might have to start doing things a little earlier or perhaps some other way.

USE OF LIGHT THERAPY ON MAIDEN AND BARREN MARES

Light therapy is the use of artificial illumination to trick a mare into believing that spring has arrived and to start her normal reproductive cycle. Beginning November 15, or by December 1, start turning on the lights at dusk and leave them on until midnight. This process should be continued until around mid-April. I prefer to use lights in individual box stalls. I use a 150-watt incandescent bulb located in the center of the stall over the mare. I have also used fluorescent fixtures and cannot really tell much difference between them and a regular incandescent bulb.

A great many farms will utilize lights in outdoor settings. Many prefer to get a large group of mares together in an outdoor catch-pen or very small paddock, and subject them to floodlights over the entire area. I have no problem with this. It is less labor intensive than getting mares up in individual stalls. But whichever light therapy method you choose, it is a useful tool in your breeding program.

FIELD TEASING MARES — THE MOST NATURAL SETTING

Field teasing is an art-form, and I learned the basics about teasing from Luther Figgs, who did most of the teasing at Castleton for many years. He always claimed that he could just look at a mare and tell if she was in heat.

I prefer field teasing for all mares because I think it is a much more natural setting and duplicates what is found in nature. I know that a great many breeders will tease mares at a bar or teasing chute. Others like to do their teasing in a stall. I learned to field tease, and have had great results over the years. Mares are more comfortable in such a setting. Again, I think it duplicates what would happen in a natural setting with a herd of mares and a stallion.

My teaser is a cold-blooded horse, the son of a horse I used previously. He is small and easier to handle than a big, aggressive horse. I also like a teaser who is smooth and knows his business. A smart teaser is so beneficial to a breeding program. My teaser will actually tease a group of mares with foals differently than he will barren mares. In a group of mares and foals he is more subtle, whereas with the barren mares he is more aggressive.

It is very important that the horse used for teasing be manageable. He should never be allowed to bite or kick a mare. A mare has the privilege of acting that way, but the teaser does not. A mare who is not in heat may wheel around and try to kick, so, in field teasing, you have to be careful to

The author recommends teasing mares in the field. The teaser can elicit reactions from mares at a distance, thereby lessening the possibility of injury to either the teaser, the mares or their young foals. In this photo, the mare at the right is "showing" to the teaser, indicating that she may be ready to breed. The mare shows this by spreading her hind legs and urinating.

avoid injury to all concerned.

Luther taught me that a maiden mare should learn to come up and meet the teaser, and not be afraid. It is especially important that a young mare develop good habits and have a good teasing experience. This will benefit both you and the mare throughout her breeding years.

Many mares will have foals at their side, so it is very important that the teasing process be conducted as selectively as possible to avoid situations where a mare or foal can be hurt.

LEARN A MARE'S HABITS—DEVELOP A ROUTINE

It is essential to know the habits of each mare, and the only way to do that is to keep good records. I keep detailed records on teasing mares, and I also make mental notes on each mare's habits in the field. After teasing each day, I come in and record my results and observations while they are still fresh in my mind.

It is also important to establish a teasing routine. I do my teasing in the afternoon or at the end of the day, just before dusk. In this way I get good, consistent observations on each mare in the field. This is more a matter of my preferred routine than anything else. If I feel that a mare is far enough along in her heat that she would warrant breeding soon, I then have that mare examined the following morning to determine her breeding status.

I don't tease a mare every day; I normally use an every-other-day schedule. However, if a mare shows me she is in heat for the first time, I will tease her again the following day to confirm the heat cycle. If I determine she is just coming into heat, this means the mare will need to be bred sometime within the next three to five days.

Once you have been around a mare for a while, she will generally show you some indication that she is in heat. The mare who comes up to the horse readily, urinates frequently, and has a flushed, relaxed vulva is easy to determine that she is in heat. Different mares will react differently. You have to learn what each mare's signals are.

For instance, a mare might normally act pretty aggressive toward a teaser and refuse him by squealing or kicking, but as soon as she comes in heat she will act differently. Or, she may be just the opposite. She may be initially disinterested most of the time, but still will come up willingly to the horse when she is coming into season. There are others who act about the same all the time. These are the ones you have to study to detect any subtle difference in their behavior.

Unfortunately, a great many mares do not "show" that readily, and you simply have to determine their habits. Sometimes I have found that a mare won't come up to the teaser, but she won't walk away, either. She just sort of hangs around, and might even follow the horse around while I am teasing other mares. This type of mare might never show an outward sign of being in heat, but often a mare who behaves this way is found to have a heat cycle in progress and is near ready or is ready to be bred.

We do have some mares who do not show they are in heat, and this comes from the fact that many mares are the result of successive generations of mares who have been bred without natural service. I have mares on the farm whose dams, grandams and great grandams were all bred artificially. A family of horses may be evolving and losing the ability to show they are in heat. Even in the warmth of early spring when nature's systems are stuck on "go," these mares will not show you they are in heat.

MARE HEAT CYCLES

Mares are bred based on showing in heat to the teaser and rectal examination, to determine if an active follicle exists.

The average mare will have a heat cycle every 18 to 22 days. The period of heat, technically called estrus, ideally lasts about five to seven days. During this heat cycle the normal mare will produce a follicle on one of her ovaries. The follicle contains the egg produced by the mare's ovaries. The egg will normally be released from the ovary (a process called ovulation) in the latter days of the heat period. Since the heat cycle ideally runs about five to seven days, ovulation normally occurs around the fourth to sixth day of the cycle.

The normal mare will produce a follicle on only one of her ovaries. Occasionally a mare produces a follicle on both ovaries, and this can lead to a twin pregnancy.

A mare is most likely to conceive just prior to ovulation. For that reason, I want to breed a mare as close to ovulation as possible. Most mares will not conceive if bred after ovulation.

Ideally, I would like to deal with mares on the textbook five-to-seven-day heat cycles, but to be honest, the mares have not read the textbooks. One mare's heat cycle may last only four days; another mare may stay in heat for more than a week. Some mares are in heat only for five days, and will ovulate on the fourth day. A mare like this will have to be bred prior to her ovulation on the fourth day of her cycle.

If you are teasing and you run across a maiden mare and she is very good, I wouldn't wait a couple of days to check her because you may lose her. She may be very close to the point of ovulation right when she initially shows. Until I develop a history on a maiden, I do not like to take a chance on waiting to check her.

The potency of the stallion must be taken into consideration also. Some stallions have very potent sperm which is long-lasting, and they can impregnate a mare anywhere from 24 to 36 hours after insemination. A stallion with less potent sperm has to be bred as close to ovulation as possible. Some semen is so strong and potent that it can survive in a mare for up to 72 hours. In a lot of cases, the mare may conceive a few days after she has been bred to a very potent sire. This can also produce some twin pregnancies where the mare conceives early on the most active follicle, and then conceives again a day or two later on another follicle.

On the morning of the day when a mare is to be bred, I will have her checked rectally and breed her in the afternoon, if she has a good follicle and appears ready. My aim is to breed as close to ovulation as possible. This is the tricky part where your experience and knowledge will come into play. I don't want to breed after ovulation, where the chances of pregnancy are very slim.

SEMEN TRANSPORT

Transported semen is getting to be a big thing in our industry. When the idea of using transported semen was first discussed, I was opposed to it mainly for two reasons. I thought the conception rate would be poor and I thought that it would seriously hurt the boarding business. But after three years of hindsight, I have changed my mind about transported semen as it has become very successful. I think it will be even more important when all the Sire Stakes programs adopt it.

Semen transport allows me to keep mares here on the farm that had been seasonal boarders; that is, they formerly left during the breeding season. Now they are full-time residents and are inseminated without leaving the farm. You don't have to ship mares and you don't have to take chances with foals being hurt during shipping or in unfamiliar surroundings. For the farm standing the stallion, transported semen also

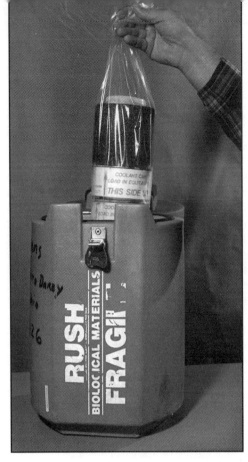

One advancement in the technology of breeding is the use of transported semen. The shipping envelope is shown here as well as the proper way to enclose the semen in the coolant canister.

allows a reduction in both the acreage required and the help needed.

I have two recommendations concerning transported semen. First, you have to be dealing with a stallion whose fertility is very good. If you try to ship semen from a horse with a low fertility rate, you will not have much success.

Second, you need to have a qualified person doing your inseminating, just as the major farms do in their breeding sheds. This person could be your veterinarian, or someone who has been trained in artificial insemination. Although I will still inseminate an occasional mare, most of the mares on my farm are inseminated either by my daughter Teresa, or by Dash, my secretary. Their arms are smaller than mine, and because most mares are sutured, it is easier for them to insert the semen. They are quite adept at doing this.

Transported semen is generally shipped overnight (occasionally same-day air) in what is called an "Equitainer." This is a device which allows semen to be transported under cooled conditions to the farm where the mare is boarded. Unless you have shipped same-day, the mare is then inseminated the day following the collection of the semen.

The important thing about handling transported semen is to use it immediately. If you pick up a shipment at the airport or if it is delivered to you by a commercial delivery service, you want to have plans in place to use it as quickly as possible. You don't leave it sitting around the barn or in someone's vehicle. It should not be subjected to adverse conditions such as heat and light.

You should only order semen when you have a mare who is ready to breed. Keep in mind that it will take a day or two before the semen will be shipped to you, so you will have to take that fact into consideration when checking your mares and when ordering semen. It can be a tricky process when timing your mare's readiness to be bred with the shipping days of the farm where the stallion is standing. This is a situation where your knowledge of the mare's breeding cycles, her response to teasing and the help of a good veterinarian can be very useful.

BREEDING ON THE FOAL HEAT

Another common practice, which sounds good in theory but is not applicable in all cases, is the practice of breeding a mare on her "foal heat."

The practice of breeding on the foal heat is based on the fact that the mare may begin to show what appears to be a regular heat cycle as early as seven to nine days after foaling. I do not recommend breeding on the foal heat, because the record on these breedings is not very good. The in-foal percentage is low (around 25 percent), because the mare often is just not ready for another pregnancy. She may conceive on the foal heat, but ends up losing the foal within the first 60 days.

I don't like breeding on the foal heat, but in some cases, if it is the only way a mare will conceive regularly, I will use it.

Another mare who might be bred on her foal heat is one who does not readily show she is in heat. With a few mares, this is about the only time you can actually tell they are in heat. If I think such a mare will be tough to get in foal under normal circumstances, I may breed her on the foal heat.

Mares who had trouble with their pregnancy or with the delivery of foals are not good candidates for foal-heat breeding. A mare with infection resulting from foaling is not going to be a good candidate either. And, of course, any mare who sustained bruising from a difficult foaling is going to need time to recover before she can be bred again.

Again, I do not like breeding on the foal heat and would recommend that it be utilized only if the mare is foaling late and there is little time left in the breeding season. If a mare is foaling after May 15, it may be desirable to try to get her back in foal on her foal heat, in an attempt to advance her foaling date every year.

If she does not conceive on the foal heat, she will probably be barren, and this allows you to start the next breeding season early with her and get her on a much better schedule.

However, even with a late-foaling mare, you may want to breed right to the virtual end of the breeding season. Some breeders, and I would include myself in this category, believe that even a late foal is better than no foal at all. I have sold a lot of June foals for $100,000, or more. Most breeding sheds at the commercial farms do not close until July 10-15, and a mare who foals late can still be bred if a late pregnancy is desirable. As I indicated, I believe a late pregnancy is better than no pregnancy.

FAILURE TO CONCEIVE

I am always disappointed if I do not get a mare in foal from her first breeding. The failure to conceive can be attributed to a number of factors, including infection or a problem with the mare's reproductive tract. There are also a number of mares who will not conceive while they are nursing a foal. These are the infamous "every-other year" mares. These mares are a problem because, economically, it is almost impossible to keep a mare who is only going to get in foal every other year.

A great number of these mares are first-timers. They have their first foal, then after foaling, their reproductive systems simply shut down. I am not sure why this happens, but nature is probably saying to us that this mare wants a little time before her next pregnancy.

I feel that a great deal of this reproductive problem is hereditary. A lot of the problem mares are daughters of mares who were problem breeders as well. Another factor is simply hormonal: the mare's reproductive system is not getting the cues it needs to resume normal activity.

Another reason for the inability to conceive is that many first-time mares have trouble foaling and need some extra time to recover. Nature knows this, and simply tells us that the mare should not conceive again for a while.

I have also noted that if a mare is bred on two good heat cycles — where everything appears normal, she has good follicles and yet she does not conceive — it is a pretty good bet that she is not going to get in foal for you that year if you just continue to breed her each successive heat. I do not have a clinical explanation for this phenomenon, but I have seen it happen a lot. This is like a baseball hitter who is ahead three balls and no strikes in the count. It is time to take a pitch, so to speak.

I recommend passing her on the third consecutive heat cycle if it is early in the season. I would flush her out with a saline and betadine solution and check her over to see if there is a reason for not conceiving. If no problems were found, I would breed her on her next heat.

Owners may not understand when you tell them that you have skipped a heat period with their mare. But, I have had great success with this procedure and I have seen a high conception rate from the very next cycle.

It is important to note that this can only be done if it is early in the breeding season. This is not recommended once June arrives because there is not much time left. At that point, I would just keep breeding her

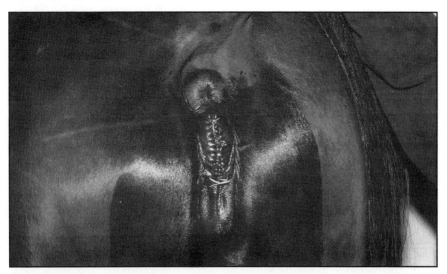

This photo shows the correct way to suture a mare. The suture should begin just below the anus and stop at a point leaving just enough room for the mare to urinate. Suturing in this way will cut down on the risk of infection.

each heat until the end of the breeding season, hoping that she might get in foal.

HORMONE THERAPY

If a mare exhibits no outward signs of showing heat, I normally try to help her along with an injection of prostaglandin, which is a hormone intended to stimulate activity in the ovaries. I find this often stimulates a mare into showing heat and producing a good follicle. Such a mare can be bred within a matter of days, and the conception rate is often good.

Another use of hormone therapy would be in the case of a mare who is going to be shipped for breeding to a different location and who is barren from the previous breeding season.

A mare such as this can be prepared for the upcoming breeding season by the oral administration of Regumate, a synthetic hormone, or by using a series of P & E (Progesterone and Estrodiole 17 Beta) shots. Check with your veterinarian for the proper dosing and use of these drugs.

This hormone therapy causes the mare's ovaries to get ready for breeding by suppressing follicular activity. As soon as the hormones are stopped, the mare should come in heat and produce a follicle naturally, within a week, and a high conception rate normally results. It is important to note that hormones are most effective when the mare has already exhibited some reproductive action. If there was no evidence of ovarian activity prior to the therapy, this hormone treatment may not produce a heat cycle.

I also want to stipulate here that hormone therapy of this kind should be used strictly as a last resort or as a means of minimizing costs when shipping mares away, since I do not believe that nature should be tampered with when it is not necessary.

THE PRACTICE OF "SHORT CYCLING"

Another method used to get a mare back in foal quickly after foaling, particularly late in the breeding season, is to "short-cycle" her. This technique involves the use of a hormone injection of prostaglandin after the period of the foal heat, but before the onset of a normal cycle.

The practice requires waiting for approximately five days after the mare has ovulated on her foal heat, then giving her a one-time injection of prostaglandin. This should cause the mare to come back into heat within 3-5 days, which is why it is called a short cycle, and will save about 10 days, which could be critical late in the breeding season. It gives the mare a little extra time after foaling to recover, and there is a much better chance she will conceive and carry the fetus to full term.

Short cycling can also be used on any type of mare if you should happen to, for some reason, miss getting her bred before she ovulates during a heat.

SUTURING MARES

Most of the mares I see are sutured, even the young mares coming to my farm right off the racetrack. This is good. I recommend that mares be sutured because it helps them stay free of infection. Let me explain why suturing is important.

One of the more common problems results from the conformation of the mare's vulva. Many mares will not have a good, flat vulva and anus. In some cases, the anus is sunk lower than the vulva, and there is a tendency for some of the mare's feces to enter her vagina when she defecates. A mare built this way must be sutured, because otherwise she will be prone to infection. This occurs a great deal in older mares who may have had a number of foals.

Other mares aspirate through their vagina, a tendency which we refer to as "sucking air." A mare who does this can actually suck in foreign material, such as airborne bacteria, and create infection. This is a common problem, and suturing helps to overcome it.

When I refer to suturing the vulva, I mean the labia of the vagina should be sewn together. This does not affect the mare's ability to be bred, unless of course, she is to be bred by natural cover. If that is the case, she should either not be sutured until after she is bred or should have the so-called "breeding stitch" which will allow her to be bred while she is still sutured. If the mare is to be bred artificially, suturing will not affect her ability to be bred. Even with a sutured labia, she can still be inseminated.

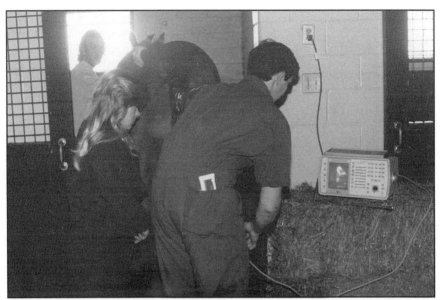

This photo illustrates the correct way to use ultrasound. The technician inserts the scope rectally, allowing the ovaries and the mare's uterus to be scanned. The image is then seen on the screen.

It is important to note that a mare who has been sutured will have to be "re-opened" before she foals. If a mare foals with a sutured vagina, she can cause great damage by tearing her vulva. This should be avoided, of course, but a labia can be repaired without affecting the mare's future ability to be bred.

ULTRASOUNDING

Ultrasounding (scanning) for breeding purposes is the use of a machine to evaluate a mare's reproductive tract. The veterinarian uses the machine, which sends sound waves out that are then bounced back to the machine by the mare's tissues, such as her uterus, ovaries or even a fetus. The computer in the ultrasound machine will then generate a picture which allows the veterinarian to "see" the mare's reproductive tract. Scanning allows you to check a mare's reproductive tract for problems. If you have a mare that doesn't show, it allows you to visually check to see if a follicle is developing. Ultrasounding is also a very useful tool in determining if a mare is carrying twins or has cysts.

PREGNANCY

At about 14-18 days after the mare is bred, it can be determined by ultrasound if she is in foal or has twins. While the ultrasound can determine within three weeks of conception that an embryo exists, some

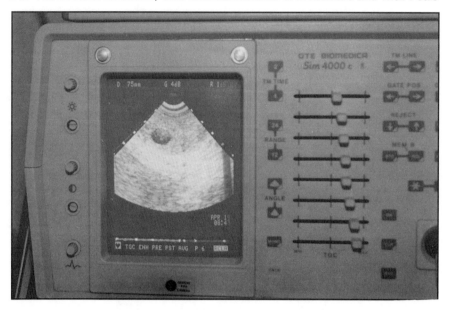

Ultrasound technology has greatly enhanced a breeders ability to detect an early pregnancy. Ultrasound images show the presence of a fertilized ovum in the mare's uterus. (Indicated here by a dark mass in the upper left portion of the pie-shaped image.)

of these embryos do not attach and are absorbed by the mare's system. I prefer to wait until I have the mare examined rectally around 40 days to determine that she is actually in foal.

Although the occurrence of twins is a small percentage of all pregnancies, it does occur on occasion. In many cases, nature takes over and the weaker embryo is expelled naturally.

The veterinary practice of "pinching a twin" can be employed if it is very early in the pregnancy and a mare has twins which are easily discernible. This practice is an area of veterinary science which has greatly improved. With this method the healthiest embryo is saved and the other embryo is "pinched" off. The remaining embryo can continue to develop.

If a mare has a history of "coming up empty" after being checked in foal, or is tested for proper hormone levels and has a problem, administration of the drug Regumate may help maintain the hormone level necessary for pregnancy.

Some mares are managed throughout their pregnancy by the daily administration of Regumate through the tenth month of pregnancy. With the average mare, the Regumate is given during the first 120 days of her pregnancy. The necessity of using Regumate on your mare and the proper dosage can be determined by your veterinarian.

FETAL GENDER DETERMINATION

Ultrasonography has evolved to the point where it is possible to determine the sex of the equine fetus at approximately 60 to 70 days of gestation. This is a non-invasive procedure similar to the ultrasound examinations used to determine pregnancy at earlier stages of gestation. The technique involves careful examination of the fetus by a veterinarian trained in this area, and allows him to, in most cases, accurately diagnose the sex of the fetus.

SPONTANEOUS ABORTION

Experience has taught me that little can be done to prevent abortions. In most cases, nature has a pretty effective way of eliminating a fetus which is malformed or malnourished.

If a mare has significant problems with a pregnancy, there is little that can be done to help her keep the foal beyond the use of antibiotics and possibly an increased dosage of Regumate. You just do everything you can do, but in most cases nothing will help. In 90 percent of the incidents, the mare will abort because there is something wrong with the fetus.

Another tactic that can be tried with a mare who is in some distress, particularly a mare who begins to start to make a bag long before she is scheduled to foal, is to remove her from the field and put her up in a box stall to monitor her condition. If she has not been on hormone therapy, I might start her on a daily program to attempt to save the pregnancy. Since many abortions are the result of infections, multiple strong doses of antibiotics—usually penicillin—may be effective in sustaining a pregnancy. We can also take a blood test to determine progesterone levels, and begin progesterone therapy if indicated.

Through the administration of vaccines, we have cut down greatly on the number of viral abortions, but there has not been much advancement in helping a mare who is having serious trouble with a pregnancy. A mare cannot be treated and immobilized like a human. A great many of these serious problems result in abortions, and normally we find that the fetus is malformed in some significant way.

MAINTENANCE OF THE IN-FOAL MARE

After a mare has been bred and conceives, it is important that you continue to monitor her condition to ensure that she has a successful pregnancy.

A routine of regular de-worming should be continued along with normal vaccinations. My mares receive rhinopneumonitis and flu shots bimonthly. I de-worm my horses every other month and any necessary vaccines are administered at the same time.

There is little else to be done for the balance of the term of the normal pregnancy, although we continue to examine the mares rectally each month throughout the breeding season to determine if their pregnancy is continuing. Once the breeding season is over, I do not normally check my pregnant mares again until the fall.

While mares are in foal, we keep their diets on a maintenance level. I don't like a mare to get too fat during a pregnancy. If I have good pasture for her, I make sure she gets a little grain, depending upon her physical condition. It is also very important that a mare have access to free-choice minerals and salt, and plenty of good water. The decisions in this area must take into account the weather, the character of the pasture, and the physical condition of the mare.

Many mares tend to get a little heavy during a pregnancy because their appetites increase and they get less exercise, just like a human. But, if a mare is being kept in a lot where there is little grass available, she will need to be supplemented with hay and grain in order to provide the kind of nutritional elements needed to sustain her and her foal during the pregnancy. I believe that some weight gain is desirable. The mare will soon be asked to provide nutrition directly to her foal, and the foaling process will stress her body, so a little extra weight won't hurt.

I believe that pregnant mares should stay outside, because the exercise they get in the field is very important to maintaining their physical condition. A mare should have access to shelter, although most times she will stay out in the weather, if given a choice. The major advantage of shelter is that you can feed the mare in a dry environment and this gives you the maximum benefit of your feed products. A horse does not like to eat wet feed. I feed a pelleted grain product, and it will break down and crumble if it gets too wet.

It is also desirable to pay attention to a mare during the final three months of her pregnancy, because this is a critical period in foal development. As much as half of fetal growth occurs in the last several months of pregnancy, so access to good feed and water is vitally important at this time.

THE LAST MONTH BEFORE FOALING

Most mares are put into the barn for their pre-foaling shots and pre-foaling blood test about 30 days before their due date. We will give the mares vaccinations against botulism, Eastern and Western encephalitis, influenza, Potomac Fever, rabies and tetanus. By administering these shots within 30 days of foaling, it helps build up some resistance in the foal's blood against those diseases.

A pre-foaling blood test called an NI screening (Neonatal Isoerythrolysis), is done at this time to check for the possibility of the mare delivering a jaundiced foal. This is a simple and relatively inexpensive test to run and well worth doing since it can save your foal's life. Jaundice in a foal is caused by antibodies in the mare's milk attacking the foal's red blood cells. The antibodies are present in the mare's milk only for the first few days after foaling. The foal ingests the antibodies through nursing the mare. Once a foal becomes jaundiced, it seldom lives.

If the test shows that the newborn foal will be jaundiced, you need to make plans to muzzle the foal at birth to prevent it from nursing its mother and you should have an alternate supply of colostrum and milk on hand to feed the foal for a few days. The colostrum and milk you will use should also be tested for jaundice reaction before administering to the foal. Further information on caring for a jaundiced foal is listed in the section on newborn foal care.

THE FOALING PROCESS — SIGNS AND SIGNALS

A great deal of the horse business, such as foaling, is a visual experience. You have to be able to read the signs, to understand the signals the horse gives you as to whether everything is O.K.

The important thing to remember is that no two mares are alike. There is no set pattern that you can read about in the textbooks to prepare yourself for foaling. Certain mares will develop certain habits and go through the same physical cycle, and this will allow you to make an educated guess as to what is happening.

As a mare gets closer to her due date, I am continually examining her udder development. When her udder or "bag" starts to enlarge, it means that nature's foaling system is beginning to kick into gear.

The mare may also begin to "wax up," a term used when a white, chalky substance appears on her bag. When this occurs, I know the mare is getting closer to foaling. Under normal circumstances, a mare in this condition can be anywhere from one day to one week from foaling. However, when the bag turns dark and has a slick, transparent look to it, the mare is due to foal within hours.

There are mares who will fool you. I have seen situations where I have examined a mare at feeding time and determined that she was still a few days from foaling, only to receive a call from the foaling barn hours later that the mare's water had broken and she was foaling. I have also seen situations where I was turning a mare out for her regular time in the field and her water broke on the way to the field. In foaling, as in so many other things, mares do not always do what you expect.

There is some debate about how big a foaling stall needs to be. I don't like a small, racetrack-size stall that is only about 10' x 12', because you do not have adequate room to get in and help a mare in the event of trouble. A foaling stall ideally should measure about 14' x 16'. I prefer a stall of that size because a mare will almost invariably lie down against a wall and this will give you most of the remaining stall area to get help to her in the event that she has trouble.

One of the most ominous signs of trouble with a mare's foaling is when she starts into labor, and then stops. This may happen once, and I will not be alarmed, but if it persists for a couple of days, I know that the mare is in trouble. Something is not right; the mare's natural instincts are being stopped. In many cases, this results in either a stillborn foal or a very difficult delivery.

The majority of mares, however, go through a pretty normal labor and foaling process. Once labor begins, most mares will start to walk excessively and will begin to scratch their tails. Her stool will become soft and she will empty out often. As she nears foaling, a mare may break out in a sweat and start a repeated pattern of laying down and getting up. This is especially true with maiden mares who are experiencing their first foaling. They do not know what is happening and can become a little agitated.

A maiden mare will always take longer to foal, so you have to learn to be patient. If the mare was a high-caliber racehorse and is in foal to a top stallion, it takes a lot of restraint on my part to stay out of her stall. A lot of times a maiden mare will get up and down repeatedly before she begins to foal, but this is not a cause for concern. The mare is simply trying to help get the foal into the correct position to be born. I am especially careful with maiden mares, however, because I don't want them attempting to get up once the foal has started to deliver and cause possible harm to the baby.

After a mare's water breaks, things begin to happen pretty quickly. If the mare is not already laying down, she will normally do so soon after her water breaks, and then the birthing process begins. In many cases, only 10 to 15 minutes elapse from the moment the water breaks until foaling is completed. If a mare's water breaks, and she does not foal in the next 15 minutes or less (in most cases), the chances are pretty high that you have a very serious problem.

By the time the mare lies down to foal, you will often be able to see the front legs and head of the foal emerging from the birth canal. The head should be resting on the two front legs; this is the correct position for foaling. This is the first sign that everything is proceeding in a normal fashion. If a mare is not in a lot of distress, and everything is proceeding normally, I will allow her to foal all by herself. I want to let a mare do all she can on her own in the foaling barn. I want nature to take its course.

The temptation is pretty strong to run right in to help a mare who lies down and starts foaling, but a great many mares are pretty smart and would learn to wait on human assistance. If a mare has had help for a couple of years in foaling, I think she figures this out and will wait on us to come pull the foal out of her.

With the young mares, I am very careful, therefore, not to be too quick to jump in and provide assistance, unless there is an obvious problem. Also, a great many young mares will start into labor and have everything going O.K. but will stop the minute a human comes into the stall.

TROUBLE DURING FOALING

The first real sign of trouble is if the foal's front legs and head do not appear simultaneously. There are many variations of trouble and one of the most common is to see one front leg and the head emerging. In this instance, you must push the foal back in, find the other leg and put it in the correct position. The foal cannot clear the birth canal past its shoulders with a leg bent under.

Another sure sign of trouble is when the legs appear, but the head does not. Normally, in this instance, the head is bent back to one side or another. You have to reach in and get the head into the correct position before foaling can continue.

The foal may also be presented breach, which is the worst possible scenario. The foal may be presented sideways, or can even be upside down. The chances of a successful foaling in a breach birth are very slim.

CARE OF THE NEWBORN FOAL

Providing everything went well during foaling, the foal should be examined closely to confirm that everything is O.K. and to make sure that any of the afterbirth or fluid is clear of its nostrils and mouth. This can be accomplished simply by putting two fingers above the nose of the foal and rubbing down over the nostrils.

Many people are quick to break the umbilical cord, but I like to leave the foal attached to the mare for as long as the mare stays down. If the mare stays down for too long, I may move the foal around to the front of the mare. This will break the cord; however, I like it to be as natural a process as possible. The foal and the mare need time to recover from the trauma of the birthing process, and valuable nutrients are still being passed through the umbilical cord. During this "down time," the foal should be dried off with a towel.

Immediately after the umbilical cord breaks, we put iodine on the foal's navel for the first time, and continue this once a day, for five days, to induce healing.

Before the mare gets up, I like to examine the placenta to make sure the mare has expelled all of the birth sac. Tie up the placenta to insure that it does not break off or that she doesn't step on it. The weight of the tied placenta will also help speed the cleaning process. A mare should "clean" or expel the entire placenta in an hour or so.

The average foal will be up on its feet within two hours. The foal instinctively gets up to nurse and will muddle its way around until it finds the mare's udder. Some foals may require a little assistance and you may have to guide them to the mare's udder.

An assessment of the mare's ability to provide the foal with colostrum must be made. Colostrum is the mare's first milk after foaling and it is rich in antibodies and nutrition, vital for the health of the newborn foal.

Most farms try to build up a good supply of colostrum for emergencies. It is obtained from foaling mares who have an ample supply and can be collected after a mare has nursed her new foal once or twice. The collected colostrum is frozen and kept on hand in the foaling barn to supplement those foals whose mothers can't provide it for them.

To check for the presence of colostrum, we do a one-time test called a Gamma-Check-C on the mare's milk immediately after foaling. The test checks for good clotting ability which shows that colostrum is present containing the vital ingredients that the newborn foal needs. If the clotting results are poor, the foal should be supplemented with good colostrum from another mare, hopefully from the supply you have frozen ahead of time.

If colostrum must be administered to a foal, I prefer to do so via a stomach tube, although the same process can be accomplished using a bottle. I prefer the tube because feeding from a bottle can discourage a foal from nursing a mare. Feed the foal about a pint of colostrum which has been thawed to room temperature ahead of time. The colostrum can be thawed in warm water but do not heat it or use a microwave since this kills the antibodies in the milk.

As discussed in the section on maintenance of the in-foal mare, if the pre-foaling blood test on your mare was positive for jaundice, the newborn foal must be muzzled immediately to prevent it from nursing the mare, generally for the next 24 to 48 hours. The foal will need to receive colostrum which has been checked for a jaundice reaction to the foal. After the foal has received colostrum (I feed it to them two times), you can then begin to feed the foal milk, either tested milk from another mare, foal-lac powder, or goat's milk. The foal will have to be fed every one and a half to two hours and the mare will need to be milked out at the same interval.

In order to test to see when it is safe to remove the muzzle and allow the foal to nurse the mare, blood will have to be drawn from the foal and a tiny sample of the mare's milk will have to be taken. The test is called jaundice foal agglutination, or JFA test, and it is usually done at 12 to 24 hour intervals by your veterinarian until the antibody level in the mare's milk has lowered far enough for the foal to safely nurse. A safe antibody level will usually be reached within 48 hours after foaling, at which time the care of the mare and foal can resume to normal.

During the first few hours after a foal's birth, we perform either a warm-water or mineral-oil enema in order to get rid of its first feces. This is very important with a foal who was late in coming, because it is very common for the late foal to suffer from a bowel impaction. We also give a newborn about 5 cc's of antibiotics daily for three days.

Within the first 24 hours, I want a mare and foal outside, if possible. If the weather is really poor, I leave them out for only a couple of hours, but the exercise is important.

It is often necessary to use a nurse mare with young foals. Nurse mares are used when the foal's natural mother must be shipped away to be re-bred, or there is a risk of injury from the natural mother. The foal in the picture is an Artsplace sister to world champion pacing colt Jenna's Beach Boy.

When the foal is 24 hours old (not before), its blood should be checked for the proper level of antibodies. These antibodies help the foal fight off disease and infection during its early days of life. Your veterinarian will draw some blood from the foal and perform an IgG (immunoglobulin G) test which indicates the antibody count. If the count is too low, the foal will need to receive plasma.

NURSE MARES

I am very careful to note how a mare behaves with a foal. Most mares are very good mothers; they are very protective and willing milkers. But there are mares who do not perform these tasks as you would like, and a decision has to be made about using nurse mares.

One of the mares with whom I am very familiar is Five O'Clock Cindy, the dam of the world champion colt pacer Jenna's Beach Boy. This mare is really a problem because she is so over-protective of her foals. I think she would be an excellent mother if she could just be turned out with her foal and left alone, but of course, that is not possible. The foal has to be handled to be trimmed and de-wormed and she just would not allow that. I am afraid that in her desire to protect her foal, she would step on it or hurt it in some way. In the last two years, I have taken her foals away from her at birth. When they come out of her, I just keep going with them and never even let her see them. I get them on a nurse mare immediately.

Nurse mares are valuable because they readily supply a quantity of milk for the foal and assure that the proper nutritional requirements are met. Nurse mares also are generally very docile and readily adopt almost any foal. Injury to a foal from a fractious mare is something that has to be avoided. If I think a mare is just too fractious for her foal's own safety, I will remove her foal and put it on a nurse mare.

I know that a lot of breeders do not like nurse mares because they want a foal getting the milk and the socialization from its real dam. I agree with this to a point. The whole question turns on potential harm to the foal. What good is it for a foal to get the dam's milk if the foal is injured in the process? In the case of a potentially valuable foal, you cannot afford the risk of injury, so the use of a nurse mare is advised.

Another case where a nurse mare might be indicated is with a foal of potentially high value whose dam is going to be shipped to be re-bred somewhere else. In many cases, I want to keep that foal on the farm where I know it can be watched, instead of sending it to another farm where it might have to survive strictly as a number. This is really a matter of economics. If a foal potentially is a $100,000 yearling, I am very cautious about sticking it on a truck at a young age and sending it off for three to four months away from me.

The other situations where nurse mares are indicated revolve around mares with poor udder output, or where the mare dies in foaling.

FOAL MANAGEMENT

Foal development should be monitored very closely. A foal should show regular weight gain almost immediately, and you should be able to assess any conformation faults within a matter of weeks. The young foal is so crooked normally, that it is virtually impossible to see any minor faults. Most young foals look awkward and ungainly.

Within the first six weeks, however, you can begin to make an assessment of the foal's conformation, and can begin corrective trimming when the foal is about two to two-and-a-half months old. I also recommend that de-worming begin at about six weeks of age and continue on a monthly basis. I try to perform de-worming and trimming at the same time. It is not possible to trim a horse until his hoof wall is developed sufficiently, and that generally is at the age of two to two-and-a-half months.

Although the very first de-worming may be done with a paste given orally, I prefer tube de-worming for the balance of a young horse's development. In this way, I am assured that the various de-worming products are getting into the horse's stomach, and in the proper quantities. For the various types of de-worming products, please consult the list of de-wormers which accompanies this chapter. And please ask your local veterinarian about the kinds of parasites that are most common to your area of the country. The main thing with de-worming is to make sure you do it, and do it religiously.

I do think it helps to handle foals as much as possible, to teach them to lead and be around people. This process is formally called "imprinting" now, but it's the same thing we have been doing for years: Getting the foals used to people and comfortable with being handled.

When a foal and its dam are turned out, I keep a halter on the mare but not on the foal. Most larger farms use some type of freeze brand for identification purposes, or, if necessary, neck straps or chains can serve. I have a manageable number of mares and foals that I see on a daily, hands-on basis so I do not have trouble with identification. I don't like to keep halters on young foals that are out all the time because they can get into trouble in the field with one on. I have seen foals injured by getting a halter caught on a fence or gate. After a foal is weaned, and goes into a field with a group, then a halter with ID is added.

WEANING—A STRESSFUL TIME

Every fall at my farm, a very important ritual occurs—the process of weaning foals from the mares. I have seen this done in several different ways and I have tried doing it any number of ways. I have developed a set of circumstances that I find to be the least stressful.

When it is time for weaning in the fall (around October 15), I like to pull a truck and four-horse trailer into a field of mares and foals. In most cases, I will have already separated the colts and fillies that I plan to run together. In one field, for instance, I will have mares with colts who will grow up together, and in another field I will have mares with filly foals who will stay together through the next year.

I catch and load the mares and truck them out of the field until only one mare remains. The last mare to be removed is one who generally is of advanced age and whose temperament is very docile. By leaving the older mare in the field, the amount of stress to the young foals is somewhat lessened. The presence of at least one mare gives the foals some security. In a day or two, the older mare can be removed as well.

Many breeders like to wean foals by putting the mare and foal in a box stall, then removing the mare. In my opinion, this is too traumatic for the mare and foal and is not a good practice, because it risks injury to the foal. The foal is generally going to be very agitated and want to get to his dam and will do a lot of bouncing around in a box stall. It is not uncommon in this situation for a foal to be injured.

By doing the weaning outside in the field, I allow an agitated foal to simply run around the pasture, and the risk of injury is lessened considerably.

START FEEDING HAY AND GRAIN

Weaning occurs in the fall of the year when the foals are at least five months of age. Depending on what kind of late-summer and early-fall weather has prevailed, the grass in most pastures is waning, and it is very important to start the weaned foals on a regular ration of grain and hay.

Young horses who will be asked to begin competitive training in a little over a year need every advantage we can give them. Access to high-quality grain and good hay is very important at this stage of development. I prefer either clover or alfalfa hay for my young horses. I do not recommend giving timothy hay to young horses, as most timothy hays do not have enough protein and nutrients. I do use timothy hay on my farm, but it is generally reserved for barren mares or pensioners. Given a choice, a horse will not eat timothy hay if he is also presented with clover or alfalfa.

As the weather worsens in early winter, I want to keep a high-quality hay in front of my young horses at all times. It is important to remember that horses are grazers; a young horse should have access to hay at all times.

I want to group likes together, that is, same sizes and rate of development. I try to feed according to how many are together and what they look like. It is very much an individual thing. For instance, if I had ten yearlings together I would feed a 50 lb. bag of pelleted feed plus ear corn. No plan really offers a fail-safe guarantee that a yearling is getting what it needs, and I really feel that if I see the yearlings every day, I can assess their growth and condition just by looking at them.

A rapid period of growth comes with the arrival of spring. It is important to remember that, with the young horses, weight gain is gradual, but growth comes in spurts.

It is inevitable that some of the yearlings will get a little heavy, especially the ones who are not very active. It is also inevitable that some of the foals will be too thin. The metabolism of some of them is so fast it is impossible to put weight on them. These problems, however, afflict a very small portion of the entire yearling population.

As a guide, I try to give my weanlings/yearlings about 8 to 10 pounds of grain daily during the winter months, and to keep high-quality hay in front of them at all times. I prefer a pelleted grain with a 14- percent protein count. I used to feed grain with a 16-percent protein rate, but finally determined it was too high in protein when used in concert with feed supplements or when the grass was plentiful.

I try to keep tabs on each yearling to determine its development. If a colt is timid and is in a field of bullies who won't let him eat, I transfer him to another field where he can get what he needs. Such a situation is very important and needs to be monitored, because every yearling needs to get the proper ration to develop to the fullest.

CORRECTIVE TRIMMING

Proper hoof maintenance is a very important item in the raising of foals, because the old adage of "no-foot, no horse" is as true today as it ever was. One of the most common problems with young foals,

An important lesson taught to young foals is the proper way to lead. This is accomplished by handling the foals. One of the most successful methods, as shown here, is to place a hand on the foal's rump and encourage it to walk along ahead of its mother. You may also employ the use of a butt rope.

particularly during a hot, dry summer, is that the hooves will not have enough moisture to encourage proper hoof growth. In the early spring when there is a heavy dew each morning and lots of rain, hoof problems are not as common. During the summer, though, when the weather turns hot and dry, I have to be on the lookout for hoof trouble.

Unless I have a foal with exceptionally poor conformation, I will trim about every one-and-a-half to two months. For a foal with relatively serious conformation flaws, I try to trim every month to give it the best chance for proper growth and development.

There are two things that can help you with this problem. One occurs naturally; the other is man-made.

If there happens to be a spot which seems to collect water and stays wet most of the time, I don't necessarily get rid of it. This creates a natural mud hole, and it is a very healthy place for hoof development. When I built my farm in Kentucky, there were several areas that stayed wet most of the time which could have been alleviated by moving some dirt, but I knew the value of having a place where a horse's hooves could get wet. Horses naturally gravitate toward the mud hole because the wet, cool mud helps cool them off in hot weather and encourages healthy hoof development.

If I have a run-in shed with sawdust or pine bark on the floor, I try to keep it wet with a hose. In this way, a young horse stands in moisture while he eats, and the moisture is very good for healthy hoof development.

If a colt or filly needs special attention with regard to corrective trimming, I like to tack on a pair of shoes around the fourth or fifth month. Many foals who naturally toe-in or toe-out can be corrected, but the problem will recur each month because of the way the horse travels. His natural gait in the field will accentuate any problem present. A colt who toes out, for instance, will wear down his hoof that way. What I like to do is keep returning a horse to level, and let nature help to remedy the problem. I have seen a great many cases where a foal with what I thought were significant conformation problems remedy themselves over time. You have to be patient. You must not overreact and do something drastic.

Generally speaking, however, I do not encourage any drastic measures with corrective trimming during the early months of life. I have found that a lot of mistakes can be made in trying to overcompensate for conformation flaws in a young foal. In many cases, it is better to live with the problem and not do anything drastic.

If I have a weanling or yearling who needs corrective shoeing, I will also encourage the growth of the foot by using some counter-irritant therapy on the coronary band. What I prefer is a compound using regular Reducine hoof treatment laced with a little venus of turpentine and DMSO. Reducine alone generally does not create the kind of irritation I am looking for. That is why I add the turpentine solution to develop a good amount of irritation. I know I am getting results when I see a scurf develop around the coronary band. I usually apply the counter-irritant each day for about five to six days, then wait and see what happens.

If I am attempting to correct a weanling or yearling, I want the foot growing as rapidly as possible. I also use mud therapy a lot with yearlings, keeping their feet packed regularly with mud to which Epsom salts and vinegar have been added.

CORRECTIVE SURGERY FOR MORE SERIOUS PROBLEMS

If a weanling has more serious problems of a skeletal nature, it may be necessary to use corrective surgery. One of the more common problems with young horses is the presence of OCD lesions (debris or very small bone chips) in the ankles, hocks and stifle joints. This is easy to detect since fluid will build up in the affected area.

If this condition is present, it will be necessary to X-ray the suspicious areas to determine the nature of the problem. Ideally, this should be done when the weanling is between the ages of six to eight months of age, or during the fall of the year, the earlier the better.

OCD surgery is not dangerous for the weanling or yearling, and the success rate of the surgery has developed to the point where it is no longer seen as a negative for development.

There are surgeries on foals, such as periosteal stripping, stapling of

The author's preference in a creep feeder is shown in this photo. The round design encourages safety as the risk of injury is diminished. This pen is approximately 35 feet in diameter, with openings about 24 inches in width. This allows the foals access to the feed, which is distributed in ground feed tubs. The small openings prevent mares from entering.

offset knees, etc.,that are available to correct some subtle conformation flaws. In most instances, if there is a serious conformation problem, you will just have to admit that it is something veterinary science cannot address.

CREEP FEEDERS

A number of farm managers have forsaken the use of creep feeders in their fields for young horses, but I have always had great success in using creep feeders and recommend them highly. I do not think a foal gets fat too quickly if his ration is correct, and I think it is very desirable for a young foal to eat grain as soon as it is able.

Creep feeders got their name originally from the fact that a foal was able to "creep" under a railed obstruction which prevents access to a full-grown horse, in this case the dam of the foal as well as the other mares in that field. The foal can get under the rail, but the mares cannot. However, my creep feeders are designed a little differently. First, they are circular in design and about 30-35 feet in diameter, and can accommodate about 12-15 foals. Instead of the foal passing under a railing, I have created gaps in the fence about 24 inches in width. This prevents the mares from getting in, and the foals generally are not subject to injury in a circular pen.

I also do not use a feeding trough in my creeps. I prefer plastic or rubber feeding tubs that are placed on the ground. Wooden troughs will hold water, and any grain that is not cleaned up by the foals is left to spoil.

If such grain is ingested later by a young horse, this can create a serious problem. On the other hand, the plastic or rubber tubs can be picked up and cleaned regularly and do not present a safety hazard to the foals if stepped on.

I also would recommend the construction of a small gate in the circular creep enclosure, because invariably there is a foal who finds himself alone in the creep and cannot find his way out. A mare also may find her way into the creep, and the gate makes it easy to retrieve her if necessary.

I feed foals twice a day, but I am very careful not to overfeed them. This is a management issue where I watch the development of each foal and assess their growth and weight-gain. I want to keep young foals aggressive at the creep feeder and am careful to never give them as much as they really want. Generally speaking, I feed a group of foals an amount that they will clean up between feedings (about two quarts of pelleted grain each) twice a day until it is time for weaning. I feel this is usually adequate to supplement the mare's milk and whatever grass is present in the late spring and early summer.

I do not recommend that a foal have free access to grain. The ration should be monitored according to the overall condition and age of the foal. I always tell my help to not feed a weanling if he did not clean up his morning ration. I think a horse who is underfed is a bigger problem than one who is overfed. With one who is fat, at least you know he is getting everything you want him to have—and then some. The underfed foal, however, is not getting what you want it to receive, and its growth and overall development may be stunted.

Creep feeders are a very valuable tool in creating a transition between the foals being sustained entirely on mare's milk and grass and their starting on a full ration of grain and hay.

When the foal is weaned, the creep feeder is no longer necessary, and a foal can be fed with the rest of its buddies in the fields and run-in sheds.

RUN-IN SHEDS

The size of run-in sheds and their design will depend greatly on the size of the pasture where the horses are to be raised. 1 prefer to have anywhere from 12 to 15 yearlings in one field together. I separate colts and fillies as a matter of course.

Run-in sheds normally are built adjacent to a barn so the yearlings can be caught easily when they are to be de-wormed and/or trimmed. My run-in sheds for 12 to 15 yearlings are 32' by 70', with a feed trough through the middle to allow access from both sides.

FEED AND WATER—IMPORTANT FACTORS

I use a pelleted feed and a commercial feed supplement for my weanlings and yearlings, as well as free-choice minerals such as dicalcium phosphate and mineralized block salt. This guarantees that

Socialization is an important aspect of raising a young foal. The author believes that young horses should be raised together with other youngsters. A pasture mate for a young horse does not necessarily have to be another foal, as quite often an older horse makes quite an acceptable pasture buddy for a young foal.

proper nutrition levels are maintained and the total feeding program is sustained throughout the critical periods of development.

Yearlings, as well as all horses, should have access to plenty of clean, fresh water of high quality. I use automatic electric waterers in all my fields on the farm, thus ensuring access to water at all times and in all climactic conditions. In bad weather a horse can still thrive if he can eat and drink water.

HOW MUCH PASTURE IS NECESSARY?

I am often asked to provide a guide to how much land is necessary to raise horses. This is a question which has many facets.

During my tenure at Castleton Farm earlier in my career, we had access to a lot of pasture, with huge, rolling fields where yearlings could run and exercise through acres and acres of lush Kentucky bluegrass.

This is a rare situation, unfortunately.

Most breeders are faced with tough economic decisions, and land is one of the most valuable commodities in a horse breeding and raising operation. In some parts of the country, especially in the East, land is so valuable for development that using it for horses is not even an option.

Ideally, I would prefer a situation where the ratio of land to each horse was about 3:1 (three acres for each horse). Realistically, however, a 2:1 or 1 1/2:1 ratio is more normal. This whole subject really turns on the quality of the pasture. If the grass has not been overgrazed and is of high quality, a horse can be sustained quite nicely in a small pasture. If the grass is of poor quality, or has been depleted by overgrazing, a 50-acre field could be inadequate. Fortunately, in Kentucky, the grass in our pastures is of a high quality with a high protein count. If we get ample rain and good growing conditions, Kentucky grass is just about perfect for raising horses in concert with high-quality grains and hays. If horses are boarded on sandy pastures with little grass, it is absolutely imperative that the grains and hay they receive are of the highest quality.

It is also very important that grass pastures be maintained properly. Soil samples should be taken frequently to determine the mineral levels available from the soil in order to determine the fertilization and liming needs. Grass should be mowed on a regular basis as this is very important for proper weed control.

Pasture should be dragged with a field harrow in the spring and fall to break up manure piles. I do not drag the field in the summer months because this tends to open the pasture to the air and it will dry out even more than normal. You want to retain as much moisture as possible in the summer grass.

The quality of land can be easily determined by soil analysis. In Kentucky, we are fortunate that our soil is naturally very high in the basic nutrients, mainly large deposits of limestone, so important to the development of young horses. However, some pastures are better than others, even when in close proximity. I would urge anyone who is raising Standardbreds to have their soil evaluated and to use liberal applications of fertilizer and lime to ensure that young horses receive every possible advantage in development.

FENCING—WHAT TYPES ARE BEST?

Another frequent question concerns the best type of fencing for horses.

Most of the larger horse farms in the country use a three or four-board wooden fence. This is largely a matter of economics, although certainly the four-board fence is very attractive. It also happens to be the most cost-effective method of fencing.

I suppose, if cost were no object, then the miles of fencing required for a horse farm of any consequence would be chain-link or diamond-mesh fencing with a top rail or top-board. However, in most cases, this is cost prohibitive.

A board fence is the most economical way to fence horse farm acreage and it provides adequate protection in most cases. It is not as inherently safe as chain-link or diamond-mesh fencing, but is more than adequate.

I do recommend that three or four-board fences be constructed with posts set on about eight-foot centers, using 16-foot boards, and that all corners be rounded, if possible. The fence should be anywhere from 48 to 52 inches in height. Posts should be set in the ground as deep as possible; certainly below the frost line in your area. If the posts are not set in the ground deep enough, the fence will not be strong enough and will become a maintenance problem.

A number of injuries occur each year in fields where the fences meet at right angles. I recommend that all corners be rounded off so a horse never encounters a sharp dead-end. A horse naturally follows a fence line, and thus the rounded corner is very useful in preventing injury.

The question of gates also arises with pasture layout. I firmly believe it is desirable to use as few gates as possible. Most horse acreage will have 12-foot gates, but this really is determined by how much width is needed for access to the fields by heavy equipment and trailers. There should be as few gates as possible and they should be located so they provide easy access from the adjacent barns and fields.

Gates also should be designed to fit snugly to gate posts, and there should be no room for a young horse to get caught between a gate and a gate post. When a gate is closed, it should fit snugly up against a gate post. If there is any way for a young horse to hurt himself, he will find it. Every precaution should be taken to avoid this, because many young horses have been trapped between a gate and gate post that fit poorly, and have been injured or killed in an attempt to extricate themselves.

SUMMARY

In summary, it is all but impossible to cover every facet of broodmare and foal management in just one chapter. I have tried to stick with the generalities and with the good practices I have learned over the past 35 years.

Remember, a good horseman is an everyday horseman. Being a practicing horseman is more art than science. Almost every decision requires that you trust your instincts, your previous experience, and acquired knowledge.

It also requires your vigilance, your observation and lots of common sense. I take a great deal of pride in what I do and how I do it. It is the way I was taught and it is the only way I can imagine operating in the horse business today.

1. **DE-WORM**

   A) Anthelcide/Equipar (Oxibendazole)

   B) Benzelmin   (Oxfendazole)

   C) Eqvalan/Zimecterin (Ivermectin)

   D) Febantel   (Rintal)

   E) Panacur   (Fenbendazole)

   F) Strongid-T/Imathal (Pyrantel Pamoate)

   G) TBZ-Piperazine

2. **FOAL - DE-WORM** (Same as mare, See #1)

3. **VACCINES**

   A) Botulism toxoid

   B) E/W, Flu, Tet.

   C) Encephalitis (EEE & WEE)

   D) Flu

   E) Potomac Fever

   F) Rabies

   G) Rhinopheumonitis/PBK

   H) Strangles

   I) Tetanus

4. **FOAL-VACCINES** (Same as mare-See#3)

7. **CULTURE**

   A) Negative

   B) Positive

8. **SPEC**

   A) Normal

   B) Bruised

9. **RECTAL EXAM**

   A) Activity on right

   B) Activity on left

   C) Follicle on right

   D) Follicle on left

   E) No follicle

10. **SUTURE VULVA**

12. **TREAT UTERUS**

   A) Betadine

   B) Furicin

   C) Gentomycin

   D) Penicillin

   E) Saline

   F) Sodium Penicillin

13. **HORMONE INJECTION**

   A) H.C.G.

   B) Progesterone

   C) Prostaglandin

16. **PRE-FOALING BLOOD**

17. **U.S.T.A. BLOOD TYPE - MARE**

   A) Foal

32. **COGGINS**

"cb" = could be; "p" = early pregnancy; "P" = pregnant; "B" = barren

NOTE: This is a copy of the legend used at Peninsula Farm to record Breeding and Health Records for all mare. For example, a notation of 9C on a Breeding/Health Record would indicate that a rectal exam (9.) as above, was performed and a follicle was present on the right ovary (C). These notations are used in the charts in the pages which follow.

1—SNEAKER BY

This shows the record of a mare who was in foal, foaled successfully and was re-bred only once after foaling. The single breeding produced a pregnancy. The mare foaled on May 6, did not have a foal heat, was given an injection of prostaglandin on May 23 and came in heat a few days after that. She was bred on May 28, went out of heat immediately thereafter, and had a pregnancy confirmed by ultrasound on June 11.

.129.........

NAME. SNEAKER BY

19 94 BREEDING/HEALTH RECORD

IN FOAL to Die Laughing DUE TO FOAL 4/17/94 TO BE BRED TO Die Laughing DATE OF FOALING 5/6/94. COLOR Bay IN 19 94 SEX Colt 17

Peninsula Farm

Examined for Pregnancy 7/5/94 Pregnant + 7/13 Preg. Due Date for Next Year 4/28/95

This is an example of a mare that was to be shipped away to breed so she was short cycled in order to cut down on the time she would have to be boarded, plus, it gave her extra time after foaling to recover.

2—MORIA ALMAHURST

This mare foaled on March 23 and came back into heat 31 days later, on April 24. She had a very active heat period, and was bred twice on the second and fourth days of her estrus. She did not conceive, however. She came back in heat on May 20, was bred once on May 21, ovulated almost immediately thereafter, and was pronounced in foal by ultrasound on June 6.

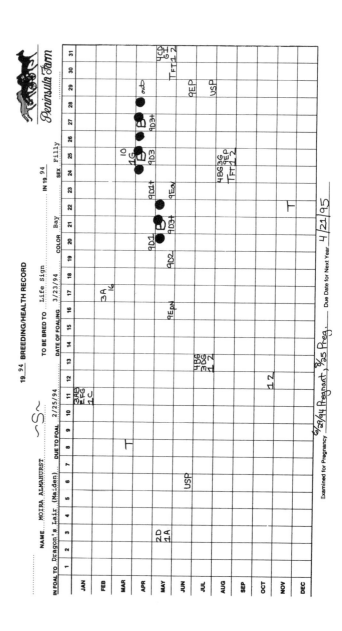

19 94 BREEDING/HEALTH RECORD

Peninsula Farm

NAME MOIRA ALMAHURST DUE TO FOAL 2/25/94 TO BE BRED TO Life Sign 3/23/94 IN 19 94

IN FOAL TO Dragon's Lair (Maiden) DATE OF FOALING COLOR Bay SEX Filly

Examined for Pregnancy 6/28/94 Pregnant, %5 Preg. Due Date for Next Year 4/21/95

3—ARMBRO DESIRE

This is the case of a barren mare who came into heat on March 26 for the first time in the season, had good follicle activity, was bred once on March 28 and conceived.

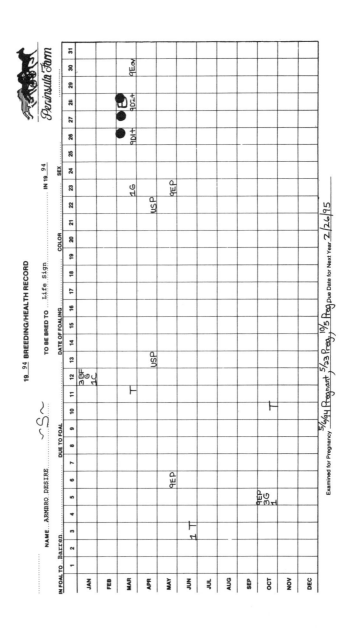

4—A LOT OF URGE

Here is a mare who was a real challenge. She first came in heat on March 20 but was not bred. She was a maiden mare and had insufficient follicular activity. Her second heat period, which began on April 7, was of short duration but was a poor estrus, and she was not bred, either. Early in May, she was bred for the first time and immediately went out of heat, but came back in heat later in the month. She was bred once again on May 21, ovulated and looked to be in foal. But she was not. She came back in heat on June 7, was bred on June 8, went out of heat on June 10 and was confirmed in foal via ultrasound on June 27.

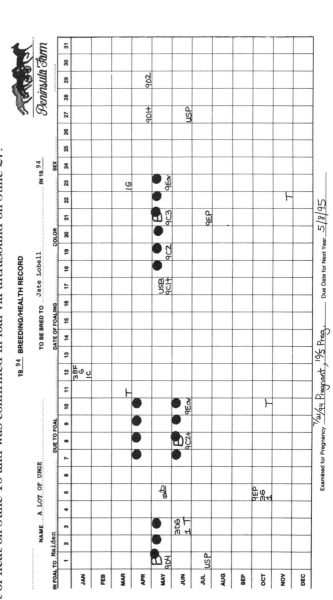

NAME A. LOT. OF. URGE.

IN FOAL TO Maiden.

19. 94 BREEDING/HEALTH RECORD

TO BE BRED TO Jate Lobell   IN 19 94

Peninsula Farm

Examined for Pregnancy 7/2/94 Pregnant, 19/5 Preg.   Due Date for Next Year 5/8/95

When Carter Duer walked onto Castleton Farm in the spring of 1961, he thought he had died and gone to heaven. It was everything he had dreamed about while working with his father's horses back in Exmore, VA. Castleton Farm was a wonderful facility for breeding and raising horses and the horses at Castleton included some of the best Standardbreds in the world.

Duer began working at Castleton under the supervision of William S. Brown and was later chosen to develop a new farm that Castleton acquired near Trenton, FL. In 1970, Duer was named to manage Castleton's splendid main farm in Lexington.

During his tenure at Castleton, Duer supervised the stud careers of Good Time, Bret Hanover, Speedy Scot, Race Time, Noble Gesture, Strike Out and many other stallions who have left a lasting imprint on the breed.

After leaving Castleton, Duer managed Kentuckiana Farms for several years. He now operates his own Peninsula Farm, a boarding and breeding facility near Lexington. It is a family-run operation with wife Helen, daughters Teresa and Donna and son John all actively involved, in one way or another, with the day-to-day operation of the farm. Duer has also operated his own training stable, using The Red Mile as a base.

Duer is respected by his peers for his uncanny knowledge of horses, particularly broodmares. Many of the sport's leading breeders have entrusted the care of their mares to Duer, knowing he is a master of every small detail associated with horse care.

Duer is also known for his ability to prep yearlings, bringing them to peak form the moment they walk into a sales ring. Each year he serves as agent for the owners of some of the best-bred yearlings in the sport.

LEADING MATERNAL FAMILIES

Peace Corps is the leading money-winning Standardbred of all time and hails from the Medio family branch which emanates from the famed Miss Bertha Dillon, who is Peace Corps' sixth dam. Shown with regular U. S. driver John Campbell on the night she established a world record of 1:57.1f in the Breeders Crown at Pompano Park, Peace Corps raced successfully on two continents and won the Kentucky Futurity, World Trotting Derby, International Trot, Elitlopp and four Breeders Crowns.

MEDIO (Miss Bertha C.)

The Medio family is closely tied to the history of Hanover Shoe Farms.

When Lawrence Sheppard acquired Miss Bertha Dillon for Hanover from the A.B. Coxe estate in the 1920's, he could not have imagined the impact that act would have on the history of the Standardbred. This became the breed's largest and most famous family, owing nearly its entire existence to Miss Bertha Dillon, a daughter of Dillon Axworthy foaled in 1914. This prolific great grand-daughter of Medio was the first mare to produce three 2:00 trotters and had seven daughters who each founded a family branch.

The Medio family is most remarkable because, in more than one instance, it has produced the fastest horses in the history of the breed—*at both gaits!*

The most accomplished branch of this family is the trotting stronghold that emanates from Miss Bertha Dillon's 1926 foal, Miss Bertha Hanover 4,T2:00. From her daughters came such luminaries as Hambletonian winners Egyptian Candor, Green Speed, Mack Lobell and American Winner, as well as the European star Sea Cove. This branch is also responsible for Peace Corps, the richest Standardbred in history and Arndon, sire of Pine Chip.

Trotters are also prominent in the family of Miss Bertha Dillon's 1927 foal, Hambletonian and Kentucky Futurity winner Hanover's Bertha 3,T1:59 1/2, whose daughter Shirley Hanover also captured trotting's biggest prize. Hanover's Bertha is the grandam of Hambo champ Blaze Hanover in a branch represented by the $1 million-winning Britelite Lobell, international star Giant Force and Breeders Crown filly champions Lookout Victory and Imageofa Clear Day.

Noted pacers were developed in the branches descending from Miss Bertha Dillon's 1925 daughter Miss Bertha Worthy; her 1928 filly Charlotte Hanover 3,T1:59 1/2; and her 1930 foal Bertha Hanover.

The Miss Bertha Worthy group produced world champion racehorse and sire Bret Hanover, his siblings Baron Hanover and the ill-fated filly Bonjour Hanover, 1973 Horse of the Year Sir Dalrae, and millionaire pacing mare Delinquent Account.

Charlotte Hanover's wing found fame for producing world champion pacer Dragon's Lair, as well as Hambletonian winners Timothy T and Christopher T, and the top trotter Cold Comfort.

Pacers in the Bertha Hanover branch of the family tree include millionaire world champions Artsplace p,4,1:49.2 and Cambest p,T1:46.1; the filly sensations Areba Areba and Stienam; and other stars such as Little Brown Jug winners Merger and Best Of All.

Two prominent Medio family branches do not pass through Miss Bertha Dillon. One goes through Jane Dillon, a 1919 sister to Miss Bertha Dillon. This is the family of 1993's two-year-old pacing star Armbro Mackintosh. The other branch emerged from Ariel Wilkes, an 1899 daughter of the foundation mare Medio. This group traces to the trotting matron Duchess Faye and her offspring, including Breeders Crown champ Delray Lobell.

MINNEHAHA (Thompson Sisters)

The Minnehaha family is also known as the Thompson Sisters, referring to Tillie Thompson, a foal of 1890, and Madam Thompson, born in 1891. A third sister, Lydia Thompson, a foal of 1892, had a single foal and did not make the impact that her famous sisters did. However, her only offspring, the gelding Peter Thompson, was the winner of the 1911 Kentucky Futurity.

The Thompson Sisters name for this family is misleading since there are branches that do not descend from either of the mares, both daughters of Guy Wilkes and granddaughters of Minnehaha. One of the non-Thompson sisters branches produced the Electioneer stallion Chimes, an important link in the siring family which eventually led to Good Time, Adios and Meadow Skipper. Another produced FFA stars C K S and Empty Feeling.

Tillie Thompson, oldest of the sisters, produced a large group whose profound legacy includes pacing performers Armbro Feather, Follow My

Shady Daisy is the richest money-winning pacing female of all time, and is a great granddaughter of the legendary sire Bret Hanover. Her maternal roots are very strong, and she hails from one of the breed's strongest outposts of female racing class, the family of Minnehaha.

Star, So Cozy, Caesars Jackpot, Amneris, Shady Daisy and Cinnamon Reel, and trotting stars Miss Tilly, Duenna, Crevette, Davidia Hanover, Filet Of Sole and Desert Wind. This branch may be home to more top racing fillies than any other in the breed. Colts are not without representation in the Tillie Thompson branch, however, with top males such as Hoot Mon, Spartan Hanover, Steve Lobell, Nobleland Sam, Race Time, Storm Damage, Warm Breeze, Harold J., Thorpe Hanover, Dancer Hanover, Speed Bowl, Brisco Hanover, Kentucky Spur and French Chef all accounted for here.

The Madam Thompson branch is smaller, but accounts for trotting stars such as Hambletonian winners Speedy Somolli, Victory Dream, Legend Hanover and Diller Hanover, and Breeders Crown winners Workaholic, Royal Troubador and Wesgate Crown. Pacing champions in this branch include Little Brown Jug winners Happy Escort, Overtrick, Bullet Hanover and Ensign Hanover, world champion and Breeders Crown winner Jenna's Beach Boy, and stakes performers, Village Connection, Flight Director, Happy Chatter, OK Bye and Slapstick.

Among those who have benefited from nurturing this family are such noted breeders as C.W. Phellis, Hanover Shoe Farms, Castleton Farms, Kentuckiana Farms, Lana Lobell Farms and Norman Woolworth.

JESSIE PEPPER

Anyone who has spent any time at all in the history books has heard of Jessie Pepper, an 1861 daughter of Mambrino Chief.

The principal line of descent comes through Jessie Pepper's grand-

Armbro Flight was one of those rare racing fillies that sent historians into the thesaurus for adjectives. The Star's Pride mare was a daughter of Hambletonian winner Helicopter and is one of the most successful trotting broodmares. She produced the Hambletonian-winning Armbro Goal.

daughter Estabella, leading to the famous McKinney sisters Roya McKinney, Regal McKinney and Queenly McKinney. Roya McKinney is the dam of Scotland and his full sisters Rose Scott and Elsie Scott. Rose Scott's family produced Tar Heel, Hickory Smoke, Hickory Pride, Armbro Flight, Armbro Goal and the Canadian star Earl, while Elsie Scott is the fifth dam of Cane Pace winner Falcons Future and the sixth dam of No Nukes.

Another of Roya McKinney's daughters was her 1926 foal La Roya, a daughter of Guy Axworthy. This branch leads directly to the mega-producer Maggie Counsel, who is the third dam of the world champion pacing filly Silk Stockings in a branch that includes two-time Breeders Crown champion Village Jiffy. The world champion racehorse and sire Falcon Seelster also descends from La Roya.

Jessie Pepper is the fifth dam of inaugural Hambletonian winner Guy McKinney, a son of Queenly McKinney. This branch also includes the Canadian sire Run The Table and Coleman Lobell. Jessie Pepper also established the family leading to the storied racemares Belle Acton and Miss Conna Adios, and to champion trotters Doublemint and Worthy Bowl.

The Regal McKinney branch is represented by Guy Abbey, sire of the champion Greyhound, and by the midwestern trot star Pronto Don. Yet another branch of the family comes through the champion mare Mabel

Three Diamonds was one of the top racing daughters of her sire Albatross, and an outstanding representative of her Miss Duvall maternal family. Raced for George Segal by Bruce Riegle (as seen here) Three Diamonds was a daughter of the Bret Hanover mare Ambiguity. Her most noted foal was the 1993 Little Brown Jug winner, Life Sign.

Trask, who at 2:01 3/4 was the fastest trotter sired by Peter The Great. This branch produced Jug heat winner Easy Goer and juvenile Breeders Crown trotting champion Crysta's Best.

Among the many who have sprinkled Jessie Pepper's spices are family founder C.J. Hamlin of Village Farm, Henry Oliver (breeder of Scotland and Rose Scott), Bowman Brown, Sr. (breeder of Hickory Pride and Hickory Smoke), the Armstrong Brothers, Delvin Miller, Lana Lobell Farm and Castleton Farm.

MISS DUVALL / (Romola)

One of the largest families, the Miss Duvall group, expanded dramatically in the 1960's and again in the 1980's, as the females descending from a pair of sisters etched their way into the record books.

The sisters, Romola and Nora Adele, both daughters of the Peter The Great stallion The Senator, are the main family sources although they are a full six generations removed from Miss Duvall. The Romola branch dominated pacing in the 1960's, while Nora Adele's family has more contemporary success. The Romola group has been maintained exclusively by Hanover Shoe Farms. Romola Hanover, a granddaughter of Romola, is one of the breed's most successful matrons, being the dam of nine in 2:00, including classics winners Romeo Hanover and his full brother Romulus Hanover. Romola Hanover has four producing daughters, headlined by the multiple stakes winner Romalie Hanover. Romola Hanover also has four successful full sisters, making this family one of the deepest in *The Register*.

Rochelle Hanover, a younger sister to Romola Hanover, established the branch that accounts for Cane Pace winner Chairmanoftheboard, Jugette winner Misty Raquel, Sweetheart winner Efishnc, and millionaire Robust Hanover.

The Nora Adele branch primarily owes its success to the breeding instincts of William R. Shehan, whose wizardry changed the course of family history. Shehan's pioneering efforts have been nurtured and expanded by both Kentuckiana Farms and Brittany Farms. There are five millionaire pacers in the Nora Adele branches that descend from the Knight Dream mare K. Nora, and the Wilmington mare Miss Norah. This quintet includes Little Brown Jug and Breeders Crown winner Life Sign, the ill-fated Breeders Crown champion Naughty But Nice, Breeders Crown champion Leah Almahurst, the sensational Nadia Lobell and the Ohio sire Tucson Hanover.

The Miss Norah branch of Nora Adele, which produced Nadia Lobell, also includes a trio of world champion females—the Jug-winning Fan Hanover, the Breeders Crown winner Central Park West, and the aged world champion Too Much Trouble. This branch of the family was established and maintained by Vernon Dancer.

This is the only major maternal family that has no significant trotting credits, which is interesting since family founder Miss Duvall does not descend from Hambletonian.

KATHLEEN / (Ethelwyn)

The Kathleen family is reproduced here because of the overall importance of several prominent family members. All major family branches descend from Kathleen's 1882 daughter Ethelwyn, sired by Harold, a son of Hambletonian.

Ethelwyn had five producing daughters, chief of which was her 1896 foal Extasy. Pacing star Good Time is found here, and is easily the most interesting member of this family because his ancestors were all trotters, including the world champion mare Nedda, who trotted in 1:58 1/4 in 1922! Nedda is the third dam of Good Time.

The same branch of Extasy's family leads to the successful pacing stallion Big Towner through Olympia, a granddaughter of Nedda. Meda won the Kentucky Futurity, but appears prominently in the pedigrees of world champion pacing females Handle With Care and Tender Loving Care. Meda's granddaughters Sue Adios and Meadow Connie founded successful family branches as well. An older limb of the family tree, through Ethelwyn, gave us Hambletonian and Kentucky Futurity winner Bill Gallon.

A daughter of Extasy, the Binvolo matron Ethel Volo, produced two significant families. Ethel Volo's daughter Ethelinda won the Kentucky

Handle With Care p,3,1:54.2 (shown with Peter Haughton) was one of the most sensational race fillies in the history of the breed. She was unde-feated at two in 1973, won 53 races and more than $800,000. A daughter of Meadow Skipper, she has a fascinating pedigree, since her seventh dam is the 1920's trotting star Nedda 1:58 1/4.

Futurity, and the latter's son McLin Hanover won the Hambletonian and Kentucky Futurity. Both were exported. A half-sister to Ethel Volo produced 1928 Hambletonian and Kentucky Futurity winner Spencer.

The other family branch includes three successive generations of world champion trotting fillies, led by the noted Stenographer. A full sister to Stenographer, the 1958 foal Hostess, has an active branch going as well, and has produced females whose maternal trail leads to the world champions Star Investment and Express Ride. There is, also, a successful pacing branch emanating from Ethel Volo, through her 1941 granddaughter Pick Up and Pick Up's daughter, the famed Dottie's Pick.

MAMIE

As far back as the early part of the 1900's, offspring tracing their maternal heritage to Mamie have been blessed with exceptional speed and class. The family has two principal branches descending from the half-

Fresh Yankee, a daughter of Hickory Pride, was the first American-bred trotter to earn $1 million, racing for Joe O'Brien. She hails from the same branch of the same maternal family as Valley Victory, trotting's wonder-sire of the 1990's, a female lineage also responsible for pacing millionaires Nihilator and Runnymede Lobell.

sisters Criterion and Rose Leyburn, daughters of Mamie.

The Criterion branch is important to us as the family of Albatross. This limb of the family tree also produced Little Brown Jug winners Dudley Hanover and Henry T. Adios, and was founded at Hanover Shoe Farms.

The Rose Leyburn tribe is more noteworthy because it is much deeper and has produced some of the breed's most outstanding horses. Dartmouth, Nihilator, Mystic Park, Sugarcane Hanover and Valley Victory all owe their maternal heritage to this tribe which descends from the famed Margaret Parish, a great granddaughter of Rose Leyburn.

This branch of the family was prominent in the mid-1930's due to the exploits of Margaret Arion, whose get included such prominent winners as Protector, the exported The Marchioness and Princess Peg, a trio of Kentucky Futurity winners. The modern trail from Margaret Arion traces to Breeders Crown juvenile winner Valley Victory and to the accomplished trotting mares Killbuck Mary and Fresh Yankee. Margaret Arion is the sixth dam of Valley Victory and the fourth dam of both Killbuck Mary and Fresh Yankee. Margaret Castleton, a daughter of Margaret Parish, appears as the granddam of Hambletonian winner The Intruder and as the fifth dam of millionaire pacing champions Nihilator and Runnymede Lobell.

This family branch is closely tied to Walnut Hall Farm.

Rosalind was one of the truly gifted racing trotters of her time. Bred, trained and raced by Ben White, Rosalind is one of the enduring matrons of the trotting breed. An outstanding representative of her Mambrino Beauty maternal family, her third dam was the fabled Volga E, an unbeaten race filly who was a full sister to Peter Volo. Rosalind's half-sister was the dam of Worthy Boy.

MAMBRINO BEAUTY

The first glimpse of quality in the Mambrino Beauty family was the birth in 1911 of Peter Volo. His full sister Volga (Volga E.) was born two years later. Peter Volo and Volga E. are out of Nervolo Belle, a granddaughter of Mambrino Beauty.

Peter Volo sired Volomite, while Volga E., unbeaten in her racing career, founded an active maternal line that led directly to the world champion Rosalind, a trotting mare so gifted that the world record she set in 1938 lasted 36 years! Rosalind's half-sister Warwell Worthy is the dam of Worthy Boy in what is one of trotting's most famous families.

Classic trotters descended directly from Volga E.'s daughter Jane Revere include Triple Crown winner Scott Frost, the world champion two-year-old TV Yankee, and the multiple stakes-winning two-year-old Cumin.

Two other daughters of Volga E. — Volga Hanover and Nervola Hanover — each established their own famous family trees, principally on the pace. Volga Hanover's group includes Little Brown Jug winners Lehigh Hanover, Vicar Hanover, Laverne Hanover and Colt Fortysix. The Nervola Hanover family comes through the full sisters Quilla Byrd, Aquila Byrd and Aquiline Byrd, and their half-sister Quilla Adios, and includes Breed-

Cassin Hanover (with Fred Egan at Lexington in 1957) was a stakes winner who became founder of the breed's most productive families. A foal of 1954, the Hoot Mon filly was a granddaughter of the foundation mare Little Lie. Cassin's daughter Elma is considered one of the elite trotting mares in history, and her full sister produced Triple Crown winner Ayres.

ers Crown champion Kingsbridge and Tattersalls Pace winner Beastmaster.

Peter Volo and Volga E. also had a full sister, The Great Miss Morris, who was foaled in 1917. She is the fifth dam of World Trotting Derby, Kentucky Futurity and Elitlopp winner Napoletano.

MIDNIGHT / (Emily Ellen)

For many years, this family was known just as Emily Ellen. This leads to some confusion, because to focus on Emily Ellen is to overlook a branch that does not pass through that famous mare.

The two family branches descend from the half-sisters Noontide, a foal of 1874, and Lady Kerner, born in 1882, both daughters of Midnight. The Noontide branch, where Emily Ellen is a prominent link in the maternal chain, has a few pacers, but it is the Noontide trotters who have established the high ground.

Trotters in this family include such names as Spencer Scott, Emily's Pride, Noble Victory, Keystone Pioneer, Florida Pro and the world champion Pine Chip. This most successful branch was established by famed breeder Charles W. Phellis. The Lady Kerner branch does not pass through Emily Ellen. Little Lie is the key female, as she is the granddam of Cassin

Impish was one of the most legendary two-year-old trotting fillies in history, racing in 1:58.3 for Frank Ervin. A daughter of The Intruder-Ilo Hanover, Impish was one of those rare racing fillies who also became a celebrated broodmare as well. Her son by Florican, Pay Dirt, became a successful sire in Europe and her daughter Canny Imp became a modern-day foundation producer. Impish is the fourth dam of classics winner Bullville Victory, and her full sister is the dam of Noble Gesture.

Hanover and Arpege, two sisters who produced the international star Elma and Triple Crown winner Ayres, respectively. A full sister to Elma is the third dam of European star Coktail Jet. The family of Little Lie was established by Charlotte Sheppard and maintained by Mrs. Sheppard and John Simpson, Sr.

There is a successful pacing branch of Noontide emanating from the noted world champion pacing filly Stand By. This family has been maintained by Castleton Farm.

There is a second Lady Kerner pacing branch which does not pass through Little Lie. This family blossomed from Castleton Farm's Knight Dream mare Hickory Jane, and includes Breeders Crown champion Glow Softly and Ohio sensation C'mon Ashley.

LIZZIE WITHERSPOON / (Isotta)

This is one of the oldest maternal lines tracing to the very origins of the Standardbred. Family founder Lizzie Witherspoon was a foal of 1865. Every prominent horse in this family descends from Isotta, a 1917 daughter of Peter The Great. Isotta is six generations removed from the tap root mare.

Carlisle and Hambletonian winner Sharp Note are the chief representatives of Isotta's daughter Isonta, while Isotta's 1929 foal Isabel Hanover is the third dam of classics winner Duke Rodney.

The Isabel Hanover group is more noted because her daughter Ilo Hanover produced the world champion Impish and her two full sisters, Important, dam of Noble Gesture, and Impudent, dam of former world champion trotting gelding I'm Impeccable. Impish produced a wave of champion trotters from only two daughters, chief of which is the Florican matron Canny Imp. This is one of trotting's most venerable families, and includes such noted stars as Yonkers Trot, World Trotting Derby and Kentucky Futurity winner Bullville Victory.

A 1930 daughter of Isotta, the Dillon Axworthy mare Irene Hanover established what could be called the stallion branch of this family. Noted males Falcon Almahurst, Overcomer, Kimberly Kid, Sampson Hanover and General Star all trace to Irene Hanover. Chief filly credit for the Irene Hanover clan is the accomplished pacing mare White Ruffles.

Isotta's 1933 daughter Easter Hanover is the granddam of Painter, while Isotta's 1937 daughter Melba Hanover, by Calumet Chuck, is the third dam of Triple Crown champion Nevele Pride. The final Isotta daughter is her 1938 foal Faith Hanover, who is the fourth dam of Nero.

This entire historic family, founded at Hanover Shoe Farms, has benefited many of the leading breeders, including Walnut Hall Farm, Castleton Farm, Almahurst Farm, Lana Lobell Farm and the Armstrong Brothers.

MISS COPELAND

When Lamon Harkness founded Walnut Hall Farm just before the turn of the 20th Century, one of the mares that contributed mightily to the emerging reputation of the famous Kentucky nursery during the first quarter century of farm operation was Fruity Worthy, a 1906 daughter of Axworthy and great granddaughter of Miss Copeland.

Fruity Worthy's daughter, The Real Lady, won the Kentucky Futurity for Thomas W. Murphy before being exported. However, the entire family traces through three other daughters of Fruity Worthy, the first foaled in 1910 and the last in 1925. These mares accounted for such noted performers as Titan Hanover, Nibble Hanover and Speedster. For instance, Fruity Worthy is the fourth dam of Titan Hanover, the first 2:00 two-year-old, and is the third dam of Nibble Hanover, an important sire. Fruity Worthy's 1922 daughter Fruity Volo established the family leading to Oil Burner, an important link in the Most Happy Fella male line.

The trotting full brothers Speedster and Speedy Rodney also trace maternally to this Kentucky family through Fruity Worthy's 1925 foal Lexington Maid. This family also includes Hambletonian winner Flirth; Breeders Crown sire Crysta's Crown and the European sire Madison Avenue.

Lexington Maid's daughter Beams Hanover founded a family that in-

Lushkara (shown with Mike Lachance), a foal of 1979, is a modern representative of the Miss Copeland family. A p,3,1:54.3 stakes-winning daughter of Albatross, Lushkara's first foal was the $2 million-winning Camtastic p,4,T1:49.3, by Cam Fella. Lushkara's branch of Miss Copeland passes through the celebrated Lexington Maid branch of the family tree.

cludes Sampson Direct, sire of Direct Scooter, 1987 Pacer of the Year Camtastic and Meadowlands Pace winner Carlsbad Cam.

Among the successful breeders who have waded in Miss Copeland's waters are Walnut Hall Farm, Almahurst Farm (breeder of Oil Burner) and Hanover Shoe Farms. The latter had great success at both gaits, developing the trotting family that produced Crysta's Crown and the pacing family that accounts for Camtastic and Carlsbad Cam.

MAGGIE H.

The Maggie H. family is home to the world champion mare Beat The Wheel 4,1:51.4, the fastest racing trotter in history, and represents one of the purest trotting groups in the entire breed. This rather remarkable status has been achieved while nearly every other family has succumbed to the development of active pacing branches. The only significant pacers

Beat The Wheel is history's fastest racing trotter with her 1:51.4 effort at The Meadowlands for Cat Manzi in 1994. A granddaughter of Speedy Crown, Beat The Wheel's maternal lineage places her in the Maggie H. family, one of trotting's strongest tribes.

in this family are Amity Chef and Horton Hanover, and both have pedigrees with large doses of trotting blood.

The Maggie H. family has two major tributaries. The first descends from a granddaughter of Maggie H., the Peter The Great mare Sienna, a foal of 1909. Sienna's dramatic impact can be best summarized by saying her family produced females that ultimately yielded such trotters as Armbro Keepsake, Me Maggie, Firm Tribute, Worldly Woman, Speed In Action, Imperfection, Royal Prestige, Nearly Perfect and Donerail. Sienna's half-sister Maggie Onward is the granddam of world champion Mr. McElwyn, and Sienna's daughter Sumatra is the dam of Calumet Chuck.

A second branch of the family, traces from Maggie H.'s daughter The Gaiety Girl, and produced the world champion trotting stallion Lee Axworthy T1:58 1/4. It also leads to the 1925 mare Princess Gay, whose daughters Fionne, Fiesta and Gay Sonata founded successful mini-families of their own. The Fionne group is the largest. This is where we find Beat The Wheel and other trotting stars such as Hambletonian champ Nuclear Kosmos, Crowning Point, Armbro Blush, Baltic Striker, Sierra Kosmos, Dayan and Big John.

The major breeders that have benefited from a sprinkling of Maggie H.'s trotting magic include William Shehan, Armstrong Brothers, Castleton Farm and Kentuckiana Farm.

SIRE FAMILIES

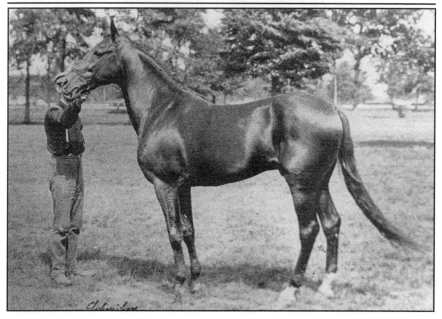

Peter The Great, a foal of 1895, was a great grandson of Hambletonian. His male family, descending from his famous sons Peter Scott and Peter Volo, is the source of nearly all of the major trotting stars, and a few pacing heroes as well. He was also a dominant broodmare sire. Peter The Great is ten generations of males removed from modern trotting sire Valley Victory.

THE FAMILY OF PETER THE GREAT

The Peter The Great line of sires has produced the fastest three-year-olds at both gaits: Mack Lobell, with a record of 1:52.1 is the fastest racing male trotter of all time and on the pace, Matt's Scooter, who time-trialled in 1:48.2 in Lexington.

Mack Lobell traces directly to Peter The Great through the Volomite line established by Victory Song and leading to Noble Victory, Noble Gesture and Mystic Park, the sire of Mack Lobell. Matt's Scooter is also found here, but through the pacing branch founded by Volomite's son Sampson Hanover, leading to Sampson Direct and finally to Direct Scooter, sire of Matt's Scooter.

Star's Pride and Speedster each founded significant trotting branches of this sire line. Star's Pride, the leading sire of Hambletonian winners, left the breed a whole slate of champion sons and grandsons to carry on, most notably the Triple Crown champion Super Bowl. The Star's Pride group belongs to the family founded by Peter The Great's 1911 foal, the legendary Peter Volo. The Star's Pride's line descends through Peter Volo's grandson Worthy Boy.

Speedster sired Triple Crown champion Speedy Scot, whose own son Speedy Crown transformed this family and the breed. Speedy Scot's influence has also been felt through his sons Arnie Almahurst and Speed In Action. Arnie Almahurst sired the world champion Arndon, and that fast horse in turn sired Pine Chip, the fastest trotter in history. Speed In Action ruled Ohio for all of the 1980's and brought his own brand of aggressive speed to Buckeye breeders. The Speedster line owes its paternal heritage to another son of Peter The Great, his 1909 foal Peter Scott. Two of Europe's top trotting stars, Ourasi and Ideal du Gazeau, trace paternally to the exported Sam Williams, a son of Peter Scott.

The pacing Peter The Great-line horses have only the Direct Scooter branch to their credit today. Direct Scooter's success bodes well for the continuation of the Volomite pacing influence coupled with Bye Bye Byrds significant contribution as a broodmare sire. The Bye Bye Byrd male line was dealt a cruel blow with the early death of Armbro Nesbit, who sired but three crops in the 1970's at Hanover Shoe Farms. Armbro Nesbit made a significant contribution in his short time at stud, siring the dams of 1990 Horse of the Year Beach Towel and the world champion pacing filly Amneris.

THE FAMILY OF ELECTIONEER

The key males in the Electioneer family are Hal Dale and Bert Abbe. Hal Dale founded the branches of the family responsible for Good Time, Adios, Meadow Skipper, and Bert Abbe, the family branch which produced Big Towner.

Good Time and Adios each had successful, productive stud careers. Good Time, one of the greatest racehorses in the history of the breed, sired Race Time, Best Of All, Columbia George and Crash, but that famous quartet could not produce any notable sons to carry on for their famous ancestor.

Adios gave us the charismatic Bret Hanover, one of the most popular and famous Standardbreds in history, bringing to a close Adios' reign as the sport's leading sire. Bret Hanover, had the most success of any of Adios' sons and also found great fame as a broodmare sire. Nihilator, Three Diamonds, Sonsam, Troublemaker, Miss Easy, Town Pro, Barberry Spur, B.G's Bunny, Jaguar Spur, Cam Fella and Fan Hanover, a most remarkable group, all have dams by Bret Hanover.

The Adios male line enjoyed a tremendous resurgence in popularity through the mid-1980's and the early 1990's with the siring efforts of Abercrombie, a grandson of Henry T. Adios.

Meadow Skipper, a son of Dale Frost, became a sire of incomparable quality who produced a number of prolific sons, including such champions as Most Happy Fella, Albatross, Nero, Governor Skipper, Falcon Almahurst, Landslide and French Chef.

Each of these horses made tremendous contributions, with the Most

Hal Dale founded a male line which came to dominate world pacing. He sired Good Time, Adios and Dale Frost, three sons whose progeny eventually produced the stars of the late 20th century. Bret Hanover, Meadow Skipper, Most Happy Fella, Albatross and Cam Fella trace in their male line to this one stallion.

Happy Fella male line appearing to be the dominant blood. There are three active branches of the Most Happy Fella male line emanating from his sons Cam Fella, Tyler B and Oil Burner.

Albatross' influence is most felt as a broodmare sire. He is the most successful broodmare sire in the history of the Standardbred. Albatross' sons have not enjoyed the success of his daughters, with noted males such as Niatross, Sonsam and B.G's Bunny apparently failing to leave a horse capable of perpetuating Albatross' male legacy.

Big Towner's paternal trail does not pass through the Hal Dale male line, but comes down through Bert Abbe and his son, Gene Abbe, the sire of Big Towner. The successful males in this branch of the Electioneer siring family are Walton Hanover, the millionaires Dorunrun Bluegrass and Totally Ruthless and Apache's Fame, a grandson of Big Towner.

THE FAMILY OF AXWORTHY

The Axworthy family has been given up for dead on more than one occasion, but it keeps coming up with a fresh horse to give everyone hope that it will continue to survive into the 21st Century.

The Axworthy line has long been known for its purity of gait, best exemplified in the trotting males emanating from Florican, whose grandson Nearly Perfect appears the most likely descendant to carry on the

Guy Axworthy was the sire of the inaugural Hambletonian winner Guy McKinney, a foal of 1923. Guy Axworthy's male line has endured the past seventy years despite the lack of depth similar to the Peter The Great and Electioneer families. Guy Axworthy stood in Kentucky at Walnut Hall Farm and established the family of males which eventually produced 1992 trotting star Sierra Kosmos 3, 1:53.4.

family genes. Nearly Perfect's son Sierra Kosmos was the fastest trotter of 1992.

In the early part of this century, Axworthy male line stallions were the dominant trotting horses of the breed, sending forth a steady stream of classic winners.

Most noted of these was Guy Axworthy, whose sons Lee Axworthy and Mr. McElwyn were both world champion trotters. However, Lee Axworthy died at the age of seven after only two seasons in the stud. One of those seasons did produce the Kentucky Futurity champion Lee Worthy, sire of the dam of world champion Rosalind. Mr. McElwyn, one of the most famous champions of his time, was not a factor in the continuation of his male line. His Hambletonian-winning son McLin Hanover was exported to Italy. Mr. McElwyn did, however, sire the dam of Star's Pride.

Guy McKinney, another of Guy Axworthy's sons, was the winner of the inaugural Hambletonian and is the grandsire of Florican, in whose sire line we find Nearly Perfect. Guy Abbey, another of Guy Axworthy's sons, had a blueblood pedigree and sired the gelding champion Greyhound, a horse decades ahead of his time.

The pacing Axworthy lines descending through Nibble Hanover's Jug-winning son Knight Dream has also had problems. The latter's sons Duane Hanover, Torpid and Adora's Dream all had their moments, but failed to

Tar Heel, shown with John Simpson, Sr., at Lexington's Red Mile, was a coarse, rough-gaited horse who nevertheless became one of the leading sires. He is best remembered as a broodmare sire. Among the breeding stars he left behind was Brenna Hanover, dam of Bret Hanover.

leave sons of their own capable of carrying the family torch. Duane Hanover is noted as the sire of the dam of Abercrombie.

The same branch of the family which produced the pacing Knight Dreams also begat the sport's first 2:00 two-year-old, the legendary trotting wonder colt Titan Hanover, whose best performer was the Hambletonian winner Hickory Smoke.

THE FAMILY OF DIRECT

The Direct sire line has not produced a significant male since the early 1970's, the last being the handsome Armbro Ranger, a great-grandson of family patriarch Tar Heel. The male-line blood of the Billy Direct sires appears headed for the history books. Billy Direct did sire Little Brown Jug winners Ensign Hanover, Dudley Hanover and Tar Heel. Neither Ensign Hanover nor Dudley Hanover left a notable son, however.

Tar Heel sired a number of quality sons over a long and successful siring career, but all of them lacked the firepower to become successful sires. Most notable of his sons was the world champion two-year-old and Little Brown Jug winner Laverne Hanover. Tar Heel also sired the Jug-winning Nansemond, but he, too, failed in the stud. This sire line did enjoy a brief moment in the limelight when Steady Star, the free-legged pacing wonder, became the breed's first 1:52 pacer in a memorable Red Mile time trial for Joe O'Brien in 1971. Steady Star was a son of Steady Beau and grandson of Tar Heel.

The major contribution of the Direct blood has been on the female side, since broodmares by Billy Direct and Tar Heel accounted for many of the breed's top horses in the 1960's and 1970's. Billy Direct produced the dams of such stars as Bye Bye Byrd, Sampson Direct, Adios Butler and Bullet Hanover. Tar Heel was the sire of the dams of Bret Hanover, Tyler B, Landslide, Silent Majority, Romeo Hanover, In The Pocket and Keystone Ore, among others. During the mid-1960's until late in the 1970's, Tar Heel was the sport's leading broodmare sire.

It is interesting to note historically that from this male line Direct, Walter Direct, Napoleon Direct, Billy Direct and Steady Star all took their records free-legged, evidencing a purity of gait that should have allowed this sire line to perpetuate itself.

LEADING SIRES THROUGHOUT THE WORLD

The influence of the Standardbred has spread throughout the world, most notably in Europe and in Australia and New Zealand.

The Scandinavian countries have long fancied North American trotting blood, and it is not surprising to learn that many American-bred sires are doing quite well in continental Europe.

In most cases, the U.S. imports are the leading sires.

SWEDEN—Star's Pride line imports went early to Sweden, including the likes of Kentucky Futurity winner Quick Pay, a son of Star's Pride who has been a top sire throughout his career. Sons of Nevele Pride were also prized in Sweden, including Zoot Suit and Pershing who were the most successful. Zoot Suit, who narrowly missed winning the Hambletonian in his U.S. campaign, has been the top sire in Sweden for some time. His best son is the Swedish Criterium winner Zoogin.

Among the young horses sent to Sweden are Napoletano, Sugarcane Hanover, Super Arnie and Spotlite Lobell. Speedy Somolli and Florida Pro were exported to Sweden as well. Several sons of Tibur, a French-bred horse, have also raced well and have begun successful stallion careers, including Ata Star L., Big Spender and Callit. Mack Lobell began his stud career in Sweden with great success. He was voted Sweden's top sire for 1995. This award came after he was sent back to the U.S. for the 1996 breeding season. Mack Lobell left six crops in Sweden.

DENMARK—The leading modern sire in Denmark has been Pay Dirt, a son of Florican and the world champion filly Impish. His most prominent son has been Vokal N. Another U.S. export who did well in Denmark is Frosty Hanover, a son of Star's Pride, and a half-brother to the dam of Hambletonian winners Timothy T and Christopher T.

The leading young sires in Denmark are former U.S. stars Buckfinder (Super Bowl), Crown's Best (Speedy Crown) and Speed Merchant (Speedy Somolli). Little Devil and Why Not, sons of Speedy Crown, have both done well. Why Not, for example, is the sire of Rudolf Le An, called the best homebred Danish trotter ever.

NORWAY—The leading sires in Norway are imports like Gunslinger Spur, a son of Florida Pro. Others are Speedy Tomali, a son of Speedy Somolli, sire of Norwegian star Tamin Sandy, who defeated Pine Chip in the 1993 Orsi Mangelli. Everglade Hanover (Florida Pro) and Songcan (Florican) both began their stud careers in Norway, but Everglade was exported to Germany and Songcan will finish his stud career in Sweden.

FINLAND—The leading sires in Finland are Choctaw Brave (Speedy Crown) and Barbeque (Nevele Pride). Choctaw Brave is sire of the Finnish star Houston Laukko.

GERMANY—Diamond Way is the outstanding sire in Germany's stud paddocks. He is a son of Super Way, who is by Super Bowl from the world champion filly Noble Gal. Graf Zeppelin, a son of Noble Victory, had a brief, but very successful siring career. Another who succeeded in the stud was Abido, a son of Ayres and the great trotting mare Elaine Rodney. Cheetah, a full brother to Bonefish, also did well. Hambletonian winner Prakas was exported to Germany in the early 1990's. His final American crop was foaled in 1993.

ITALY—Only Italy can boast a dominant sire who has withstood the onslaught of the U.S. imports, this the brilliant Sharif di Iesolo, who is a grandson of Victory Song, but was bred in Italy. Sharif di Iesolo, a son of the exported U.S.-bred Quick Song, has also produced a number of young sons who look to be successful sires, as well, including Zebu, Argo Ve, Esotico Prad, Indro Park, Lancaster OM and Lurabo Blue. The most successful young U.S. import to Italy has been Park Avenue Joe, a son of Speedy Somolli from the international trotting star Delmonica Hanover. Supergill and Royal Prestige were exported to Italy at the close of 1994.

The richest Italian-bred trotter ever is Mint di Iesolo, a son of the exported Gator Bowl, a son of Super Bowl. Mint di Iesolo has won more than $2 million.

FRANCE—The French stud book had been closed for many years and U.S. imports had not made the dramatic inroads there that had been seen in the rest of Europe. Florestan, however, was a success in France and he was a result of breeding the great French mare Roquepine with

Star's Pride. The French, for a short period of time, allowed a French mare to go to an American horse, but no American horse could stand in France. Florestan's son, Quito de Talonay, was his best, although the Franco-American cross proved quite valuable in invigorating the French breed.

These restrictions were rescinded for a short period in the 1980's and the Breeders Crown winner Workaholic now stands in France servicing a full book of mares, although the French stud book is again closed. French trotting received a cruel blow when the outstanding trotter Fakir du Vivier died after only two seasons in the stud. His two crops have raced with great success.

The leading French-bred sires are Kerjacques and his sons Chambon P and Jiosco. The champion Ourasi, one of the great French trotters, has embarked on a stud career, but is suffering from poor fertility. Some young French champions such as Tenor du Beaune, Mon Tourbillon and Ultra Ducal are the most successful young sires.

Tenor du Beaune and Mon Tourbillon represent trotting blood which does not trace to Hambletonian. Mon Tourbillion is from the same sire line which produced Roquepine, two-time winner of the Roosevelt International. The French-bred Tibur, who became a Swedish siring star, is also a non-Hambletonian line trotter, as was the Yonkers International winner Reve d'Udon. Tibur is from the same male line which produced the sensational Oriolo, but is from a different branch of that family descending through the noted sire Fandango.

Ideal du Gazeau, three-time winner of the Roosevelt International, and Ourasi each have a distinctly American heritage, since their male line traces to the foundation sire Peter Scott through his son, the 1920's French export Sam Williams.

AUSTRALIA & NEW ZEALAND—U.S. pacing exports dominate the stallion picture Down Under just as the American expatriates control trotting in Europe. Most of the top stallions in Australia have American ties.

One of the leading young sires in Australia is Golden Greek, a son of Abercrombie. Other successful stallions with U.S. roots are Torado Hanover (Albatross), who has been the leading Australian sire in the late 1980's and early 1990's; What's Next (Most Happy Fella); French Chef (Meadow Skipper); Windshield Wiper (Meadow Skipper) and Woodrow Wilson winner Land Grant (Meadow Skipper). Other American-bred horses who did well in Australia are Vance Hanover, an unraced son of Albatross and Hilarion, a Meadowlands Pace-winning son of Strike Out.

Kentucky, a son of Tar Heel, was very successful during the 1970's and early 1980's, as was Hilarious Way, a son of Bret Hanover. Hilarious Way is the leading broodmare sire in Australia in the early 1990's. French Chef, as noted above, was an immediate success after his importation from the U.S., but died after only four seasons in Australia. He was heavily patronized with many of Australia's better mares and quickly became the leading juvenile sire with his initial Down Under crops.

The top "Colonial-bred" is Classic Garry, a son of Garry Rowan and grandson of Garrison Hanover, a Billy Direct horse who stood in New Zealand. Classic Garry raced in the U.S. before becoming a successful stallion in Australia. Smokey Hanover, another Billy Direct line pacer, also had success Down Under. The paternal line of Volomite has also fared well for many years in the southern hemisphere through the offspring of Volomite's son, Light Brigade.

PEDIGREE SECTION

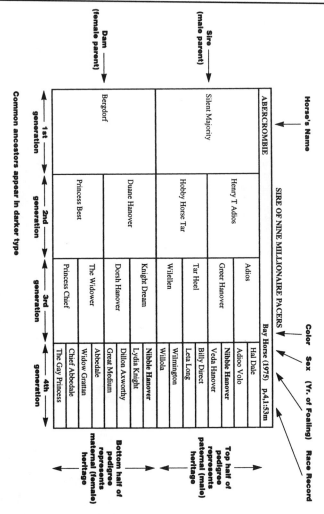

Here is a sample tabulated pedigree. The pedigree is a linear, generational representation of a horse's family tree. The horse's immediate parents appear in the first generation, the second generation represents grandparents, the third generation the great-grandparents, and so on. These pedigrees have been selected to show common, successful breeding theories or patterns, or to illustrate the parentage of prominent horses.

In pedigrees where the same parents are represented more than once, darker type indicates what is called a "common cross." A 2X4 cross, for instance, occurs where a common ancestor appears in the second and fourth generations. A 3X3 cross would have a common parent in the third generation. A "multiple cross" occurs when a common ancestor appears more than twice in a pedigree.

REPRESENTATIVE OF 4x4 LINEBRED CROSSES

4x4 TO SCOTLAND; 3x3 SIBLING CROSS (VICTORY SONG IS A 3/4 BROTHER TO PETER SONG)

ARNIE ALMAHURST			Bay Horse (1970) 3,T1:57.2m
Speedy Scot	Speedster	Rodney	Spencer Scott
			Earl's Princess Martha
		Mimi Hanover	Dean Hanover
			Hanover Maid
	Scotch Love	**Victory Song**	Volomite
			Evensong
		Selka Scot	**Scotland**
			Selka Guy
Ambitious Blaze	Blaze Hanover	Hoot Mon	**Scotland**
			Missey
		Beverly Hanover	Mr. McElwyn
			Hanover's Bertha
	Allie Song	**Peter Song**	Peter Volo
			Evensong
		Josephine Knight	Protector
			Josephine Brewer

4x4 CROSS TO ADIOS & KNIGHT DREAM FOR LITTLE BROWN JUG CHAMP

LIFE SIGN			Bay Horse (1990) p,3,1:50.3m
Abercrombie	Silent Majority	Henry T. Adios	**Adios**
			Greer Hanover
		Hobby Horse Tar	Tar Heel
			Wilellen
	Bergdorf	Duane Hanover	**Knight Dream**
			Dorsh Hanover
		Princess Best	The Widower
			Princess Chief
Three Diamonds	Albatross	Meadow Skipper	Dale Frost
			Countess Vivian
		Voodoo Hanover	Dancer Hanover
			Vibrant Hanover
	Ambiguity	Bret Hanover	**Adios**
			Brenna Hanover
		K. Nora	**Knight Dream**
			Adora

4x4 CROSS TO PETER VOLO FOR SIRING SUPERSTAR

MEADOW SKIPPER			Brown Horse (1960) p,3,1:55.1m	
Dale Frost	Hal Dale	Abbedale	The Abbe	
			Daisydale D.	
		Margaret Hal	Argot Hal	
			Margaret Polk	
	Galloway	Raider	**Peter Volo**	
			Nelda Dillon	
		Bethel	David Guy	
			Annotation	
Countess Vivian	King's Counsel	Volomite	**Peter Volo**	
			Cita Frisco	
		Margaret Spangler	Guy Axworthy	
			Maggie Winder	
	Filly Direct	Billy Direct	Napoleon Direct	
			Gay Forbes	
		Calumet Edna	Peter the Brewer	
			Broncho Queen	

TOP SIRE & BROODMARE SIRE HAS 4x4 MATERNAL CROSS TO SCOTLAND

SPEEDY CROWN			Bay Horse (1968) 3,1:57.1m	
Speedy Scot	Speedster	Rodney	Spencer Scott	
			Earl's Princess Martha	
		Mimi Hanover	Dean Hanover	
			Hanover Maid	
	Scotch Love	Victory Song	Volomite	
			Evensong	
		Selka Scot	**Scotland**	
			Selka Guy	
Missile Toe	Florican	Spud Hanover	Guy McKinney	
			Evelyn The Great	
		Florimel	Spencer	
			Carolyn	
	Worth a Plenty	Darnley	**Scotland**	
			Fionne	
		Sparkle Plenty	Worthy Boy	
			The Gem	

TOP YOUNG SIRE HAS FOUR CROSSES TO STAR'S PRIDE

VALLEY VICTORY			Bay Horse (1986) 3,1:55.3m	
Baltic Speed	Speedy Somolli	Speedy Crown	Speedy Scot	
			Missile Toe	
		Somolli	**Star's Pride**	
			Laurita Hanover	
	Sugar Frosting	Carlisle	**Hickory Pride**	
			Good Note	
		Karen's Choice	The Intruder	
			My Tip	
Valley Victoria	Bonefish	Nevele Pride	**Star's Pride**	
			Thankful	
		Exciting Speed	Speedster	
			Expresson	
	Victorious Lou	Noble Victory	Victory Song	
			Emily's Pride	
		Lou Sidney	Darnley	
			Lucy Abbey	

PROMINENT SIRES

SIRE OF NINE MILLIONAIRE PACERS

ABERCROMBIE			Bay Horse (1975) p,4,1:53m	
Silent Majority	Henry T Adios	Adios	Hal Dale	
			Adioo Volo	
		Greer Hanover	**Nibble Hanover**	
			Veda Hanover	
	Hobby Horse Tar	Tar Heel	Billy Direct	
			Leta Long	
		Wilellen	Wilmington	
			Willola	
Bergdorf	Duane Hanover	Knight Dream	**Nibble Hanover**	
			Lydia Knight	
		Dorsh Hanover	Dillon Axworthy	
			Great Medium	
	Princess Best	The Widower	Abbedale	
			Widow Grattan	
		Princess Chief	Chief Abbedale	
			The Gay Princess	

GENE ABBE'S SON BECAME PROMINENT FILLY SIRE

BIG TOWNER			Brown Horse (1974) p,4,1:54.4m	
Gene Abbe	Bert Abbe	The Abbe	Chimes	
			Nettie King	
		Miss Ella H.	Mack H.	
			Nelly Patch	
	Rose Marie	Martinos	Cochato	
			Queen Audubon	
		Lady Permilia	Coastman	
			Virginia Alta	
Tiny Wave	Shadow Wave	Adios	Hal Dale	
			Adioo Volo	
		Shadow Grattan	Silent Grattan	
			Peacedale	
	Tiny Gold	Guinea Gold	Frisco Dale	
			Goldie Grattan	
		Cynthiana	Protector	
			Olympia	

LEADING BROODMARE SIRE OF $1 MILLION WINNERS

BRET HANOVER			Bay Horse (1962) p,4,T1:53.3m	
Adios	Hal Dale	Abbedale	The Abbe	
			Daisydale D.	
		Margaret Hal	Argot Hal	
			Margaret Polk	
	Adioo Volo	Adioo Guy	Guy Dillon	
			Adioo	
		Sigrid Volo	Peter Volo	
			Polly Parrot	
Brenna Hanover	Tar Heel	Billy Direct	Napoleon Direct	
			Gay Forbes	
		Leta Long	Volomite	
			Rosette	
	Beryl Hanover	Nibble Hanover	Calumet Chuck	
			Justissima	
		Laura Hanover	The Laurel Hall	
			Miss Bertha Worthy	

PROMINENT SIRE'S SECOND DAM IS A SISTER TO ADIOS

BYE BYE BYRD			Bay Horse (1955) p,5,T1:56.1m
Poplar Byrd	Volomite	Peter Volo	Peter the Great
			Nervolo Belle
		Cita Frisco	San Francisco
			Mendocita
	Ann Vonian	Grattan at Law	Grattan Royal
			Daisy at Law
		Margaret Vonian	Favonian
			Margaret C. Brooke
Evalina Hanover	Billy Direct	Napoleon Direct	Walter Direct
			Lady Erectess
		Gay Forbes	Malcolm Forbes
			Gay Girl Chimes
	Adieu	**Hal Dale**	Abbedale
			Margaret Hal
		Adioo Volo	Adioo Guy
			Sigrid Volo

PROMINENT PACING SIRE HAS LINEAGE DOMINATED BY TROTTING BLOOD

DIRECT SCOOTER			Bay Horse (1976) p,3 ,1:54m
Sampson Direct	Sampson Hanover	Volomite	**Peter Volo**
			Cita Frisco
		Irene Hanover	**Dillon Axworthy**
			Isotta
	Dottie Rosecroft	**Billy Direct**	Napoleon Direct
			Gay Forbes
		Beams Hanover	**Calumet Chuck**
			Lexington Maid
Noble Claire	**Noble Victory**	**Victory Song**	Volomite
			Evensong
		Emily's Pride	**Star's Pride**
			Emily Scott
	Scotch Claire	**Scotland**	**Peter Scott**
			Roya McKinney
		Abbey Claire	**Guy Abbey**
			Jean Claire

SIRE OF THE DAM OF LEADING SIRE ABERCROMBIE

DUANE HANOVER			Bay Horse (1952) p,4,1:58m
Knight Dream	Nibble Hanover	Calumet Chuck	Truax
			Sumatra
		Justissima	Justice Brooke
			Clarie Toddington
	Lydia Knight	Peter the Brewer	Peter the Great
			Zombrewer
		Guy Rosa	Guy Axworthy
			Rosa Lake
Dorsh Hanover	Dillon Axworthy	Axworthy	Axtell
			Marguerite
		Adioo Dillon	Sidney Dillon
			Adioo
	Great Medium	Peter the Great	Pilot Medium
			Santos
		Dorsh Medium	Red Medium
			Vicanora

TOP SIRE OF EARLY SPEED; WAS SENSATION AT TWO ON TRACK

JATE LOBELL			Bay Horse (1984) p,3,1:51.2m
No Nukes	Oil Burner	Most Happy Fella	Meadow Skipper
			Laughing Girl
		Dottie Shadow	Shadow Wave
			Diana Streak
	Gidget Lobell	Overtrick	Solicitor
			Overbid
		GoGo Playmate	Tar Heel
			GoGo Playtime
J. R. Amy	Blaze Pick	Gene Abbe	Bert Abbe
			Rose Marie
		Susan Wayne	Orphan Wayne
			Miss Wayne Hal
	Good Time Minnie	Good Time	Hal Dale
			On Time
		Minnewashta	The Widower
			Minnehaha

STRONG BROODMARE SIRE HAD FOUNDATION MATERNAL BACKGROUND

TAR HEEL			Black Horse (1948) p,4,T1:57m
Billy Direct	Napoleon Direct	Walter Direct	Direct Hal
			Ella Brown
		Lady Erectress	Tom Kendle
			Nelly Zarro
	Gay Forbes	Malcolm Forbes	Bingen
			Nancy Hanks
		Gay Girl Chimes	Berkshire Chimes
			Miss Gay Girl
Leta Long	Volomite	Peter Volo	Peter The Great
			Nervolo Belle
		Cita Frisco	San Francisco
			Mendocita
	Rosette	Mr. McElwyn	Guy Axworthy
			Widow Maggie
		Rose Scott	Peter Scott
			Roya McKinney

PACERS WITH COMMON CROSSES TO HAL DALE

3x4 CROSS TO HAL DALE FOR LEADING BROODMARE SIRE

ALBATROSS			Bay Horse (1968) p,4,1:54.3f
Meadow Skipper	Dale Frost	**Hal Dale**	Abbedale
			Margaret Hal
		Galloway	Raider
			Bethel
	Countess Vivian	King's Counsel	Volomite
			Margaret Spangler
		Filly Direct	Billy Direct
			Calumet Edna
Voodoo Hanover	Dancer Hanover	Adios	**Hal Dale**
			Adioo Volo
		The Old Maid	Guy Abbey
			Spinster
	Vibrant Hanover	Tar Heel	Billy Direct
			Leta Long
		Vivian Hanover	Guy McKinney
			Guesswork

UNDEFEATED (16 FOR 16) AT 4; STILL FASTEST 2 YEAR-OLD EVER

ARTSPLACE			Bay Horse (1988) p,4,1:49.2m
Abercrombie	Silent Majority	Henry T. Adios	**Adios**
			Greer Hanover
		Hobby Horse Tar	Tar Heel
			Wilellen
	Bergdorf	Duane Hanover	Knight Dream
			Dorsh Hanover
		Princess Best	The Widower
			Princess Chief
Miss Elvira	Albatross	Meadow Skipper	**Dale Frost**
			Countess Vivian
		Voodoo Hanover	**Dancer Hanover**
			Vibrant Hanover
	Ladalia Hanover	Columbia George	**Good Time**
			Mitzi Eden
		Lady Kacne	Duane Hanover
			Lady Lunken

LEADING SIRE IS DOUBLE LINEBRED TO HAL DALE (4X4X4X4)

CAM FELLA			Bay Horse (1979) p,4,1:53.1m
Most Happy Fella	Meadow Skipper	**Dale Frost**	**Hal Dale**
			Galloway
		Countess Vivian	King's Counsel
			Filly Direct
	Laughing Girl	Good Time	**Hal Dale**
			On Time
		Maxine's Dream	Knight Dream
			Maxine Abbe
Nan Cam	Bret Hanover	Adios	**Hal Dale**
			Adioo Volo
		Brenna Hanover	Tar Heel
			Beryl Hanover
	Nan Frost	**Dale Frost**	**Hal Dale**
			Galloway
		Mynah Hanover	Ensign Hanover
			Betty Mahone

WORLD CHAMPION 2 YEAR-OLD HAS MULTIPLE HAL DALE-LINE INFLUENCES

DIE LAUGHING			Brown Horse (1988) p,3,1:51.1f
No Nukes	Oil Burner	Most Happy Fella	**Meadow Skipper**
			Laughing Girl
		Dottie Shadow	**Shadow Wave**
			Diana Streak
	Gidget Lobell	Overtrick	Solicitor
			Overbid
		GoGo Playmate	Tar Heel
			GoGo Playtime
Makin Smiles	Albatross	**Meadow Skipper**	**Dale Frost**
			Countess Vivian
		Voodoo Hanover	**Dancer Hanover**
			Vibrant Hanover
	Real Hilarious	Shadow Wave	**Adios**
			Shadow Grattan
		Seascape	Painter
			Way Wave

$1 MILLION WINNER HAS MULTIPLE CROSSES TO HAL DALE SIRES

IMMORTALITY			Bay Mare (1990) p,3,1:51m
No Nukes	Oil Burner	Most Happy Fella	**Meadow Skipper**
			Laughing Girl
		Dottie Shadow	**Shadow Wave**
			Diana Streak
	Gidget Lobell	Overtrick	Solicitor
			Overbid
		GoGo Playmate	Tar Heel
			GoGo Playtime
Jef's Eternity	Albatross	**Meadow Skipper**	**Dale Frost**
			Countess Vivian
		Voodoo Hanover	**Dancer Hanover**
			Vibrant Hanover
	Time Goes Bye	Bye Bye Byrd	Poplar Byrd
			Evalina Hanover
		Time Out	**Good Time**
			Rilda Guy

LEADING SIRE HAS MULTIPLE CROSSES TO HAL DALE SIRES

NO NUKES			Brown Horse (1979) p,3,T1:52.1m	
Oil Burner	Most Happy Fella	Meadow Skipper	**Dale Frost**	
			Countess Vivian	
		Laughing Girl	**Good Time**	
			Maxine's Dream	
	Dottie Shadow	Shadow Wave	**Adios**	
			Shadow Grattan	
		Diana Streak	Red Streak	
			Diana Mite	
Gidget Lobell	Overtrick	Solicitor	King's Counsel	
			Jane Reynolds	
		Overbid	**Hal Dale**	
			Barbara Direct	
	GoGo Playmate	Tar Heel	**Billy Direct**	
			Leta Long	
		GoGo Playtime	**Good Time**	
			Dell Siskiyou	

SEVEN OF EIGHT MALES IN 4TH GENERATION FROM SAME MALE LINE!

SHADY DAISY			Brown Mare (1988) p,3,1:51m	
Falcon Seelster	Warm Breeze	Bret Hanover	**Adios**	
			Brenna Hanover	
		Touch of Spring	**Good Time**	
			Breath O Spring	
	Fashion Trick	Overtrick	Solicitor	
			Overbid	
		Meadow Child	**Adios Butler**	
			Midway Lady	
Tika Belle	Skipper Walt	Meadow Skipper	**Dale Frost**	
			Countess Vivian	
		Barbara Eden	**Good Time**	
			Mitzi Eden	
	Tika Hanover	Best of All	**Good Time**	
			Besta Hanover	
		Time Wave	**Shadow Wave**	
			Vixen	

COMMON CROSSES TO THREE SONS OF HAL DALE

TYLER B			Bay Horse (1977) p,3,1:55.1m
Most Happy Fella	Meadow Skipper	**Dale Frost**	**Hal Dale**
			Galloway
		Countess Vivian	King's Counsel
			Filly Direct
	Laughing Girl	**Good Time**	**Hal Dale**
			On Time
		Maxine's Dream	Knight Dream
			Maxine Abbe
Tarport Cheer	Tar Heel	Billy Direct	Napoleon Direct
			Gay Forbes
		Leta Long	Volomite
			Rosette
	Meadow Cheer	**Adios**	**Hal Dale**
			Adioo Volo
		Betty G.	Wilmington
			Betty Crispin

A TRIO OF FAST THREE-YEAR-OLDS

THE BREED'S FASTEST THREE-YEAR-OLD

MATT'S SCOOTER			Bay Horse (1985) p,3,T1:48.2m
Direct Scooter	Sampson Direct	Sampson Hanover	Volomite
			Irene Hanover
		Dottie Rosecroft	Billy Direct
			Beams Hanover
	Noble Claire	Noble Victory	Victory Song
			Emily's Pride
		Scotch Claire	Scotland
			Abbey Claire
Ellens Glory	Meadow Skipper	Dale Frost	Hal Dale
			Galloway
		Countess Vivian	King's Counsel
			Filly Direct
	Gloria Barmin	Greentree Adios	Adios
			Martha Lee
		Adept Hanover	Tar Heel
			Arbutus Hanover

THE FIRST 1:55 TROTTER

NEVELE PRIDE			Bay Horse (1965) 4,T1:54.4m
Star's Pride	Worthy Boy	Volomite	Peter Volo
			Cita Frisco
		Warwell Worthy	Peter the Brewer
			Alma Lee
	Stardrift	Mr. McElwyn	Guy Axworthy
			Widow Maggie
		Dillcisco	San Francisco
			Dilworthy
Thankful	Hoot Mon	Scotland	Peter Scott
			Roya McKinney
		Missey	Guy Abbey
			Tilly Tonka
	Magnolia Hanover	Dean Hanover	Dillon Axworthy
			Palestrina
		Melba Hanover	Calumet Chuck
			Isotta

WORLD CHAMPION RACE COLT; GRANDSIRE OF VALLEY VICTORY

SPEEDY SOMOLLI			Bay Horse (1975) 3,1:55m
Speedy Crown	Speedy Scot	Speedster	Rodney
			Mimi Hanover
		Scotch Love	Victory Song
			Selka Scot
	Missile Toe	Florican	Spud Hanover
			Florimel
		Worth A Plenty	Darnley
			Sparkle Plenty
Somolli	Star's Pride	Worthy Boy	Volomite
			Warwell Worthy
		Stardrift	Mr. McElwyn
			Dillcisco
	Laurita Hanover	Hoot Mon	Scotland
			Missey
		Lark Hanover	Dean Hanover
			Leading Lady

REPRESENTATIVE 3x3 INBRED CROSSES

INBRED 3x3 CROSS TO TAR HEEL; LINEBRED 4x4 TO ADIOS AND BILLY DIRECT

DRAGON'S LAIR			Bay Horse (1982) p,5,1:51.3m
Tyler B	Most Happy Fella	Meadow Skipper	Dale Frost
			Countess Vivian
		Laughing Girl	Good Time
			Maxine's Dream
	Tarport Cheer	**Tar Heel**	**Billy Direct**
			Leta Long
		Meadow Cheer	**Adios**
			Betty G.
Sandy's Sable	Race Time	Good Time	Hal Dale
			On Time
		Breath O Spring	Worthy Boy
			Lady Scotland
	Carolonda	**Tar Heel**	**Billy Direct**
			Leta Long
		Adios Onda	**Adios**
			Onda Hanover

3x3 TO SPEEDSTER CROSSES MALE LINE OF DAM w/BROODMARE SIRE

MACK LOBELL			Brown Horse (1984) 3,1:52.1m
Mystic Park	Noble Gesture	Noble Victory	**Victory Song**
			Emily's Pride
		Important	The Intruder
			Ilo Hanover
	Mystic Sign	**Speedster**	**Rodney**
			Mimi Hanover
		Mystical	Worthy Boy
			Mystie Win
Matina Hanover	Speedy Count	**Speedster**	**Rodney**
			Mimi Hanover
		Countess Song	**Victory Song**
			The Viscountess
	Matora Hanover	Nibble Hanover	Calumet Chuck
			Justissima
		Mignon Hanover	Spencer Scott
			Madge Hanover

INBRED 3x3 TO HAL DALE; LINEBRED 4x4x4 TO ABBEDALE; 4x4 VOLOMITE

MOST HAPPY FELLA			Bay Horse (1967) p,3,T1:55m
Meadow Skipper	Dale Frost	Hal Dale	Abbedale
			Margaret Hal
		Galloway	Raider
			Bethel
	Countess Vivian	King's Counsel	Volomite
			Margaret Spangler
		Filly Direct	Billy Direct
			Calumet Edna
Laughing Girl	Good Time	Hal Dale	Abbedale
			Margaret Hal
		On Time	Volomite
			Nedda Guy
	Maxine's Dream	Knight Dream	Nibble Hanover
			Lydia Knight
		Maxine Abbe	Abbedale
			Maxine Direct

TOP DOLLAR MALE IS INBRED TO SUPER-SIRE MEADOW SKIPPER

NIHILATOR			Bay Horse (1982) p,3,1:49.3m
Niatross	Albatross	Meadow Skipper	Dale Frost
			Countess Vivian
		Voodoo Hanover	Dancer Hanover
			Vibrant Hanover
	Niagara Dream	Bye Bye Byrd	Poplar Byrd
			Evalina Hanover
		Scoot	Scamp
			Doris Spencer
Margie's Melody	Bret Hanover	Adios	Hal Dale
			Adioo Volo
		Brenna Hanover	Tar Heel
			Beryl Hanover
	Pretty Margie	Meadow Skipper	Dale Frost
			Countess Vivian
		Margie's Storm	Storm Cloud
			My Margie

PROMINENT AXWORTHY MALE HAS INBRED DAM (3x3 PETER VOLO)

SONGCAN			Bay Horse (1969) 3,1:58.3h	
Florican	Spud Hanover	Guy McKinney	Guy Axworthy	
			Queenly McKinney	
		Evelyn the Great	Peter the Great	
			Miss Deforest	
	Florimel	Spencer	Lee Tide	
			Petrex	
		Carolyn	Mr. McElwyn	
			Harvest Gale	
Ami Song	Victory Song	Volomite	**Peter Volo**	
			Cita Frisco	
		Evensong	Nelson Dillon	
			Taffolet	
	Hollyrood Amity	Hollyrood Harkaway	**Peter Volo**	
			Hollyrood Nimble	
		Hollyrood Ann	Hollyrood Prince	
			Hollyrood Diana	

3X3 TO VOLOMITE; 4x4 CROSS TO PETER VOLO

SUPER BOWL			Bay Horse (1969) 3,1:56.2m	
Star's Pride	Worthy Boy	**Volomite**	**Peter Volo**	
			Cita Frisco	
		Warwell Worthy	Peter The Brewer	
			Alma Lee	
	Stardrift	Mr. McElwyn	Guy Axworthy	
			Widow Maggie	
		Dillcisco	San Francisco	
			Dilworthy	
Pillow Talk	Rodney	Spencer Scott	Scotland	
			May Spencer	
		Earl's Princess Martha	Protector	
			Mignon	
	Bewitch	**Volomite**	**Peter Volo**	
			Cita Frisco	
		Bexley	Clever Hanover	
			Santos Express	

HORSES WITH 2x4 TROTTING CROSSES

2x4 CROSS TO STAR'S PRIDE FOR FASTEST HAMBO CHAMP

AMERICAN WINNER			Bay Horse (1990) 3,1:52.3m	
Super Bowl	**Star's Pride**	Worthy Boy	Volomite	
			Warwell Worthy	
		Stardrift	Mr. McElwyn	
			Dillcisco	
	Pillow Talk	Rodney	Spencer Scott	
			Earl's Princess Martha	
		Bewitch	Volomite	
			Bexley	
B J's Pleasure	Speedy Somolli	Speedy Crown	Speedy Scot	
			Missile Toe	
		Somolli	**Star's Pride**	
			Laurita Hanover	
	Matina Hanover	Speedy Count	Speedster	
			Countess Song	
		Matora Hanover	Nibble Hanover	
			Mignon Hanover	

2x4 CROSS TO FLORICAN; DAM IS LINEBRED TO RODNEY

NEARLY PERFECT			Bay Horse (1982) 4,1:54m	
Songcan	**Florican**	Spud Hanover	Guy McKinney	
			Evelyn The Great	
		Florimel	Spencer	
			Carolyn	
	Ami Song	Victory Song	Volomite	
			Evensong	
		Hollyrood Amity	Hollyrood Harkaway	
			Hollyrood Ann	
Exciting	Super Bowl	Star's Pride	Worthy Boy	
			Stardrift	
		Pillow Talk	**Rodney**	
			Bewitch	
	Gypsy Slipper	Speedy Scot	**Speedster**	
			Scotch Love	
		Golden Link	**Florican**	
			Kashaplenty	

2x4 CROSS TO VOLOMITE; STRONG PATERNAL/MATERNAL LINEAGE

NOBLE VICTORY			Brown Horse (1962) 4,1:55.3m
Victory Song	Volomite	Peter Volo	Peter the Great
			Nervolo Belle
		Cita Frisco	San Francisco
			Mendocita
	Evensong	Nelson Dillon	Dillon Axworthy
			Miss Pierette
		Taffolet	Guy Axworthy
			Taffeta Silk
Emily's Pride	Star's Pride	Worthy Boy	Volomite
			Warwell Worthy
		Stardrift	Mr. McElwyn
			Dillcisco
	Emily Scott	Scotland	Peter Scott
			Roya McKinney
		May Spencer	Spencer
			Guyellen

2x4 STAR'S PRIDE; SIRE INBRED TO VOLOMITE; DAM INBRED TO SPEEDSTER

SUPERGILL			Bay Horse (1985) 3,1:53.3m
Super Bowl	Star's Pride	Worthy Boy	Volomite
			Warwell Worthy
		Stardrift	Mr. McElwyn
			Dillcisco
	Pillow Talk	Rodney	Spencer Scott
			Earl's Princess Martha
		Bewitch	Volomite
			Bexley
Winky's Gill	Bonefish	Nevele Pride	Star's Pride
			Thankful
		Exciting Speed	Speedster
			Expresson
	Lassie Blue Chip	Speedy Scot	Speedster
			Scotch Love
		Lady Jamie	Jamie
			Lady Ann Reed

LINEBRED TROTTERS

4x3 CROSS TO STAR'S PRIDE FOR ONTARIO-BASED TROTTING STAR

BALANCED IMAGE			Bay Horse (1978) 3,1:58.4m	
Noble Gesture	Noble Victory	Victory Song	Volomite	
			Evensong	
		Emily's Pride	**Star's Pride**	
			Emily Scott	
	Important	The Intruder	Scotland	
			Mighty Margaret	
		Ilo Hanover	Nibble Hanover	
			Isabel Hanover	
Well Molded	Speedster	Rodney	Spencer Scott	
			Earl's Princess Martha	
		Mimi Hanover	Dean Hanover	
			Hanover Maid	
	Tarport Farr	**Star's Pride**	Worthy Boy	
			Stardrift	
		Meadow Farr	Kimberly Kid	
			Split	

THE SIRE OF VALLEY VICTORY & PEACE CORPS; 3X4 STAR'S PRIDE

BALTIC SPEED			Bay Horse (1981) 3,1:56m	
Speedy Somolli	Speedy Crown	Speedy Scot	Speedster	
			Scotch Love	
		Missile Toe	Florican	
			Worth A Plenty	
	Somolli	**Star's Pride**	Worthy Boy	
			Stardrift	
		Laurita Hanover	Hoot Mon	
			Lark Hanover	
Sugar Frosting	Carlisle	Hickory Pride	**Star's Pride**	
			Misty Hanover	
		Good Note	Phonograph	
			Rosemary Hanover	
	Karen's Choice	The Intruder	Scotland	
			Mighty Margaret	
		My Tip	My Birthday	
			Lawful Tip	

LINEBRED FEMALE IS TOP MONEY-WINNING STANDARDBRED

PEACE CORPS			Bay Mare (1986) 3,1:52.4m	
Baltic Speed	Speedy Somolli	Speedy Crown	Speedy Scot	
			Missile Toe	
		Somolli	**Star's Pride**	
			Laurita Hanover	
	Sugar Frosting	Carlisle	Hickory Pride	
			Good Note	
		Karen's Choice	The Intruder	
			My Tip	
Worth Beein'	Super Bowl	**Star's Pride**	**Worthy Boy**	
			Stardrift	
		Pillow Talk	Rodney	
			Bewitch	
	Aunt Hilda	Noble Victory	Victory Song	
			Emily's Pride	
		Worth Seein	**Worthy Boy**	
			Jen Hanover	

FASTEST TROTTER'S SIRE & DAM FROM SAME MALE LINE

PINE CHIP			Bay Horse (1990) 4,T1:51m	
Arndon	Arnie Almahurst	**Speedy Scot**	Speedster	
			Scotch Love	
		Ambitious Blaza	Blaze Hanover	
			Allie Song	
	Roydon Gal	Super Bowl	**Star's Pride**	
			Pillow Talk	
		Blythesome	Demon Rum	
			Blythe Sampson	
Pine Speed	Speedy Somolli	Speedy Crown	**Speedy Scot**	
			Missile Toe	
		Somolli	**Star's Pride**	
			Laurita Hanover	
	Piney Hanover	Harlan Dean	Harlan	
			Lydean Hanover	
		Posey Hanover	Nibble Hanover	
			Precious Hanover	

FAST 3 YEAR-OLD HAS 4X3 CROSS TO VICTORY SONG; 4X4X4 TO STAR'S PRIDE

SIERRA KOSMOS			Brown Horse (1989) 3,1:53.4m	
Nearly Perfect	Songcan	Florican	Spud Hanover	
			Florimel	
		Ami Song	**Victory Song**	
			Hollyrood Amity	
	Exciting	Super Bowl	**Star's Pride**	
			Pillow Talk	
		Gypsy Slipper	Speedy Scot	
			Golden Link	
Sunkiss Bel	Noble Victory	**Victory Song**	Volomite	
			Evensong	
		Emily's Pride	**Star's Pride**	
			Emily Scott	
	Sunday Hill	B.F.Coaltown	Galophone	
			Sis Rodney	
		Starlette Hill	**Star's Pride**	
			Gay Hill	

OTHER EXAMPLES OF STRONG LINEBREEDING

FASTEST MARE HAS DOUBLE LINEBRED CROSS TO ADIOS

CAESARS JACKPOT			Bay Mare (1986) p,5,T1:49.2m	
Walton Hanover	Big Towner	Gene Abbe	Bert Abbe	
			Rose Marie	
		Tiny Wave	**Shadow Wave**	
			Tiny Gold	
	Wendy Sue Hanover	Best Of All	Good Time	
			Besta Hanover	
		Wendy Hanover	**Bullet Hanover**	
			Wayblaze	
Tracy's Jackpot	Albatross	Meadow Skipper	Dale Frost	
			Countess Vivian	
		Voodoo Hanover	**Dancer Hanover**	
			Vibrant Hanover	
	Perky Mindy	Adios Vic	**Adios**	
			Miss Creedabelle	
		Prelude Lobell	Tar Heel	
			Hodge Podge	

FAST, RICH FEMALE HAS TRIPLE CROSS TO ADIOS (4x3x4)

MISS EASY			Bay Mare (1988) p,3,1:51.1m	
Amity Chef	French Chef	Meadow Skipper	Dale Frost	
			Countess Vivian	
		LaPomme Souffle	Nevele Pride	
			Pompanette	
	Hush A Bye	Bye Bye Byrd	Poplar Byrd	
			Evalina Hanover	
		Helenca Hanover	**Adios**	
			Helen's Heel	
Pleasure Seeker	Bret Hanover	**Adios**	Hal Dale	
			Adioo Volo	
		Brenna Hanover	Tar Heel	
			Beryl Hanover	
	Phyllis C.	Duane Hanover	Knight Dream	
			Dorsh Hanover	
		Little Fanny	**Adios**	
			Phantom Lady	

TOP TROTTER IS DOUBLE LINEBRED TO VOLOMITE

NAPOLETANO			Bay Horse (1984) 3,1:53.2m	
Super Bowl	**Star's Pride**	Worthy Boy	**Volomite**	
			Warwell Worthy	
		Stardrift	Mr. McElwyn	
			Dillcisco	
	Pillow Talk	Rodney	Spencer Scott	
			Earl's Princess Martha	
		Bewitch	**Volomite**	
			Bexley	
Noble Sarah	Noble Victory	**Victory Song**	**Volomite**	
			Evensong	
		Emily's Pride	**Star's Pride**	
			Emily Scott	
	Miss Sarah Rodney	Rodney	Spencer Scott	
			Earl's Princess Martha	
		Victory Miss	**Victory Song**	
			Miss Sarah Abbey	

PRINCIPAL LINES OF DESCENT OF THE EUROPEAN TROTTER

The charts on the next four pages set forth the male lines of descent of the European trotter, and are updated from charts which appeared in the original Care and Training book. Prominent European trotters descend from some of the same sources as those in North America, namely tracing through Hambletonian's prominent sons. North American influences on the European trotter have become more significant due to heavy export activity over the past 30 years. There are, however, several successful European trotting strains that do not trace in their male line to Hambletonian, and those are indicated on these pages. European trotters who do not descend from Hambletonian still trace in their male lines to the same horses from which all racing breeds trace their origin, that of the Darley Arabian, the Godolphin Arabian and the Byrely Turk. These male lines, most notably the Darley Arabian, for example, produced the modern Thoroughbred through the famed Eclipse.

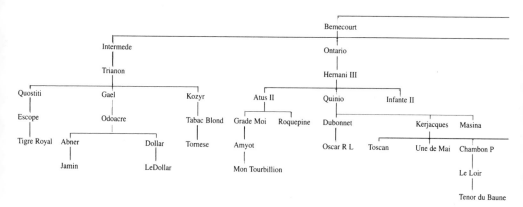

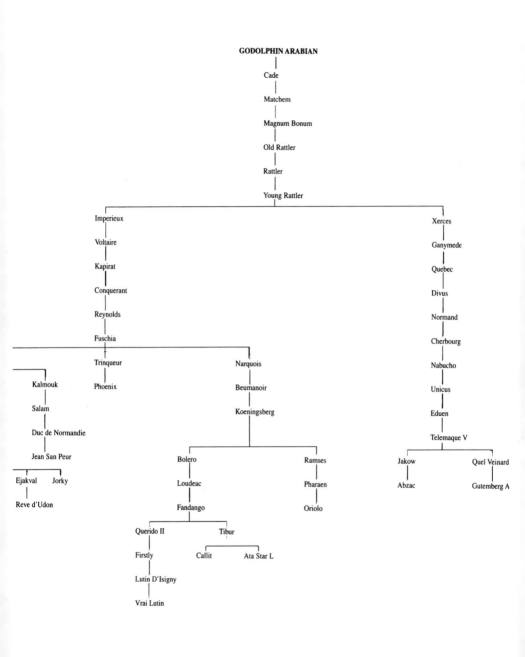

GODOLPHIN ARABIAN

Cade

Matchem

Magnum Bonum

Old Rattler

Rattler

Young Rattler

Imperieux   Xerces

Voltaire   Ganymede

Kapirat   Quebec

Conquerant   Divus

Reynolds   Normand

Fuschia   Cherbourg

Trinqueur   Narquois   Nabucho

Kalmouk   Beumanoir   Unicus

Salam   Phoenix   Koeningsberg   Eduen

Duc de Normandie   Telemaque V

Jean San Peur   Bolero   Ramses   Jakow   Quel Veinard

Ejakval   Jorky   Loudeac   Pharaen   Abzac   Gutemberg A

Reve d'Udon   Fandango   Oriolo

                    Querido II   Tibur

                    Firstly   Callit   Ata Star L

                    Lutin D'Isigny

                    Vrai Lutin

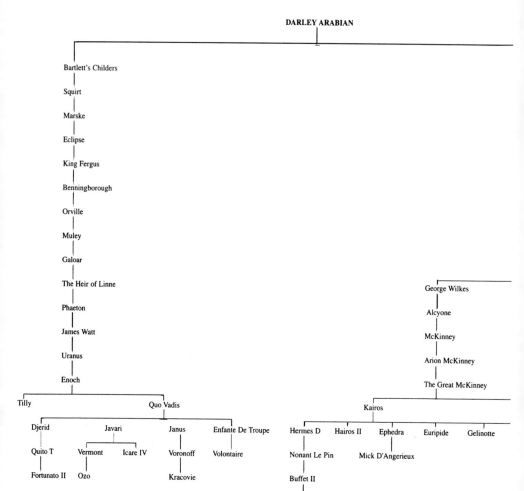

DARLEY ARABIAN

Bartlett's Childers

Squirt

Marske

Eclipse

King Fergus

Benningborough

Orville

Muley

Galoar

The Heir of Linne

Phaeton

James Watt

Uranus

Enoch

Tilly

Quo Vadis

Djerid — Javari — Janus — Enfante De Troupe

Quito T — Vermont — Icare IV — Voronoff — Volontaire

Fortunato II — Ozo — Kracovie

George Wilkes

Alcyone

McKinney

Arion McKinney

The Great McKinney

Kairos

Hermes D — Hairos II — Ephedra — Euripide — Gelinotte

Nonant Le Pin — Mick D'Angerieux

Buffet II

Ultra Ducal

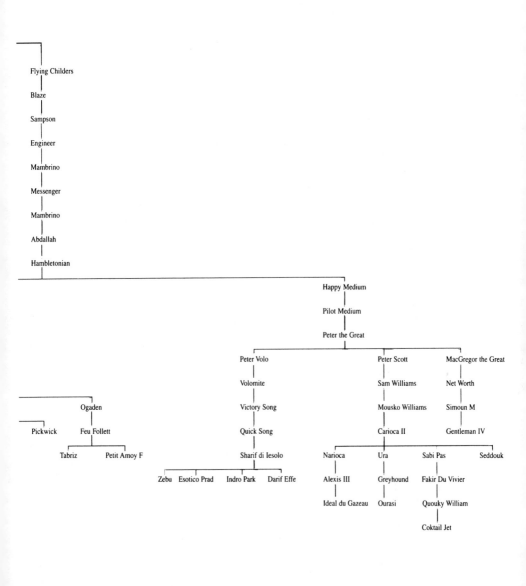

Peter Manning, 40

Peter Scott: bloodline, 40—44, 50; sire family, 680, 681

Peter The Brewer, 52, 63

Peter The Great: bloodline, 40, 51, 63; illus., 680; Maggie H. line, 679; sire family, 680—81; sire of Isotta, 676; sire of Mabel Trask, 670

Peter Thompson, 667

Peter Volo: bloodline, 40, 51, 52; maternal family, 674; sire family, 680

Pettersson, Bjorn, 45

Pharynx, 619

Phellis, Charles W., 71, 668, 675

Phosphorus-calcium balance, 624

Physical therapy, 612

Physical type, breeding for, 71—72

Pick Up, 672

Pierce, Ron, 58

Pine Chip: accomplishments, 260—63; aggressiveness, 249, 512; bloodline, 40, 41, 47; J. Campbell, 539; illus., 49; maternal family, 666, 675; pedigree, 709; shoeing, 232, 265; sire family, 47—50, 681; training, 259

Pine Speed, 48

"Pink center candy," 381

"Pipe cleaner" ("straw" roll), 214

Placenta, 647

Plain bell boot: illus., 226

Plain shoe, 159

Plastic rim pads, 176

Plastic shoes, 163, 167

Play The Palace, 368

Plutocrat, 71

Poor eaters, 308—9, 320. See also Feeding; Nutrition

Poplar Byrd, 61

Porterhouse, 41

Position in a race, 502—3; increasing importance of, 542; not worrying about, 550—52; post positions, 516; winning positions, 530—32, 533

Post positions, 516

Potency, 635

Potomac fever, 579, 644

Poultice, 420

Power cart, 278—79; building up stifles, 597; illus., 278, 597; knuckling over, 287; three-year-olds, 292; trotters, 282

Power Seat, 48

Powers, Larry, 405, 421

Pownall, Harry, 52

Prakas: accomplishments, 301; bloodline, 47; in Germany, 686; line-gaited trotter, 288; training, 277—78, 279; trotter history, 73

Pre-race checklist for drivers, 509

Pre-race routine, 457

Precious Bunny, 20, 21, 22, 23, 24, 31, 36, 377

Preferential, 403

Pregnancy, 641—45

Presidential Ball: bloodline, 16, 20, 21; Breeders Crown, 522; illus., 519; Life Sign and, 354; Little Brown Jug, 518, 519; North America Cup, 548, 563

Princess Gay, 679

Princess Peg, 52, 673

Probe, 56, 563

Progesterone and Estrodiole 17 Beta (P & E), 639

Programmed, 39

Prolific Lady, 83—84, 115; illus., 83

Pronto Don, 669

Proportion, 87—90; illus., 88—89

Prostaglandin, 639, 640

Protector, 673

Protein levels: and the growing horse, 316—17; mare's milk, 317

Prudy Hanover, 277

Pull-down blinds, 557

Pullers, 512, 515

Q

Quarter boots, 339, 413

Quarter cracks, 577—78; illus., 577

Queenly McKinney, 669

Quick-hitch harness: breaking the yearling, 126, 132; illus., 127, 330; pacers, 329

Quick Pay, 685

Quick Song, 686

Quilla Adios, 674

Quilla Byrd, 674

Quito de Talonay, 687

R

Rabies vaccine, 644

Race driving: See Driving strategy

Race lines, 494

Race program, 505

Race scheduling: training between races, 255—58, 295—97, 454—57; for two-year-olds, 354—56

Race secretary, 489